Cases in
Strategic Management
and Business Policy

Peter M. Ginter   *Linda E. Swayne*

Cases in Strategic Management and Business Policy

PRENTICE HALL
Englewood Cliffs, New Jersey 07632

Library of Congress Cataloging-in-Publication Data

Cases in strategic management and business policy / [edited by] Peter
M. Ginter, Linda E. Swayne.
    p. cm.
  ISBN 0-13-116229-2
  1. Strategic planning—Case studies. I. Ginter, Peter M.
II. Swayne, Linda E.
HD30.28.C4 1990
658.4′012—dc20
                          89-29209
                             CIP

Editorial/production supervision: Peggy M. Gordon
Interior design: Karen Buck
Cover design: Wanda Lubelska Design
Manufacturing buyer: Peter Havens

 © 1990 by Prentice-Hall, Inc.
A Division of Simon & Schuster
Englewood Cliffs, New Jersey 07632

Printed in the United States of America
10 9 8 7 6 5 4 3 2 1

ISBN 0-13-116229-2

Prentice-Hall International (UK) Limited, *London*
Prentice-Hall of Australia Pty. Limited, *Sydney*
Prentice-Hall Canada Inc., *Toronto*
Prentice-Hall Hispanoamericana, S.A., *Mexico*
Prentice-Hall of India Private Limited, *New Delhi*
Prentice-Hall of Japan, Inc., *Tokyo*
Simon & Schuster Asia Pte. Ltd., *Singapore*
Editora Prentice-Hall do Brasil, Ltda., *Rio de Janeiro*

Contents

Preface

College education must be directed toward preparing students to enter complex decision-making environments. Yet no definitive answers for tomorrow's business problems are found in today's classrooms. For new managers, there will be few situations to which they can apply "classic" solutions developed in the college classroom. Rather, students will need to learn to apply an independent critical intelligence to make judgments in a complex world of differing and competing points of view. Therefore, the task of business education is to develop students' abilities to raise relevant questions and to stimulate students to develop creative solutions.

Stanford University's President, Donald Kennedy, commented that education should "prod people ceaselessly to acquire more insight and knowledge." Further, he stated, "I tend to respect institutions that raise more questions than they answer. That's what produces people who have a drive to know and to understand."

Cases typically raise more questions than they answer, and in analyzing them students gain an understanding of the interdependence of business functions and the complexities of the business environment. Cases and the case instructor provide the context and impetus to raise questions and to seek understanding and through this process develop the student's ability in the science and art of management.

Realizing the importance of the case method, strategic management and business policy instructors have adopted the case approach to provide situations in which students may integrate and apply their management knowledge to gain experience. The case approach has proven successful in allowing students to practice decision-making skills without financial risk to an employer. Yet students must learn a systematic approach to address complex strategic situations. Therefore, *Cases in Strategic Management and Business Policy* includes case studies that provide a variety of strategic decision-making situations and appendixes that concern case analysis, financial analysis, oral presentations, and sources for business information.

The Strategic Management or Business Policy Course

This book is designed for use in the strategic management or business policy course, which is usually the capstone course in a program of study for a business degree and is typically required for all business majors and minors. The general objective of the capstone course is to pull together business theory and practice into a broad understanding of enterprise management. Other business courses generally provide an overview of the field, as in the principles course, or an in-depth study of one of the functional areas such as human behavior in organizations, marketing, production, or financial management. The strategic management or business policy course asks students to solve problems and develop comprehensive business strategies in situations not clearly predetermined as management, marketing, or finance. Using a top-management perspective, students must consider all of an organization's systems and interrelationships in developing recommendations.

Organization and Approach

This book contains strategy and policy cases that provide the organizations and environments for analysis, decision-making, and recommendations plus four appendixes that provide guidance in developing and presenting case analyses.

The Cases.   In order to effectively use cases, both students and instructors must understand the nature of case studies and their teaching objectives. A case typically is a record of a business situation actually faced by business executives, together with surrounding facts, opinions, and prejudices upon which executive decisions must depend.

A case study places students in a managerial position in which they will have to "size up" the situation and suggest some action for the organization. The action is typically a plan (set of decisions) which will address the key issues of the case. Therefore, the case most often provides some degree of focus as well as the environmental context. Seldom does the student have all the information necessary to make the best decision. Additionally, extraneous data must be identified and discarded.

The objective of the case approach is not to provide the "right" solution, or rote knowledge, that the student will apply to a future situation. Rather, the case approach provides the student with perspective concerning the complexity of the issues that organizations face, application of theory, practice in discerning critical issues, an understanding of the interrelatedness of business functions, and discussion concerning important issues facing modern enterprise. Case studies provide the student an in-depth learning experience in a given business situation that is difficult to obtain elsewhere.

The objective of this casebook is to provide a mechanism to integrate business theory and practice. The case studies developed and chosen for the casebook offer students a broad exposure to a cross section of strategic business situations. We think you will find this collection of twenty-nine cases to be pedagogically sound, appealing to students, stimulating to teach, and on target with respect to relevant contemporary issues.

All the cases included here are current and are supported with extensive industry information to provide background material necessary to understand and assess an organization's environment. However, the cases, as with tomorrow's business decisions, are not listed under predetermined categories that may indicate the nature of the problem or opportunity facing the organization. In addition, the book contains many new cases that have not previously appeared in business policy casebooks or texts.

Among the twenty-nine cases, eighteen deal with well-known national organizations; five are international operations, five are moderately sized regional companies, and eight may be classified as entrepreneurial businesses. These companies produce a variety of products and services and are in various stages of growth. The book also has excellent balance with regard to market position. The cases are multidimensional and comprehensive in that all of the elements of strategic management (strategy formulation, implementation, and evaluation and control), as well as the organization's environment, must be considered in the analysis of the case. In addition, many of the cases have related issues involving resource management, ethics, corporate culture, leadership, and so forth.

The Appendixes. The first two appendixes provide an orientation to case analysis through a practical analytical framework for addressing strategic management issues (Appendix A) and fundamentals for financial analysis (Appendix B). The third appendix assists the student in developing an oral presentation, and the fourth appendix provides a comprehensive reference for sources of business information. This appendix is provided for professors who require additional research for case analysis and for the student who has been motivated "to acquire more insight and knowledge."

The text portion of the book is designed for the student's benefit when initially approaching case analysis and to lend some structure to the process of strategic analysis. Because some instructors prefer a different format for case analysis, these sections have been placed after the cases. The instructor can assign those appendixes considered appropriate to personal teaching style. In addition, with this approach, instructors have the flexibility of using the case-only approach or supplementing the casebook with their own materials, a collection of strategic management and business policy readings, or a traditional textbook.

This casebook will work particularly well with many of the new paperback treatments of strategic management and business policy, collected readings, or broader policy approaches which use materials by such authors as Peter F. Drucker, Thomas J. Peters, Michael E. Porter, Henry Mintzberg, and others. The instructor's manual accompanying this casebook provides perspective concerning the industry, the scope, and the elements of the strategic planning process emphasized in each case.

ACKNOWLEDGMENTS

We are deeply indebted to many individuals for their assistance and encouragement in the preparation of this casebook. First, we would like to thank the appendix contributors—W. Jack Duncan (Appendix A), Bennie H. Nunnally, Jr. (Appendix B), and Carol M. Baxter and Gary F. Kohut (Appendix C). Their work provides structure and pedagogical guidance. Also, a special thanks to Dean M. Gene Newport of the School of Business at the University of Alabama at Birmingham and Dean Richard E. Neel of the College of Business Administration at the University of North Carolina at Charlotte who have always been supportive of our efforts. An additional thanks to all the fine people at Prentice Hall for their constant help and guidance, especially Alison Reeves, who provided encouragement, ideas, and enthusiasm. We would also like to thank the Prentice Hall reviewers. These colleagues were particularly helpful in balancing the types of cases and identifying "teachable" cases. Also, thanks to the companies included in the cases. They have given a great deal of time to contribute to the education of tomorrow's business leaders. Finally, this book would not have been possible without the case writers. Case writing is a difficult art, requiring many hours of library research, personal interviews, and detailed analysis. The case contributors listed in this text represent some of the finest case researchers anywhere. We think you will appreciate and enjoy their craft.

Peter M. Ginter
Linda E. Swayne

Case Abstracts

None of the sportswriters or other competing cities gave Charlotte much of a chance to win one of the new National Basketball Association franchises. But George Shinn, local entrepreneur, put together such an attractive package that the expansion committe had to consider the application. Despite the smaller city size and the predominance of the college game in the area, Charlotte was awarded the first of the expansion franchises and began play in the fall of 1989. The opening night crowd was a sellout, but what strategies should the fledgling franchise pursue to develop long-term profitability?

In 1979, Chrysler received a loan guarantee from the federal government. The corporation was near bankruptcy and had severe problems with products, management, dealer distribution, and labor. The case covers the recovery period for Chrysler Corporation under the leadership of Lee Iacocca. Strategy and progress through the 1980s are covered, including Iacocca's management, marketing, labor relations, dealers, diversification, and financial performance. The corporation had to not only get back on track but also prepare for the future in an intensely competitive environment both domestically and internationally. The strategic rationale for the American Motors Corporation acquisition and future problems must be related to Chrysler's changing external environment and internal strengths and weaknesses.

Case 3: **FARED Robot Systems, Inc.**   **38**

James W. Clinton, *University of Northern Colorado*

FARED Robot Systems was formed in 1981 by an entrepreneur who believed that manufacturers needed an integrated systems approach to factory automation. FARED initially marketed consulting services pertaining to robotics and factory automation but in response to customer demands added the development and manufacture of related systems hardware. The long-term prospects for the industry are favorable because manufacturers recognize that worker productivity must increase if they are to compete effectively with foreign manufacturers. However, FARED experienced significant financial problems and found it difficult to obtain sufficient working capital to pursue desirable strategies and developmental projects. Competition, both domestic and international, in the machine tool industry, the presence of large inventories of unsold factory equipment, and the 1986 Tax Reform Act, which makes the purchase of new plant and equipment less attractive, have combined to reduce the attractiveness of factory automation in the short-term.

Case 4: **Liz Claiborne, Inc.**   **53**

Barbara A. Spencer, *Mississippi State University*
Lisa K. Rowe, *Mississippi State University*

Started in 1976 with $250,000 in borrowed capital, Liz Claiborne, Inc. has grown to be included in the *Fortune* 500 list of the largest industrial companies. Concentrating on providing apparel for professional women in a business environment, the company designs apparel that meets the customer's need for style and practicability at an affordable price. The clothing is manufactured by independent suppliers, most of which are outside the United States. Fashion is a fickle industry and largely driven by the economy. Maintaining success in such a competitive environment requires creativity, diligence, and luck. Liz Claiborne seems to have all three—corporate growth has outpaced the industry. Further growth is being pursued by related diversification into cosmetics and retail stores and product development.

Case 5: **Brown-Forman, Inc. and The California Cooler Revolution**   **70**

Per V. Jenster, *IMEDE*

California Cooler virtually created the wine cooler category in the early 1980s. Guided by two young entrepreneurs, California Cooler arose from a small operation into the fourth largest wine shipper in the state of California in just three years. Since its incorporation in 1981, California Cooler has experienced phenomenal sales growth and is one of the few success stories in the flat wine industry. In 1985, Brown-Forman, Inc. used approximately $98 million in cash and future payments contingent upon sales to acquire California Cooler in an attempt to invigorate its wine and spirits division. Although California Cooler held the number one market position when acquired in 1985, competition continued to mount as market share fell. Awaiting the strategic plan from California Cooler's management, W. L. Lyons Brown, Jr., Chairman and CEO of Brown-Forman, knew it would be critical for the longer-term success of the new operation.

Plastic Suppliers, Inc. began operations in April 1986 as a maquiladora supplier for injection molded plastic parts. The plant began with the six investors working as co-owners and department heads (and everything else). In less than two years, PSI had doubled production, hired over eighty employees, and doubled the number of injection molding machines. Rapid expansion resulted in accounting and management problems. A newly appointed CEO had resigned over conflicts with the Board of Directors. The bank would not lend more money needed for cash flow, the plant was operating at 100 percent capacity, and the owners wanted to expand operations again.

Delta was the fourth largest air carrier providing scheduled air transportation for passengers, freight, and mail over a network of routes throughout the U.S. and overseas. Changes in top-level management in the company during the summer of 1987 included the retirement of Delta's CEO, David Garrett, who had exhibited tremendous leadership. There were several new senior executives, promoted from within, and a new CEO, Ron Allen. Delta was voted best airline by readers of *Travel Holiday* magazine. The company had an outstanding record for customer service but ranked poorly for on-time flight arrivals. The crash of Flight 191 and the near mishaps in early 1987 generated much negative publicity. Can Delta survive in such a dynamic environment without Garrett, especially in light of a possible reregulation in the industry?

Applied CAD Knowledge, Inc. was a small circuit board design service bureau in an industry which was changing rapidly along competitive and technological dimensions. For some years, the cost of computing equipment for PCB design had fallen rapidly. Barriers to entry collapsed, primarily because low-cost software permitted circuit design on personal computers. Applied CAD had always been subject to "feast or famine" cycles. Now sales were even harder to predict in advance. Lead times in the industry were short; when customers needed a board designed, they usually wanted it yesterday. Fast delivery, reliability in design, and low cost were vitally important. Owner Jeff Stevens, like many small business owners, had done most of his own marketing and sales, as well as a major share of the actual circuit design work. For several years, Jeff and his board discussed hiring a marketing vice-president and producing a promotional brochure. Sales continued their feast-or-famine cycle, however; when busy, Jeff had no time to recruit and work with a high-level person. When slow, he lacked the confidence in future abilities to support another salary.

The second part of the study describes a four-month recruiting process, leading to Jerry

King's hiring as marketing vice-president in December 1987. King's glowing predictions promised a chance to reach $1 million in sales in 1988. After working together for one month, Stevens and King predicted sales of $100,000 each for February and March. Stevens had finally found the "partner" he needed.

Case 9: Comshare, Inc.   140

Donald W. Scotton, *Cleveland State University*
Bernard C. Reimann, *Cleveland State University*
Allan D. Waren, *Cleveland State University*

The computing industry has experienced truly explosive growth in the last decade. Along with this growth there has been an interesting evolution in the structure and competitive dynamics of the market. Particularly interesting is the trend away from time-sharing to in-house computing and the rapid expansion of special purpose applications software markets. Comshare is an entrepreneurial firm which seems to have adapted quite successfully to these fundamental changes in its environment. In the process it has transformed itself from a major time-sharing vendor to an emerging, serious contender in the rapidly growing subset of corporate financial planning DSS (Decision Support Systems) software.

Case 10: Apple Computer, Inc. Targets Desktop Engineering   156

Robert O. Lewis, *M.B.A. Student, University of North Carolina at Charlotte*
Linda E. Swayne, *University of North Carolina at Charlotte*
Peter M. Ginter, *University of Alabama at Birmingham*

Matthew Robertson, previously a member of the highly successful development team for desktop publishing, had a new assignment. The engineering workstation market had been identified as having considerable potential for Apple's Macintosh II microcomputer. In terms of features and price, the Mac II was ideal for low-end workstation applications. Yet engineers were going to be hard to convince that the Mac II was more than a toy and could handle sophisticated engineering software. Because the engineering workstation market was already established and included several formidable competitors, Matthew knew this new assignment was going to be more challenging than desktop publishing, a market that Apple established.

Case 11: Honeywell, Inc. in Brazil   177

Delbert C. Hastings, *University of Minnesota*

Honeywell had operated in Brazil since 1958 and had built its business on selling control products and systems, made or assembled in its Sao Paulo plant from imported or locally made parts. However, increasing protectionist legislation by Brazil was threatening the importation of parts and the business itself. The Brazilian legislation called for domestic development of computers, chips and their applications, all sizes and varieties of hardware and components, software, telecommunications and digitalized equipment, and instruments in many lines. The aim of the legislation was to put Brazil's computer technology, skills, and products on a level with the leading countries of the world by impeding foreign firms operating in Brazil. The situation had become increasingly difficult as the regulatory bodies denied a series of Honeywell's license applications but approved arrangements with selected competitors. Though Honeywell's annual revenue in Brazil had never exceeded $15 million, Honeywell's top managers were convinced that Brazil was a country that would repay strenuous efforts to "stay in."

Peter M. Ginter, *University of Alabama at Birmingham*
Linda E. Swayne, *University of North Carolina at Charlotte*

Baldor Electric manufactured electric motors for the industrial market. Company growth had exceeded industry growth dramatically. Baldor ranked third in the industry, with sales of $200 million. After twenty-two years of progressive growth, and despite an increasing market share, dollar and unit sales declined from 1982 through 1986. By 1988 the company appeared to be back on target. The company's product line included electric motors sold through distributors and to original equipment manufacturers. The primary comparative advantage was energy efficient motors at competitive prices. Recent diversifications into motor starters and motor drivers had broadened the company's opportunity for growth.

Peter M. Ginter, *University of Alabama at Birmingham*
Linda E. Swayne, *University of North Carolina at Charlotte*

The electric motor industry is extremely concentrated, with the top eleven (of 340 nationally) companies accounting for over 80 percent of industry sales. The various kinds of motors, motor applications, major competitors, major markets, and market niches as well as industry forecasts are included as background material for the student.

John M. Gwin, *University of Virginia*
Per V. Jenster, *IMEDE*
William K. Carter, *University of Virginia*

Ira Rimerman, Group Executive, Consumer Services Group, International, Citicorp, was in his third-floor office at Citicorp's headquarters in New York City early in 1986 when he received notice from the Board of Citicorp that his proposal to acquire the British National Life Assurance Company, Ltd. (BNLA) in England had been approved. For a total investment of $33.3 million, Citicorp was now in the life underwriting business. Although pleased with the Board's approval, several issues were on Mr. Rimerman's mind as he thought back over the last few months when his staff analyzed and developed suggestions for a business strategy for BNLA. Soon he must recommend a sound strategy for BNLA along with supporting key policies, tactics, and organizational changes.

The state of Mississippi was determined to further its economic development. Strategic plans for the state's growth were being developed by the new governor. John O'Shea, Director of Economic Development, was investigating the opportunity for the state to expand catfish production. Mississippi was the leading grower and producer of farm-raised catfish. The objective was to concentrate on the development of the state through the catfish industry and not just on the industry alone.

K mart is the second largest retailer in sales volume and the largest discount department store chain in the United States. By the mid-1980s, the discount department store industry was characterized by a reduced number of store openings and diminished sales growth. K mart had continued to grow in sales volume but return on investment reflected industry-wide stagnation. K mart management placed heavy emphasis on corporate planning "to make decisions now to improve performance tomorrow." The Director of Planning and Research believed that K mart had been very successful in the area of strategic planning in the past. He felt that strategic planning used intelligently by management would be the key to corporate growth in the future.

In 1985 Goodyear was the world's largest manufacturer of tire and rubber products with net sales of over $10.9 billion. Goodyear's grand strategy at that time was to have tires and related products account for approximately one-half of sales, Goodyear Aerospace Corporation account for approximately one-fourth, and Celeron Corporation (natural gas and pipeline network) for one-fourth. The strategy was abandoned in late 1986 when Goodyear stock began being traded heavily on the New York Stock Exchange. A group led by Sir James Goldsmith, a global financier, was attempting to take over Goodyear. The company's efforts were directed toward thwarting the attempt. Management was eventually successful; however, Goodyear emerged a very different company.

LOTUS, developer of 1-2-3 microcomputer spreadsheet software, was faced with a serious market challenge. The company had 70 to 80 percent of the market for IBM PC and

PC-compatible spreadsheet programs. Numerous competitors established spreadsheet entries in the current market and were continually providing updated versions. LOTUS's updated version 3.0 for 1-2-3 would not debut until 1989. Meanwhile, its competitors introduced 1-2-3 compatible products with advanced features not available in current versions of 1-2-3 at the same price or at lower prices. LOTUS must decide how to maintain its competitive position without sacrificing the simplicity and familiar interface provided to existing users in an environment featuring slower growth rates for spreadsheet sales and more intense price and product competition.

Case 19: Chaparral Steel Company   343

John W. Simmons, *University of Texas at Tyler*
Mark J. Kroll, *University of Texas at Tyler*

Chaparral Steel, a wholly owned subsidiary of Texas Industries, Inc., selected Midlothian, Texas, for its steel mini-mill. The company used new technology and new managerial approaches to the steel industry to create the tenth largest steel firm in the United States. Contrasting integrated steel firms with the specialty firms and the relatively new mini-mill firms, the case outlines the relative advantages of the mini-mill technology in general and some of the unique approaches to the industry by Chaparral specifically. The company must develop a strategy for growth in a mature industry, which necessitates wresting away market share from both established domestic and foreign producers.

Case 20: Zenith Data Systems: The Trials and Tribulations of a Corporate Repositioning Strategy   365

Paul H. Meredith, *University of Southwestern Louisiana*

Zenith CEO, Jerry Pearlman, had much to contemplate: hostile takeover attempts, slow growth in the television business, entrance into the minicomputer industry by way of the microcomputer segments, launching the number one laptop microcomputer, and channel conflict that would require resolution. John Frank, President of Zenith Electronics subsidiary Zenith Data Systems (ZDS), was pressing for strategic change. Architect of the current strategy while Vice-President of marketing for Zenith Electronics, Frank now wanted Zenith to get out of the low-growth TV and appliance market and concentrate on computers. The computer segment strategy had been to capture the government and education markets. Now he was directing ZDS into the retail (consumer) and OEM markets. Pearlman knew that Frank's vision would require significant retrenchment in some areas and explosive growth in others. Such a move would change the strategic direction of the company and require dramatic organizational changes at Zenith. Repositioning would have to be guided by an effective and clear strategy.

Case 21: Saunders System, Inc. (1916–1986): The End of a Tradition   388

Peter M. Ginter, *University of Alabama at Birmingham*
Linda E. Swayne, *University of North Carolina at Charlotte*
John D. Leonard, *M.B.A. Student, University of Alabama at Birmingham*

Saunders System, Inc. was one of the nation's major truck transportation service companies competing with the giants of the industry such as Ryder and Hertz. The early 1970s were a time of great pressure on Saunders because of rising fuel costs and high inflation. These influences were reduced by industry regulation which allowed for higher costs to be passed on to customers. The 1980s brought deregulation to the trucking industry, creating an intensely competitive market with fewer entry controls. In 1986 Saunders was pursuing a strategy of geographic and product expansion, offering a wide variety of services. However, it was management's opinion that without additional capital resources, or repositioning of the firm, they would no longer be able to compete effectively. Therefore, in 1986, Kidder, Peabody investment bankers were engaged to investigate the sale of the company. Later that year, negotiations and competitive bids culminated in an agreement whereby Ryder Systems, Inc. would buy Saunders for $12.50 per share.

Case 22: Motor Carrier Transportation   404

Peter M. Ginter, *University of Alabama at Birmingham*
Linda E. Swayne, *University of North Carolina at Charlotte*

The trucking industry is comprised of a variety of types of companies supplying America's transportation needs. Private trucking, common carriers, and contract carriers are explored in order to understand the number of products that transportation companies can offer since industry deregulation. General industry problems as well as opportunities are included as background information to enable the student to focus on developing a strategy for Saunders.

Case 23: Chili's Restaurant   419

Sexton Adams, *University of North Texas*
Adelaide Griffin, *Texas Woman's University*

Chili's, which started operations in 1975, became a very successful midscale dinnerhouse restaurant chain. Sales had continually risen since the inception, and Chili's had increased its number of restaurants to eighty by 1986. This expansion was a result of dynamic and innovative management strategy, effective financial planning, good marketing research, and publicity. However, changing industry patterns, including direct competition from restaurants, indirect competition from carry-out food products, and increasing frozen food choices to be eaten at home, impacted the small chain. In 1986 Chili's management had to plan for the future.

Case 24: The United States Army Health Services Command   437

William F. Koehler, *Jacksonville State University*

The Army Health Services Command (HSC), a major command of the Department of the Army, was formed in 1973 with responsibility to provide Army health care in the mainland United States, Alaska, Hawaii, Panama, Puerto Rico, and Guam and Johnston Island in the Pacific. Since its organization HSC has been faced with an increasing patient load due to the aging of the retired Army population and a greater number of married active duty soldiers. This patient load, the rising costs of medical technology and professional personnel, and the high usage of the Army health care system, raised the HSC budget to $3.2 billion annually. The HSC was also faced with a significant rate of patient dissatisfaction and an environment in which Congress and the administration were looking for ways to control health care costs and concurrently maintain quality of care.

Case 25: Kraft, Inc.   456

Charles W. Boyd, *Southwest Missouri State University*

The objective of Kraft, Inc. was to become recognized as the leading food company in the world. To accomplish this objective, the company's management team had to contend with a decline in the U.S. population growth rate, changing dietary habits, and a worldwide restructuring of major food processing companies. Kraft's top managers were coping with these changes through the product mix, including retrenchment in fluid milk products and growth in frozen desserts, such as the acquisition of Frusen Gladje, a premium ice cream. In 1986, Dart and Kraft, Inc. were separated into Kraft, Inc. and Premark International, Inc. which controlled Tupperware, West Bend, Hobart, and Wilsonart. As a result, Kraft, Inc. is now composed of the food lines and the Duracell Battery Division. To gain the top position in the world food-processing industry, Kraft had to develop outstanding strategies.

Case 26: Purba-Paschim Trading Company: A Small Business Considers Expansion to Bangladesh   477

Hafiz G. A. Siddiqi, *Mankato State University*

Purba-Paschim Trading Company (PPTC) was a small business that imported seasonal garments and frozen fish from several developing countries. As the sources of supply began to diminish when the developing countries began marketing the products rather than selling them to trading companies and because quota restrictions were encountered, PPTC investigated the possibility of establishing its own manufacturing facility. The Chittagong Export Processing Zone in Bangladesh seemed to offer the opportunity the trading company was seeking; however, it would require approximately $3 million and considerable management time.

Case 27: Morningstar Bakery, Inc.   488

D. Michael Fields, *University of North Carolina at Charlotte*

From a standing start, Morningstar achieved a moderate level of success in developing a customer base of restaurant and foodstores which sold a wide range of products from the bakery's "all natural" line. Since the firm's inception, sales have continued at a steady but unspectacular rate. As a result of Morningstar's receptiveness to new product requests from customers, the product line grew to eighteen items which required numerous short production runs. As the firm approaches profitability, the long hours required to produce these multiple products have caused the Pollards to reevaluate their strategy. Terri has developed a gourmet brownie that the Pollards believe is "no ordinary product." Certain that their brownie is clearly superior to any on the market, John foresees the brownie being mass produced for a national market. A successful reception at the local level would allow the firm to produce brownies exclusively—dropping other products which are both time consuming and have lower growth potential.

Peter M. Ginter, *University of Alabama at Birmingham*
Linda E. Swayne, *University of North Carolina at Charlotte*
Patricia A. Luna, *Golden Enterprises, Incorporated*

Golden Flake Snack Foods accounted for 95 percent of the revenue and 96 percent of the operating profit of Golden Enterprises, Inc. Golden Flake is a full-line manufacturer of salted snack food products manufactured in Alabama, Tennessee, and Florida. With products currently distributed in thirteen southeastern states, company revenues in 1988 were over $128 million. Golden Flake has been able to double sales every five years throughout its history. However, as the company moves farther from its home market, management is finding this objective increasingly more difficult to accomplish. Intense competition against the industry giant, Frito-Lay, and multiple smaller companies has spurred management into renewed efforts to develop an effective strategy.

Elyce G. Warzeski, *M.B.A. Student, Tulane University*
Jeffrey A. Barach, *Tulane University*

PRINTECH was started by Elyce and Bob Warzeski when Bob was part of the massive layoffs in the oil industry. He wanted to use his Ph.D. in geology to do research and to teach; however, hundreds of similarly misplaced geologists were seeking the same positions. When his grandmother died, and left Bob an inheritance, the Warzeski's purchased a Macintosh computer. Working together as business partners was challenging for the married couple, but neither had the skills to run PRINTECH independently. The business developed slowly but word-of-mouth was excellent, and soon the couple was faced with a decision of whether to expand the business. Bob still had hopes of landing a university teaching position. If they made a substantial investment in equipment, it would be difficult to move.

The Charlotte Hornets NBA Franchise

The excitement was contagious. It was the first home game for Charlotte's first major league, professional sports team, the Charlotte Hornets—the National Basketball Association's (NBA) newest team (along with the Miami Heat). "It has been worth it all," thought George Shinn, as he looked out over the opening night sell-out crowd.

He remembered the times that it seemed there was no possibility of Charlotte winning an NBA franchise—when the national press carried the comment that the only franchise Charlotte would be awarded would have golden arches. "Ah, but there were great times, too," thought Shinn, "like when the city banned together and purchased tickets and surpassed any other expansion team's season ticket sales and when the city had the ticker-tape parade downtown after we were awarded the franchise and showered us with 32.5 million shredded dollars from the Federal Reserve. . . ."

The planning and execution of the pursuit of a major league NBA franchise had been nearly flawless. But most people laughed about the possibility of Charlotte being selected. On the advice of Max Muhleman, a sports marketing consultant, Shinn contacted Norm Sonju, general manager of the Dallas Mavericks, the newest franchise in the league. Following the advice of Sonju, Muhleman, and others, Shinn approached the league with a business-oriented proposal. Facts concerning Charlotte's market—its size, its location in the Carolinas, and its distance from the four Atlantic Coast Conference (ACC) schools known for their basketball programs—were outlined as well as the city's support for the franchise (the city-owned coliseum built for basketball was leased to Shinn for five years at $1 per game), city official support, and local media coverage.

Charlotteans were tired of their city being considered small time and wanted big city status. Winning a major league franchise was considered a way to earn that status.

THE CITY

Founded by Scotch-Irish farmers around 1748, the city was named after Queen Charlotte of Mecklenburg-Strelitz, wife of King George III of Great Britain. In 1988, Charlotte was the largest city in the Carolinas with a population of 374,000;

This case was prepared by Linda E. Swayne and Peter M. Ginter. It is intended as a basis for class discussion rather than to illustrate either effective or ineffective handling of an administrative situation. Used by permission from Linda E. Swayne.

the Charlotte Metropolitan Statistical Area (MSA) contained 1.07 million, and more than 5.5 million people lived within a 100-mile radius.

A particularly sensitive issue with the residents of Charlotte was the confusion over what has been dubbed the "Ch" factor. Charlotte has been confused with Charlottesville (Virginia), and Charleston (South Carolina and West Virginia). As a result, whenever Charlotte was mentioned in the national media it was always stated as Charlotte, North Carolina. Locals complained that Miami, Minneapolis, Chicago, or other major cities did not have to be identified by state and felt strongly that Charlotte was a big city that could stand alone. City officials believed that a major league franchise would build recognition so that people across the nation would know where Charlotte was located without having to identify the state.

Centrally located in the state of North Carolina near the South Carolina border, the city had often been called the financial center of the South. Three super-regional banks had major offices in Charlotte. The largest, NCNB Corporation, had just completed a buy-out of Texas Republic Bank. Because of the large banks, other financial services had located in the city as well, including accounting firms, insurance companies, and law practices.

Charlotte was also known for its transportation industry which developed because of access to Interstates 85 and 77. Companies had the ability to reach approximately 70 percent of the nation's population within twelve hours from Charlotte transportation terminals. As a result, distribution was also a major industry.

Charlotte's central location in the tenth most populated state of the nation (6.4 million), its airport which served as a hub for USAir (formerly Piedmont) airlines, and mild climate enticed 298 *Fortune* 500 companies to locate offices in the city. One *Fortune* 500 company located its headquarters in Charlotte. Companies with a significant presence in Charlotte included USAir, IBM, AT&T, DuPont, Apple Computer, Coca-Cola Bottling, NCNB, First Union Corporation, Royal Insurance, Home Mortgage, and Duke Power.

The surrounding area had many textile manufacturers; however, the city and its suburbs tended to have service and support facilities for textile operations rather than textile manufacturing plants.

Charlotte's growth during the previous ten years had been fueled by the influx of both companies and people to the Sunbelt. During the summer of 1988, the unemployment level was at a record low of 2.9 percent while economic growth was forecasted to outpace GNP by 2 percent over the next five years. The per capita income level was above $13,000 in 1988.

The Charlotte Uptown Development Corporation estimated that between 1971 and 1986 there had been $700 million in private investment and $58 million in capital expenditures by the city of Charlotte. More than $382 million of construction was planned or in progress, including the $300 million NCNB/Charter Properties/Lincoln Property complex with a fifty-story office tower which would include a performing arts center.

The magnitude of this expansion had caused Charlotte to seek "big city" recognition and prompted taxpayers to approve a $68 million municipal bond referendum for the construction of a new coliseum.

PURSUING THE TEAM

First and foremost, George Shinn has been an astute businessman. He felt that Charlotte was ready for a professional team. Since he loved baseball as a child, he initially sought to establish a professional baseball team. Meeting with resistance to expansion and little movement of major league baseball franchises, Shinn next pursued a professional football franchise. Several exhibition games were played in Charlotte in a small, ill-equipped high school stadium. At about that time, there were some indications that the NBA might be considering expansion. Shinn began investigating the NBA and the possibilities of a franchise for Charlotte.

THE NATIONAL BASKETBALL ASSOCIATION

The NBA started in 1946 with 11 teams. In 1980, the NBA was composed of 22 teams (Exhibit 1-1). Four of these teams—the Denver Nuggets, Indiana Pacers, New Jersey Nets (formerly the New York Nets), and the San Antonio Spurs—had been incorporated into the NBA in 1976 following the demise of the American Basketball Association (ABA), which had started in 1967. In 1981, the Dallas Mavericks were added to the league and became the most successful expansion franchise, setting an expansion attendance record of over 7,500 fans per game.

Exhibit 1-1   **NBA Teams by Conference in 1981 (includes franchise year)**

Eastern Conference	Western Conference
Atlantic Division	**Midwest Division**
Boston Celtics	Dallas Mavericks (1980–1981)
New Jersey Nets (1976–1977)	Denver Nuggets (1976–1977)
New York Knicks	Houston Rockets (1967–1968)
Philadelphia 76ers	Sacramento Kings
Washington Bullets	San Antonio Spurs (1976–1977)
Central Division	Utah Jazz (1974–1975)
Atlanta Hawks	**Pacific Division**
Chicago Bulls	Golden State Warriors
Cleveland Cavaliers (1970–1971)	LA Clippers (1970–1971)
Detroit Pistons	LA Lakers
Indiana Pacers (1976–1977)	Phoenix Suns (1968–1969)
Milwaukee Bucks (1968–1969)	Portland Trail Blazers (1970–1971)
	Seattle Supersonics (1967–1968)

Although Dallas was successful, many teams were operating at substantial losses due to poor attendance. To offset the falling revenues from ticket sales, television revenues were increased, but only through increasing the number of games televised. The net effect was overexposure for professional basketball and further decline in ticket revenues. "You are not going to improve your situation if you have a lot of poor events that do not titillate your audience," according to former NBA Commissioner Lawrence F. O'Brien. In 1983, 13 of the 23 teams were operating in the red and at least six franchises were for sale.

The better teams, generating the greatest revenue dollars and operating profitably, were able to offer salaries that would attract the best players. Thus, the best teams became better and the weaker teams tried to find buyers. The disparity escalated when the players won the right to be free agents; they could sell their services to the highest bidder. Player salaries rose drastically and only the richest teams could afford to hire the "stars." The richer franchises dominated the game, a problem common to all professional sports, not just basketball.

Further exacerbating the problem was payment for televised games. Pay TV added to the coffers of the better teams. Teams in the largest metropolitan areas generated more revenues because of the population available to subscribe to pay TV. In other areas, such as Utah and Portland, the number of pay TV subscribers would never be sufficient to induce paid coverage.

The Stern Solution

Under the leadership of David J. Stern, NBA General Counsel, 1978 to 1982, Executive Vice-President and General Manager, 1982 to 1984, and Commissioner 1984 to the present, the NBA developed a unique strategy that the owners and players thought would ensure the long-term viability of the league. Stern determined that the problem was that poor teams were detrimental to the health of the entire league. By putting a "cap" on the amount a team could pay in player salaries, the NBA hoped to develop greater parity between teams, improve competition, and increase interest from fans.

The Stern salary "solution" went into effect in the 1984–1985 season. Each team was able to determine how the salary pool would be allocated among the players. Thus, if a team wanted to "buy" a superstar, less money would be available for other players on the team. The cap for each team was a fluctuating amount determined by the success of the league in the previous season. Players agreed to the solution as they would receive 53 percent of the league's gross receipts, equally divided among the 23 teams. The player pool of nonsuperstars would have increased salaries, and a grandfather clause allowed the teams to continue paying current superstars super salaries.

The second phase of Stern's plan was to improve NBA ratings on television by reducing the number of games shown on network and cable TV. It was hoped that by limiting the NBA's exposure, the value of commercial time would be increased. As a result of Stern's strategy, the league experienced a 16 percent increase in TV revenues in 1982–1983 while airing half as many games as in the previous season.

Basketball is the smallest of the "big three" professional sports. Despite increasing revenues, it lags behind professional baseball and football. In 1984 the NBA had total revenues of $192 million compared with baseball's $625 million and football's $700 million. Slightly over 10.5 million basketball fans attended 943 regular season games, whereas 14 million football fans attended 224 NFL games and 44.7 million fans attended 2,106 baseball games.

THE NBA EXPANDS

The NBA, under the leadership of Commissioner Stern, experienced strong revenue growth after 1983. Exhibit 1-2 shows the increase in attendance for the 23

Exhibit 1-2   **Regular Season Attendance by Team Ranked by Overall 1987–1988 Total (In millions)**

Team	Capacity	1983–84	1984–85	1985–86	1986–87	1987–88
Detroit Pistons	21,519	.653	.692	.695	1.405	1.626
Chicago Bulls	17,500	.261	.487	.469	1.326	1.415
Boston Celtics	14,890	.607	.611	.610	1.329	1.375
LA Lakers	17,505	.622	.614	.689	1.296	1.358
Atlanta Hawks	16,339	.293	.300	.378	1.138	1.221
Dallas Mavericks	17,007	.583	.684	.693	1.206	1.219
Houston Rockets	16,279	.436	.569	.605	1.199	1.218
New York Knicks	19,591	.496	.457	.592	1.081	1.151
Philadelphia 76ers	18,168	.588	.572	.513	1.267	1.098
Portland Blazers	12,666	.519	.519	.519	.993	1.040
Cleveland Cavs	20,900	.208	.324	.391	.924	1.034
Denver Nuggets	17,022	.462	.449	.532	.963	1.026
Indiana Pacers	16,912	.421	.438	.461	.999	1.022
Milwaukee Bucs	18,600	.414	.423	.443	1.001	1.012
Seattle 'Sonics	14,250	.447	.303	.329	.836	1.010
Utah Jazz	12,444	.408	.374	.478	.949	.998
New Jersey Nets	20,039	.512	.502	.483	.960	.983
Golden State Warriors	15,025	.338	.301	.401	.900	.977
Washington Bullets	18,643	.325	.383	.374	.991	.975
Phoenix Suns	14,471	.446	.493	.456	.916	.951
Sacramento Kings[a]	16,400	.370	.263	.424	.885	.911
San Antonio Spurs	15,770	.376	.364	.336	.800	.853
LA Clippers[b]	15,310	.229	.384	.342	.766	.836
Total		10.014	10.506	11.213	24.130	25.309

[a]Moved before '85–'86 season.

[b]Moved before '84–'85 season.

Source: NBA Guide annual editions, 1983–1987.

teams. The health of the league improved so dramatically that in 1985 Mr. Stern organized a league expansion committee, headed by Norm Sonju of the Dallas Mavericks, to study the feasibility of adding new teams. Stern commented, "Because we're trying to balance the needs of the league—which I suppose could be best served by, say, 12 teams—with a keen appreciation for the fact that when you present yourself as a major league, and bona fide cities request to join your league, you had better take them seriously."

In 1986, after carefully considering the requests from potential owners in seven cities, the NBA voted to expand the league by one to as many as three teams, depending on the number of worthy candidates. Critics believed that just when the NBA problems were being resolved, expansion would rekindle the financial troubles of many of the teams. However, since each of the expansion franchises would pay $32.5 million, as much as $97.5 million would be divided among the 23 teams, resulting in improved finances of $4.24 million for each franchise, if three teams were added.

The Race for Selection

The principle contenders for an NBA franchise were Charlotte, Miami, Minneapolis, Orlando, Tampa Bay, Toronto, and Orange County, California. Each team had to forward a $100,000 application fee to the league expansion committee. Once selected, the expansion team owners would pay $32.5 million as the franchise fee. The owners of the last expansion team, the Dallas Mavericks, paid approximately $12 million for their franchise awarded in 1980.

The NBA expansion committee established three standards of quality for the competition: ownership, television potential, and playing facility. The winning cities could be playing as early as the 1988–1989 season, which was two years away.

At the outset, Charlotte was generally rated as the least likely city for selection. "The biggest thing Charlotte had to overcome was its perception," said Norm Sonju, vice-president and general manager of the Dallas Mavericks and member of the expansion committee. "George Shinn and the city had plenty of things to offer, but they had to get the message across. They had to change the perception that the market was too small and was dominated by the colleges."

The principal hurdle for Charlotte was the area's well-known passion for college basketball. Four in-state ACC teams—University of North Carolina, North Carolina State, Duke, and Wake Forest—regularly played to sell-out crowds and had strong television ratings. Even though major professional NBA stars such as Michael Jordan, James Worthy, Ralph Sampson, Mike Gominski, Walter Davis, Bobby Jones, and Johnny Dawkins had emerged from the ACC, the NBA owners were skeptical.

In October 1986, George Shinn and his management team made a critical presentation to league owners in Phoenix. They used a map of North and South Carolina to highlight the facts that major colleges were two hours away and a population of 5.5 million was located within one and one half hours drive of the Charlotte coliseum. Charlotte was still thought to be a long shot to win a franchise, but the city had not been eliminated from consideration.

As the year passed, both Tampa Bay and Orange County had trouble developing interest in season ticket sales and in building an arena. Toronto fell behind due to the lack of basketball tradition, either professional or collegiate. Exuberantly, Charlotte was one of the final four teams, although most analysts still viewed the city as a long shot because of the market size and the strength of college basketball, which was viewed as a substitute for a professional team. The expansion committee still had not publicly announced how many franchises would be awarded.

The next critical test was the sale of season tickets which the NBA would use as a measure of "true" fan support. Miami had 7,250 tickets sold, requiring a $95 deposit; Orlando had 11,900 tickets spoken for with a mix of pledges, $50, and $100 deposits; Minneapolis had 6,450 tickets sold, requiring a $50 deposit; and Charlotte had 5,900 tickets sold, requiring a $250 deposit. In their presentation to the expansion committee, Shinn's delegation stressed the importance of the larger deposits required in Charlotte as compared to the other cities, in an effort to illustrate the intensity of fan support.

The Competition

By March 1987, the race had clearly defined competitors (Exhibit 1-3 gives statistical comparisons of the four cities). Miami had sold over 10,000 season tickets and its co-owner, Julio Iglesias, was being toasted as the answer to Miami's perceived weakness. With a large Hispanic audience, approximately 800,000 of Miami's

Exhibit 1-3   **Demographics of the Major Contenders**

	Charlotte	Miami	Minneapolis	Orlando
Population, MSA	1,110,273	1,827,891	2,347,088	957,776
Population, city	362,478	429,828	353,996	155,850
Growth (1980–1986)	10.3%	9.8%	8.7%	28.5%
Projected growth (1980–1991)	17.4%	17.0%	14.4%	47.3%
Per capita income, city	$15,225	$9,878	$16,266	$13,092
Per capita income, MSA	$12,748	$13,886	$15,589	$14,853
Percent black	19.98	14.90	2.34	12.94
Percent Hispanic	0.77	23.50	1.05	3.71
Median age	30	36.3	28.9	30.3
Males to 100 females	92.6	89.9	94.7	94.1
Pro teams (prior to NBA, major league)	0	1	3	0

1.8 million population, which was relatively unfamiliar with basketball, many analysts saw Iglesias becoming the "Jack Nicholson of the LA Lakers" for Miami. The city's major strengths were its new arena and the excellent history of the Miami Dolphins pro football team.

Orlando was felt to have less of a chance to be selected because its arena would be difficult, if not impossible, to complete in time for the upcoming season. Its advantages were 25 million Disney World visitors and a cable television network of over a million customers.

Minneapolis also ran into scheduling problems with the Metrodome. Many believed that intense competition would develop among its pro football, baseball, and hockey teams with the addition of an NBA franchise. Additionally, the low deposit required for season tickets might have inflated fan commitment to an NBA team.

Charlotte's weakness, potential market size, was overcome by selling over 15,000 season tickets which required large deposits. The city rallied behind Shinn, determined to win a pro franchise. The other major advantage was the Charlotte 23,500-seat coliseum, completed during the summer of 1988.

On April 22, 1987, NBA Commissioner David Stern announced that the league would expand by four teams. Charlotte was awarded the first expansion franchise, to be joined by Miami during the 1988–1989 season. Minneapolis and Orlando would participate in the 1989–1990 season.

The Driving Force Behind the Franchise—George Shinn

George Shinn grew up in the Charlotte area. At the age of eleven, his father died of a heart attack. His mother was forced to sell the family business and other properties to pay debts from an ongoing real estate venture. Only their home was saved.

"I'll never forget the crushing humiliation of those auctions, watching other people make bids on what had been my father's life work," comments Mr. Shinn. His mother told him later, "Being poor is nothing to be ashamed of. But I'll be ashamed of you if you don't make something out of yourself so you can stop being poor."

After high school, Shinn worked at Cannon Mills, a major textile manufacturing company. At the suggestion of his mother, he enrolled in a two-year business college in Concord, North Carolina, a small town just outside Charlotte. He worked as a janitor to pay part of his tuition and by the time he was 23 he was running the school. Subsequently Shinn became the sole owner of Rutledge Education System which includes 26 schools in ten states. In 1975, Shinn was the youngest to win a Horatio Alger Award for rags-to-riches success. He was one of 11 honored, and was selected from among 2,000 nominees.

Shinn credits his positive attitude, motivation, and strong faith for his success. He has written several books on the subject, including *The American Dream Still Works* and *The Miracle of Motivation*. It is this level of motivation, analysts note, that has brought an NBA franchise to Charlotte. According to John A. Tate III of First Union Corporation (a major Charlotte-based bank), "George is the living, breathing example of the power of positive thinking."

Often cited as the turning point in the decision to select Charlotte as an expansion city was Mr. Shinn's negotiation of the new 23,500-seat municipal coliseum lease at $1 per game for the next five years. "That really got the owners' attention," relayed an NBA representative. "The members of the expansion committee had been staring at the ceiling or looking out the window while politely listening to Charlotte's pitch. Then they heard the lease terms, and they got whiplash."

While Mr. Shinn was credited with bringing the franchise to Charlotte, he never overlooked the importance of the support of the city and the area fans. When the team's original name, the Spirit, drew snickers and critical remarks from both fans and the press, Shinn launched a campaign for the fans from North and South Carolina to rename the team. Later, polls and contests had the fans name the mascot and win prizes by guessing the Hornets' top picks in the expansion and college drafts.

HISTORY OF PRO SPORTS IN CHARLOTTE

North Carolina has never supported a major league professional sports team. Football fans rooted for the Washington Redskins (which was the closest football team until the Falcons were established in Atlanta) and baseball fans rooted for the Atlanta Braves because owner Ted Turner televised all Braves games on his cable network, which was one of the major stations broadcast in Charlotte for many years. No pro basketball team had been able to corral enthusiasm, as local fans supported the numerous college teams that played in the area.

Previous attempts at establishing professional sports have not been successful. The Carolina Lightning soccer team, the Charlotte Hornets of the World Football League, and the Charlotte Checkers of the Southern Hockey League are recent teams that folded. In 1969, an ABA basketball team, the Carolina Cougars, a regional franchise, was shared by Greensboro, Charlotte, and Raleigh. The Cougars played their last game in the Carolinas in the spring of 1974, after which the franchise was moved to St. Louis. The ABA folded in 1976 (four of the franchises were accepted into the NBA). Many sportswriters and others concluded that the city could not or would not support major league, professional athletics.

Wrestling and NASCAR racing are the area's "professional" sporting events that have been financially successful. The Charlotte Motor Speedway draws the nation's second largest crowd for a single sporting event, The World 600 Race. Only the Indianapolis 500 has a larger single-event crowd.

"Charlotte has had a tremendous outpouring of public support and has, in my mind, completely justified its recommendation," proclaimed NBA Commissioner David Stern. But would the tremendous outpouring of public support continue if the Hornets weren't winners? The average expansion team wins 26 percent of its first season games which translates into a 21-61 record. The Dallas Mavericks, the most recent expansion team, won 15 games its first year and the league has become even more competitive since the statistics were compiled. Many agree that winning 20 games would be an outstanding rookie season for the Charlotte Hornets.

THE CHARLOTTE HORNETS

Many decisions concerning the team have been made with press coverage in mind. When the fans and the press denigrated the original name, "Spirit," a new name was chosen. Hornets have particular meaning to the independent minded citizens of North Carolina. When the British commander Lord Charles Cornwallis attempted to fight the revolutionary soldiers in North Carolina at the battle of Kings Mountain, a large part of his troops were slaughtered. Then he encountered Nathanael Greene's forces at Guilford courthouse. Cornwallis likened the North Carolina troops to a swarm of hornets that they could not escape, more hostile to England than any in America, and the war in North Carolina was abandoned. "Hornets Nest" is a common designation for the piedmont area of North and South Carolina.

Basketball uniforms do not generally draw much attention, but Shinn made sure that the Hornets' uniforms were talked about and written about in the press. He hired Alexander Julian, a native North Carolinian, to design the team's uniform. The Hornets are the first professional team in sports history to have their uniforms created by a nationally known fashion designer. The teal and white colors were chosen to blend with the purple and teal colors of the Charlotte coliseum.

When asked what kind of statement he was trying to make, Julian replied: "We've got a team that has style; we've got a team that has class. We've got a team that has energy and is going to be a winner." Paid in regular deliveries of barbecue from his home state, Shinn also awarded Julian the first jersey. National coverage started in New York City with a press conference in the morning and continued with a press conference in Charlotte in the afternoon.

The Charlotte coliseum is often referred to as a jewel in Charlotte's crown. Financed by $68 million in bonds that won overwhelming support from the voters, the coliseum holds up to 23,500 seats. It was designed for basketball (23,388 seats of which 22,919 seats are revenue producing). There was general consensus that no seat was really bad.

Pricing for season tickets was done for the old coliseum with the anticipation that one season (1987–1988) might be played there. The NBA was astute in awarding the franchises in early 1987 and then waiting until late 1988 for the two new teams to begin playing. According to Shinn, "We needed every minute to prepare properly for our first season." The new coliseum was completed in the summer of 1988 and had several events (including one preseason Hornet's game) to be thoroughly ready for the opening of professional basketball in Charlotte.

Only season tickets were sold until October 17, 1988. Prices for the forty-one home games varied from $287 to $2,050. Exhibit 1-4 illustrates the location and cost

Exhibit 1-4   **Charlotte Coliseum Seating Plan and Prices**

Price/Season	Price/Game	No. Seats	Location	Per Game Sold-Out Revenue
$ 287	$ 7	2,668	F	$18,676
410	10	3,048	E	30,480
533	13	2,600	D	33,800
656	16	4,564	C	73,024
820	20	5,689	B	113,780
1,025	25	3,126	A	78,150
1,435	35	700	BB	24,500
2,050	50	524	AA	26,200
		22,919		$398,610

of the various seats. After October 17, individual game tickets were sold at the per game price listed in Exhibit 1-4. Tickets to the Chicago Bulls (Michael Jordan, a guard on the Chicago Bulls team is a North Carolinian), and the champion LA Lakers games were sold out within two days.

If all 41 home games were played to sell-out crowds (an unlikely event) ticket sales revenue would be $16,343,010. In addition, twelve sky boxes were sold for the season for $90,000 each. Eight of the boxes have 10 seats and four of the boxes have 18 seats for a total of 152 seats. They are sold on a per season basis only. The remaining seats are non-revenue producing and are used for the press (courtside) and the Hornets players.

A teal and purple (coliseum colors) bee was designed by Jerrell Caskey of Hendrick Sportswear as the team mascot (Exhibit 1-5). The challenge was to design a friendly but fierce "Hornet" that would be used constantly to identify the team.

The team mascot, Hugo the Hornet, was designed and created by Cheryl Henson, daughter of Muppet's creator Jim Henson. Named by a fan in a contest, the mascot was to be used at all Hornet's home games and special promotional events.

Hornet's Administrative Organization

George Shinn became the managing partner of a group of owners. Rick Hendrick, owner of a number of automobile dealerships across the country, Felix Sabates, the former owner of a Charlotte semipro soccer franchise, and Cy Bahakel, current owner of a local, independent TV station, became the minority partners.

Carl Sheer was hired as vice-president and general manager of the Hornets on June 25, 1987. He started his management career with the Carolina Cougars of the ABA, then was selected as general manager for the Denver Nuggets (initially the Denver Rockets of the ABA). He was instrumental in the transition for the Nuggets

Exhibit 1-5   **The Charlotte Hornet**

into the NBA. After holding that position for ten years, Sheer joined the LA Clippers for two years before becoming the commissioner of the Continental Basketball League in 1986.

For six months, Carl Sheer continued his duties as commissioner of the Continental Basketball League while preliminary Hornets activities were being completed. He started working full-time for the Hornets on January 1, 1988. His responsibilities included hiring a director of player personnel, scouts, a coach, and an administrative team for the organization (Exhibit 1-6).

The Coaching Staff

Gene Littles, an ABA standout who played five years for the Carolina Cougars and one year for the Colonels, was hired as director of player personnel and quickly assembled a team of scouts to cover the NBA and college games during the 1987–1988 season. Littles began his coaching career as an assistant coach at Appalachian State University in Boone, North Carolina, and then as head coach at North Carolina A & T University. In the NBA, he performed assistant coaching duties with the

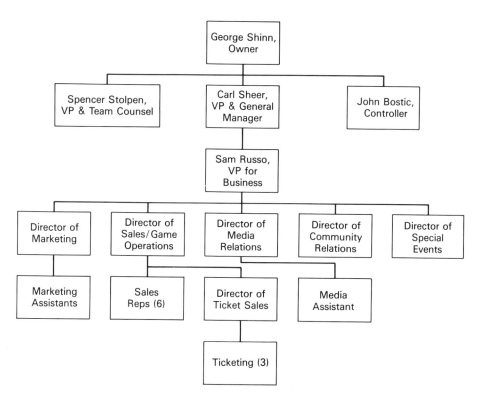

Exhibit 1-6   **Charlotte Hornets Administrative Staff**

Utah Jazz, Cleveland Cavaliers, and most recently, the Chicago Bulls. He was assigned additional duties as assistant coach for the Hornets in June 1988.

Shinn, Sheer, and Littles teamed together to hire the Hornets' first coach. Many speculated that Larry Brown, coach for the 1988 national champion University of Kansas, was the top choice. He was offered the coaching position at UCLA, accepted, and then several days later, declined the offer. He claimed he wanted to stay with his national championship team and repeat that performance. Shinn demands loyalty and forthrightness. When Brown changed his mind about the UCLA offer, many knew there would not be a place in the Hornets organization for him. Several weeks later he accepted the head coaching position with the San Antonio Spurs.

Dick Harter, previously an assistant coach for the Detroit Pistons and then the Indiana Pacers of the NBA, was selected as the first Hornets head coach. His seventeen-year college coaching career included positions as head coach at Penn State (1978–1983), Oregon (1971–1978), University of Pennsylvania (1966–1971), and Rider College (1965–1966).

The Team

Harter, Shinn, Sheer, and Littles, with recommendations from the scouts, selected the team from the expansion draft, the college draft, free agents, and trades. Each of the existing NBA teams could protect eight of their twelve players from the expansion team draft. A coin toss determined whether Charlotte or Miami would be the first to select in the expansion draft or the college draft. When Charlotte won the coin toss, the staff decided to take first choice in the college draft (which was actually the eighth choice after choices by the seven regular teams that did not make the play-offs). Miami then had the first choice in the expansion draft.

Various strategies for developing an expansion team are debated. One school of thought is to go for young, inexperienced players and "grow your own" team. Obviously this strategy will mean that the first season will have few wins. Poorer performance by rookies may mean loss of attendance and fan support, but may be the better long-range strategy. The opposing viewpoint is to trade and pay for veterans who will be able to win at least some games in the first season. The weakness of this strategy is that veteran players in the NBA do not play that many seasons before they retire. A six-year veteran may only play a few more years, and then new players must be recruited.

The Hornets team was selected on the basis of being clean cut, hard working on the court, and active in the community. Two veteran free agents were signed: Kurt Rambis of the LA Lakers and Earl Cureton of the LA Clippers. Robert Reid was obtained in a trade from the Houston Rockets for Bernard Thompson (obtained in the expansion draft from the Phoenix Suns) and a 1990 second-round draft choice. Kelly Tripucka was obtained in a trade from the Utah Jazz for Michael Brown (obtained in the expansion draft from the Chicago Bulls).

Tyrone Bogues (Washington Bullets), Dell Curry (Cleveland Cavaliers),

Rickey Green (Utah Jazz), Michael Holton (Portland Trail Blazers), David Hoppen (Golden State Warriors), and Ralph Lewis (Detroit Pistons) were selected in the expansion draft.

Rex Chapman (University of Kentucky) was the Hornets' first-round college draft choice (eighth pick) and Tom Tolbert (Arizona) was the second-round choice (34th pick). Tim Kempton and Brian Rowsom were signed as free agents after the Hornets preseason camp. Both had played in Europe the previous season.

The Hornets as a Business

The financial outlook for the Hornets' first year was considered impressive by expansion team standards. Benefitting from the $1 per game coliseum rental and the salary cap, the Hornets expect revenues to exceed expenses by $3.93 million, although the interest on one-half of the $32.5 million franchise fee which was borrowed was not included (Exhibit 1-7).

It has been estimated that the Hornets passed up $3.6 million in concession and parking revenues for the five-year $1 per game coliseum rental. According to George Shinn, "A good deal is a good deal for everyone involved." The $1 a game rental for the coliseum is estimated to be approximately $500,000 a year savings for the Hornets.

The NBA has mandated a $4.6 million cap on player salaries for the 1988–1989 expansion teams for two years to facilitate early profitable operations. Veteran teams have salaries capped at $6.7 million for the 1988–1989 season. However, some teams, such as the LA Lakers, have much higher salaries due to the grandfather

---

Exhibit 1-7   **Charlotte Hornets Projected Revenue and Expenses 1988–1989 (In millions)**

Revenue	
Season ticket sales	$ 9.84
Individual ticket sales	1.97
National/cable TV	2.72
Local TV	1.5
Coliseum signage	.9
Total revenue	$16.93
Expenses	
Player salaries	$4.6
Coaching staff salaries	
Administrative staff salaries	
Travel expenses	8.4
Marketing/advertising	
Miscellaneous	
Total expenses	$13.0

clause for superstars already on the payroll when the cap went into effect. Charlotte's salaries can rise to the cap of veteran teams by the third season (1990–1991).

During the off-season and before the start of the 1988–1989 season, the NBA negotiated major new television contracts with CBS-TV and Ted Turner's "Superstation" WTBS cable (Exhibit 1-8). The WTBS contract called for $23 million to be split equally among the 25 teams (including Charlotte and Miami) during the 1988–1989 season. During the 1989–1990 season, WTBS will split $27 million among the 27 teams (includes the two newer expansion teams, Minneapolis and Orlando).

The average NBA franchise can expect to earn 60 percent of its revenue through ticket sales and the remainder from the franchise's share of league licensing of broadcast advertising sponsorship rights.

Additional revenue can be generated by the sale of advertising space within the coliseum, sponsorship of promotional nights, souvenirs, and advertising space in the Charlotte Hornets' magazine *The Sting*.

Doing Things Right

It had been a long, busy, but satisfying day. George Shinn looked around the now-deserted coliseum. "It would have been really great if we won our first game, but at least we have a team and the opening night is behind us," he thought. "On to the next game." He remembered Carl Sheer's recent comment.

"It takes no genius to do the business we'll do in year one," Sheer had said. "We have to sustain the initial interest and enthusiasm we've had early on. . . ."

Shinn walked toward the exit and contemplated the future of his franchise. "Really, the first phase is over," he thought. "We need to enter a new phase. It's more than just maintaining momentum . . . The Hornets must be run like a business. A fun and exciting business, but a business nonetheless. We must not only do the right thing, we've got to do things right. It's time to determine where we want to go with this thing and focus on the three or four critical factors for success. We need an innovative strategy for sustained growth."

He turned around and gazed at the coliseum floor, the "Home of the Charlotte Hornets," but his thoughts went beyond the Hornets. "For the last couple of years we have been so focused on getting this franchise that we haven't really devel-

---

Exhibit 1-8   **Broadcast Revenue for the Hornets' 1988–1989 Season**

NBA (per team)	
CBS-TV	$1.8 million
WTBS-Cable TV	$0.92 million
Local broadcast	
WCCB	$1–1.5 million

oped and communicated a broader vision of the future for our management team, employees, fans, or for that matter, the public.''

"What should we be doing five years from now? Should I get into some other form of entertainment? Baseball after all is my favorite sport and it's becoming profitable again. An NFL franchise is still a possibility. Nothing is really out of the question.''

Shinn once more headed for the door. "It's late. . . . Tomorrow we'll make time to think about the future." He left the coliseum with innovative ideas swirling in his head, ideas for initiatives to make his dreams reality.

Case 2

Chrysler: The Road Back

INTRODUCTION: THE CHRYSLER CRISIS

In August 1979 Chrysler's market share had fallen by almost one-and-a-half percent over a two-year period. The inventory of large, unsold automobiles had grown considerably. Furthermore, a huge loss of $700 million was expected by the end of 1979. The situation for Chrysler was desperate; cash flow was a serious problem.

What the nation observed at this time was a startling departure from political convention. The American public and government representatives were shocked when Chrysler petitioned the United States government for $1 billion in aid through the Treasury Department.

After several months of negotiation, Chrysler submitted a plan that included an aggregate of non-federally guaranteed assistance of $1.43 billion. In response, Congressional and administration leaders agreed to a total of $1.2 billion in federal loan guarantees and created the Loan Guarantee Board to oversee specific activities. President Carter signed the Loan Guarantee Act in December 1979.

This case was prepared by Cyril C. Ling of the University of Wisconsin–Whitewater with the assistance of Kathleen Kautzer, Anne Lowder, Marie Marx, Randish Uppal, and Donna Verhein, as a basis for class discussion rather than to illustrate either effective or ineffective handling of an administrative situation. Used by permission from Cyril C. Ling.

TERMS OF THE LOAN GUARANTEE ACT

The Chrysler Corporation Loan Guarantee Act of 1979, enacted after intense debate and much opposition, provided aid subject to certain conditions.

The following is a summary of the conditions.

1. Chrysler Corporation had to give proof that there was no plan for it to be absorbed by or merged with any foreign entity; in addition, it was to be shown that the prospective earning power of the company reasonably assured payment of the interest-bearing loan on or before December 31, 1990.

2. The federal loans had to be matched by at least $1.43 billion of non-federally guaranteed assistance from the following:

   A. Concessions from parties with an existing economic stake, namely:
      - Employees represented by labor unions would take wage and benefit reductions totalling $462.5 million over a three-year period.
      - Employees not represented by a labor organization would accept at least $125 million reduction in wages and benefits.
      - Suppliers and creditors would waive their rights under any prior commitment unless approved by the Loan Board.

   B. Capital obtained from sale of securities.

   C. Cash obtained from the disposition of company assets.

   D. Issuance of common stock to employees and labor organizations connected with the company.

3. Chrysler Corporation was required to pay out an annual guarantee fee sufficient to compensate for specified administrative expenses incurred by the government. In addition, Chrysler was required to share a portion of its gains with the government in the form of warrants.

4. Any major changes in the operating or financing plan of the company required approval by the Loan Board.

5. The Department of Transportation was directed to do a long-term planning study to assess the auto industry as a whole and Chrysler Corporation's viability in the industry. It would then report directly to the Loan Board.

Passage of this plan to assist Chrysler was due in large part to the forceful efforts of chief executive Lido Anthony Iacocca.

LEE IACOCCA: MANAGERIAL IMPACT ON CHRYSLER

Lee Iacocca was hired as president of Chrysler Corporation by Chairman John Riccardo in late 1978. Iacocca had established himself as an effective communicator as well as a highly regarded product developer and marketer. Throughout his career at Ford, Iacocca took advantage of opportunities, being willing to accept risk to get ahead. This self-confidence had made him a convincing salesman, not only of cars but also of ideas.

Throughout the crisis of 1978–1979, Lee Iacocca became increasingly associated with Chrysler's viability in the automobile industry. His magnetic, direct, and dominant personality was an important force in dealing with the government, employees, creditors, suppliers, dealers, and labor organizations.

Iacocca's first priority was to concentrate on the K-cars, due out in 1980. He put three retired Ford colleagues in charge of product planning, purchasing, and quality control. He also separated manufacturing from sales and product development in order to better assess each department. Then, he turned to staffing concerns.

At the beginning of his car career, Iacocca adopted a tough approach toward subordinates, evaluating performance records and demanding improvement whenever necessary. This eventually led to the quarterly review in which he constantly graded and reviewed performance based on the goals set for the various managers. Each manager received thorough criticism if goals were not met. While at Ford, Iacocca had recorded these quarterly review evaluations. When he left Ford, he was allowed to take his personal papers, these reviews included. He relied on these data to select key staff for Chrysler, starting with his finance executive, followed by sales, public relations, and manufacturing managers. Coupled with this information was Iacocca's salesmanship, enabling him to persuade several excellent executives to join a company that faced an enormous loss and a questionable future. With a new management team, Iacocca then began to centralize the operations, specialize the staff, and reduce the staff by approximately 8,500 white-collar workers.

The next problem addressed was the enormous buildup in car inventory. Iacocca informed dealers they would have to help get rid of the inventories. They would no longer be able to pick and choose the cars they wanted. Also, Iacocca became involved at dealer meetings and conventions and became more responsive to dealer suggestions.

Lee Iacocca thus started to bring order and control into the "helter-skelter" manner in which Chrysler had been operating. For example, before Iacocca stepped in, the comptroller had allowed twenty-five different departments to handle billing, making it nearly impossible to calculate costs accurately. The problem was most serious in regard to warranties. The company had no clear idea how much money was being paid on the warranties. Further, there was no systematic communication back through quality control to manufacturing and, consequently, no improvement of the product. Even worse, budget averages went uncontrolled.

After passage of the Loan Guarantee Act, Chrysler's financial crisis was lessened, but obtaining the concessions necessary under the Act was difficult. At first, the banks were unwilling to extend credit to Chrysler, but they conceded when Iacocca pointed out that their failure to do so would cause Chrysler to file Chapter Eleven. Iacocca was a consummate opportunist when it came to exploiting the fear of bankruptcy, and he used this technique on creditors and suppliers many times.

Iacocca was a forceful speaker and soon began to appear in commercials promoting Chrysler products. Sales started to rise. Surveys showed that buyers were becoming converts due to their increasing faith in the credibility of Iacocca.

Under Iacocca's guidance, in late 1982 (fourth quarter), Chrysler showed its first net profit in five years; in 1983 it repaid the $1.2 billion in guaranteed loans and bought back the government's warrants for $311 million.

PRODUCTS, MARKETING, AND TECHNOLOGY

The marketing strategies used by Chrysler since 1980 have concentrated on quality, performance, and value, the key concerns of a customer buying a car or truck today, according to industry market research studies.

Products

Chrysler's strategy of reducing costs was met by using its K-car as a foundation for future models. Virtually all of its other cars were derived from the K-car's platform, including the LeBaron, Chrysler E Class, Dodge 600, the New Yorker, and to a smaller degree its GT-type cars, Dodge Daytona and Chrysler Laser. This technique saved the company money and allowed more efficient use of technical resources.

Chrysler did well by developing autos for special market segments. These "niche" cars, as they are known in Detroit, competed in small but profitable markets where other automakers were not as numerous. The introduction in 1982 of the Chrysler and Dodge convertibles was just one example of this tactic. From 1976, when American producers stopped convertible production, only very expensive imported convertibles were available to consumers. Contrary to the views of other Detroit automakers that Chrysler's convertible was just a fad, the new product was successful. Industry researchers predicted sales to be 3,000 in the first year: 24,000 cars were sold. These results prompted Ford, GM, and AMC to reintroduce convertibles to compete with Chrysler.

Another example of marketing to a small segment was the "minivan." Chrysler again was the first United States company to introduce this product, one year ahead of Ford and almost two years ahead of General Motors. Chrysler researchers observed that families were growing, and education and income levels of these families were rising. These consumers were driving station wagons, sedans, or vans. Accordingly, Chrysler planners developed a vehicle that incorporated the characteristics of all three—space enough for a family, fuel efficiency, the capability to transport goods, and front wheel drive. Chrysler's Dodge Caravan and the Plymouth Voyager captured 52 percent of the market segment.

Another market Chrysler targeted was the "baby boomer" market. These potential customers drove subcompact cars in the 1970s but upscale cars in the 1980s. They, too, were well educated, reasonably affluent, and intensely value conscious.

Furthermore, research suggested they discriminated among products on quality, not price. To aim at their tastes and incomes, Chrysler introduced 4-door sedans that gave the comfort and convenience of American cars with quality and affordability associated with Japanese cars.

Warranties and Incentives

Marketing strategies were also developed to support Chrysler's theme of building the "best quality" cars in America. Each car purchased since 1981 carried a five-year/50,000-mile warranty (increased to 7 years/70,000 miles in 1987). Prior to 1987, no other United States automaker had such an offer on all of its passenger cars. Even today, Chrysler remains the leader in warranty protection plans, although other American producers have increased their coverages substantially.

Instead of offering factory-directed cash rebates, Chrysler began its "Thank You America" campaign in 1985 by mailing a $500 certificate good toward the purchase of a new car or van to all consumers who had purchased one of Chrysler's domestically built vehicles since 1979. Iacocca did not consider this a rebate because it was targeted only to purchasers of a Chrysler product since 1979. This campaign was so successful that a similar campaign, "Thanks Again, America," followed in 1986.

Technology

Another strategy Chrysler followed was to compete in every major segment of the market with contemporary products. To carry out this strategy, Chrysler continued to modernize and build new plants. In 1983, it revised upward its original five-year, $6.5 billion investment plan established in 1980, to $8 billion in order to build and design products that would stay abreast of changing consumer tastes. Again in 1985, Chrysler estimated spending $12.5 billion through 1990 for plant and tooling.

A further step in the area of technology was the Chrysler Pacifica Advanced Product Design Center in California. The center's body shops are completely "robotized." Its plants have advanced automated test equipment and one of the most sophisticated computer-aided design (CAD) systems in the auto industry.

In 1984, its Sterling Heights Assembly Plant was opened; this plant had over 80 robots and over 150 lasers and cameras to inspect the car's body in more than 300 areas. In the late 1970s, Chrysler had, at most, 16 robots in *all* its plants. This plant also began using just-in-time (JIT) delivery to reduce inventory costs and in-line sequencing to assure the quality of the car being produced. By 1988, Chrysler hoped to have these advanced systems in all its plants. Sterling Heights was expanded to produce not only Chrysler's Euro-style, 4-door sedans, the Dodge Lancer, and the Chrysler LeBaron GTS, but also to produce two new subcompacts, the Plymouth Sundance and Dodge Shadow.

A Technology Advisory Council was organized in 1986. The scientists and engineers on the Council collect information from independent sources about new technologies and advise Chrysler people on how to incorporate this data into their products. The results suggest the company's proactive stance on technology has been productive. Concern for modern technology is one important explanation for market share growth from 8.8 percent in 1980 to 11.8 percent in 1985. Also, the company leads the American auto industry in fuel economy and has the lowest safety recall rate among autos built in the period from 1982 to 1984. Chrysler's projected 1984 sales were one million cars; demand pushed sales to 1.8 million.

All of Chrysler's plants have the joint UAW-Chrysler Product Quality Improvement Program which consists of plant-level teams to identify and solve quality problems. Quality training programs are incorporated at plants with the new technology. Technical training at Chrysler Corporation requires approximately 800,000 man-hours a year, almost nine times the amount spent five years ago.

Joint Ventures and Acquisitions

The technological change which Chrysler experienced in the 1980s created the need to look at outside business opportunities to maintain and strengthen its position in the area of technology. This goal has been met through a number of partnerships and joint ventures. Chrysler has strengthened ties with its Japanese partner, Mitsubishi Motors Corporation, by signing a joint venture agreement, under the name Diamond-Star Motors, to produce a new, small auto for the United States market. Production for this new vehicle is to begin in 1988. It also renewed its contract with Mitsubishi to import V-6 engines which will be incorporated in future cars.

In addition to its efforts with Mitsubishi and the creation of Diamond-Star Motors, Chrysler has entered into an agreement with Samsung, a Korean automaker, to manufacture parts and components and has established two important linkages with Italian car companies. Chrysler purchased Lamborghini, a maker of expensive sports and grand touring cars and has purchased a portion of Maserati, which is producing a new two-seat coupe-roadster for Chrysler priced in the $30,000 to $40,000 bracket.

A recent nonautomotive acquisition has both technological and marketing significance. The company purchased Gulfstream Aerospace Corp., a successful builder of corporate jet aircraft and an important defense contractor. Gulfstream was attractive for its technical capabilities, but in addition, it offered Chrysler a two-year backlog of jet orders and reentry to the defense business.

Chrysler's strategy in advertising its automobiles has been aggressive since 1982. Slogans, direct competitive comparisons, special financing, warranty features, and Mr. Iacocca have all been used to attract the public's attention. Like most auto companies, Chrysler advertising used a mix of media but unlike others the company made extensive use of its chief executive in print, television, and occasionally, in person.

PERSONNEL AND LABOR RELATIONS

An important part of Chrysler's survival strategy involved its labor force. One of the first steps the company took to lower expenses was to dramatically reduce its work force. Sixteen of 52 plants were closed. In 1978, the company had 157,000 employees, and in 1983, there were 74,700. The remaining workers were asked to make concessions to enable the company to qualify for the government loan guarantee. The agreement called for union member wage concessions totalling $462.5 million plus an additional $125 million in concessions from nonunion workers. Also, pension fund deferrals totaled $342 million in savings. Ultimately, the wage and benefit sacrifices made by laborers totalled $1.2 billion. The concessions included:

1. Delay of scheduled wage increases.
2. Sacrifice of all paid personal holidays.
3. Temporary forfeiture of cost-of-living adjustments.
4. Deferrals and cuts in pension plans.
5. Sickness and accident insurance benefits frozen until 1982.

These sacrifices created a $2.50 hourly pay differential between Chrysler workers and General Motors and Ford workers. Each employee forfeited roughly $14,500 in wages and benefits.

Chrysler had to agree to certain demands from workers to obtain approval of these concessions. Some of the company concessions agreed to by management were:

1. Labor representation on the board (Douglas Fraser, then president of United Auto Workers [UAW]).
2. Agreement not to invest pension funds in five companies with operations in South Africa.
3. Ten percent of pension funds earmarked for "socially desirable investments" such as residential mortgages, nursing homes, and day care centers in Chrysler communities.
4. Workers age 50 and older displaced by plant closings eligible for early pension benefits.

The agreement had no provision for recovery of lost wages and benefits, but it did promise equality with Ford and General Motors by the time the three-year labor contract expired. Also, workers were granted an equity stake; $250 million in new shares were issued in an employee stock ownership plan. It was hoped that employees who owned a part of the company would feel more a part of the system and would be willing to work harder to further the company. A separate profit-sharing plan was negotiated in 1981 which promised workers stock worth 15 percent of the company's profits beyond a minimum return of net worth. This plan went into effect only when and if Chrysler earned $100 million in one year, and the plan ceased in September 1983.

The wage freeze to which union members agreed saved Chrysler an estimated $800 per car, an improved production cost position vis-à-vis Ford and General Motors. Iacocca's challenge was to maintain these competitive advantages long enough to enable Chrysler to become profitable once again.

Iacocca cut his own salary to $1 in a symbolic gesture, but when his pay was retroactively raised to $324,000 in 1981 as the company's position improved, union workers grew discontented. Two levels of management were awarded perquisites, which was interpreted by union members as a breach of good faith. In retaliation to executive pay and benefit increases, UAW leaders ended a moratorium on authorization of local strikes.

At the 1982 labor contract negotiations, Chrysler sought to limit the cost of health care benefits and to continue to hold down wages, despite its promise to restore parity in three years. Workers, on the other hand, sought to restore the cost-of-living allowance and to reduce the pay gap that existed between Chrysler and Ford and General Motors. Negotiations began in July. In October workers voted on an agreement containing provisions making pay raises contingent upon profits and instituting health care cost controls designed to save the company $10 million by 1983. Health care costs per year per active employee were about $6,000, in contrast to $1,250 for an average U.S. company. But health insurance was so important to union members that the contract was the first major contract to be voted down in UAW history.

Although the company's original plan had been to convince the union that it could not afford an increase, the threat of a strike forced management to rethink its position. Workers were asked to vote for either a strike or a new round of negotiations. Most workers chose a new round, but the Canadian workers struck, costing the company an estimated $15 million. In December an agreement was finally reached to end the five-week strike. United States workers received a $.75/hour increase plus cost-of-living adjustment. Canadian workers received $1.15/hour because of higher inflation rates in Canada. In return for the wage increases, workers forfeited the profit-sharing plan that had been negotiated in 1981. Although health care benefits remained the same, the UAW agreed to eliminate $10 million by curbing abuses in the system. This contract, which cost the company $155 million, expired in January 1984.

A strategic move to prevent Canadian workers from striking during U.S. company-wide negotiations was to alter the contract expiration dates. Chrysler negotiated a three-year U.S. pact and a two-year Canadian pact so that only one union had to be dealt with at a time.

Discontent among workers was triggered again in June 1983 when the company repaid one-third of its government guaranteed loan, seven years early. Pressure was exerted to reopen the contract instead of waiting until October. Workers felt that wage increases would be fair in light of the company's obviously improved cash position.

Lee Iacocca, again concerned about the effects of a strike, agreed to reopen the contract. He calculated that a 60-day strike would bankrupt the company. An agreement which restored $2.42/hour to workers was signed in August and enabled Chrysler to plan on two years of labor stability. It cost the company about $1 billion and raised projected total labor costs 29 percent by 1985.

In order for the company to afford the increases brought about by the 1983 contract, Chrysler had to further improve productivity. Part of this effort came in the form of a new absenteeism policy implemented in 1983. Each employee began with a "clean slate" upon implementation. A six-step process concluded with discharge if an employee was found to be a chronic offender.

A critical diversion of Chrysler's strategy has been to remain less integrated than General Motors or Ford. Chrysler bought 70 percent of its components from outside sources while Ford and General Motors purchased 50 percent and 30 percent, respectively. Wage rates in supplier firms not governed by the UAW contract with automakers were considerably lower. Management used this "outsourcing" technique to encourage workers to increase productivity. When the union demanded higher wages, Chrysler has countered with the threat of outside subcontracting and possibly plant closings or loss of jobs.

Outside sources have also provided the company a stable supply during strikes. Certain parts are made only in Canada; thus, it is important for Chrysler to have other sources so that production in American factories does not have to be interrupted because of a Canadian strike.

The labor contract negotiated in late 1985 demonstrates still another labor strategy which Chrysler has sought to implement. This contract created a pilot program to study more than 50 job classifications at four plants to determine whether reducing this number to six would increase productivity and improve competitiveness. Although the union has long opposed decreasing the number of job classifications, union leaders have come to clearly understand the result of low productivity—increased outside subcontracting.

Management's main goal in the 1985 bargaining sessions was to achieve a three-year contract so that costs would be known for three years instead of two and the contract expiration date would not match that of GM and Ford. Chrysler's success in these negotiations carried a high price—workers won the restoration of an annual improvement factor. This was a three percent across-the-board raise which had been abandoned by all automakers in favor of scaled increases and lump-sum payments. The move alarmed management of other automakers because it was viewed as a separation of performance and profit from wage increases and bonuses.

DEALERS

Dealers' and suppliers' three percent contribution to the aid package came in the form of a purchase of $78 million in convertible debentures. This figure would have been higher, but many of the dealers were near bankruptcy themselves, and thus, reneged on their pledges to purchase the issue.

Lee Iacocca was successful in greatly strengthening Chrysler's dealer base. One thousand of 4,800 outlets were lost in 1979–1980 but 300 new dealers were recruited in 1982. To stimulate dealer wholesale orders, Chrysler introduced incentive programs for dealers, sales managers, and salespeople. In these programs, customers could receive rebates or cash; dealers, sales managers, and salespeople were eligible for cash payments; and sales managers could win trips.

DIVERSIFICATION

To effectively insulate annual earnings and financial health from dependence on worldwide auto sales and to broaden the base of operations and achieve corporate growth, Chrysler embarked on an aggressive diversification campaign. Aerospace technology and financial services were the two principal sectors targeted for expansion.

Entry into the advanced technology arena was accomplished through the purchase of Gulfstream Aerospace Corporation in August 1985 for $654 million. Regardless of the condition of the new car market, Gulfstream's large order backlog for corporate jets would provide an excellent source of revenue for Chrysler in future years. Gulfstream's product line, engineering, design, and manufacturing capabilities would make it feasible for Chrysler to compete successfully as a defense contractor.

Further entry into the financial services sector of the economy was accomplished through the diversification of Chrysler Financial Corporation (CFC), which:

- Purchased EF Hutton Credit Corporation (now Chrysler Capital). The addition of Chrysler Capital enabled Chrysler to finance capital equipment by arranging leases, securing loans, and conditional sales contracts for customers and dealers.
- Purchased Finance American and BA Financial Services (now Chrysler First). The addition of Chrysler First enabled Chrysler to enter the direct consumer lending, private wholesale and retail financing and insurance markets.
- Entered into a joint venture with General Electric Credit Corporation.

As a result of its expansion, CFC became the fourth largest nonbank financial company in the nation. Chrysler Financial plans to achieve annual sales of $25 billion by 1990, with approximately 50 percent of assets and revenue engaged in nonautomotive business equalling the entire current consolidated sales revenue for Chrysler Corporation. Development of CFC will enable Chrysler to enter credit markets on favorable terms and stabilize corporate earnings.

FINANCE

The Year 1983

Chrysler's return to financial health began in 1983. Net sales increased from $10.1 billion in 1982 to $13.3 billion in 1983, an increase of 32 percent. This increase was due, in large part, to improvement in the product mix and modest price increases. The rapid turnover of inventory (far above industry standards) would suggest that the product mix appealed to the consumer. Net income of $700.9 million in 1983 was also 312 percent higher than that reported in 1982.

Chrysler's financial strategy in 1983 was anchored by important shifts in assets and liabilities. The company sold its European operation to Peugeot, invested substantially in plant modernization in St. Louis and Windsor, and reduced interest burden by early repayment of $1.2 billion of guaranteed loans. The size of the work force was reduced and brought additional savings in benefit and pension costs. Debt was restricted, Chrysler Defense was sold to improve liquidity, and preferred stock was reduced to eliminate the future drain of dividend payments. Continued efforts to reduce inventories, manufacturing costs, and number of employees succeeded in bringing the break-even point down from 2.3 million units to 1.1 million units.

The Year 1984

In 1984 Chrysler had another year of prosperity. Net income was $2.38 billion (240 percent above the 1983 net income level). Chrysler's real success was illustrated when various measures of profitability (return on sales, return on assets, and return on net worth) were compared with industry standards. In all cases, Chrysler had consistently outperformed the rest of the industry. Rapid inventory turnover (also well above industry norms) indicated that Chrysler continued to identify and supply what consumers wanted to buy.

Financial strategies continued to focus on reduction of debt made possible by improved earnings; reduction of inventories through JIT techniques and improved coordination with suppliers; improved relationships between interest income and interest expense; further plant modernization (including opening of the new Sterling Heights plant) bringing increased depreciation benefits; new credit arrangements to strengthen working capital; and the purchase of a share of Maserati, the Italian car maker.

The Year 1985

Another record year was established in 1985 when net sales were 9 percent ahead of 1984 net sales. Record earnings were due to an increase in worldwide sales, improvement in product mix, moderate price increases, and consolidated sales from

Gulfstream Aerospace. Chrysler remained more profitable than the rest of the industry measured by return on sales, assets, and net worth.

As a result of strengthening the balance sheet and improving overall corporate financial health in 1983 and 1984, Chrysler was in a position to capture additional market share. This more aggressive posture was most clearly illustrated in the significant increase in investments in associated companies and unconsolidated subsidiaries. There was an increase of approximately 6 percent from 1984 to 1985. The increase was due to investments made in the following areas:

1. Increase of equity holding in Mitsubishi Motors. The number of cars and engines to be imported by Chrysler would be increased.
2. Formation of a joint venture with Mitsubishi (called Diamond-Star Motors) to produce 180,000 small cars in the United States.
3. Formation of a joint venture with Samsung of Korea to provide low-cost, high-quality parts and components.
4. Formation of a joint venture with Maserati Motors to import a luxury sports car.
5. Formation of a joint venture with Lotus Cars Ltd. to develop a 16-valve engine.

Establishment of the various joint ventures along with the increase in domestic research and development expenses and design work positions the company to be more competitive in a variety of market segments, from subcompact economy model to full-size luxury car.

Due to Chrysler's previous rapid repayment and restructuring of long-term debt, the company has been able to releverage itself under a more favorable interest rate structure. During 1985, Chrysler issued $1.83 billion in long-term debt. At first glance it may appear that this was contrary to one of the strategies listed earlier. However, the proceeds from the long-term debt were used to help implement two other strategies, namely:

1. Increase production efficiency and product quality.
2. Diversify into nonautomotive related businesses.

Production efficiency and product quality were enhanced by the continued modernization or expansion of plants. This effort included:

- Dodge City Plant in Warren, Michigan ($500 million).
- Sterling Heights Plant in Sterling, Michigan ($160 million).
- Kokomo Transmission/Casting Plant in Kokomo, Indiana ($350 million).
- Trenton Engine Plant in Trenton, Michigan ($150 million).
- Outer Drive Tech Center in Detroit, Michigan ($58 million).
- McGraw Glass Plant in Detroit, Michigan ($53 million).

The net working capital position of the firm was enhanced in 1985. This is evidenced when comparing Chrysler's sales to net working capital ratios between

1984 and 1985 with the rest of the industry. Working capital was increased due to the issuance of long-term debt, increased sales, and use of revolving credit lines. The level of inventories on hand continued to drop as more production facilities switched to JIT inventory management.

Cost of goods manufactured increased during the year due to two factors:

1. Modernization and retooling of plants. Some of the cost had to be absorbed as overhead.
2. Increase in labor rates. The agreement with the UAW (signed in 1983) was in effect during 1985 and added $1 billion to the cost of wages and benefits.

Increases in the cost of manufacturing put additional pressure on the break-even point and profitability. For the break-even point to be maintained at 1.2 million units, increases in labor and overhead costs had to be offset by increases in sales, efficiency, and quality of materials.

Income tax expense increased in 1985. Because all the tax loss carryforwards had been used in 1984, no portion of the 1985 net income could be offset by prior losses. However, a portion of the net income was offset with investment tax credit carryforwards. Tax consequence had to become a consideration in strategic planning for Chrysler once again.

The Year 1986

Chrysler Corporation's continued growth reached a record $22.59 billion in sales in 1986, a 6.26 percent increase over 1985. Growth was attributed to continued expansion in the product mix and the use of sales incentives. In the U.S., market share increased from 11.4 to 11.7 percent of the U.S. retail car and truck market. Chrysler's share of the North American truck market reached 12.3 percent. Chrysler was the only one of the big three automakers to increase its market share in 1986; however, net earnings fell to $1.4 billion as compared with $1.64 billion in 1985. Return on equity fell to 26.3 percent, net profit on sales decreased to 6.2 percent, and return on assets decreased for the second consecutive year to 9.7 percent.

To meet its five-year $12.5 billion modernization plan, Chrysler invested over $3 billion in capital improvements in 1986. Major expenditures included:

- Chrysler Technology Center in Auburn Hills, Michigan ($675 million).
- Sterling Heights Assembly Plant, Sterling, Michigan ($577 million).
- Dodge City Truck Assembly Plant in Warren, Michigan ($490 million).
- St. Louis II Assembly Plant in St. Louis, Missouri ($475 million).
- St. Louis I Plant in St. Louis, Missouri ($455 million).
- Trenton Engine Plant, Trenton, Michigan ($280 million).
- Mountain Road Engine Plant, Detroit, Michigan ($70 million).
- Outer Drive Manufacturing Tech Center in Detroit, Michigan ($56 million).
- McGraw Glass Plant in Detroit, Michigan ($41 million).

The Liberty Project, designed to reduce the cost of each vehicle manufactured by $2,500, continued in 1986. Part of this project included the company's own component business operations (CBO) supplier plant group which competed with other suppliers for Chrysler business. Seventy percent of Chrysler's parts were sourced from outside suppliers, while GM sourced 30 percent and Ford 50 percent. This enabled Chrysler to remain flexible and to develop close, long-term supplier relationships, supporting the JIT program's success.

To achieve the goal of market share expansion, Chrysler executed several aggressive strategies. The company introduced the new luxury LeBaron Coupe and Convertible, Plymouth Sundance and Dodge Shadow sport sedans, and the Dodge Dakota (which was the first midsize pickup offered by any manufacturer). Additionally the sticker prices on the Dodge Omni and Plymouth Horizon were reduced $700 to undercut comparable Japanese models. Later, in response to the low financing rate offered by other manufacturers, Chrysler offered as low as 2.4 percent APR financing and provided customers with a rebate plan option if they desired to purchase with cash.

The CFC became North America's fourth largest nonbank finance company as it achieved record net earnings of $200 million, a 30 percent increase over 1985. Its diversified portfolio contributed to earnings and was expected to enhance future stability.

Gulfstream Aerospace became one of the aviation industry's most profitable companies. Chrysler expected to benefit greatly in 1987 from the advance orders placed in 1986 for Gulfstream IV aircraft. The level of the advance orders set an aviation record for dollar value.

Chrysler divested itself of Peugeot S.A. and posted a net-of-tax gain of $132 million.

In 1986, the company's break-even point increased to 1.4 million units, which Chrysler attributed to the capital investment program.

The Year 1987

The Chrysler Corporation again achieved record sales with a 16.3 percent increase over 1986 to $26.28 billion. Contributing factors included the additional sales from newly acquired American Motors Corporation (AMC), higher average price per vehicle, and increased revenue from Gulfstream Aerospace. According to Ward's 1988 Automotive Yearbook, whereas 1986 share had remained steady (cars and trucks combined), 1987 share rose to 13.29 percent. The North American truck market share increased to 19 percent (both figures include the postacquisition AMC sales). However, net profit ($1.29 billion) decreased for the third consecutive year as did return on equity (19.83%), return on assets (6.47%), and profit margin on sales.

Chrysler revised its capital spending plan slightly for the period from 1988 to 1992 with a budget projected to exceed $14 billion. The company made several major acquisitions in 1987: American Motors Corporation, Electrospace Systems, and Lamborghini. American Motors (AMC) was acquired to strengthen the company's product mix and manufacturing flexibility. Electrospace and Gulfstream were expected to enter into joint ventures in both technology markets and government contracts. The Italian automaker, Lamborghini, was acquired to complement Chrysler's upscale product strategy.

Chrysler and AMC jointly developed and marketed the Eagle, the first new automotive division introduced by a U.S. company in thirteen years. The midsize Eagle Premier, and the full-size New Yorker, New Yorker Landau, and Dodge Dynasty were introduced and positioned for the upscale market. The Dodge truck line experienced strong continued demand and benefitted from the acquisition of the Jeep brand.

Chrysler Financial Corporation posted record net earnings of $225.8 million, an increase of 12.9 percent. Gulfstream Aerospace continued operating in a strong marketplace as advance orders totaled $1.2 billion for the Gulfstream IV and military defense contracts.

After the acquisitions of AMC and Lamborghini, Chrysler's break-even point rose to 1.8 million units, which is approximately 73 percent of the full year combined unit sales from the consolidated motors groups, a level too high for Chrysler to safely sustain over a period of years. (The company's postbailout break-even had been cut to 1.1 million units and AMC's 1986 production was less than 300,000 units.)

A LOOK TO FUTURE OBJECTIVES

Chrysler is seen as pursuing its unique "idea" of what an American car company should be. It has been offering fewer nameplates and resisting the temptation to grow just for growth's sake. This was reflected clearly in Iacocca's own words when he said, "We can be a first-rate company as long as we respect our size and don't try to have any delusions of grandeur."

Resourcefulness is one of the key strategies that helped Chrysler get through the recent troubled years. For instance, when Chrysler contracted with American Motors, which had excess capacity, to build the Gran Fury, Diplomat, and Fifth Avenue cars, it was using its own St. Louis plant to make longer versions of its popular minivans, the Plymouth Voyager and Dodge Caravan. According to one observer, the payoff for this resourcefulness was that Chrysler could build cars in its United States plants up to $500 cheaper than that of their rivals.

The company will continue to avoid building more plants for several reasons. First, the existing joint venture with Mitsubishi in central Illinois will be on-line in 1988 with capacity for 180,000 vehicles. Second, counting both foreign and domestic producers, substantial excess capacity will exist in the industry in the United States by the start of the next decade. Third, and possibly, most obvious, the purchase of

AMC provides Chrysler with substantial capacity for new as well as current products.

In a further attempt to use domestic capacity efficiently and avoid adding risky new capacity, Chrysler plans to reenter the European market by building cars in the U.S. or by leasing space in Europe. Chrysler has claimed that it has already pulled ahead of the European car makers by cutting 25 hours from the time needed to build a car. This means that Chrysler has cut in half the advantage that was enjoyed by Japanese car makers, and it plans to be on par with Japanese costs by 1990. Chrysler's immediate hopes for Europe are quite conservative. Robert A. Lutz, who joined Chrysler as executive vice-president in June 1986, and who headed Ford in Europe, implied that there was no compelling strategic or tactical incentive for Chrysler to broaden its base beyond the United States, but that it would serve as a good insurance policy to cover all eventualities.

In the more immediate future Chrysler is looking toward exploiting its hard-won position in the United States. Since fierce price-cutting and financing incentives resulted in lower earnings in the first half of 1986, changing the product mix to more expensive, higher margin cars became an important strategy. For example, the 1987 models included the sporty Shadow and Sundance compacts, "stretched" minivans, and a midsize Le Baron sports coupe and convertible; by the end of 1987, the new $30,000 plus sports car by Maserati (actually delayed until 1989 by the break between Chrysler and Maserati); and in 1988 the new Chrysler and Dodge luxury sedans. By 1990, the Imperial nameplate will likely reappear in the company's line on a stretched New Yorker. To focus this domestic attack, Chrysler has realigned its product development and marketing staffs. The mandate for the future is to develop and market vehicles around key themes for each line: Plymouth for value and integrity, Dodge for performance, Chrysler for luxury and comfort, and Dodge trucks for quality and toughness.

Chrysler's present businesses are divided into three operating subsidiaries: automotive, financial, and aerospace. Chairman Iacocca is forming a fourth unit— Chrysler Technologies Corporation. The ideal target is a defense company costing $1 billion or less. This new unit is being created out of existing high-tech operations within the company. Iacocca plans to capitalize the new organization with approximately $1 billion and give it the autonomy to develop its own strategy and identify potential takeover candidates.

Chrysler Financial Corporation also sees a promising future. In 1983, CFC was a $5 billion subsidiary wholly dedicated to financing cars and trucks. By 1986, it was almost four times that size and offered much broader commercial and retail services. Robert S. Miller, Jr., the chairman of this subsidiary, expects to expand the company by a further 50 percent, to $30 billion in assets, by 1990. Most of this expansion is to come from nonautomotive business.

The goal that has been dubbed the Liberty Project is to slash manufacturing costs by 30 percent or $2,500 per car, by 1995. Most of Chrysler's current cost advantage comes from "shopping" for cheap services and components rather than making parts internally.

AMERICAN MOTORS CORPORATION

Chrysler and AMC had continued negotiations from late 1986 into 1987 in an attempt to expand production at the Kenosha plant to include Omni and Horizon models. Talks broke down frequently and the governor of Wisconsin, Tommy Thompson, intervened to keep the parties together. Just as negotiations were about to cease for what appeared to be the final time, Chrysler announced its intention to purchase AMC by acquiring the 46 percent interest of Renault and exchanging stock for other AMC shares.

The acquisition has matched well with existing Chrysler strategy—improving plant and technology and strengthening product lines. Essentially, Chrysler bought AMC productive capacity and the Jeep product line. The AMC facilities have added between 850,000 and 900,000 units annually to Chrysler's capacity. Approximately 100,000 units were already devoted to Chrysler rear-drive models at Kenosha. The Kenosha facilities (230,000 capacity) and the Toledo Jeep plant (280,000 capacity) were built decades ago and are difficult to improve; however, the new Bramalea, Ontario plant (150,000 capacity) has been regarded by experts to be the most modern production facility in North America. It will be devoted to production of the Renault Premier for at least a few years while Chrysler faces decisions on the older plants, whether (and how) to make them suitable for the intermediate term.

The Jeep product line has been an important and interesting acquisition for Chrysler. The company was probably the only one of the big three automakers that could truly benefit from the acquisition—both Ford and GM already had solidly established truck lines. The identity of the Jeep product has been well established—the nameplate goes back over forty years to World II—and the line has been redesigned with a new, larger capacity cylinder engine.

Chrysler-Plymouth dealers have been handling Renault Medallion and Premier lines, and Dodge dealers have handled Jeep along with Dodge trucks and Mitsubishi 4WD lines. When the new Chrysler/Maserati TC appears, it will replace the cancelled Renault Alpine as the "sport" category leader for the company. The Alliance ceased production in Kenosha, and Chrysler continued rear-drive model production for a time. The facilities have been redesigned for limited engine manufacturing in the near future.

The total acquisition cost of approximately $1.2 billion included Renault's 46 percent (at $9.50/share), other outstanding shares, plus bonds and cash. For that substantial price of admission, Chrysler gets to attack numerous challenges such as old plants; the selling of Renault products which have never been especially successful in the United States; working out with the UAW simplified labor agreements for

Exhibit 2-1 Chrysler Corporation and Consolidated Subsidiaries Balance Sheets, 1982–1987 (In millions)

Assets	Dec. 31, 1982	Dec. 31, 1983	Dec. 31, 1984	Dec. 31, 1985	Dec. 31, 1986	Dec. 31, 1987
Current Assets						
Cash and time deposits	$ 109.7	$ 111.6	$ 75.2	$ 147.6	$ 285.1	$ 355.4
Marketable securities	787.5	957.8	1,624.9	2,649.9	2,394.3	2,054.6
Net accounts receivable	247.9	291.2	332.2	207.5	372.5	577.6
Inventories	1,133.0	1,301.4	1,625.9	1,862.7	1,699.6	2,552.1
Prepaid pension expense	—	—	243.0	260.0	348.9	54.1
Prepaid insurance, taxes and other expenses	91.0	91.8	78.7	185.8	263.6	577.0
Total Current Assets	2,369.1	2,753.8	3,979.9	5,313.5	5,364.0	6,170.8
Investments and Other Assets						
Investments in associated companies	352.4	128.5	128.5	283.0	317.7	371.8
Investments in and advances to unconsolidated subsidiaries	886.0	733.8	1,112.4	1,787.4	1,989.6	2,349.1
Intangible assets	—	—	—	—	386.6	2,136.7
Other noncurrent assets	182.3	101.2	128.7	581.8	287.5	604.3
Total Investments and Other Assets	1,420.7	963.5	1,369.6	2,652.2	2,981.4	5,461.9
Property, Plant and Equipment						
Land, buildings, machinery and equipment	3,950.6	4,469.8	5,163.8	5,942.0	7,081.5	8,938.9
Less accumulated depreciation	2,255.2	2,334.0	2,534.5	2,664.8	2,767.5	3,089.8
	1,695.4	2,135.8	2,629.3	3,277.2	4,314.0	5,849.1
Unamortized special tools	778.3	919.2	1,083.9	1,362.4	1,803.8	2,462.8

…property, plant and equipment	8,311.9	6,117.8	4,639.6	3,713.2	3,055.0	2,473.7
Total Assets	$19,944.6	$14,463.2	$12,605.3	$9,062.7	$6,772.3	$6,263.5
Liabilities and Stockholders' Equity						
Current Liabilities						
Accounts payable—trade and other	$ 3,721.7	$ 2,958.3	$ 2,504.5	$2,323.0	$1,628.7	$ 897.8
Short-term debt	73.4	82.2	195.3	6.7	361.1	79.4
Payments due within one year on long-term debt	211.9	119.8	101.6	42.8	55.7	21.0
Accrued liabilities and expenses	2,630.9	1,960.7	1,927.8	1,743.2	1,408.4	1,114.4
Total Current Liabilities	6,637.9	5,121.0	4,729.2	4,115.7	3,453.9	2,112.6
Other Liabilities						
Accrued employee benefits	749.3	289.6	298.4	362.3	417.6	635.7
Other noncurrent liabilities	1,525.5	661.3	604.5	497.0	431.5	335.1
Deferred taxes on income	1,195.8	712.4	391.8	21.7	—	—
Total other liabilities	3,470.6	1,663.3	1,294.7	881.0	849.1	970.8
Long-term debt	3,333.2	2,334.1	2,366.1	760.1	1,104.0	2,189.0
Shareholder's Equity						
Preferred stock	.3	—	—	—	225.0	1,320.9
Common stock	244.7	229.8	153.2	123.9	121.8	501.4
Additional paid-in capital	2,374.3	1,866.6	1,943.2	2,325.3	2,276.4	692.5
Retained earnings (deficit)	4,581.3	3,503.9	2,153.3	921.2	(1,255.1)	(1,523.7)
Treasury stock	(697.7)	(319.1)	(34.4)	(64.5)	2.8	—
Total Shareholder's Equity	6,502.9	5,281.2	4,215.3	3,305.9	1,365.3	991.1
Total Liabilities and Shareholder's Equity	$19,944.6	$14,399.6	$12,605.3	$9,062.7	$6,772.3	$6,263.5

35

Exhibit 2-2 Chrysler Corporation Consolidated Statement of Earnings, 1982–1987 (In millions)

	1982	1983	1984	1985	1986	1987
Net sales	$10,056.5	$13,263.8	$19,572.7	$21,255.5	$22,586.3	$26,276.5
Equity in earnings of unconsolidated subsidiaries	(5.8)	90.8	126.1	255.9	298.6	348.9
Other income	19.6	32.9	18.4	41.7	120.7	6.1
Total Net Revenue	10,070.3	13,387.5	19,717.2	21,553.1	23,005.6	26,631.5
Costs, other than items below	8,606.2	10,861.2	15,528.2	17,467.7	18,635.2	21,301.8
Depreciation	195.9	183.3	271.6	263.7	236.8	463.7
Amortization of special tools	236.7	273.9	282.8	212.6	306.8	411.5
Selling and administrative expenses	669.8	804.9	987.7	1,144.4	1,376.8	1,634.3
Pension plans	271.7	254.7	267.3	219.8	236.3	470.3
Interest (income) expense—net	158.0	82.1	(50.7)	(124.9)	32.7	170.2
Gain on sale of investment in Peugeot, S.A.	—	—	—	—	(144.3)	—
Total Net Costs	10,138.3	12,460.1	17,286.9	19,183.3	20,680.3	24,451.8
Operating earnings (loss)	(68.0)	927.4	2,430.3	2,369.8	2,325.3	2,179.7
Writedown of investment in Peugeot, S.A.	—	223.9	—	—	—	—
Earnings (loss) from continuing operations before taxes and extraordinary items	(68.0)	703.5	2,430.3	2,369.8	2,325.3	2,179.7
Taxes on income	.9	401.6	934.2	734.6	921.7	890.0
Earnings (loss) from continuing operations	(68.9)	301.9	1,496.1	1,635.2	1,403.6	1,289.7
Gain on sale of Chrysler Defense, Inc. (net of $66 million of taxes)	172.1	—	—	—	—	—
Earnings before extraordinary items	103.2	301.0	1,496.1	1,635.2	1,403.6	1,289.7
Extraordinary item effect of utilization of tax loss carry forwards	66.9	399.9	883.9	—	—	—
Net Earnings	$170.1	$700.9	$2,380.0	$1,635.2	$1,403.6	$1,289.7

the AMC facilities; marketing the Jeep abroad; and integrating former AMC President Joseph Cappy into Chrysler operations.

SOME POTENTIAL PROBLEMS

If these challenges are not sufficient, Chrysler is significantly more dependent on the North American car buyer than General Motors and Ford. It expects some 97 percent of its sales revenues to come from the United States and Canada. Although Chrysler has increased its share in Mitsubishi Motors Corporation from 15 percent to 24 percent and expects to acquire Maserati by 1995, it still lacks the worldwide cushions of Ford and General Motors. This obstacle is further intensified by Iacocca's plan *not* to alter Chrysler's geographical focus. He has declared that Chrysler is not interested in "playing conglomerate" and becoming a large global company.

Chrysler is planning to spend $12.5 billion developing new vehicles and overhauling plants by 1990. The company plans to do this without borrowing, despite the industry-wide sales slump analysts are expecting in late 1988 or 1989. Furthermore, the company has to match Japanese production costs, regardless of whether the dollar is strong or weak against the yen.

Chrysler has yet to achieve customer satisfaction levels associated with that of Japanese cars. This could take many years since the Japanese producers are shifting toward the high end of the market at the same pace as Chrysler. There is a prediction from the Motor Vehicle Program at the Massachusetts Institute of Technology that a collision will take place in the late 1980s when Japan's United States-based auto plants begin to bring out more than a million upscale vehicles of their own each year. This competitive threat will receive significant attention from all of the big three auto firms in the United States.

Clearly, Iacocca and Chrysler are moving beyond survival to a more secure, profitable niche in an industry where the competition comes from every corner of the globe. The long-run success of Chrysler, however, will depend on the approach and success Chrysler management can bring to the broad array of challenges it faces.

FARED Robot Systems, Inc.

THE COMPANY

FARED Robot Systems, Inc., was incorporated in the state of Colorado on May 20, 1981, to provide consulting services to industrial customers who wished to adapt robotics technology to their manufacturing processes. (The name of the company is an acronym for *F*lexible *A*utomation, *R*obotic *E*ngineering, and *D*istribution.)

FARED quickly learned that customers were less interested in learning from FARED's salesmen about equipment specifications than they were in obtaining the equipment hardware. FARED's customers, therefore, wanted both consulting services and automated equipment provided by the same vendor. FARED responded by changing both product and service mix to accommodate these customer preferences.

By the summer of 1987, FARED provided custom design of precision assembly automated equipment focusing on four major industries: (1) automotive manufacturers and their suppliers, (2) home appliances, (3) electronics, and (4) ordnance (munitions and weapons systems). FARED currently was creating assembly systems for General Motors for use in the manufacture of automobile instrument gauges. The company also was developing a system to manufacture ice cube makers for the Whirlpool Corporation, as well as a $5 million system (the third of its kind) to produce washing machines.

FARED can provide customers with a "one-stop" or turnkey automation capability of robotic equipment that the company manufactures itself, assembles from parts and components manufactured by others, or obtains from other manufacturers and distributes as complete systems. FARED has the capability to custom design and manufacture assembly systems to the specifications of customers who wish to automate assembly of precision parts and components used in applications such as computer keyboard products, home appliances, and automobile assembly. All of FARED's systems involve computerized controls.

In addition to providing robotics and automated hardware equipment to customers, FARED offers software and communications systems that create a completely integrated macrosystem of hardware, software, control, and communications. FARED's 1986 annual report states that:

> A typical FARED system assembles a product by using programmable conveyors which direct product flow to as many as one hundred functional tasking elements. These

---

This case was prepared by James W. Clinton, University of Northern Colorado, as a basis for class discussion rather than to illustrate either effective or ineffective handling of an administrative situation. Used by permission from James W. Clinton.

elements include custom-designed automation, standard machinery, and robotic cells that have the ability to self-correct many assembly problems. The systems also use elements of FARED's generic automation equipment, such as robot hands, pallet iden-tification systems and precision–part tray handlers, which allow us to increase system reliability while reducing costs. Pertinent information generated at these cells can be stored, retrieved or passed to other operating elements within the system, to diagnostic centers, or to a plant host computer.

We know of no other assembly-systems integrator in the world, within the areas in which we compete, that has achieved the degree of hardware/software integration and in-process control typically found in FARED-developed products.

FARED Robot Systems has undergone a transformation during its history through acquisition and the formation of subsidiaries (Exhibit 3-1). A discussion of these transactions follows.

In February 1982, FARED incorporated a separate and wholly owned subsidi-ary, FARED Automation, Inc., in the state of Michigan. FARED Automation was created primarily to acquire Intec Corporation, an automation design engineering company. FARED Automation acquired Intec on March 1, 1982 through the issue of FARED common stock and promissory notes.

In November 1982 FARED formed a subsidiary, FARED Drilling Technolo-gies, Inc. to research the feasibility of an automated pipe-handling system. In 1984, however, FARED Robot Systems reduced the company's ownership to approxi-mately 13 percent of FARED Drilling's outstanding stock. A decline in oil prices and cutbacks in both onshore and offshore oil and gas drilling during 1985 and 1986 further reduced the potential demand for an automated pipe-handling system. In addition, development of this pipe-handling system required several millions of dol-lars—money that FARED believed could be better applied to its core businesses.

FARED Robot Systems acquired Automated Robotic Systems (ARS) on Sep-tember 15, 1983, in exchange for 2.2 million shares of FARED's common stock. A holding company, ARS, consisted of two wholly owned subsidiaries (Equus Auto-mated Systems, Inc. and Equus Robotic Systems). On January 1, 1983, ARS ac-quired both of these subsidiaries for a combined purchase price of $4.984 million.

Exhibit 3-1   **Major Transactions, FARED Robot Systems, 1981–1984**

Date	Transaction
May 20, 1981	Incorporated in Colorado
February 1982	Created Michigan subsidiary, FARED Automation
March 1982	Acquired Intec
November 1982	Formed subsidiary, FARED Drilling Technologies, Inc.
1983	Disposed of FARED Automation assets
September 1983	Acquired Automated Robotic Systems
1984	Reduced ownership in FARED Drilling

This purchase price included $3.7 million in goodwill—the difference between the fair market value of assets acquired and their purchase price.

According to current FARED President Harold Spidle, "I wasn't here at the time, but I question that FARED could have survived without this merger. A steep price was paid in additional debt; but, in exchange, Equus, which wanted to go public, saved the expense that would have been involved with a public offering of stock through an investment banker." As a result of the merger, according to President Spidle, "Instead of two companies with major problems, there resulted one larger company—with even larger problems."

During fiscal 1984, FARED Robot Systems relocated corporate offices to Arlington, Texas and consolidated most of its operations among facilities located in the Dallas–Fort Worth area. The move was made because the Texas market appeared to offer more growth potential than that found in the Rocky Mountain region around Denver.

In 1985, FARED constructed a new plant in Fort Worth which consolidated the company's offices and manufacturing facilities under one roof. The plant and offices were built to the company's specifications as part of a ten year lease obligation. FARED was offered attractive terms that President Spidle considered "a gift." The developers of the property were committed to the economic development of the Fort Worth area and, in their wish to emphasize high technology enterprise, viewed FARED as a desirable tenant. In an adjoining part of the industrial park, the University of Texas was building a Robotics Research Center. FARED believed that there was the potential for synergy between the company and the university's research center.

MARKETING

FARED Robot Systems (FRS) markets its products and services within the continental United States through a company sales force. Its marketing is focused on the central and western states.

Target customers of primary interest to FARED are manufacturers who: (1) assemble small precision devices, (2) produce machine components or parts, (3) move or reposition mechanical assemblies, or (4) make electronic circuit boards. These production processes, for robotics to be economically feasible, require a volume or frequency of 50,000 operations per week.

FARED advertises its products and services in trade journals, participates in robotics trade shows, and is a member of several trade associations committed to the promotion of robotics and automation applications.

Several major customers account for a substantial portion of FARED's consolidated sales. In fiscal 1986, Whirlpool Corporation and IBM Corporation accounted for 69 and 18 percent, respectively, of FARED's sales. In the previous year, Apple Computer, IBM Corporation, Whirlpool Corporation, and Xebec accounted for 11, 42, 14, and 13 percent, respectively, of the company's total sales. Equipment built by FARED for IBM is shown in Exhibit 3–2.

For IBM, FARED designed and built one of the world's largest robotic assembly systems, containing more than 80 automated work stations. This system is a part of one of the most advanced typewriter and letter-quality printer manufacturing facilities in the world.

Exhibit 3-2   **An Example of a FARED-Designed and Built Product as Shown in a FARED Marketing Brochure**

FARED's marginal financial condition adversely affects the company's marketing efforts, according to Mr. Spidle.

> Some potential customers won't consider entering into a contract unless they clearly believe that FARED has the resources to complete, e.g., a $150,000 or $1 million contract. Customers' progress payments sometimes are awfully slow. We've lost contracts because we just didn't have a good enough balance sheet.

OPERATIONS

FARED uses a "mixed technology assembly," consisting of robotics, machine tools, and manual operations, which are electronically monitored. Concurrent with all assembly processes are integral inspection systems that monitor production efficiency and product quality and also create a data base for reference, control, and assessment. FARED has produced an electronic console that displays a complete manufacturing system as presently functioning in FARED's plant facility and as it is intended to be installed in the customer's plant. The console display shows reject frequencies and sources of problems and significantly reduces adding value to defective assemblies, thus reducing cost of goods sold and improving production efficiency.

FARED's manufacturing operations include materials arrival; materials processing, including machining, welding, and painting; product assembly; and finished goods packaging and shipment.

FARED is attempting to develop generic robotic applications for use in common industrial manufacture and assembly operations. Such recycled applications will permit the company to spread research and development costs over more units and enable management to price systems and products more competitively.

Several of FARED's major contracts experienced cost overruns in 1985. These contracts, for which FARED either will experience a loss or achieve minimal profit, continue to place a strain on FARED's working capital. However, the company hopes to develop standard hardware and software applications so that it can apply the learning curve to comparable systems, parts of systems, or processes, and thus spread developmental costs over a greater number of applications and minimize the likelihood of future cost overruns.

FARED designed and built one of the world's largest robotic assembly systems for IBM to manufacture typewriters and letter quality printers. The total system included more than 80 automated workstations, and cost $13 million to produce.

FARED provides assembly cells for an automated assembly line designed to build the Apple IIc computer. This robotic system assembles a computer every 16 seconds.

FARED built a system for General Electric to drill multiple holes simultaneously through steel discs. The system drills the discs at a rate of 108 discs per minute. FARED also designed and built a machine for the Whirlpool Corporation that assembles washing machine parts and detects and rejects improperly assembled parts at a rate of 150 assemblies per minute. FARED also designed and built a machine that automatically cuts, seals, and ties a rope on the starter used in McCulloch chain saws.

Frank Romeo, Executive Vice-President, offered the following comments:

> Recently we completed a robotic application that can replace eight people working 16 hours a day. The rapid ROI is there—just as a university would replace an instructor if it could develop a robot that could perform all of the instructor's teaching functions and have it pay off within a year.
>
> We're doing what we can to advance the technology and make it cost effective for our customers. The first unit of a robotic cell we recently constructed cost $180,000; the second $120,000; and the third $90,000. We developed a circuit board to replace a complicated set of wires and connections. The improved grasping and control element is significantly lighter and reduced costs by 75 percent.
>
> The computer industry has yet to capitalize upon the potential of automated assembly of its products. We built and entire assembly operation for Apple Computer at their Dallas plant. Apple, however, in an economy move, closed the plant before it became operational. As a result, FARED lost the opportunity to point to a local operating facility that used FARED technology. The plant was state of the art in automation and robotics. We have, nonetheless, a videotape of the operation which we use as a marketing tool.

MANAGEMENT

None of the original founding officers and directors of the company presently is associated with the company. All have been replaced by present management.

FARED's current President, CEO, and Chairman, Harold D. Spidle, was appointed in June 1984, as noted in the 1984 *Annual Report,* " . . . to address various operational problems within the company and gain the confidence of customers, creditors, and prospective investors." President Spidle said that he was particularly attracted by the caliber of the company's employees and was very impressed by the quality of equipment being produced for IBM, using FARED-developed systems. Prior to coming to FARED, he had been president of a California company that manufactured equipment for the transport of liquid nitrogen and oxygen. That company, however, sold out to the Richmond Tank Car Company of Houston, Texas, and Spidle was transferred to Houston as an executive for Richmond, but he was not comfortable with this new parent company and was anxious to run his own company. In his search for acquisition opportunities, he attracted the attention of several venture capitalists, including the venture department of Texas Commerce Bank which had invested $1 million in FARED. Through their efforts, he was offered the presidency of FARED, which he accepted. Spidle has an undergraduate degree in engineering and a graduate degree in fluid mechanics. According to the president:

Investors come to this plant, are enthusiastic about what they see, and want to invest in the company. For example, Caterpillar Tractor invested $2 million in the company in December 1985. They are interested for the long term in the things that we are doing.

We're disappointed in the market performance of the company's common stock. We believe that the company and the industry are experiencing a temporary malaise which will turn in the future. Manufacturers know that robotics and automation must be considered; it's just a matter of when.

Competition is fierce. All competitors have underbid to obtain contracts. Furthermore, it's difficult to accurately estimate engineering time and develop a customized manufacturing application. Regardless, however, we've got to make money. After all, that is what enables us to operate and attract investors. In regard to planning, we would like to look down the road two or three years, as is typically done in strategic management, but under our present situation we can take only one year at a time.

Frank Romeo, Executive Vice-President, came to FARED from Mooney Engineering where he had been an engineer and designer. Scott Musselman, Chief Financial Officer, joined FARED in 1982. He previously worked for a Big Eight accounting firm. Don Jackson, Manager of Support Services, previously worked for Mooney Engineering.

The directors of the company are:

- Harold D. Spidle, President, CEO, and Chairman;
- Nolan Lehmann, President, Equus Corporation International;
- Fred R. Lummis, II, Vice-President, Texas Commerce Investment Company;
- Robert L. Powers, President, Caterpillar Venture Capital, Inc., and
- Thomas W. Wright, President, Sunwestern Venture Group.

ORGANIZATION

FARED uses what Frank Romeo terms a modified matrix organizational design. Technical management consists of: (1) mechanical engineers, (2) software engineers, (3) controls engineers, and (4) CAD/CAM systems specialists (Exhibit 3-3). Technical specialists and engineers are assigned to project managers as needed. FARED, as of August 14, 1986, had 130 employees—about 45 percent of whom were engineers, 40 percent tradesmen and technicians assigned to manufacture and assembly, and 15 percent management.

FINANCE

FARED Robot Systems has yet to earn a profit in five years of operations (Exhibits 3-4 and 3-5). FARED went public in 1982, issuing 16 million shares of common stock at $.25 per share. On October 18, 1983, the company declared a re-

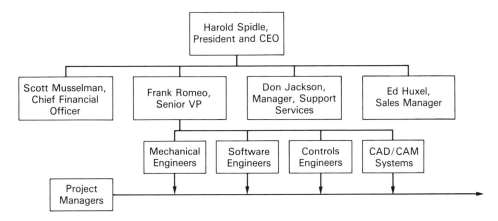

Exhibit 3-3   **Organization Chart, FARED Robot Systems**

Exhibit 3-4   **Consolidated Income Statement, 1983–1986 (In thousands)**

	11 mos. 9/30/83	Fiscal 1984	Fiscal 1985	Fiscal 1986
Sales	$9,942	$16,151	$16,771	$12,677
Cost of goods sold	8,582	15,495	15,497	11,264
Gross margin	1,360	656	1,274	1,413
Sales, administrative, and general expense	3,628	3,431	2,397	2,618
Research & dev. expense	1,746	909	—	—
Operating loss	(4,014)	(3,684)	(1,123)	(1,205)
Interest expense	(585)	(1,007)	(741)	(666)
Other income (expense)	162	(1,248)	(130)	(162)
Gain from sale of subsidiary stock	1,255	—	—	—
Acquisition costs	(192)	—	—	—
Net loss before minority interest	(3,374)	(3,443)	(1,994)	(2,033)
Minority interest in net loss of consolidated subsidiary	395	241	—	—
Net loss	$(2,979)	$(3,202)	$(1,994)	$(2,033)
Net loss per common share	$(.33)	$(.30)	$(.12)	$(.12)
Weighted average common shares outstanding (000)	8,925	10,770	16,179	17,379

Exhibit 3-5   **Consolidated Balance Sheet, 1983–1986 (In thousands)**

| | September 30 | | | |
	1983	1984	1985	1986
Cash	$ 746	$ 253	$ 470	$ 232
Accounts receivable	1,924	2,403	2,618	756
Costs/earnings in excess of billings on uncompleted contracts	1,687	2,121	1,733	305
Inventories	549	368	326	209
Other	176	28	41	41
Total Current Assets	5,082	5,173	5,188	1,543
Net property/equipment	3,096	2,223	1,639	1,755
Net intangible assets	3,804	3,622	3,498	3,375
Other	238	220	288	233
Total Long-Term Assets	7,138	6,065	5,425	5,363
Total Assets	$12,220	$11,238	$10,613	$ 6,906
Notes payable	3,140	—	—	17
Accounts payable	2,051	2,218	1,031	335
Billings in excess of costs and earnings on uncompleted contracts	319	1,065	513	182
Current portion of long-term debt	614	712	847	828
Accrued interest payable	53	245	339	209
Other	459	509	692	496
Total Current Liabilities	6,636	4,749	3,422	2,067
Notes payable to bank	1,200	4,683	1,134	785
Subordinated notes payable	3,178	465	2,928	3,150
Capital lease obligations	614	459	281	82
Minority interest in consolidated subsidiaries	277	—	—	—
Other	41	29	142	—
Total Long-Term Liabilities	5,310	5,636	4,485	4,017
Total Liabilities	11,946	10,385	7,907	6,084
Stockholders' Equity				
Common stock	47	67	86	87
Additional paid-in capital	4,742	8,504	12,331	12,480
Retained earnings (Deficit)	(4,515)	(7,718)	(9,711)	(11,745)
Stockholders' Equity	274	853	2,706	822
Total Liability and Stockholders' Equity	$12,220	$11,238	$10,613	$ 6,906

verse stock split, exchanging one share of the newly issued stock for five shares of previously issued stock. The highest bid prices for the company's stock during 1984–1986 were:

Year	High Bid Price
1984	12 13/16
1985	2 15/16
1986	5/8

On May 26, 1987, the stock sold at $.06 bid and $.09 asked.

Throughout 1986, President Spidle attempted to obtain an additional $6 million in venture capital to add to the company's working capital so that:

> . . . we can do those things that we haven't been able to do because of the company's constrained financial condition. The funds would be used for increased marketing and additional research and development, as well as for possible acquisitions of vertically integrated companies.

In early June 1987, Spidle indicated that he expected to secure an additional $1.3 million in financing from four venture capitalists and the owner of the plant which FARED presently is leasing. Of this amount, $950,000 is scheduled to be subordinated debt; the remainder, $350,000, will be in stock.

Under terms of a debt agreement with a bank creditor, FARED cannot pay a dividend without prior consent of the bank. FARED also is required to maintain a minimum working capital of $1 million, a minimum stockholders' equity of $2 million, and a current ratio of at least 1.2 to 1.

Standard and Poor's *Stock Reports* noted on February 28, 1986, that FARED Robot Systems:

> . . . reported to the Securities and Exchange Commission that . . . (FARED's) operations reflected low gross margins resulting from cost overruns; also, its level of backlog had declined. Should possible resulting demands placed upon Company's liquidity cause delayed payments to creditors (Company not having access to working capital credit facilities), Company might have delays in shipments from suppliers, causing additional project delays and cost overruns which could have a material adverse effect on future operations.

In the 1985 *Annual Report* "Notes to Financial Statements," the following information is stated concerning FARED's notes payable to bank:

> The $4,770,309 notes payable to bank at September 30, 1984, consisted of $2,396,992 borrowed under a $3,000,000 revolving line of credit, $873,317 borrowed under a $1,500,000 bridge loan, and a $1,500,000 term loan. These loans had been in default and were restructured concurrent with the issuance of $2,800,000 of 14 1/2% Convertible Subordinated Debentures. The bank converted $1,700,000 of debt into 1,700,000 shares of FARED common stock, received $1,500,000 in cash from the proceeds of the

debenture, and structured the $1,570,309 balance of the debt as a long-term note requiring quarterly principal payments of $87,239 commencing September 30, 1985.

FARED presently is leasing various computer equipment, software, and related peripheral equipment as part of a computer-aided design system. FARED was obligated to make lease payments of $213,927 for 1986 and 1987 and $92,059 in 1988. FARED also has noncancellable leases for additional facilities and equipment. Under these operating leases, FARED is obligated to pay $781,054 in 1986, $735,763 in 1987, $498,089 in 1988, and $478,885 in 1989 and 1990. According to President Spidle, leases shown on the balance sheet for Computer Assisted Design (CAD) can presently be duplicated for one-half FARED's original outlay for these leases. FARED committed itself to these lease agreements to obtain equipment necessary for research. Unfortunately, the technology changes so rapidly in this field that management continually is confronted with the dilemma of either waiting for the price of the technology to drop or taking current technology and initiating developmental effort.

FARED has leased 95,000 square feet of office and manufacturing space in Fort Worth for a ten-year period. Lease payments are $390,000 the first year, increasing to $520,000 in the tenth year. The lessor has agreed to finance leasehold improvements of $590,000. FARED issued a note of $100,000 for a one-year period, a $340,000 promissory note payable over ten years, and issued the lessor 200,000 shares of FARED's common stock to pay the remaining $150,000.

LEGAL

In September 1985 a customer terminated its contract with FARED, alleging that FARED had defaulted on the contract by failing to deliver equipment that operated as specified in the contract. The customer indicated that he planned to correct deficiencies in the equipment and bill FARED for the expense. FARED has initiated legal action to recover the amount billed to the customer and unpaid—$251,430. FARED, according to a note in the company's 1986 *Annual Report,* ". . . does not anticipate any losses with respect to this lawsuit." No other major legal issues are pending or anticipated.

COMPETITION

FARED's competitors are varied and possess substantial resources. They consist of: (1) domestic assembly automation manufacturers, (2) foreign robot manufacturers, (3) distributors of assembly equipment components, including those manufactured overseas, (4) robot consulting and service companies, and (5) major American manufacturers who produce robots as an incidental part of their operations.

Domestic Manufacturers.   Important manufacturers of automation equipment (and considered by FARED executives to be the company's major domestic competitors) are Cincinnati Milacron, Unimation (a division of the Westinghouse Corporation), and Adept Technology, Inc. (which, according to Dun & Bradstreet's 1987 *Million Dollar Directory,* had sales of $7 million in 1986 and 170 employees). Cincinnati Milacron's sales in 1985 were $732.2 million. Milacron spent $36.6 million in 1985 on research and development.

Foreign Manufacturers.   Fujitsu of Japan, ASEA of Sweden (the largest robot manufacturer in the world but who has only a small share of robots used in the United States and makes robots for the spray painting of automobiles and larger operations), Sankyo/Seiki of Japan, which manufacturers robots for IBM (Japanese manufacturers of robots are concentrated in the field of small parts assembly), KUKA and Volkswagen of Germany, and Automatic Tooling Systems of Canada are major international manufacturers and distributors of robots.

Domestic Distributors.   Esab/Heath distributes the Swedish-made ASEA robot in the United States.

Robot Consulting and Service Companies.   There are numerous companies that offer robot and automation consulting and service. These include:

1. Productivity Systems, Inc., Detroit, Michigan: develops robot applications, conducts training seminars on robots, and evaluates vendor robot proposals.
2. LTI, Inc., Los Angeles, California: develops robot applications, conducts training seminars in robotic systems, and evaluates candidate robotic products for users.
3. Robotics Systems, Inc., Atlanta, Georgia: a subsidiary of Brown and Sharpe Manufacturing (also a manufacturer of robots), offers services similar to those provided by FARED; Robotics has operated a robot demonstration facility since 1981.
4. Kohol, Dayton, Ohio.
5. Finch Robotics Company, Philadelphia, Pennsylvania.
6. D. Appleton Company, Manhattan Beach, California: specializes in integrating computer systems such as those used in factory automation.
7. Automatix, Burlington, Massachusetts.
8. Electronic Data Systems (EDS) Corporation: a subsidiary of General Motors Corporation, acquired by GM in 1984 for $2.5 billion.

Other American Manufacturers.   The following manufacture robots for use in company-related manufacturing operations and also for sale to others. These manufacturers are:

1. General Motors: with the Japanese manufacturer, Fanuc, formed the joint venture, GMF, which was the world's largest robot supplier in 1985, with sales that were almost three times those of Cincinnati Milacron.
2. General Electric: joined with Fanuc of Japan in a $200 million joint venture in June 1986, called GE Fanuc Automation Corporation.
3. Westinghouse: acquired Unimation, Inc. for $107 million in 1983.
4. IBM.

THE INDUSTRIAL ENVIRONMENT

Major United States manufacturers are increasing their use of factory automation systems, more than doubling such systems from $7.4 billion in 1980 to $18.1 billion in 1985, and are expected to double 1985 levels by 1990 (Exhibit 3-6). Several major manufacturers plan to spend billions of dollars on factory automation that include substantial use of robotic systems. Investment in computer aided manufacturing is more than doubling every five years (Exhibit 3-7). Between 1985 and 1990, IBM expects to invest more than $15 billion in automation. General Electric will spend $1 billion on automation during this same five-year period. American manufacturers' investment in factory automation, nevertheless, is only about one-half the amount spent by Japanese companies for similar automation systems.

Robotics and automation are expected to be of increasing importance to American manufacturers as they attempt to raise worker productivity, lower costs, and compete with both foreign manufacturers and other American firms that have relocated manufacturing facilities overseas. According to *Value Line Investment Survey,* August 22, 1986:

> The industry's mix of incoming orders already appears to be gradually shifting from relatively standard stand-alone machine tools (like lathes) to highly sophisticated manufacturing systems made up of several machine tools linked by material handling devices, the entire system controlled by computers. And the high-tech content of even stand-alone machines seems to be rising. More incorporate robots, lasers, and the like than they did several years ago.

Exhibit 3-6   **U.S. Domestic Investment in Automation, 1980, 1985, and 1990 (In millions)**

	1980	1985	1990 (est.)
Computer-aided design (CAD)	$ 389	$ 2,456	$ 6,500
Computer-aided manufacturing (CAM)	6,853	15,375	32,300
Communication links, misc.	113	264	800
Total	$7,355	$18,095	$39,600

Exhibit 3-7 U.S. Domestic Investment in Computer-Aided Manufacturing 1980, 1985, and 1990 (In millions)

	1980	1985	1990 (est.)
Factory computers and software	$ 935	$2,861	$6,500
Materials handling systems	2,000	4,500	9,000
Machine tools and controls	3,000	4,800	7,000
Programmable computers	50	550	3,000
Robots and sensors	68	664	2,800
Automated test equipment	800	2,000	4,000
Total	$6,853	$15,375	$32,300

The machine tool companies (rather than their potential customers) bear the cost of designing these manufacturing systems, and even after proposals to build such systems are drafted, there are no assurances that all of the work that went into developing the proposal will result in a firm order.

Advantages of Factory Automation. Factory automation offers the following benefits:

1. Faster turnaround on product design and manufacture. Integrated computer systems are used to design, engineer, manufacture, package, and ship products tailored to customer specifications.
2. Improved information exchange, access, and storage.
3. Improved accuracy of manufacturing and operations data.
4. Lower labor costs to process manufacturing information, including materials requirements planning information.
5. Reduced inventory costs where automation is related to just-in-time (JIT) inventory planning and control.
6. Improved reliability of manufacture that can improve product quality.
7. Improved manufacturing flexibility that allows smaller batches of product to be manufactured more quickly and economically. Lower break-even points in production are possible. Computer-integrated manufacturing (CIM), which is also known as flexible automation or manufacturing, allows machines to make different products without time-consuming retooling or setups. Manufacturers will be able to respond more quickly to changing consumer tastes as well as concurrently responding to multiple customer segments. Factory automation will cause learning curve theory to be reevaluated because economies are realized without the need for large volume production.

8. Manufacturers are encouraged to adopt a more integrative approach to their total operation and identify, for example, marketing benefits associated with improved responsiveness of factory automation, and long-term production economies obtained at the expense of major short-term capital investment. Automation affects every functional area of the firm and requires extensive coordination if potential benefits are to be realized.

9. Factory automation will reduce labor costs to the degree that companies will find it just as economical to manufacture in the United States as they would in a lower cost overseas location. Consequently, according to Patrick A. Toole, vice-president for manufacturing, as reported in *Business Week,* "... the ideal location for the factory of the future is in the market where its products are consumed."

Current Industry Situation.   According to *Value Line Investment Survey,* February 20, 1987, prospects for the machine tool industry:

> ... for 1987 remain highly uncertain. Continued weakness in domestic industrial growth and the existence of inventories of Japanese machine tools suggest that orders won't pick up much. . . . Earnings prospects for just about all of the companies in this group are dismal.
>
> By the late Eighties, interest in factory automation systems ought to be considerably stronger, supporting a partial earnings recovery for those companies able to survive until then.
>
> ... There's a lot of interest in sophisticated, unmanned factory automation systems. . . . We expect the move to full factory automation to get underway by the 1990s.

General Electric announced in January 1987 that it will close its robotics plant in Florida. The company said, "The robotics industry is taking longer than expected to develop and the segment in which it (GE Fanuc Automation Corporation) concentrated, automated welding, is much smaller than originally anticipated." According to *Business Week,* robotics accounts for less than 2 percent of GE's total revenues from factory automation.

In August 1986, GMF Robotics, a joint venture of General Motors and Fanuc of Japan, reduced its workforce from 700 to 200 and cancelled plans to build an automated factory designed to build robots that build robots. General Motors also has experienced difficulty in introducing automated systems within a major automobile assembly plant that is considered to be state-of-the-art. General Motors' difficulty has affected the entire field of robotics since most of the capital expenditures in robotics have been in the automotive industry. *Business Week* reported that the auto industry accounted for "nearly two-thirds of 1985 investments in automation, and GM spent more than half of that."

The 1986 Tax Reform Act eliminated the investment tax credit and extended depreciation periods, discouraging investment in new plant and equipment. Decline in demand for factory automation systems caused the Eaton Corporation, for example, to withdraw from this segment of the machine tool industry.

Value Line Investment Survey, August 22, 1986, reported that, ". . . there still are large inventories of low-priced Japanese machine tools in the United States . . . waiting to be sold." Similarly, *Business Week,* January 12, 1987, noted that, "A big U.S. inventory of low-cost, foreign-made machines must be worked off before orders of domestic manufacturers pick up."

Business Week, in a special report of September 29, 1986, reported that:

> The great wave of automation that has swept through offices and factories since 1980 is losing momentum, largely because not enough companies are adopting the innovative work practices that get the most out of automation. Many managers are reluctant to run the kind of social revolution at work that is needed to make technology pay for itself . . .

According to an article which appeared in *The Wall Street Journal* on May 14, 1987:

> Factory automation lags expectations as firms take a piecemeal approach. . . . the University of Michigan Business School . . . puts the 1985 market at $24 billion . . . most automation is done on a machine-by-machine basis rather than through companywide planning. Moreover . . . the yen's rising value may make manufacturers slower to automate because they believe they're getting a 'breather' from Japanese competition.

Case 4

Liz Claiborne, Inc.

At 20 years of age, a young woman determined to enter the fashion industry won a *Harper's Bazaar* design contest and headed for New York to begin a new career. After working in the apparel industry for 26 years, Elisabeth Claiborne Ortenberg and her husband, Arthur Ortenberg, started Liz Claiborne, Inc. on January 19, 1976, with $50,000 of their own savings and another $200,000 from family and friends. In 1986, Liz Claiborne, Inc. moved into the *Fortune* 500 list of the largest industrial companies in the United States. Today, Claiborne (as she is known professionally) is one of the most successful entrepreneurs in the world.

The Claiborne company concentrates primarily on providing apparel that meets the needs of the professional woman in a business environment. It offers its

This case was prepared by Barbara A. Spencer and Lisa K. Rowe, Mississippi State University, as a basis for class discussion rather than to illustrate either effective or ineffective handling of an administrative situation. Used by permission from Barbara A. Spencer.

customers an array of related separates including blouses, sweaters, skirts, jackets, tailored pants, and matching accessories. On a more casual basis, Claiborne customers can find jeans, jumpsuits, knit tops and skirts, dresses, and sportswear. In 1985, the company introduced a menswear collection that has been making steady gains in the marketplace.

The company's clothing lines are designed by its own staff under Ms. Claiborne's personal supervision. Most items are manufactured by independent suppliers, about 12 percent in the U.S. and the remainder abroad, mainly in the Far East. Claiborne's products are marketed under various trademarks to over 3,500 accounts throughout the United States, operating approximately 9,000 department and specialty stores. Sales are also made to direct mail catalog concerns, foreign customers, and other outlets.

In addition to its apparel lines, Claiborne has licensees in such areas as shoes (Marx and Newman), eyewear (Tropi-Cal), hosiery (Kayser Roth), optics (Pal Optical), and patterns (McCall). These licensing agreements allow other firms to use the Claiborne trademark on their products. Generally, licensees pay a fixed sum when signing the agreement and then pay a royalty over the life of the contract. In 1986, the company acquired the Liz Claiborne Accessories division of Wickes Cos., Inc., which had previously operated under a licensing agreement. Later that year, in a joint venture with Avon Products, the firm introduced a Liz Claiborne perfume with its first national advertising campaign. In yet another venture, Claiborne announced the establishment of a new retail operation in 1987.

The common threads underlying each of these product lines are style and practicality. Claiborne believes that a limited number of clothing items can be arranged into a multitude of different outfits with the help of accessories like belts, hats, shoes, and scarves. The result is clothing that meets the needs of the New York customer and the middle American customer as well. As one industry expert notes, "It's not the cutting edge of fashion, but it's where fashion really sells."[1]

This formula has pushed Liz Claiborne, Inc. to the top of the apparel industry. Since the firm went public in 1981, sales have grown at an average compounded annual rate of more than 40 percent, while earnings have soared tenfold[2] (Exhibit 4-1).

THE APPAREL INDUSTRY STRUCTURE

The apparel industry includes the manufacture of children's clothing; men's and boy's sportswear; men's, youth's and boy's trousers and slacks, shirts, nightwear, suits, coats, and overcoats; womens', misses', and junior blouses, dresses, suits, skirts, coats, sportswear, undergarments, and sleepwear. It has an enormous structure with millions of employees whose main objectives are to generate profits

---

[1] R. Skolnik, "Liz the Wiz," *Sales and Marketing Management,* September 9, 1985, pp. 36–38.
[2] K. Deveny, "Can Ms. Fashion Bounce Back?" *Business Week,* January 16, 1989, pp. 64–70.

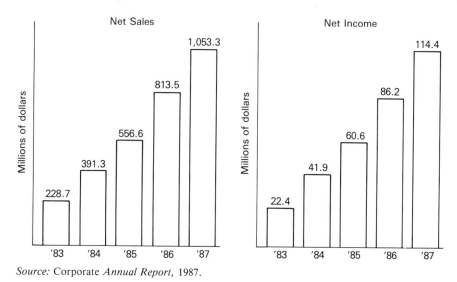

Source: Corporate *Annual Report*, 1987.

Exhibit 4-1   **Claiborne Company, Five-Year Growth in Sales and Income**

and keep customers in suspense from season to season. The industry is only a little over 100 years old but has already developed into a multimillion dollar business that allows individuals to express themselves to the world. The apparel industry's trends, as well as its clothing designs, are almost constantly changing to cater to a society of self-expression, imagination, and power. It is one of the few industries whose success is determined by so many environments: social, economic, political, and cultural.

The U.S. Department of Commerce estimates that the domestic apparel manufacturing industry consists of about 5,000 firms using 21,000 facilities throughout the United States. Of the 21,000 operating units, nearly 25 percent employed fewer than five workers, and more than half employed fewer than 50 workers.[3] Most of these companies produce a narrow range of products, frequently under contract for a large diversified firm or retailer. The domestic and foreign competition is fierce. This has kept apparel prices relatively low with price increases consistently lagging behind inflation.[4]

New York City is the main market center for the apparel industry. An estimated 5,000 apparel firms, where almost all of the leading fashion designers work, are located in the city. Overall, about 60 percent of the apparel industry is concentrated in New York, California, Pennsylvania, and New Jersey.[5] Most high-fashion and tailored clothing producers are located in the metropolitan areas of the mid-

[3]*Standard and Poor's Industry Surveys,* August 27, 1987, pp. T82–T88.
[4]Ibid.
[5]Ibid.

Atlantic states and in California. Factories making products such as jean-cut casual slacks are usually located in the South and Southwest.

As apparel manufacturing has shifted overseas, the population of U.S. apparel companies has been shrinking through bankruptcies and acquisitions.[6] According to the American Manufacturers Association, failures of companies making apparel and related products have been increasing since the late 1970s. Because they frequently provide labor cost savings, imports have been increasing.

The apparel industry has been particularly vulnerable to foreign competition because of the high labor content of its products. Because detailed and often repetitive tasks are the norm in this industry, semiskilled or unskilled workers are typically employed. Until recently, wage rates in such textile and apparel nations as Taiwan, China, Hong Kong, and South Korea have ranged from twenty cents to less than two dollars per hour. Moreover, many importers say that they cannot get the quality, reliability, price, and quick delivery from domestic sources that are available abroad.

Yet in 1988, the falling dollar and trade agreements that sharply restrict growth in Asian clothing imports may provide apparel makers with incentives to return to the United States. Production expenses, especially in the Far East, have risen sharply. And importing is becoming more challenging. For example, Chaus Inc., a New York based women's clothing maker, recently had $12 million dollars worth of blouses barred from entering the United States because of import quotas.

The domestic apparel manufacturing industry does have at least one advantage over foreign producers—direct access to U.S. markets. Domestic producers are capitalizing on this asset by using new techniques and technology to shorten the long channel from supplier to producer to retailer. Not only does new technology enable the industry to speed up the manufacturing process and shorten the channel, it also reduces labor time per garment. Presently, larger manufacturers use technological innovations because of their great impact on labor costs. Computer-aided garment design is being upgraded and refined using better software and faster computers. Computer inspections of fabrics, scanning and measurement of fabric-width variance, and automated marker-making systems are widely used. In the fabric cutting area, water-jet and laser methods have been used with some success. New programmable sewing units utilizing microprocessors are faster and more flexible, thereby reducing labor costs even more.

More than half of the U.S. apparel industry production workers are union members. The two major unions are the International Ladies Garment Workers Union (ILGWU) and the Amalgamated Clothing and Textile Workers Union (ACTWU). Workers earned about $5.85 an hour in 1986, an increase of almost 28 percent since 1980.[7] Despite these increases, apparel workers' earnings are significantly less than those of the average manufacturing worker. Possible explanations for this discrepancy include the low wage rates paid by foreign apparel-producing

[6]Ibid.
[7]Ibid.

countries, the low level of skill required for the job, and the fact that 81 percent of all apparel production workers are women.

Entrance into the apparel industry is not easy. Start-up costs and capital required for inventories and fixed facilities are relatively low compared with those of other industries; yet, the new competitor must have a sufficiently large financial base to overcome the effects of product differentiation and strong brand loyalty among consumers. For apparel to sell, it must have better quality and price than that existing in the market. In the fashion industry, a company must be knowledgeable about production procedures, marketing, research and development, and monitoring structural and cultural changes. If a new competitor lacks these qualities, the company will likely lag behind the industry. A new entrant may gain access to a distribution channel, but if it is not the right channel at the right time, profit will be hard to realize.

Suppliers of raw materials, particularly fabrics, abound. Almost 7,000 fabric-producing plants operate in the United States, yet no particular plant controls the industry. Furthermore, inexpensive textiles can be imported easily to the United States from numerous countries.

It is difficult to pinpoint competitors in the apparel industry because of the large number of different target markets, price levels, and quality levels. Liz Claiborne products, for example, are marketed as "designer" items as are those of Donna Karan, Ralph Lauren, Yves St. Laurent, and Giorgio Armani among others. Yet Claiborne prices its clothing in the "better" apparel range, which is generally less expensive than many designer lines. Mass market styles like those of Bernard Chaus fall slightly below Claiborne in price.

Ralph Laren targets upper income buyers but does not have a strong career focus. His line has a more casual, relaxed look than that of his competitors. Lauren's outfits are basically separates, which can be mixed and matched, unlike the fully coordinated outfits many working women desire.

Donna Karan learned design from Anne Klein and became chief designer of Anne Klein and Company after Klein's death in 1974. Later she began her own business. Two of Karan's key strengths are convenience and knowledge of what the consumer wants. She markets her entire line, including accessories, at a single location. Karan's clothes are expensive: a blazer costs about $250 or more, and a crocodile purse can cost as much as $2,000.[8]

While still employed at Anne Klein and Company, Karan played a big part in the development of a collection called Anne Klein II, considered a major competitor for Liz Claiborne. In 1985, a typical blazer from the former Anne Klein collection cost about $115 to produce and sold to the consumer for twice that amount. In contrast, Anne Klein II blazers cost the company about $45 to make and retailed for $175.[9] Anne Klein II and other derivative lines save money by using cheap labor and less expensive fabrics. They sometimes leave out linings and add fewer details,

---

[8]J. Fierman, "High Fashion Names Knock Themselves Off," *Fortune,* June 10, 1985, p. 73.
[9]Ibid.

making clothing items less expensive.[10] The moderate prices of Liz Claiborne and Anne Klein II appeal to their target markets because these women desire affordable clothing with the style, sophistication, and comfort to be worn in an everyday working atmosphere.

The level just below Liz Claiborne has a large target market which demands good quality clothing at a lower price. Bernard Chaus's designs fit into this category and can be found in the same department stores as Liz Claiborne and Anne Klein. His womenswear line targets business and professional women who cannot afford to pay high prices for clothing. His clothes have great appeal to this market because they are well made and are not trendy but can be worn from year to year.

ENVIRONMENTAL TRENDS

The Bureau of Census estimates that from 1960 to 1990 the number of women in the labor force will more than double, with the largest gain among women ages 24 to 44.

For apparel makers, the influx of women into professional occupations has resulted in the sale of billions of dollars a year in clothes. In the past, designers took a man's pin-striped suit and modified it so that it would fit a woman.[11] These days, clothes in the workplace are becoming more feminine, reflecting women's security in business, as well as their quest for individualism and personal identity. The majority of these women work in jobs that do not require extremely formal executive wear. Many can go to work more casually dressed in a wider range of styles. At the same time, the daily task of dressing for work requires a wardrobe with depth and versatility as well as affordability.[12]

With the growing number of two-income families, shoppers are finding their time to be increasingly valuable. One way that apparel makers are attempting to reach these busy consumers is through the mail order business. Direct marketing appeals to the needs of consumers who are less interested in going into stores because of traffic and parking problems. In 1984, according to a Direct Marketing Association study, at-home mail and phone orders brought in $170 billion to retailers, double the amount of five years before.[13]

Today, direct mail sales are growing so fast that some industry observers expect direct mail to be pulling in 20 percent of general merchandise sales by 1990.[14] More and more companies are getting in on the action. Bloomingdale's, for example, started sending catalogs to customers after finding that mailings designed to increase store traffic actually resulted in a considerable increase in phone and mail

[10]Ibid.

[11]A. Smith, "How Liz Claiborne Designed an Empire," *Esquire,* January 1986, pp. 78–79.

[12]Liz Is Big Biz," *Madison Avenue,* October 1986, pp. 28–31.

[13]J. Schneider, "Direct to the Consumer," *Nation's Business,* June 1985, pp. 29–32.

[14]Ibid.

sales.[15] Recently, however, so many new catalogs have appeared that some consumers have reached their limit. They may carefully peruse a few favorites, while discarding the rest.

The retail industry is also experiencing problems that directly affect apparel firms. First, many stores lack a clear identity. Because consumers can choose from a large number and variety of stores, retailers need apparel that differentiates them in the mind of the consumer. Consequently, they are putting pressure on manufacturers to shorten time cycles to provide more varied and timely deliveries. They feel that the manufacturing process must be accelerated to keep up with the constantly changing tastes of customers. This has also increased the pressure to shorten the lead time from ordering to delivery.

Second, in 1988, many department stores found themselves saddled with excess inventory due to sluggish sales. Female customers, in particular, stopped buying in the summer of 1987. Some say that they rebelled against the resurrection of the miniskirt. As of mid-1988, they had not yet returned to former buying levels, and both retailers and manufacturers were faced with declining orders (Exhibit 4–2).

Third, many stores are increasingly emphasizing house brands, placing them in direct competition with makers of designer-label goods. As a result, some manufacturers are cutting wholesale prices. Others are abandoning their own labels and becoming contractors for retailers' private label clothing. Moreover, analysts predict that many smaller apparel makers will be forced out of the business altogether.[16]

Fourth, there has been a growing trend toward consolidation among retail department stores. Larger stores place larger orders and favor vendors who can meet their needs. They are also likely to seek "one-stop shopping," buying from manufacturers who provide a broad range of styles and sizes, as well as give assistance in

---

Exhibit 4-2 **Unit Purchases of Women's Sportswear (First 5 months of 1988 compared with first 5 months of 1987)**

Category	Change in Units	Change in Dollars
Women's shirts/blouses	−10%	−10%
Sweaters	−14	−16
Slacks	−6	0
Blazers	−31	−24
Jeans	−7	+1
Skirts	−5	−13
Total (women's sportswear)	−9	−10

Source: The Wall Street Journal, August 3, 1988.

---

[15]Ibid.

[16]T. Agins, "U.S. Apparel Makers Face Tough Times," *The Wall Street Journal,* August 3, 1988, pp. 20, 22.

merchandising the goods in the store.[17] Manufacturers who do not meet these needs are being dropped.

To reduce their dependency on department stores, some of the larger manufacturers are opening their own retail stores. Ralph Lauren, for example, has over 70 stores that showcase his entire collection under one roof, providing exposure he would never get in a department store. Other newcomers to retail include Calvin Klein, Christian Dior, Adrienne Vittadini, Williwear, and Liz Claiborne. Vertical integration has already proven to be quite successful for such firms as Esprit, Benetton, Laura Ashley, and The Gap.

INTERNAL ENVIRONMENT

Elisabeth Claiborne Ortenberg was born in Brussels to American parents and spent much of her childhood traveling in Europe with her banker father. Claiborne later lived in New Orleans and Baltimore but returned to Europe before completing high school.[18] After studying art for several years in Paris, she won a *Harper's Bazaar* contest at age 20. She then moved to New York where she found work drawing and modeling and married an art director from the Bonwit Teller specialty store.

Claiborne met Arthur Ortenberg in the mid-1950s when he was running the junior dress division of a women's sportswear company. He hired her as a designer. They ended their first marriages and wed each other.[19]

Elisabeth then went to work as chief designer of Jonathan Logan's junior dress division. In that capacity, she continually tried to convince her bosses to create clothes for highly paid working women. She made limited progress, but remained dissatisfied. She wanted to strike out on her own, but she waited until her son, Alex, turned 21. In her words, "If we were going to lose everything we had, I wanted him to be old enough to handle it."[20] Her fears were unfounded. The business showed a profit in the first nine months.

Presently, Claiborne serves as chairman, president, and CEO of the organization. Although she no longer designs clothes herself, a point she regrets, she personally oversees all design. Her past experience in art and her keen eye for fashion serve her well in these roles. Within the industry, she is widely credited with having a deep understanding of her working woman customer.[21]

Claiborne's husband, Arthur Ortenberg, has served in various senior executive positions and as one of the directors of the company since its incorporation in 1976. His 20 years of experience in textiles and apparels include a stint as director of Fashion Products Research, Inc., a textile consulting firm. His strengths in finance,

[17]Ibid.

[18]P. Sellers, "The Rag Trade's Reluctant Revolutionary," *Fortune,* January 5, 1987, pp. 36–38.

[19]Ibid.

[20]Ibid.

[21]"Liz Claiborne's Pattern for Success," *Sales and Marketing Management,* June 1987, p. 54.

administration, and organization have been an asset to the firm. In 1985, he was elected vice-chairman of the board, along with the third key member of the management team, Jerome (Jerry) Chazen.

Chazen formally joined the company in May 1977. With 20 years' experience in the women's sportswear area, Chazen's major strengths are in sales and marketing. He has served in various executive positions including executive vice-president for marketing. In addition to his position as vice-chairman, he presently is a member of the board.

Leonard Boxer served as the fourth senior executive, and as a director of the firm, from 1976 to 1985. With seven years prior experience in running production at Susan Thomas Apparel Company, he had the contacts to help organize overseas manufacturing operations. Although Boxer is officially retired, he still serves as a director and as a special consultant to the corporation.

The top managers at Liz Claiborne have always worked as a team. Claiborne and Ortenberg particularly seem to complement each other in many ways. She is shy, and he's outgoing. She looks at details, whereas he sees the big picture.[22] The marketing of Liz Claiborne, Inc. reflects both of their personalities. Both are intense, a bit arrogant, and obsessed about the high quality image of Liz Claiborne clothes.[23]

Claiborne and Ortenberg describe their most important mission as preparing successors.[24] Ortenberg is developing managers who will be able to run the company with the same team approach that has worked so well from the beginning. Claiborne is working with several designers to take her place.

Structure/Culture

Liz Claiborne, Inc. is well managed without being extremely formal. Many of the employees are young, and many sport Liz Claiborne's hippest attire.[25] Claiborne's personal style can be felt throughout the organization—from the decor to the creative process.[26]

Generally, managers and designers use their own discretion when carrying out their tasks. Few restrictions are needed because Claiborne believes in hiring employees who are the best at what they do. Claiborne, Ortenberg, and Chazen oversee the vice-presidents of all divisions with Chazen having more authority over the men's line. Until recently, the structure was comprised of three levels with the Board at the top, the management team in the middle, and a horizontal level of product

[22]Sellers, "Rag Trade's," pp. 36–38.

[23]Ibid.

[24]Ibid.

[25]Deveny, "Can Ms. Fashion?" pp. 64–70.

[26]Ibid.

and design divisions (Collection, Lizsport, Lizwear, Dresses, Dana Buchman, Accessories, Cosmetics, Menswear, and Retail).

In 1987, the three sportswear divisions, Collection, Lizport, and Lizwear, were brought together as the Sportswear Group and placed under the direction of a single president. This move was intended to bring a sharper focus and more dynamic direction to the major portion of the business on a daily basis.[27]

A number of other structural changes were also made in 1987. First, the Executive Committee, which had advised the Board on strategy and policy issues, was replaced by a new pared-down Policy Committee.[28] The old Executive Committee had grown fairly large partially because it had been used as a development tool for younger managers who served alongside seasoned executives. In addition, a Strategy Planning Committee was established to evaluate new business opportunities, monitor market share, and identify growth areas within the business. This committee includes employees from key areas throughout the company.

Two additional executive positions were also created, again to help train new managers for their eventual role in replacing the original Claiborne team. The first position, executive vice-president for operations and corporate planning, consolidates all production planning, raw materials acquisition, manufacturing, and distribution in one office.[29] The second, senior vice-president for corporate sales and marketing, coordinates these efforts across divisions.[30]

Liz Claiborne, Inc. considers its staff as one big family. It devotes more time and effort to the development of employees than any other activity. In training, great emphasis is placed on understanding the consumer and seeing clothing through "Claiborne eyes."[31] Claiborne herself believes in hard work and conveys this belief to her employees through her own actions on the job.

Marketing

The first commandment at Liz Claiborne is "Satisfy thy Consumer." The second is "Support thy Retailer."[32] Yet, the company has no sales force on the road. From the beginning, retailers have come to New York several times a year to get Liz Claiborne merchandise. This enables Claiborne's marketing team to deal directly with top executives and to be readily accessible to major customers. It also adds a measure of control to the company's sales operation. Each of the company's divisions is responsible for marketing its own products, but the entire sales effort reflects the format of the buying organizations of its major customers.

[27]*Liz Claiborne Annual Report,* 1987.
[28]Ibid.
[29]Ibid.
[30]Ibid.
[31]Ibid.
[32]Skolnik, "Liz the Wiz, pp. 36–38.

Many of the salespeople at Liz Claiborne have worked as buyers for retail outlets. Because the company often helps department stores in planning their merchandising programs, the salespeople have to be at least as knowledgeable as the buyers they work with. Moreover, most of the salespeople are women who "look like the typical Claiborne customer."[33]

The company claims that its salespeople are not pushy. But in one sense, they are demanding. Buyers are required to take an entire line, not selected items from those shown. Liz Claiborne's clout with retailers stems from the fact that its clothes generate annual sales of more than $400 per square foot, while the average is 50 percent less. As a result, the company claims that it is the number one or two vendor at most of the department stores it supplies.[34]

In yet another innovative move, Claiborne was the first to transcend industry standards by offering six seasonal lines per year as opposed to the usual four. As a result, retailers can buy six smaller chunks of fresh merchandise a year instead of four larger ones. This not only cuts inventory costs for the stores, but also enables Claiborne's overseas suppliers to operate more efficiently with two extra cycles filling their slack period.[35]

Although Claiborne has no travelling sales force, the company does provide a group of retail consultants who travel from store to store and work with retail salespeople. According to Jerry Chazen, one of the biggest problems in retail today is the "lack of trained people on the floor."[36] Claiborne's consultants try to combat this problem by running seminars and clinics for store employees. They explain the company's goals and fashion perspective and stress good customer service.

Liz Claiborne maintains a cooperative advertising program under which it generally matches a customer's advertising expenditures up to 2 percent of their apparel purchases and up to 3 percent of their accessories purchases (Exhibit 4-3). The company does no significant direct advertising to the public other than this cooperative advertising. In fact, the firm actually discourages retailers from listing the Liz Claiborne label in sale ads. Moreover, Claiborne rarely gives credits or discounts that other apparel companies typically offer. Still Chazen estimates that 60 percent of the company's clothes are sold at full price versus about 40 percent for the average apparel firm.[37]

In 1987, the company opened its first store-within-a-store in the Jordan Marsh department store in Boston. Organized like a women's specialty shop, it is a personalized selling space where knowledgeable salespeople can help shoppers find the Liz Claiborne products they need to complete their wardrobes. Several more of these shops are planned for the future.

[33]"Liz Claiborne's Pattern," p. 54.

[34]Deveny, "Can Ms. Fashion?" pp. 64–70.

[35]H. Rudnitsky, "What's in a Name?" *Forbes,* March 12, 1984, pp. 43–44.

[36]Skolnik, "Liz the Wiz," pp. 36–38.

[37]"Liz Claiborne's Pattern," p. 54.

Exhibit 4-3   **Liz Claiborne, Inc. Co-op Advertisement with McRae's Department Store**

Research and Development

Claiborne regularly makes trips across the country to visit department stores and talk to customers. This gives her immediate feedback on how customers view her clothing. Information is also gathered using the firm's systematic updated retail feedback (SURF) system. In this system, reports come in weekly from a sample of department stores across the country that represent a cross section of store sizes and geographical locations. Using these data, computer programs generate outputs that indicate how consumers are reacting to recent merchandise shipments. Claiborne has discovered that there is often no relationship between what the retailers think and what the consumers buy.

As noted earlier, Claiborne personally oversees the creation of new designs. She has the ability to sense various moods in her mostly female, business-oriented target market, and creates her design statements accordingly. To assist her in this task, the company is planning to open a limited number of Liz Claiborne prototype and presentational specialty shops in key markets across the United States. The stores will allow consumers to view a specially coordinated selection of Liz Claiborne merchandise in an ideal setting. They will also allow the firm to track sales, styles, colors, and customer perceptions to better plan future offerings.

Manufacturing

In the manufacturing area, Liz Claiborne has been able to stabilize production prices over the years because it owned no factories. Instead, company managers have made agreements with independent suppliers located mostly in the Orient. All finished goods are shipped to the company's New Jersey facilities for reinspection and distribution.

Currently, manufacturing operations are run by a production administration staff which oversees product engineering, allocation of production among suppliers, and quality control. This staff constantly seeks additional suppliers throughout the world. Liz Claiborne, Inc. does not have formal or long-term arrangements with the suppliers who manufacture its products. Because it is often the largest customer of many of its manufacturing suppliers, its power over them is relatively high.

The Claiborne company buys materials, such as the fabrics and trimmings used in its apparel, in bulk from various suppliers in the United States and abroad. Until recently, the company has criticized U.S. textile mills for their reluctance to produce small orders of custom fabrics. To get such materials, used in 80 percent of its clothes, it had to go abroad, usually to Asia. Now the company is buying more fabrics custom-ordered from U.S. mills and has renovated two factories in New York's Chinatown to sew women's shirts, skirts, and slacks. Although it costs more to make the clothes in Chinatown, the New York location permits better quality control and faster turnaround.[38]

[38]"Claiborne Comes Home," *Business Week,* January 11, 1988, p. 73.

The company schedules a great portion of its products and manufacturing commitments late in the production cycle in order to deliver clothes that reflect current tastes on time. By doing this, it favors suppliers who can make quick adjustments in response to changing production needs. To support and continue sales growth, Claiborne has to make substantial advance commitments with its suppliers, often as much as seven months prior to the receipt of firm orders from customers for the items to be produced. Yet, management is very careful when doing this because misjudging the market could cause the company to face excess inventory supplies or manufacturing commitments.

Human Resource Management

As of December 1987, Liz Claiborne, Inc. had approximately 3,800 full-time employees. Claiborne feels that all jobs are important, and she has good relations with her employees. This reflects the company's informal, decentralized structure which allows for smoother operation and communication between employees.

Liz Claiborne, Inc. is a member of the Manufacturers' Association and has been bound by a collective bargaining agreement with an affiliate of the International Ladies' Garment Workers Union. The company also has an agreement with the Joint Board of Shirt, Leisurewear, Robe, Glove, and Rainwear Workers Union of the Amalgamated Clothing and Textile Workers of America.

Finance

In 1987, the company's net sales were $1,053 million, up from $813 million in 1986 and $557 million in 1985. Net income expressed as a percentage of net sales in 1987, 1986, and 1985 was 10.9, 10.6, and 10.9 percent, respectively. The increase in 1987 as compared to 1986 was due primarily to a reduced provision for income taxes as a percentage of net sales. The decline in 1986 as compared to 1985 was caused by lower gross profit margins and higher selling, general and administrative expenses, offset by a reduced provision for income taxes. Liz Claiborne's balance sheet and income statement are shown in Exhibits 4-4 and 4-5.

CURRENT SITUATION

The Liz Claiborne company has been moving forward on a number of fronts. In September 1986, the company entered the "bridge" sportswear market with a new "Dana Buchman" clothing label. This category bridges the gap between designer and better sportswear.[39] Although the distinctions among these categories are

_____
[39]P. Gill, "Bridge-(Wo)manship," *Stores,* October 1987, pp. 20–25.

Exhibit 4-4   Liz Claiborne, Inc. and Subsidiaries Consolidated Balance Sheet
(In thousands)

	12/28/85	12/27/86	12/26/87
Assets			
Cash	$ 955	$ 2,628	$ 2,704
Short-term investments	55,225	101,441	157,762
Accounts receivable	58,940	57,718	80,591
Inventories	72,846	114,879	156,375
Deferred income tax benefits	—	2,861	6,563
Other current assets	12,109	14,860	19,994
Total Current Assets	200,075	294,387	423,989
Property and Equipment			
Building	—	13,702	15,002
Machinery and equipment	6,341	13,599	22,085
Furniture and fixtures	4,124	6,007	8,916
Leasehold improvements	8,447	14,608	23,900
	18,912	47,916	69,903
Less accumulated depreciation and amortization	7,721	11,118	16,763
	11,191	36,798	53,140
Investment in Joint Venture	3,460	3,392	3,767
Other Assets	7,838	925	1,473
Total Assets	$222,564	$335,502	$482,369
Liabilities			
Long-term debt due within 1 yr	—	—	357
Note payable	—	4,900	—
Advances from developer	—	2,409	—
Accounts payable	26,804	39,820	53,044
Accrued expenses	15,574	26,166	43,374
Income taxes payable	3,527	7,921	6,412
Total Current Liabilities	45,905	81,216	103,187
Long-term debt	10,000	—	14,464
Deferred income taxes	3,930	6,499	7,762
Stockholders' Equity			
Common stock, $1 par value, authorized shares— 250,000,000 in 1987 and 125,000,000 in 1986	42,904	43,279	87,136
Capital in excess of par value	12,865	21,404	29,889
Retained earnings	106,960	183,104	239,931
Total Stockholders' Equity	162,729	247,787	356,956
Total Liabilities and Stock- holders' Equity	$222,564	$335,502	$482,369

Exhibit 4-5   **Liz Claiborne, Inc. and Subsidiaries Consolidated Income Statement (In thousands except per share data)**

	Fiscal Year Ending		
	1985	1986	1987
Net Sales	$556,553	$813,497	$1,053,324
Costs and Expenses			
Cost of goods sold	341,700	502,247	655,569
Selling, general admin. expenses	97,325	146,289	194,686
Interest expense	71	1,122	670
Interest and other income	(2,143)	(5,463)	(5,626)
	436,953	644,195	845,299
Income (before income taxes)	119,600	169,302	208,025
Income taxes	59,020	83,108	93,611
Net Income	$60,580	$86,194	$114,414
Earnings per common share	$ .71	$ 1.00	$ 1.32
Dividends per common share	$ .08	$ .12	$ .16

somewhat fuzzy, bridge merchandise is priced lower than designer labels, while still providing a fashionable designer look. The Dana Buchman line earned over $5 million in sales in its first four months in the marketplace. Company executives are pleased with these results because through "Dana Buchman," they have gained entry into a new price category with a name not associated with Liz Claiborne and a product line that can be developed independently.[40]

The menswear division is also growing rapidly. When first introduced, the men's clothes, particularly the pants, were too baggy. With this problem taken care of, sales of men's clothing increased 79 percent in 1987. In 1988, the company expanded its offerings in this area with a new line of dress shirts, ties, hosiery, and underwear.

In December 1987, Claiborne ended its joint venture with Avon. The company charged that Avon failed to meet its obligations for the Fall/Christmas seasons which together account for over 70 percent of annual sales. In a suit filed in the State Supreme Court in Manhatten, Claiborne, Inc. complained that this gaffe would "irreparably harm and likely destroy the business."[41] Despite these problems, however, the Liz Claiborne fragrance is selling well. A men's cologne is now being developed, but industry analysts caution that a second success is not automatic.

In February 1988, Liz Claiborne, Inc. opened the first of a chain of stores called First Issue Boutiques. These stores sell a collection of relaxed sportswear bearing the merchandise label First Issue. Although the clothes are said to have the Liz

[40]*Annual Report,* 1987.

[41]Liz Claiborne, Inc. (Business Brief), *The Wall Street Journal,* March 1, 1988, p. 44.

Claiborne look, they are priced just below the Liz Claiborne collections. Ideally, the new stores will compete with The Limited, The Gap, and Banana Republic while not antagonizing retailers who already carry the Claiborne line. Like Dana Buchman, First Issue provides Claiborne with an entrance into a new market and a new label to develop and expand. Jerome Chazen predicts that the stores could eventually become a bigger part of Liz Claiborne than apparel. The company opened 13 stores in 1988 and about 20 more are planned for 1989.

The company also plans to introduce a line of large-size women's clothing in 1989. The line, which will be named "Elisabeth," will be aimed at the 40 million U.S. women who wear a size 14 or larger. With its strong presence in department stores across the country, Liz Claiborne hopes to gain a major share of this market.

Although all of these moves appear to be positive, not everything the company touches turns to gold. In 1987, Claiborne phased out its Girls' Sportswear Division which could not compete with the lower prices charged by other children's clothing producers. In addition, the company brought out a line of miniskirts, midriff-baring tops, and prewashed denim clothing that customers rejected.[42]

Problems with the clothing line combined with flat sales throughout the industry caused the company to predict that its full-year 1988 earnings would fall 10 percent from 1987. It indicated that the abundance of inventory in the industry had made it unable to obtain anticipated prices.[43] Management addressed the problem by maintaining price points for fall 1988 by absorbing higher costs (particularly for fabrics) and so narrowing operating margins. As a result, for the first time in its seven years of covering Liz Claiborne, *Value Line* ranked Claiborne stock as a likely below-average performer in 1988.[44]

Although sales did rebound during the holiday season at the end of 1988, there are indications that the Liz label may be maturing. The tremendous growth rates of the past may no longer be feasible. Given the present conditions in the apparel industry, continued diversification may be required if growth is to continue. Yet there are numerous risks.

One obvious risk is that management may not have the skills to prosper in industries outside of apparel. The First Issue stores, for example, compete in a market that has been even more lackluster than the company's core business.[45] Moreover, the competition from such entrenched firms as The Limited and The Gap is fierce. Does Claiborne's management team have the expertise to beat these players at their own game?

Another risk is that the Claiborne name may become over-used. The use of the Dana Buchman and First Issue labels seems to reveal a sensitivity to this matter. But do these new products actually serve different market segments or will they simply cannibalize the original Claiborne line?

[42]Deveney, "Can Ms. Fashion?" pp. 64–70.

[43]Agins, "U.S. Apparel Makers," p. 20.

[44]*Value Line,* June 3, 1988, p. 1608.

[45]Deveny, "Can Ms. Fashion?" pp. 64–70.

Another question to consider is whether the company can continue to prosper without the guidance of Elisabeth and Arthur Ortenburg. Recently, they have been trying to limit their role in daily operations. They had hoped to shift to a one-month-on, one-month-off schedule, but the plan fell through when the stock market crashed in October 1987.[46] Another sign that they may be reducing their involvement with the firm was their sale of over 900,000 shares of their company stock in 1988. Some analysts are worried about this large sale, whereas others note that their holdings in the firm (valued at $82 million) are still substantial.

Elisabeth Claiborne Ortenberg and her company appear to have reached a critical juncture in their development. What strategies should they utilize to maintain their number one position in the apparel industry? How can they convince skeptical investors that the bloom is not off the rose?

[46]Ibid.

Case **5**

Brown-Forman, Inc. and the California Cooler Revolution

On December 5, 1985, W. L. Lyons Brown, Jr., chairman and CEO of Brown-Forman, Inc., was faced with the future prospect of the firm's recent acquisition of California Cooler, Inc. Although California Cooler held the number one market position when acquired earlier that fall, competition continued to mount as market share fell. Awaiting the 1986 strategic plan from California Cooler's management, Mr. Brown knew it would be critical for the long-term success of this new acquisition.

THE HISTORY OF CALIFORNIA COOLER

California Cooler virtually created the wine cooler category in the early 1980s. Guided by two young entrepreneurs and nicknamed the "Apple Computer" of the

This case was prepared by Per V. Jenster, IMEDE, as a basis for class discussion rather than to illustrate either effective or ineffective handling of an administrative situation. Used by permission from Per V. Jenster.

wine industry, California Cooler arose from a small bathtub operation into the fourth largest wine shipper in the state of California in just three years. Since its incorporation in 1981, California Cooler had experienced phenomenal sales growth. July 1984 shipments of over 3.6 million gallons marked a 350 percent increase over the previous year. Total shipments for 1984 equaled 20 million gallons, more than four times the number of 1983 shipments. One of the few success stories in this decade's flat wine industry, California Cooler paved the way for an exploding new market segment.

The firm was founded in August 1981 by two high school friends, Michael Crete and R. Stuart Bewley. While working for a California wine distributor, Michael Crete realized he was onto something when a home-brewed concoction poured into long neck, returnable beer bottles outdrew a keg of Michelob at a party. Whipped up by Crete for beach parties during his college days, the popular recipe soon created a new drink phenomenon. Crete then contacted Bewley. After collecting $150,000 from friends and relatives, the two young California natives opened makeshift production quarters in an old farm labor camp building in Stockton, California. Distributed from the back of a pickup truck, the California Cooler product achieved sales of 3,000 nine-liter cases in 1981. The following year, however, several local Adolph Coors beer distributors agreed to handle the new product and sales reached 800,000 cases. Even with no advertising for the original drink, distributors discovered that it sold well. The president of Bay Area Brewing Company commented, "It developed a mystique." Another distributor noted that, although his company expected demand for California Cooler to pass in 90 days, it continued to grow.

By 1984, California Cooler had a 60 percent market share. Its annual sales of $95 million totaled more than all of its competitors combined. The firm sometimes had three West German bottling lines working night and day churning out 125 cases per minute to meet production demand. Jon A. Fredrikson, editor and publisher of the *Gomberg Report,* one of the wine industry's top marketing publications, praised California Cooler's success in early 1985:

> *Talk about a successful effort—it's mind-boggling.* Nothing in the wine industry has done this from such a low base with no capital requirements. It's a gold mine. They buy bulk wine, mix it, and add carbonation, running the line around the clock. It's a production man's dream, a one product line. Their sales are incredible, given how tough it was to sell wine last year for the big guys (Exhibit 5-1).

MARKETING STRATEGY

Product and Price

California Cooler's effective marketing strategy contributed to its dramatic sales growth. The very nature of the lightly carbonated drink, composed of 50 percent white wine and 50 percent fruit juices, enhanced its initial appeal. California

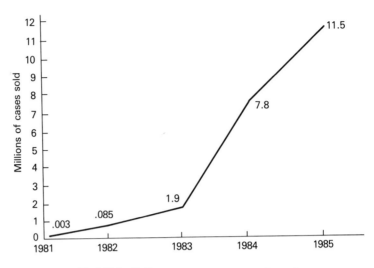

Exhibit 5-1   **California Cooler Growth**

Coolers contained only 5 to 6 percent alcohol, ensuring that the product remained in line with the decade's temperance movement. It was thirst quenching and therefore appealed to adults who wanted a little kick out of a soft drink. Furthermore, as a result of its 50 percent citrus juice content, the California Cooler was perceived as healthier than many other products. The fruit pulp was left in the bottle, and its presence was stressed on the brand's label. This enabled the firm to distinguish its new product from the clear, sipping wine category and thus broaden its potential customer base.

Even the packaging was appropriately conceived. Sold in a single-serving drink, the cooler offered the versatility of a beer, which a consumer could take anywhere and drink out of a bottle. Moreover, Crete and Bewley desired a quality package and believed nothing beat a Heineken bottle. Thus, the California Cooler was marketed in a green-tinted, twist top, short-necked bottle. A gold foil top was added and the new drink was sold in four-packs for under $4. In this way, Crete and Bewley hoped beer drinkers would be enticed to try California Coolers.

Initially targeting younger generation, natural thinking customers, California Cooler exploded onto the beverage scene with more force than either diet soft drinks or light beers. Selling for just under $1 per bottle, California Cooler offered fat profit margins for distributors. The drink was rarely discounted. It earned a 33 percent wholesale margin, typical of California wine distributors, but considerably above the 20 to 22 percent average margin obtained by beer distributors. Distributors and retailers often increased profits even further by marking up cooler prices to match those of imported beer.

Distribution

Although product characteristics and pricing methods promoted sales, California Cooler's distribution policy unlocked the door to initial success. Crete and Bewley borrowed beer distribution tactics. Their drink was not only packaged like beer but was also sold chilled. Convinced the movement in beverages was out of the cold box and not off the racks, the two entrepreneurs wanted California Coolers to be sold in the refrigerator of a sales account. Crete rationalized that beer distributors knew cold boxes like the palm of their hand and could therefore store, merchandise, and move California Coolers like beer. "Most wine distributors," he explained, "come in three-piece suits and wouldn't dream of entering a cold box." Aside from their expertise in moving refrigerated products, beer distributors possessed more accounts than their counterparts in the wine industry. Involved in virtually all accounts, beer wholesalers blanketed territories and serviced their accounts more frequently. Furthermore, they carried fewer products compared to the larger portfolios typical of wine wholesalers. Thus, Crete reasoned that beer distributors would "have time to work on California Cooler and wouldn't bury it." Besides, as good ole' boys, beer distributors would better represent the informal product.

Advertising

For more than a year California Cooler operated without an advertising budget. Relying on word-of-mouth promotion and brewery devices such as bin displays and cold box decals, distributors found that the new cooler product sold well. Late in 1982, however, California Cooler ran radio spot jingle advertisements sung to the tune of the Beach Boys song, "California Girls." Although narrow in scope, this advertising effort received praise from distributors and competitors. The firm was one of the few wine cooler producers to spend money on itself early in the game.

In 1983, 18 months after incorporation, the company broke even and began shopping for an advertising agency to help broaden sales from its northern California base. McCann-Erickson joined the team at the close of the year. The agency developed a $6 million national advertising campaign for 1984. The introductory ads ran on television and radio and were placed on billboards west of the Mississippi. They positioned California Coolers, not as a beer or wine, but rather as "beyond ordinary refreshment." Although the ads helped California Cooler survive the onslaught of competition, they were inappropriately targeted. Michael Crete explained, in retrospect, "They were a little too symbolic for the everyday consumer we were trying to reach."

In a further attempt to make its brand stand out among the many market newcomers, California Cooler spent $300,000 on an advertising campaign aimed at retailers. Ads ran in trade publications such as *Convenience Store News, Supermarket Business,* and *Nation's Restaurant News.* Direct mail pitches were also sent to bars. Hired as Director of Marketing in December 1983, Thomas M. Gibbs, III commented, "We were one of the few companies that made an effort to go after the retailer. We wanted as much of that door (the cold box) as we could get.'' Despite this promotional push, however, California Cooler's market share fell from 70 percent in 1983 to 60 percent by the end of 1984. See Exhibit 5-2 for advertising expenditures.

The Orange-Flavored California Cooler

The market share decline sparked two offensive moves in early 1985. To help save cold box facings, or shelf space, the company (1) expanded its product line and (2) increased its advertising budget for national network television commercials, spot radio ads, and promotional tools. In February, testing began on an orange-flavored version of the California Cooler. Four western test markets were used— Austin, Phoenix, San Diego, and Seattle. Like its precursor, this product consisted of a blend of white wine, orange juice, and a few other ingredients. The packaging remained similar as well. An orange and gold color scheme, however, replaced the original green and gold one. The orange-flavored product thus acquired a more soft drink-like appearance.

The firm developed its spin-off product only after studying the popularity of the orange-flavored soft drink, orange juice, and the mimosa, a breakfast drink consisting of orange juice and champagne. The success of 20/20, an orange-flavored cooler already on the market, also helped spark California Cooler's decision to introduce its own version. After hitting the marketplace in the spring of 1983, 20/20 leaped into second place in the wine cooler category with a 9 percent market share by the end of 1984. California Cooler aimed to attract healthy living, young consumers who were not big wine drinkers with its new product line extension. The product's promotion consisted of a $7 million national advertising campaign created

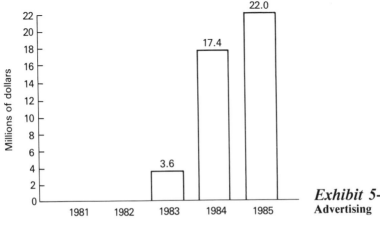

Exhibit 5-2   **California Cooler Advertising**

by Fabrinic and McCullough, a San Francisco–based advertising agency. Scheduled to air in the late spring of 1985, the ads rested on high expectations. The new orange California Cooler was depicted as "Rookie of the Year" and was escorted by the original California Cooler designated as the "Most Valuable Player."

THE 1985 NATIONAL ADVERTISING CAMPAIGN

As the undisputed champion of the wine cooler category in 1984, California Cooler faced an altogether different marketplace in 1985. The cooler market was due to erupt as big names such as Ernest and Julio Gallo, and Seagram and Sons prepared to introduce new products supported by extensive national advertising programs. Acknowledging this formidable competition, Crete admitted, "There's real financial strength out there, and they are out there to knock us off." In response to these market threats, California Cooler hired one of America's hottest advertising agencies, Chiat-Day, to help maintain market share and thwart competition.

The strategy underlying the $10 million national campaign was to get as much exposure as possible before Gallo and Seagram blitzed the media with huge advertising budgets and household names. The slightly whacky ads were entitled "One More Reason to Hate California" and aired as two separate 30-second commercials, one for television and the other for radio. The ads contained funny putdowns of the hot tubs, health food fetishes, and all-around casual lifestyles of Californians, including their namesake drink. The radio version of the ads featured original music and a comedian who delivered lines mocking Californians and their native state.

Market research in 1984 showed that 20 percent of California Cooler's consumers were substituting the product for beer, whereas only 5 percent were substituting it for wine. These findings guided Chiat-Day's strategy formulation for the 1985 national advertising campaign. Jon Vost, Vice-President and Director of Account Management at Chiat-Day, explained, "The strategy now is to embrace beer. The product delivers many of the same elements of the beer drinking experience." Thus, the ads were appropriately shot at bars, not outdoors as previously done. Furthermore, Chiat-Day strove to elevate California Cooler to "an American Institution." Confident in the product's mainstream potential, the agency felt, given the right advertising over time, that it could make consumers regard the product as the best thing since beer.

The advertisements were targeted to both men and women between the ages of 18 and 35. Commercials ran on shows equally skewed to male and female viewers. The list included shows such as "Remington Steele," "Riptide," and "Foxfire."

Heavy promotions supplemented California Cooler's advertising efforts. Held in the early spring, a $10,000 California beach party served to kick off the national campaign. Rock music played as party goers made use of an indoor-outdoor bar linked with palm trees. A "Why I Hate California Sweepstakes," which awarded a two-week vacation in the state to the winner and a one-week trip to the runner-up, was the main attraction. Other promotional schemes included a national Summer Sailboating Sweepstakes as well as the sponsorship of an official California Cooler car at the annual Long Beach, California Grand Prix.

Although creative, the ads received mixed reviews at first. Chiat-Day counted on eliciting a feeling of admiration and envy of things from California. Some people, however, felt the humor failed to outweigh the negativeness. California Cooler distributors seemed to be uncertain of the campaign's future. One distributor pictured the campaign as either a "smashing success or a dismal failure." Yet most agreed that the humor and outrageousness would at least make viewers notice, and hopefully remember, the product. The ads sought to raise California Cooler above the crowd.

As California Cooler concentrated on positioning its product as an informal, mainstream drink, competitors started to position their products differently. Well-established wine producers such as Gallo and Seagram and Sons began marketing a clear, wine look-alike cooler to more upscale customers. Both firms initiated extensive national advertising campaigns. Gallo's ads used more traditional humor, whereas Seagram's commercials (aired in 16 markets before its national rollout in May 1985) took the cooler outside in life-style executions. Moreover, believing the market was turning female, Seagram's directors and advertising agents geared their advertisements toward women.

COOLER UNCERTAINTY

The burgeoning wine cooler market appeared to be reaching maturity by the summer of 1985. A shakeout was inevitable. Much of the new category's success still depended on the heavy marketing of Gallo and Seagram and Sons. Industry experts remained unclear about the fate of the wine cooler segment. One industry analyst articulated his confusion: "I don't know if it's a passing fancy or if real industry needs are being satisfied by this type of beverage." Likewise, the future of California Cooler's strongest competitors was yet undetermined. Jon Fredrickson wondered whether Gallo and Seagram and Sons would carve out another market niche with their clear coolers aimed more at Yuppies than the "cloudy, funky, down to earth, blue-collar beverages" offered by 1985 market leaders.

Despite industry doubt, California Cooler remained confident in the future of its market. Considering their 12-month headstart on rivals, Crete and Bewley felt their firm could ride out an industry shakeout. The company had already successfully competed against big corporations such as Heublein, Inc. and Heileman Brewing Company. An early market entrant targeted to an upscale wine market as a Perrier substitute, Heublein's Citronent Cooler had acquired only a 2 percent market share by 1984 despite heavy advertising. Heileman's Country Cooler was also selling relatively poorly.

Although California Cooler was the undisputed victor in the wine cooler category since its incorporation, it continued to report declining sales growth during the first half of 1985. Hungry for a bite of the leader's success, well-known companies possessing considerable financial and marketing strength continued to enter the market. Plus, rumor had it that Anheuser Busch was also preparing to market a wine cooler. Regardless, California Cooler was determined to remain number one in 1985. At the start of the year, cofounder R. Stuart Bewley affirmed, "We'll have tough competition, but bigger isn't necessarily better. Other companies' coolers are sidelines. Ours is the mainline."

THE BIRTH OF BARTLES AND JAYMES

By the summer of 1985, however, management's determination to remain atop the wine cooler category had disappeared. As Crete and Bewley assessed the seriousness of their competitors, they soon realized that California Cooler lacked the financial and marketing resources necessary to maintain its leadership position. California Cooler's number one ranking in the industry had become more vulnerable as its market share fell to 51 percent and Ernest and Julio Gallo hit the market at full speed. Bartles and Jaymes was spending almost $20 million on a series of 20 national television commercials for its "premium wine cooler." These successful ads featured two small-time midwestern businessmen, Ed Bartles and Frank Jaymes, who had their life savings riding on a wine cooler that they claimed would go with everything but "Kohlrabi and candy corn." Along with these creative advertisements, Gallo offered volume discounts on its cooler, a tactic never used by California Cooler. Bartles and Jaymes was already capturing the most sales in a number of important markets, including northern California, Chicago, and Texas.

BROWN-FORMAN ENTERS THE PICTURE

In the heat of competition, the intentions of California Cooler's cofounders and top executives changed. Anxious to cash out of the wine cooler market they had created, Michael Crete and R. Stuart Bewley sold California Cooler in early July to Brown-Forman, Inc., a profitable, well-diversified, and resourceful corporation.

Two weeks prior to the September 5, 1985, settlement, California Cooler's marketing director resigned. Although Mr. Gibbs claimed his departure was not a bitter one, he admitted that California Cooler "lacked direction" since announcing the sale, and that it was not making necessary marketing decisions. Furthermore, Crete and Bewley had refused to share the cash they received from the sale with Gibbs and other top company executives.

Brown-Forman placed Vice-Chairman William Street in charge of California Cooler operations. Mr. Street participated in the selection of Jon Shastid, who would replace Gibbs. Mr. Shastid would assume the more expansive title of Vice-President of Sales and Marketing Director for Brown-Forman's newly acquired California Cooler. Former marketing director for Ernest and Julio Gallo Winery, Modesto, Shastid would bring considerable wine industry experience and expertise to the position. Even so, California Cooler had still not made plans for the important, upcoming 1985 holiday season. Granted, Brown-Forman could provide the vital resources required to remain competitive in a high status market share battle. Nevertheless, California Cooler was unsettled by its changing management structure while in the midst of the wine cooler market share war.

INDUSTRY OVERVIEW

The wine, beer, and distilled spirits industry has been feeling the effects of the shift in Americans' perceptions of alcoholic beverages. Not only have consumers become obsessed with the new health craze, emphasizing "clean" living, but the government has been stressing the importance of getting drunk drivers off the road. Both the enforcement of strict drunk driving laws and the increase of the legal drinking age have caused a dramatic decrease in the consumption of alcoholic beverages. As a result, the wine cooler provided a healthier alternative to beer, wine, and spirits.

The traditional categories of alcoholic beverages, composed of beer, wine, and spirits, were showing unfavorable sales figures in the early 1980s. In response to the condition of the industry, many distilleries justified their declining sales to shareholders by issuing such statements as the following: "Consumption of distilled spirits declined for the third consecutive year in fiscal 1985, as a trend towards further moderation of drinking habits continued in the United States. Domestic consumption of wine, however, increased modestly due primarily to the rapid growth of sparkling wines and wine coolers."

In the face of an overall declining industry, the wine cooler sparked the beginning of a new era in the wine market. In fact, demand, profit potential, and product definition of wine coolers together have led to long-term business building in the industry. Due to the steadily increasing sales of wine coolers, the volume of wine sold in the U.S. has been increasing in the past few years. Wine coolers accounted for about 6.4 percent of the U.S. wine market in 1984, having grown in volume by nearly 500 percent that year, and 1900 percent in 1983.

This success resulted in the birth of a completely new category in the alcoholic beverages industry. California Cooler became an immediate consumer hit and proved that the cooler category was here to stay. The dramatic success of California Cooler attracted competition from the major wine-producing companies. By 1984, 40 cooler brands were on the market, but the major competitors were:

- California Cooler.
- Bartles & Jaymes (Ernest & Julio Wines).
- Sun Country (Canadaigua Wines).
- Seagrams Cooler (Seagram Wines).
- Calvin Cooler (Jos. Victori Wines).

Exhibit 5-3 outlines the market share data.

As the sales volume of wine coolers continues to increase by 65 percent per year, the level of competition will remain fierce; only the strong will prevail. For example, the number of competitors with established brands has increased 86 percent from 1981 to 1985.

The wine cooler has even attracted the attention of giant beer-producing companies, a further indication that this new beverage segment is not a fad, but rather a provider of potential sales volume. The cost to play in the "cooler game" is growing at a phenomenal rate. Some companies are now spending 30 percent of sales on advertising to maintain their current position in the market. The amount of advertising dollars spent has increased 96.6 percent from 1984 to 1985. Competitive intensity continues to increase. As a result of continually increasing competition, profit margins are quickly shrinking. The average price of a four pack (the main package of the industry) had dropped from $3.69 to $1.99. See Exhibit 5-4 for wine cooler sales, advertising expenditures, and competition.

BROWN-FORMAN, INC.

Brown-Forman, Inc. was founded in 1870 as a producer, importer, and marketer of wines and distilled spirits. Its ability to react quickly and astutely to changing public tastes and market conditions transformed Brown-Forman into a diversified producer and marketer of fine quality consumer products. It has maintained and continued to emphasize its all-important quality image across the firm's diversified markets.

Throughout the years, the growth strategy of the company has been to acquire products with strong brand names. Hence, a firm is considered for acquisition only if it is (or has the potential to be) a leader in its category. In addition, companies considered for acquisition must have a return on investment of 14 percent.

Exhibit 5-3   **Depletions[a] (Thousands of nine-liter cases)**

Brand	1981	1982	1983	1984	1985E
California Cooler	3	85	1,900	7,800	11,500
Bartles & Jaymes	—	—	—	—	7,500
Sun Country	—	—	—	1,590	5,000
Seagram's Cooler	—	—	—	5	4,000
Calvin Cooler	—	—	—	630	2,800
Total	3	85	1900	10,025	30,800

[a]Depletions are net sales from wholesalers to retailers.

Exhibit 5-4   Wine Cooler Category Growth

	1981	1982	1983	1984	1985
Cases sold (In thousands)	4	130	2,600	15,000	43,000
Advertising dollars spent (In thousands)	0	0	$ 2.2	$ 6,700	$65,000
Late comers to the category (est. brands)	9	19	19	49	63

Wine and Spirits Division

Until July 1983, Brown-Forman remained only in the wine and spirits industry. Adhering to its strict acquisition policies, it has built a solid portfolio of products in the domestic spirits, imported spirits, and wine and specialty liquors markets. Major brands of the firm include Jack Daniels Tennessee Whiskey, Canadian Mist Canadian Whiskey, Early Times Style Kentucky Whiskey, Bolla and Cella Italian Wine, Southern Comfort, Korbel Champagnes, Martell Cognacs, and the recently acquired California Cooler.

All of the liquors and wines have maintained top positions in their markets. Despite their premium status, however, several brands suffered sales declines resulting from the overall industry's slower growth. Exhibit 5-5 presents the major brands' worldwide depletions in fiscal 1985. For example, Jack Daniels had a 2 percent decrease in volume due to the lower per capita consumption of liquor. While

Exhibit 5-5   Major Brands' Worldwide Depletions in Fiscal 1985

Brands	9-Liter Case	Change
American Spirits		
Jack Daniels	3,930,000	(2%)
Early Times	1,940,000	—
Old Forester	500,000	(3%)
Imported Spirits		
Canadian Mist	4,265,000	7%
Usher's	580,000	7%
Wine and Specialties		
Bolla	1,690,000	(3%)
Cella	2,750,000	(4%)
Southern Comfort	1,700,000	2%
Korbel Champagnes	910,000	22%

Source: Brown-Forman, Inc. *Annual Report,* 1985.

maintaining premium positions in their markets, Bolla and Cella wine sales also decreased 3 to 4 percent because of changing market tastes. Although such brands as Canadian Mist and Korbel Champagnes achieved higher sales levels, Brown-Forman was, nevertheless, concerned about stagnating sales within the industry and the slowing growth of some products.

The success of Canadian Mist and other Brown-Forman products is partly a result of the firm's brand management program. This program fulfills the company's desire for tight internal control and is seen as the most efficient means of positioning its brands in the competitive market. The system gives the brand manager authority over everything from advertising to packaging. The manager, however, must maintain the 14 percent return on investment criteria. If he fails, both the brand and his job could be in danger.

Another factor attributing to Brown-Forman's success in maintaining market leadership is the firm's emphasis on advertising. Senior brand manager Bud Ballard says:

> We believe in brand building. Rather than having many, many brands, we believe in having a few good ones and then advertising them heavily. We try to build a quality bridge for a long-lasting effect. The life cycle in liquor products is extremely long compared to other products that are in today and gone tomorrow, like the hoola hoop. If you're making whisky—where you have to age it for three to four to ten years—then you can't live with a one-year life cycle.

This philosophy and Brown-Forman's advertising campaigns have helped the wine and spirit brands achieve high market positions.

Brown-Forman as a Diversified Firm

Despite Brown-Forman's success in the wine and spirits industry, W. L. Lyons Brown, chairman of the company, saw a need to diversify into other markets in 1983. The need stemmed from declining consumption and changing consumer tastes in the industry. As a hedge to this problem, he opted to acquire Lenox, Inc., a producer of fine china, crystal, and giftware. Although Lenox's markets and distribution system differed dramatically from Brown-Forman's, Lenox possessed the quality image, high market position, and profitability that Brown-Forman sought. Since the acquisition, Brown-Forman greatly expanded distribution and increased sales. Despite the presently inflated prices of Lenox abroad (due to the high value of the dollar), sales are high in the foreign markets.

Diversification has also led to the creation of Brown-Forman's personal use products division. It is comprised of the Hartmann luggage and the Keepsake and ArtCarved jewelry divisions. Hartmann is the premier brand in the upper-end American luggage category with a market share more than double its nearest competitor. The recently combined Keepsake and ArtCarved jewelry division markets quality bridal jewelry. ArtCarved also manufactures and markets high school and college class rings.

During the fiscal year ended June 1985 (prior to the California Cooler acquisition), revenues and operating income of the different segments were:

	Revenue	**Percentage**
Wine and spirits	$905 million	74.9
Home furnishings	$156 million	12.9
Personal use products	$147 million	12.2

	Operating Income	**Percentage**
Wine and spirits	$167 million	84.8
Home furnishings	$ 17 million	8.6
Personal use products	$ 13 million	6.6

Exhibits 5-6 and 5-7 are Brown-Forman's consolidated financial statements for fiscal years ended 1984 and 1985.

Exhibit 5-6   Brown-Forman, Inc. Consolidated Balance Sheet (In thousands)

	April 30, 1984	April 30, 1985
Assets		
Cash and short-term investments	$ 24,787	$ 23,362
Accounts receivable	166,493	157,276
Inventories		
Barreled whiskey	162,755	140,224
Finished goods	83,251	80,916
Work in process	30,331	29,876
Raw materials and supplies	31,104	29,709
Total inventories	307,441	280,725
Other Current Assets	31,111	27,922
Total Current Assets	529,832	489,285
Property, Plant and Equipment, at Cost		
Land	14,512	15,267
Buildings	90,486	93,859
Equipment	122,787	133,773
	277,785	242,899
Less accumulated depreciation	(75,374)	(89,438)
Net Property, Plant and Equipment	152,411	153,461
Intangible assets	272,955	264,820
Other assets	27,629	27,817
Total Assets	$982,827	$935,383
Liabilities		
Notes payable to banks	$ 9,856	$ 183
Accounts payable and accrued expenses	95,799	106,869
Current portion of long-term debt	33,741	28,031
Accrued taxes on income	33,921	28,357
Total Current Liabilities	173,297	163,440

Exhibit 5-6   (continued)

	April 30, 1984	April 30, 1985
Long-term debt	264,411	266,162
Deferred income taxes	26,819	39,949
Total Liabilities	464,527	469,551
Stockholders' Equity		
Capital Stock:		
Preferred $.40 cumulative, $10 par value redeemable at Company's option at $D10.25 per share plus unpaid accrued dividends; 1,177,948 shares authorized and outstanding	11,779	11,779
Class A common stock, voting, $15 par value, authorized shares, 18,000,000; issued shares, 8,041,268	1,206	1,206
Class B common stock, nonvoting, $15 par value; authorized shares, 36,000,000; issued shares, 17,776,210	2,667	2,667
Capital in excess of par value of common stock	91,146	91,156
Retained earnings	417,645	477,940
Cumulative translation adjustment	(2,221)	(2,492)
Less common treasury stock, at cost	(3,922)	(116,424)
Common Stockholders' Equity	506,521	454,053
Total Stockholders' Equity	518,300	465,832
Total Liabilities and Stockholders' Equity	$982,827	$935,383

Exhibit 5-7   Brown-Forman, Inc. Consolidated Statement of Income (In thousands)

	Year Ended April 30,	
	1984	1985
Net sales	$1,146,343	$1,208,113
Excise tax	282,550	278,721
Cost of sales	437,718	457,687
Gross profit	426,075	470,705
Selling, advertising, administrative, and general expenses	250,627	282,627
Operating income	175,448	188,088
Interest income	2,975	1,945
Interest expense	34,969	35,749
Income before taxes	143,454	154,284
Taxes on income	69,900	72,600
Net income	$ 73,554	$ 81,684
Earnings per common share	$ 2.90	$ 3.43

The Acquisition of California Cooler

In early 1985, attention turned to the firm's wine and spirits division. Brown-Forman's management was concerned about the continued drop in the division's profitability. The wine and spirits division, the company's major line of business with 75 percent of total sales, was suffering from a sharp decrease in demand for alcoholic beverages.

The well-diversified company, however, was not on the verge of financial calamity. In fact, its consolidated financial statements showed 27 consecutive years of sales increases and earning gains. With a large pool of cash at its disposal, management opted to make an acquisition. The search for a growing company to reinvigorate the division culminated with the purchase of California Cooler on September 5, 1985.

Brown-Forman used approximately $98 million in cash to acquire California Cooler. Future payments were contingent on the level of future case sales volume. If volume remained at present levels, additional payments would total $83 million. Given the strong growth in total demand for wine coolers, however, future payments were likely to exceed this level.

Brown-Forman saw the new life it needed in California Cooler. The acquired firm was the foremost brand in the fastest growing segment of the alcoholic beverage industry. With its sales volume doubling to 750 million cases in 1985, a strong 51 percent market share, and a lofty 40 percent pretax margin, California Cooler would immediately impact Brown-Forman's financial statements. Brown-Forman hoped to become the major worldwide force in the alcoholic beverage industry.

California Cooler, however, was not without its problems. Its initial monopoly quickly degenerated into an intensely competitive market. As the number of firms in the industry continued to swell, success became a function of the company's marketing and distribution capabilities. California Cooler had to compete against large beverage companies with more marketing muscle. The intermediate result of this competition was falling market share and a loss of competitive advantage in costs. The end result was the sale of the company to Brown-Forman at the depressed price.

Brown-Forman's management had carefully reviewed all the cost-benefit reports at the time of the acquisition. California Cooler was a profitable and growing firm, but its performance was slowing. Management, nevertheless, concluded that Brown-Forman's greater financial resources and management experience would be sufficient to recapture lost market share and improve the company's bottom line. Furthermore, California Cooler met Brown-Forman's two main acquisition criteria: first, the firm had a strong product image; and second, it had the potential to be (and in this case, it was) the best product in the market.

Management recognized three trends that could lessen California Cooler's profitability.

1. Marketing costs have increased sharply. The fight for market share is concentrated on advertising, and a $20 million ad budget is required just to compete.

2. The existing high margin on sales has begun to fall. As sales volume continues to increase, beverage producers are introducing new competitive products, which will adversely affect the favorable price structure.

3. The sustainability of present demand levels is unknown. It is never easy to maintain a 100 percent annual growth rate.

Brown-Forman's strategy is to maintain a strong presence in the market by applying its high level of advertising and distribution expertise to the California Cooler product. Because California Cooler's sales have historically originated more from beer than from wine drinkers, Brown-Forman plans to continue focusing its promotional efforts at the retail level on beer drinkers. The company is willing to spend up to $30 million on advertising to maintain its 51 percent market share.

The conglomerate feels that California Cooler's original distribution strategy, one of dispersing the product to the points of sale via beer distributors, is effective. However, it will experiment with cutting prices to wholesalers to increase shelf space and visibility.

In the fall of 1985, William Street officially assumed corporate responsibility for the market champion. Maintaining California Cooler's leadership position, however, would become increasingly difficult. Armed with a capable and qualified new marketing chief, Mr. Street prepared to battle with the formidable competition. Confident and aggressive, Mr. Street affirmed at the close of 1985, "We're putting our ducks in a row in terms of promotion in 1986. I have no doubt we'll be a viable competitor for the number one position throughout next year."

With these prospects in mind, Mr. Brown was awaiting Bill Street's strategic plan for the upcoming year. One question remained, however. Would this strategy assure Mr. Brown of California Cooler's continuing dominance in the wine cooler market and of its long-term contribution to Brown-Forman's diversified portfolio?

Plastic Suppliers, Inc.

COMPANY HISTORY

Plastic Suppliers, Inc. (PSI) commenced operations in April 1986. The company was an offshoot of its founder's lifelong dream of owning his own business by providing services which he enjoyed and was highly qualified to perform. At the onset he was designated the CEO and the two other people who joined him were part owners and heads of the various functions within the organization. All three were friends who had worked in the plastics business as technicians for many years and shared the founder's personal objective of being their own boss.

Mr. Edmunds, the founder, had a 16-year career at IBM, where he started from the bottom and worked his way up till he became head of the new products division. Despite his position with IBM, Mr. Edmunds's entrepreneuring spirit could not hold him down to a job at a prestigious internationally acclaimed company like IBM. Therefore, he and his friends invested their lifetime savings in a small business, PSI, and started operations in McAllen, Texas.

Several advantages accrued because of the choice of location in South Texas. First, Mr. Edmunds was a native of South Texas. Second, most of the existing plastics injection molding outfits were located in the northeastern or midwestern United States, and the nearest (a very small facility) was in Dallas, some 550 miles north of McAllen. Third, the maquiladoras were located just across the border in Mexico, some 12 miles away. Maquiladora plants are usually one-half of twin plant operations, normally U.S. owned, with one plant on each side of the U.S.–Mexican border. Parts and technical operations are performed on the U.S. side, and manual operations are performed on the Mexican side. Mr. Edmunds realized that the maquiladora industry was rapidly growing, with a need for various plastic parts for many operations.

Having a supplier that was nearer to the maquiladoras could cut delivery time enormously. Inventory levels could be kept low resulting in lower investments in inventory and all the pluses and minuses of just-in-time (JIT) inventory methods. The distance alone was an advantage for PSI as a supplier. If for any reason problems occurred about the supplied parts, customers (maquiladoras) had the convenience of easily crossing the border into the United States and correcting any problems.

Maquiladoras choose suppliers from the United States rather than Mexico pri-

This case was prepared by Walter E. Greene, Pan American University, with the assistance of Mark E. George and Carminia D. Oris, as a basis for class discussion rather than to illustrate either effective or ineffective handling of an administrative situation. Used by permission from Walter E. Greene.

marily because of the higher quality and available service. Finally, in the Rio Grande valley region of Mexico alone, there had been a 43 percent increase in maquiladoras in the nine-year period from 1978 to 1986, increasing from 49 to 70 plants. Mr. Edmunds had projected, barring any drastic changes, a 10 percent annual growth rate for PSI, with 95 percent derived from the Mexican maquiladoras.

During the first two years of operations, growth had been tremendous. The first operation was equipped with four 150-ton plastics injection molding machines (similar to the plastic injection molding machines that make toy soldiers, etc., only much larger). Recently, four additional machines had been installed, three 150-ton and one 500-ton machines. The plant had been expanded to accommodate the new equipment and the work force had grown from the original six to 86.

COMPANY OBJECTIVES

Aside from Mr. Edmunds's personal desire to run his own business, the company had one major objective. All owners agreed that the company was to become a full-service supplier of plastic injection molding parts to local manufacturing firms on both sides of the Mexican border, in U.S. plants and in the maquiladora operations.

An organization chart is shown in Exhibit 6-1. The company was Mr. Edmunds's dream of a lifetime; he had worked hard and put his life savings into founding PSI. As a technician his major concerns were meeting client specifications and providing quality services and products. His cohorts were also technicians who wanted to be their own bosses. During its first two years, PSI found a niche in the market and grew at a tremendously fast pace. As was common with entrepreneurs, they outgrew their original investments, and venture capitalists from both the United States and Mexico stepped in and provided much needed capital.

PRODUCTS AND SERVICES PROVIDED

The company had three profit generating departments, namely, engineering, tooling and production. The engineering department created mold designs, the tooling department made the actual molds and did mold repairs, and the production department ran the mold to produce the various plastic parts.

Although each department's function could be considered a continuous flow from mold design to parts production, clients came in needing one or two or all of the services that PSI offered. Some clients had their own molds (which they brought down from northern locations, so that delivery would be faster) so all that PSI had to do was produce the plastic parts and maintain the molds. Other customers came with specifications for the part they needed, requiring PSI to design and make the mold, then produce the parts. Added to all these functions, PSI was also capable of rendering local delivery services after it purchased a small delivery van.

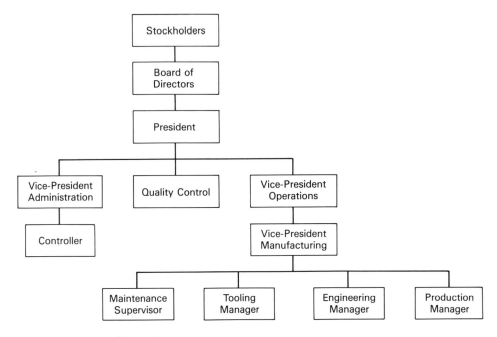

Exhibit 6-1   **Organization Chart[a] Plastic Suppliers, Inc.**

Engineering was responsible for designing the molds that would be used to make the parts. Its head was one of the original three men who had started the business. He had two assistants who prepared drawings showing all details of the mold. The drawings were made through a computer using CAD (computer assisted design) software, thus making the task easier than when done manually. Designing the molds required highly skilled people, unavailable in the local job market area.

Tooling, supervised by one of the three founders, made the molds based on the drawing specifications from the engineering department. Making a mold took anywhere from a couple of weeks at the very least to three months or more. Skilled personnel were required for this department because of the complexity of the tasks involved. However, as was the case with engineering, skilled personnel were unavailable in the local job market. After the molds were built, they were moved to the production floor for preliminary testing. If any flaws were discovered, the molds were sent back to tooling for adjustments.

Adjusted and tested molds were turned over to production, manned mostly with semiskilled operators. The only skill required was in setting up the machine specifications to turn out the right number of plastic parts. Knowledge of cycle times, water levels, and so forth were important. Apart from this the machines did most of the work. Each machine was manned by a worker who made certain the

[a]Taken from a report issued to third parties (suppliers, bankers, and prospective investors).

parts were produced according to the quantity on the specification sheet and the machine did not run out of water. This task did not require any special skills. Normally the only way big production schedules could be met was by second shift operations in the department and on rare occasions a third shift (24-hour operations).

QUALITY CONTROLS AND PROBLEMS

Mr. Edmunds realized that quality control (QC) was of the highest priority with maquiladora operators. Since PSI produced plastic parts which became part of larger components, all parts had to fit perfectly. One of PSI's customers, which used a large portion of PSI capacity, was a maquiladora plant that manufactured parts for automobile seat belts. This maquiladora plant produced all seat belts required by one of the big three U.S. automobile manufacturers. This required strict measurement and material quality controls. Therefore, a QC department was added.

Frequently, problems arose concerning a job. Usually time schedules were set up to ensure that the parts reached the customer on time and to maximize the utilization of personnel and machines. However, delays could, and did often, occur due to:

1. Too much time spent on designing the molds (engineering), or in making the molds (tooling), or in producing the parts (production).
2. Sometimes parts did not conform to QC standards, and then each of the departments blamed the other department for the failure.
3. Sometimes the molds broke or did not work correctly even if they passed QC checks.
4. Finally, machine breakdowns were a frequent problem.

ECONOMIC ENVIRONMENT

The company's economic environment was greatly influenced by the fact that it was situated in the Rio Grande valley of South Texas. While the U.S. national unemployment rate was about 7 percent, as was that in the state of Texas, unemployment in the valley area was between 15 and 18 percent during this period. Starr County (one of the four counties in the valley) had the dubious honor of being one of the four poorest counties in the United States with an average annual income of $3,300. Poor health, low educational achievement, and limited job opportunities characterized this region. The local economy was highly influenced by what happened to the oil industry and the Mexican economy. Mexico's rate of inflation during the first years PSI was in operation was 160 percent and had averaged over 100 percent for the past three years.

Most Mexicans residing near the border brought business to the area by purchasing goods on the U.S. side. With the Mexican peso devalued a few years earlier, the high rate of Mexican inflation, the bottom dropping out of the oil market, and the killing freeze that destroyed the valley's citrus crop three years before, business on the U.S. side of the border was basically at a standstill.

Unfortunately, in view of the area's past economy, local banks were geared to agriculture, oil, and small retail establishments. The failure rate of Texas banks during this period had been one of the highest of any state in the United States. Bankers were scared, and in addition, none had any experience with manufacturing establishments like PSI.

Public officials in the region exhorted the development of a manufacturing sector. With high unemployment, firms of any kind were encouraged to relocate to the valley from the industrial north. Aware that the economy had to become multifaceted to lessen the impact of drastic changes in the local economy, a strong desire developed to encourage the manufacturing sector to grow in the valley region.

FAST EXPANSION

Rapid expansion was triggered by the increased demand from maquiladora operators. At the onset, PSI was doing small jobs and one big project (to manufacture bag handles). One machine was devoted entirely to the plastic handles. The other three machines were almost always idle because of small production runs. Then when the word spread that PSI was located in the valley, jobs came pouring in. Two maquiladora plants, Zenith Televisions and TRW (seat belts), alone took practically all of the original capacity. Expansion was inevitable, and the four additional machines were acquired. The production department's capacity in terms of machine hours had more than doubled during its first two years. Raw materials were stacked in boxes alongside the machines due to lack of space. A small nearby warehouse had been leased for extra storage. A small office for the engineering personnel had to be added because of overcrowding in the administrative office.

FINANCIAL PROBLEMS

During the first 20 months no accurate financial reports were maintained. However, new stockholders were concerned about the lack of accounting information to support decision-making. The original bookkeeper was just that, a bookkeeper. Mr. Earl, a CPA with consulting and work experience in one of the major accounting firms, was hired. He set up the accounting system from scratch (Exhibits 6-2 and 6–3).

As the controller, Mr. Earl performed functions like financial sourcing, financial information analysis, and general accounting. He secured several short-term and long-term loans.

Cash flow problems had beset PSI from the start. Collections were very late.

Exhibit 6-2   Plastic Suppliers, Inc. Balance Sheet[a] Last Month

Current Assets

Cash	$ (8,689)	
Accounts receivable	146,547	
Inventory	266,449	
Prepaid expenses	3,765	
Deposits	579	
Total Current Assets		408,651

Fixed Assets

Autos and trucks	75,880	
Furniture and fixtures	14,191	
Equipment	2,084,960	
Building	283,246	
Less accumulated depreciation	(98,470)	
Land	81,383	
Leasehold improvements	49,525	
Less accumulated amortization	(3,186)	
Total Fixed Assets		2,487,529
Total Assets		$2,896,180

Current Liabilities

Notes payable	152,049	
Accrued payable	22,590	
Taxes payable	91,519	
Other payable	52,421	
Current portion long-term debt	343,487	
Deferred income	67,771	
Total Current Liabilities		729,837

Long-Term

Mortgage payable	361,154	
Notes Payable	1,694,265	
Total Long-Term Liabilities		2,055,419
Total Liabilities		2,785,256

Stockholders' Equity

Common stock	466,575	
Paid-in capital	579,236	
Treasury stock	(180,432)	
Retained earnings	(754,455)	
Total Stockholders' Equity		110,924
Total Liabilities and Equity		$2,896,180

[a]Taken from a report issued to third parties (suppliers, bankers, and prospective investors).

Exhibit 6-3   **PSI Income Statement (For the year ended December 31)**

	Department			
	Production	**Mold Build**	**Repairs**	**Total**
Sales	$120,000	$140,000	$34,000	$294,000
Cost of sales				
Materials used	68,345	20,496		88,841
Direct labor	32,492	123,932	566	156,990
Overhead	31,433	26,058	3,515	61,007
Total Cost of Sales	132,271	170,486	4,081	306,838
Gross Profit	(12,271)	(30,486)	29,919	(12,838)
General and Administrative Expenses				
Payroll				108,232
Maintenance				24,289
Depreciation				36,114
Amortization				1,213
Rents and leases				311
Insurance–assets				7,887
Travel and entertainment				11,546
Shipping				507
Taxes				741
Consulting fees				30,428
Office supplies				7,324
Telephone and telegraph				5,622
Mail/postage/courier				2,596
Electricity and water				19,835
Fuel and oil				122
Contributions and donations				51
Licenses and permits				491
Memberships, dues and sub-scriptions				1,418
Total General and Administrative Expenses				258,728
Operating Income				(271,565)
Less Other Expenses (Revenues)				
Financial expenses				42,083
Other expenses				3,824
Net Income				$(317,471)

To meet current expenses (such as payroll, and regular monthly payments) short-term loans had been obtained. However, as loans matured, interest and principal payments became too high for PSI to handle. Eventually the debt grew so large that the debt-to-equity ratio and the debt-to-asset ratio precluded conventional debt financing. Long-term loans were hard to obtain because of the banking system's reservations about lending to manufacturing organizations.

When Mr. Earl derived job costs and compared them against the revenues, he discovered that PSI was barely making a profit on most of their contracts. In the absence of cost standards and a cost accounting system, the price quotations given to clients were not enough to cover costs of manufacturing the parts. A consulting team was hired to determine the standard costs for labor, raw materials, and overhead and to set up a system to monitor expenses on a per job basis. The study was completed, however, the resulting cost accounting system was not implemented because Mr. Edmunds, the CEO, was too busy searching for more sales and financial sources for borrowing.

With the existing plant already filled to capacity, management had plans for a bigger facility that could accommodate 20 plastic injection molding machines in the production department and offices for each of the departments. The number of jobs had increased and the company was producing at maximum capacity. Therefore, management believed that the proposed new facility was a must, yet no financing was available.

CHANGE OF MANAGEMENT

Mr. Edmunds relinquished his position as CEO to Mr. Earl. Mr. Edmunds felt that the administrative duties were too much for him to handle and all sorts of paperwork was accumulating. Besides, Mr. Edmunds was a technician and not fond of paperwork, and Mr. Earl had done an outstanding job of compiling PSI's financial statements.

Almost immediately, conflict of opinions arose about strategic policies between Mr. Earl and the Board.

At the board meeting, Mr. Earl tendered his thirty-day notice of resignation. Mr. Edmunds stated in the meeting that he would not resume duties as CEO, as he had more than he could handle generating sales (technical marketing).

TAKEOVER PROBLEMS

Aware of the financial problems of PSI and of their prospects as a maquiladora supplier, one of PSI's newest clients had become interested in acquiring the company. This client firm was one of the larger maquiladora operators, and its intention was to integrate vertically and thus ensure an adequate supply of plastic parts at cheaper prices. This potential acquirer saw a definite advantage of a supplier located as close as PSI.

To prevent the takeover, the existing stockholders had infused additional equity of approximately twice their original investments. Despite this, PSI still needed additional financing to start the new facility.

Delta Air Lines, Inc.

It was 6:40 P.M. on August 2, 1985, when the first officer of cabin crew Flight 191 spotted lightning. The flight proceeded into the thunderstorm and was caught by a sudden downburst of air blowing from the opposite direction. The cockpit voice recorder quoted the captain as saying, "Push it up! Push it up!" followed by, "togo!" which means to take the plane up to a higher altitude and go around the other direction.[1]

However, eight seconds later the aircraft struck a hill, emerged from the thunderstorm, touched down on state highway 114, and struck a vehicle. The plane then burst into flames and collided with a water tower on the airport grounds. Ron Allen, recently appointed CEO of Delta, was relieved that the tragedy, the worst aircrash in Delta's history, was finally behind the company. But was it really? Recent news stories indicated that some families of the 137 who died in the crash were trying to reopen the case.

Delta Air Lines, Inc. was the fourth largest air carrier providing scheduled air transportation for passengers, freight, and mail over a network of routes throughout the United States and overseas. Delta served 132 domestic cities in 42 states, the District of Columbia, and Puerto Rico, and operated flights to 20 international cities in nine foreign countries.

The airline industry was extremely competitive. Problems with government deregulation resulted in a proliferation of routes, fare wars, and increasing concentration.

INDUSTRY OVERVIEW

We have not seen the total results of deregulation, by a long shot. The experiment in deregulation is not completed yet.[2]

Airports these days can be an exciting place especially for the people at an airline desk right after they have announced a flight cancellation. Riots, police, and

[1]James Ott, "Recorder Reveals Lightning Preceded Delta 1-1011 Crash," *Aviation Week and Space Technology,* October 7, 1985, p. 26.

[2]"Delta's Soft Landing," *Management Today,* July 1985, p. 71.

This case was prepared by Michele Boren, Regina Bruce, Barron Green, and Victor Khoo under the direct supervision of Sexton Adams, University of North Texas, and Adelaide Griffin, Texas Woman's University, as a basis for class discussion rather than to illustrate either effective or ineffective handling of an administrative situation. Used by permission from Sexton Adams.

arrests are not uncommon. The situation is becoming so bad that some of the major airlines are training their employees in crowd control.[3]

The airline industry has undergone tremendous changes since deregulation in 1978. Increased demand has caused serious problems for the industry in terms of service. In 1987, 126 million adults, 72 percent of the population, had flown at least once in their lives as compared to only 10 percent in 1967. Fifty-three million adults made at least one airplane trip in 1986 as compared to 38 million in 1977.[4] As a result of this increase, congestion problems have occurred.

Several factors have caused the congestion. Deregulation has made flying affordable for the average citizen. According to the Air Transport Association, the average fare fell 9.6 percent in 1986, the largest one year drop ever.[5] Combine the drop in general fares with the discount wars and a very attractive ticket price ensued. Another problem is the fact that airlines are changing their routes to a hub and spoke system. Hubbing means that several flights converge on the same location at the same time, resulting in additional congestion. When a delay occurs in the hub, the spoke location will also have a delay, causing a domino effect throughout the system.

Government Regulation

The process of airline deregulation began in 1978 under President Jimmy Carter. Prior to deregulation, competition among airlines was limited by the Civil Aeronautics Board (the CAB ceased to exist by 1985) in two of the three major areas of airline marketing—route authority and pricing—leaving only the amount of capacity (number of flights) up to the judgment of individual carriers. Also, there was tight control over the entrance of new airlines.

The results were predictable—a fairly small number of major airlines, flying medium to large size jets, served a broad network of large cities and small towns. In many cases, an airline's dealings with the CAB were more important than its dealings with customers. However, after the deregulation acts permitting airlines to compete in all three areas, customer service was viewed as the crucial element in any airline success story.

Fare Wars

Prior to deregulation, the pricing of airline fares was controlled by the CAB, which allowed no price competition. After deregulation, pricing strategies became an important factor. Deregulation allowed many new entrants into the industry,

---

[3]Jonathan Dahl, "Battling Crowds at the Airports," *The Wall Street Journal,* October 19, 1987, p. 29.

[4]Holman Jenkins, Jr., "Setting Course for Smoother Skies," *Insight,* October 26, 1987, p. 8.

[5]"Merger Myopia," *The Wall Street Journal,* October 19, 1987, p. 27.

many of which had lower cost structures enabling them to offer substantially discounted fares. The major carriers had to respond to these low fares to maintain market share. The first "fare war" occurred during the winter of 1982. In addition, various approaches such as frequent flyer programs and advance discount tickets were initiated.

Because most of the airline management teams had been trained during the period of regulation, they lacked the experience to deal with these complex pricing strategies. Consequently, the prices of fares varied greatly within the industry and even within a given flight. Fare wars severely damaged many of the major carriers who suffered decreased passenger revenues without a corresponding increase in the number of passengers.

With the advent of highly sophisticated computer systems, major carriers were tackling the pricing game much more effectively.[6]

Economic Factors

The economy has clearly had a major impact on the airline industry. Many of the major airlines performed poorly during the recessionary period of 1980 to 1982. In 1985, the economy began to improve, and oil prices reached record lows. These factors, coupled with the increased numbers of passengers, led to record profits for some of the major carriers. But the profits in 1986 were lower than 1985 due to the reduced prices brought on by the fare wars. Fares were going down while operating expenses were going up (Exhibit 7-1 provides industry averages).

Exhibit 7-1   **Composite Industry Statistics: Air Transport Industry (In millions)**

	1984	1985	1986	1987 (est.)
Revenues	$42,059	$45,826	$42,405	$45,800
Load factor	58.2%	56.0%	57.7%	57.0%
Operating margin	11.6%	10.3%	10.8%	11.0%
Depreciation	$ 2,584.2	$ 2,881.8	$ 3,006.0	$ 3,320.0
Net profit	$ 913.3	$ 584.7	$ 143.9	$ 525
Income tax rate	42.5%	40.6%	NMF	35.0%
Net profit margin	2.2%	1.3%	0.3%	1.1%
Long-term debt	$12,173	$15,452	$17,593	$19,000
Net worth	$ 9,587.4	$11,930	$13,020	$14,500
% Earned total capital	7.0%	4.7%	2.5%	14.5%
% Earned net worth	9.5%	4.9%	32.0%	3.5%

Source: Marilyn M. McKelling, "Air Transport Industry," *Value Line,* July 3, 1987, p. 251.

---

[6]Kenneth Labich, "Winners and the Air Wars," *Fortune,* May 11, 1987, p. 74.

Exhibit 7-2 **Classification of Airlines**		
Major Airlines	**National Airlines**	**Regional Airlines**
American	Alaska	ASA
Delta	Aloha	Aspen Airways
Northwest	American West	Business Express
Pan Am	Braniff	Comair
Texas Air	Hawaiian	Florida Express
TWA	Midway	Metro Airways
United	Southwest	Skywest
USAir		

Source: James P. Woolsey, "Airlines Enjoy Modest Traffic, Financial Gains, Benefits of Lower Fuel Costs," *Air Transport World,* June 1987, p. 64.

During the first half of 1987, the economy continued to grow at a moderate pace. The Dow Jones Industrial Average had more than tripled since 1982. The energy and agriculture sectors had begun to regain strength. Although the trade imbalance had improved slightly and the value of the dollar had begun to rise, economists were still concerned that the trade balance might worsen and that the value of the dollar would fall, pushing the United States into a recession. On October 19, 1987, the Dow Jones Industrial Average fell 508 points, 22.6 percent of market value.[7] The stock prices of several airline carriers were adversely affected. If the predictions of a recession were coming true, how damaging would the effects be for the airline industry?

Industry Concentration

The airline industry is comprised of three different leagues: major, national, and regional airlines although this delineation fluctuates (Exhibit 7-2). The best example of this is Braniff changing from a major airline to a national airline.

The merger game has been prevalent during deregulation. Between 1985 and 1987, there were eight mergers which decreased the number of major carriers from 20 to eight. The acquisitions were not cheap, however. The majors spent or borrowed nearly $6 billion to buy each other.[8]

The number of independent major airlines was shrinking. Eight megacarriers existed and represented 91.7 percent of the nation's scheduled jet air travel.[9] This

[7]Amy Stromberg, "How Panic Swept Wall Street," *The Dallas Times Herald,* October 20, 1987, p. 7-A.

[8]James P. Woolsey, "Airlines Enjoy Modest Traffic, Financial Gains, Benefits of Lower Fuel Costs," *Air Transport World,* June 1987, p. 64.

[9]Donald L. Pevsner, "Merger Mania is Putting Lower Air Fares in Tailspin," *The Dallas Morning News,* October 11, 1987, p. 10-G.

growth came at the expense of the national and regional lines. Many were either bought out by larger airlines or made marketing agreements with them. In 1986, 75 airlines in this group were involved in code-sharing or other arrangements with a larger airline. The numbers of these lines has dropped by 59, from a high of 238 in 1981 to a low of 179 in 1985.[10]

The major airlines constituted most of the domestic flights between the large metropolitan areas as well as most of the international flights. They were by far the most expensive lines and recorded the most passenger miles and revenues. The national lines consisted mostly of domestic flights, concentrating on the major metropolitan areas as well as the smaller hubs such as Cincinnati and Charlotte. The national price structure is lower than the majors, in general, with some airlines going strictly no-frills. The regional lines are the low-cost carriers of the industry. They usually operate only a few routes and act as feeders to the larger lines.

Flight Schedules

Competing with each other in flight schedules was not new to airlines. Since deregulation, airlines have expanded their routes and increased the frequency of flights. This has been achieved by acquiring additional aircraft. As a result, traffic at several major airports is increasingly congested with more planes on the runways and terminals than can be accommodated. This problem has triggered a new call for a possible reregulation of flight schedules at several major airports.

According to Department of Transportation (DOT) officials, there has been an increasing trend in flight delay problems since December 1986. Delays at 22 airports were increased by 22.4 percent to 376,000 delays in 1986, and for the first three months of 1987, more than a third of customer complaints against airlines were contributed by delays and cancellations.[11] The delay problems prompted the DOT to take some steps against flight scheduling at several major airports. The department chose Hartsfield Atlanta International Airport as the first of 13 airports to be investigated.

DELTA'S STRATEGY IN A COMPETITIVE MARKETPLACE

Management

The attitude of our people is unusual. Delta people pitch in where they are needed.[12]

Ron Allen was elected Delta's Chairman and CEO on August 7, 1987. He succeeded David Garrett who reached mandatory retirement age after having served

---

[10]Woolsey, p. 59.

[11]James Ott, "Airlines View Flight Adjustments as Trend Toward Regulation," *Aviation Week and Space Technology,* February 9, 1987, p. 34.

[12]Delta's Soft Landing," p. 70.

Delta for 41 years. Garrett exhibited strong leadership and guided Delta through some troubled times into a healthy, growing airline. His management style brought Delta through uncertainty and a changing environment caused by the Deregulation Act of 1978. Delta experienced its first major net loss of $86.7 million in 1983, after 36 years of profitable operations. Nevertheless, the airline was quick in responding to this crisis situation and bounced back in 1984 with a net income of $175.6 million, a $262.3 million turnaround from 1983.

According to Garrett, several factors contributed to this turnaround in profitability: improvement in marketing strategy, increased computer application in travel agent programs by using the DATA II automated reservation system, significant fleet change, and greater dependence on commuter carriers in feeding passengers to Delta's major hubs. Garrett retired on July 31, 1987, but he planned to remain active as a member of the Board and served as Chairman of the Executive Committee.

Allen was a veteran in the airline business. He had been with Delta for 24 years, beginning in personnel and moving to the position of Senior Vice President for Administration and Personnel. By November 1983, he was promoted to President and Chief Operating Officer (COO), and four years later, he became the new CEO.

Allen's successor as president and COO was Hollis Harris, a Delta veteran of 33 years. He worked his way up the corporate ladder from transportation agent, through Technical Operations, Operations, Passenger Service, to Senior Vice-President of Operations before being named COO.

Delta's organization was set up with seven functional divisions—finance, marketing, personnel, technical operations, operations, information services and properties, and general counsel and secretary. Each of these divisions was supervised by a senior vice-president and a chief financial officer who reported to the president and COO. Several subdivisions existed in each functional area, which were supervised by either vice-presidents or assistant vice-presidents (Exhibit 7-3).

Even though the organization was very centralized, the senior management group was accessible to the rest of the company. Ron Allen and his senior management group always made the critical decisions; however, Delta's management maintained an "open door" policy for employees to discuss problems and concerns. In addition, Delta's management had generally maintained a policy of delegating the maximum degree of responsibility to its crew members.

Operations

The competitive environment today is to have a strong, high-frequency operation in major centers. You have to control a good deal of traffic in order to survive in a very volatile, competitive environment.[13]

---

[13]Bruce A. Smith, "Delta Agrees to Acquire Western for $860 Million," *Aviation Week and Space Technology,* September 15, 1986, p. 31.

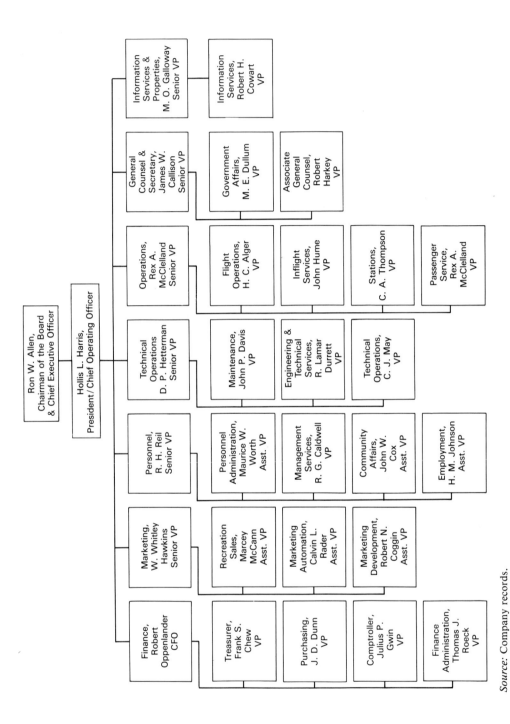

Exhibit 7-3 **Delta Air Lines, Inc., Organization Chart**

Source: Company records.

100

Delta, in compliance with its strategic plan to become a major international airline, acquired Western Airlines. This acquisition increased Delta's presence in areas where it previously lacked strength. Forty-four new cities were added, including cities in Alaska, Hawaii, western Canada, and Mexico. New hubs were added at Salt Lake City and Los Angeles (Exhibit 7-4 illustrates Delta's operations).

Delta invented and operated under the hub and spoke system which became the keystone of route development in the airline industry. The hub and spoke system required fewer planes than if each regional base had to be connected with all others by a direct flight. Major hubs for Delta were Dallas–Fort Worth, Atlanta, Salt Lake City, and Los Angeles. More than half of all Delta flights either began or ended at one of these cities.

In addition to the new routes added by the merger with Western, Delta added new service from Atlanta through Portland, Oregon, to Tokyo, Japan and Seoul, South Korea. New service was also added from Cincinnati to London. The Cincinnati hub was expanded and upgraded to compete head-on with other major carriers in the Midwest. Delta more than doubled its daily flights to Cincinnati.

Delta used four regional carriers to increase the efficiency of its hub operations: Atlantic Southeast Airline, Comair, Business Express, and SkyWest. These carriers served 93 cities and operated more than 1,400 flights per day.

Exhibit 7-4   **Delta's Operations**

Cargo operations and mail carrier service continued to increase in 1987. Delta signed a new agreement with the U.S. Post Office for the carriage of mail, which was expected to increase the number of mail ton miles throughout 1988. Delta continued its push into the special passenger markets such as conventions and groups, military and government, tour and cruise passengers, and family and senior citizen travelers.

In an effort to support continued growth, Delta expanded several facilities during 1987. Federal Inspection Service facilities were added in Atlanta and Dallas–Fort Worth, and plans were to add one in Cincinnati. Gate expansion occurred in Cincinnati, Dallas–Fort Worth, Portland, and Los Angeles. New terminal facilities were opened in Mobile and Fort Lauderdale.

Aircraft

To facilitate this expansion, Delta received delivery of 35 new aircraft in addition to 92 aircraft gained in the acquisition of Western. The company had 59,000 passenger seats available in 368 planes: 132 B-727s, 36 DC-9s, 9 DC-10s, 12 DC-8s, 35 L-1011s, 22 B-767s, 86 B-737s, 28 B-757s, 8 MD-82/88s.[14] To be prepared for future expansion, Delta had 63 aircraft on order and options on another 101 aircraft from 1988 through 1992.

During 1987, Delta decreased its average cost per seat mile by 14 percent. This decrease along with reduced fuel prices and greater productivity from personnel, helped Delta decrease its unit costs and increase its operating revenues.

Customer Service

We will resist in every appropriate way any implication that Delta misleads the public.[15]

According to U.S. government records, Delta offered the best customer service for the thirteenth consecutive year. Delta was voted the best airline by the readers of *Travel Holiday* magazine.[16] In addition, Delta had one of the best records in overbooking. Overbooking results in bumping some passengers from a flight, usually late arrivals. Delta did this to 1.3 passengers of every 1,000 on an involuntary basis, and 6.4 passengers of 1,000 on a combined voluntary and involuntary basis. These numbers were second and first in the airline industry.[17]

Flight delays have continued to plague Delta. The airline had one of the worst

---

[14]Marilyn M. McKellin, "Air Transport Industry," *Value Line,* July 3, 1987, p. 259.

[15]Laurie McGinley, "U.S. Weighs Penalizing Delta, Eastern Over Scheduling at Airport in Atlanta," *The Wall Street Journal,* April 10, 1987, p. 3.

[16]Delta Airlines, Inc., *Annual Report 1987,* p. 10.

[17]Francis C. Brown, III, and Jonathan Dahl, "New Data on Airline Performance May End Up Misleading Travelers," *The Wall Street Journal,* November 23, 1987, p. 25.

records for on-time arrival of reported flights. In September 1987, Delta had 72.3 percent of reported flights that arrived on time. The company ranked eleventh of 13 major airlines. Delta also had 4.7 percent of its regularly scheduled flights arriving late 70 percent or more of the time, which was the third worst percentage. Finally, Delta had six flights which arrived late 96 to 100 percent of the time—the most of any airline.[18]

Upon investigation of flight delays at Atlanta's Hartsfield airport, Transportation Secretary Elizabeth Dole accused Delta of setting unrealistic flight schedules. The department said its investigation showed that more than 55 Delta flights to and from Atlanta arrived at least 15 minutes late 70 percent of the time during a thirty-day sampling period. In addition, two Delta flights were late 100 percent of the time.[19]

Delta was "appalled" by Ms. Dole's accusation that it might be engaging in deceptive practices. The carrier maintained that its Atlanta schedules had not increased significantly since 1984. Delta said the DOT was engaged in "a misguided effort to shift responsibility for airline delays away from the government's failure to staff and maintain an adequate air traffic control system."[20]

Finance/Accounting

Financial strength is very important in a marketing war. It permits you to create an unprofitable price to fight off interlopers in a market.[21]

Delta's balance sheets and income statements are shown in Exhibits 7-5 and 7-6. For the fiscal year ending June 30, 1987, Delta had operating revenues of $5.3 billion. Net income was $263.7 million compared to $47.3 million in fiscal 1986. In addition earnings on common stock was $5.90 per share.

Debt has long been used by Delta to finance its fleet expansion programs. As of June 30, 1983, Delta's long-term debt was in excess of $800 million. The debt generated approximately $62 million in interest expense for fiscal 1987.

On December 31, 1986, Delta purchased all 61,331,334 outstanding shares of Western Airlines stock for $787 million by paying $384 million in cash and issuing 83 million shares of Delta stock for the balance. In addition Delta assumed Western's long-term debt of $228 million, capital lease obligations totalling $199 million, and other noncurrent liabilities of $29 million.

Delta's operating financial strength was demonstrated in the significant decrease in its unit cost during fiscal 1987. As shown in Exhibit 7-7, the average cost

---

[18]Laurie McGinley and Jonathan Dahl, "Delay Date: Airlines' Figures Hold Surprises—And Spark Controversy," *The Wall Street Journal,* November 11, 1987, p. 22.

[19]McGinley, p. 3.

[20]Ibid.

[21]"Delta's Soft Landing," p. 71.

per available seat mile was 7.12 cents, down 14 percent from the 8.3 cents average in fiscal 1986. The decline in seat mile cost was extremely important as airlines struggled to compete by providing the lower fares to travelers.

Delta continued to use lease financing to acquire new aircraft since the company had a significant amount of investment tax credit and net operating loss carryovers. During fiscal 1987, all new aircraft acquired were sold and leased back from the purchaser using operating leases.

Exhibit 7-5 **Consolidated Balance Sheets June 30, 1986 and 1987 (In thousands)**

Assets	1986	1987
Current Assets		
Cash and temporary cash investments	$ 61,315	$ 379,928
Accounts receivable, net of allowance for		
uncollectible accounts	425,912	626,139
Refundable income taxes	10,485	—
Maintenance and operating supplies, at average		
cost	35,503	42,337
Prepaid expenses and other current assets	49,660	131,170
Total Current Assets	582,875	1,179,574
Property and Equipment		
Flight equipment owned	4,174,632	4,485,898
Less accumulated depreciation	1,939,205	1,951,494
	2,235,427	2,534,404
Flight equipment under capital leases	—	221,811
Less accumulated amortization	—	16,307
	—	205,504
Ground property and equipment	965,980	1,078,185
Less accumulated depreciation	390,324	451,643
	575,656	626,542
Advance payments for new equipment	323,399	307,461
	3,134,482	3,673,911
Other Assets		
Investments in associated companies	37,976	55,427
Cost in excess of net assets acquired, net of		
accumulated amortization of $5,529	—	371,756
Funds held by bond trustees	7,677	8,308
Other	22,452	53,407
	68,105	488,898
Total Assets	$3,785,462	$5,342,383

Exhibit 7-5   (continued)

Liabilities and Stockholders' Equity	1986	1987
Current Liabilities		
Current maturities of long-term debt	$ 10,921	$ 8,406
Current obligations under capital leases	—	12,921
Short-term notes payable	9,000	11,000
Commercial paper outstanding	41,055	14,836
Accounts payable and miscellaneous accrued liabilities	270,445	455,686
Air traffic liability	286,579	506,669
Accrued vacation pay	88,595	110,835
Transportation tax payable	39,342	60,705
Total Current Liabilities	745,937	1,181,058
Non-Current Liabilities		
Long-term debt	868,615	837,201
Capital leases	—	181,216
Other	38,949	80,320
	907,564	1,098,737
Deferred Credits		
Deferred income taxes	427,339	590,876
Unamortized investment tax credits	150,594	98,525
Manufacturers credits	146,844	137,611
Deferred gain on sale and leaseback transactions	104,742	297,050
Other	496	614
	830,015	1,124,676
Total Liabilities	2,483,516	3,404,471
Stockholders' Equity		
Common stock, par value $3.00 per share— Authorized 100,000,000 shares; outstanding 48,639,469 shares at June 30, 1987, and 40,116,383 shares at June 30, 1986	120,349	145,918
Additional paid-in capital	93,333	484,398
Reinvested earnings	1,088,264	1,307,598
Total Stockholders' Equity	1,301,946	1,937,912
Total Liabilities and Stockholders' Equity	$3,785,462	$5,342,383

Source: Delta Air Lines, Inc. *Annual Report,* 1987.

Exhibit 7-6   **Consolidated Statements of Income for the years ended June 30, 1985, 1986, and 1987 (In thousands, except per share amounts)**

	1985	1986	1987
Operating Revenues			
Passenger	$4,376,986	$4,132,284	$4,921,852
Cargo	235,199	240,115	280,271
Other, net	71,930	87,663	116,049
Total Operating Revenues	4,684,115	4,460,062	5,318,172
Operating Expenses			
Salaries and related costs	1,856,243	1,963,575	2,228,814
Aircraft fuel	892,182	796,883	672,004
Aircraft maintenance materials and repairs	66,022	91,590	127,856
Aircraft rent	57,090	68,518	150,653
Other rent	92,839	109,778	145,473
Landing fees	60,908	65,879	89,519
Passenger service	170,163	180,409	219,834
Passenger commissions	350,690	359,299	432,066
Other cash costs	422,840	425,723	569,453
Depreciation and amortization	349,128	363,920	277,975
Total Operating Expenses	4,318,105	4,425,574	4,913,647
Operating Income	366,010	34,488	404,525
Other Income (Expense)			
Interest expense	(84,081)	(79,113)	(94,000)
Less interest capitalized	22,028	23,758	32,092
	(62,053)	(55,355)	(61,908)
Gain on disposition of aircraft	94,343	16,526	96,270
Miscellaneous income, net	6,863	7,775	8,312
	39,153	(31,054)	42,674
Income before income taxes	405,163	3,434	447,199
Income taxes (provided) credited	(186,624)	2,228	(219,715)
Amortization of investment Tax credits	40,914	41,624	36,245
Net Income	$ 259,453	$ 47,286	$ 263,729
Net Income per Common Share	$6.50	$1.18	$5.90

Source: Delta Air Lines, Inc., *Annual Report,* 1987.

Exhibit 7-7   Delta Operating Statistics

	1986	1987	% Change
Revenue plane miles (000)	311,347	407,773	+31
Available seat miles (000)	53,336,135	69,013,669	+29
Available ton miles (000)	6,934,047	8,999,668	+30
Fuel gallons consumed (000)	1,126,876	1,435,801	+27
Average fuel price/gallon	$ .707	$ .468	−34
Passenger load factor	56.48%	55.66%	− 1
Break-even load factor	56.01%	51.09%	− 9
Cost/available seat mile	$ .083	$ .071	−14

Cost per Available Seat Mile (in cents)

'87
'86
'85
'84
'83
'82
'81
'80
'79
'78

       2¢   4¢   6¢   8¢   10¢

Source: Delta Air Lines, Inc., *Annual Report,* 1987.

Marketing and Sales

We have determined that much of Delta's future success will depend on the imagination and skill we bring to the use of fast-paced developments in the information management technologies.[22]

Delta had recently taken several actions to enhance its competitive situation for the future. The company's marketing plan called for expansion of the Dallas-Fort Worth and Cincinnati hubs. On July 30, 1986, Delta announced that it would double its operations at the Cincinnati airport by the end of the 1986 calendar year.

In September 1987, Delta launched a new marketing campaign to counteract some of the negative press resulting from the crash of Flight 191 and the near mishaps that occurred in early 1987. The theme "We love to fly and it shows" (Exhibit 7-8) replaced the two-year old theme, "Delta gets you there." The company was expected to spend about $70 million on the new campaign.[23]

[22]Ibid., p. 69.

[23]Dennis Fulton, "Delta Wheeling Out New Ad Campaign," *The Dallas Morning News,* November 27, 1987, p. 1-F.

Source: Delta Air Lines, Inc., 1987.

Exhibit 7-8   **Delta Promotion**

Acquiring Western Airlines provided Delta with a significant improvement in its route system. Western added 44 cities to the 108 already served by Delta. Western's domestic operations were centered in the western half of the U.S. in areas where Delta did not have substantial operations.

Delta Airlines signed a ten-year agreement to become the official airline of Walt Disney World. (Struggling Eastern Airlines had been the official airline.) Many marketing opportunities are expected as a result of the association with Walt Disney World.

COMPETITOR PROFILES

Delta's direct competitors included the other seven major airlines, but national and regional carriers could not be disregarded.

Texas Air Corporation

Texas Air was ranked as the largest multiairline corporation in the United States. The corporation was made up of Continental, Eastern, Frontier, People Express, New York Air, and Texas International. Texas Air's major hubs were Houston, Denver, Atlanta, Miami, Kansas City, and Newark. The airline served primarily the domestic corridor. The massive growth that this company had undergone in the past year had caused several problems. First, Texas Air was the owner of the most complained about airline—Continental.[24]

Continental posted a passenger load drop to 56.2 percent from 60.4 percent a year earlier. Traffic increased 83.3 percent which reflects Continental's merged operations with People Express and New York Air. Eastern also reported a decline in traffic while reducing the available seat miles. Eastern's load factor improved to 58.2 percent from 54.4 percent a year earlier.[25]

Continental reported that its September 1987 on-time performance was 80 percent. It completed 98.9 percent of flights and transported 99.3 percent of its passenger bags to the right airport at the right time.[26]

Labor disagreements plagued Eastern. Service and schedule disruptions, along with misplaced luggage, had driven many passengers to other airlines.[27]

[24]Laurie McGinley, "Consumer Gripes About Air Service Fell in September," *The Wall Street Journal,* October 12, 1987, p. 29.

[25]Paulette Thomas, "Texas Air's Continental Unit Posts Drop in September Passenger Load to 56.2%," *The Wall Street Journal,* October 7, 1987, p. 6.

[26]Dennis Fulton, "Continental Reports September Performance." *The Dallas Morning News,* October 16, 1987, p. 4-D.

[27]McKellin, p. 268.

United Airlines

United Airlines was the largest single domestic airline in the United States. United had hubs in Chicago, Denver, San Francisco, and Washington, D.C., with flights serving North America as well as Europe, Mexico, and the Far East.

United Airline's parent company changed its name from UAL Inc. to Allegis Corporation and altered its original strategy that was designed to give the company a full line of services to meet all passenger needs. To protect the company from hostile takeovers, Allegis decided to divest the Hertz operations, the Westin and Hilton International hotel chains, and all or part of their computerized reservations system (CRS). The Hilton International chain was sold to Ladbroke Group PLC of Britain for $1.07 billion.[28] Hertz was sold to a group including Ford Motor Company and Hertz management for $1.2 billion.[29] The proceeds of the sale went to Allegis Corporation shareholders.

American Airlines

American was the second largest domestic carrier. It had major hubs in Dallas–Fort Worth, Chicago, Nashville, Raleigh–Durham, and San Juan. American had international service to Canada, Mexico, the Caribbean, and Europe. In 1987, new routes were established to Zurich, Geneva, Paris, Frankfurt, and Tokyo.

American had been very profitable over the past four years, posting total profits of $1.09 billion. In 1986, American purchased AirCal for $225 million. This was the major event of 1986 for the company and represented a new and stronger push into the West Coast area.[30]

American filed suit in 1987 against Texas Air claiming that corporation illegally induced travel agencies to break contracts with American's "Sabre" reservation system. The suit sought millions in actual claims that Texas Air used illegal methods to coerce travels agencies into abandoning the Sabre system.[31]

Third quarter results for AMR, the parent company of American Airlines, showed a 27.8 percent drop in earnings. Revenues were up to $1.97 billion while operating income was down $7.1 million.[32] Traffic increased almost 15 percent, but the load factor, or percentage of seats filled, was unchanged at 66 percent.[33]

[28]"Allegis Completes Hilton Sale," *The Wall Street Journal,* October 15, 1987, p. 5.

[29]James P. Miller, "Ford to Acquire U.S. Leasing for $68 a Share," *The Wall Street Journal,* October 12, 1987, p. 2.

[30]"U.S. Majors," p. 110.

[31]Dennis Fulton, "American Files Suit Against Texas Air," *The Dallas Morning News,* October 16, 1987, p. 1-D.

[32]Dennis Fulton, "AMR Earnings Sag 27.8% in Quarter," *The Dallas Morning News,* October 15, 1987, p. 6-D.

[33]AMR's American Air Traffic," *The Wall Street Journal,* October 12, 1987, p. 6.

American placed a large aircraft order in 1987, agreeing to purchase fifteen 767-300FRs from Boeing and 25 A300-600Rs from Airbus. Both deals were leased with easy-return provisions.[34] American was reportedly going to use the Airbus planes in the Caribbean and use the replaced jets for domestic expansion. The Boeing jets were to be placed in service in North America for European routes.

Northwest Airlines

By acquiring Republic Airlines, Northwest became the fifth largest airline company in the United States. The carrier serviced all the major metropolitan areas in the United States, the Far East, and Canada.

Northeast was preparing to upgrade its fleet by ordering 100 Airbus A320s. The company would order up to 20 Airbus A340 widebodies in 1987 with delivery expected to occur in 1992.[35]

Northwest earned $76.9 million in 1986, up from 1985. Yields had increased with the integration of Republic and were considered to have a good chance of increasing in 1987. Northwest appeared to be in a good position with its marketing agreement with TWA to use the PARS computer reservation system, which would enable Northwest to have the travel agent leverage needed to compete with the other computer reservation system giants.[36]

TWA

Trans World Airlines was the sixth largest domestic airline, servicing the continental United States, Europe, Mideast, India, and the Caribbean. Ownership of Ozark Airways gave it a major hold in St. Louis. Since international service was very cyclical, Ozark gave TWA some stability in the domestic market.

In March 1986, TWA's flight attendants went on strike over wage cuts imposed by the controlling owner, Carl Ichan. Management eventually won by hiring new replacements, which cut costs by 10 percent.[37]

Despite the strike and the decreased international passenger mileage caused by anti-American terrorism, TWA still posted a net profit of $85 million in the fourth quarter of 1987, which reduced the airline's overall deficit by $76 million.[38] Both 1985 and 1986 had been poor years for TWA. With renewed interest in transatlantic travel and a stronger position in the midwestern market, TWA was expected to rebound and continue to improve its profitability.[39]

[34] "U.S. Majors," p. 100.

[35] Ibid., p. 108.

[36] Ibid.

[37] Ibid., p. 115.

[38] Ibid.

[39] McKellin, p. 270.

Pan Am Corporation

Pan Am was the seventh largest airline in the United States. The airline recently sold its Pacific routes to United Airlines in order to concentrate its efforts on the Atlantic and European routes. In 1987, Pan Am had relatively good growth with increased demand from the Europeans due to the weaker dollar.[40] Improved feeder systems through agreements with regional airlines to serve the JFK and Miami hubs also helped increase growth.

Pan Am was determined to improve in the future. Management felt that reduced labor costs was the key to the long-term survival of the airline. Pan Am attempted to secure labor savings of $180 million during the period from 1985 to 1987.[41]

A group of airline experts and a coalition of Pan Am's unions negotiated a company takeover. The airline experts, led by Kerk Kerkorian, wanted greater concessions from the union than current management. The situation was placed on hold until a more viable solution could be worked out.[42]

USAir

USAir was the ninth largest domestic carrier. USAir recently purchased PSA, a West Coast carrier, and owned 51 percent of Piedmont Airlines. USAir enjoyed a strong West Coast presence and with the addition of Piedmont, USAir's East Coast network was greatly enhanced. These acquisitions gave USAir a very competitive strategy.[43]

When the acquisitions were completed, USAir became the seventh largest domestic carrier. In 1987, USAir was developing a new hub in Philadelphia and started service to Atlanta, Jacksonville, Manchester, and Portland.

USAir increased its passenger boarding as well as load factors and revenues. USAir had to perform adequately in order to service its increased debt.[44]

DELTA'S PROBLEMS

While we would like to put the series of safety incidents behind us, we will not and cannot allow ourselves to forget them, but rather we must learn from experience.[45]

---

[40]Ibid., p. 265.

[41]Ibid.

[42]New York Times News Service, "Pan Am Proposal Requires Greater Worker Concessions," *The Dallas Morning News,* October 15, 1987, p. 3-D.

[43]McKellin, p. 271.

[44]Ibid.

[45]David Tarrant, "Delta 191 Pilot Used Tranquilizers," *The Dallas Morning News,* December 9, 1987, p. 1.

According to the Federal Aviation Administration (FAA) investigation of Delta's training program for flight safety, numerous problems were uncovered with pilot-crew coordination, lapses in discipline, and poor cockpit communication. The investigation was triggered by a series of safety incidents at Delta during June and July 1987. The report indicated the shortcomings primarily were due to a lack of clear-cut, definitive guidance from those responsible for developing and standardizing cockpit procedures. The inspection team also blamed the airline's management philosophy for the crew problems.[46]

Delta's management philosophy was to delegate a maximum degree of responsibility to its crew members. According to the FAA, this philosophy worked well in the past, but there was a limit to this approach due to an increasingly complex and stressful environment. The report suggested that the philosophy caused crew members to work independently rather than functioning as a team.[47]

The following safety incidents were recorded in 1987:

June 18, 1987. A Delta jet had to abort its takeoff run as another jet passed 100 feet overhead while taking off in the opposite direction on the same runway.

June 30, 1987. The crew of a Delta jet accidently turned off the engines while climbing over the Pacific Ocean after leaving Los Angeles. The pilot managed to restore power 600 feet above the ocean.

July 7, 1987. A Delta pilot heading for Lexington, Kentucky, mistakenly landed twenty miles away at Frankfort, Kentucky.

July 8, 1987. A Delta jumbo jet flying from London to Cincinnati strayed 60 miles off course and came within 100 feet of a Continental Airlines jet off the coast of Newfoundland.

Delta was the brunt of much negative publicity due to the intense media coverage of the preceding events. Delta identified breakdown of cockpit communication as the primary cause of the safety incidents. The firm took corrective action and individuals were disciplined in response to the incidents.

While the negative coverage of these events was short-lived, Delta had been and continued to receive negative coverage in connection with the August 2, 1985, crash of Flight 191. The National Transportation Safety Board reported the probable cause of the accident, which left 137 dead, as the flight crew's decision to initiate and continue the approach into a cumulonimbus cloud that they observed to contain lightning; the lack of specific guidelines, procedures, and training for avoiding and escaping low-altitude wind shear; and the lack of definitive, real-time wind shear hazard data.[49]

Recent reports regarding the pretrial events (the trial was scheduled for Febru-

[46]Ibid.

[47]Ibid., p. 28-A.

[48]Clemens P. Work, "The Gremlins in the Sky," *U.S. News and World Report,* July 20, 1987, p. 12–13.

[49]"NTSB Documents Observations of Weather Prior to Delta Crash," *Aviation Week and Space Technology,* November 10, 1986, p. 89.

ary 1, 1988, to determine liability in the incident) stated that an expert witness for the plaintiffs (families of the accident victims) would testify that the pilot, Captain Edward M. Connors, had been taking a prescription tranquilizer called Stelazine and that it affected his flying.[50]

Delta spokesman, Jim Lundy, defended Connors by stating, "There is no indication that Capt. Connors was on medication at the time of the accident."[51] The National Transportation Safety Board said that if enough new evidence was revealed they might reopen the crash investigation.[52] Coverage of the Flight 191 accident would continue until all the lawsuits have been settled. What effect would this have on Delta operations?

[50]Anne Reeks, "Tranquilizer Affected Captain of Flight 191, Witness Contends," *The Dallas Morning News,* December 9, 1987, p. 29-A.

[51]Tarrant, p. 37-A.

[52]Ibid.

Case 8

Applied CAD Knowledge, Inc. (A)

Something is seriously wrong with this planet. Look at us. I'm working a hundred and twenty hours a week or more, and not catching up. I've got these two friends—both recently divorced, like me—who aren't working at all: they're living off their girl friends, and loving it. One of them is basking in Hawaii. But here I am, busting my ass and giving my customers problems anyhow.

Some guys go on television and say, "Send money now," and people *do.* I ask my best customer to send money, and he goes bankrupt instead. What's wrong with this picture?

Jeff Stevens, owner and president of Applied CAD Knowledge, Inc., was reporting on current sales and production levels to the two business school professors who comprised his Board of Directors. It was late August 1987, and the three men sat in a booth at Bogie's restaurant. The waitress, Patty, was accustomed to these

This case was prepared by John A. Seeger, Bentley College, and Raymond M. Kinnunen, Northeastern University, as a basis for class discussion rather than to illustrate either effective or ineffective handling of an administrative situation. Used by permission from Raymond M. Kinnunen.

monthly meetings; she offered another round of Lite Beer. "Make mine cyanide," said Stevens. "On the rocks, please."

Applied CAD, a small service bureau which designed electronic circuit boards, was experiencing the highest sales levels in its three-year history. June sales had reached $50,000—leaving a backlog of $90,000; July shipments had set a record at $58,000; August would be nearly as high. The problem facing Stevens through the summer of 1987 was a shortage of good designers, either as full-time workers or as part-time freelancers. The surge in business resulted in Stevens sitting at the computer consoles himself, doing design work on second and third shifts, six or seven days a week. After eight weeks of this schedule, the strain was showing. One director asked about the longer-range sales picture, and Stevens summed it up:

> Can I borrow a .45 automatic? I'd like a good game of Russian Roulette.
>
> There's nothing on the books at all for late fall, and not much likely. Every major customer we have is in "busy phase" right now. When the designs are finished, it will be another four to six months before their next generation of product revisions. In the meantime, everybody is burned out. All I'm hoping for right now is a front porch, a rocking chair, a lobotomy, and a drool cup.

THE ELECTRONICS INDUSTRY AND CIRCUIT BOARD DESIGN

The United States electronics industry in 1987 was a sprawling giant, some of whose sectors were growing while others remained in a protracted slump. In 1986, total industry size was estimated by *Electronic Business* magazine (December 10, 1985) as $100.5 billion to $182 billion. The same article projected industry revenues for 1995 to be $295.4 billion to $512 billion. The magazine concluded that its industry represented a major driving force for the American economy. The *Value Line* investment service reports separately on four segments of the electronics industry (Exhibit 8-1).

Exhibit 8-1   **Electronics Industry Revenues (In billions)**

Industry Sector	Number of Companies	1982	1983	1984	1985	1986	(est.) 1987
Electronics	35	$16.4	$17.7	$ 21.6	$ 21.2	$ 22.0	$ 24.0
U.S. semiconductors	14	11.4	13.0	17.2	15.6	16.0	17.8
Computers/peripherals	34	78.6	88.4	104.4	110.5	115.0	127.5
Electrical equipment	25	50.9	51.2	54.9	56.5	64.7	72.0

Source: Value Line, May 8, 1987.

Printed Circuit Boards

A basic part of nearly every electronic product, whichever segment of the industry produced or used it, was the printed circuit board to which a variety of electronic components were attached. These components ranged from old-fashioned resistors, capacitors, and vacuum tubes to transistors and the most modern integrated circuit chips. All components needed some sort of platform to sit on and some way to make connection with the other components of the circuit.

In the 1930s and 1940s, circuit boards were made from thin, nonconducting fiberboard with metal pins and sockets attached. Assembly operators wound the wire leads of the circuit's resistors, capacitors, and so forth around the proper pins and soldered them in place. By the 1960s, the technology of wiring boards and assembling components had advanced to a highly automated stage. Numerically controlled machines positioned components and connected pins to one another with wires. During this decade, electronic components became increasingly miniaturized and more reliable, complex, and powerful. With these technological developments, the printed circuit board (PCB) was developed; its use and technical sophistication accelerated rapidly.

In a printed circuit, the wires leading from one pin to another are replaced by electrically conductive lines "printed" or plated onto (or under) the surface of the board itself. The pins themselves are gone; wire leads from electrical components are inserted through small holes in the board and soldered on the underside. By the 1980s, components could be counted directly on the board's surface, in contact with the printed "wires."

The increasing complexity of electronic circuits presented a problem for PCB technology. When connections were made with wires, assemblers simply attached one end, routed the wire over the top of everything between the two pins involved, and attached the other end where it belonged. With printed circuits, however, designers are constrained to two dimensions on a flat board; they must route the line between two pins without touching any other lines, and they cannot go "over the top" without leaving the surface of the board. Furthermore, efficient design calls for the components to be tightly packed together, grouped by function. Designers frequently find situations where they cannot lay out a trace from one point to another without interfering with other traces.

"Multilayer" PCBs eased this problem by providing "upstairs" layers on the board, allowing the designer to go over the top. Multilayer boards contain at least three layers of traces, and sometimes more than twenty layers. Skilled designers seek to minimize the number of layers required for a given circuit in order to reduce manufacturing costs of the board. Multilayer PCBs are far more expensive to manufacture. In 1983, multilayer boards had sales of $900 million, or 26 percent of the PCB market. By 1993, they were forecast to reach sales of $5.6 billion, or 41 percent market share. Exhibit 8-2 shows PCB sales and projections by type of board.

Board design was made more complicated by increasing density of components, by sensitivity of components to heat (some threw off large amounts of heat,

Exhibit 8-2   Sales and Projections for PCBs by Type of Board

PCB Type	1983 Sales (In millions)	1983 Market Share	Annual Growth Rate	1993 Sales (In millions)	1993 Market Share
Multilevel	$ 900	25.2%	20%	$ 5,600	41.0%
Double-sided	2,000	56.1%	13%	6,700	49.0%
Flexible	353	9.9%	10%	916	6.7%
Single-sided	307	8.8%	4%	454	3.3%
	$3,560	100.0%		$13,670	100.0%

Source: *Electronic Business,* February 1, 1985, p. 87.

and others would go haywire if their operating temperature was disturbed), and by radio-frequency interference (some components generated static; others might "hear" the noise and try to process it). The layout of components on the board had tremendous impact on how well the finished product worked, as well as on its manufacturing cost.

Printed circuit boards offered many technical advantages over the previous method for fashioning circuits.

1. *Greater miniaturization.* PCBs can be highly miniaturized, allowing progressively more powerful and complex electronic circuits for smaller, lighter products.
2. *Improved performance.* Product reliability is much greater than in pin-to-pin circuitry, permitting application in extreme environmental conditions.
3. *Manufacturing advantages.* For high volume products, manufacturing costs are greatly reduced. Applications range from simple consumer products to the most powerful mainframe computers.
4. *Maintenance advantages.* Designers could "package" electronic systems into discrete modules which, if not functioning properly, could be replaced without the immediate need of determining where the problem was within the board.

Frost and Sullivan, Inc., a New York market research firm, estimated (in "The Printed Circuit Board Market in the U.S.," July 1986, quoted by permission) that total U.S. PCB market reached $3.7 billion in sales in 1985, a decrease of 12 percent from 1984 production. The PCBs were projected to grow to a likely $6.5 billion by 1990 and to $10.8 billion in 1995. Multilayer PCBs were expected to be the fastest-growing type, averaging 15.7 percent annual growth. A little over half the market was served in 1985 by independent PCB makers, as opposed to captive suppliers, according to Frost and Sullivan.

Trends in Circuit Board Design Equipment

Originally (and still, for simple circuits), an engineer or technician worked from a "schematic" drawing of the circuit, which showed how the various components were connected. On a large layout table, the PCB designer manually drew in the components and linked them with black tape (or ink), to produce a "photo master" film which was in turn used to project the design photographically onto the base material of the circuit board. As circuits became more complex, the manual process bogged down.

Specialized computer hardware and software began to help designers and engineers solve complex design problems. By the mid 1970s, system vendors began to offer CAD systems specifically developed for PCB designing. Racal-Redac, Inc., a British firm, was the first to offer a powerful special purpose PCB-oriented system. Based on Digital Equipment Corporation's PDP-11 computer, the Redac product was the first to permit PCB designers to interact with the computer, trying various routings of traces and seeing how they looked on the graphic display. This approach competed well against established systems such as Computervision, whose general purpose equipment was priced in the $500,000 class and still lacked the interactive design capability.

By 1982, prices of PCB design systems had fallen below $100,000. New CAD equipment makers entered the field, with automated routing or documentation features which carried substantial advantages over the established Redac software. Calay and Cadnetix, as examples, introduced strong entries—neither being compatible with the Redac or Sci-Cards equipment already in the field. Racal-Redac Ltd., however, had perhaps taken the greatest strides to tailor its software to run on a variety of hardware platforms. Said Ian Orrock, chief executive of Redac's electronics CAD division in England, "We're all going to end up being software houses."

Another important feature of the new CAD equipment was ease of use; the older CAD/CAM systems might require months of learning time before a designer became proficient. In the late 1970s, with high equipment costs and low availability of trained designers, only the largest electronics firms designed and produced their own PCBs. Service bureaus took advantage of the market opportunity, acting as the primary design resource for smaller clients and as peak load designers for firms with in-house capacity. As electronics firms purchased and began to use the newer systems, however, they wanted service bureaus to be equipped with similar or compatible machines. Service bureaus felt the pressure to acquire the most up-to-date hardware and software available in order to qualify as bidders.

Service Bureau Operations

When a service bureau invested in CAD equipment, the sheer size of the investment created pressure to use the equipment intensively. Multishift operations were common, but the supply of designers to operate them was severely limited. Typically, a service bureau did not hire permanent staff for all three shifts because the work load was too unpredictable. Service bureaus generally hired moonlighting designers from established electronics firms to staff their second and third shifts.

Printed circuit board design requires a peculiar combination of skills, primarily in spatial geometry, circuit insight, memory, and persistence. A talented designer, perhaps capable of completing a complex design in three weeks of console time, might be several times more productive than a "journeyman." In the early 1980s, talented designers willing to work odd shifts were earning over $100,000 per year; few of them had college educations.

Most customers requested separate quotations for each board; often, customers asked for bids from several service bureaus. Design clients always ran on tight schedules, Jeff Stevens observed, wanting their work to be delivered "yesterday":

> Circuit board design is usually one of the last steps before a new product goes into production. Our design time is the customer's time-to-market. It's natural for them to be in a hurry.

For the design of a large, complex, four-layered PCB a client might pay from $10,000 to $15,000. Such a project might require five to six man-weeks of labor input (two-thirds of which might be designer's time); it might involve extensive communication between Applied CAD and a wide variety of the client's technical personnel, and it would often require Applied CAD personnel to work through the night at various project stages to make deadlines. In such a typical project, much of Applied CAD's time would be spent sorting out and coordinating conflicting information and directions from different technical people in the client company. Stevens noted,

> Even our clients themselves won't always know completely what they want. When we take their directions to their logical conclusions, problems often occur. Then we have to show them what developed. You spend a lot of time on the phone with clients, sometimes at 3 A.M. Often, I wind up making decisions for the client, so the work can go ahead; later, I have to convince the client the decision was right.

Design reliability remained a key attribute of a service bureau's reputation, since whole product lines (or engineers' jobs) might depend on the PCB design's working properly, and on its prompt delivery. He continued,

> We had one job, in the old days, where a satellite was literally sitting on the launch pad. waiting for a corrected module design. The engineers had discovered a design flaw. They flew into town with the specs, and then took turns sitting behind the designer at the scope, or sitting beside their hotel room telephone, waiting to answer any questions that might come up. In this business, you have to deliver.

When the design phase of a job was finished, the computer tape or disk would be carried to a second service bureau for creation of the film photoplots needed for manufacturing. The equipment for photoplotting was far more complex and expensive than the computer systems needed for design. Only a few design shops in the New England area had their own photoplotting capability; they performed this work for other service bureaus and in-house design departments as well as for their own design clients.

The actual production of PCBs might be done by the client company itself or by a fabrication shop which specialized in the work. The New England area was home to some 80 to 100 fab shops, many of which offered design as well as manufacturing services. A few large firms (Hadco at $125 million in sales) were equipped to service very large orders—100,000 or more boards of a design—but most fab shops fell in the $1 to $2 million size range, with an average order size of 25 to 30 relatively small boards. One shop estimated its average PCB was priced at $22 each, with a set-up charge of $150.

Trends in PCB Design

By the end of 1986, a number of vendors had developed PCB design packages to run on personal computers, primarily the IBM XT or AT machines. These software systems, some including automatic routing, were priced as low as a few hundred dollars or as high as $13,000, and varied widely in their features and capabilities. In-house design capability became practical for most electronics firms, although many lacked the PCB expertise that still marked the better service bureaus. Freelance designers, too, could acquire their own equipment. Exhibit 8-3 compares the features and prices of 24 such software packages.

Clients were inclined to stay with their existing service bureaus, unless they were severely burned. Good relationships between service staff and engineering personnel helped minimize communication errors, and availability of the data base from the original job allowed for revisions or modifications at a much lower cost.

In the 1980s, as the cost of entering the service bureau business dropped, many new firms appeared. Jeff Stevens observed, "When I started at Redac in 1978, there were three service bureaus in New England. By 1983 there were maybe a dozen. Now there might be 75 and it could reach 100 in another year." In 1987, several competing service bureaus in the area were owned by former employees of Racal-Redac, where Jeff himself had learned the business. Exhibit 8-4 lists the major competitors in the northeastern United States in 1986.

For the longer run, some industry analysts speculated that constant advances in miniaturizing electronic circuits might permit semiconductor technology to reduce certain whole PCBs (such as those developed for computer memory) into a single chip.

APPLIED CAD KNOWLEDGE, INC.

History

Jeff Stevens had learned the rudiments of circuit board design in his first job after high school graduation, as a technician in a five-person product development laboratory. One of his duties was to prepare enlarged prints of circuits, using black tape on white mylar. In another concurrent job as a technician in an electronics manufacturing firm, he learned how the circuits themselves worked.

In 1977, Stevens left his two technician jobs for an entry-level design position with Racal-Redac in Littleton, Massachusetts. Redac operated a service bureau to complement its sales of DEC hardware and British software. As a pioneer in the field, Redac at the time boasted a near-monopoly in powerful systems dedicated to PCB design. Stevens, in a training rotation, joined Redac's service bureau as a data-entry technician.

> We had three computer systems and about 20 people altogether. A system then cost about $200,000 and a lot of companies didn't have enough design work to justify buying one.
>
> In data entry, you prepare code to represent all the terminals and components on the board. I refused to code the first job they gave me, and nearly got fired. Finally I convinced them that the job *shouldn't* be coded: the turkey who engineered it had the diodes in backward, and the circuit wasn't going to work. About a week later, they put me in charge of data entry, supervising the guy who had wanted to fire me.

Stevens became a designer, then a lead designer, then operations manager of the service bureau. Under his leadership, the operation dramatically improved its reputation for quality and on-time delivery, as well as its financial performance.

> When I took over in October of 1981, monthly sales were $50,000 and monthly expenses were $110,000. In six months we turned it around: monthly sales were $110,000 and expenses were $50,000. There had been a tremendous amount of dead wood. We had a big bonfire with it, and went from 26 people to 16. In some ways, it was a brutal campaign, I guess.

In June 1983, Stevens left Racal-Redac to work as a consulting designer, helping electronics firms with their CAD decisions as well as doing freelance design work. He had developed design and management expertise and established a reputation in industry circles which he could now broker directly to clients who were familiar with his previous work.

In December 1983, Jeff established Applied CAD while still working from his home in Pepperell, Massachusetts. By purchasing used computer equipment and installing it himself in his living room, Stevens was able to hold his initial investment to $35,000; the largest expense was $28,000 for the software purchased from his former employer. (Financial data for Applied CAD's latest three years of operation are shown in Exhibit 8-5.)

> The equipment pretty well filled up the living room, and through the summer I couldn't run it during the daytime: we didn't have enough electricity to cool it down. Winter solved that problem, though; I heated the house with a PDP-11.

In late 1984, applied CAD leased a 1,000 square foot office suite on the ground floor of a new building near the Merrimack River in Tyngsboro, Mass. Jeff Stevens designed the interior space to have a central computer room (with special air conditioning), a darkened "console room" for the actual design work, and a large front

Exhibit 8-3   **Representative Low-Cost PCB Layout Packages**

Company	Product	Base Price	Required Hardware	Operating System	Auto-Router	Auto-Router Price
Abacus Software	PC board designer	$195	ATARI 520ST or 1040ST	GEM	•	
Accel Technologies	Tango-PCB	$495	IBM PC/XT or PC/AT	MS-DOS	•	
Aptos Systems	Criterion II	$4,000	ARTIST 1 CARD and IBM PC/XT or PC/AT	MS-DOS	•	$5,000
Automated Images	Personal 870	$8,000	IBM PC/XT or PC/AT	MS-DOS		
B&C Microsystems	PCB/DE	$395	IBM PC/XT or PC/AT	MS-DOS (and the Autocad drafting package)		
CAD Software	PADS-PCB	$975	IBM PC/XT or PC/AT	MS-DOS	•	$750
Case Technology	Vanguard PCB	$4250	IBM PC/AT, SUN-3 or DEC MICROVAX	MS-DOS, UNIX, or VMS	•	$5,500
Daisy Systems	Personal Boardmaster	$8,000	IBM PC/AT or DAISY PL386	DNIX		
Dasoft Design	Project: PCB	$950	IBM/PC/XT or PC/AT	MS-DOS	•	
Design Computation	Draftsman-EE	$1,147	IBM PC/XT or PC/AT	MS-DOS	•	$2,450
Douglas Electronics	Douglas CAD/CAM	$395	Apple Macintosh	Macintosh		
Electronic Design Tools	PROCAD	$2,495	IBM PC/XT or PC/AT and 68000 coprocessor	MS-DOS	•	$2,495

Exhibit 8-3   (continued)

Auto-Placement	Compatible Net Lists	Maximum Number of Colors	Maximum Number of Traces	Maximum Number of Components	Maximum Number of Layers	Packaging Technologies
		2	1,100 lines	250	2	
	Accel, Omation, Orcad	16	26,000 lines	1,000	9	SMD
•	Aptos, Futurenet, P-CAD	16	2,000 nets	1,000	50	SMD, ECL, Analog
	Applicon, Futurenet, ORCAD	16			16	SMD, Hybrid
	B&C	16				
•	Futurenet	16	4511 nets	764	30	SMD, Fine-line
•	Case	16	2000 nets	1000	256	SMD
	Daisy	7	14,000 lines	14,000	256	SMD
	Dasoft	6			4	SMD
•		16	4000 nets	300	20	Fine-line
		2				SMD, Analog
•	Electronic Design Tools	16	10,000 nets	3,000	56	SMD, Constant-impedance

(*continued*)

Exhibit 8-3 (continued)

Company	Product	Base Price	Required Hardware	Operating System	Auto-Router	Auto-Router Price
Electronic Industrial Equipment	Executive CAD	$11,000	IBM PC/XT or PC/AT	MS-DOS	•	
Futurenet	Dash-PCB	$13,000	IBM PC/AT and 32032 coprocessor	UNIX	•	
Hewlett-Packard	EGS	$7,000	HP 9000	HP-UX		
Kontron	KAD-286	$10,400	IBM PC/AT	MS-DOS		
Personal CAD Systems	PCB-1	$6,000	IBM PC/XT or PC/AT	MS-DOS	•	$6,000
Racal-Redac	Redboard	$12,000	IBM PC/XT or PC/AT	MS-DOS	•	
Seetrax (in U.S. circuits and systems)	Ranger	$5,000	IBM PC/AT	MS-DOS	•	$2,000
Softcircuits	PCLOPLUS	$1,024	Commodore AMIGA 1000	AMIGADOS	•	
VAMP	McCAD	$395	Apple Macintosh	Macintosh	•	$995
Visionics	EE Designer II	$1,875	IBM PC/XT or PC/AT	MS-DOS	•	$1,475
Wintek	Smartwork	$895	IBM PC/XT or PC/AT	MS-DOS	•	
Ziegler Instruments (in U.S. Caddy)	Caddy Electronic System	$2,495	IBM PC/XT or PC/AT	MS-DOS	•	$2,500

Source: EDN, March 18, 1987, pp. 140–141. Used by permission.

Exhibit 8-3   (continued)

Auto-Placement	Compatible Net Lists	Maximum Number of Colors	Maximum Number of Traces	Maximum Number of Components	Maximum Number of Layers	Packaging Technologies
•	Electronic Industrial Equipment	16			4	SMD, ECL
	Futurenet	4			10	Fine-line
	HP	15			255	Hybrid
	Kontron	64	5,300 lines	3,200	255	ECL, SMD, Hybrid
•	P-CAD, Futurenet	16	1,000 nets	300	50	SMD
•	Racal-Redac	16	1,900 nets	511	16	SMD
•	Seetrax	16	10,000 lines	1,400	16	SMD
		16				
•	VAMP	2	32,000 lines	32,000	6	SMD, Metric
•		16		999	26	SMD
	Wintek	3			6	
	Ziegler	16			128	Analog

Exhibit 8-4 **PC Design Service Bureaus in New England**

Design Houses by Sales Volume, $0–$1 Million/Year

Abington Labs	P C Design Company
Berkshire Design	PAC-LAB, Inc.
CAD TEC	Packaging for Electronics
Cadtronix, Ltd.	PC Design Services
Computer Aided Circuits, Inc.	Point Design, Inc.
Dataline PCB Corp.	Power Processing, Inc.
Design Services	Product Development Co.
Energraphics	Qualitron Corp.
Graphics Technology Corp.	Quality Circuit Design, Inc.
Herbertons, Inc.	Research Labs, Inc.
HET Printed Circuit Design	Scientific Calculations, Inc.
High Tech CAD Service Co.	Tracor Electro-Assembly, Inc.
Jette Fabrication	Winter Design
LSI Engineering	

Design Houses by Sales Volume, $1–$2 Million/Year

Automated Images, Inc.	TECCON
Automated Design, Inc.	Tech Systems & Design
CAD Services, Inc.	Kenex, Inc.
Antal Associates	Alternate Circuit Design Technology
Multiwire of New England	Photofabrication Technology, Inc.

Design Houses by Sales Volume, $2–$5 Million/Year

TEK-ART Associates	Eastern Electronics Mfg. Corp.
Strato Reprographix	Datacube, Inc.
Altek Co.	Owl Electronic Laboratories, Inc.

Design Houses by Sales Volume, $5–$10 Million/Year

Triad Engineering Co.	Photronic Labs, Inc.

Design Houses by Sales Volume, $10+ Million/Year

Algorex Corp.	Racal-Redac Service Bureau
ASI Automated Systems, Inc.	Synermation, Inc.
Augat Interconnection Systems Group	

Source: Mass. Tech. Times, *New England Printed Circuit Directory.* Copyright © 1985. Reprinted by permission.

Exhibit 8-5 Financial Statements of Applied CAD Knowledge, Inc.

Balance Sheet

	1985	1986	1987
Assets			
Current assets			
Cash	$128,568	$ 14,148	$ 33,074
Accounts receivable, trade	18,865	15,375	14,250
Prepaid taxes and other current assets	4,853	1,200	5,074
Total Current Assets	152,286	30,723	52,398
Property and equipment	174,079	190,079	203,079
Less accumulated depreciation	48,697	86,357	124,062
Total Property and Equipment	125,382	103,722	79,017
Total Assets	$277,668	$134,445	$131,415
Liabilities and Stockholders' Equity			
Current liabilities			
Accounts payable, trade	$127,685	$ 9,025	$ 21,823
Current maturities of long-term debt	13,300		
Income taxes payable	4,008		2,303
Other current liabilities	5,000	5,373	70
Total Current Liabilities	149,993	14,398	24,196
Long-term debt, less current maturities	41,121	83,247	53,663
Stockholders' Equity			
Common stock, no par value; authorized 15,000 shares, issued and outstanding 1,000 shares	25,000	25,000	25,000
Retained earnings	61,554	11,800	28,556
Total Stockholders' Equity	86,554	36,800	53,556
Total Liabilities and Stockholders' Equity	$277,668	$134,445	$131,415

Statement of Income and Retained Earnings

	1985	1986	1987
Net Revenues	$328,262	$232,540	$346,627
Cost of Revenue			
Salaries, wages and outside services	134,686	116,835	209,998
Research and development	14,154	7,551	13,731
Software costs	65,131	18,864	
Total Cost of Revenue	$213,971	$143,250	$223,729
Gross Profit	114,291	89,290	122,898
Selling, general and administrative expenses	72,320	143,051	77,732
Operating Profit	41,971	(53,761)	45,166
Bad Debt Expense			(28,660)
Interest income (expense), net	2,331	3,176	(10,103)
Income before Income Taxes	44,302	(50,185)	6,403
Income Taxes	4,508	0	0
Net income	39,794	(50,185)	6,403
Retained earnings, beginning of year	21,760	62,385	22,154
Retained earnings, end of year	$ 61,554	$ 11,800	$ 28,557

office. By January 1985, the computing equipment was installed and operating. The console room was furnished with two Recaro ergonometric chairs (at $1,100 each) for the designers' use; the front office held a large reception desk and a sparse collection of work tables, file cabinets, and spare hardware.

Organization

Jeff oversaw all operations in his company, did all the high level marketing and sales contact work with clients, and did much of the technical design work as well. Another full-time designer was hired in May 1985 but had to be terminated in September 1986 due to persistent personal problems. Steve Jones, Jeff's data manager and former assistant at Redac, became a full-time employee in January 1986. Among other duties, Steve covered the telephone, coordinated technical work done by freelance contractors in Jeff's absence, and performed various administrative duties. Steve had a B.S. in Engineering and, before Redac, had worked for other PCB electronics companies. In April 1987, Jeff hired John MacNamara, a former subcontract designer, on a full-time salaried basis.

In May 1987 Jeff also hired a part-time person to keep the books, write checks, and handle other office-related matters. For her first three months she focused on straightening out the books and tax-related items. She was also trying to find time to set up an accounting package on the personal computer. The package had been purchased in August 1986 (at the request of Board members) for the purpose of generating accurate monthly statements. Since the company's founding, the Board had been asking for accurate end-of-month data on sales, accounts receivable, cash balance, backlog, and accounts payable. They also wanted monthly financial statements, although Stevens himself saw little point in them: cash flow projections served his immediate needs. The accounting package was chosen by one of the Board members, based partly on its broad capabilities. For example, it could assist in invoicing and aging receivables.

Jeff had other capable designers "on-call"—available for freelance project work when the company needed them. Depending on the market, there were time periods when Jeff could obtain the services of several contractors to meet peak work loads. In general, design contractors worked on a negotiated fixed-fee basis for completing a specific portion of a design project. In July 1987, however (after sales in June reached approximately $50,000 and the backlog reached $90,000), Jeff found it difficult to attract contract designers with free time. The backlog consisted of about 15 boards ranging in price from $800 to $15,000. The electronics industry had turned upward and in busy times everyone was busy. Consequently, freelance designers were committed to their own customers or employers who were also busy.

Jeff's board consisted of Jeff and two college professors at well-known institutions in the Boston area. Since the fall of 1985 they had met monthly for three to four hours, usually during the first week of the month. At most meetings they first discussed the previous month's sales and current levels of cash, accounts receivable, backlog, and payables. Other typical agenda items ranged from the purchase of new equipment or software to marketing to personnel problems.

At most meetings, they spent considerable time discussing the current business climate and the future sales outlook. This usually led to a discussion of hiring someone to take over the marketing and sales function. It was generally agreed that such a person could not only contribute to the company's growth in sales but also free up a considerable amount of Jeff's time that could be devoted to design and operational matters. When Applied CAD was busy, however, Jeff had very little time to devote to finding, hiring, and working with such a person. When the firm was not busy, Jeff's concerns over the reliability of future cash flows made him hesitant to make the major salary commitment that a marketing professional would require. He was aware of the contrary pressures: "I can't get out of the 'boom-splat' syndrome," he said.

To Jeff, the "splat" came when backlogs and cash balances fell. The winter of 1987, for example, had felt to him like hitting a wall. (Exhibit 8-6 shows monthly

Exhibit 8-6 Monthly Sales and Month-End Receivables, Backlogs, Cash Levels (In thousands)

	Accounts Receivable	Sales	Backlog	Cash
1986				
January	$18	$20	$20	$98
February	*	10	*	*
March	18	10	12	62
April	18	10	20	28
May	24	20	26	26
June	*	10	*	*
July	14	25	*	18
August	70	50	30	15
September	90	40	*	8
October	50	30	*	26
November	19	5	10	17
December	24	10	18	14
1987				
January	13	3	*	7
February	40	21	*	8
March	35	28	22	6
April	32	22	37	11
May	25	22	50	5
June	50	50	90	10
July	90	58	30	10

*Not available

totals of sales, accounts receivable, backlogs, and cash balances, as estimated by Jeff at monthly Board meetings.)

Hardware and Software

After moving into his new quarters, Jeff Stevens located another PDP-11/34 computer, this one for sale at $7,000. Adding it to his shop required purchase of another Redac software package, but the added capacity was needed. Other competing CAD systems were now available, but the decision to stick with Redac seemed straightforward to Jeff:

> Racal-Redac systems had several advantages. They were specifically dedicated to PCB design work and they had software that was brutally efficient. They were familiar to most of the freelance designers in the area. Wide acceptance of Redac's software makes it easier to get overflow work from companies who demanded compatibility with their own equipment. Not to mention that I know this gear backward and forward, and could keep several machines busy at once.

The Redac software was originally developed in 1972, which made it very old by industry standards. Jeff pointed out, however, that because machines were slower in 1972 and had much less memory, their software *had* to be extremely efficient. Having used this software for a long time, he said, "I've been able to make process modifications to improve its efficiency, and I know all its intricacies." Jeff had developed some proprietary software for PCB design work which he believed kept him at the cutting edge of the competition. At times, he wondered about the possibilities of licensing his proprietary software to other PCB design firms. He concluded, however, that the small market for this type of software product would probably not justify the necessary marketing and additional product development costs.

In addition to the original equipment purchased by Jeff in 1983, the company purchased a VAX Model 11/751 and a Calay Version 03 in December 1985 at a cost of approximately $170,000. (See Exhibit 8-7 for the cash flow statements prepared for the bank to obtain a loan.) The VAX was intended to be used as a communication and networking device and as a platform for developing new software. The Calay was a dedicated hardware system that included an automatic router which could completely design certain less complex boards without an operator. On more complex boards it could complete a major percentage of the board, leaving a designer to do the remainder. In September 1986, a software upgrade to Calay Version 04 was purchased at a cost of approximately $28,000. Although bank financing was available, Jeff decided to pay cash for this equipment to avoid raising his monthly fixed expenses. The new purchases gave Applied CAD enough machine capacity to support some $2 million in annual sales.

When the Calay machine was purchased Jeff and his directors felt that its automatic routing capability might open a new market for the company for less complex boards. Because the Calay was virtually automatic on certain applications, the final price of these boards could be much less than if they were done by hand.

Exhibit 8-7 Applied CAD Knowledge, Inc., Cash Flow Projections as of December 16, 1985 (In thousands)

	Dec. 1985	Jan. 1986	Feb. 1986	March 1986	April 1986	May 1986	June 1986	July 1986	Aug. 1986	Sept. 1986	Oct. 1986	Nov. 1986	Dec. 1986	Total 1986
Sales	25	30	30	30	30	30	30	30	30	30	30	30	30	360
Expenses[f]	20	24	29.5	29.5	29.5	29.5	29.5	29.5	29.5	29.5	29.5	29.5	29.5	348.5
Profit	5	6	.5	.5	.5	.5	.5	.5	.5	.5	.5	.5	.5	11.5
Opening Cash	141	148	102	102.5	88	88.5	89	89.5	90	90.5	91	91	91.5	
Receivables	37	17	30	30	30	30	30	30	30	30	30	30	30	
Disbursements[e]	30	24[a]	29.5[c]	29.5	29.5	29.5	29.5	29.5	29.5	29.5	29.5	29.5	29.5	
Taxes[d]		29[b]		15										
Closing Cash	148	102	102.5	88	88.5	89	89.5	90	90.5	91	91	91.5	92	

[a]Includes loan payment of $4,000 per month.

[b]25% of equipment costing $156,000.

[c]Includes new employees at $66,000 per year.

[d]Taxes based on the following assumptions: 1985 profit of $150,000; $50,000 software expense on new equipment; $20,000 depreciation on new equipment; $10,000 misc. expenses; investment tax credit of $15,000.

[e]Figures do not include depreciation which would only influence total profit.

[f]Expenses include rent, heat, light, power, salaries, contract work, telephone, etc. This level of expenses will support sales double those projected.

Due to the lower price to the customer, the Calay was also appropriate for designing boards that would be produced in smaller quantities. Finally, Jeff believed the manufacturer of the Calay as well as the Calay user group would supply new customer leads. Some of these expectations had been met.

The VAX, however, was not being fully used as originally intended—to allow hands-off automation of the firm's varied pieces of computing equipment, as well as providing batch data processing capacity. In its ultimate form, the VAX might actually operate the older, more cumbersome systems. It would be able to juggle dozens of design tasks between workstations and autorouters, queueing and evaluating each job and calling for human intervention when needed. One director, visualizing robots sitting in Applied CAD's Recaro chairs, called this the "Robo-Router plan." To carry it out would require an additional investment of approximately $15,000 in hardware and another $10,000 to $20,000 in programming, along with a significant amount of Jeff's time. The investment would result in very substantial cost reductions and reduced dependence on freelance designers, but it would only pay for itself under high volume conditions.

Current Business Options

In August 1987 Jeff was contemplating the current business climate, his accomplishments with Applied CAD over the past three years, and where the company was headed. His major objective was growth. Jeff and the Board had discussed many times the need for a marketing person and a promotional brochure for the company. On occasion, he had talked with marketing people about Applied CAD's needs, but most of these prospective employees lacked the level of skills and PCB experience Jeff hoped to acquire. He had also talked with commercial artists about design of a brochure. Jeff and his Board felt that a "first class" brochure would cost $5,000 to $10,000.

Marketing in the PCB business, especially among companies with sales of under $1 million, was characterized as informal. Very few companies had full-time people devoted to the marketing task; in most cases it was the owner-president who handled marketing and sales. Most small companies had their own list of faithful customers, and new customers tended to come by word of mouth. In the under $1 million segment it was not uncommon for a company, when extremely overloaded with work, to farm out a task to a competitor. Also, certain other services, such as photoplotting, were done by shops that also did design work. Consequently, there was considerable communication among the competitors; the players seemed to know who received what jobs.

The marketing job at a company like Applied CAD consisted mainly of coordinating the advertising and a sales brochure, calling on present customers, and attempting to find new customers. Such a person needed a working knowledge of PCB design, which required experience in the industry. People with the qualifications necessary normally earned a $40,000 to $50,000 base salary plus commissions; frequently their total compensation exceeded $100,000 per year. Of major concern to Jeff was Applied CAD's erratic history of sales and cash balances, and the difficulty of predicting sales volume any further than two months in advance (see Exhibit 8-6). He balked at taking on responsibility for an executive level salary, lacking confidence in the future. "This would probably be somebody with kids to feed or send to college," Jeff said. "How could I pay them, in slow times?"

Still marketing appeared to be the function most critical to generating the growth rates Jeff Stevens and his board hoped to achieve. It was key, also, in meeting the major potential threat posed by the recent availability of inexpensive software which could enable personal computers to design printed circuit boards (see Exhibit 8-3). Jeff had heard that some of that software could perform almost as well as the more expensive equipment that was being used by Applied CAD. He wondered how the advent of PC-based design might be viewed as an opportunity, not a threat.

Four possible responses had occurred to Jeff and his people: Applied CAD could ignore the PC software, adopt it, distribute it, or sell its own software to the PC users. Ignoring the new technology might work in the short run, since the complex boards designed by Applied CAD would not be the first affected; in the long run, however, failure to keep up with technology would leave more and more jobs subject to low-cost competition.

By adopting the new software for his next equipment expansion, Applied CAD could take a proactive stance. Jeff could buy a system or two to see how good they were and hire people to work on the new systems on a freelance basis. Of course, he would need a flow of jobs to experiment with. A variation of this alternative was to sit back and wait, being ready to move quickly if he saw something developing.

A third alternative, acting as a distributor for the PC software, would give Applied CAD a product to sell to prospects who insisted on doing their own design. This could establish relationships with people who might later need overload capacity.

Fourth, Applied CAD could proceed with development of its proprietary software, creating a product to sell to PC users. Jeff estimated that his automated design review system (ADRS) could save both time and grief for other designers. In some tasks, it could cut the required design time in half. In all jobs, the capability to check the finished design against the original input automatically and completely could improve quality. The ADRS already existed in rough form; it was one of the elements which would make up the "Robo-Router" system, if that were implemented.

Many of these options seemed to require significant marketing skills—strengths—where the company was presently weak. The technical questions could be answered, if Jeff had the time to work on them. But the marketing questions called for a person with extensive industry experience, broad contacts, a creative imagination, and the ability to make things happen.

Amid all the other problems facing the owner of a small business, Jeff was trying to figure out how to shape his business for the long-range future, and how to attract the kind of person he could work with to assure growth—and survival.

Applied CAD Knowledge, Inc. (B)

In September 1987, as the summer rush slowed, Jeff Stevens began to talk seriously with Jerry King, Regional Sales Manager of Calay Systems, Inc., about the marketing problems of Applied CAD Knowledge, Inc. Stevens wanted someone to become, in effect, a co-owner and officer of the small firm. King had been a principal in his own service bureau in the very early days of automated PCB design and retained friendships and contacts with high level personnel in many electronics firms. (Exhibit 8-8 shows King's resume.)

Exhibit 8-8   **Resume**

Resume

Married
Four Children
Excellent Health

JERRY KING

Education:

FAIRLEIGH DICKENSON UNIVERSITY, Madison, New Jersey
Major: Business Administration

U.S. NAVY, Electronics "A" School, Pearl Harbor, Hawaii

CONTINUING EDUCATION, including numerous seminars and workshops in Corporate Finance, Power Base Selling, Territory Time Management, The Art of Negotiating, Computer Graphics in Electronics, Sales Management and Marketing Techniques.

Experience:

GENERAL BUSINESS MANAGEMENT: Establishing policies and procedures for high volume cost efficient business operations, planning promotions for new business development, hiring, training and supervising personnel, including management level, designing and conducting management, sales, marketing and CAD/CAM training seminars internationally.

TECHNICAL BACKGROUND: Twenty-one years of direct Printed Circuit Design, Fabrication and Electronics CAD/CAM marketing experience. Helped to create detailed business plans for three start-up companies including a high volume printed circuit design service bureau and raised five million dollars in venture capital used to purchase state-of-the-art CAD/CAM systems and other related equipment. Managed the development and marketing of a PCB Design Automation turn-key system which was sold exclusively to Calma/GE in 1977 and integrated with their GDS1 TRI-DESIGN system. Very strong market knowledge in Computer Aided Engineering (CAE), Computer Aided Design (CAD), Computer Aided Test (CAT), and Computer Aided Manufacturing (CAM).

Exhibit 8-8   **(continued)**

Accomplishments:

Particularly effective in areas of personnel management, motivation and training, thereby increasing sales volume production flow, productivity and employee morale. Significant career accomplishments in customer relations, marketing and sales leadership and management.

Employment History:

1986–Present   Calay Systems Incorporated, Waltham, Massachusetts.
SENIOR ACCOUNT MANAGER.

Responsible for a direct territory consisting of Northern Massachusetts, Vermont, New Hampshire, Maine and Quebec.

1985–1986   Automated Systems Incorporated, Nashua, New Hampshire.
EASTERN REGIONAL SALES MANAGER.

Responsible for regional design and fabrication service sales with a regional quota in excess of $5 million.

1981–1985   Engineering Automation Systems, Inc., San Jose, California.
WESTERN REGIONAL SALES MANAGER.

Responsible for new Printed Circuit Design CAD/CAM system. Set up regional office, hired and trained sales and support staff of twelve people. Western regional sales were in excess of fifty percent of the company's business.

September 1984 PROMOTED TO NATIONAL SALES MANAGER.

1978–1981   Computervision Corporation, Bedford, Massachusetts.
NATIONAL PRODUCT SALES MANAGER.

Responsible for all electronic CAD/CAM system sales and related products. Provided direct sales management and training to the national field sales team, conducted sales training internationally, assisted in developing competitive strategy, technical support and new product development. Reported to the Vice President of North American Division.

March 1980 PROMOTED TO MANAGER, CORPORATE DEMONSTRATION AND BENCHMARK CENTER.

Managed team of 38 people who performed all corporate level demonstrations and benchmarks. Supported field offices with technical information and people worldwide. Reported to the Vice President of Marketing Operations. THIS WAS A KEY MANAGEMENT POSITION FOR THE COMPANY.

1966–1978   King Systems, Inc., San Diego, California. (A Printed Circuit Design CAD/CAM and NC Drilling Service Bureau.)
FOUNDER, PRESIDENT, CHAIRMAN and MAJOR STOCKHOLDER.

Served as Chief Executive Officer in charge of all aspects of the operation. Primary activities in sales management, direct field sales and customer relations. Responsible for financial administration, production operations and personnel administration. Assessed future needs and created business planning for increasing market share, facilities capability and penetrating new market opportunity. Developed a new concept in contract services for blanket sales to large government and commercial prime contractors.

Exhibit 8-9   **Excerpts from Jerry King's December 9, 1987 Board Presentation**

Introduction

The plan is a detailed road map for taking Applied CAD Knowledge, Inc. from the current sales volume to more than $3 million annual sales volume over the next three years. It identifies target markets, competitive environment, and sales tactics which will be used for achieving the sales projections during the plan period from January 1, 1988, through December 31, 1990. The projections show a monthly breakdown for 1988 and a yearly number for 1989 and 1990. The monthly projections were created on Lotus and provide for projected, forecasted, and actual sales bookings for each month. As each month passes the actual numbers are entered and a goal status report is generated as part of the end of month reporting. At the end of each quarter a new quarter will be added so that there will always be four consecutive quarters of monthly projections.

The aggressive growth which is outlined will require significant expansion of facilities, personnel and equipment in order to maintain consistent *quality* and *on time* deliveries and insure *repeat business* from established customers. It is required that the management and the Board of Directors of Applied CAD provide the necessary production controls and capital–operating budgets to support expansion commensurate with sales volume increases over the term of the plan.

The PCB design service market can be divided into three major segments. Each of these segments will include companies who design and manufacture electronic equipment for commercial, industrial, aerospace and military vertical market areas.

Major Accounts and Government Subcontractors

Major accounts are *Fortune* 1000 companies. They present a significant opportunity for multiple board contracts and blanket purchase agreements. Any one company could fill Applied CAD's capacity.

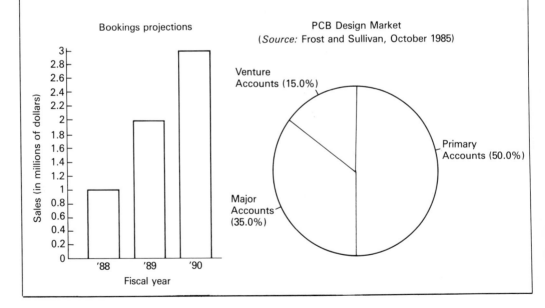

Bookings projections

PCB Design Market
(*Source:* Frost and Sullivan, October 1985)

Exhibit 8-9   (continued)

Primary Accounts

Primary accounts are companies who have been doing business for more than three years (not a start-up) and typically do between $5 and $500 million in annual sales. These companies represent the most consistent level of business. The type of contracts available from this market segment are usually on the level of one to four board designs per month. Typically, each board or project has to be sold separately at the project engineering level.

Venture Start-up Accounts

Venture start-up companies usually are operating on stringent budgets. They typically have no internal CAD capability and therefore must rely on outside service. The business potential for this market segment is very significant. This market represents a high risk and therefore is avoided by the major competitors, leaving more opportunity for the smaller operation. It is not unusual to obtain sole source product level contracts from companies in this market.

After a month of conversations and negotiations, including a meeting with the board, the two men reached a tentative agreement on employment terms which would give King a 3 percent commission on all company sales, a car allowance, and a base salary of $40,000 per year. Since the marketing person would be influential in pricing many jobs, it was important to preserve his regard for profitability; King was offered a stock interest in Applied CAD, contingent on the bottom line at the end of 1988. With a handshake agreement, Stevens set out to reduce the terms to an employment contract letter.

Exhibit 8-10   Sales Projections Presented to the Board, January 8, 1988

Forecast Q1 1988: Sales by Customer in Thousands of Dollars

Account Name	Jan. 50%	Jan. 90%	Feb. 50%	Feb. 90%	Mar. 50%	Mar. 90%	Tot. 50%	Tot. 90%	Grand Total
Customer A	0.0	20.0	0.0	8.0	20.0	0.0	20.0	28.0	48.0
Prospect I	0.0	7.0	0.0	0.0	0.0	0.0	0.0	7.0	7.0
Prospect II	5.0	0.0	2.0	0.0	2.0	0.0	9.0	0.0	9.0
Customer B	0.0	0.0	12.0	0.0	0.0	0.0	12.0	0.0	12.0
Customer C	12.0	0.0	0.0	0.0	0.0	0.0	12.0	0.0	12.0
Customer D	0.0	0.0	12.0	0.0	0.0	0.0	12.0	0.0	12.0
Customer E	0.0	30.0	0.0	0.0	20.0	0.0	20.0	30.0	50.0
Prospect III	0.0	0.0	15.0	0.0	20.0	0.0	35.0	0.0	35.0
Prospect IV	0.0	0.0	15.0	0.0	20.0	0.0	35.0	0.0	35.0
Prospect V	0.0	6.5	0.0	0.8	0.0	3.8	0.0	11.1	11.1
Customer F	0.0	0.0	0.0	7.0	0.0	0.0	0.0	7.0	7.0
Total	$17.0	$63.5	$56.0	$15.8	$82.0	$3.8	$155.0	$83.1	$238.1

(continued)

Exhibit 8-10   (continued)

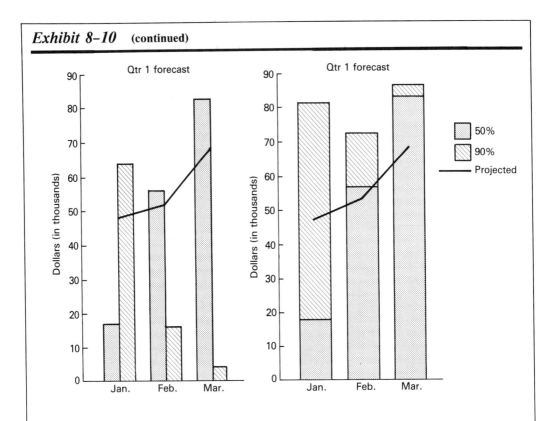

Forecast FY 1988: Bookings by Product Type

	Service	Software	Total	Accum Total
January	33	15	48	48
February	48	5	53	101
March	53	15	68	169
Total Quarter 1	124	35	169	
April	60	5	65	234
May	68	15	83	317
June	75	5	80	397
Total Quarter 2	203	25	228	
July	80	15	95	492
August	85		85	577
September	88	15	103	680
Total Quarter 3	253	30	283	
October	90	8	98	778
November	95	15	110	888
December	98	15	113	1001
Total Quarter 4	283	38	321	

The following night, Jerry King called Stevens to express his regret that he would be unable to accept the position after all because he had just received an offer from AT&T to set up Australian operations for a new venture. It was simply too good an offer to refuse, King said. A dejected Jeff Stevens reported the development at the next board meeting; "We're back to square one," he said. "And the next 'splat' is just about to arrive."

Applied CAD's monthly sales dropped to half their mid-1987 level, and the backlog dropped to near zero. On December 8, however, Jerry King called Jeff to say he had just decided against Australia, and would like to apply again for the marketing vice-president position, if it were still open. Jeff agreed, and the next day Jerry presented to Jeff and the board a plan for reaching $1 million in sales in 1988, and for growing by $1 million per year in the following two years. (This plan is

Exhibit 8-11	Monthly Sales and Month-End Receivables, Backlogs, Cash Levels (In thousands)			
	Accounts Receivable	**Sales**	**Backlog**	**Cash**
1986				
January	$18	$20	$20	$98
February	*	10	*	*
March	18	10	12	62
April	18	10	20	28
May	24	20	26	26
June	*	10	*	*
July	14	25	*	18
August	70	50	30	15
September	90	40	*	8
October	50	30	*	26
November	19	5	10	17
December	24	10	18	14
1987				
January	13	3	*	7
February	40	21	*	8
March	35	28	22	6
April	32	22	37	11
May	25	22	50	5
June	50	50	90	10
July	90	58	30	10
August	*	25	*	10
September	34	25	50	21
October	62	48	9	8
November	50	24	*	*
December	14	34	9	33
1988				
January	8	6	*	19

*Not available

partially reproduced in Exhibit 8-9). Concerned with the timing of cash flows, one of the directors asked how long it would take to generate enough new sales to cover their added marketing expenses. King responded, "If I couldn't provide more than enough sales to cover my pay, I wouldn't take the job."

Although not officially joining Applied CAD until January 4, Jerry spent the rest of December in joint calling with Jeff on customers where Calay and Applied CAD shared some interests. In these first weeks, the "chemistry" Jeff Stevens had hoped for became readily apparent. The two men's skills complemented each other well; this would be a highly effective team, Stevens felt.

As 1988 began, King and Stevens continued to work closely together. Since Applied CAD's office layout did not provide the privacy needed for telephone prospecting, Jerry worked out of his home, joining Jeff several times per week on joint sales calls. At the January 8 meeting of the board, the two men presented detailed sales projections for the first quarter and broader estimates for the entire year (Exhibit 8-10). One account alone, California PrinCo, held the promise of $250,000 in sales over the next four months. An old and steady customer of Applied CAD, PrinCo was nearing a decision on a major expansion in their use of circuit boards.

January sales totalled only $6,000 but many prospects seemed close to signing for large orders. At the February 19 board meeting, Jeff and Jerry predicted sales of $100,000 per month for February and March; it appeared a 1988 sales goal of $1 million might still be reachable. Exhibit 8-11 shows monthly sales and backlogs through January 1988.

Case 9

Comshare, Inc.

Comshare, Inc. was a computer service firm that began operations in 1966. It was a "high tech" company offering time-sharing services to industry, government, and other nonprofit organizations. These services included network access to computers owned and operated by Comshare. Users were able to communicate with the Comshare computers located at Ann Arbor, Michigan, via sophisticated communication networks of telephone lines. The system was designed to provide very rapid, apparently instantaneous, response to most simple requests. It appeared to the user

This case was prepared by Donald W. Scotton, Bernard C. Reimann, and Allan D. Warren, Cleveland State University, as a basis for class discussion rather than to illustrate either effective or ineffective handling of an administrative situation. Used by permission from Bernard C. Reimann.

that he had access to his own computer. All of the usual data processing and accounting functions could be performed on data stored at the computer center. Users could access their data from any of their plant locations for use in dealing with organizational problems.

During the period from 1966 until 1982, many advances occurred in the use of time-sharing and in the services offered by Comshare. These included the addition of sophisticated data bases, better methods for retrieving information, and the development of modeling methods for solving business and financial problems. Comshare was a leader in the industry in developing concepts and products to make possible this advanced technology for problem solving.

The latest and most significant of these developments was System W, an advanced Decision Support System (DSS) software product, which Comshare introduced late in 1982. This software made it possible for executives to enter or retrieve data from either mainframe or personal computers, build models to simulate their businesses, make forecasts, do statistical analyses, test assumptions or alternative "scenarios," and even display their results in customized reports or graphs. Although a substantial number of competitive products existed, Comshare executives considered System W to be a technological breakthrough in that it greatly facilitated modeling in multiple dimensions. Most of the competitive products were either limited to two-dimensional "spreadsheets," or required extremely complex programming to achieve multidimensional modeling and analysis.

Comshare had recently signed a marketing agreement with IBM concerning System W. IBM was interested in making highly sophisticated software available to its customers to complement its offerings of mainframe and personal computers. The arrangement included the agreement for IBM salespeople to recommend that users and prospects interested in DSS software consider System W. When feasible and desirable, IBM representatives could make joint sales calls with Comshare salespeople.

Shortly after this arrangement was made, Comshare executives were reflecting upon this action and its implications. Richard L. Crandall, President of Comshare, indicated:

> We will utilize our complete organization to make this arrangement successful; and we will modify and adapt System W to the changing needs of users. We are no longer only a computer-based time sharing corporation. An important part of our future lies in the development of Decision Support Systems that permit business executives to make better decisions through the interactive use of mainframe and personal computers.

THE INDUSTRY

Product Evolution

Initially computers were developed primarily for scientific computing. Their ability to store and manipulate any information was recognized and led to more and more business-oriented applications. Information could be stored, processed, and returned to users in manageable and meaningful reports and graphs. The rapid acceptance of computers led to the development of improved computers and ancillary equipment, such as terminals for entering data and calling it out, printers and plotters to provide "hard copy" output, and supporting networks and hardware to transmit and receive information. A vital complement to the hardware configuration was the appropriate software (program) to tell computers how to process the information.

An early trend toward specialization in the computing industry occurred in the mid 1960s, at which time it was recognized that not every firm or branch operation needed its own large mainframe computer. Rather, access through a communications network to a remote computer could meet user needs more economically, with little or no capital investment. Specialists developed the time-sharing concept whereby many different firms, as well as the many branches of each firm, could share a common computer in such a fashion that it appeared to each individual user as though he had sole access to the machine. Initial reception of this approach was best among the scientific and engineering community, and these groups were initially seen as the natural market for time-sharing. Concurrent with this phase was the development of communication networks that utilized telephone lines and supporting hardware to transmit and receive data.

By the late 1960s, it was recognized that it was the business needs of private firms, nonprofit groups, and government that comprised the most significant market of computer services. There was a growing requirement for better ways to record, store, retrieve, and manipulate information about organization functions such as accounting, finance, production, personnel, marketing, and research. Therein lay the challenge for developers of software packages, that is, to provide the means to perform these functions with the aid of computers. Software specialist firms emerged to supplement the efforts of the large hardware developers such as IBM and Digital Equipment Corporation.

Since hardware manufacturers tended to focus their efforts on systems software, a profitable and growing niche became available in the area of applications software. As a result, a variety of "software houses" emerged to provide high quality applications software with an emphasis on "user friendliness," or ease of use, as well as on efficiency. Typical applications included material requirements planning, accounting and financial reporting, and data base management.

Another important factor contributed to the accelerating growth of this specialized software market in the 1970s. This was the inability of the data processing function, in most firms, to keep up with the burgeoning demand for its services. The resulting backlog of data processing projects led to an urgent need for highly sophisticated software which would be so easy to use that nonprogrammers, such as financial or marketing executives and their staffs, could develop their own, custom-made applications.

At the same time, the increasing competitiveness and uncertainty of the business environment were creating a growing interest in strategic planning. This in turn led to a strong need for information systems to help top executives and strategic planners make decisions. One answer to this need was DSS (Decision Support System) applications software. This highly sophisticated software made possible the bringing together of relevant information from both internal and external data bases, and the use of complex models to simulate and analyze strategic alternatives before they were implemented.

The Market

There were fewer than 2,000 international computer software and service firms as reported in the 1982 Comshare *Annual Report.* Comshare, Inc. was one of the largest of these firms involved in the marketing of DSS software, which included data management, financial modeling, forecasting, analysis, reporting, and graphics. These DSS products were used by time-sharing customers via a worldwide computer network, as well as by customers who licensed the products for use on their mainframe computers or microcomputers.

The market for corporate and financial planning DSS software and processing services was reported as follows in the 1983 Comshare *Annual Report:*

1981 Sales	$549 million
1982 Sales	729 million
1987 Forecast	3.1 billion

The report also indicated that 1981 industry sales of all types of software totalled $4.2 billion. Richard L. Crandall, President of Comshare, reported in an interview for this case that 17 percent, or $714 million, came from data management and financial software sales, the two main predecessors of DSS. He indicated also that "in 1975 barely one-half billion dollars of industry sales were in software." *Business Week,* in its February 27, 1984 issue, published a special report on "Software: the New Driving Force." In it they forecast that software sales in the U.S. would "keep on growing by a dizzying 32% a year, topping $30 billion in 1988."

Competition

Mr. Kevin O.N. Kalkhoven, Group Vice President, estimated that the 1983 DSS industry leaders, their products, and sales were as follows:

Execucom	IFPS	$20 million
Management Decision Systems	Express	7–8 million
Comshare	System W	7–8 million
EPS, Inc.	FCS/EPS	6–7 million

It should be noted that, prior to the introduction of System W, Comshare had been a vendor of FCS/EPS on its time-sharing service. It still supported those time-sharing customers who were not willing to switch to System W.

There were more than sixty other competitors, at least twenty of whom had entered the business in the last two or three years. Two software products were identified as being particularly significant to Comshare. These were IFPS, a product originally developed for financial risk analysis, and Express, which was originally developed for marketing research functions. Both products had subsequently been enhanced and were being marketed as full function DSS systems. Comshare viewed IFPS as being particularly easy to use but lacking integrated functionality in areas such as data management, whereas Express was seen as a very hard to use product which was functionally well integrated and quite powerful.

In order to compete effectively in this market, Comshare felt it was essential to develop a product which was easier to use than IFPS and had more capabilities and was better integrated than Express. Thus System W was designed to take advantage of this opportunity for product positioning relative to the industry leaders.

Another potential threat that Comshare management had noticed was that a number of other firms were waking up to the huge potential of the market. These firms were redoubling their efforts both in improving their products and in marketing them. Several firms had decided to "unbundle" their prices for total systems in order to be more competitive. Thus a customer interested only in modeling, for example, could buy a "starter" system for as little as $10,000. If other capabilities, such as forecasting or graphics, were desired, each of these additional modules could be purchased separately for $5,000 to $15,000 each. Another aspect of product pricing was the increasing willingness of some vendors to discount the prices of their software, especially for multiple purchases.

Life Cycle

Time-sharing sales were of continuing importance to Comshare. A recent issue of Data Communications revealed that time-sharing expenditures in the United States were $3.1 billion in 1982 and $3.8 billion in 1983. Projected expenditures in 1984 were $4.2 billion. The bulk of Comshare's revenue continued to be realized from time-sharing services.

Mr. Kalkhoven made the following comments about the time-sharing portion of the industry:

> In the mid and late 1960s there were 800 time-sharing companies and now there are less than 100. There are 600 microcomputer manufacturers today and they will follow the same pattern as time-sharing. There will be very few in the future. I have been involved in this industry (high computer technology) since 1970. It has undergone an interesting life cycle pattern.

He proceeded to draw the diagram shown in Exhibit 9-1 on a blackboard. Then he described the three phases in the life cycle of a high-technology, computer-oriented firm as follows:

> 1. *Entrepreneurial Phase.* Normally the computer high tech firm remains in this phase for about five years. It takes from three to five years to realize a profit. There is a fast change in products, and a heavy capital investment is required. Management is largely drawn from technological people who are involved in the innovation of the

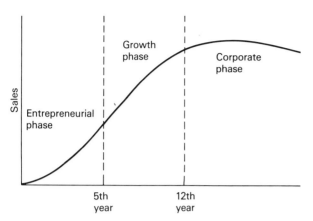

Sales

Entrepreneurial
phase

Growth
phase

Corporate
phase

5th
year

12th
year

Exhibit 9-1 **Life Cycle of a
High-Technology, Computer-
Oriented Firm**

products and concepts, for example from engineering. A large number of firms fail
and drop out because they run out of capital and cannot meet the rapidly changing
technology.

2. *Growth Phase.* This period extends from about year six through twelve. Market
leaders evolve. The number of competitors is reduced dramatically. For example, in
the time-sharing portion of the computer field, the number of firms was reduced
from approximately 800 to 100. During this growth period, technical and management stabilities emerge. The firms begin to develop corporate missions and policies;
they establish planning and marketing management approaches to guide their des-
tinies.

However, signs of what will happen later also emerge. These include a technological slowdown where profit is realized on existing technology rather than on new
product developments. As an example, Comshare enjoyed profits and the fruits
of a number of innovations associated with time-sharing networks. The need for
significant capital becomes urgent in this phase. Furthermore, the economic climate
is likely to suffer a recession at some point over this period of years. By the latter
1970s time-sharing technology had passed its period of rapid development, and the
onset of a recession confronted young management with new and unanticipated conditions.

3. *Corporate Phase.* During the corporate phase the strategic management and marketing process, initiated in the Growth Phase, is implemented fully. Marketing opportunities are identified more specifically. Strategic and tactical planning reach maturity. Operational programs and controls are developed as the bases for achieving
objectives. At this stage the firm must pick a product and go . . . you must pay for
its development and introduction with the cash cows. The initial mission, technology, and products may change. For many members of the industry the corporate
phase is just emerging. They must decide whether they will be hardware manufacturers, specialists in mainframes or microcomputers, time-sharing providers, systems consultants, limited software developers and purveyors, or decision support
system businesses.

COMSHARE BACKGROUND

Antecedents

The firm was founded in 1966 at Ann Arbor, Michigan. The founding president was Robert F. Guise, an independent consultant. He was joined in this venture by Richard L. Crandall, at that time a graduate student at the University of Michigan, and by four other persons.

Mr. Crandall studied computer applications under Professor Westervelt and taught computer courses at the university. In 1965, he learned about some exciting developments at Berkeley involving the design of a time-sharing operating system. He joined a group with members from Tymshare and from the University of California at Berkeley to work on this project. Crandall said:

> This was a stimulating group with which to work. We completed the operating system development and then I returned to Ann Arbor in 1966 to rejoin Comshare. [He returned as Research Director.]

Time-sharing was the first service to follow Comshare's consulting activities. Their first network consisted of direct dial access from customers to the Comshare computer. Mr. Crandall was involved in the technical aspects of developing time-sharing and the facilitating network hardware. In 1967 he became vice-president of research and development and also assumed operating responsibilities, including marketing. Mr. Crandall continued his remarks:

> We went public in 1968 and took in over $5 million. It was used within one year to open offices around the country. By January 1970 we had $3-4 million sales volume but were losing so much money that there was concern about the employees and the future of the firm. At the time of our March 1970 board meeting, I was chief operating officer and serious discussions took place as to the survival of the company. In August 1970 I was given the Presidency. We were $6 million in debt and losing $3 million a year.

Acquisitions and Divestitures

Comshare reacted to its changing environment through a variety of strategies. First there was a series of acquisitions and divestitures as indicated in Exhibit 9-2. These were carried out in the desire to gain new, related products, market entry, and knowledge about technical products and their adaptation to the markets.

Opportunities and complexities occurred with some acquisitions. Mr. Crandall commented:

> Computer Research Company was acquired in 1980 to learn about their use of IBM equipment and software. They were essentially a vendor of raw computer time and we did not understand the myriad of implications and options, including such items as pricing and IBM operating systems. Initially there was a culture shock between the two firms. Integration was difficult and eventually was achieved by absorbing the entire

Year	Event
	Exhibit 9-2 **Chronological Activities of Comshare, Inc.**
1965	Start-up and time-sharing operating system development
1966	Incorporation as a Michigan company
1968	Public offering of stock (traded over the counter)
	Start-up of Canadian affiliate (Comshare, Ltd.)
1970	Start-up of European operations as Canadian subsidiary (Comshare International, BV)
1974	Purchase of 30% interest in Comshare International, BV
	License agreement to provide services in Japan (Japan Information Service, Ltd.)
1977	Acquisition of Systematic Computer Systems Inc. (individual income tax processing services)
1978	Acquisition of Valuation Systems Corporation (consultants in current measurement systems)
	Acquisition of Trust Management Systems, Inc. (bank trust department services)
	Acquisition of 100% Comshare International, BV
1979	Acquisition of Digitax, Inc. (individual and fiduciary tax return processing services)
	Stock split (three for two)
1980	Acquisition of Computer Research Company (supplier of large-scale IBM computer processing services)
	Expansion into France with a wholly owned subsidiary (after receiving French government permission)
	Start-up of Hardware Systems Division (to provide services to users of large-scale Xerox computer systems)
	Secondary public offering of shares (net $10.1 million)
1981	Sale of individual income tax processing services (including those of Systematic Computer Systems and Digitax)
	Acquisition of Advance Management Strategies Inc. (microcomputer software now sold as COMSHARE Target Software)
	Increase in ownership of Comshare Ltd. (now owns 37.3% of Canadian affiliate)
1982	New product release: Planner Calc and Target Financial Modeling (microcomputer-based DSS products)
	Sale of the fiduciary income tax processing services
1983	New flagship product release: System W (DSS system for large-scale IBM computers)
	Sale of Trust Management Systems (accounting software for bank trust departments)
	Sale of Trilog Associates (balance of bank trust department services)
1984	Consummation of marketing agreement with IBM

Source: Comshare, Inc., annual reports.

operation into the main business of the parent, Comshare. We finally learned the IBM environment, from the executive office through to the salesmen. In the meantime, Computer Research Company has been completely integrated.

T. Wallace Wrathall, Group Vice President, Finance and Administration, discussed some of the acquisitions and divestitures as follows:

> The 1978 acquisition of Valuation Systems Corporation gave us their software for computing the current values of assets based on replacement costs. These financial systems products fit into the Comshare family of products and thus made the merger attractive. The corporation was eventually merged into Comshare. Currently these specific financial reports are no longer required by the Securities and Exchange Commission. However, the merger was successful.
>
> Later it was evaluated as belonging to the bank market rather than the domain of human resources, and it was sold.
>
> We were in the tax processing business and had purchased Systematic Computer Services to add to our line of services for CPA firms and their needs. To provide national coverage for our income tax processing services we then acquired Digitax in 1979. These firms were then sold in 1981. They were not profitable and, to offset this trend, more product development would have been required.

Mr. Crandall commented that the acquisitions of the Canadian, British, and European affiliates had been highly beneficial in extending markets, integrating operations, and furthering innovation and product development. As shown in Exhibit 9-2, this effort extended from 1968 forward.

STRATEGY LEADING TO SYSTEM W

Introduction

Comshare had been a planning-oriented company since the early 1970s. In 1972 they first formulated a long-range strategic plan. This plan enumerated corporate goals in broad terms and specified detailed objectives that were quantified as possible. Strategies were developed to meet these objectives and thus the corporate goals. In general terms these goals were: (1) to be a profitable growth company, and (2) to be the best firm in their market segment.

As a direct result of this planning process, Comshare changed its emphasis from general purpose time-sharing sales to providing more specialized, business problem-solving assistance. This was achieved by (1) making appropriate software tools available on their time-sharing network and (2) utilizing their customer support representatives to help customers solve business problems using these software tools. As Kevin Kalkhoven stated, "It was no longer appropriate to be everything to everyone."

In 1979 Comshare undertook a major review of their current plans and strategies. Mr. Kalkhoven further commented:

We saw three important things in 1979: (1) we had not changed—we were still primarily a time-sharing company; (2) we had not anticipated the rapid changes in hardware costs and performance; and (3) we had not anticipated the marketplace being dominated by the demand for microcomputers and software. Moreover, Comshare was experiencing the effects of the recession and the accompanying reduced revenues. Although we were one of the market leaders, we were in a period of technological stagnation.

Richard L. Crandall, reflecting on the results of this review, said, "We were satisfied that the corporate goals spelled out in 1972 were still valid; however, the environment had changed and we needed to reassess it and its impact on our strategies."

Environmental Review

Comshare management reviewed the environment and company position in terms of strengths, weaknesses, opportunities, and threats, and they observed the following:

A. *Strengths*
  1. The firm was well developed and represented on the international market. Its international sales force provided a strong competitive advantage.
  2. The talent existed to solve business problems. Experienced people had worked on these problems in the sale of time-sharing services.
  3. Market position was established in time-sharing.
  4. A product gap in inquiry and analysis software had been identified, and Comshare had the research and development capability to resolve it.
  5. The firm had a good cash flow and cash position. It could operate at a break-even position for several years.

B. *Weaknesses*
  1. Comshare had no identifiable image in software.
  2. The marketing organization did not have selling skills in software.
  3. The business recession and lack of a software product prevented Comshare from taking immediate market action.

C. *Threats*
  1. As software firms and products became more prevalent for in-house computer use, the demand for time-sharing services diminished.
  2. Service firms reduced prices to compete for market share.
  3. The advent of personal computers caused both computers and software to become available to users at lower costs.

D. *Opportunities*
  1. There was an increased demand for productivity software. Certain packages were available for data management applications. Also there

were "first round," relatively unsophisticated financial modeling packages. There was a need for a more functional product to solve a variety of problems for a broader group of users.

2. Existing software was relatively difficult to use and not as integrated and functional as it could be. Thus, Comshare had a market opportunity for a more functional and easier to operate DSS.

New Strategies

The environmental review led to a number of conclusions that were significant for the development of new strategies to achieve corporate goals. Comshare observed that:

1. Its value and importance to the customer were based on the skills of the Comshare employees and on the capabilities of the software it provided.
2. Time-sharing was only a delivery mechanism for providing access to software, which was used to solve business problems.
3. Software could also be delivered to the customer by selling mainframe software for use on customers' computers.
4. Personal computers were potentially important software delivery vehicles.

As a result of further analysis, Comshare decided that DSS was its primary product and should be delivered to customers in as many ways as possible. Time-sharing, as a delivery mechanism, remained an important aspect of the business; however, future development emphasis would be on DSS software.

To provide a finer focus for these efforts, Comshare determined that its best approach lay in the development and marketing of DSS software specifically designed for IBM computers. Thus the decision was made to develop a comprehensive, easy-to-use DSS optimized to run on IBM systems.

The developmental work was carried out in the European headquarters in London and resulted in a software product named Wizard. At present this DSS is marketed in Europe under the name of Wizard and in the United States as System W. Comshare had planned to use the name Wizard in the U.S. However, they discovered that a small software vendor had obtained an earlier trademark of Wizard for his product. To avoid infringement, Comshare was forced to change the name, at considerable expense, because sales brochures and other documentation had been printed bearing the designation Wizard.

Complementary Marketing Arrangement with IBM

A letter was received from IBM in September 1982 in which an invitation was extended to approximately 100 computer firms to attend an IBM-hosted conference. The purpose of the conference was to consider strategy for dealing with end users of computers and related services. The emphasis was on application software rather than data management and operating system software. Mr. Crandall attended the conference and noted that most representatives of attending firms did not seem to take the new IBM direction seriously.

However, he felt that IBM was very serious in its desire to have outsiders provide application software, while IBM concentrated on further developing its hardware—both mainframe and personal computers. This was a central part of IBM's new "Information Center" strategy, conceived to meet the pent-up demand among executives to use computers to satisfy their needs for relevant information. This concept required the development of "user friendly" software which would allow nonprogrammer executive users to develop their own DSSs. Since IBM did not itself have any strong offerings in this type of DSS software, Mr. Crandall envisioned a desire on the part of IBM to work closely with a firm capable of developing and marketing superior DSS software.

Discussion continued between IBM and Comshare, and in early January 1984 a two-year complementary marketing arrangement was reached. As indicated in the January 9, 1984, issue of *Computerworld*, IBM would recommend System W for use in Information Centers using IBM 4300 computers. IBM and Comshare sales representatives would refer prospects to each other. In addition, provision was made for joint sales calls of IBM and Comshare personnel to prospective users of DSS. The potential advantage to IBM was the prospect of increased hardware sales resulting from the availability of Comshare's DSS software. Finally, Comshare would continue its responsibility to users to install System W and conduct training programs.

FINANCIAL CONSIDERATIONS

Comshare was founded much as other entrepreneurial firms. Capital contributions by the six founders and the Weyerhauser family provided the impetus for the firm's start. There was a public offering of the firm's stock in 1968, and it was followed by a secondary offering in 1980 which netted $10 million. Exhibits 9-3 and 9-4 contain income and balance sheet data from 1978 through fiscal year 1983. These data reveal revenue increases until 1981, at which time recessionary influences were evident.

T. Wallace Wrathall, Group Vice President, Finance and Administration, commented:

> There are notable differences in the financial management of Comshare versus industry at large. Some of these include:
>
> 1. We have no inventory—only software tapes with low unit production cost. (This does not include the cost of research and development.)
> 2. There is a short life cycle of plant and products because of the rapidly changing technology.
> 3. Investment decisions have a short life cycle. So we need a high rate of return.

Exhibit 9-3   Comshare's Six-Year Trend Selected Financial Information[a]

			Year Ending June 30			
	1978	1979	1980	1981	1982	1983
Revenue	$23,404	$46,049	$68,579	$79,837	$78,453	$76,337
Income from operations	$ 3,791	$ 8,292	$10,672	$ 8,163	$ 1,406	$ 2,453
Interest expense	$ 450	$ 752	$ 1,486	$ 1,291	$ 1,240	$ 1,039
Interest income	$ 70	$ 116	$ 156	$ 370	$ 1,278	$ 1,052
Income before taxes	$ 3,943	$ 7,711	$ 9,146	$ 7,535	$ 1,591	$ 2,458
Income from continuing operations	$ 2,682	$ 4,383	$ 5,346	$ 4,374	$ 829	$ 1,331
Per share income	$ 1.00	$ 1.31	$ 1.41	$ 1.03	$ .18	$ .31
Average number of shares outstanding (thousands)	$ 2,675	$ 3,334	$ 3,791	$ 4,251	$ 4,542	$ 4,340
Research and development expense	$ 1,857	$ 3,289	$ 4,539	$ 5,916	$ 6,109	$ 6,135
As a percentage of revenue	7.9%	7.1%	6.6%	7.4%	7.8%	8.0%
Working capital	$ 1,107	$ 3,208	$ 5,584	$12,244	$12,350	$ 9,378
Capital expenditures	$ 3,081	$11,277	$13,685	$10,516	$ 8,684	$ 6,377
Total assets	$21,663	$47,275	$62,581	$70,919	$66,842	$59,381
Long-term debt	$ 3,825	$ 9,553	$14,415	$ 8,485	$ 9,960	$ 2,067
Shareholders' equity	$12,537	$22,086	$27,736	$40,735	$37,745	$38,192
Number of employees at year-end	538	1,100	1,282	1,215	1,164	1,084

[a]Dollar amounts in thousands of dollars except per share data.

In fiscal 1982, the company, in compliance with Statement No. 52 of the Financial Accounting Standards Board, changed its method of accounting for foreign currency translation adjustments. Financial data for periods prior to fiscal 1982 has not been restated for this change in accounting principle.

Information regarding Results of Operations excludes discontinued operations.

The average number of shares outstanding and income-per-share data have been adjusted to reflect a three-for-two-stock split in July 1979.

Source: Comshare, Inc., 1983 Annual Report.

4. Research and development expenditures are high compared to other industries.

5. Capital requirements are declining and are relatively low compared to the remainder of the industry.

6. Operating, selling, and development costs are largely people costs and will go up more rapidly than industry averages.

Mr. Wrathall reflected on other aspects that affect the firm:

1. Accounting rules can cause us to buy rather than make. . . . The manner in which we are required to report research and development costs is all important.

2. One-third of our sales are in markets outside of the United States. Because of the declining value of the British pound sterling, transferred earnings and investments are reduced. Continued decline in the value of the pound could result in a real loss.

3. System W was developed in the United Kingdom (under the name of Wizard) and sold to Comshare in the U.S. This developmental policy can result in the parent firm paying less for R and D because of favorable exchange rates and possibly more favorable tax rates.

Mr. Kalkhoven spoke on the necessity for a combination of product and financial policy to finance the marketing of System W and other new products. He alluded to the Boston Consulting Group's explanation of classifying products according to their growth and market share rates. Those products that no longer have a high growth rate but have retained a favorable market share can be marketed successfully for revenues to support the introduction and market development of new products under the so-called Cash Cow Strategy. The executives of Comshare had its time-sharing product line as a Cash Cow that would be useful in supporting the introduction of System W, its development, and the development of other DSS products as well. Moreover, Comshare's substantial time-sharing customer base gave it an easily accessible and somewhat captive market for System W and related products.

MANAGEMENT CONSIDERATIONS

Early in 1984, the top management group consisted of the following relatively young but highly qualified executives:

Richard L. Crandall, 41, became President and CEO in 1970. He was one of the original six founders of the firm in 1966. In 1978 he had served as president of the Association of the Data Processing Service Organizations. He was also a frequent speaker and author of numerous articles related to issues pertinent to the computer industry.

Kevin O. N. Kalkhoven, 39, was Group Vice President in charge of marketing product development and sales. He had been with the company since 1971. Prior to that he worked for IBM as an analytical services manager, and in sales management for SIA, Ltd. in the U.K. He lectured frequently on the subject of decision support

Exhibit 9-4   **Comshare, Inc. Consolidated Balance Sheet**

	As of June 30	
	1982	**1983**
Assets		
Current Assets		
Cash	$ 3,059,300	$ 3,407,500
Temporary investments, at cost	7,507,000	4,413,800
Accounts receivable, less allowance for doubtful accounts of $570,700 in 1983 and $550,400 in 1982	13,301,000	13,221,900
Prepaid expenses	2,512,900	2,154,200
Total Current Assets	26,380,200	23,197,400
Property and equipment, at cost		
Land	999,200	964,400
Computers and other equipment	42,408,200	42,983,700
Building and leasehold improvements	6,152,000	6,221,800
Property and equipment under construction	3,530,700	2,518,800
	53,090,100	52,688,700
Less accumulated depreciation	23,694,200	26,605,200
Property and Equipment, Net	29,395,900	26,083,500
Other Assets		
Investment in affiliate	2,020,500	1,905,700
Goodwill, net of accumulated amortization of $766,200 in 1983 and $567,300 in 1982	6,486,300	6,242,800
Purchased software, net of accumulated amortization of $1,101,600 in 1983 and $496,000 in 1982	1,948,600	1,521,000
Deposits and other	610,700	430,600
Total Other Assets	11,066,100	10,100,200
Total Assets	$66,842,200	$59,381,100

systems to such groups as the American Marketing Association and the Planning Executives Institute.

T. Wallace Wrathall, 47, Group Vice President for Finance and Administration, had joined Comshare in 1975. Prior to that he had 17 years of broad experience in finance and accounting. His previous employer, Varian Associates, was also in the computer high technology business and also had extensive foreign operations. Other employers included Del Monte Corporation, Optical Coating Laboratory, and Eldorado Electrodata.

Ian G. McNaught-Davis, 54, became Group Vice President in 1978 and managed the European operations. He was also a director of Comshare Limited. Mr. Davis was the founding chief executive of Comshare Limited (U.K.) in 1970. He was employed earlier for nine years with General Electric Information Systems. His

---

Exhibit 9-4   (continued)

	As of June 30	
	1982	**1983**
Liabilities and Shareholders' Equity		
Current Liabilities		
Current portion of long-term debt	$ 1,039,000	$ 345,200
Notes payable	1,151,700	1,857,700
Accounts payable	3,437,200	3,709,600
Accrued liabilities		
Payroll	2,391,600	2,722,600
Taxes, other than income taxes	1,162,400	992,400
Discontinued operations	1,720,500	98,500
Other	2,601,300	3,186,100
Total Accrued Liabilities	7,875,800	6,999,600
Accrued Income Taxes	526,300	907,500
Total Current Liabilities	14,030,000	13,819,600
Long-term debt	9,959,900	2,067,300
Deferred income taxes	5,086,900	5,302,500
Deferred credits	20,900	—
Shareholders' Equity		
Common stock, $1.00 par value; authorized		
10,000,000 shares; outstanding 4,281,414		
shares in 1983 and 4,599,604 shares in 1982	4,599,600	4,281,400
Capital contributed in excess of par	25,871,200	24,368,400
Retained earnings	10,415,200	12,624,200
Currency translation adjustments	(2,377,200)	(3,082,300)
	38,508,800	38,191,700
Less treasury stock, at cost (119,000 shares in		
1982)	764,300	—
Total Shareholders' Equity	37,744,500	38,191,700
Total Liabilities and Shareholders' Equity	$66,842,200	$59,381,100

Source: Comshare, Inc., *1983 Annual Report.*

---

last position with G.E. was Director of Marketing. He has been the moderator of approximately 20 one-hour television programs for the British Broadcasting Corporation concerning computers and their uses. Also, he lectured throughout the United Kingdom and Europe at universities and professional conferences.

These men exercised management and intellectual leadership throughout the organization. They were innovative in the development of solutions to everyday business problems and issues. During the early years the overriding concern was bringing together people who were innovative, self reliant, and results oriented. In this way computer services and software could be developed by a group of imaginative and dedicated people.

Richard Crandall was a leader and model for personnel involved in this activity. He became involved at the age of 18. He was president at the age of 26. He indicated that this was a young man's sphere of activity populated by those who shared common levels of intelligence, curiosity, innovativeness, and the pleasure of working diligently to achieve results to be enjoyed psychologically and materially. At the present time the average ages of Comshare employees were:

Nonmanagers	26 years
Managers	32 years
Executives	38 years

Kevin Kalkhoven pointed out that successful persons at Comshare were socially adept, got on well with others, and had excellent senses of humor. They had a natural curiosity about management practices. This led them to study and adapt business management approaches to planning, programming, operating, and controlling the firm's activities.

Mr. Crandall summarized the management philosophy and direction of Comshare as follows:

> The future of our business is in knowledge based software, and we must organize and operate properly to maintain success. We are a marketing oriented company. Our Research and Development effort is directed to meeting market needs in creative ways. New technology can spur innovation and creativity. We must attract talented people to Comshare who can work successfully in our environment. Top management is the key to innovation and the strategic management and marketing process. The approach and philosophy must permeate from the top of the organization.

Case 10

Apple Computer, Inc. Targets Desktop Engineering

Matthew Robertson was reviewing the first quarter sales figures for the Macintosh II. It seemed amazing to him that the most challenging problem Apple faced today was how to keep up with the demand for Mac IIs. The corporate first quarter

This case was prepared by Robert O. Lewis, Linda E. Swayne, and Peter M. Ginter as a basis for classroom discussion rather than to illustrate either effective or ineffective handling of an administrative situation. Some facts have been altered to protect confidentiality of company information. Used by permission from Linda E. Swayne.

results were impressive. Not only were sales up 35 percent compared to first quarter results a year ago but net earnings increased more than 20 percent (Exhibit 10-1).

The phone rang suddenly and broke Matthew's concentration. "Hello Matthew, this is Jan." "Hi Jan, how's it going?" "Crazy, of course. Listen, I'm not going to be able to make this afternoon's meeting. Can we reschedule for tomorrow morning—first thing?" "Sure, no problem. I was just looking over the quarterly report. Have you seen it?" "I heard it was great, but did you hear that Sun is finally shipping their low-end workstation? And there's been a lot of press about our evolving the Mac as opposed to introducing new revolutionary machines." "Yeah, we've got a lot to talk about, don't we? Look, I'll call Tom and reschedule for tomorrow, okay? . . . All right, see you tomorrow."

Matthew looked around his office and saw the mountains of information he had been collecting and analyzing for the past three weeks. Tomorrow morning he'd compare notes with his other team members, Janice Latham and Tom Kelly, and together they would come up with a program for Apple's formal entry into the engineering workstation market. Introducing the Mac II to Apple's new market would be a lot like his previous assignment as a member of the tremendously successful Desktop Publishing Market Development Team (MDT), but it would also be more challenging, Matthew thought. And Matthew realized *he* was now responsible for the success of this team—desktop publishing had been pioneered by Apple, but the engineering workstation market was already established. The competition would be ready.

APPLE COMPUTER'S BACKGROUND

Apple manufactures and markets two principal lines of personal computers, related software, and peripheral products. The first, which fueled the company's growth into 1986, was the Apple II product line. This line was geared to the educational (preschool through high school) and home computing markets. The second and the platform for the future growth of Apple was the Macintosh product line. Macintosh was developed for the business market (productivity and desktop publishing) and the higher educational market. See Exhibit 10-2 for a chronological history of Apple. Apple had not escaped the industry-wide computer slump of 1984–1985. However, through a well-organized restructuring, Apple emerged in 1986 as a leaner, more market-sensitive company and went on to record sales and profits.

Exhibit 10-1 **Apple Computer, First Quarter Sales and Earnings**			
	1988	**1989**	**% Change**
Sales	$1.042 billion	$1.405 billion	+35%
Net earnings	$121 million	$140 million	+20%

Exhibit 10-2   **Chronological History of Apple Computer, Inc.**

March	1976	Apple Computer was founded by Steven Wozniak (26) and Steven Jobs (21). They produced a hobbiest computer that contained 16 times the memory of any other such computer. It was priced at $666.66. Officially formed on April Fools' Day.
Jan.	1977	Jobs, Wozniak, and Mike Markkula incorporate Apple Computer and draft the first formal business plan.
April	1977	Apple II is introduced.
Dec.	1977	First year sales are $774,000.
Feb.	1980	Annual sales reach $100,000,000.
Dec.	1980	Apple offers public stock.
Aug.	1981	IBM introduces the PC.
Jan.	1983	The Lisa is introduced (forerunner of the Macintosh).
April	1983	John Sculley becomes President and CEO.
Dec.	1983	Apple annual sales reach $1 billion.
Jan.	1984	Fully automated Macintosh factory begins operation. Less than 1% of the cost of a Macintosh unit can be attributed to labor.
March	1984	Apple ships the Macintosh.
June	1985	Steven Jobs is removed from operations at Apple.
Dec.	1985	Annual sales reach $1.52 billion.
Feb.	1986	Apple purchases a Cray supercomputer to assist in the design of new products.
April	1987	Apple announces a 2-for-1 stock split and a first-ever cash dividend.
May	1987	Apple introduces the Macintosh II. This machine is positioned for the power-user in markets such as corporate MIS departments and desktop publishing.
Sept.	1987	U.S. sales organization splits into three regional divisions—Western, Central and Eastern.
March	1988	Apple begins shipping A/UX (UNIX software interface for engineering workstations).

When they founded Apple in 1976, Wozniak and Jobs had very specific ideas about what they wanted. The first business plan was written by retired Intel founder, Mike Markkula. The original corporate objectives and key strategies are included in Exhibit 10-3.

In 1987, Apple's CEO, John Sculley, set corporate objectives that included achieving $4 billion in sales by 1990, spending $300 million on research and development by 1990, and maintaining the entrepreneurial spirit of a small company. He and the Apple employees were committed to the corporate mission: "To produce innovative products that place the individual, not the mainframe, at the center of the computing universe."

Organizational Structure

Apple's organizational structure was designed to meet the corporate objective of maintaining the entrepreneurial spirit of a small company. It is best described as

---

Exhibit 10-3   **Apple's Corporate Objectives and Strategies, 1976**

Objectives

- Obtain a market share greater than or equal to two times that of the nearest competitor.
- Realize equal to or greater than 20% pretax profit.
- Grow to $500 million annual sales in 10 years.
- Establish and maintain an operating environment conducive to human growth and development.
- Continue to make significant technological contributions to the home computer industry.
- (Possible) Structure company for easy exit of founders within five years.

Key Strategies

- It is extremely important for Apple to be the first recognized leader in the home computer marketplace.
- Continually market peripheral products for the basic computer, thereby generating sales equal to or greater than the initial computer purchase.
- Allocate sufficient funds to R&D to guarantee technological leadership consistent with market demands.
- Attract and retain *absolutely* outstanding personnel.
- Rifle-shot the hobby market as the first stepping stone to the major market.
- Maintain significant effort in manufacturing to continually reduce cost of production.
- Grow at the same rate that the market grows.
- Design and market the computer to be more economical than a dedicated system in specific applications, even though all features of the Apple are not used.

Source: John Sculley, *Odyssey: Pepsi to Apple,* New York: Harper & Row, Publishers, Inc., 1987.

---

a hybrid design—neither centralized nor decentralized, it's actually a network. The network stems from the board and the single layer of upper management (six senior executives). It is given structure with functional areas like operations, marketing, finance, and so on. Senior members of the functional departments will recognize a problem or opportunity that needs to be addressed. Knowledge of the problem (or opportunity) comes from either a member of a functional department or someone in the network. Then modular groups are set up to solve that specific problem or develop that opportunity and later disbanded when the task is completed and re-formed into other groups to take on new projects.

The marketing functional area stems from the corporate marketing and sales managers, to one of the three regional marketing managers, then to separate managers within the region for education, retail, and direct sales. Reporting to the sales managers are sales representatives of varying capacities as well as sales support people.

Apple believes that the network is a superior format because it is a natural way for communication to flow. Inside the network, idea exchange is not inhibited by functional boundaries or management levels. Creativeness, flexibility, innovation, and individuality are all fostered in the network schema. The high-technology industry is subject to rapid change; therefore, the company and its personnel must be able to quickly share ideas about any change, develop alternatives, make a decision, and implement it. Another chief advantage of the network design is its efficiency. Apple's annual sales per employee was roughly $400,000—based on 1988 sales. Therefore the network structure allows Apple to operate leaner and achieve a corporate objective—to preserve its entrepreneurial spirit.

Through this network, Apple has identified the engineering workstation market as a lucrative target for the future. A task group was formed to analyze the situation and develop strategies to be implemented through the marketing channels. They would also recommend the direction for product development to meet the future needs of the identified target market.

Organizational Philosophy

Apple considers itself to be a "Third Wave" company (as opposed to a "Second Wave" company which sees the future as an extension of the past and therefore focuses on ritual) and focuses on the individual. Exhibit 10-4 illustrates the difference between a "Third Wave" and "Second Wave" company.

Exhibit 10-4   **Contrasted Management Paradigms**

Characteristic	Second Wave	Third Wave
Organization	Hierarchy	Network
Output	Market share	Market creation
Focus	Institution	Individual
Style	Structured	Flexible
Source of strength	Stability	Change
Structure	Self-sufficiency	Interdependencies
Culture	Tradition	Genetic code[a]
Mission	Goals/strategic plans	Identity/directions/values
Leadership	Dogmatic	Inspirational
Quality	Affordable best	No compromise
Expectations	Security	Personal growth
Status	Title and rank	Making a difference
Resource	Cash	Information
Advantage	Better sameness	Meaningful difference
Motivation	To complete	To build

[a]Genetic coding is a term describing how a third-wave company refers to the past only for a sense of direction.

Source: John Sculley, *Odyssey: Pepsi to Apple,* New York: Harper & Row Publishers, Inc., 1987.

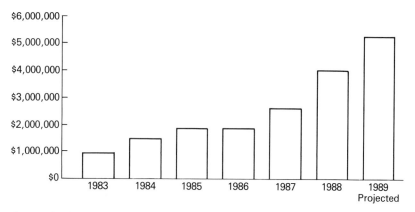

Source: Apple Computer, Inc.

Exhibit 10-5   **Apple Computer, Inc. Annual Sales**

APPLE AND THE MICROCOMPUTER INDUSTRY

With a revenue increase of 53 percent in 1988, Apple Computer is in a strong position in the computer industry. Analysts project 1989 revenues to approach $5.4 billion, a 30 percent increase (Exhibits 10-5 and 10-6).

The key to this success was the introduction of the Macintosh II, a machine that is equal to or better than (depending on the application) the high-performance machines offered by IBM, Compaq, and other similar microcomputer manufacturers. The Mac II features superior color graphics, extremely fast processing speed, and an advanced 32-bit architecture with the ability to run multiple operating systems. One operating system of importance to the engineering marketplace is UNIX. The Macintosh II can be configured to operate this complex system while maintaining its user friendly interface.

The power of the Mac II gained the awareness of MIS professionals, many of whom had regarded the original Macintosh as a "toy." With the introduction of the Mac II, many business/MIS decision makers realized that Apple could compete with IBM and would remain a key player in the computer industry. The user interface Apple had touted was now on a powerful system and, to give Apple even more credibility, IBM copied it in the form of the OS/2 presentation manager (operating system).

On March 18, 1988, Apple filed suit against Microsoft Corporation and Hewlett-Packard for copyright violations concerning the Macintosh Operating System. The suit directly charged that Microsoft's Windows 2.03 software copied the Macintosh interface.[1]

According to technical analysts, the Macintosh operating system is at least two years ahead of IBM's OS/2 in the evolutionary process (capabilities, upward

[1]Jim Forbes, Daniel Lyons and Gregory Spector, *PcWeek,* March 22, 1988, p. 1.

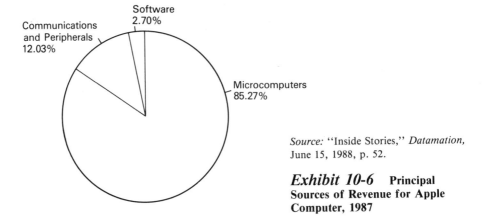

Source: "Inside Stories," *Datamation,* June 15, 1988, p. 52.

Exhibit 10-6   **Principal Sources of Revenue for Apple Computer, 1987**

expansion, and available software), and Apple's future depends on its ability to maintain that lead. Currently IBM leads the industry although its share eroded considerably from August 1987 to January 1988 (Exhibit 10-7).

Marketing research indicates that among potential buyers (those planning to buy within the next year), over the time periods shown in Exhibit 10-8, Apple's "share of year-ahead planned purchases" has grown consistently while IBM's (though still large) has faltered. Among respondents who have considered purchasing a specific brand, some have not tried the brand (Exhibit 10-9). Of those respondents who have tried the brand they intended to buy, the percentage who actually bought that brand is somewhat less than the trial (Exhibit 10-10).

TARGET MARKET

Apple's primary markets are designated higher education, business, government, K-12 education, and international. International sales currently account for nearly 30 percent of the company's annualized revenue. Apple has designated desktop engineering as the next target market.

The engineering workstation (desktop engineering) market consists of the various engineering fields—electrical, chemical, mechanical, civil, industrial, and architectural. Apple had segmented the market into two principal submarkets—the engi-

Exhibit 10-7   **Microcomputer Market Share**

	August 1987	January 1988
IBM	66%	47%
Apple	8%	17%
Compaq	6%	12%
Compatibles	20%	24%

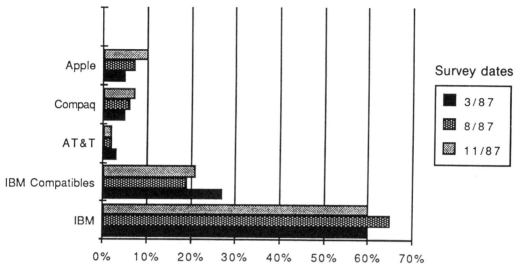

Source: Richard Stromer, *PcWeek,* January 12, 1988, p. 138.

Exhibit 10-8 **Share of Year-Ahead Planned Purchases**

neering workplace and engineering higher education. The UNIX workstation market is not limited to the United States, or engineers, and independent research has projected the world-wide market potential to be more than $20 billion by 1990. Apple has beefed up its international presence, implementing a strategy called *multilocal focusing* in recognition of this and other growing markets. Multilocal is Apple's term for regionalizing corporate communications as well as the ability to customize the product line for the end user.

Apple's present objective is to secure a strong foundation within the two mar-

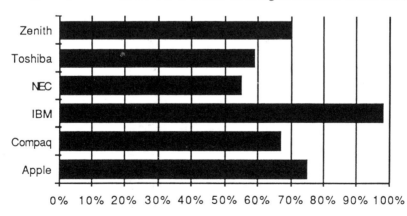

Source: Richard Stromer, *PcWeek,* March 22, 1988, p. 146.

Exhibit 10-9 **Percentage of Respondents Considering a Brand Who Have Tried that Brand**

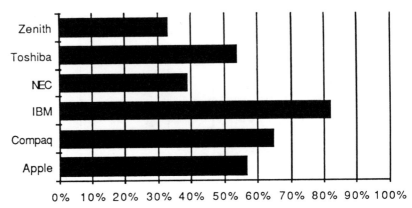

Source: Reprinted from *PcWeek,* January 12, 1988 and March 22, 1988. Copyright © 1988, Ziff Communications Company.

Exhibit 10-10   **Percentage of Respondents Who Have Tried a Brand and Have Purchased that Brand**

ket segments in the more narrow scope of the engineering workstation market. Apple plans to leverage resources for long-term growth and development of the two targets. Once Apple has established itself as a major workstation manufacturer, they will expand the objective to include all UNIX environments and applications.

Workstation Defined

In 1987, the U.S. engineering-specific workstation market, only eight years old, accounted for over $3 billion in sales. An engineering workstation is a micro-computer that is positioned in the market between a minicomputer and the tradi-tional personal computer. A workstation has become a high-performance personal computer that typically uses a programming language called UNIX, which is a so-phisticated operating system that controls the workstation and communicates with other computers of different manufacture.

UNIX has become the preferred system because it supports networking (tying many different computers together through the use of electronic hardware and soft-ware), allows the use of more than one application at a time, has full graphics sup-port, and is not a proprietary system (meaning that with some adjustments most any computer can operate UNIX, allowing the use of any application software program written under UNIX). Engineers use this system to perform tasks that range from scientific analysis to product design simulation. With the decreased cost of comput-ing, engineers and scientists are realizing the benefits that were once limited to the mainframe computer. And the computers can now sit on their desk.

COMPETITION

Sun Microsystems, IBM, Digital Equipment, Apollo Computer, and NeXT make up the principal competitors in the engineering market. Hewlett-Packard is

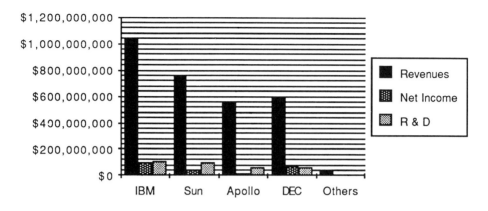

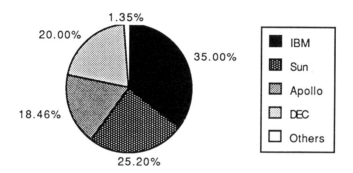

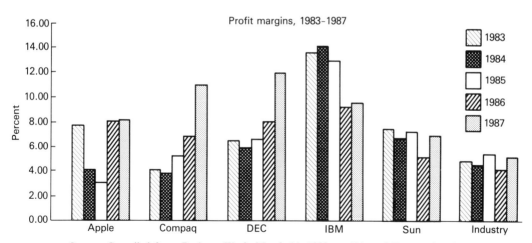

Source: Compiled from *Business Week,* March 14, 1988, p. 134, and *Datamation,* November 15, 1987, pp. 61–76.

Exhibit 10-11   **Major Competitor Revenue, Market Share and Profitability—Engineering Market**

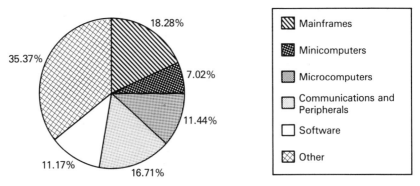

Source: "Inside Stories," *Datamation,* June 15, 1988, p. 42.

Exhibit 10-12   **IBM Principal Revenue Sources, 1987**

expected to bring its Spectrum computer to the UNIX marketplace soon. Apollo Computer pioneered the engineering workstation market in 1980. In 1985, it had a 40 percent market share that has since eroded to around 18 percent. Revenues, market share, and profitability information for the major competitors are illustrated in Exhibit 10-11.

IBM

John F. Akers, Chairman of IBM, instituted a complete reorganization to reestablish IBM as the most profitable company in the world. Analysts expected the changes to help IBM become more innovative and to move products out into the market more rapidly. "IBM has been taking too long bringing systems to the market," said Michael Geran, Vice-President for Nikko Securities International, a New York brokerage firm. "This is an evolutionary step by IBM to use an organizational change to speed up product releases and get closer to the marketplace."[2]

The change was to be accomplished through decentralization. Mr. Akers planned to push decision-making power down to the younger managers, fostering an entrepreneurial spirit.[3]

The IBM strategy is a full product and service line offering approach. Faced with flat growth projections (revenues) for both mainframe and minicomputer products, IBM has targeted personal computers, software, and services as the new and continued high growth markets (Exhibit 10-12).

The machine IBM has positioned for engineers is the Model 80. It is based on the 80386 Intel microprocessor with a speed of up to 20 MHz (a measure of raw processing speed). It operates with OS/2 and DOS system software, however, the computer has proprietary hardware set up to reduce the cloning potential (competitors who copy or purchase the same parts that IBM uses).

---

[2]Steven Burke, *PcWeek,* February 9, 1988, p. 127.

[3]*Business Week,* February 15, 1988, and *Business Week,* July 18, 1988.

The Model 80 can be categorized into IBM's new computer line as the Personal System 2 (PS/2). As of March 1988, IBM reported sales of 1.5 million PS/2 units and the Model 80 represents roughly 82,500 units sold. Due to the market's resistance to proprietary hardware, IBM has instituted tough quotas for its dealer network (many of the same dealers carry the Apple line). This has resulted in almost wholesale pricing—the Model 80 started out retailing for over $10,000 but now sells for approximately $7,000.[4]

Sun Microsystems

Sun manufactures a line of computers that range from desktop supercomputers to low-end workstations. These computers have all been positioned into the engineering market. Sun has not had the means to expand beyond that market. The company announced in February 1988 that their Triad Strategy was to be comprised of three different computers all featuring the UNIX operating system and a user-friendly graphic interface similar to the Mac interface. Sun is well known for its marketing savvy (oriented toward personal selling) in the engineering market and is one of the fastest growing computer manufacturers.

A principal component of Sun's success has been the fact that their computers have been built with widely accepted computing standards like Ethernet network protocols, Motorola's 68000 series processors, Intel's 80386 processor and AT&T's UNIX operating system software. Another is Sun's ability to take off-the-shelf components, like those mentioned above, to produce a high performance machine at a lower price than other competitors.

This practice is a double edged sword for Sun. Using off-the-shelf components enables them to take advantage of technological breakthroughs as they reach the market. On the other hand, this approach forces Sun to provide state-of-the-art machines constantly in order to keep margins up. As competitors continually match Sun (or eventually outguess the next off-the-shelf high-tech buy) customers may switch vendors for the very reasons they chose Sun—pricing and cutting-edge technology.[5]

With a UNIX operating system, Sun was seen as a "safe buy." But Sun is not without weaknesses; it is apparently vulnerable to manufacturing inefficiency (most of the system components are purchased) and has had a lack of financial clout.[6] Sun recently announced the sale of a 20 percent block of stock to AT&T.[7] Analysts view this as a sign of the impact of larger companies entering and expanding the market. The smaller companies will have to rely on their responsiveness to changing technology and market needs in order to succeed or survive.

AT&T is not new to computers; they lost between $800 million and $1.2 billion in 1986 alone and laid off thousands of employees. AT&T was the original developer

---

[4]*PcWeek*, March 29, 1988, pp. 10–11.

[5]Stuart Gannes, "America's Fastest-Growing Companies," *Fortune*, May 23, 1988, p. 30.

[6]"Mid-Range Shootout: Mini/Micro Survey," *Datamation*, November 15, 1987, pp. 61–76.

[7]*PcWeek*, January 12, 1988, p. 1.

of the UNIX operating system and had seen many companies profit from it while they were regulated by the government and not permitted to sell computers until the early 1980s. Industry analysts expect several effects of the agreement between Sun and AT&T. Sun will gain the distribution channel AT&T was using (dealers), and Sun will get financial resources to fuel its rapid growth. Analysts consider the price for Sun's 20 percent block of stock to be a bargain at $300 million, giving AT&T the opportunity to recoup previous losses.[8]

Sun's alliance with AT&T has developed another problem. Customers and competitors are suspecting that UNIX will no longer be as "open" to all computer systems as it has been. DEC, IBM, and others have grouped together to develop an alternative to UNIX.[9]

Sun's newest computer, the Sun 386i, uses a 80386 Intel microprocessor that is also purchased by IBM, Compaq, and others for use in their high-performance machines. The Sun 386i will be positioned against the IBM Model 80, Compaq 386, and the Macintosh II. Using a "386" processor will allow the Sun system to run DOS applications within the UNIX operating system software, giving the user access to all programs written for the IBM world. Jeff Elpern, manager of sales development for alternative distribution channels for Sun, has been quoted as saying that MicroAge, Entre Computer, and other independent dealers have been signed to distribution agreements. Mr. Elpern expects to have 100 dealers signed by the end of June 1988. Andrew Neff, an analyst with Bear, Stearns & Co., a New York investment company, said, "Last year, it was IBM who was getting eaten up by Compaq at the high end and by everyone else at the low end. Now it's Compaq's turn." (Note: reference to IBM's "high-end" is equivalent to the "low-end" Sun workstation.)[10]

William O'Shea, Executive Director of AT&T's Information Technology Division, stated, "It is key that we recognize the existence of DOS and OS/2 and that we operate effectively in environments that include those systems as well as UNIX."[11]

Apollo Computer

While Apollo established the workstation market, recent competition with more financial resources and better marketing expertise has contributed to Apollo's decline. Sales are still increasing, but not at a rate in proportion to the growth of the market. Apollo's low-end workstation is the DN 3000. Their principal market for this system is the previous Apollo customer.

Digital Equipment Corporation (DEC)

Within 30 years, DEC has grown to be approximately the world's second largest computer systems supplier. Exhibit 10-13 illustrates the principal revenue sources

[8]Ibid.

[9]Richard Brandt, Phane Peterson, and Geoff Lewis, "Getting Computers to Dance to the Same Music," *Business Week*, May 23, 1988, pp. 112–114.

[10]Kenneth Siegmann, *PcWeek*, March 29, 1988, p. 139.

[11]Steven Burke, *PcWeek*, March 29, 1988, p. 139.

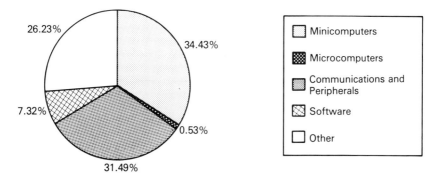

26.23%

34.43%

7.32%

0.53%

31.49%

- ☐ Minicomputers
- ▨ Microcomputers
- ▨ Communications and Peripherals
- ▧ Software
- ☐ Other

Source: "Inside Stories," *Datamation,* June 15, 1988, p. 42.

Exhibit 10-13 **Principal Revenue Sources for DEC, 1987**

for DEC. As of 1987, no revenue was attributed to the sales of mainframe products.

The DEC strategy is to move from the role of a minicomputer vendor to one of a full-line supplier. DEC has embarked on a new product development campaign which includes mainframes, communications, software, services, and individual workstations (high performance PCs). DEC has also developed relationships with Apple Computer, Compaq Computer, and Northern Telecom.

DEC has made the most competitive progress against IBM in the mini-computer market. DEC has successfully sold its VAX Cluster through the benefit of two main points. One, if a single VAX unit goes down, service can continue without interruption. Two, additional VAX units can be added as more processing power is required. Under an IBM mainframe, service is lost when it breaks down and if the IBM customer outgrows the system, management must sell the old at market price and purchase a larger, more expensive system, often requiring software changes.

Analysts currently feel DEC's move into the mainframe product area is "anti-thema." Another problem facing DEC is the increasing power of personal computers which are now making inroads into individual workstation market share. The principal firms marketing such PCs are Apple, Compaq, IBM, and Sun Microsystems. Even more threatening to DEC is the fact that when better communications software is available from these competitors, PC customers will be able to connect their PCs together and form a system very comparable to the DEC VAX Cluster—at a substantial discount.[12]

Overall, analysts project a conservative 15 percent revenue increase, but DEC will try to use its product expansion strategy to actualize a larger revenue gain.

In 1988, Apple Computer and Digital Equipment reached a marketing agreement for strategically aligning their products. Analysts expected DEC to concentrate

---

[12]Leslie Helm, John Verity, Geoff Lewis, Phane Peterson, and Jonathan Levine, "What Next for Digital?" *Business Week,* May 16, 1988, p. 91.

on the high end of the engineering market and Apple to focus on the low to middle end. However, in late 1988, DEC announced it would market Tandy manufactured PC clones and would manufacture a full line of workstation micros based on RISC (Reduced Instruction Set Computing) technology. It was unclear whether or not DEC would position these products directly against Apple.

Compaq

Compaq's strategy has evolved into one similar to that of Sun Microsystems. Compaq is now introducing machines of greater performance and of at least equal quality to that of IBM machines. Compaq machines are priced consistently below comparable IBM models, but above competitors. The use of a high quality image has enabled Compaq to become a "next best alternative" to IBM and represents a "better value" to many computer customers.

The principal threat to Compaq is the "new standard" touted by IBM called the PS/2 or Personal System/2 computer line. If this eventually becomes the new PC standard, Compaq may be forced into an adoptive strategy that could result in a margin decline. However, analysts feel Compaq will have at least two years of healthy sales and income growth.

Currently, Compaq is positioning its "386" machine as superior in performance, quality, and value compared to the IBM models. They have been very successful. It is unknown what impact the Sun entry into the broad dealer channel will have upon Compaq's strategy.

Hewlett-Packard

The HP Vectra RS/20 computer is based on the 80386 microprocessor and operates on DOS similar to the IBM models.

The HP Spectrum is reported to use a RISC processor, a type of processor where 20 percent of all computer instructions are executed in four-fifths the time of a normal processor. It is reported that the price will be near that of a low-end workstation, and that it will operate UNIX and run DOS similar to the Sun 386i. The graphic interface used on this computer is the subject of the Apple lawsuit.

NeXT, Inc.

Founded by Steve Jobs three years ago, NeXT introduced its first computer in late 1988. While not scheduled to ship in quantity until late summer of 1989, and most application software not expected until early 1990, industry analysts viewed the NeXT machine as the "next" leap in technology.

The main processor was the 25 MHz Motorola 68030 (5 mips) which is somewhat faster than Apple's Mac IIx (based on the 16 MHz Motorola 68030 chip) and operated on a version of UNIX called Mach. The machine utilized separate microprocessors for operations such as video, sound, and input-output information processing. This enabled information to be handled much faster, from beginning to end, than any currently available micro using a comparable main processor. Technical analysts consider this "mainframe on a desktop" approach to be the key advantage of the NeXT machine.

Mr. Jobs has stated the current strategy of NeXT will focus on higher education, primarily to the engineering and computer science markets and did not rule out the possibility of entering the business market in the future. Mr. Jobs also announced IBM has entered into a license agreement with NeXT for the use of its graphic interface and programming environment to run on all IBM UNIX machines. Analysts considered this to be a hedge on the possible failure of IBM's OS/2.

THE MEETING

Tom Kelly, a software engineer and software market analyst, and Janice Latham, a hardware engineer and hardware analyst, were seated with Matthew as they began to discuss the decisions they would have to make.

Apple's marketing research team in conjunction with their product development team had determined that an unmet need existed in the engineering workstation market. Research indicated that engineers would request a computer that would do more than scientific applications especially if they were already using a high-end system or were seeking a system for subordinate engineers. Exhibit 10-14 illustrates engineer preferences when selecting a workstation.

Apple also recognized that MIS directors relied on input from engineers concerning workstation requirements, but MIS directors were still responsible for the results of the purchase decision. Exhibit 10-15 indicates the purchasing criteria used by MIS directors. Jan and Tom agreed that the surveys were fairly representative of customer attitudes.

Matthew reminded them that the market for engineering workstations was $3 billion in 1987. Projections for the low-end segment of the workstation market were $1.1 billion in sales for 1988, $1.15 billion in 1989, and $1.3 billion in 1990. Jan said, "Those projections seem conservative to me. Looking over this quarter's sales figures, we are selling all we can make, yet we don't know if we're meeting our potential." "You're right," Matthew responded, "We don't even know the real potential of this market. It might be just like desktop publishing where we found that any small business could benefit from using the product. Every engineering applica-

Exhibit 10-14 **Ranked Criteria for Workstations by Engineers**	
Power, benefits, features	1
Support	2
Compatible/networkable	3
Learning curve	4
Cost effectiveness	5

Exhibit 10-15	**Ranked Criteria for Workstations by MIS Directors**
System quality/reliability/performance	1
Compatibility/networkable	2
Vendor reputation/financial strength	3
Application software availability	4
Price	5

tion could conceivably be performed on the Mac II and there are numerous types of engineers . . .'' (Exhibit 10-16).

Next, Matthew brought up the point that support was ranked highly by engineers. Apple's primary salespeople would come from the dealer organization. Jan said, "There are different kinds of engineers, each with a certain need, and they're different primary markets. Yet electrical engineers are electrical engineers although some are employed in business, some in government, and some in higher education. I think we're kidding ourselves if we believe our dealer network can easily handle the more sophisticated installations.''

"I can see that and yet we can't ignore the dealer network," commented Matthew. "I can't think of a way to reach as many engineering prospects as we did desktop publishing prospects.''

Apple uses a direct sales force primarily to sell to large corporations (approximately 100 accounts), all universities, and to the dealer network. The dealer network is divided into two types—retail accounts and independent resellers. The retail accounts are usually national chains like Computerland and MicroAge. The independent resellers are individual stores that combine a retail plan with an outbound sales program.

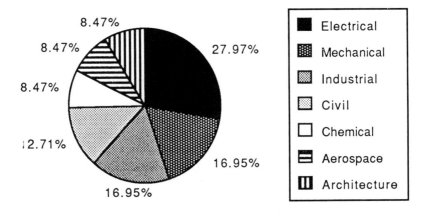

Exhibit 10-16   **Engineers by Discipline**

Exhibit 10-17   **Computer Performance Comparison**

IBM Model 80	Compaq 386	Sun 3/50	Sun 386i	Apollo DN 30
16 MHz 80386 1.5 mips[a]	20 MHz 80386 2 mips	16 MHz 68020 2 mips	25 MHz 80386 3 mips	16 MHz 68020 2 mips

[a]mips (million instructions executed per second) is a benchmark used to compare processing power.
Source: PcWeek, March 29, 1988, p. 139.

Something else was bothering Tom, "Take a look at this computer comparison from *PcWeek* for low-end engineering workstations. Everybody's here except us."

"We should have been there! The Mac II has virtually the same performance as those in the article," said Jan. "We have the 68020 processor with a 2 mips rating and look at this price comparison." (See Exhibits 10-17 and 10-18.)

Matthew concentrated on another hurdle Apple would have to overcome. "Our image is very strong as a home computer marketer and the Macintosh seems to suffer from an image of being so easy to use it must lack power and sophistication." Jan jumped in, " Several participants in my hardware focus group study kept saying they didn't believe sophisticated software was available, even though they knew the hardware was powerful." "Even Seymour Cray, the Cray supercomputer designer, uses a Mac II to design his new systems. But it's expensive to change attitudes," exclaimed Tom.

"There's one more issue we've got to weigh," Matthew slowly leaned forward. "Jan mentioned to me yesterday the revolution vs. evolution press we've been getting. I'm concerned about how this will affect our plans." Tom interrupted, "Matt, I was talking with Tim Morgan last night and he's involved with an assessment on that with public relations. I'm sure he's got some ideas and I'll talk with him as soon as we're finished."

"Okay, Tom, that sounds good. Our marketing budget for the engineering workstation segment has tentatively been set at $16 million. (Exhibits 10-19 and 10-20 present the financial statements.) That has to be allocated for the workstation in all our primary markets—engineers in business, government, and higher educa-

Exhibit 10-18   **Price Comparison**

	IBM Model 80	Compaq 386	Sun 3/50	Sun 386i	Apollo DN 30	Mac II
Price	$7000	$7000	$7995	$8500	$8295	$6500
Price/mips	$4500	$3500	$4000	$2800	$4000	$3250

Source: PcWeek, March 29, 1988, p. 139.

Exhibit 10-19 Apple Computer, Inc., Balance Sheet, 1980–1988 (In thousands)

	1980	1981	1982	1983	1984	1985	1986	1987	1988
Assets									
Current assets									
Cash & short-term investments	$ 363	$ 72,834	$153,056	$143,284	$114,888	$337,013	$ 576,215	$ 565,094	$ 545,717
Accounts Receivable	15,814	42,330	71,478	136,420	258,238	220,157	263,126	405,637	638,816
Inventories	34,191	103,873	81,229	142,457	264,619	166,951	108,680	225,753	461,470
Prepaid expenses	NA	NA	NA	27,949	26,751	70,375	53,029	48,798	88,711
Other	3,738	8,067	11,312	18,883	23,055	27,569	39,884	62,143	48,280
Total Current Assets	54,106	227,104	317,075	468,993	687,551	822,065	1,040,934	1,307,425	1,782,994
Property, plant and equipment	4,779	22,371	34,483	67,050	75,868	90,446	107,315	130,434	207,357
Other assets	6,465	5,363	6,229	20,536	25,367	23,666	11,879	40,072	91,735
Total Assets	$65,350	$254,838	$357,787	$556,579	$788,786	$936,177	$1,160,128	$1,477,931	$2,082,086

Liabilities and Owners' Equity

Current liabilities									
Notes payable	$ 7,850	$ 10,745	$ 4,185	$ 37,321	$ 71,094	$121,702	$ 124,550	$ 168,992	$ 127,871
Accounts payable	14,495	26,613	25,125	52,701	109,038	74,744	118,053	205,929	510,475
Income taxes payable	8,135	8,621	15,307	0	11,268	27,800	14,652	20,242	62,465
Other current liabilities	7,300	24,301	41,139	38,764	63,784	71,179	71,280	83,585	126,282
Total Current Liabilities	37,780	70,280	85,756	128,786	255,184	295,425	328,535	478,678	827,093
Long-term debt	671	1,909	2,052	1,308	0	0	0	0	0
Deferred income taxes	951	5,262	12,887	48,584	69,037	90,265	137,506	162,765	251,568
Owners' Equity									
Par value	0	0	0	0	0	0	0	0	0
Capital in-excess of par value	8,342	120,361	138,760	182,855	206,097	229,749	220,766	263,347	226,972
Retained earnings	17,606	57,026	118,332	195,046	258,468	320,738	473,321	573,141	776,453
Total Equity	25,948	177,387	257,092	377,901	464,565	550,487	694,087	836,488	1,003,425
Total Liabilities and Equity	$65,350	$254,838	$357,787	$556,579	$788,786	$936,177	$1,160,128	$1,477,931	$2,082,086

Exhibit 10-20 Apple Computer, Inc., Consolidated Statement of Income, 1979–1988 (In thousands)

	1979	1980	1981	1982	1983	1984	1985	1986	1987	1988
Sales	$47,867	$117,126	$334,783	$583,061	$982,769	$1,515,280	$1,918,280	$1,901,898	$2,661,068	$4,071,373
Cost of goods sold	27,450	67,329	170,124	288,001	505,765	878,586	1,117,864	891,112	1,296,220	1,990,879
Gross Profit	20,417	49,797	164,659	295,060	477,004	637,290	800,416	1,010,786	1,364,848	2,080,494
Operating Expenses										
Research and development	3,601	7,282	20,956	37,979	60,040	71,136	72,526	127,758	191,554	272,512
Marketing and sales	4,097	12,110	55,369	119,945	229,961	392,866	478,079	476,685	655,219	952,577
General and administrative	2,617	6,820	22,191	34,927	57,364	81,840	147,043	132,812	146,637	235,067
Total Expenses	10,315	26,212	98,516	192,851	347,365	545,842	690,157	737,255	993,410	1,460,156
Operating Income	10,102	23,585	66,143	102,209	129,639	91,448	102,768	273,531	371,438	620,338
Interest and Other Income, net	3	567	10,400	14,563	16,483	17,737	17,277	36,187	38,930	35,823
Net income before tax	10,105	24,152	76,543	116,772	146,122	109,185	120,045	309,718	410,368	656,161
Taxes	5,032	12,454	37,123	55,466	69,408	45,130	58,822	155,755	192,872	255,903
Net Income	5,073	11,698	39,420	61,306	76,714	64,055	61,223	153,963	217,496	400,258
Earnings per Share	$0.12	$0.24	$0.70	$1.06	$1.28	$1.05	$0.99	$1.20	$1.65	$3.08

tion," replied Matthew. He went on, "As I see it, we have three challenges: the image of the Macintosh being too easy to use, the perception that sophisticated software packages are not available, and the sales of engineering workstations through our current dealer network. Add to that the unknown effect of the press about how we're evolving the Mac rather than breaking new technological frontiers. Given these issues, Corporate still expects us to make the Mac II a major player in the workstation market."

Case 11

Honeywell, Inc. in Brazil

"How can we stay in Brazil?" was the question put rhetorically by John May, Honeywell's Vice-President and General Manager for Latin America, one day in early 1981 at the firm's Minneapolis headquarters. "Their informatics policy and protectionist exclusions are driving us into Guanabara Bay."

"Yes, but we've got to hang on," responded Edson Spencer, Chairman and CEO of Honeywell. "The long-run prospects are still very promising and I doubt we could get back in if we withdraw."

Brazil's actions of 1979 and succeeding years had indeed made Honeywell's situation in that country precarious. In 1979, Brazil had established regulations and a regulatory body aimed at quickly boosting Brazil's position and capabilities in a field they called "informatics." The term covered anything having to do with computers, chips and their applications, all sizes and varieties of hardware and components, software, and digital telecommunications, digitalized equipment, and instruments in many lines. The regulatory bodies, the regulations, and their applications were developed and extended year by year in the 1980s.

The informatics product lines were at the heart of Honeywell's business, and Brazil's computer development policies might therefore have been expected to benefit Honeywell in Brazil. But aims of the regulations were highly restrictive. *Domestic* development of technology in these lines was the keynote: Brazilian firms, Brazilian products, Brazilian technical expertise. The ultimate aim was to put Brazil's com-

This case was prepared by Delbert C. Hastings (with the assistance of Esra Cendturk) as a basis for class discussion rather than to illustrate either effective or ineffective handling of an administrative situation. Used by permission from The Case Development Center, University of Minnesota.

puter technology, skills, and products on a level with the leading countries of the world.

Brazil's development strategy in this field involved making selective use of foreign firms and technology. The regulations were designed to impede international and foreign firms operating or seeking to operate in Brazil in the product lines in which Brazil wanted domestic expertise. Foreign firms were permitted to operate in Brazil only to the extent that technological knowledge, skills, and productive capabilities were transferred to or built up in Brazil.

Foreign and international firms were controlled by issuance or denial of licenses to operate in a desired product or service line. Denial of a license forced the firm out of that product line and perhaps out of Brazil. This was the situation that Honeywell found itself facing. The situation had become increasingly difficult as the regulations and regulatory bodies were developed and modified in the early 1980s, and as the regulatory bodies denied a series of Honeywell's carefully prepared applications but approved arrangements with selected competitors.

In part Brazil's government policies were *defensive,* due to endemic problems of capital shortage, inflation, and shortages of foreign exchange. In part they were *forward-looking,* as Brazil sought to boost its people's welfare by speeding economic development. And in part they were *aggressive,* as Brazil sought the capability of keeping up with world technology.

Honeywell's top managers were convinced that Brazil was a country that would repay strenuous efforts to "stay in." Brazil is a major country, with a huge area and a large, growing population. It has vast resources, even now not fully explored, and it is well along in industrialization. Though Honeywell's annual revenue in Brazil had never exceeded $15 million, Brazil's promise as a future industrial power could not be ignored.

Honeywell had operated in Brazil since 1958. It built its business on selling control products and systems, made or assembled in its Sao Paulo plant from imported or locally made parts. The business itself and the importation of parts were now being severely threatened. A complex web of factors involving Honeywell and its Brazilian subsidiaries, the Brazilian government agencies enforcing the informatics policy, and the history, culture, and politics of Brazil must be grasped to understand the situation fully.

THE COMPANY: HONEYWELL'S CORPORATE ORGANIZATION AND OPERATIONS

Organization

Honeywell, operating in 85 country markets in its centennial year of 1985, has been an international company at least since 1930, when it acquired an office in Toronto (though it had begun exporting a decade earlier). In recent decades it has become one of the world's leading business firms, providing computer, control, and communication systems and services to customers around the globe. Its main business falls into four industry segments. These segments constitute the firm's macro-organizational structure. Honeywell's *1984 Annual Report* describes them as follows:

> Aerospace and Defense includes the design, development, and production of guidance systems and controls for military and commercial aircraft, space vehicles, missiles, naval vessels, and military vehicles.
>
> Control Products includes microelectronic and electromechanical components and products for residential, commercial, and industrial applications which are marketed on an individual product basis to wholesalers, distributors, and original equipment manufacturers.
>
> Control Systems includes sophisticated commercial building and industrial systems, both analog and digital computer based, which are designed for data acquisition, monitoring, control, and management of customer processes and equipment.
>
> Information Systems includes products and services related to electronic data processing systems for business, governmental, and scientific applications.

In addition to these four, the organization includes an International Controls unit, operated as a separate unit but related in products to both the Control Products and the Control Systems units. International Controls is subdivided into four geographical divisions. The Information Systems has its own international group, and the Aerospace and Defense division also handles its own international matters. Numerous foreign subsidiaries exist. The skeleton organizational structure of Honeywell Inc. is set out in Exhibit 11-1.

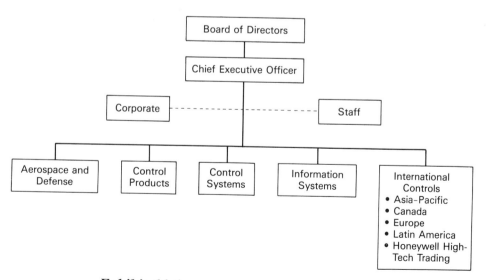

Exhibit 11-1   **Honeywell Inc.'s Corporate Structure**

Honeywell High-Tech Trading Inc. is a recent (1984) addition to the International Controls division. Organized as an export trading company under recent U.S. law, High-Tech Trading exports products of clients, engages in various forms of countertrade, and represents Honeywell products in countries not otherwise covered.

In 1984, the International Controls division operated plants in 33 locations, had offices in 40 countries around the world, and had distributors in 52 additional countries. Its factories are located in Australia, Belgium, Brazil, Canada, France, Germany, Japan, Mexico, the Netherlands, Singapore, Spain, Switzerland, Taiwan, and Thailand. In 1984 the International Controls division had 14,934 employees among the Honeywell corporate total of 93,514. International Controls is headed by J. E. Chenoweth, an Executive Vice-President of Honeywell.

International Controls, Latin America division, is of special interest here because it includes Brazil. The division has plants in Sao Paolo, Brazil, and in Chihuahua and Mexico City, Mexico. It also operates 100-percent-owned subsidiary companies in Argentina, Brazil, Mexico, Puerto Rico, Venezuela, and Uruguay.

In this case it is necessary to distinguish carefully between Control Products and Control Systems, as well as between the commercial and industrial applications of such products.

Control Products manufactures high-unit-volume individual products and markets them through direct sales or through distributor networks. These products become original equipment in many applications. The catalog of Control Products' Microswitch division lists over 50,000 sensors, switches, and controls used in manufacturing, materials handling, automotive ignition, commercial products, business machines, aerospace, ordnance, and marine equipment. Control Products' Energy Products division specializes in controls and systems for retail stores, offices, restaurants, and supermarkets (referred to as "light commercial" applications). The Residential division specializes in air-quality-and-comfort controls and systems for homes. Thus, Control Products markets individual products both to industrial users and to commercial and residential applications. In general, Control Products does not sell systems for heavy industrial use.

In contrast, Control Systems emphasizes systems rather than individual parts. This division commonly contracts with buyers to provide complete custom-designed control systems for large industrial and commercial uses. A control system might be a complex set of sensors, valves, meters, and communications lines to a central microprocessor to control a complete steel mill as well as to display and record results, or to provide controls over heating and cooling, air purification, fire detection, security, and other aspects of a major office building or building complex. Process control and process management functions are major industrial applications. Control Systems has been expanding into communications systems, including internal telephone, telecommunications, and computer network systems. This division includes the Honeywell/Ericsson Development Company, a research and development joint venture with the Ericsson Group of Stockholm, Sweden. Control Systems is thus centrally involved in investments to increase efficiency and quality and to effect technological improvement in both industrial and commercial operations. The Control Systems division also markets to both industrial and commercial users, but is more involved in industrial process control and in large projects.

Both Control Products and Control Systems (and hence International Controls) depend for their main markets on their buyers' capital investment projects (though the replacement market is also important). Hence the investment climate and availability of investment capital in their market areas are highly important.

Honeywell's Financial Performance

Honeywell's 1984 revenues totalled $6.07 billion, moving the firm into fifty-sixth place among *Fortune* 500 U.S. industrial companies, up from sixtieth in 1983. Exhibit 11-2 provides a financial and operating overview by line of business from 1980 through 1984. Exhibit 11-3 gives data by major geographical area.

Honeywell's Corporate Policies

Honeywell's business philosophy is rooted in the marketing concept. Its 1984 *Annual Report* states, "Honeywell is an international corporation whose mission is to work together with customers to help them achieve their goals through leadership in automation and control."

Honeywell's commitment to leadership in its product lines and market areas is firm. As stated in its 1983 *Annual Report,* Honeywell intends to participate in market segments only where it can serve the needs of its customers as leader or—at worst—sharing leadership. A statement to a prospective joint-venture partner set this out as follows: "Honeywell is willing to take risks in new products, new businesses, and new markets, but always with the long-range objective of leadership in mind. After a period of time operating in the risk mode, if such a goal is unattainable, we may withdraw from such segments."

The company's long-term financial objectives include an 18 percent return on equity and a 14 percent return on investment, with a debt ratio not to exceed 30 percent.

Guided by this philosophy, Honeywell believes that its long-term success can be assured only through the effectiveness of its products, through cost controls, and through continuously developing new technology so as to ensure maintenance of its leadership position.

Achievement by Honeywell of its leadership in Brazil has been in question in recent years. Persistent inflation, devaluations, currency shortages, and the emergence of protectionist regulations implemented through Brazil's "informatics" law have made it hard, if not yet impossible, for Honeywell to continue its business operations there. Some background in Brazil's history, culture, and political development is useful for understanding Honeywell's strategic moves during the first half of the 1980s and their ill-fated outcomes.

Exhibit 11-2   **Honeywell, Inc. Consolidated Corporate Financial and Operating Data by Major Product Lines, 1980–1984 (In millions)**

	1980	1981	1982	1983	1984
Revenue					
Aerospace and Defense	$ 996.3	$1,103.5	$1,258.3	$1,540.5	$1,608.0
Control Products	888.1	854.7	822.0	890.4	1,024.5
Control Systems	1,351.2	1,529.4	1,622.1	1,570.8	1,615.8
Information Systems	1,634.1	1,773.7	1,684.7	1,666/1	1,825.3
	$4,869.7	$5,261.3	$5,387.1	$5,667.4	$6,073.4
Operating Profit					
Aerospace and Defense	$ 62.1	$ 77.2	$ 87.4	$ 109.0	$ 116.2
Control Products	132.9	82.1	79.3	83.0	141.1
Control Systems	150.4	175.0	187.2	134.9	135.9
Information Systems	183.5	158.3	79.8	130.8	179.7
Operating Profit	528.9	492.6	433.7	457.7	572.9
Gain on sale of interests in Cii-Honeywell Bull and GEISCO	—	—	90.8	—	—
Unallocated items	(119.7)	(135.9)	(133.5)	(100.2)	(142.0)
Income before Income Taxes	$ 409.2	$ 356.7	$ 391.0	$ 357.5	$ 430.9
Assets					
Aerospace and Defense	$ 367.1	$ 478.1	$ 674.4	$ 701.8	$ 800.5
Control Products	600.2	584.3	584.6	661.5	671.3
Control Systems	815.0	899.7	930.7	972.9	1,074.1
Information Systems	1,340.6	1,371.4	1,369.1	1,322.6	1,310.4
Corporate	701.5	893.8	769.8	885.3	841.9
Discontinued operations	60.4	86.7	126.8	119.6	61.6
	$3,884.8	$4,314.0	$4,455.4	$4,663.7	$4,759.8

Source: Honeywell, Inc., *Annual Report,* 1984.

THE COUNTRY: BRAZIL

Brazil has been transforming itself from a primarily agricultural into a major industrial nation, producing iron and steel, heavy machinery, automobiles, weaponry, electronics, food products, and consumer goods. It is now the eighth largest free world economy (GNP equal to about US$250 billion or $2,000 per capita in 1981, a recession year). Its estimated 131 million people made it the world's sixth most populous country in 1985. In area, its 3,286,000 sq. mi. make it just smaller than the United States (3,615,000 sq. mi.), and fifth largest country in the world. It extends 2,965 miles north to south, 2,691 miles east to west, occupies nearly half of

Exhibit 11-3 **Honeywell, Inc. Corporate Financial Information by Geographical Area 1982, 1983, and 1984 (In millions)**

	1982	1983	1984
External Revenue			
United States	$3,885.3	$4,179.9	$4,514.3
Europe	1,022.4	1,059.0	1,059.7
Other areas	479.4	428.5	499.3
Totals	$5,387.1	$5,667.4	$6,073.6
Transfers between Geographical Areas			
United States	$ 241.9	$ 220.6	$ 265.3
Europe	16.6	22.9	29.9
Other areas	14.1	24.7	19.5
Totals	$ 272.6	$ 268.2	$ 314.7
Total Revenues			
United States	$4,127.2	$4,400.5	$4,779.9
Europe	1,039.0	1,081.9	1,089.6
Other areas	493.5	453.2	518.8
Eliminations	(272.6)	(268.2)	(314.7)
Totals	$5,387.1	$5,667.4	$6,073.6
Operating Profit			
United States	$ 259.7	$ 320.6	$ 417.9
Europe	128.8	80.6	108.0
Other areas	30.9	50.9	54.9
Eliminations	14.3	5.6	(7.9)
Operating profit	433.7	457.7	572.9
Gain on sale of interests in Cii-Honeywell Bull and GEISCO	90.8		
Unallocated items[a]	(133.5)	(100.2)	(142.0)
Income before income taxes	$ 391.0	$ 357.5	$ 430.0
Identifiable Assets			
United States	$2,675.1	$2,794.4	$2,900.2
Europe	791.2	783.7	812.8
Other areas	356.9	357.1	363.7
Corporate	769.8	885.4	841.9
Eliminations	(137.6)	(156.9)	(158.8)
Totals	$4,455.4	$4,663.7	$4,759.8

[a]Interest expense, and general corporate income and expense.

Source: Honeywell, Inc., *Annual Report, 1984.*

the South American continent, and borders every South American country except
Ecuador and Chile (Exhibit 11-4). It has vast quantities of minerals, agricultural
land, forests, and fisheries as well as human resources.

1968 to 1974—The "Economic Miracle" Years

With vast human and natural resources, Brazil has been portrayed by many
as the land of the future. Such contentions were further reinforced between 1968
and 1974, referred to in Brazil as the "Economic Miracle" period, when Brazil's
GNP increased at the impressive annual rate of 11.5 percent and manufacturing
output rose at the even higher rate of 18.9 percent. These high rates resulted in part

Exhibit 11-4   **South America**

from expansionary government policies and from reemployment of manufacturing capacity idled in 1967. In addition, a substantial expansion of world trade and a high level of capital inflow created a favorable international environment. Brazil's exports increased an average of 27 percent a year while exports of manufactured products rose 38 percent annually. Moreover, this rapid economic growth was accompanied by declining inflation and only a modest rise in external debt.

Brazil's current situation is best understood in terms of history and political background. Brazil's history starts in Europe in the 1400s.

Historical and Political Background

The discovery of Brazil occurred as part of the "Age of Exploration" in the late fifteenth and early sixteenth centuries, with the discovery of sea routes around Africa, Columbus's voyage to the Caribbean, and extended exploration of the New World. The original chief participants were rivals, Spain and Portugal. Potential and actual conflicts in territorial claims between the two countries were settled in 1494 by the Treaty of Tordesillas which gave Portugal the lands east of and Spain the lands west of a dividing line 370 leagues west of the Cape Verde Islands. This treaty made Brazil the only Portugese-speaking country in the New World.

In 1500 Admiral Pedro Cabral discovered and claimed for Portugal the territory of Brazil (its coast lay east of the Tordesillas line). Early development by a system of "captaincies" was followed by crown colony status under a royal governor-general. A sugar industry based on African slave labor soon flourished; by 1600, 120 sugar mills were operating in Brazil. The native Indians were also enslaved, but their numbers were soon decimated by disease. Jesuit missionaries sent to convert the Indians soon became their advocates in both Brazil and Portugal. Inflow of Europeans began.

Exploration of the interior continued, especially by the legendary Bandeirantes of Sao Paulo. Their explorations and settlements pushed Brazil's western boundary to the Andes foothills, far beyond the Tordesillas dividing line. A frontier economy based largely on cattle-raising developed. The sugar plantations and cattle ranches gave rise to the typical elite owner class and working/slave class.

French, Dutch, English, and Spanish incursions into Brazilian territory were fought off. When the conflicts were finally settled, the recognized territory of Brazil extended to the Andes foothills on the west, the River Plate on the south, and nearly the entire Amazon basin on the north. Spain ruled Portugal from 1580 to 1640. Afterward conflict with Spain over territory in Brazil's south continued until a final division created the country of Paraguay. This conflict recurred sporadically for years.

Gold and diamonds, discovered and mined since 1693 in Minas Gerais state, enriched Portugal's royal coffers. The Jesuits, opposing Indian enslavement, were judged too influential and were expelled in 1759. Cotton and coffee became important exports during the 1700s. Immigration from Europe continued.

The year 1789 (notable in the United States and Europe as well) brought initial stirrings for independence in Brazil. The Portugese royal family fled to Brazil in 1807 during Napoleon's invasion of their kingdom. When the royal court was able to return to Lisbon in 1820, it sought to reestablish Brazil's former colonial status. The Brazilians again sought independence and achieved it peaceably in 1822. A constitution adopted in 1824 made Dom Pedro legitimate emperor but also set the precedent, continued in all Brazilian constitutions, of indirect election (via "electors") of some officials. This system diluted popular participation and is now much disputed.

Brazil remained an empire until 1889. The first emperor, Dom Pedro I, authoritarian and unpopular, was soon forced to abdicate. The second, Dom Pedro II, ruled well and popularly for his first 25 years. However, a disastrous war with Paraguay put him in a bad light and had the unexpected effect of raising the Brazilian army as a permanent political force. Slavery was abolished in 1888, but the process weakened Dom Pedro's standing. His deposition in 1889 ended the empire. A republic was then formed, and a constitution modeled on that of the United States was adopted in 1891. But strife continued, and government was under military dictatorships until 1893. A revolt then permitted a civilian president to take office; this form of government endured until 1930. During that period, Brazil sided with the Allies in World War I.

In 1930 Getulio Vargas overthew the civilian government and set up a dictatorship which lasted until 1945. After several Brazilian ships were sunk by German submarines, Brazil entered World War II on the Allies' side. Brazil lent airfields and naval facilities, and Brazilian troops fought valiantly in the Italian campaign.

Vargas was deposed by the military in 1945. A succession of elected presidents then held office until 1964. Pressures toward more effective mass participation in the political system continued. The latter three presidents—Kubitschek, Quadros, and Goulart—were increasingly leftist, and a socialist revolution of uncertain variety seemed imminent. In 1964 the military forces and two state governors, acting to forestall such an outcome, declared a (nonviolent) revolution and deposed Goulart. These nonradical "revolutionaries" undertook to restore economic and financial order, to remove Communists from government and to bring about "moral regeneration." Union officers, mayors, governors, bureaucrats, legislators, and former presidents were arrested. Democracy, respectability, and legal status of the government were, however, stated goals of the military revolutionaries.

This military government lasted 21 years, from 1964 to 1985 (Exhibit 11-5), with five army generals ruling in turn. But the economic troubles of the 1970s, skyrocketing oil prices, increasing foreign debt, and intractable inflation ended confidence in military leadership. In the later years, the military did aim at restoring civilian rule (under the term "abertura" or "opening") and ultimately planned and carried out an election. With the decisive Electoral College vote of January 15, 1985 Tancredo Neves was elected president, to succeed General Figueiredo. Jose Sarney was chosen vice-president. But Neves, aged 75 and in poor health, was hospitalized on inauguration day (March 15, 1985), and died on April 21, 1985. He was quietly succeeded by Sarney.

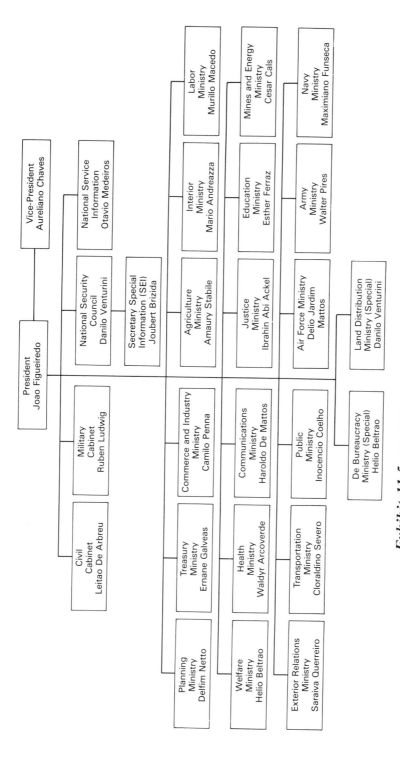

Exhibit 11-5 **Brazil Government Organization (as of 1984)**

President
Joao Figueiredo

Vice-President
Aureliano Chaves

Civil Cabinet
Leitao De Arbreu

Military Cabinet
Ruben Ludwig

National Security Council
Danilo Venturini

National Service Information
Otavio Medeiros

Secretary Special Information (SEI)
Joubert Brizida

Planning Ministry
Delfim Netto

Treasury Ministry
Ernane Galveas

Commerce and Industry Ministry
Camilo Penna

Agriculture Ministry
Amaury Stabile

Interior Ministry
Mario Andreazza

Labor Ministry
Murillo Macedo

Welfare Ministry
Helio Beltrao

Health Ministry
Waldyr Arcoverde

Communications Ministry
Haroldo De Mattos

Justice Ministry
Ibrahin Abi Ackel

Education Ministry
Esther Ferraz

Mines and Energy Ministry
Cesar Cals

Exterior Relations Ministry
Saraiva Querreiro

Transportation Ministry
Cloraldino Severo

Public Ministry
Inocencio Coelho

Air Force Ministry
Delio Jardim Mattos

Army Ministry
Walter Pires

Navy Ministry
Maximiano Funseca

De Bureaucracy Ministry (Special)
Helio Beltrao

Land Distribution Ministry (Special)
Danilo Venturini

Observations Arising from Brazil's History

Brazil's political-cultural background has been elitist. Adhering to a strict class system, Brazilians follow the tradition of honorable, generous, and responsible behavior associated with high rank. The country has slowly evolved toward a democratic political structure, with impulses toward rapid and extreme political change mediated by the guiding presence and frequently the overt action of the military forces. The social conflicts implicit in this process are important factors in the continuing instability of the Brazilian political system.

The all-important military has long had and continues to have a special position, role, and ideology in Brazil. Under the constitutions of 1891, 1937, 1946, and 1967, the military was recognized as a guardian of Brazil not only externally but internally. After 1889 the military asserted its role as guarantors of constitutional government, in the name of the people, although often violating constitutional status in the guarantee process. Meanwhile, the military forces evolved (primarily in the officer corps) from elitist toward middle class (but not lower class). Officer training and schooling is thorough and rigorous. The process has produced many able officers and, through a system of selective attendance at upper level military schools by civil officials, has strongly influenced the higher levels of the civil administrations also.

The military governments have stood for both stability and change, pushing economic development perhaps more successfully than do civilian governments. The extended military intervention from 1964 to 1985 may have forestalled conversion to some form of socialism. Although accompanied by a modest level of resistance and strife, this special military role is accepted in Brazil more than in other Latin American countries.

Strong government interventions in and guidance of the Brazilian economy, including government establishment and continued ownership of significant firms, is also of long standing, and is considered normal. Current interventions in the economy are in no way unusual. For a "nonsocialist" country, the list of government-owned firms is extensive but not unusual for Latin America.

Prohibitions against foreign firms in specific operations or industries have been present since colonial times. Thus current prohibitions against multinationals are not unusual.

Although Brazil has tremendous natural resources, it has had and continues to have a tremendous concomitant need for capital to develop these resources. Because of the country's vastness and lack of significant petroleum deposits, its transportation system (railroads, roads, and highways) and its energy and power sources are insufficient for current operations and future development. Consequently it has put its capital into large infrastructure projects—electric power, development of alcohol production as a substitute for petroleum, development of offshore oil fields, development of iron mines for exports—all holding significant promise for the future but not yielding immediate increases in needed consumption goods or exports (except in the case of iron ore).

Internally generated capital has met only a fraction of the country's needs. Forced to draw on external sources, Brazil has accumulated large foreign debts. Debt service requirements bring the inevitable shortages of foreign exchange, import restrictions (even when imports of capital and capital goods would be to its great advantage), and export campaigns (even when its lower classes need homes and food). These forces have rendered Brazil highly vulnerable to world economic downturns such as that of the early 1980s.

Throughout its history, Brazil has suffered successive boom-and-bust swings in sugar, cotton, cocoa, rubber, and coffee. Capital has been accumulated in such industries only to be dissipated in the downswings. Economic stability has been a stranger to Brazil.

Despite all these difficulties, Brazil has achieved major industrial growth in recent decades, especially in iron ore, steel, automobiles, machinery, soy beans, and military goods.

Population growth has been rapid during the past 50 years (2.47% in the early 1980s; United States, under 1%). The 1980 census showed Brazil, with a population of 119 million (United States, 228 million), to have 17 million wage earners (U.S. employment of 101 million) out of a work force of about 50 million (United States, 108 million). Brazil's population is skewed to preworking-age children and young adults. While Brazil has large areas to be populated, its economic development has lagged, yielding high unemployment and inadequate housing, education, and social services. High infant mortality and illiteracy continue. This imbalance between population growth and economic development is perhaps Brazil's greatest enduring problem and, with the political features cited above, the source of much of its continuing instability.

An estimated 90 percent of the population is baptized Roman Catholic; Brazil is the largest Roman Catholic country in the world. The clergy has been a force for amelioration of the conditions of the poor but, with a few notable exceptions, has not been highly active politically.

By at least the 1930s Brazil perceived itself as having a "manifest destiny" to become a leading nation. Its size and resources and its able people and significant accomplishments have led outside observers to the same conclusion. Although achievement has been difficult, the goal strongly influences current Brazilian public policy.

Brazil's national pride runs high. Brazil seeks self-development and independence from foreign countries, institutions, and firms. In Senator [Roberto] Campos' view,

> Support for the [1984 Informatics] protectionist legislation was so overwhelming because of Brazilian national pride and the country's anger at its dependence on foreigners.
>
> When our country feels it has suffered external humiliation, for instance, bankers at the door, the IMF imposing austerity measures, the result is an outburst of nationalism—an outburst against those imposing the humiliation.[1]

---

[1] *Financial Times*, November 5, 1985.

But this understandable pride and self-confidence runs counter to Brazil's needs for capital, for economic development, and for the technology available only in the more highly developed industrial countries. These conflicting and emotionally charged goals have created major internal stresses in government policy setting as well as restrictions laid on foreign and multinational firms. In external affairs the same conflicts recur with foreign banks, with the IMF (International Monetary Fund), and with multinational enterprises striving to operate in Brazil.

Despite the facts that Brazil's development runs perhaps a half century behind that of the United States and that its southern European flavor creates significant contrasts to the stronger northern European influences in the United States, Brazil and the United States share distinct similarities. The two are sibling New World countries of European parentage, with large areas and great natural and human resources, with admixtures of African and native American racial stocks and cultural attributes. Both adopted the goals of industrialization and, broadly speaking, of democracy. Brazil's constitutions and military organization have been patterned significantly on those of the United States. Both performed on the Allied side in two world wars. It is little wonder that ties between the two countries have been and continue to be strong.

Current Economic Conditions in Brazil

Brazil's five and one-half years of miracle growth came to a sudden halt during the latter part of 1974. Economic problems beginning then (and still continuing) stemmed in large part from the quadrupling of oil prices, which induced general world recession and financial problems in many countries. These problems were most severe in underdeveloped countries and in those without domestic oil sources. World inflation resulted, since oil was so important an input to all economies. The grossly higher oil prices caused oil-poor Brazil immediate difficulties in paying for its imports.[2]

Thus, in the mid 1970s Brazil's balance of payments stringencies imposed constraints on growth while inflation accelerated to unprecedented levels. The major recourse to sustain growth was to borrow from abroad. Brazil's foreign indebtedness increased sharply in the 1970s, expanding nearly fourfold between 1973 and 1978. Gross external medium- and long-term indebtedness totaled US$53.8 billion in 1980.

---

[2]*Note:* About half of Brazil's imports have been of crude oil and products, since Brazil had very low oil production until the offshore developments of 1983 to 1985. *Financial Times* data of November 5, 1985, show that in 1973 total Brazilian consumption of crude oil ran at 790,000 barrels per day [b/d] and domestic production was about 175,000 b/d, 22 percent of consumption. By 1984 consumption was about 960,000 b/d and domestic production was 460,000 b/d, 48 percent of consumption. Thus, Brazil is gradually improving its oil situation.

The Second Oil Crisis and the 1980–1981 Recession

The second-round (1979–1980) oil crisis, coupled with high interest rates accelerated Brazil's already mounting debt. Each year more loans were rolled over rather than repaid. Brazil suddenly developed a need for new earning power for foreign currencies, a need not yet fulfilled by late 1982. The total medium- and long-term external debt stood at US$61.4 billion at the end of 1981. This trend continued at an accelerated rate: Brazil entered 1983 with a foreign debt of over US$83 billion; it rose in 1984 to $90 billion, and in early 1985 to about $100 billion, the largest foreign debt of any Third World country.

Brazil was not alone. An international financial crisis loomed at this time, since other Third World countries such as Yugoslavia, Poland, Mexico, and Argentina were also deeply in debt. International aid was required, with the IMF, BIS (Banking International Settlements), and groups of developed countries striving to avoid breakdown of the world monetary system and debt repudiations. A "cartel of debtors" was proposed. But with global private and public cooperation debts were stretched out, payments postponed, and a crisis was averted. The IMF credits were arranged, but reduced government spending and other austerity measures were enforced as a prerequisite to the actual advance of funds to countries.

Brazil's Debt Management Problems

The country's growing foreign debt, balance of payments difficulties, and economic instability planted the seeds for its current austerity program and import curbs. In 1974, at the end of Brazil's miracle growth period, the trade balance turned sharply negative by US$4.7 billion. Restrictions on imports and export incentives were implemented. In 1980 the nominal average tariff on manufactured imports was boosted from 47 percent to a range of 23 to 203 percent, averaging just above 100 percent. As a result, Brazil's trade deficit was reduced to US$2.8 billion by 1980. In 1982 a trade surplus of $775 million was achieved because of government policies that further restricted imports, encouraged exports, and induced domestic recession.

In the same year, President (General) Figueiredo reaffirmed the government's commitment to a US$6.0 billion foreign trade surplus in 1983. The goal was overmet by 1984's trade surplus of US$13 billion. But by 1985 Brazil had been in a severe recession for five years, and its debt problems persisted.

> Brazil is scheduled to resume talks with bankers early next month on the package to stretch over 16 years some $45 billion in principal foreign debt payments falling due between 1985 and 1991. The current democratic government inherited . . . the pact from the previous military regime.
>
> More pressing is an agreement with the IMF on an economic austerity program that must underpin any bank accord. The IMF suspended emergency credits to the country last February, after Brazil repeatedly failed to meet economic targets stipulated by its three-year, $4 billion IMF agreements.

Inflation, just under 100 percent at the end of 1982, was again in triple digits in 1983. The consumer price index rose by 210 percent in 1983, 220 percent in 1984, and an estimated 250 percent in 1985. Brazil continued indexation of wages, prices, and interest rates to offset the effects of inflation.

Brazil's currency is nominally tied to the U.S. dollar. But inflation required a policy of weekly minidevaluations of the cruzeiro (CR$), averaging 2.5 percent and with occasional larger devaluations.

Exhibit 11-6 gives summary figures on Brazil's balance of payments for the period 1977 to 1980; Exhibit 11-7 gives estimates for Brazil's balance of trade for the years 1982 through 1985.

Role of Government in the Brazilian Economy

Brazil's near hyperinflation traces to the public finance imbalance of its miracle growth years. In striving for faster growth than permitted by domestic capital

Exhibit 11-6 Brazil's Balance of Payments, 1977–1980 (In millions US$)

	1977	1978	1979	1980
Current Account[a]				
Exports (+)	$12,120	$12,659	$15,244	$20,132
Imports (−)	12,023	13,683	18,084	22,961
Balance on Merchandise Trade	97	−1,024	−2,840	−2,829
Interest payments (net) (−)	2,462	3,344	5,347	7,150
Other payments for service (net) (−)	1,672	1,647	1,834	2,200
Balance on Current Account	−4,037	−6,015	−10,021	−12,179
Capital Account				
Direct foreign investment (net inflow) (+)	810	1,071	1,491	1,202
Brazilian loans abroad (net)	−267	−357	−610	568
Medium- and long-term loans (net inflow) (+)	940	988	759	1,011
Financial credits (net inflow)	3,690	7,857	4,606	4,440
Other capital movements	−506	718	560	1,459
Balance on Capital Account	4,667	10,277	6,806	8,680
Change in Currency Reserves	630	4,262	−3,215	−3,499

[a]A plus sign in parentheses indicates a source of foreign exchange; a minus sign indicates a use.
Source: Adapted from *Brazil, A Country Study*, U.S. Army, 1983.

Exhibit 11-7   **Brazil's Exports and Imports, 1982–1985 (In millions US$)**

	1982	1983	1984	1985 (est.)
Exports	$20,175	$21,900	$26,500	$26,000
Imports	NA	15,400	13,500	14,500
Balance on Merchandise Trade	NA	6,500	13,000	11,500

Sources: 1982, 1983, International Monetary Fund, *Financial Times,* November 5, 1984. 1984, 1985 estimates, *The Wall Street Journal,* April 19, 1985.

and resources, the government had run high budget deficits. Part arose from subsidies required to cover losses of the 500 or so companies (called ''parastatals'') wholly or partly owned by the federal government. Some states (similar to the United States) also formed companies, particularly banks, to aid and steer development in their areas. Governments at various levels also took over and frequently subsidized other firms so as to provide essential goods and services at low cost. But curbing hyperinflation called for even greater reductions in government expenditures. Thus, the 1982 austerity measures included reductions in credit and subsidy programs, fixed interest rates, and changes in the salary law, which had indexed salaries to inflation.

The parastatals, however, still played a dominant role in Brazil's economy. Of the top 200 Brazilian firms in 1980, 82 were under partial or total government control. Furthermore, these parastatals accounted for 76 percent of the total net worth of the top 200 firms. These firms accounted for a large part of Brazil's new investment, and many private Brazilian firms depended heavily on them for business.

Foreign firms also continued to find that their largest customers were among the nearly 500 parastatal bodies. Hence, although the austerity program was designed to reduce the investment spending by the Brazilian government in 1981, the parastatals were responsible for about one-half of the nation's foreign debt and 29 percent of fixed investment. The public sector deficit, which Brazil expected to reduce to 8.8 percent of GDP (Gross Domestic Product) in 1983, was nevertheless continuing at the 1982 level of 15.5 percent. As noted above, many of the public firms were unprofitable (steel, nuclear energy), and their subsidies added to the public deficit.

Investment by private Brazilian companies and multinational firms was expected to dampen the recession caused by the austerity program. However, private investment slowed during the mid 1980s because of the economic and political uncertainties. Net direct investment inflow into Brazil, US$1.5 billion in 1979, was down to $1.2 billion in 1980 and was estimated to be under $500 million in 1983.

Brazil's stated policy was to encourage foreign investment for its impetus to growth, industrial development, and contribution to the balance of payments. The policy has favored joint ventures, and gave additional advantages (e.g., in credit arrangements) to joint-venture firms with majority local capital. This policy line had induced a number of multinational firms to take on Brazilian partners.

However, the austerity measures and the growing distaste for direct foreign participation and investment in high technology industries created political uncertainty for foreign firms. In 1983, the third year of Brazil's recession, the economic and politically hostile environment created major concerns among the multinationals in Brazil.

Brazilianization

The austerity program also included various measures to lessen foreign participation in markets considered priority industries for the growth of a modern Brazilian economy. Before 1979 industries reserved for Brazilian firms only included the merchant marine, information media, and petroleum refining and exploration. Foreign firms were also legislated out of banking, petrochemicals, mining and, in 1979, informatics. Since it hit their major area of business, closure of the informatics sector was seen as potentially fatal by most multinationals in Brazil.

INFORMATICS

The term "informatics" is used in Brazil in a very broad sense, referring to virtually any product with an electronic digital component, as well as to the software and services involved. Semiconductors, electronic instruments, computer and telecommunications equipment, and the software associated with this equipment were included. As Henry V. Eicher, President of Burroughs Electronics put it, "This ban would theoretically apply even to digitalized toys and watches."

History of the Current Policy

The Brazilian government first became involved in the informatics sector in 1972 by creating CAPRE (Coordinating Commission for Electronic Processing Activities) under the Planning Ministry (SEPLAN; see Exhibit 11-5). CAPRE was expected to contribute to managing Brazil's severe balance of payments problems.

However, with the late 1970s economic slump, the Brazilian government decided that a national informatics industry was a prerequisite for the country's modernization. This initiative originated in the Brazilian Navy's inability to utilize fully British ships it had purchased, because of lack of domestic computer expertise. The informatics policies and programs have since had a strong military and national security component, an impediment to the flexibility needed for economic and technological development. Thus the government's overall objectives, to serve both military-political and economic objectives, were to create indigenous technological design and production capabilities.

Government authorities further believed that technologically and financially dominant foreign firms—most multinationals in Brazil—even though operating as joint ventures, controlled the national informatics industry through their control over technology. Hence regulation of informatics and other high technology was rooted in three needs: (1) to modernize the entire Brazilian industrial base; (2) to maintain national security; (3) to ensure that scarce currency reserves were not expended on technologies either inappropriate for Brazil or remaining under foreign control.

Viewing informatics in strategic (with a large military component) rather than economic terms, in late 1979 the Brazilian government created the Secretaria Especial de Informatica (Special Secretariat of Informatics or SEI) to replace CAPRE. Underlining this concern, rather than remaining in the Planning Ministry, SEI was placed directly under the National Security Council, with a direct reporting line to the (military) president. SEI's early 1984 organization chart appears as Exhibit 11-8.

Though formulating and administering Brazil's informatics policy since 1979, SEI's outlook became much more protectionist and nationalistic in May 1984 when Colonel Ediso Dytz replaced Colonel Joubert Brizida as Executive Secretary. Dytz served in this post until Sarney became president in 1985. Dytz had long advocated and defended 100-percent-Brazilian ownership of computer firms. To meet the objectives of the new Brazilianization campaign, SEI imposed and continued to expand a wide array of restrictions that limited foreign investment and participation in informatics.

This policy became known as "Market Reserve." In July 1981 as SEI announced its strategy, it reserved to national firms (defined as 100-percent-Brazilian ownership, public or private) the exclusive right to manufacture and sell products within 18 high-technology categories. In 1983 the market reserve list was extended to five additional product categories. Exhibit 11-9 lists these product categories under market reserve.

The market reserve policy was implemented by requiring all import license applications and manufacturing proposals involving market reserve products or products with electronic features or end uses to be submitted to SEI for approval or disapproval. The SEI had full authority to deny production by foreign firms or importation by either foreign or domestic firms of any product within its mandate if it believed that the product or a close substitute was or could be available from a Brazilian source. A product was considered a substitute if it could accomplish the same task regardless of cost or loss of efficiency.

Technology transfer through licensing was also dependent on SEI approval. Such transfers were controlled by constraints on royalty payments. Foreign firms

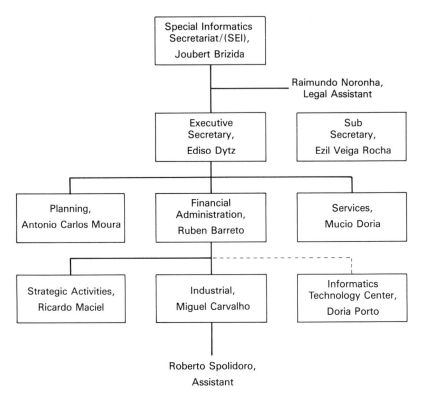

Exhibit 11-8   SEI Organizational Chart 1984

operating in Brazil were not allowed to sell informatics products in the country unless they satisfied the "no national substitute" rule. Thus, SEI expanded its coverage to sectors related to informatics.

In May 1985, shortly after Jose Sarney became President of Brazil, Colonel Dytz was replaced as Executive Secretary of SEI by Jose Rubens Doria Porto, former leader of the Informatics Technology Center. Colonel Dytz endorsed the new head as representing "continuity of the former team."

"Pirating" Intellectual Property

Brazil has avoided having laws or international agreements protecting "intellectual property"—patents, copyrights, trademarks—and does not act to prevent "counterfeiting" of packaging, corporate, professional, or brand names, or making use of trade secrets. A U.S. government publication, *Business America,* in early 1985 stated: "Disrespect for intellectual property rights is firmly entrenched in Brazil. . . . There is little support for copyright protection of software." A bill introduced

---

Exhibit 11-9   **Product Categories Under Market Reserve in Brazil**

Original List 1981
  *Minicomputers, Microcomputers
   Electronic cash registers
  *Electronic data processing machines
   Electronic accounting machines
   Financial terminals and controls
   Electronic authenticators, ticket preparers
   Analog and digital equipment, modems
   Video terminals
   Remote access terminals for data banks
   Data-entry equipment
   Electronic communications processors
  *Digital multiplexers for data communications
  *Digital concentrators for data communications
   Teleprinters
   Facsimile equipment
  *Process control instrumentation; programmable controllers
  *Numerical control equipment
   Secrecy and cryptotechnological equipment

Added in 1983
  *Microcomputer software
  *Biomedical instrumentation
  *Analytical instruments
  *Measuring and testing instruments
   Superminicomputers

---

  *Affecting Honeywell most directly.

---

in the Brazilian Congress would require all software brought into the country to be listed in a public registry, with source codes included.

A *Financial Times* story of November 5, 1985, reported that certain Brazilian firms simply disregard international patents. Twenty firms were making counterfeit Apple IIs and three IBM PCs. In the absence of law and regulations, these Brazilian firms' operations were quite open and seemed to enjoy the implicit blessing of SEI. Both Apple and IBM were rebuffed when they sought to register their products with SEI for protection.

An Exception

One Brazilian firm operating legitimately appeared to have promise. Itautec of Sao Paulo, subsidiary of the important Banco Itau, spent four years from its founding in 1979 developing its staff and its technology. It sold 270 of its own-design microcomputers in 1984 and projected sales of 6,000 in 1985, with revenues going from US$5 million to US$50 million. Its work force grew from 400 to 1,900 and it expects to export soon to Third World countries.

Effects of Informatics Policies on Foreign Firms

In general, Brazil's informatics policy either excluded foreign firms from markets or restricted them to licensing technology. Denial of import requests and manufacturing proposals forestalled their new product lines. These adverse effects pushed some foreign firms to divert investment to other countries. On the other hand, Philco (Ford Motor's consumer electronics subsidiary), closed its $30 million plant barely two years after it started producing chips in Brazil. Similarly the German firm Siemens announced its intention to close its Brazilian subsidiary and withdraw from Brazil since its major business—digital controls—was reserved by SEI. Others, including IBM and Burroughs, chose to "dig in" for the duration of market reserve, believing that withdrawing from this key Third World market would be irreversible.

As its policies bit, Brazil apparently began paying a high price, in cutoff of foreign capital inflows, in technological lag, and in higher consumer costs. A 1984 U.S. government publication states, "Brazilian firms are generally not able to supply state-of-the-art technology at competitive prices." And "Foreign experts view Brazilian technology in the computer area as being outdated by at least five years. . . . [A]dvances in technology are so rapid in this industry that it will be difficult for Brazil to make the major leaps required to make its industry competitive on a global basis."

Despite these costs, foreign firms, large or small, lost ground in Brazil regardless of their strategies. If not yet forced to leave, they found their survival more and more challenged. Even the most tenacious felt their survival unlikely without changes in informatics policy.

The 1984 Informatics Legislation

On October 3, 1984, the Brazilian Congress passed a national informatics law which institutionalized the existing system. A *Business America* article explained:

> The law's provisions will continue to limit foreign access to Brazil's informatics market by extending market reserve for eight years and by broadening product coverage.
>
> The law transfers policymaking authority from the Special Secretariat for Informatics (SEI), which is controlled by the National Security Council, to a new organization—the National Council for Informatics and Automation (CONIN). CONIN will be comprised of representatives from ten Executive agencies and eight members from the private sector. This membership should balance the interests of the national security-conscious SEI with commercial and economic concerns of other government agencies and industry. CONIN will be required to develop a three-year national informatics plan that will require Presidential and Congressional approval. Furthermore, the Congress has been vested with annual oversight responsibility involving the plan's implementation.
>
> For the first time, "national company" is officially defined. The definition is essentially unchanged from the practical definition that has been in place for several years, i.e., 100 percent Brazilian ownership. "Effective" national control is required, mean-

ing autonomy of the firm from foreign sources of capital and technology, and full voting control by resident Brazilians. Although this represents a change in language from 'exclusive' Brazilian control, the Brazilian government has already indicated that it will prohibit joint ventures. . . .

Although the restructuring of informatics policymaking to include representatives from the executive branch and private industry, and vesting Congress with oversight authority, could lead in a more flexible and practical application of market reserve, it is unlikely to lead to the policy's demise. Market reserve has strong, broad-based domestic support, demonstrated in part by the virtually unanimous Congressional approval of the new law. Brazil is likely to keep market reserve in place and accommodate demands by modifying its application in areas where there is a strong domestic constituency for change, such as industrial process controls and digital input for unrelated industries (e.g., automotive industry). Much will depend on the implementing regulations that are now being developed, on the inclination of the new Brazilian government that takes office next March 15 [1985], on the national informatics plan proposed by CONIN, and on the evaluation of that plan by the Congress. However, the outlook for imports and foreign direct investment is not likely to improve in the short- to medium-term.

Some U.S. firms already in Brazil are prepared to "dig in" for the duration of market reserve, in the hope that the policy will be abandoned or at least modified, in the 1990s. They view the new legislation as simply a codification of the existing system, which they have learned to live with. Others think the new legislation "regularizes" the current system, and suggest that this may result in application of more objective standards to government investment/import decisions. Still others see the legislation as an indication that restrictive policies will be more effectively enforced.

Looking back over the past several years at the application of informatics policy, apparent inconsistencies between policy and practice are evident. For example, in spite of restrictions on foreign equity investment, foreign and national companies actively court each other as potential partners, in anticipation of SEI eventually allowing joint ventures. SEI is regularly receptive to project proposals that include foreign participation, and some have been approved. SEI tends to look more favorably on proposals that: 1) link small manufacturers with strong financial institutions; 2) propose establishing R&D centers in Brazil; and/or 3) indicate a positive trade balance. Follow-up is essential because SEI's small staff is frequently unable to review detailed proposals thoroughly. In addition, although SEI originally argued that only two Brazilian firms would be authorized to produce super-minicomputers, eight proposals were ultimately approved. The super-minicomputer will be produced by three Brazilian firms which intend to develop their own technology based on previously acquired foreign know-how, and four additional Brazilian firms using newly licensed foreign technology. This market has been estimated at $1.5 billion over the next five years.[3]

The *Financial Times* commented on the October 1984 informatics law as follows:

Colonel Ediso Dytz, of the SEI government agency agrees: "The fact that you import foreign products does not mean that you learn the technical expertise yourself.

[3]*Business America,* December 10, 1984, p. 44.

Not surprisingly, ABICOMP, the Brazilian association of computer manufacturers, totally supports the legislation.[4]

HONEYWELL'S OPERATIONS AND STRATEGIES IN BRAZIL

Honeywell first entered the Brazilian market in 1958 based on the belief that Brazil would be a key economy in the world by the end of this century. As is common, it entered by forming a subsidiary under Brazilian law. As it turned out, use of organizational alternatives became a central feature of Honeywell's Brazilian strategy.

Honeywell Controles, Limitada and its Operations

With the establishment of a wholly owned control systems subsidiary in 1958—Honeywell Controles, Ltda, (HCL)—the company made substantial investments in Brazil to develop a leadership position. It concentrated on four product categories: (1) residential controls, (2) commercial building systems, (3) components, and (4) process control instruments.

Residential control's business included safety, environmental, and energy conservation systems for residences and apartment buildings. This line accounted for 9 percent of HCL's 1981 sales. Because the Brazilian residential controls market was not yet developed, only a limited number of burner safety devices and gas controls could be marketed locally, the majority being exported.

Commercial building systems covered instruments, systems, and services for comfort controls, security, fire protection, and energy conservation in large buildings such as hotels, airports, offices, and hospitals. This line represented 14 percent of HCL's 1981 sales. Again, without a fully developed Brazilian market for these systems, the majority sold by HCL were imported, only manufacturing locally control valves, flow switches, electromechanical temperature controls, and panels. The market for these products was largely limited to simple, unsophisticated applications that could be supplied by local manufacturers or imported by small distributor companies. Lacking a local market for its imported advanced systems, HCL was not able to import solid state spare parts, microchips, or printer circuit cards, or to capitalize on its technology to differentiate its products from those of local firms.

The components business, accounting for 13 percent of HCL's 1981 sales, included electric and electronic switches and components. These products were used by manufacturers of consumer and capital goods and were also sold through authorized distributors and replacements. Some of the component products were assembled from U.S. imported parts.

Process control instruments had been HCL's biggest and fastest growing prod-

[4]*Financial Times,* November 5, 1985.

uct line, accounting for 64 percent of 1981 sales. This line included analog and digital control systems and control panels. The engineering and services accompanying these products were directed at petrochemical industries, steel plants and mineral processing, electric utilities, and most of the smaller direct user manufacturing and processing plants in Brazil. An overview of HCL's business is presented in Exhibit 11-10.

Of HCL's four business lines, only components and process control instruments concentrated primarily on local needs since they served well-developed markets in Brazil.

THE COMPONENTS AND PROCESS CONTROLS MARKET IN BRAZIL

The Brazilian economy offered a substantial market for components and industrial process controls, with sales totaling some US$85 million in 1979 and $89 million in 1980 (but declining in 1981) as set forth in Exhibit 11-11.

While estimates of the number of Brazilian producers of process controls ranged from 44 to 200, trade sources indicated that 17 leading firms accounted for 95 percent of production in 1980. Seven local subsidiaries of U.S. companies supplied about a third of this total while three operations owned by other foreign manufacturers (two German, one Japanese) contributed 17 percent.

Domestically owned companies, including Engematic and Fujinor, together supplied 20 percent of locally built instruments, and Encil, Engro, Hiter, IEF, and Transmitel, each supplying about 5 percent. A number of U.S. firms either had technology licensing agreements with local companies or operated Brazilian subsidiaries. In addition to Honeywell, other American firms with Brazilian factories included Bailey, Bristol and Babcock, Fisher and Porter, Foxboro, Masoneilar, and Taylor. Other competitors were manufacturers from Japan, Germany, France, and the United Kingdom.

Exhibit 11-10   **Sales of Honeywell Controles, Ltda (Brazil), 1981 (100% owned by Honeywell, Inc.)**

Business Lines	Sales (In millions US$)		% of Total
Residential controls	$1.05		9
Commercial building systems	1.70		14
Components	1.62		13
Industrial process controls			
Sold through HCL 3.73		31	
Imported by customers 3.93		33	
Total industrial process controls	7.66		64
Total	$12.03		100

Exhibit 11-11   **Brazil: The Total Market for Industrial Process Controls**[a]
Selected years, 1974–1981 (In millions US$)

	1974	1977	1979	1980	1981
Production	$28	$64	$24.8	$27.4	$30.5
Imports	50	73	62.0	63.5	53.2
Exports	1	4	1.4	1.6	2.0
Domestic market size	77	133	85.4	89.3	81.7

[a]Figures include process control valves (36% of total in 1981) which are locally manufactured and whose importation is prohibited.
Source: "Industrial Process Controls: Brazil," *Country Market Survey,* 1979, 1984. U.S. Department of Commerce.

The high concentration and dominance of foreign firms in the industrial process controls and components market were largely attributed to Brazil's need for upgrading its process industries. Improved process controls and components that increased efficiency were essential if Brazil was to boost exports and generate revenues to meet the country's huge debt service and oil bills. Hence, process control sales were projected at $112 million in 1987, a 5.4 percent annual growth rate. Exhibit 11-12 summarizes expected growth by product categories.

HONEYWELL AND SEI REGULATIONS

Despite anticipated growth, SEI questioned the role of foreign firms in the industrial process control and components industry. Considering it critical for national security and local technology, in 1981 SEI brought industrial process controls and components under informatics market reserve. Foreign firms were thus banned

Exhibit 11-12   **Brazil: The Market for Specific Industrial Process Controls**
1981 and 1987 (In millions US$)

	1981	1987
Control valves	$29.8	$37.5
Nonelectric/nonelectronic instruments	23.4	31.5
Electric/electronic instruments	28.5	42.9
Total	81.7	111.9

Source: U.S. Department of Commerce, International Trade Administration, Office of Trade Information Services Research Report. (This information is in chart form in the original.)

from making and selling or importing such control products, and Brazilian firms were required to obtain SEI licenses to import foreign equipment. Predictably, the number of local firms and domestic production increased at the expense of imports and local manufacturing by multinationals. HCL's components and process controls business was hard hit.

HCL's components business was severely hurt by SEI's import restrictions because HCL imported most components from Honeywell USA. The SEI restriction nearly choked off all such imports. It was the closing of the process control sector to foreign firms that endangered HCL's survival.

In 1979, before SEI's rulings, HCL's sales of process control instruments reached US$8.2 million, while in 1981 they were down to $7.7 million, and have steadily declined since. Banned from selling its most profitable line—advanced digital process controls—which would have given it leadership in Brazil's process control market, HCL's financial position deteriorated. The exclusion from the digital controls market reduced HCL to offering only outmoded analog systems. Demand for these high cost–low efficiency systems was shrinking as government policy encouraged automation and digital technology. Consequently, HCL incurred a one-time write-off loss in 1982 (though it broke even every year thereafter). By 1984 HCL's total sales were down to US$4 million compared with $12 million in 1981.

As a 100-percent-foreign owned company, HCL was of course the very type of firm that SEI policies and regulations were intended to affect. Although Honeywell had anticipated emergence of a protected market for informatics when SEI was established in 1979, the consequences of SEI restrictions were unexpectedly severe.

Honeywell Transcontrol Automacao, Limitada

During SEI's initial days in 1979, when the Brazilianization campaign was just beginning, Honeywell formed a 55-percent-Brazilian-owned (45-percent-Honeywell-owned) joint venture called Honeywell Transcontrol Automacao, Ltda (or HTAL). This strategic step was part of Honeywell's response to uncertainty about SEI's future policy actions. Honeywell planned to use HTAL to enter the protected markets by having the joint venture recognized as a company with majority national capital and ownership.

In 1980 four firms were selected and approved by SEI as Registered Manufacturers to provide selected analog (old technology) control instruments in Brazil. The chosen firms (and the technology they were to use) were Engematic (Hitachi, Japan); Bristol (Bristol & Babcock, United States); Fujinor (Fuji, Japan); and Ecil (Leeds & Northrup, United States). In exchange for agreeing to Brazilian majority ownership and to the requirement that they manufacture (i.e., assemble) in Brazil 95 percent of the controls sold locally, the four were to be assured import licensing for all necessary components, an 80 percent reduction in import duties, exemption from the 15 percent tax levied on duty-paid value, and exclusive access to the 50 to 70 percent of the market controlled by the government. (Later, observers found these firms to be less than successful.)

Honeywell's joint venture HTAL was thus not included on the 1980 list. But the expected lockout of all other importers did not occur; despite the rules some rejected manufacturers were given import licenses at times. And in 1981 a government commission reported that process controls required by major Brazilian industries were beyond the capabilities of domestic manufacturers.

Until 1981, HTAL existed very nearly in name only, having little business of its own. However, in 1981 when SEI further restricted imports and foreign manufacturing in informatics, it became impossible for Honeywell to operate in the reserved process control market through its wholly owned subsidiary HCL. But the Brazilian process control market offered too large an opportunity for Honeywell to abandon it, especially when the company had achieved modest growth and had invested effort and money in this sector for 20 years.

With no opportunity to operate in the industrial process controls market through either HCL or imports, Honeywell decided to seek SEI approval through its joint venture HTAL. In 1981 HTAL prepared several proposals for SEI's review. However, even by 1982 SEI had yet to issue its appraisal. The SEI views regarding such joint ventures were not encouraging either. Colonel Brizida had made clear SEI's stand.

> Whenever foreign capital, which holds technology control, participates in joint-ventures (even with only 10 percent ownership) the technology is not effectively transferred to Brazil. SEI makes clear its disapproval of the participation in "reserved market areas" by companies where foreign investors hold any kind of equity, even nonvoting capital.

Greatly discouraged but still reluctant to leave the Brazilian market, in 1982 Honeywell began closing down HCL's local process control business, trimming its local personnel and investment, and redirecting its analog process control business to a new Brazilian distributor firm formed by its former process control division employees.

Honeywell then tried one more organizational alternative in an attempt to stabilize its position.

The Digidata Licensing Arrangement

In late 1981, with HTAL's proposals languishing in SEI's files, Honeywell opened negotiations toward a licensing agreement with a small Brazilian company named Digidata in another attempt to get its advanced digital control systems into Brazil. Honeywell's strategy was to license its advanced digital control technology to this 100-percent-Brazilian company which would then perform final assembly, sale, and installation of the systems.

The negotiations were successful. In early 1982 SEI announced an important action, in which it would select Brazilian producers of advanced digital process control instruments incorporating licensed foreign technology. Digidata-Honeywell prepared a proposal and presented it to SEI. Despite its previously failed attempts,

Honeywell was optimistic about this proposal. First, Digidata met SEI's 100-percent ownership and control requirement for participation in this reserved market. Also, Honeywell's advanced digital process control technology was acknowledged to be the world's leader.

The SEI evaluations took over a year. Finally, in July 1983 SEI announced the firms to which it was granting permission to manufacture control instruments with licensed foreign technology. The chosen firms with proposed foreign technology source were Electronica Brasileira (Leeds & Northrup, United States); Ecil and P&D-Sistemas Electronicos (Yokogawa, Japan); Unipar, Unipar Quimica, and Brascontrol Industria e Comercio (Fisher, United States); Prologo (Asea); and Industrias Villares (Hitachi, Japan). Digidata's name was not on the list.

With this latest outcome, Honeywell found itself virtually locked out of both licensing and import privileges, and out of the reserved markets in which it once had had the majority of its Brazilian business. And in 1982, Professor Jose de Jesus Mendez' statement in front of Colonel Dytz was pointed: "We want Honeywell's technology for the next two or three years, but after that we expect Honeywell to get out of Brazil."

Honeywell entered 1984 with greatly scaled down Brazilian operations, having adjusted as best it could (largely during the year 1982) by several drastic changes in its Brazilian operations:

- Dissolution of the joint-venture firm Honeywell Transcontrol Automacao, Ltda (HTAL).
- Closing down the local process control business of Honeywell Controles, Ltda (HCL), and turning the remaining business over to HCL's former process control division employees.
- Scaling down local personnel, with more than 50 percent of its employees already laid off.
- "Fire Sale" of all inventory of products in the reserved markets.

With these steps, which flowed from both SEI's regulations and Brazil's continuing economic problems, Honeywell's early 1984 presence was reduced to a bare minimum. The company was represented by a small corps of support personnel for economically feasible import sales and services not specifically regulated or prohibited by government decrees. Although Honeywell still believed in Brazil's long-range future, the five years of continuous struggle and deteriorating conditions since 1979 forced the question whether Honeywell would have a place in Brazil's future. Thus Honeywell was faced with hard choices regarding further operations in Brazil.

THE FUTURE

The SEI actions over the five years, 1979 to 1984, were marked by continuously increasing restrictions on imports and production by foreign firms of products within the 23 reserved product areas. Continuation of discrimination against manufacturing and service companies not qualifying as "national firms" was expected. Strong approval of SEI's policies by the Brazilian Congress in 1981 and 1984 pointed to possible future expansion of SEI's activities and broadening of its product and market restrictions. Brazil's historic regulatory and protectionist philosophy left no sector immune from potential future decrees.

Yet there were a few rays of hope, if only hope, remaining. Brazil's foreign debt situation, though still shaky, had not deteriorated into abrogation of foreign debt, though Brazil chafed under IMF restrictions. A transition of government from the 1964 to 1985 military regime to a civilian president had occurred quite smoothly, though the president-elect's untimely death had thrust the vice-president-elect precipitately into the presidency. Brazil showed it could change a negative trade balance into a positive one by pushing exports and restricting imports, though the balance of payments problem remained, due to high debt service requirements. And the continued import restrictions underlay much of Honeywell's problem. Finally, the change to the civilian-dominated policy board, CONIN, overseeing the informatics program and SEI, as well as the Congressional oversight program, both set up by the 1984 law, offered the possibility of a more sympathetic view of involvement of foreign firms in the lines of business served by Honeywell. But government actions during 1985 indicated that an unbending stance was still the politically most rewarding attitude.

In view of the expected economic and political conditions in Brazil and the magnitude of losses already incurred, Honeywell knew that the problem would not solve itself. The situation required immediate and forceful action, and Honeywell's top management in Minneapolis, together with its international and South American executives began a critical examination of Honeywell's options in Brazil.

Case 12

Baldor Electric Company: Positioning for the Twenty-First Century

As Greg Kowert, Vice-President for Strategic Planning, looked at the quarterly report, a broad grin spread over his face. First quarter sales were $55.1 million, an increase of 17 percent over the same period last year. The strategic initiatives

This case was prepared by Peter M. Ginter and Linda E. Swayne as a basis for class discussion rather than to illustrate either effective or ineffective handling of an administrative situation. Used by permission from Peter M. Ginter.

were paying off. After several disappointing years, 1987 had been a record year for Baldor Electric with sales breaking the $200 million level for the first time. And the first quarter results for 1988 were even better.

Kowert felt that previous strategies had enabled the company to maintain 21 straight years of growth at a rate about twice that of gross national product (GNP). However, the environment changed in the 1980s. Baldor's customers were not growing, and they were inundated with foreign competition, resulting in declining sales. Therefore, Baldor sales declined as well.

In retrospect, the management team had identified the "strong dollar" as the major problem causing the decline in sales. A trade-weighted average indicated that 1985 was a peak year which resulted in many industries suffering losses (Exhibit 12-1). Many of Baldor's customers were negatively impacted as were machine tool sales.

Negative Impact of the "High" Dollar

Woodworking machinery	− 80%
Machine tools	− 55%
Textile machinery	− 54%
Semiconductor equipment	− 40%
Chemical processing equipment	− 40%
Packaging machinery	− 35%

Source: Adapted from U.S. Department of Commerce data.

Additionally, a correlation was identified between the strength of the dollar and the amount of exports although it was delayed (Exhibit 12-2). Fortunately, the environment was improved in 1987 and Baldor, as well as the company's customers, had improved results.

The following comparative advantages were considered by management to be

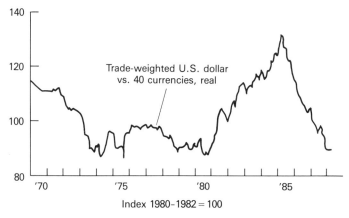

Index 1980–1982 = 100

Source: Federal Reserve Bank and Morgan Guaranty Trust Company.

Exhibit 12-1   **Exchange Rates**

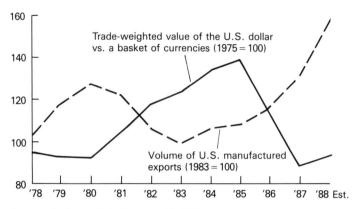

Source: *Business Week,* January 18, 1988.

Exhibit 12-2   **The Dollar's Delayed Impact on Exports**

responsible not only for Baldor's transition from a small to midsized company but also for Baldor's increased market share.

- Concentration on industrial electric motors—By manufacturing only electric motors for industrial markets, Baldor had been able to focus its resources on a highly specialized market.
- Most committed to the industry—Baldor had the largest percentage of its sales in electric motors. Many of the competitors were divisions of larger companies and had to compete with other divisions for allocations of resources.
- Energy-efficient motors—Through the years the company had followed the strategy of providing better products at competitive prices. For Baldor, this translated into better materials and superior engineering directed at durability and energy efficiency.
- Diversification into closely related products—By purchasing small companies that manufactured electric motor starters and adjustable-speed drives, Baldor enhanced its ability to sell its industrial motors.
- Independent representative sales organization—The company sold all of its products through independent representatives. Many reps derive most of their income from Baldor, and thus the selling task has been accomplished by a group of semiautonomous entrepreneurs compensated by direct incentives.
- Availability—Baldor attempted to sell as many items as possible as stock products and carried heavy inventories positioned close to customers in 28 warehouses around the country. This inventory policy was unique in the industry.

- Backward integration—Baldor manufactured more of its component parts than the competition.
- Management team—Experienced managers from the field were brought in when several key managers retired.

BALDOR ELECTRIC COMPANY PROFILE

Edwin C. Ballman founded Baldor Electric Company in St. Louis, Missouri, in 1920 as a manufacturer of industrial electric motors. Baldor has expanded primarily through internal growth. The company opened a plant in Fort Smith, Arkansas, in 1957, and subsequently moved the corporate headquarters there. Today 16 plants employ more than 2,400 people.

From the very beginning, Baldor emphasized production of motors that delivered maximum output while consuming a minimum of energy. Management felt that the energy crisis in the early 1970s increased the interest in energy efficiency and led to rapid growth for the company.

Baldor has been the fastest growing company in the electric motor industry. During the period between 1971 and 1981, Baldor's growth was approximately 22 percent annually, almost 80 percent faster than the industry as a whole. As illustrated in Exhibit 12-3, Baldor's market share increased about 15 percent during the 1975 recession, by 20 percent during the 1982 business contraction, and doubled during the period between 1973 and 1982.

In 1978, Baldor was the tenth largest producer of industrial motors. By 1983, the company had moved to fifth largest and in 1987, Baldor became the third largest in the business. Craig W. Fanning of Dean Witter attributed the increased market

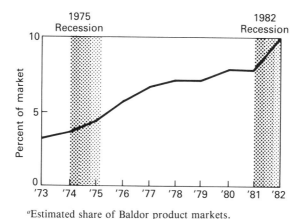

*a*Estimated share of Baldor product markets.

Exhibit 12-3   **Baldor's Market Share 1973–1982*a***

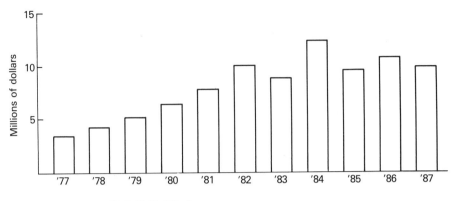

Exhibit 12-4   **Baldor's Capital Investments**

share to "entering new, growing markets with innovative products, an outstanding record of product quality and efficiency, strong distribution, the industry's broadest product line in the 1/50 to 250 HP range, and responsiveness to customer needs."[1]

The period between 1983 and 1986 was particularly difficult for the industrial market, and Baldor was no exception. In 1983 the first ever sales decline prompted the company to develop a strategic response. During this period, when customers in three key industries—agriculture, mining, and energy—stopped buying motors, and other traditional markets were negatively affected by the recession, Baldor was able to replace lost sales.

Rather than retreating as some companies (such as Westinghouse) did, or moving production to foreign or offshore facilities, Baldor maintained production in the United States, worked at developing new markets, and attacked costs. Capital investments were increased $89 million from 1977 to 1987 in order to improve production efficiencies (Exhibit 12-4).

New markets were developed in food processing, electronic manufacturing equipment, and electronics. The "wash down" motor was introduced in 1985 in response to customer needs in food processing for a motor that could withstand daily cleaning. Baldor purchased three small companies that "doubled their opportunity spectrum" by establishing the company in the electric motor starter, adjustable speed drive, and large DC motor businesses. The company made an increasing commitment to research and development (Exhibit 12-5).

The Mission

The company's management is proud of the mission statement, which they consider to be the basis for their success: "BALDOR is to be the best (as determined

---

[1]Craig W. Fanning, *Dean Witter Research Report on Baldor Electric,* September 1, 1987, p. 3.

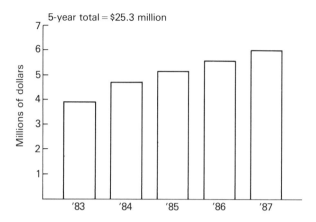

Exhibit 12-5   **Research and Development Expenditures**

by our customers) marketers, designers, and manufacturers of high-quality electric motors and related electronic products." According to CEO Roland S. Boreham, Jr., "We were one of the first to recognize that 'best' or 'quality' only has real meaning when it is defined as being determined by the customer. Other than the last four words which were added recently, this statement is many years old."

In 1985, Baldor started developing the superstructure on which to build the company into a world class manufacturer. The first element was automated information flow, sometimes called computer-integrated manufacturing. The second was continuous-flow manufacturing as contrasted to batch manufacturing, and the third was a total quality system.

The company has been a leader in automating information flow but has been adding to that lead with a state-of-the-art material planning system and a new data processing operating system. A new data processing center, scheduled for completion in 1989, will allow the company to improve information capabilities as well as substantially reduce the cost of processing information.

The changeover for the two largest plants from batch to flexible-flow manufacturing was completed late in 1987. The costs and time involved were greater than anticipated, but the benefits derived also have been greater than anticipated— improved quality, more reliable delivery, lower costs, and less inventory.

The company hired Crosby Associates, a major consulting firm, to work with the total organization to achieve world-class quality. In independent surveys of customers, Baldor typically rates first or second in quality.

The Market

Baldor's products are sold to a variety of industries. Although agriculture, mining, and energy had been major customers for the company, electric motors have applicability in most manufacturing situations. To meet company growth objectives, many industries were studied to see how Baldor could change and improve its product line to meet the needs of potential customers. Exhibit 12-6 lists the markets served by Baldor.

Product Line.   Industrial electric motors, varying in size from 1/50 through 250 horsepower (HP), have been the principal product line, accounting for over 90 percent of Baldor's sales. The company built motors to customer specification (custom) and for general purposes (stock) for the industrial rather than consumer (home appliance motors, etc.) market. About one-third of the business consisted of making motors to order and the other two-thirds were stock products of which the company had over 2,000 items. Exhibit 12-7 identifies the major product lines produced by Baldor.

All Baldor's motors have been manufactured in accordance with industry standards supplied by the National Electrical Manufacturers Association (NEMA). The smallest, most precise motors were added in the late 1970s when a Connecticut company, Boehm, was purchased. In 1982, Baldor had vigorously expanded its new product development program that increased both the depth and breadth of the company's line. In 1983, Baldor introduced a new superefficient line called the Baldor Super-E. As shown in Exhibit 12-8, the efficiency of the new Super-E line is considerably higher than the average "premium" motor.

In 1986 two small firms that produced DC servomotors were purchased. Servomotors, and the servodrivers which control them, offer precise speed and motion control and complete programmability. Manufacturing robots, among other things, are driven by servomotors. The other acquisition in 1986 was a company that had developed a state-of-the-art solid-state motor starter—a device that turns motors on and off with less damage to the motor and the systems they power. Although Baldor had a very small share in each of these industries, servomotors and motor starters represented a $2 billion dollar market.

Another new line introduced by Baldor in June 1987 was brushless DC motors. "Brushless DC motors have been used in aerospace, aircraft, and computers. They

---

Exhibit 12-6   **Markets Served by Baldor Electric**

Packaging equipment	Textile machinery
Motion controls	Pollution control
CAD/CAM	Heating, ventilation, air conditioning
Graphic arts	Mining
Energy—oil, gas, coal, etc.	Materials handling
Distribution/replacement	Electric vehicles
Agribusiness	Food processing
Power transmission	Medical equipment
Chemical processing	Woodworking
Design/construct/engineer	Pulp and paper
Machine tools	

Exhibit 12-7   **Baldor Product Lines**

Explosion-proof motors—The company supplies explosion-proof motors designed to operate in atmospheres containing combustible dust and vapors. Ranging to 100 HP, including models with all performance characteristics required for service on offshore drill rigs and crop drying.

Hostile environment motors—From 1 HP to 200 HP motors of cast iron frames to be used in chemical processing, dirty duty, and wash down duty (food service) applications.

Agribusiness—Baldor's line of agriduty motors traditionally has been considered one of the industry's broadest and most diversified. To further strengthen its position in this market, Baldor added a series of specialized models such as a centrifugal fan motors, confinement house motors, vacuum pump motors, and grain stirring motors.

Fractional and subfractional horsepower motors—Baldor has been active in small motors as well. More than 70 models are offered in the subfractional (1/50 to 1/4 HP) motor category used in such applications as kidney dialysis and heart pumping.

Heavy-duty motors—The company also markets a variety of heavy-duty cast iron motors ranging in size from 1 1/2 HP to 15 HP in the 300 and corrosion-protected lines.

Super-E series—The Super-E line (super energy efficient) is designed primarily for applications where energy consumption is unusually high and motors are operated continuously for extended periods.

Custom motors—The company works with customers to design motors to fit unique applications.

Servomotors, servodrivers, and tachometers—Top-of-the-line technology in adjustable-speed drives has enabled Baldor to enter this market. The company's market share is small by design as only the high end customers have been targeted.

Additional lines—Other product lines include close-coupled pump motors and motors specifically designed for use with six-step and pulsewidth-modulated inverters.

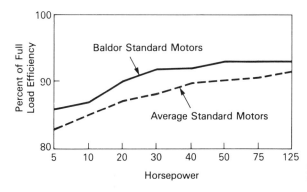

Source: U.S. Department of Energy, November 1980.

Exhibit 12-8   **Standard Motor Efficiencies**

have not been used much in industry. But we intend to change that,'' stated Chairman Boreham.

The newest line consisted of ''smart motors,'' those motors that will operate as directed. According to Boreham, ''Not only will a 'smart motor' start when you tell it to, but will run at the speed you tell it to run at, it'll accelerate as you wish and decelerate as you wish, or even position where you wish it to. So it'll do a lot more for you than a standard motor, which enables the user of the motor to make his machine or the device that he is running more useful.''

Sales and Marketing.   The products of the company were marketed in all 50 of the United States and in 40 foreign countries. Baldor's motors were sold through 27 district managers who are independent manufacturer's representatives. They had responsibility for 32 warehouses in the United States and Canada (Exhibit 12-9) and sold to over 2,000 distributors. A sophisticated computer network, capable of checking the status of customer orders and inventory counts, maintained communication between sales offices, plants, and corporate headquarters. Baldor did use a direct sales force for some OEM motor sales.

Because Baldor sold to such varied markets, the industrial distributor developed a more important role. Better design, increased applications, higher speeds, and greater reliability broadened the use of electric motors to various new industries. Distributors developed greater familiarity with their markets and through constant contact, with current and potential customers, were able to identify new opportunities.

The new acquisitions in servomotors and motor starters required Baldor to institute a new channel of distribution. Because customers needed significantly more

Exhibit 12-9   **Baldor's Sales Offices and Warehouses**

From BALDOR: a broad line of electric motors for a broad range of textile applications.

Looking for relief from high utility bills that have made the cost of manufacturing textiles skyrocket since the mid 1970's? Baldor markets two lines of high-efficiency motors—plus 575-volt and special textile motor "retrofit" kits.

Considering automation? Baldor also manufactures servo-motors, servodrivers, and motion-control systems that can help make you more competitive by increasing your productivity.

Looking for ways to protect textile manufacturing and processing equipment from mechanical shock during start-up or sudden speed changes? Baldor/Lectron solid state motor starters can solve this problem.

Just as important, we go to great lengths to make sure you get the product you need—where and when you need it. Baldor products are available from more than 2,000 local distributors and a network of 25 strategically-placed ware-

houses across the country.

If you manufacture textile machinery in the U.S., and export it, we'll support you overseas, too. In fact, Baldor now serves motor buyers on five continents and in the Pacific.

For more information about the nation's best and broadest line of industrial electrical motors, or special motors for special textile applications, contact BALDOR, Fort Smith, Arkansas 72902. Phone 501-646-4711.

We help sharpen American industry's competitive edge

Exhibit 12-10   **Baldor Advertisement**

Exhibit 12-11   **Baldor Consolidated Balance Sheets (In thousands)**

	December 31, 1986	January 2, 1988
Assets		
Current Assets		
Cash and cash equivalents	$ 15,787	$ 12,047
Receivables, less allowances of $700,000 and $640,000, respectively	31,989	35,000
Inventories		
Finished products	27,564	31,445
Work in-process	7,015	7,552
Raw material	16,577	17,129
	51,156	56,126
LIFO valuation adjustment (deduction)	(15,762)	(18,051)
	35,394	38,075
Other current assets	3,543	4,193
Total Current Assets	86,713	89,315
Other Assets	3,682	3,004
Property, Plant and Equipment		
Land and improvements	1,907	1,922
Buildings and improvements	12,575	13,070
Machinery and equipment	63,740	70,932
Allowances for depreciation and amortization (deduction)	(31,985)	(38,477)
	46,237	47,447
Total Assets	$136,632	$139,766
Liabilities and Stockholders' Equity		
Current Liabilities		
Accounts payable	$ 6,724	$ 7,350
Employee compensation	1,808	2,771
Profit sharing	1,589	1,419
Anticipated warranty costs	2,300	2,250
Other accrued expenses	4,021	7,594
Income taxes	2,906	
Current maturities of long-term obligations	1,030	1,050
Total Current Liabilities	20,378	22,434
Long-Term Obligations	8,808	7,743
Deferred Income Taxes	13,185	13,821
Stockholders' Equity		
Preferred stock, $.10 par value		
Authorized shares: 5,000,000		
Issued and outstanding shares: None		
Common stock, $.10 par value		
Authorized shares: 25,000,000		

Exhibit 12-11   (continued)

Issued and outstanding shares:		
1987—6,302,725; 1986—6,429,664		
(less shares held in treasury:		
1987—308,776; 1986—142,993)	643	630
Additional capital	11,314	8,825
Retained earnings	82,304	86,313
	94,261	95,768
Total Liabilities and Shareholders' Equity	$136,632	$139,766

"help in buying" and service both before and after the sale, a new subsidiary was formed—the Motion Products Group. Baldor used direct selling for this technical and more sophisticated market.

Advertising and trade promotion traditionally have been important elements in Baldor's marketing mix, serving as a direct line of communication to an extremely broad and growing audience of customer and sales prospects as the company has expanded through market penetration. In addition, these efforts directly supported the selling activities of Baldor's representatives and distributors.

Advertising objectives have been to develop brand recognition and brand preference. The investment in advertising and promotion has continued to increase, in part due to the number of new products introduced to the various markets. The energy efficiency and savings of Baldor motors are prominent in advertising to the trade (Exhibit 12-10).

After four extremely competitive years with no price increases, Baldor's selling prices for motors were raised 3.5 percent in the fall of 1987 and 4 percent in April 1988. However, the 7 percent increase just covered the cost increases for raw materials, particularly copper, aluminum, and steel. Because all the domestic producers of motors generally priced their motors similarly, the other companies had had price increases as well; however, Baldor's motors were more energy efficient.

Manufacturing.   Baldor had sixteen manufacturing plants. All were located in the United States except for one plant in West Germany. Within the last two years, steps had been taken to improve the production processes.

The conversion of the two largest plants to continuous-flow manufacturing had resulted in direct cost savings, lower inventories, and a more productive work force. Each job was dated, which made it easy to determine if it were behind schedule. Quicker turnaround time had been achieved as well as improved quality—approaching 95 percent. Conversion of two more plants was in progress and scheduled for completion by 1989.

Management did not think they needed to open any more plants to fill the increased demand as current plants converted to continuous-flow manufacturing had doubled capacity by freeing up floor space and using previously unavailable space.

Because the 32 warehouses must maintain adequate motor inventories, careful production scheduling was critical. The inventory level and customer orders for each warehouse were on-line to facilitate communication with all Baldor plants. Total inventory was monitored daily and used to develop the production schedule at the

---

Exhibit 12-12 Baldor Statement of Consolidated Earnings (In thousands, except share data)

	Year Ended		
	December 31, 1985	December 31, 1986	January 2, 1988
Net sales	$174,710	$181,656	$200,099
Other income—net	987	1,172	1,086
	175,697	182,828	201,185
Cost and Expenses			
Cost of goods sold	124,831	131,568	148,240
Selling and administrative	33,568	35,846	39,335
Profit sharing	2,016	1,814	1,417
Interest	891	816	745
Restructuring			4,600
	161,306	170,044	194,337
Earnings before income taxes and cumulative effect of accounting change	14,391	12,784	6,848
Income taxes	6,200	5,840	2,870
Earnings before cumulative effect of accounting change	8,191	6,944	3,978
Cumulative effect of accounting change for income taxes			2,970
Net Earnings	$8,191	$6,944	$6,948
Earnings per Common Share			
Earnings before cumulative effect of accounting change	$1.26	$1.07	$.62
Cumulative effect of accounting change for income taxes			.46
Net Earnings	$1.26	$1.07	$1.08
Weighted average common shares outstanding	6,524,609	6,514,068	6,432,090

plants. The investment in computers had provided Baldor comparative advantages in avoiding stock-outs and reducing manufacturing lead time.

All labor is nonunion. "We don't even consider that we have labor relations; we have employee relations—without a third party," claims Chairman Boreham. Plants are located in small towns (except for the St. Louis location). Although Baldor's wages and benefits are about half those of unionized industrial laborers, the wages are considered high when compared to other small town employers. Even during the difficult years of 1983 to 1986, employees were maintained and large-scale layoffs were avoided. Baldor's stable work environment made it a highly desirable company to work for and company turnover was low.

Financial Position.   The company was in a strong position as evidenced by the financial statements (Exhibits 12-11 and 12-12). According to R. L. Qualls, Executive Vice-President of Finance, "Over the past several years, we have been able to essentially finance all of our operating needs out of the cash flow of the company." (See Exhibit 12-13.)

Record sales were achieved in 1987 amounting to $200.1 million—an increase of 10.2 percent over 1986. "The 1987 increase in sales growth is about double the annual growth rate we experienced in the 1983–1986 period," stated Qualls.

The company has maintained a conservative capital position. Long-term obligations were 15 percent of total capitalization on December 31, 1982—down from 18 percent in 1981. The ratio was reduced to 7.5 percent at the end of 1987. No new long-term financing was sought in 1987. Exhibit 12-14 presents a ten-year summary of important financial data for Baldor. Exhibit 12-15 shows the changes in Baldor's financial position, and Exhibit 12-16 provides a statement of stockholder's equity.

Penetration of International Markets.   For many years at Baldor, international sales were handled by an export management company. In 1982, when sales were dropping in the United States, Baldor completely changed its method of mar-

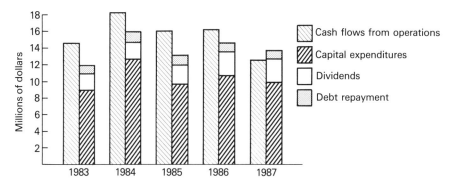

Exhibit 12-13   **Baldor's Cash Flows 1983–1987**

Exhibit 12-14 Ten-Year Summary of Baldor Financial Data (In thousands, except per share data)

	Net Sales	Cost of Goods Sold	Net Earnings	Per Share Data		Stockholders' Equity	Total Assets	Long-Term Obligations	Working Capital
				Net Earnings	Dividends				
1987	$200,099	$148,240	$ 6,948	$1.08	$.46	$95,768	$139,766	$ 7,743	$66,881
1986	181,656	131,568	6,944	1.07	.41	94,261	136,632	8,808	66,335
1985	174,710	124,831	8,191	1.26	.37	91,677	136,650	9,834	66,170
1984	183,716	132,067	9,740	1.50	.33	85,887	128,670	10,833	59,706
1983	148,661	107,078	7,756	1.20	.32	77,364	114,742	11,805	54,885
1982	150,031	108,242	8,518	1.33	.32	70,844	106,065	12,610	53,639
1981	160,162	110,425	11,733	1.84	.29	63,470	102,276	13,497	52,217
1980	146,454	102,155	9,409	1.50	.24	52,448	81,973	10,318	43,733
1979	140,018	98,173	9,331	1.50	.193	42,985	74,112	11,210	36,310
1978	120,105	81,120	8,642	1.40	.14	33,929	60,466	7,427	28,462

Exhibit 12-15   **Baldor Statement of Consolidated Cash Flows (In thousands)**

	Year Ended		
	December 31, 1985	**December 31, 1986**	**January 2, 1988**
Cash flows from operations			
Net income	$ 8,191	$ 6,944	$ 6,948
Depreciation and amortization	7,115	8,314	8,890
Deferred income taxes	3,427	2,195	636
Cash flows provided by (used for) changes in current assets and liabilities (see table below)	(3,554)	(135)	(4,366)
Other—net	929	(982)	603
Net cash provided by operating activities	16,108	16,336	12,711
Cash flows from investments			
Additions to property, plant and equipment	(9,758)	(10,920)	(9,965)
Cash flows from financing			
Reduction of long-term obligations	(972)	(995)	(1,045)
Repurchase of company stock		(1,785)	(3,119)
Dividends paid	(2,411)	(2,664)	(2,939)
Stock option plans	10	89	617
Net cash used in financing	(3,373)	(5,355)	(6,486)
Net increase (decrease) in cash and cash equivalents	2,977	61	(3,740)
Cash and cash equivalents at the beginning of the year	12,749	15,726	15,787
Cash and cash equivalents at the end of the year	$15,726	$15,787	$12,047
Cash flows provided by (used for) changes in current assets and liabilities			
Accounts receivable	$ 1,813	$(1,849)	$(3,071)
Inventories	(1,937)	3,515	(2,681)
Other current assets	(3,165)	2,001	(650)
Accounts payable	(2,792)	(351)	626
Accrued expenses	930	(1,975)	4,316
Income taxes payable	1,597	(1,476)	(2,906)
	$(3,554)	$ (135)	$(4,366)

Exhibit 12-16   **Statements of Consolidated Stockholders' Equity (In thousands)**

	Common Stock		Additional	Retained	
	Shares	**Amount**	**Capital**	**Earnings**	**Total**
Balance at January 1, 1985	6,516	$652	$12,991	$72,244	$85,887
Stock option plans	1		10		10
Net earnings				8,191	8,191
Common stock dividends—$.37 per share				(2,411)	(2,411)
Balance at December 31, 1985	6,517	652	13,001	78,024	91,677
Repurchase of common stock	(91)	(9)	(1,776)		(1,785)
Stock option plans	4		89		89
Net earnings				6,944	6,944
Common stock dividends—$.41 per share				(2,664)	(2,664)
Balance at December 31, 1986	6,430	643	11,314	82,304	94,261
Repurchase of common stock	(160)	(16)	(3,103)		(3,119)
Stock option plans (net of shares exchanged)	33	3	614		617
Net earnings				6,948	6,948
Common stock dividends—$.46 per share				(2,939)	(2,939)
Balance at January 2, 1988	6,303	$630	$ 8,825	$86,313	$95,768

keting to foreign countries. Each international market was studied individually, rather than collectively as in the past, to determine the best method of distribution. As a result, Baldor established representatives in many targeted countries and was seeking representation in others. In 1983, representatives were established in such markets as Latin America, Australia, the United Kingdom, West Germany, the Middle East, and Singapore. By 1987 additional offices were established in the Philippines, Thailand, South Korea, Taiwan, the Netherlands, Brazil, Spain, Austria, France, and Saudi Arabia.

Baldor had increased its product capability in the international markets by introducing motors with standards that were interchangeable with those outside the

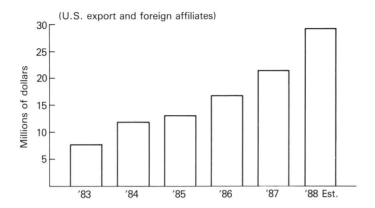

Exhibit 12-17   **Baldor's International Sales**

United States. In addition, Baldor was increasing international advertising and participation in foreign trade shows.

In 1987, international sales represented 10 percent of Baldor's sales (Exhibit 12-17). According to CEO Boreham, "Our export business is now growing at about twice the rate of our domestic business and we believe that can continue. Our goal is to aim for 20 percent. We have sales offices pretty well around the world."

BALDOR LOOKS TO THE FUTURE

The company has been extremely successful in differentiating its products from competitors by offering energy-efficient motors at competitive prices and diversifying its product line to include electronic servomotors and starters. Moving from the number five position to the number three position seemed to validate the company's commitment to satisfying customers with a quality product. "Is the number one position an unreasonable goal for Baldor?" questioned Greg. "What would it take to move to the number two position?"

Greg knew there were several options open to Baldor to aggressively pursue the leading position in the market. The electric motor market continued to offer opportunities because many small competitors had not been able to completely serve the market. A major competitor, Westinghouse, had dropped out of the market, and others were having difficulty competing. New products could be developed to meet the needs of new markets, which have been projected to grow rapidly, and international markets presented good opportunities. The lines between motors, controls, and the devices they control have blurred; thus, Baldor has the opportunity for further diversification into the areas of computers or robotics.

Greg Kowert wondered which one or what combination of opportunities he should recommend for the continued growth of Baldor. He supposed he should start with a review of the electric motor industry.

The Electric Motor Industry

The U.S. electric motor industry can be divided into two primary segments—industrial motors and consumer, or appliance, motors. A few of the big manufacturers, like General Electric and Westinghouse, supply both markets. Some producers like Baldor make only industrial motors. Still others specialize in consumer motors.

The industrial/consumer distinction is ordinarily used to identify the difference between motors made in extremely high volume (usually fractional HP consumer market motors) and those usually manufactured in lower volume (higher HP motors designed for special and heavy usage). Generally, consumer motors are made with less durable, lower quality parts, while industrial motors are manufactured for greater durability and more rugged conditions.

KEY COMPETITORS

There are approximately 340 companies in the United States involved in the production of motors. In a 1981 company study, the top three companies in the industry accounted for over 50 percent of the industry's sales, while the top eleven companies accounted for approximately 80 percent of the industry's sales. Exhibit 13-1 illustrates electric motor sales comparisons for the top eleven companies.

The electric motor industry is a growing industry with strong competitors including many of the best known companies in America (such as GE and Westinghouse). To a great degree, the relative strengths of competitors help maintain high quality products. One measure of this quality has been the industry's ability to export four times as many motors as is currently imported. The financial position and operating results of most of the top companies in the industry are very strong (Exhibit 13-2).

General Electric.   General Electric (GE) is the industry leader and the only company manufacturing a full line of electric motors. The company is also the single largest exporter of motors and generators, although its motor sales account for less than 10 percent of GE's total sales. General Electric is respected in the industry as a very well-managed company producing quality products.

This case was prepared by Peter M. Ginter and Linda E. Swayne as a basis for class discussion rather than to illustrate either effective or ineffective handling of an administrative situation. Used by permission from Peter M. Ginter.

Exhibit 13-1   **Estimated Electric Motor Sales for the Industry's Leading Firms**

Company	1969 Sales (Motor only)	Rank	1981 Sales (Motor only)	Rank	Motor Percent of Total Sales
General Electric	519	1	1200	1	4
Emerson (Incl. USEM)	285	3	700	2	20
Westinghouse	353	2	450	3	5
Exxon (Reliance)	122	4	290	4	n/a
W. W. Grainger	75	5	265	5	25
Baldor	18	11	151	6	94
Franklin Electric	30	9	150	7	94
Siemens-Allis (A-C)	70	6	125	8	n/a
Gould (Century)	60	7	120	9	7
Litton Industries (L/A)	40	8	100	10	n/a
Marathon Electric	25	10	80	11	n/a

Source: Baldor Electric Company.

Emerson Electric.   Emerson Electric is second in terms of motor sales and has maintained a rapid growth rate over the last five years. Emerson's sales comprise approximately two-thirds consumer motors distributed through Emerson Motor division and one-third industrial motors sold through U.S. Electrical Motors.

Westinghouse.   Westinghouse, third in sales among the motor manufacturers, has a broad line of electric motors. However, its growth rate has been below the average of other leaders in the industry. Baldor's management speculated that the lack of growth is likely due to a number of other concerns that have diverted management attention from motor sales in the last few years.

Reliance Electric.   Reliance, a subsidiary of Exxon since 1979, has maintained a good reputation regarding the quality of their electric motors, and continues to be a well-respected manufacturer of industrial motors and a tough competitor in the industry.

W. W. Grainger.   Grainger's expertise has been as a distributor of products to industry through its stores, its catalog the "Blue Book," and direct to original equipment manufacturers (OEMs). Motors represent about 25 percent of Grainger's sales.

Exhibit 13-2 Operating Results for Selected Electric Motor Firms, 1981

	Total Assets	Total Net Worth	Current Ratio	Long-term Debt to Total Capital	Net Earnings to Total Sales	Return on Average Total Assets	Return on Average Equity
General Electric	$20,942	$ 9,128	1.2	.104	.061	.083	.19
Emerson	2,201	1,386	2.4	.106	.080	.130	.21
Westinghouse	8,316	2,837	1.03	.180	.047	.058	.163
Exxon	62,931	28,517	1.3	.153	.049	.093	.206
W. W. Grainger	472	335	2.2	.041	.065	.119	.180
Franklin Electric	98	53	2.3	.263	.041	.074	.141
Baldor Electric	103	63	3.3	.175	.073	.127	.202
Siemens-Allis (A-C)	1,594	656	1.5	.305	—	—	—
Gould (Century)	1,597	810	2.3	.299	.052	.061	.119

Baldor Electric Company.   Baldor focuses on energy-efficient industrial electric motors and sells to distributors and OEMs. Since 94 percent of its sales are electric motors, Baldor is committed to the electric motor industry.

ELECTRIC MOTORS

Rather than being used for one purpose by a single market, electric motors are used in many types of machinery and equipment by both consumers and industrial users throughout the world. The electric motor markets can be segmented into five major product categories:

- Fractional horsepower motors—motors under one horsepower.
- Integral horsepower motors and generators.
- Prime motor sets—internal combustion engine/generator combinations.
- Motor generator sets—electric motor/generator combinations.
- Other equipment (servos, synchros, resolvers, parts, and accessories).

The electric motor is a rotating machine used for the conversion of electrical energy to mechanical power. Motors can meet a variety of service requirements such as running, starting, holding, or stopping a load.

Electric motors are the sole method of converting electrical energy to mechanical power. No matter what the source of energy, coal, oil, gas, or nuclear, an electric motor is utilized for conversion of the electric energy to mechanical power. Advantages of electrical power are ease of transportation over great distances and ease of control compared to other forms of energy. Currently 30 percent of all energy is converted to electrical power and 64 percent of that generated electricity is used to power motor-driven equipment.

The basic science used in operation of the electric motor has remained the same since its invention early in the nineteenth century. There have, however, been substantial refinements in manufacturing processes and size of the components. Exhibit 13-3 summarizes the different types of AC- and DC-powered motors and indicates the many possible market-niche strategies available to manufacturers of electric motors.

Induction motors account for approximately 90 percent of the sales in the fractional and integral horsepower ratings. This type of motor is the simplest and most rugged. The stator "induces" an electric current in the rotor, which has no wiring, resulting in a motor that is less expensive and less subject to failure than other types of motors.

The major variations for induction motors relate to the construction of the rotor (squirrel cage or wound rotor) and the operating current (single-phase or poly-phase). Most industrial systems are three-phase AC current while most consumer applications use single phase. However, the motor can be designed to run on either single- or poly-phase current.

Squirrel cage rotors utilize a laminated steel core fitted with slots into which

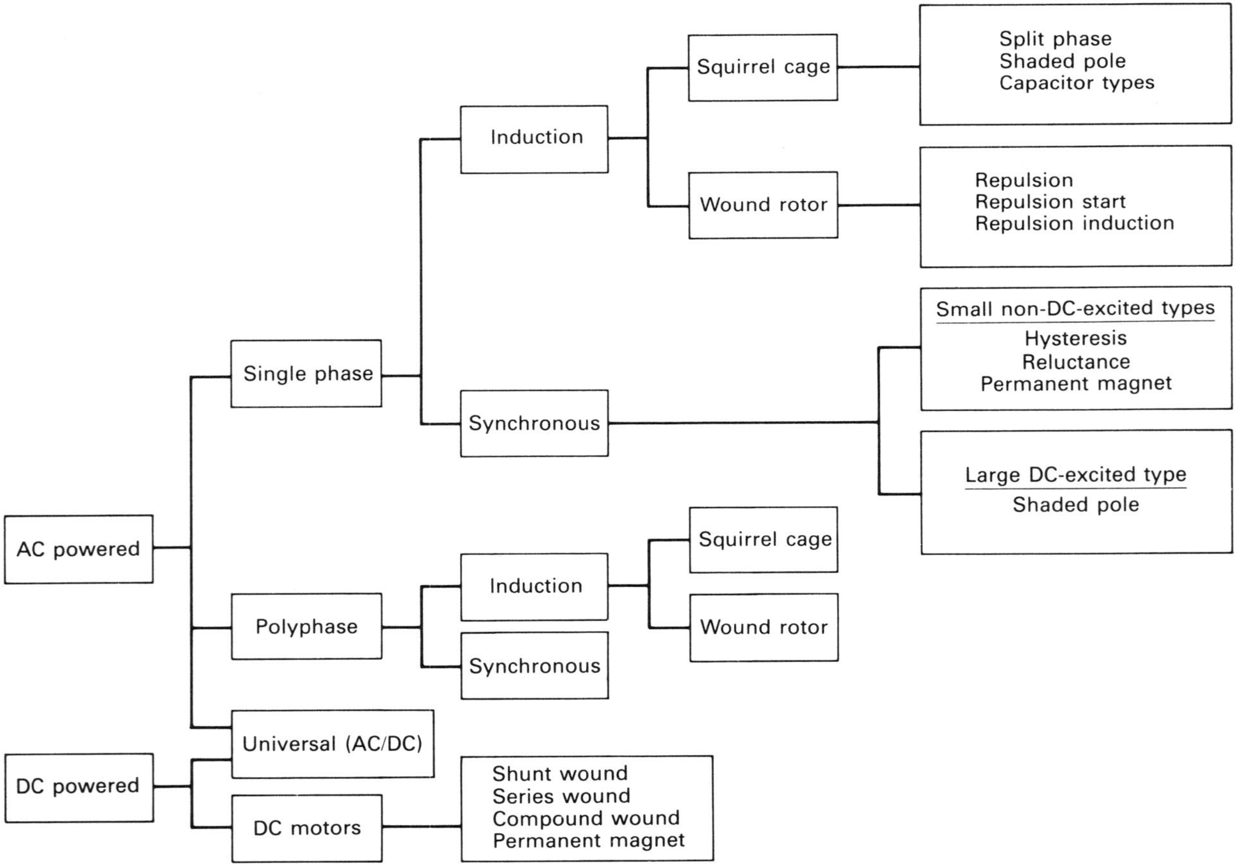

Exhibit 13-3 **Summary of Motor Types**

Source: Research Group/Predicast, Inc.

conductors are placed as the rotor. Wound rotor units use a copper winding in the rotor assembly. Wound rotor units are more expensive and usually limited to variable-speed applications (electronic control devices).

Synchronous motors are used in applications where constant operating speed is required—the AC motor operates in perfect synchronization with the frequency of the line current. They can be constructed to run on single-phase or poly-phase current. Integral horsepower synchronous motors are constructed with a rotor that must be supplied with DC current from an external source.

Commutator motors produce rotary motion through the interaction of two stationary electromagnetic fields. The commutator functions as a rotating switch that reverses the direction of current flow to the armature coil (or rotor) every half revolution of the motor. Commutator motors can be run on either AC or DC current, although most are of the DC type.

DC motors have quick signal response, can be easily operated at different speeds, and can be given precise speed-torque relationships. Applications using DC motors include those that have precise control characteristics, such as instrumentation, material handling and automation equipment, computer output devices, and word processing equipment.

ELECTRIC MOTOR MARKET GROWTH

Electric motors are fundamental to a modern industrialized society. The 1980s appear to hold many changes for the United States as well as all the world economies. Specifically, there will be increased emphasis on factory automation, electronics, and conservation of resources, which suggests greater demand for efficient electric motors. Thus it appears that the pace of change in the electric motor industry will accelerate.

Sales of motors increased from 107 million units in 1963 to over 300 million in 1978—and annual growth rate of over 7 percent. This growth exceeded the less than 5 percent growth in U.S. production of motors because of expanding mechanization and use of motorized equipment in all sectors of the economy. Although the prices of electric motors declined due to improved designs, materials, and manufacturing processes during this period, price increases have been rapid since the mid 1970s primarily because of higher rates of inflation. Growth patterns by motor type and by selected industries for electric motors are summarized in Exhibits 13-4 and 13-5.

Projected growth by motor type indicates that projected real growth is largest for integral horsepower motors (approximately 10% annual growth), whereas growth for fractional horsepower is projected to be flat, and other motor type segments are expected to have moderate growth (Exhibit 13-6). Although currently small markets, servo motors and other motors used in factory automation are expected to grow to approximately $200 million to $400 million in the 1980s.

Exhibit 13-4   **Market Growth by Motor Type (In percent)**

Motor Type	Average Annual Growth 1970–1975	Average Annual Growth 1975–1980	Average Annual Growth 1970–1980
Fractional horsepower motors	5.7	16.1	10.8
Integral horsepower motors, excluding land transportation	11.5	9.6	10.5
Land transportation motors	12.1	10.3	11.2
Prime mover generator sets, except steam or hydraulic turbine	16.3	12.2	14.2
Motor generator sets and other rotating equipment	−0.4	12.5	5.9

Source: Business Trend Analysts.

Demand for electric motors is projected to increase across all categories. Relative growth for selected electric motor markets is illustrated in Exhibit 13-7.

INDUSTRY DYNAMICS

The electric motor industry is capital intensive with substantial investments required in facilities, machinery, and tooling. The required high investments create formidable entry barriers. In addition, the industry is of a technical nature requiring sophisticated engineering skills. As a result, only one new company has entered the top eleven companies in the industry over the last fifteen years. (This company was founded by a past owner of another one of the top companies.) Finally, the sunk costs of electric motor production also make it difficult for a company to exit the market.

Major factors currently affecting the electric motor industry include rising energy costs, electric vehicles, factory automation, and technological evolution. Rising energy costs have resulted in an increased emphasis by customers for product quality and energy efficiency. Energy cost increases are projected by the federal government to continue for the foreseeable future. Many manufacturers are offering higher efficiency electric motors at premium prices to meet this demand. It is estimated that energy-efficient motors now account for 11 percent of the 5 to 20 horsepower market, compared to 1 percent in 1977.

The difference of a few percentage points in energy efficiency can result in a complete payback of the motor's purchase cost within the first year for larger horsepower units. Exhibit 13-8 illustrates the possible savings with an energy-efficient 50-horsepower motor versus an average standard motor based on different hours of

Exhibit 13-5   **Growth in the Purchase of Motors by Selected Industries (In millions)**

Industry	1972	1977[a]
Refrigeration and heating equipment	$344.5	$593.9
Household laundry equipment	94.1	141.8
Household refrigerators and freezers	76.8	98.7
Construction machinery	29.2	88.5
Electric housewares and fans	40.8	58.6
Electric computing equipment	34.1	55.2
Motor vehicle parts and accessories	9.0	41.3
Blowers and fans	23.4	37.9
Special industry machinery	25.1	37.4
Mining machinery	12.4	35.4
Machine tools, metal cutting types	20.6	33.3
Household appliances	20.5	31.0
Household vacuum cleaners	7.6	28.3
Office machinery and typewriters	6.0	28.2
Shipbuilding and repair	9.8	26.0
General industrial machinery	12.5	23.5
Conveyors and conveying equipment	9.2	22.1
Industrial trucks and tractors	10.6	19.3
Printing trades machinery	8.0	16.5
Woodworking machinery	8.6	16.1
Household cooking equipment	6.5	15.9
Machine tools, metal forming types	7.1	15.3
Measuring and controlling devices	2.2	14.6
Hoists, cranes, and monorails	8.4	13.6
Lawn and garden equipment	1.6	12.2
Elevators and moving stairways	11.7	12.0
Radio and TV sets	13.0	11.7
Power driven hand tools	10.3	11.6
Engineering and scientific instruments	5.1	11.0
Food products machinery	11.2	10.6
Metal working machinery	4.0	10.1

[a]Preliminary figures.

Source: Business Trend Analysts, Census of Manufacturers.

operation. Because of such cost savings, many users are considering replacing their less efficient motors with new, energy-efficient electric motors.

Forecasts are for electric vehicles to be used increasingly for consumer and industrial transportation. Increased usage will result from rising costs of fossil fuel, improved battery technology, and operating efficiencies of electric vehicles.

Factory automation is creating a whole new market for electric motors. This new field, electronic motors, includes the servomotors and controls used for the movement and precise positioning of robots, machine tools, and factory vehicles.

Exhibit 13-6 **Projected Growth in Motor Sales by Motor Type 1980–1990ᵃ**
(In percent)

Fractional horsepower motors	9.9
Integral horsepower motors, excluding land transportation	19.3
Land transportation motors	17.2
Prime mover generator sets, except steam or hydraulic turbine	15.0
Motor generator sets and other rotating equipment	7.8

ᵃIncludes estimated 10% annual inflation.
Source: Business Trend Analysts.

This particular portion of the industry is in its infancy and includes many small companies. The most successful of these small electric motor companies will be subject to acquisition by the larger firms in the industry.

Technological evolution has become important not only to the markets served but also to the individual companies within the motor industry. Automation of the electric motor manufacturer's factories, taking advantage of the newer production technologies, will be critical to the companies' abilities to compete as low-cost producers.

Exhibit 13-7 **Relative Growth for Selected Electric Motor Markets**

Item	1978	1985	1990
Manufacturing Production Index	147	193	230
Million motors/index point	1.82	1.99	2.12
Motor, Generator Sales (million units)	267.2	383.5	488.0
Fabricated metals	4.5	5.8	6.6
Machinery and equipment	34.5	40.5	45.9
Electrical and electronics	42.0	62.7	73.3
Transport equipment	34.4	40.7	46.2
Instruments	5.6	8.1	10.1
Toys, games, other manufacturing	43.3	64.0	76.4
Interplant transfers	102.8	161.7	229.5
$/unit	16.5	26.5	42.6
Motor, Generator Sales (million $)	4,403.9	10,170	20,780
Fabricated metals	101.9	203	290
Machinery and equipment	1,823.1	3,864	5,856
Electrical and electronics	620.5	1,427	2,250
Transport equipment	455.7	1,266	6,772
Instruments	158.2	320	485
Toys, games, other manufacturing	145.6	270	392
Interplant transfers	1,098.9	2,820	4,735

Exhibit 13-8   Possible Savings through Energy-Efficient Motors

Annual Savings 50-HP Motor

Power Cost per KWH	40-hour Week (1 Shift)	80-hour Week (2 Shifts)	168-hour Week (Continuous)
.02	$ 72.07	$144.15	$ 302.71
.04	144.15	288.30	605.42
.07	216.22	432.45	908.14
.08	288.30	576.60	1,210.85
.10	360.37	720.74	1,513.56
	50 weeks per year		

KEY FACTORS FOR SUCCESS IN THE ELECTRIC MOTOR INDUSTRY

Several factors are essential if a firm is to have long-term success in the electric motor industry. The key factors appear to include:

- Market share.
- Product differentiation.
- Product quality and reliability.
- Price/low cost production.
- Distribution.
- Research and development.
- Financial strength.

Market Share

Market share is an important factor for success in the electric motor industry because the industry is maturing and consolidation is quite likely. Firms that do not command significant share of the total market or are not firmly entrenched in a particular segment of the market may be subject to acquisition as competition becomes more intense.

Product Differentiation

Many of the larger firms attempt to compete in a number of distinct markets, whereas the smaller firms generally tend to concentrate on developing a special niche. Most of the highly successful firms in the industry have segmented the market and have developed different products to serve as many of the segments as possible. Examples of successful market segmentation include Franklin Electric—submersible pump motors; W. W. Grainger—unique distribution through catalog and company-owned stores; and Baldor—product availability and energy-efficient motors.

Although it is possible and perhaps even essential to be successful in the short run by serving specialized markets, broad market coverage may better assure long-term success as the company is not dependent on the contingencies of a single market.

Product Quality and Reliability

Because much of the industry produces motors for the industrial market, durability and reliability are quite important. Quality issues include the mechanical and electrical functions, raw materials used, durability, efficiency, and care of manufacturing. Company image concerning quality is important in the consumer market as well.

Price/Low Cost Production

In a mature industry, the low cost producers are usually the most successful. As an industry matures, competition increases (the electric motor industry has 340 companies), and it becomes more difficult to provide a unique product. Therefore as the technology of market segments stabilizes and products become relatively standardized, price becomes a major consideration. To offer low prices, manufacturers must be low-cost producers.

Distribution

The electric motor producer must have well-established distribution systems in order to meet customer needs. Important factors in electric motor distribution are:

- Availability—the ability to deliver immediately from stock.
- Delivery reliability—the ability to consistently meet delivery lead times.
- Service—a close, friendly relationship with customers (primarily OEMs).

Research and Development

In today's environment, modernized manufacturing methods and technical product developments will be needed to remain competitive. Therefore, firms in the industry will have to seriously engage in both process and product research and development.

Financial Strength

Adequate financial strength is required for companies in the industry to remain competitive and respond to possible strategic moves by other companies. Financial support is necessary for quality assurance programs, distribution system needs, and research and development requirements.

Citicorp—British National Life Assurance

Ira Rimerman, Group Executive, Consumer Services Group, International, Citicorp, was in his third-floor office in Citicorp's headquarters in New York City on January 16, 1986, when he received notice from the Board of Citicorp that his MEP (Major Expenditure Proposal) to acquire the British National Life Assurance Company, Ltd. (BNLA) in England had been approved. For a total investment of $33.3 million, Citicorp was now in the life underwriting business.[1]

Although he was pleased with the Board's approval, several issues were on Mr. Rimerman's mind as he thought back over the last few months when his staff analyzed and developed suggestions for a business strategy for BNLA, including key policies, tactics, and organizational changes.

CITICORP'S HISTORY

Citicorp's corporate history spanned 175 years, from its early inception as a small commercial bank in New York City in 1812 through its growth into one of the world's largest financial services intermediaries. A recurring historical theme seemed to be the firm's ability to identify correctly the developing trends in the marketplace and to devise appropriate strategies for taking advantage of them.

The firm first emerged as a significant bank in the latter part of the nineteenth century by responding successfully to the transition of the United States from an agricultural to an industrial economy. Since the mid 1960s, the firm had transcended the corporate treasurer and the metropolitan New Yorker as its sole funding source and found ways to attract the more than $1.5 trillion consumer savings market in the United States.

During the 1960s and 1970s, Citicorp completed two separate but integral strategic efforts that revolutionized the company and influenced the whole financial service industry. First, in 1967, the firm formed a bank holding company which

[1]All financial information related to BNLA has been changed for proprietary reasons. All dollars are U.S.$, with conversion rates provided where appropriate.

This case was prepared by John M. Gwin (University of Virginia), Per V. Jenster (IMEDE), and William K. Carter (University of Virginia). The authors gratefully acknowledge the support of the McIntire School of Commerce (University of Virginia) and the General Electric Foundation. The authors are also grateful to Citicorp for its willing cooperation. This case was prepared for the sixth McIntire Commerce Invitational, held at the University of Virginia on February 11–14, 1987. It is written as a basis for student discussion rather than to illustrate either effective or ineffective handling of an administrative situation. Used by permission from John M. Gwin.

permitted it to broaden its geographical and product bases. Second, in the early 1970s, it redefined its business from a U.S. commercial bank with branches abroad to a global financial services enterprise with the United States as its home base. By 1980, the firm had further broadened its scope by defining its business as that of providing services and information to solve financial needs. Exhibits 14-1 and 14-2 provide a summary of the firm's financial profile.

CITICORP'S STRATEGY

The firm's strategic plan called for three separate kinds of world-class banks, all of which could leverage off an unrivaled global network. By the mid 1980s, the Investment Bank, also known as the Capital Markets Group, enabled the firm to fully intermediate the capital flows of the world, with over $6 billion in transactions in the swap market. The Institutional Bank was the principal supplier of financial service mechanisms to corporations and governments worldwide. Finally, the Individual Bank served the individual consumer on a worldwide basis.

Walter B. Wriston, former Chairman of Citicorp/Citibank, explained the firm's strategy:

> Over time, it seemed to us, the institution without access to the consumer would slowly become an institution without adequate funding. In addition, consumer-led economic recoveries are becoming more the rule than the exception and we looked for ways to participate. For all of these reasons, you have often heard about this consumer transition and the identification of the consumer as a key to our strategy in the middle '70s. It was usually described as risky but there are also risks in doing nothing.[2]

Exhibit 14-1　　**Citicorp and Subsidiaries Revenues Earned and Rates of Return Achieved (In billions)**

	Revenues	ROA[a]	ROE[b]
1981	$4.0	.46%	13%
1982	$5.1	.59%	16%
1983	$5.8	.67%	16%
1984	$6.6	.62%	15%
1985	$8.5	.62%	15%

Source: Citicorp *Annual Report,* 1985.

[a]$ROA = \dfrac{\text{Net Income}}{\text{Average Total Assets}}$

[b]$ROE = \dfrac{\text{Net Income} - \text{Preferred Dividends}}{\text{Average Common Equity}}$

---

[2]*The Citi of Tomorrow: Today,* Walter B. Wriston's address to the Bank and Financial Analysts Association, New York, March 7, 1984.

The holding company structure was used to overcome the geographical constraints of the domestic businesses. It also allowed for a few acquisitions and for the creation of de novo units to build a global network which, among other things, featured a unique competitive franchise for bank cards within the Individual Bank.

Wriston also remarked:

> It costs about $150 per year to service an individual through a branch system. That number plummets to $20 if we use the credit card as our primary delivery vehicle. In short, through fees and merchant discounts, the card as a stand-alone product is a profitable endeavor. By the 1990s, it may well become the core delivery mechanism when augmented by automatic teller machines and home banking. . . . We envision a world of 35 million Citicorp customers producing earnings of $30 per customer. . . .

Exhibit 14-2   **Citicorp Financial Statements (In billions)**

Consolidated Balance Sheet
Citicorp and Subsidiaries

	December 31, 1984	December 31, 1985
Assets		
Cash, deposits with banks, and securities	$31	$40
Commercial loans	$59	$58
Consumer loans	43	55
Lease financing	2	3
Less allowance for credit losses	1	1
Net	$103	$115
Premises and other assets	17	18
Total Assets	$151	$173
Liabilities		
Deposits	$ 90	$105
Borrowings and other liabilities	39	42
Long-term debt	13	16
Capital notes and redeemable preferred	2	2
Total Liabilities	$144	$165
Stockholders' Equity		
Preferred stock	1	1
Common stock	1	1
Additional paid-in capital	1	1
Retained earnings	4	5
	$ 7	$ 8
Total Liabilities and Stockholders' Equity	$151	$173

(continued)

Exhibit 14-2   (continued)

Consolidated Income Statement
Citicorp and Subsidiaries

	1983	1984	1985
Interest revenue	$15.2	$18.2	$19.5
Less: Interest expense	11.2	13.9	14.0
Provision for credit losses	.5	.6	1.3
Net	$3.5	$3.7	$4.2
Other revenues	1.8	2.3	3.0
	$5.3	$6.0	$7.2
Operating expenses	3.7	4.5	5.5
Income before income taxes	$1.6	$1.5	$1.7
Income taxes	.7	.6	.7
Net Income	$ 0.9	$ 0.9	$ 1.0
Earnings per share:			
Common and equivalent	$6.48	$6.45	$7.12
Fully diluted	6.15	6.36	7.11

Consolidated Balance Sheet
Citibank and Subsidiaries

	December 31, 1984	December 31, 1985
Assets		
Cash, deposits with banks, and securities	$ 28	$ 40
Loans and lease financing, net	69	75
Premises and other assets	15	16
Total	$112	$131
Liabilities		
Deposits	$ 78	$ 92
Borrowings and other liabilities	26	29
Long-term debt	2	3
Stockholders' Equity		
Capital stock	1	1
Additional paid-in capital	1	1
Retained earnings	4	5
Total	$112	$131

Source: Citicorp *Annual Report,* 1985.

We had big plans for this group when it started and we can now see a time by which it will become a billion dollar business.

The 1980s also dictated a new philosophy which differed from traditional bank practice and from the media's bias for focusing on size as a measure of success. Commercial asset growth on the books of Citicorp was discouraged. In fact, management stretched its imagination to take assets off the firm's books, not to put them on. In 1983, more than $2 billion in loans generated in the United States by the Institutional Bank were sold to others by the Investment Bank. That number was expected to reach $20 billion by 1989. Wriston further explained:

> Our stockholders benefit, since we keep part of the spread while someone else keeps the assets (and the risk). But in order to make this a viable business, you must have both the asset generating capability and the distribution capability nationwide and worldwide.

The worldwide orientation was further encouraged as cross-border lending started to slow down. Citicorp predicted that individual countries would be forced to develop their own indigenous capital markets. Thus, there was an opportunity to develop a "multi-domestic" strategy which would enable Citicorp to offer full financial services in 60-80 countries before 1990.

The Five I's

In the early 1980s, Citicorp added two more "I's" to the strategic thrust which had initially included development of the Investment Bank, the Individual Bank, and the Institutional Bank. The two embryonic "I's" were the Information and Insurance businesses. According to Wriston:

> We want to be in the information business simply because we are in the information business. Information about money has become almost as important as money itself. As bankers, we are familiar with the time value of money. As investors, we must think of the time value of information. The central core of any decision making process is information. The fact that you know something relevant before, or more clearly than your competitors may lead you to act sooner, to your advantage. Herein lies the problem, determining what is relevant. Hence, the packaging of information and its distribution will be critical. . . . We eventually intend to become a main competitor, as a preeminent distributor of financial data-base services worldwide. This is only possible with a truly global system, one through which information is distributed with electrons rather than the mail.[3]

The rationale for entering the insurance business was simple: insurance accounted for fully 40 percent of all financial services in 1985. Citicorp would therefore not be a truly effective financial services enterprise without offering these products. Insurance was also a natural adjunct to the consumer business, considering

---

[3]Consistent with these plans, Citicorp acquired Quotron, a firm specializing in informational data bases.

the outmoded and expensive agency method of distribution that dominated the industry. Moreover, the firm was already a major factor in credit insurance. For example, one third of its second-mortgage customers bought credit life insurance.

The Banking Holding Company Act of 1956, and specifically Regulation Y, Section 4(c)-8 for the Board of Governors of the Federal Reserve System, prohibited banks from engaging in life insurance underwriting (with certain exceptions). Thus, the firm's insurance strategy was primarily aimed at an overseas expansion. This expansion was made possible by the Federal Reserve Board's ruling, requested by Citicorp, which enabled the firm to establish a fully competitive insurance operation in the United Kingdom. The Board concluded:

> The general activity of underwriting life insurance in the United Kingdom can be considered usual in connection with banking or other financial operations in the United Kingdom.

This shift in the Reserve Board's attitude enabled Citicorp to consider expansion into insurance, to identify the United Kingdom as a potential country in which to do so, and ultimately to pursue BNLA for acquisition.

Citicorp's goals for the five I's in 1986 can be summarized as follows:[4]

Institutional
- Trim work force from 20,000 to 17,000.
- Pull back from middle markets overseas.
- Push investment banking products more.
- Clean up loan portfolio, reduce write-offs.

Investment
- Build credible corporate finance group, especially in mergers and acquisitions.
- Hold on to investment banking talent.
- Wire 90 trading rooms around the globe.
- Improve coordination between London, Tokyo, and New York.

Individual
- Continue to grow fast in retail banking.
- Make all acquired savings and loans profitable.
- Push international consumer business.

Information
- Leave Quotron alone to calm customers.
- Develop new products.

Insurance
- Push for easing limits on banks.
- Grow overseas.
- Cross-sell more insurance products through customer base.

The 1985 sector performance is displayed in Exhibit 14-3.

[4]From information provided by Citicorp and *Business Week*, December 8, 1986.

Exhibit 14-3   Sector Performance Citicorp and Subsidiaries (In millions)

	1984	1985	% change
Individual Bank			
Net revenue	$3,107	$4,120	33
Operating expenses	2,735	3,614	32
Other income and expense	(12)	102	*a*
Income before taxes	360	608	69
Net Income	$ 222	$ 340	53
ROA	.51%	.61%	
ROE	12.7 %	15.3 %	
Institutional Bank			
Net revenue	$2,068	$2,168	5
Operating expenses	1,275	1,500	18
Income before taxes	793	668	(16)
Net Income	$ 454	$ 392	(14)
ROA	.64%	.54%	
ROE	15.9 %	13.6 %	
Investment Bank			
Net revenue	$1,241	$1,589	28
Operating expenses	587	803	37
Income before taxes	654	786	20
Net Income	$ 343	$425	24
ROA	1.33%	1.34%	
ROE	33.2 %	33.5 %	
Unallocated			
(Certain corporate-level items which are not allocated among sectors)			
Revenue	$ (79)	$ 28	*a*
Operating expenses	116	148	28
Additional provision for credit losses	68	226	132
Income before taxes	(263)	(346)	(32)
Net Income	$(129)	$(159)	(23)

*a*Not applicable

CITICORP'S STRUCTURE AND OBJECTIVES

The Investment Bank, the Institutional Bank, and the Individual Bank were each organized into a sector and headed by a sector executive. Activities related to insurance and information were under the auspices of group executives within the three sectors, until such time as they justified the creation of their own sectors.

Each of the three sectors was composed of several groups, divisions, and business families, headed by a group executive, with business managers reporting to him or her. The organization of the Individual Bank, which is of particular interest in this case, was somewhat different from the others. As dictated in John S. Reed's (chairman of Citicorp since 1985) memorandum of March 9, 1976 (internally known as the "Memo from the Beach"), the business manager was responsible for the day-to-day operation, whereas a division executive's responsibility was strategic in nature.

This meant that a branch manager in, say Hong Kong, would report to an area manager, then a country manager, a division manager, a group executive, a vice-chairman or sector executive, and then the chairman. In effect, the flat structure placed only three layers of management between the most junior branch manager and the Policy Committee (thirty senior executives) of Citicorp.

In January 1986 Reed issued a set of guidelines developed by the Policy Committee, which included Citicorp's objectives for the next ten years (Exhibit 14-4) and its values (Exhibit 14-5). Exhibit 14-6 (A and B) displays the organizational structure of the Individual Bank and Consumer Services Group, International.

The International Opportunity

In the *1985 Annual Report,*[5] the board stated:

> We recognize that, ultimately, our success will be directly attributable to our ability to offer our consumers worldwide pre-eminent service for each of their relationships with us. Our view is that by pursuing service excellence across all of our efforts, we enhance our standing with our customers and thereby the likelihood that they will choose us for a growing share of their financial needs.

Internationally, Citicorp expanded its presence in a number of markets during 1985, while maintaining returns well in excess of corporate standards. In that year, Citicorp completed significant acquisitions in Italy (Banca Centro Sud), Belgium (Banque Sud Belge), and Chile (Corporacion Financiera Atlas), as well as consumer businesses in Columbia, Guam, and India.

Richard S. Braddock, Sector Executive of the Individual Bank and Director of Citicorp and Citibank, explained:

> We view our opportunities in the international marketplace as substantial, not only because our share tends to be relatively small in most places, but also because we have the opportunity to apply lessons learned from market to market and to expand attractive and proven product packages. . . .[6]

[5]Citicorp *Annual Report,* 1985, p. 11.
[6]Ibid.

Exhibit 14-4   **Citicorp Objectives**

Citicorp's objective is to continue to build the world's leading financial services organization by creating value for our stockholders, customers, staff members, and the communities where we live and work. Creation of value is dependent on building an internal environment based on integrity, innovation, teamwork, and a commitment to unquestioned financial strength.

Value for the Shareholder

- 12% to 18% compound growth in earnings per share.
- Improving return on equity to 17% to 18% (maintaining the internal hurdle at 20%).
- A strong balance sheet including a 10% capital position and an AA+ credit rating.
- Performance profile (earnings, market position, returns) improving within the top 30 companies in the world.
- Improving market position for our businesses, defined by explicit market share reporting.
- Well-diversified geographical and business earnings, assets, and liabilities.

Value for Our Customer

Maintain and build our two customer sets, institutional and individual, through customer service excellence, professionalism, product innovation, and the energy of our response to customer needs. Regularly monitor progress through external and internal surveys.

Value for Our Staff

Maintain an open, challenging, rewarding, and healthy working environment characterized by excellence and fairness in dealing with our employees. Business unit management is responsible for maintaining this working environment and will support and adhere to the People Management beliefs outlined in the attached statement. We will regularly monitor such support and adherence with specific, measurable goals.

Value for the Communities in which We Operate

Management of each business unit and/or geographical location is part of the community within which we operate and has an obligation:

- To contribute to community values.
- To participate in appropriate ways.
- To work to change the legal and regulatory environment to enhance our "opportunity space."
- To deal with our communities in an open, straightforward manner.

Source: Company documents.

The Consumer Services Group, International (CSGI)

The Consumer Services Group, International, within the Individual Bank, was organized in separate divisions: the Asia–Pacific division had its headquarters in Tokyo; Europe–Middle East–Africa (EMEA) division, in London; the Western division in Rio de Janeiro; Payment Products Division (Diners Club), in Chicago; and Systems Division, in New York. The group employed 26,000 people in 70 businesses, located in 40 countries.

Exhibit 14-5   **Citicorp Values**

Excellence in People Management
What We Believe

The Basics

While people management is a part of our business, there are certain non-negotiable assumptions we make about how we will deal with the people who make up Citicorp. These basics must take precedence in everything we do.

- Respect for individuals.
- Treating people with dignity, openness, honesty, and fairness.

Citicorp Values

In addition to our other specific Citicorp values (innovation, integrity, and service excellence), we have a set of values related to people management. These are things we feel strongly about and which are driven by the needs of our business.

- Meritocracy. Emphasizing excellence of performance, professionalism, and effectiveness as the determining factors for selection, retention, rewards, and advancement. Recognizing good performance wherever and whenever it occurs. Appropriately exiting consistent nonperformers.
- Independent initiative. Promoting personal freedom to act and allowing people to succeed and to learn from failure.
- Listening. Creating an environment where we really hear what people say. Working together so that people throughout the organization have an impact.
- Development. Consciously building experience and talent of our people with the goal of professional growth. Creating a balance between developmental experiences and current contribution.

Working Style

Our working styles will vary in different business situations and environments. The following describe the ways in which we approach people management, each applied as appropriate to individual business conditions.

- Teamwork. Building effective business driven partnerships within the organization. Achieving a balance between cooperation and entrepreneurial spirit.
- Integration. Helping new people and new businesses to effectively and appropriately become part of the Citicorp culture.

Source: Company documents.

John Liu, Senior Human Resource Officer, Consumer Services Group, International, summarized how Citicorp's culture was reflected by the Group:

> We want to be part of the largest low-cost provider of financial services in the world. As such we don't focus only on banks such as Chase Manhattan. Rather, we look also at Sears, AMEX, and others who provide financial services. This is the stretch we hold in front of us.

In order to help achieve this, we have to find new ways of doing things. Taking insurance as an example, Citicorp practices its decentralized operational mode, sometimes referred to as the "thousand flowers" approach.

In insurance, to use a metaphor, we want to have a thousand flowers bloom. Over time, we'll put the flowers together in a bouquet, and if we don't like the shape of it, we'll take this or that flower away. However, today we just started our picking and that is why you'll find insurance activities in the Institutional Bank (commercial insurance), the Investment Bank (brokerage insurance activities), and with us in the Individual Bank (life underwriting, mortgage insurance, etc.). It's all emerging slowly out of our philosophy, and the BNLA acquisition is the first major life underwriting acquisition we have ever had.

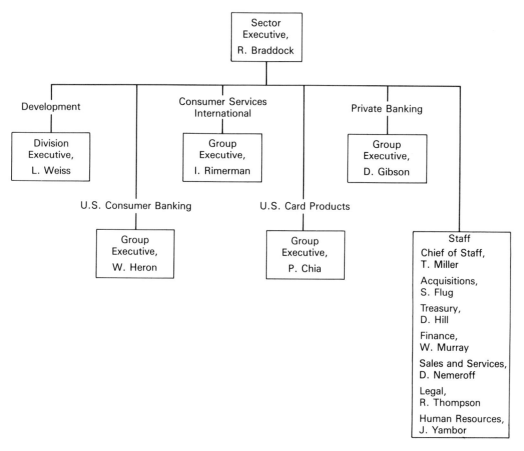

Source: Company documents

Exhibit 14-6A   **Individual Bank Organization**

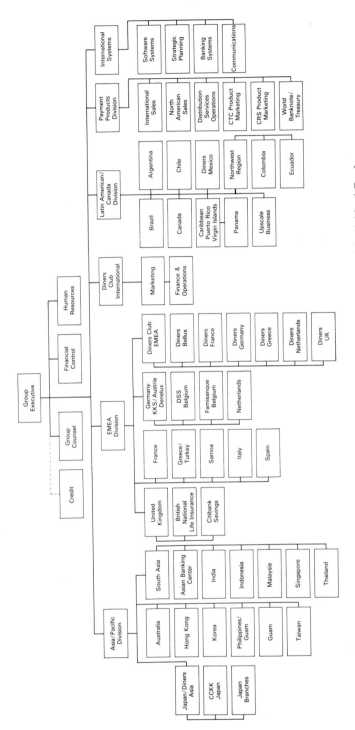

Exhibit 14-6B **Consumer Services Group, International Individual Bank**

As part of this stretch, the corporation applies certain hurdle rates to guide this vision. We have a stated hurdle rate, internally, such as a ROE of no less than 20 percent. Additionally, we also have a ROA hurdle rate of 90 basis points. In our group, we use our own internal hurdle rates as a way of managing our businesses. One such hurdle rate which comes to mind is to target a ratio of 1.5 between consumer net revenue and delivery expenses.

Within the Group, we want to more than double our earnings over the next five years. We want to do this partly through acquisitions, of which we must have done at least 10 over the past three years and added more than 6,000 people. Although we still will make acquisitions, we clearly must slow down and develop these new businesses.

The acquisitions have not been hostile and for the most part have been either "hospitalized" or unprofitable businesses. This has given us certain advantages, but also created challenges when it comes to integrating a new business into our organization.[7]

The unique culture and reward system of Consumer Services Group, International is reflected in Exhibit 14-7, which summarizes the results of an organizational survey of its senior managers.

The Search for an Acquisition

Liu further explained how the BNLA acquisition came about:

About three years ago, we started a drive to get into insurance and encouraged our people in the UK, Australia, Germany, and Belgium to start to look into insurance. As you know, there are three ways you can get into a new business. You can (a) acquire, (b) start a de novo unit, or (c) do a joint venture.

In England, which was one of the largest and most profitable markets (relatively) for life insurance, we initially identified Excelsior Life Assurance[8] as a possibility in early 1984. As an insurance company of substantial size in the UK, the acquisition would immediately bring us into this market on a large scale. However, the more we analyzed the numbers, the more concerned we got. This was a significant investment, and we had little knowledge about life insurance. So when our joint-venture partner (a large U.S. insurance company) withdrew, we reconsidered our options.

Then Citicorp's UK Country Manager and the European Division Manager of the United Kingdom sponsored (identified) BNLA as a potential candidate for our move into life underwriting insurance. After the identification of the candidate, an acquisition team was put together. The team consisted of people from across our UK businesses as well as outside consultants and were all selected for their specific skills as they related to this opportunity.

One of the most important issues for us is now to decide how to integrate the business—should we fully integrate, keep it at an arm's-length distance, or somewhere in between, and how should we do it. With this decision also comes the question of what type of person to put into the driver's seat.

---

[7]Interview with John Liu.
[8]The name has been changed to protect confidentiality.

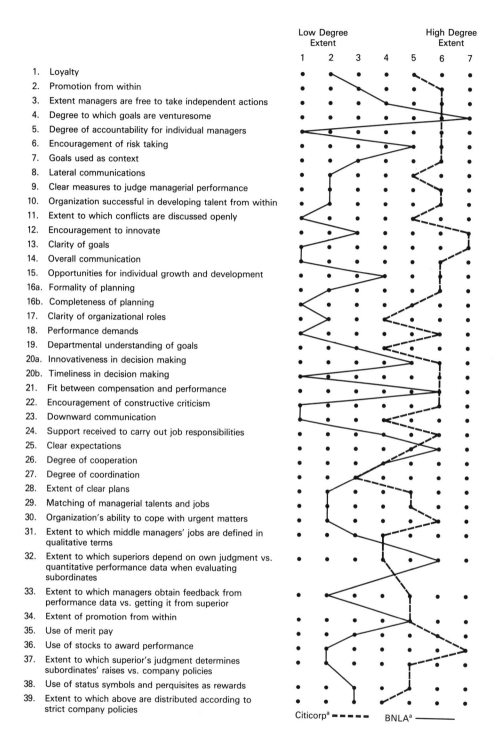

		Low Degree Extent					High Degree Extent	
		1	2	3	4	5	6	7
1.	Loyalty							
2.	Promotion from within							
3.	Extent managers are free to take independent actions							
4.	Degree to which goals are venturesome							
5.	Degree of accountability for individual managers							
6.	Encouragement of risk taking							
7.	Goals used as context							
8.	Lateral communications							
9.	Clear measures to judge managerial performance							
10.	Organization successful in developing talent from within							
11.	Extent to which conflicts are discussed openly							
12.	Encouragement to innovate							
13.	Clarity of goals							
14.	Overall communication							
15.	Opportunities for individual growth and development							
16a.	Formality of planning							
16b.	Completeness of planning							
17.	Clarity of organizational roles							
18.	Performance demands							
19.	Departmental understanding of goals							
20a.	Innovativeness in decision making							
20b.	Timeliness in decision making							
21.	Fit between compensation and performance							
22.	Encouragement of constructive criticism							
23.	Downward communication							
24.	Support received to carry out job responsibilities							
25.	Clear expectations							
26.	Degree of cooperation							
27.	Degree of coordination							
28.	Extent of clear plans							
29.	Matching of managerial talents and jobs							
30.	Organization's ability to cope with urgent matters							
31.	Extent to which middle managers' jobs are defined in qualitative terms							
32.	Extent to which superiors depend on own judgment vs. quantitative performance data when evaluating subordinates							
33.	Extent to which managers obtain feedback from performance data vs. getting it from superior							
34.	Extent of promotion from within							
35.	Use of merit pay							
36.	Use of stocks to award performance							
37.	Extent to which superior's judgment determines subordinates' raises vs. company policies							
38.	Use of status symbols and perquisites as rewards							
39.	Extent to which above are distributed according to strict company policies							

Citicorp[a] ▪▪▪▪▪   BNLA[a] ──────

[a]Questionnaires were completed by managers and outside observers. Items of the questionnaire are summarized and labeled because of proprietary reasons; values indicate average scores.

Exhibit 14-7   **Summary of Organizational Surveys Conducted by the Case Writers**

THE UNITED KINGDOM (U.K.)

The U.K. economy is the sixth largest in the world and is in transition, as is the U.S. economy, from an industrial to a service orientation. By 1985, the United Kingdom had the lowest level of legal/regulatory control for domestic and international financial activity of any developed country. However, U.K. regulation of life insurance underwriting, particularly with regard to reserves, was among the most stringent in the world. The government was considered politically stable, and the conservatives in power were committed to controlling inflation and government spending to provide a platform for economic growth. Even though 12 percent of the work force was unemployed, there was little social unrest.

The United Kingdom was expected to remain self-sufficient in oil for the remainder of the century. Inflation was expected to be controlled in the 5 to 7 percent range, and no major changes were expected in either the political system or the regulatory environment. Expected growth figures for U.K. GNP for 1986 and 1987 were 1.5 percent and 2.6 percent, respectively. Inflation was expected to be around 5.0 percent for the same two periods.

The U.K. Life Assurance Market[9]

The U.K. life assurance market was considered large and growing. Growth in new premiums went from $1.9 billion in 1980 to $4.7 billion in 1983. During the same period average growth of premium income rose from $7.8 billion to $13.2 billion, and total sums insured grew an average of 17 percent to $295 billion. There were 289 licensed underwriters in the United Kingdom. The relative size of the top twelve companies is presented in Exhibit 14-8.

Analyses showed that life assurance in the United Kingdom was seen as both a protection instrument and a consumer investment. The policies accumulated cash value and also yielded dividends to policyholders. There were basically three types of underwriters in the marketplace: industrial, orthodox, and linked life.

The industrial companies offered small value policies which were targeted at the lower socioeconomic groups. The premiums were collected in person, usually monthly, by employed agents, who did little actual "selling." The policies carried high administrative overheads and were, therefore, relatively poor values for the consumer. This sector of the market was dominated by Prudential, which wrote 65 percent of the new policies issued each year. This type of insurance had a vast customer base, with over 70 million policies in existence. At the same time, this type of policy had a declining market share, and smaller companies were retrenching because of overhead inefficiencies.

The orthodox life companies offered larger value policies which catered to the more affluent customer. This type of policy was distributed through "independent"

---

[9]In the United Kingdom "assurance" is used synonymously with the U.S. domestic word "insurance."

Exhibit 14-8 **Major Players in the British Life Assurance Market**

			Worldwide Premium Income		% Increase 1982 over 1981	% Increase 1981 over 1980	Size of Life Fund (End '82 in billions)
	Classification	Ranking	Value (In millions)	% of Total			
Prudential	Stock	1	$ 1,656	13	12	16	$ 9.4
Legal and General	Stock	2	775	6	15	10	6.6
Standard Life	Mutual	3	630	5	13	20	6.3
Norwich Union	Mutual	4	565	4	19	13	3.8
Hambro Life	Stock	5	464	4	20	32	2.1
Commercial Union	Stock	6	444	4	12	15	3.8
Eagle Star	Stock/Sub	7	414	3	21	28	2.2
Abbey Life	Stock/Sub	8	353	3	8	63	1.4
Sun Life	Stock	9	328	3	2	25	2.1
Scottish Amicable	Mutual	10	319	3	24	38	2.5
G.R.E.	Stock	11	318	3	14	27	2.8
Pearl	Stock	12	311	2	8	10	1.9
Subtotal			6,577	53	13	21	44.9 (56%)
Others		13–48	4,924	40	15	21	
Balance			823	7	5	15	36.1 (44%)
			$12,324	100	15	21	$81.0

Note: US$1.20 = £1

professionals who usually had some other relationship with the customer. These independent agents could be insurance brokers, solicitors (attorneys), accountants, banks, or estate agents. It was fairly common in the United Kingdom for all these groups to offer insurance as part of their service portfolio to their clients. These independent agents typically offered policies from three to six different underwriters. The firms which offered orthodox policies had traditionally not "marketed" to their consumer base for fear of offending the professional intermediary. There were different "classes" of agents who covered specific market segments.

The linked life policy was relatively new and was introduced in the 1960s as an alternative to the orthodox life policy. It targeted the same consumer as the orthodox policy but was sold normally by a commission-paid, self-employed sales force, much like insurance representatives in the United States. Policyholders of linked life insurance did not "participate" in the profits of the underwriter through dividends, but their investments were placed in a number of funds (similar to mutual funds) managed by the underwriter. Thus, the linked life policyholder took investment risk/return, and the underwriter provided a death guarantee. The range of products offered by the three types of underwriters is depicted in Exhibit 14-9.

Trends in the U.K. market indicated that the role of single premium life assurance was expanding. This type policy was one in which a single payment was made to the underwriter at the beginning of the policy life, and no further premiums were

---

Exhibit 14-9   **Product Range**

	Nonprofit/ Participating	Relative Importance (Low/High)	Industrial	Traditional	Linked
Protection					
Whole life	NP	L	—	✔	—
	P	L	✔	✔	✔
Term	NP	H	✔	✔	✔
Permanent health	NP	M	—	✔	—
Savings					
Endowment	NP	L	—	✔	—
	P	H	✔	✔	✔
Pensions	NP	L	—	✔	—
	P	H	✔	✔	✔
Annuities	NP	M	—	✔	✔
Single premium bonds	P	H	—	✔	✔
Group Schemes					
Pension	*a*	H	—	✔	✔

*a*Not available.

due. Before the creation of the single premium policy, most life policy premiums were paid yearly over the life of the policy. Logically, there was no single premium industrial underwriting, given the socio-economic status of most policyholders. The target for the single premium policies was the "banked homeowner"—a person who had a relationship with a bank and owned his or her own home.

In addition to the expansion of the single premium policy, there had been a decline in share of the industrial policy from 13 percent of total insurance in 1980 to 6 percent in 1983. The growth sectors of the market were linked life and personal pensions (which were similar to the Individual Retirement Account in the United States).

Premium income had generally become increasingly volatile, because single premium income had grown from 12 percent of total premium income in 1980 to 22 percent in 1983. Since 1968, the growth segments for premium income were linked life, personal pensions, and mortgage endowment. In 1983, the government introduced "Mortgage Interest Relief at Source" (MIRAS), which caused mortgage repayments on insurance linked mortgages to appear more competitive than conventional mortgages, and thus causing an increase in the mortgage endowment business. In March 1984, the British government abolished Life Assurance Premium Relief (LAPR).

In their attempt to expand their share of the market, traditional companies had begun moving into the linked life segment. Major growth was expected in pension-related policies as the most efficient (from a tax perspective) savings medium. Allied Dunbar and Guardian Royal Exchange exemplified a movement to "full financial services."

For the future, the desire of the government to increase the "portability" of pensions could open a major new market. At this time, personal pensions were sold only by life assurance companies (by law). The removal of this restriction was under consideration and would bring new banks into the market. There was some concern that the government policy of "fiscal neutrality" between savings mediums could cause further amendment to tax laws, but this was not expected in the short term.

In the future marketplace, it would be possible for banks to exploit their customer bases and "sell" insurance, instead of being passive providers. Building societies (very similar to U.S. savings and loan institutions, and responsible for writing most home mortgages in the United Kingdom) did not currently have legislative permission to function as insurance brokers as did the banks. It was expected that the societies would request that power in 1986–1987, which would bring more new players to the market. There would be an increase in the pensions business to reach the large self-employed group in the United Kingdom. Exhibit 14-10 offers a view of the current and future importance of key segments in the U.K. market.

In summary, the U.K. life underwriting market was the seventh largest in the world and was growing. Life assurance in the United Kingdom filled a dual role for the consumer—protection and savings-investment. The market was led by large and well-established players, but there were major market opportunities for other well-managed companies. The market was differentiated by distribution methods, and

---

Exhibit 14-10   Intermediaries View of Key Market Segments

	Percent Responding: Currently Important	Percent Responding: Likely to Increase in Importance
Self-employed	90	65
People of medium incomes	82	46
Owners/directors of small companies	80	57
People on high incomes	79	53
Young couples	78	57
Middle-aged couples	72	43
Women	68	51
People with free capital	66	39
Retired couples	46	38

---

the long-term profit stream generated by most firms led to high investor confidence and high share prices. The U.K. premium income in 1982 totaled $28 billion, of which $12 billion was in life assurance underwriting. The market was predominantly U.K.-owned, as were the major players, though a company did not necessarily need to be a general insurance firm to compete successfully in either market. Each market involved different legislative bases, different distribution channels, and different skills. The U.K. firms were significant in world markets, particularly non-life, where they received over 50 percent of the premium income.

The U.K. Financial Services Market

There were five major categories of financial services in the United Kingdom: transaction accounts, savings, shelter (home) financing, lending, and protection. Exhibit 14-11 is a chart of the major players and other entrants in these markets. The total savings market had grown from $124 billion in 1980 to $193.6 billion in 1983. The relative share figures for the major institutions in the savings market are shown in Exhibit 14-12. Shelter finance had grown from $62.8 billion to $108.8 billion in the same period. A synopsis of the growth and change in the unsecured loan market is shown in Exhibit 14-13.

Banks were leading the expansion into the related areas of mortgage financing, estate agency (trust), stock brokering, and life assurance underwriting. Building societies now offered checkbook access to savings and ATM (automatic teller machine) networks. Legislation intended to equalize competitive roles in the market had been passed. Technological advancements were expected at this point, but were not yet in place. The market would continue to change rapidly due to continuing deregulation and increasing technological sophistication. Traditional barriers were falling, and banks were leading the way into other sectors of the economy to satisfy con-

Exhibit 14-11   Elements of the U.K. Financial Services Market

Service	Major Players	Other Entrants
Transaction accounts	Clearing banks	N/A
Savings	Building societies	Banks
	Life assurance companies	
Shelter finance	Building society	Banks
		Finance houses
Lending	Banks	Finance houses
		In-store credit
Protection	Life assurance companies	N/A
	General insurance companies	

sumer demand. Insurance was an integral part of the market and was supported by past and present government and fiscal policy.

Citicorp in the United Kingdom

The Consumer Services Group (U.K.) was dominated by Citibank Savings, a mature business operating in four specific markets:

Finance house:	Indirect financing for autos and home improvement.
Mortgage banking:	Consumer mortgages through association with insurance firm partners.
Retail cards:	Private label card operation for London's High Street retailers, as well as the European Banking Centre, Travellers Checks, and Diners Club.

Exhibit 14-12   Market Movements—Savings "50% of Deposits with Insurance Companies"

	1980	1983
Insurance funds	45%	50%
Building society	28%	28%
Banks	13%	7½%
National savings	7%	7%
Shares, etc.	7%	7½%
Total market	$124 billion	$193.6 billion

Notes: Compound growth 16% per annum (RPI 8.3% compound).

Insurance funds ($97 million at end 1983) are not accessible.

US$120 = £1 for all years.

Consumer banking: Cross-selling a portfolio of products to
consumers, such as personal loans,
checking (transaction) accounts, mortgages, and insurance.

Citibank Savings had 39 branches in the United Kingdom, 19 of which were
recognized as direct branches within the consumer bank.

U.K. Life Assurance Consumers

The U.K. life assurance consumers were underinsured relative to those of other
developed nations. The total life coverage as a percent of yearly average wage as
compared for seven industrialized nations was:

United Kingdom	88%
France	147%
Sweden	148%
Australia	178%
United States	183%
Canada	184%
Japan	325%

The product was seen by U.K. consumers as intangible and offering no present
benefit. The contracts were viewed as a "mass of small print" and were inflexible
once purchased. The purchase pattern was characterized as infrequent and having

---

Exhibit 14-13   **Market Movements—Unsecured Loans "Not Participating
as a Principal but Providing Cover to Repay"**

	1980	1983
Finance houses	34%	29%
Bank loans	29%	37%
Bank credit cards	18%	21%
In-store cards	11%	9%
Other	8%	4%
Total market	$7.1 billion	$13.2 billion

Notes: Compound growth 23%.

An estimated 30% of bank and finance house loans are covered by life/disability insurance
to cover repayments.

New developments from 1982 on larger loans gives bullet repayments covered by endowment insurance.

Statistics exclude "loan backs" from long-term savings under an insurance policy.

Exhibit 14-14   **U.K. Consumer Behavior**

Key Product Groups	Holding %	Recent Purchase[a] %	Future Purchase[b] %
Endowment mortgage	9	17	9
Mortgage protection	16	24	16
Protection cover	35	42	19
Endowment cover	42	63	39
Total (including multi-purchase)	74	100	57

[a]Purchased in the last 12 months.

[b]Expected purchase in the next 12 months.

a high unit cost, and the consumer had a "low knowledge base" about the product. The benefits perceived were "peace of mind," a response to issues of social responsibility, and investment/tax avoidance. Seventy-four percent of U.K. households had life coverage, which included 45 percent of all adults (predominantly men). A chart of U.K. consumer behavior regarding purchase by product type is presented as Exhibit 14-14. The major reasons for purchase were "protection" and "house purchase." In general, no major alternatives were considered, and the decision to buy insurance coverage was a joint one in the family. The amount of coverage was generally based on affordability rather than need, and shopping among companies was minimal. Exhibit 14-15 characterizes the major segments of the market; required company attributes from the consumers' view are shown in Exhibit 14-16.

Exhibit 14-15   **Consumer "Types"**

	Medium	Purchase	Timing	Knowledge	Mind Set
Thinking young couple	Broker and direct to company	Buys	Regular	Sophisticated	Protection
Young family man	Agent or sales-man	Sold	Spasmodic	Low–trusting	Protection/savings
Middle-aged man	Any	Sold	Spasmodic	Low—wants known company	Protection/savings
Self-employed	Salesman or broker	Sold	Spasmodic	Learns quickly, decision maker	Savings
Late arrivals	Direct (coupon response)	Indirectly sold	Once	Low	Protection (burial policy)

> **Exhibit 14-16** **Required Company Attributes: "What to Look for in a Company" (Excludes Industrial)**
>
> | | Spontaneous Response (%) | Prompted Response (%) |
> |---|---|---|
> | Well-known | 33 | 60 |
> | Good reputation | 27 | 51 |
> | Good investment performance | 23 | 30 |
> | Good sales people | 15 | 56 |
> | Long-established | 8 | 43 |

The life assurance market was not as mature as its size might indicate. Most consumers were underinsured, and over half the adult population had no coverage at all. There was a key role to be played for protection products (distinct from investment products). Linked life companies concentrated on "investment" policies, and the benefits to the policyholder were neither fixed nor guaranteed by the company, but were invested in a separate range of funds (at the risk/return of the consumer). In this sense, linked life firms worked very much like mutual fund companies in the United States. Their sources of income were profits from insurance underwriting, a 5 percent bid/offer differential on investments in the funds, and a 3/4 percent fund management fee. The products were sold through a direct sales force, which was normally paid only by commission.

In the U.K. market, 15 percent of adults had a linked life policy (33% of adults with life assurance coverage). The policies were most popular in the under-55 age range, and in London and the southeast of England.

THE HISTORY OF BRITISH NATIONAL LIFE ASSURANCE

British National Life Assurance was a spin-off company from the British National Insurance Society. It was created in 1982 by Sir William Baltimore as a subsidiary of EXCO Corporation (a large U.S. company), when EXCO Corporation had decided to diversify into financial services. British National Insurance remained a property and casualty life underwriter, while BNLA became the life underwriting business of EXCO Corporation. The Managing Director of the new firm was Ernest Smith, a true English gentleman and skilled manager. The Sales Director was Frank Jones, a charismatic and skilled salesman with considerable experience in the insurance business.[10]

EXCO Corporation took very little interest in the performance of BNLA and allowed Mr. Smith and Mr. Jones to manage the company as they saw fit. In es-

---

[10]All names in this section have been changed to protect confidentiality.

sence, Mr. Jones controlled sales and marketing, and Mr. Smith controlled public relations and administration.

In the interim, Sir William Baltimore retired from EXCO Corporation. He subsequently became Director of Insurance Development (on a consulting basis) for Citicorp's Consumer Services Group, International EMEA Division, headquartered in London.

The consumers' view of the Citicorp/BNLA merger was that it offered wider financial services as a result, and a bank-owned insurance company was seen positively. Negative reaction to the fact that it was American-owned could be foreseen.

In January 1986, BNLA employed 392 people, 101 at its headquarters and 250 comprising the sales force from 22 branches. Each branch had a branch manager and an administrative assistant. An organizational chart and staff analysis are provided in Exhibits 14-17 and 14-18.

There were 47,600 policyholders and $305 million in life insurance in force. However, BNLA policy lapses and salesperson turnover were twice the industry average. The commission-only sales force was the major distribution method for BNLA products, and its productivity was some 75 percent below average. The sales force was inappropiately trained, and the commission structure resulted in low pay relative to the competition.

BNLA spent considerable sums of money training a sales force that was paid poorly relative to industry averages. Mr. Jones subscribed to the philosophy that a high-quality product would essentially sell itself, and that, therefore, high commissions were unnecessary. His view was that sales goals would be achieved, in the long run, as a result of high training levels and high-quality products. This became known in the organization as "Frank's Philosophy." This philosophy also constrained promotional activities to direct selling only. The marketing department was therefore mostly engaged in arranging flashy conventions and gimmicks for the sales force.

Communication between top management and the organization was generally considered poor or nonexistent. Bad news, such as the lack of profits, the low sales force performance, and information about the negative cash flows, was never passed along to the management team. Although annual budgets were compiled, their content was never shared with departments. Conversely, no formal system existed for monthly reporting on departmental activities.

Smith believed that financial reporting should be kept to a minimum, although all required disclosures were always filed on time. The financial officer had a small minicomputer at his disposal. Moreover, the firm had taken steps to automate the office environment at its headquarters by establishing a word processing pool.

Toward the end of 1984, EXCO Corporation decided that it was not going to make a go of BNLA (or of financial services generally), and put the company up for sale. The company knew that it was "on the block," and employee morale took a nose-dive. This enhanced the "rudderless" sense of the company, as performance became even less an issue and "Frank's Philosophy" became the guiding force in the firm. A culture-reward system profile of BNLA is shown in Exhibit 14-7.

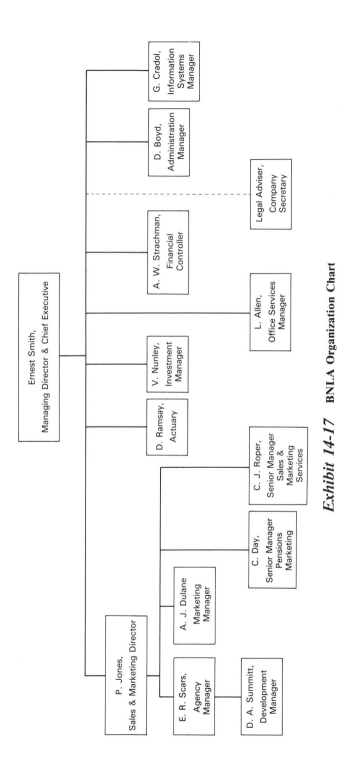

Exhibit 14-17 **BNLA Organization Chart**

259

Exhibit 14-18   **British National Life Staff Analysis**

Department	January 1986
Actuarial	5
Administration	21
Office services	10
Data processing	21
Finance	16
Investment	3
Personnel and training	—
Legal	1
Marketing	13
Sales	9
Credit insurance (from November 1986)	—
Managing director	2
Branch managers	22
Branch administrators	19
Subtotal	142
Salaried sales force	[a]
Total	142
Sales associates	250

[a]Not applicable.

BNLA Product/Market Posture

At the time of the Citicorp acquisition, BNLA was a linked life firm which offered six basic products to the market.

1. Plan-for-Life—A highly flexible policy that offered the consumer control over the content of the plan. The consumer decided what proportion of the premium to devote to savings or protection, and this could be changed as needs and circumstances warranted.

2. Plan-for-Capital—A regular savings plan with high investment content and minimum life coverage. It was ideal for someone who wanted to save dynamically for eight to ten years. The proceeds were free from basic rate income tax (the "off the top" rate in the United Kingdom), from personal capital gains tax, and, after ten years, from higher-rate tax as well. This product was quite similar to the Individual Retirement Account in its tax treatment. It differed in its small insurance cover.

3. Plan-for-Investment—A lump-sum plan to invest in the company's different funds. The capital invested was allocated a set number of units, depend-

ing on the current value of the fund. At any time, the plan had a value equivalent to the bid (sell) value of the price of units multiplied by the number of units held. This fund was very similar to the mutual funds offered through brokerage houses in the United States, except there were certain tax advantages not offered in U.S. mutual funds.

4. Plan-for-Retirement—A retirement annuity policy which was suitable for the self-employed and those who had no private pension scheme—unit-linked, but had outstanding tax advantages. This plan was similar to the Keogh plans in the United States but was free of investment limits.

5. Plan-for-Executive—An individual pension plan suitable for senior members of a trading company (brokerage house) who wished to add to their retirement benefits. This was a very specialized policy, and was, once again, similar to the IRA, except that both the executive and employer could contribute.

6. Plan-for-Pension Preservation—A specialized plan conformed to legislation passed in 1970 which allowed the transfer of vested pension funds from a previous employer into this plan without tax penalties.

In addition to these plans, a broker provided access to general insurance such as motor, house contents (homeowners), and building insurance (U.K. insurance companies are not permitted to act as insurance brokers). The BNLA product line was generally complete and well rounded, and fulfilled the needs of the consumer, from protection and investment to retirement planning.

BNLA—A Financial Perspective

Accounting standards in the United States required earnings on a life insurance policy to be recognized evenly over the years of premium payments. In contrast, U.K. life insurance regulations required maintenance of prudent reserves that resulted in a new life assurance company's generating losses or very low profits during its early years. The function of the regulations was to severely restrict dividend payments and thereby protect policyholders. The U.S. accounting was significantly less conservative; when the balance sheet of a U.K. life firm was recast to comply with U.S. accounting, the reported equity generally increased considerably.

Citicorp's customary financial goals and targets were designed for traditional banking businesses and did not lend themselves to evaluating an investment in a life insurance company. For that reason, Citicorp measured BNLA performance against a hurdle rate of 20 percent ROE on BNLA's recorded equity. Based on Citicorp's projections at the time of the acquisition, BNLA was expected to produce negative ROEs in 1985 and 1986 (Exhibit 14-19) and to achieve the 20 percent hurdle rate for the first time in 1991. To comply with U.S. accounting, BNLA's recorded equity at the time of the acquisition was adjusted as follows (in millions; please note that all BNLA financial data have been changed for proprietary reasons):

Exhibit 14-19 BNLA Operating Forecast, Including Required Synergies—Restated According to U.S. Accounting Principles (In millions)[a]

	1985	1986	1987	1988	1989
Premiums, net	$19.9	$47.0	$74.5	$109.9	$153.1
Reinsurance	.0	2.7	8.5	12.5	15.0
Investment income	3.2	8.4	12.9	19.8	30.4
Total Revenues	$23.1	$58.1	$95.9	$142.2	$198.5
Benefits paid	$3.1	$ 4.2	$ 7.2	$ 13.3	$ 34.1
Increase in reserves	12.0	40.5	66.4	96.4	119.3
Commissions	2.9	6.7	11.6	17.2	23.4
Operating expenses	5.5	7.8	7.4	9.1	12.5
Total Expenses	$23.5	$59.2	$92.6	$136.0	$189.3
Income before taxes[a]	$(0.4)	$(1.1)	$3.3	$6.2	$9.2
Income taxes	0	0	0.8	2.8	4.3
Net Income	$(0.4)	$(1.1)	$2.5	$3.4	$4.9
ROE					
On BNLA equity	(7%)	(5%)	7%	9%	12%
By Citicorp formulas	(30%)	(40%)	6%	11%	16%

[a]Reconciled with BNLA's stand-alone forecast, under U.K. accounting principles, as follows:

	1985	1986	1987	1988	1989
U.K. pretax income, without synergies	$(0.7)	$(3.9)	$(2.4)	$(0.6)	$1.5
Adjustment for U.S. accounting rules		(0.1)	(0.1)	(0.1)	(0.1)
Impact of synergies		1.1	4.0	4.9	5.6
Impact of capital infusion	0.3	1.8	1.8	2.0	2.2
Income before taxes, as reported above	$(0.4)	$(1.1)	$3.3	$6.2	$9.2

BNLA Forecast Balance Sheets, Including Required Synergies— Restated According to U.S. Accounting Principles (In millions)[a]

	As of December 31 of each year				
	1985	1986	1987	1988	1989
Securities	$91	$126	$177	$257	$363
Reinsurance receivable	0	1	7	13	15
Other assets	4	8	21	38	59
Total Assets	$95	$135	$205	$308	$437
Insurance reserves	$62	$103	$169	$266	$385
Other liabilities	1	1	3	6	10
Common stock	32	32	32	32	32
Retained earnings	0	(1)	1	4	10
Total Liabilities and Equity	$95	$135	$205	$308	$437

Exhibit 14-19   (continued)   **BNLA Historical Balance Sheets—According to U.K. Accounting Principles (In millions)**[a]

	As of December 31 of each year	
	1983	**1984**
Securities	$38	$56
Other assets	1	4
Total assets	$39	$60
Insurance reserves	$31	$56
Other liabilities	5	1
Capital	3	3
Total	$39	$60

BNLA Historical Income Statements—According to U.K. Accounting Principles (In millions)[a]

	1983	**1984**
Premiums, net	$5	$31
Investment income	3	4
Total revenues	$8	$35
Benefits paid	$3	$ 3
Increase in reserves	7	25
Commissions	1	1
Operating expenses	1	9
Total expenses	$12	$38
Income before taxes	($4)	($3)
Income taxes	0	0
Net income	($4)	($3)

[a]All balances in US$ at an exchange rate of 1 £ = $1.4.

Source: Citicorp MEP; the data have been altered for proprietary reasons.

Note: Caution should be exercised in comparing BNLA financial data with that of Citicorp, or even with that of other U.K. life assurance companies. This is because, first, there were some significant differences between traditional banking businesses and a U.K. life assurance operation, especially in rules governing the accounting recognition of earnings and in U.K. tax and regulatory requirements. Second, these differences were exaggerated in the case of a relatively new, rapidly growing U.K. life assurance company, where the reported amount of equity may have been as large as 60 percent of reported assets because of the conservatism inherent in regulatory requirements. Third, it was also difficult to make meaningful financial comparisons among different U.K. life companies. An immature firm had a financial picture bearing little resemblance to that of an older, established competitor, which may have reported equity as low as 2 percent of total assets.

Exhibit 14-20

Memorandum

TO: Group Executive

FROM: Divisional Executive

RE: U.K. Insurance Acquisition MEP (Major Expenditure Proposal)

DATE: 14th August 1985

As you know, in 1981 Citibank submitted an application to the Fed seeking permission to expand its line of insurance activities in the U.K. to write whole life in addition to its traditional base of credit life. This action was felt appropriate given that in the U.K. expanded insurance activities are considered a normal part of the banking sector with most large U.K. banks engaged in such activities through wholly owned insurance subsidiaries. Therefore for Citibank to enjoy equal footing with the competition, approval would be necessary since these activities are not otherwise permitted under Citibank's U.S. charter.

Upon receiving permission from the Fed in early 1984, we were then confronted with the business decision of how best to tackle this new opportunity. A team from within Citibank Savings was formed to evaluate the marketplace and make a recommendation on how to proceed. In this effort they were assisted by a senior insurance consultant from the U.K. who had a prior relationship with Citibank. A broad range of companies were evaluated as possible acquisition candidates and several points became clear. A direct sales force (versus mass solicitation) was considered key as well as the company's ownership structure (i.e., if publically owned, how could a takeover be affected?).

Considerations of size became important because additional Fed approval would be required for any takeover. A unique opportunity confronted us to acquire a major U.K. insurer, PQ Life Assurance, but the cost of such an acquisition was put at a figure several hundred million dollars higher than the desired size of investment. This acquisition, which would have been a joint venture, was approved internally within Citibank, but closure with our proposed partners failed.

We then shifted our thinking back to internal "de novo" growth and in so doing have reevaluated several smaller acquisition candidates which had surfaced previously. Acquiring a smaller company may be regarded as "accelerated de novo" and we are actively pursuing the acquisition of British National Life Assurance Company at a cost of $13.7 million (goodwill of $0.5 million) with a further capital increase of $19.6 million, bringing the total investment to $33.3 million. If we were to pursue the internal de novo growth route, we would also require additional capital of about $19.6 million as our current capitalization of $3 million supports the credit life business only. These capital levels are prescribed by the U.K. insurance regulatory bodies in order to meet minimum solvency margins.

The following analysis compares forecasted earnings through acquisition versus internal growth. On a cumulative basis through 1990 the acquisition route produces over $17 million in incremental earnings.

It is important to note that there is a lag in profitability in an emerging life assurance business due to the slow build up of premium income (net of commissions) which in the earlier years is not sufficient to cover the fixed costs of the distribution system. The difference in profitability between the two alternatives below is simply a reflection of this curve and that once a steady state is achieved both propositions would yield the same results.

Exhibit 14-20   (continued)

	De novo[a]	Acquisition[a]	B/(W)[a]
1985	$(.5)	$(1.3)	$ (.6)
1986	(1.3)	(2.9)	(1.6)
1987	(3.6)	.4	4.0
1988	(3.5)	1.3	4.8
1989	(2.5)	2.5	5.0
1990	(1.3)	4.9	6.2
	(12.7)	4.9	17.8

This MEP assumes no tax credit against the operating losses in 1985 and 1986. In 1987, the first full year of profitability, the loss carryforward is absorbed. In any event no current U.K. taxes will likely be payable at least until 1990, and the tax expense is therefore all U.S. deferred.

Your approval of the attached MEP is recommended.

Note: All numbers in this document have been changed for proprietary reasons.

[a]In millions of $US.

Book values of assets	$77.1	
Book amount of liabilities	66.9	
Book value of equity	$10.2	
Adjustments to comply with U.S. accounting:		
Write-downs of assets	−3.5	
	$ 6.7	
Reduction of reserves	+6.5	
Adjusted equity	$13.2	
Portion acquired	100%	
Purchased equity	$13.2	
Purchase price	13.7	$13.7
Goodwill	$ 0.5	
Additional capital infusion		19.6
Total investment[11]		$33.3

Exhibit 14-19 presents summary financial data on BNLA, including forecasts. For 1985, production of new life policies was 40 percent below forecast. Operating expenses were 50 percent higher than forecast and about 50 percent higher than the industry norms for a firm at this stage of development. This is fairly consistent with expense levels of previous years.

THE ACQUISITION

During the time when Citicorp U.K. was actively seeking an insurance company to acquire, Bob Selander was the new country manager of Citicorp's U.K. business. The acquisition of an insurance company was a part of the strategic plan

---

[11]Investment was made in pounds sterling and was fully hedged via the forward market.

Exhibit 14-21 **Inter-Office Communication, Citibank**

TO:	Office: Kensington	**SUBJECT:**	British National
	Person: Divisional Executive		Life Acquisition
		REFERENCE:	AAA/dcb
FROM:	Office: Hammersmith	**DATE:**	13th August 1985
	Person: U.K. Country Business		
	Managers		

Attached is an MEP covering the proposed acquisition of 100 percent of British National Life Assurance Company Limited (BNLA) for a price not to exceed US$13.7 million. We have also included a $19.6 million capital injection in this MEP as we anticipate this being the incremental requirement under U.K. statutory provisions prior to adequate earnings levels being achieved. Injection of this capital will also improve the companies earnings performance allowing earlier consolidation for tax purposes.

Rationale

Life insurance continues to be viewed as a key element to our Individual Bank strategy in the U.K. Consumers view life insurance not only as protection, but also as a tax planning and investment opportunity. 50 percent of total U.K. consumer savings are invested in insurance company managed funds. In order to meet the full financial needs of the U.K. consumer, we must offer life insurance related services. In order to do so, we filed in 1981 and received U.S. Federal Reserve Board approval in 1984 to sell and underwrite life insurance through our U.K. subsidiaries. To date these have been involved only in the credit life related areas complementary to our Citibank Savings lending activities.

We have been pursuing a full service life insurance sales and underwriting firm to broaden our presence in the U.K. consumer market. Due to extremely high premiums, the acquisition of a large company giving us an immediate and substantial presence has been eliminated as an option. Instead, we have decided to develop our existing insurance operations and look at BNLA as an opportunity to accelerate our de novo expansion. BNLA gives us an existing infrastructure, including systems, investment management, and a direct sales force; a reasonably capable management team and an appropriate product line. Utilizing BNLA and our existing customer base, we anticipate substantial sales/revenue synergies which could not otherwise be realized by a de novo development in less than two years.

Based on our projections, a de novo development of a direct sales insurance business involving the hiring of management, systems and product development and branch/sales force recruitment and training would require 18–24 months and US$3.5 million in expenses before any sales occur. Cumulative, after tax losses through 1990 on a start-up would be US$12.7 million. This compares with the BNLA acquisition cumulative profits of US$4.9 million through 1990.

The success of the acquisition is dependent on our providing BNLA with sales prospects from our existing U.K. customer portfolio. This will enhance sales force performance by increasing new policy sales per salesperson by 50 percent in 1986 and up to 100 percent in 1990. The resultant sales per salesperson in 1990 are expected to be at the level currently achieved by mature direct sales forces in the life insurance industry.

Company Background

The origins of BNLA date back to 1920, but true development started with the relaunch of the company as a direct selling, unit linking life company in January 1983, and today has 34 thousand policyholders with $218 million insurance in force. In 1984 premiums were $4.2 million, generated

Exhibit 14-21   (continued)

through a direct sales force of 247 operating out of 22 branch offices. Its premium income in 1984 was $17.2 million single and $3.2 million regular.

A wholly owned subsidiary of XYZ Corporation [this company's identity is altered to protect confidentiality], the firm is now being sold as part of XYZ's efforts to refocus on its nonfinancial business activities.

Financial Expectations

BNLA presently loses approximately $3.1 million pre-tax due to start-up expenses and the higher costs in the growth phase of a life insurance company. With our purchase of BNLA, the company will be able to offer insurance to the 1 million consumers with whom we have an established relationship in the United Kingdom. We expect this to nearly double sales and lead to a fifth year achievement of our corporate hurdle rates. Cumulative losses prior to break-even in year three will amount to US$4 million. Of the $1.3 million premium, goodwill is anticipated to $.5 million after allowing for a $.8 million adjustment to revalue policyholder liabilities. Details are contained in the attached MEP.

Regulatory and Other Considerations

Any agreement will be subject to U.K./U.S. regulatory approvals where we do not anticipate any objections to the acquisition given the small size and our existing permissions.

The purchase will be subject to our audit and acceptance of:

- BNLA's operating system, controls, and procedures.
- A review of contracts, leases, and other documentation.
- Personnel, legal, and regulatory compliance.
- A review of their investment portfolio.
- The financial statements and tax returns (Peat Marwick will handle).
- Current policyholder portfolio (we will retain an outside actuarial consultant for valuation purposes).

Additionally, we will require management continuity and will negotiate employment contracts with several key managers to ensure continuity after our acquisition.

The company's headquarters are approximately one hour's drive from our Hammersmith offices so I envision no management complications due to location.

The company will initially be managed independently from our other Individual Bank activities focusing on the necessary adjustments to ensure Citicorp standards are met. The building of sales momentum is the next priority with further synergies to be explored at a later date. Given the apparent strength of the BNLA management team, minimal personnel moves into BNLA are anticipated. The existing Managing Director will report to me and I will retain the insurance expertise currently on my staff.

I recommend your approval.

Note: All numbers in this document have been changed for proprietary reasons.

he inherited from his predecessor. Sir William Baltimore had previously developed a list of potential acquisitions for consideration.

The first possibility which came to light was Excelsior Life Assurance—one of the largest life assurance firms in the United Kingdom. Sir William Baltimore had been a director of Excelsior Life Assurance and knew its inner workings very well. Upon his recommendations and with the joint-venture participation of another life assurance firm, an acquisition plan was put together. Late in the process, the joint-venture partner withdrew from the deal, and Citicorp decided that Excelsior Life Assurance was too large to acquire alone. The search was reopened.

After considering several moderately sized firms, it was decided that the good-will portion of the purchase price for a moderately sized firm would never allow such an acquisition to make Citicorp's internal hurdle rates. The search was moved to smaller firms. From a list of 12 life assurance firms, BNLA emerged as the most desirable candidate. Exhibits 14-20 and 14-21 discuss Citicorp's rationale for the acquisition. Not only was BNLA of a size that permitted the acquisition to be managed, but there was fairly little to be paid for the goodwill of the company. In short, the price was right, and the potential was there. Negotiations with EXCO Corporation and with Ernest Smith continued for some time, and finally, the purchase price was agreed upon. Citicorp had its U.K. life assurance company.

Case 15

The Catfish Caper: Economic Development and the State of Mississippi

INTRODUCTION

The slamming door only added emphasis as John O'Shea suddenly realized he had been issued the mandate of his career. Mississippi's new governor had just informed O'Shea, Director of Economic Development, that not only did Mississippi's future hinge on John's work within the next week, but so did John's job. The governor, who had been in office for three months, had advanced general strategic plans for the state as a whole, but was dealing with each major department head individually to solicit detail for that plan. His "dealings" with John had just ended.

In attempting to collect his thoughts and determine how to proceed, John reviewed the governor's comments.

> One hundred and fifty years ago Mississippi was one of the richest states in the nation. Since 1929, many of the structural changes in American society and industrial organizations have bypassed us. Now the state is engaged in the process of catching up. Our

This case was prepared by Patrick A. Taylor, Shirley F. Olson, and Raymond A. Phelps, III, Millsaps College, as a basis for class discussion rather than to illustrate either effective or ineffective handling of an administrative situation. Used by permission from Patrick A. Taylor.

leaders are committed to advancing the state economically. Broad-based, grassroots support for development initiative definitely exists.

We've got five programs with the expressed purpose of fostering economic development here. So that you are not working in isolation, look over the various development agencies and their budgets, including your department's, as of late 1985.

With that the governor had handed him a brief summary (Exhibit 15-1). After giving O'Shea a chance to review the information, the governor continued:

Our efforts have yet to pay significant dividends, however. Mississippi's labor force is still largely unskilled and low paid. Average agricultural wages in Mississippi were $9,613 annually in 1984 compared to the state's all-industry average of $14,121.[1] As of late 1985 personal income in Mississippi stood at about $24 billion, allocated among the approximately 2.6 million residents of the state. And, despite the fact that a consultant from Alexander Grant and Company had rated Mississippi's industrial climate among the top ten in the nation for six consecutive years,[2] the message did not seem to be reaching the ears of industry. As one state legislator told me, the development program notwithstanding, "There doesn't seem to be a rudder on the boat."[3] And the irony, John, is that he (the legislator) was right.

The governor continued by reminding O'Shea that Mississippi finds itself trapped in a vicious cycle of circumstances which are keeping down incomes and standards of living among the state's residents. The tax base is small because the population is small and incomes are low. A small and comparatively poor popula-

---

Exhibit 15-1   **Mississippi Development Programs (In millions)**

Department	Budget
Department of Economic Development	$ 6.3
Research and Development Center	5.3
Department of Agriculture and Commerce	17
Federal/State Programs	157[a]
Institute for Technology Development	36[b]

[a]$154 million from federal grants to the state.

[b]$20 million are federal funds.

Source: Clarion Ledger, December 13, 1985.

---

[1]*Mississippi Statistical Abstract,* 1985, College of Business and Industry, Mississippi State University, December, 1985.

[2]"Problems, Image, Make State Hard to Sell," *Clarion Ledger,* December 13, 1985, pp. 1A, 6A.

[3]Ibid.

tion means the state has limited ability to raise revenue through taxes. As of the middle of 1986, sales tax collections amounted to only about $240 million for the state treasury.[4] In turn, low tax revenues mean few public services—especially education. Substandard education virtually assures that levels of skill and incomes of much of the state's populace will remain at or near the bottom among the states. The governor then told John, "The goal of those like yourself charged with planning for economic development in Mississippi is nothing less than breaking the grip of this unhappy chain of events. One of the other agency heads recently summed it up this way—'We're being left in the dust and we need to know why.'"[5]

The governor then continued, saying:

> Given our will to progress, there remains the crucial issue of how and where to look for growth. I've proposed to the legislature a general strategy for the state's development. What I want from you is a *detailed* review of the catfish industry so we can determine if it can play a role in that development. You know I personally favor this industry and believe it has so much potential for the state. But before I can take this to the legislature I need specifics of the industry: its strengths, weaknesses, opportunities, threats; where Mississippi now stands in production; an overview of the industry structure; details on the farming itself, as well as processing, marketing, and distribution. I want a report prepared for both the legislature and me to educate us on the industry and to help us determine what needs to be done to get this industry moving.

With that the governor walked away, and the next sound was the slamming of the door.

Having been the head of economic development during several administrations John knew he had been given an order, and his report had better be accurate. He immediately set out to prepare that report for presentation to the governor and the legislature.

"I better start with an overview of the state's economy and catfish production," he thought.

MISSISSIPPI—LEADING PRODUCER OF CATFISH

The state of Mississippi and the catfish industry are very important to each other. Mississippi ranks at or near the bottom of the fifty states in most measures of economic activity. But the state is the leading producer, by a wide margin, of farm-raised catfish. Mississippi annually supplies about 90 percent of the total U.S. catfish crop and has nearly 70 percent of the nation's total acreage devoted to catfish farming. Catfish farming and related occupations account for about 3,000 jobs in Mississippi with an annual payroll of some $30 million. All together the catfish industry is worth about $125 million annually to the economy of Mississippi.[6] Exhibit 15-2 makes clear Mississippi's prominence in the market.

---

[4]Mississippi State Tax Commission.

[5]"Problems, Image, p. 1A.

[6]"Catfish Industry Seeking Markets," *Clarion Ledger,* September 9, 1984, pp. 1I–2I.

Exhibit 15-2   Acreage in Catfish Ponds

State	Acres	% of Total
Mississippi	65,000	69.9
Alabama	12,000	12.9
Arkansas	9,000	9.7
All others	7,000	7.5
Total	93,000	100.0

Source: *Clarion Ledger,* September 9, 1984.

Although catfish farming is conducted in many of Mississippi's 82 counties, only about 10 percent of the state's total catfish production is raised outside of a few west-central counties (mostly Humphreys and Sharkey counties) in what is known as the Delta. Exhibit 15-3 shows the distribution of acreage in catfish production throughout the state as of 1980. The Delta is fertile, flat land lying along the Mississippi River (the shaded area on the map in Exhibit 15-3). It is also the area of the state where a large share of other agriculture is conducted. Cotton, soybeans, and rice are common Delta crops. Since catfish farms are concentrated in the Delta, processors are located there as well. For instance, Delta Catfish Processors, Inc., the largest U.S. catfish processor, is located in the Sunflower County town of Indianola. The firm's 1986 sales were about $75 million.[7]

With that phase of the report completed, John turned to the structure of the catfish industry.

STRUCTURE OF THE INDUSTRY IN MISSISSIPPI

The structure of Mississippi's catfish industry has several facets. At the farming level the industry is atomistic. There are about 400 firms or individuals raising catfish in the state. The number of growers at any point in time is difficult to determine with complete accuracy, due to differing crop rotation strategies and market conditions. It is an easier matter to identify the number of processors doing business in Mississippi.

At the processing stage the industry becomes much more highly concentrated. Though eight firms process catfish in the state, four firms account for 85 to 90 percent of production. Two of the eight, Country Skillet Company and Farm Fresh Catfish Company, are owned by very large, nationally known firms, respectively, Con-Agra, Inc. and George A. Hormel and Company. Exhibit 15-4 lists Mississippi's processors.

Analysts have estimated that catfish processors in Mississippi reached capacity

[7]"Catfish Firm Pride of the Delta," *Clarion Ledger,* December 22, 1985, pp. 1G, 7G.

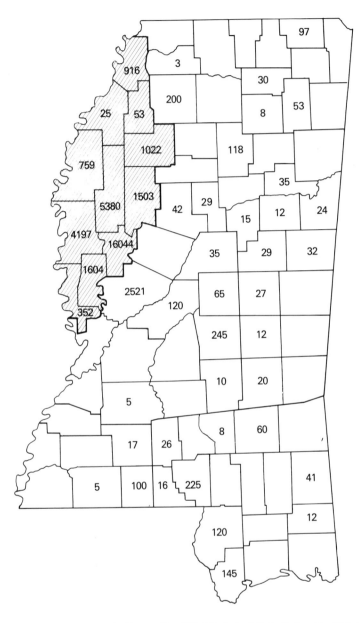

Source: Agricultural Economics Report No. 129, Mississippi State University, October, 1981.

Exhibit 15-3   **Distribution of Catfish Pond Acreage by County, 1980**

Exhibit 15-4   Processors in Mississippi

Firm	Owners	Workers
Delta Catfish Processors, Indianola, Miss.	Co-op	1050
Farm Fresh Catfish, Hollandale, Miss.	Hormel	450
Country Skillet Catfish, Isola, Miss.	Con-Agra	350
Grain Feed Fish, Itta Bena, Miss.	Partnership	420
Agriculture Products, Greenwood, Miss.	Private	87
Simmons Farm-Raised Catfish, Yazoo City, Miss.	Private	75
Magnolia Processors, Tunica, Miss.	Private	50
Humphreys County Processors, Belzoni, Miss.	Private	50

Source: Jackson *Journal of Business,* May/June 1986.

---

some time in 1986. The break-even point for catfish processors is around 60 percent of capacity.[8] Exhibit 15-5 presents some recent production and price data for the state of Mississippi. The prices noted are largely determined by market conditions despite the high level of concentration at the processing stage.

It is important to note that value added at the processing stage is large relative to the pond-side price of live fish. This, together with the fact that production costs are higher than processing costs, provides catfish farmers with an important incentive to expand forward into processing. In fact, this has already occurred in one instance in Mississippi when a coalition of catfish farmers established on a cooperative basis a processing firm, Delta Catfish Processors, Inc.

Exhibit 15-5   Catfish Production in Mississippi

Year	Average Pond Price/lb	Average Plant Price/lb	Value Added	Processed Weight (× 1000 lb)
1979	$0.61	$1.45	$0.84	24,330
1980	0.68	1.66	0.98	27,761
1981	0.64	1.68	1.04	35,137
1982	0.55	1.51	0.96	57,959
1983	0.61	1.45	0.84	72,463
1984	0.69	1.60	0.91	154,255
1985	0.73	1.65	0.92	191,930
1986	0.72	1.64	0.92	219,471[a]

[a]Estimated from part year data.

Source: USDA Crop Reporting Board.

---

[8]Booz, Allen, & Hamilton, "Report to Catfish Farmers of America," January 7, 1984.

Realizing that the governor and members of the legislature were probably not familiar with the details of catfish farming, O'Shea decided that he better provide some background in this area.

SPECIFICS OF CATFISH FARMING

Aquaculture, as its name implies, is an alternative to agriculture. In fact the USDA and the Mississippi State Extension Service publish pond design plans which allow catfish and row crops to be raised on the same land on a rotational basis. All that is required to transform a conventional farm into a catfish farm is a source of adequate supplies of clean water and the construction of levees to subdivide acreage into manageably sized ponds. Twenty-acre ponds are about the right size for efficient tending and harvesting when those tasks are balanced against construction costs.

In 1982, researchers at Mississippi State University (M.S.U.) estimated some of the cost factors involved in catfish farming.[9] Exclusive of land costs, which would be about $1500 per acre and interest rates were about 12 percent, pond construction and equipment acquisition costs were found to be in the range of $3,000 to $3,500 per acre. Operating costs were found to be in the neighborhood of $2,200 per acre, about one-half of which is feed cost. (Only two feed suppliers are located within the state of Mississippi.) The university researchers discovered that direct labor costs could be expected to be in the range of $135 to $180 per acre. These costs amount to roughly $0.60 per pound of live fish harvested. Costs, of course, were lower for larger farms. Including land costs, someone interested in going into the catfish farming business may expect to spend about $1 million for every 300 acres to be cultivated.[10] Furthermore, the M.S.U. analysis supported the fact that moderate economies of scale and learning curve effects apply to catfish farming.

The existence of levees, of course, is the major distinction between acreage used for catfish farming and land cultivated for conventional crops. Because they must be substantial enough both to hold water and support vehicle-mounted harvesting and tending equipment, levees must be fairly large. Across its base, a typical levee might be 55 to 60 feet depending on the slope of the bank. Access ways on levee tops will be about 18 feet wide. In addition to ponds and levees, provisions must also be made for filling and draining ponds. This requires that a system of ditches and piping be installed. So although the floor of a drained pond may be used to raise row crops, the system of levees and related construction diminishes the effective area available for crop rotation. Exhibit 15-6 provides a diagram of a typical levee system for one pond.

Once the farm has been prepared and stocked with fingerling fish of about one ounce in weight, it takes between 12 and 24 months for most fish to reach the

---

[9]Mississippi State University, Agricultural Economics Research Report No. 134, June, 1982.

[10]"Swimming Uncharted Waters," Jackson *Journal of Business,* May/June, 1986, pp. 14–24.

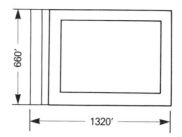

Specifications for a 20 land acre pond

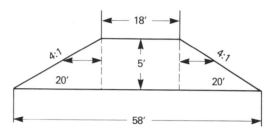

Specification for an "inside" levee

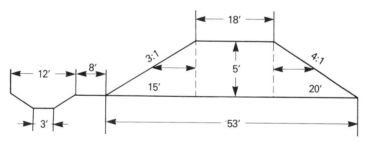

Specification for an "outside" levee, berm, and ditch

Source: "Mississippi Farm Raised Catfish," Agricultural Economics Research Report, No. 134, Mississippi State University, June 1982.

Exhibit 15-6   **Typical 20-Acre Pond Design in the Mississippi Delta, 1982**

typical harvesting size of 1¼ to 2 pounds live weight. Catfish are very efficient weight gainers, which accounts in large part for their increasing popularity as a cash crop. The average catfish weighing from 1 oz. to about 3 pounds can convert feed to body weight at the rate of 1.7:1. By comparison, conversion ratios for chicken, cattle, and pork are 2:1, 7.5:1 and 4.5:1, respectively. Large fish are unable to match the conversion rate of smaller fish, however, helping to account for usual harvest weights of under two pounds.

The primary criterion for harvesting is not weight but taste. As fish begin to reach about 2 pounds in weight, samples are taken from each pond and prepared to be eaten on-the-spot by an experienced taster. The taster evaluates the taste and texture of the samples. Tasters look for a mild, almost bland, distinctly not "fishy" taste and firm texture. If the taster determines the fish to be "on flavor," harvesting of appropriately sized fish begins at once. In the event sampled fish are found to be "off flavor," some minor adjustments may be made in water chemistry and feed composition. After a few days the pond content is again sampled. Normally, fish can be brought back "on flavor" in a short time by making a few small adjustments in food and water conditions. But there is some chance that most or all of the fish in a particular pond may never be acceptable.

When the pond is ready, harvesting may be done by the farmer, the processor, or a contract custom harvester. In any case, it costs about $.03 per pound to harvest catfish. Harvesting is accomplished by corralling the fish in a small area of the pond, using power driven seining nets. Once collected, the fish are dipped out of the pond using a truck-mounted basket with mesh openings too small to allow harvesting-size fish to escape. Fish smaller than desired fall back into the pond and are allowed to grow larger. Harvested fish are loaded on tank trucks which transport them live to processing plants. Currently the average acre in catfish farming produced between 3,000 and 5,000 pounds of live fish per year. Says one farmer, "We'll harvest 10,000 pounds to the acre once we get a handle on the disease and flavor problems and we're closing in on both of 'em." With careful management fish can be harvested year-round, providing an even supply throughout the year.

With a summary of the farming itself completed, the Economic Development Director still realized several areas were missing in his report. One of the most important was a description of catfish processing.

Catfish Processing

Normally processing of live fish into various food products is done by separate processing firms located near the catfish farms. It is unusual for a processor to transport fish more than 60 miles—20 is more common with some hauls as short as a matter of yards. Depending on the distance from pond to plant, as little as one hour may separate swimming fish from ready-to-ship products, so processing time is very short.

In the span of an hour or two, processors can transform 4,000 to 5,000 pounds of live fish into fresh and frozen ready-to-sell products. Catfish yield a rather high percentage of useful product to waste, or offal, as remains are called. Depending to some extent on the exact mix of end products, catfish can yield between 40 and 60 percent of their live weights in salable products. Offal is sometimes used in the making of livestock and other feeds; otherwise it is simply waste. Exhibit 15-7 displays useful yields by product.

The product mix currently available includes both traditional and newly developed items. The familiar products include fillets, whole, bone-in fish, steaks, strips,

---

Exhibit 15-7   **Salable Product Yields**

Product	% Useful
Steaks	58
Fillets	40
Whole dressed fish	58

Source: Mississippi Cooperative Extension Service, December 1984, pp. 18–22.

---

and nuggets. Nuggets are made of gleanings from bones and belly flaps which otherwise would be wasted. Potential new products include wieners and sausage made from catfish. These items require processing beyond what is needed to produce the more common cuts, of course, but due to the natural mildness of catfish, it is highly versatile and amenable to seasoning. By far the largest fraction, about 70 percent, of end product is in the form of fillets.

Having reviewed where Mississippi stands in catfish production, the industry structure, details of aquafarming, and processing, O'Shea realized no report would be complete without information on the distribution of the fish. He and his research assistant reviewed the details accordingly.

Distribution

Catfish products may be shipped to any one of several users in either fresh, ice-packed, or frozen form. The product mix between fish shipped frozen and fish packed in ice is about evenly divided. Processors ship to retailers, wholesalers, and other processors who make specialty products such as complete catfish dinners in frozen form. At the present time about one-third of the poundage processors turn out is allocated to each of the three channels of distribution. Most of the product shipped to downstream processors is frozen, whereas most of that shipped to retailers is fresh. A majority of those who process further are fast-food and other type restaurants. In fact, recent purchases by Church's fried chicken chain took a quarter of the crop raised in Mississippi and accounted for an increase in the pond-side price of from $.50 to $.80 per pound, according to one analyst.[11]

Sales to Church's alone in 1985 amounted to about 42 million pounds of processed catfish. Church's is not the only restaurant chain which is in the process of adding catfish dishes to the menu. Aside from many local chains or single unit restaurants, Red Lobster and Long John Silver's are both beginning to serve catfish. All of these outlets are considered to be further processors because they conduct additional transformation before selling catfish at retail.

---

[11]"Catfish Demand Explodes Since Fillets Reached Church's Fried Chicken Menu," *The Wall Street Journal,* July 8, 1985, p. 22.

In mid-1986, however, Church's encountered a problem with the way it stores cooked fish before serving it. Some of Church's fried products are stored under heat lamps to keep the food at an acceptable temperature for a short while before it is sold. But the breading Church's used in preparing catfish coatings became slightly soggy when exposed to the lamps. Though this did not involve the fish itself and posed no health hazard, it was unacceptable to Church's as a matter of quality control. They want a "crunchiness" to their catfish. As a result Church's has removed all catfish items from their menus until the problem can be corrected.

Church's feels they will be able to develop a coating which remains crisp under the lamps and is now working on the problem in their laboratories. One industry consultant says, "I expect Church's to solve the coating problems within nine months. But if they don't . . ." Until a new process is available Church's will not buy any more of the catfish crop. Losing Church's business even temporarily will depress the entire industry because of the size of Church's orders. But there is no reason to believe Church's problems will dampen other restaurants' and fast-food chains' enthusiasm for catfish. A marketing professor who consults with those in the industry noted that Church's difficulties with catfish are related to their particular coating, storage techniques, and texture requirements. Other servers do not seem to have encountered such problems with their preparations.

Although the state might be the top producer and processor, the issue of marketing still remained to be considered. This is where John personally saw the biggest void, and he gave it full attention.

Marketing Catfish

Catfish require a substantial marketing effort because most consumers think of catfish as bottom-dwelling scavengers unfit for human consumption. But, as noted earlier, fish farmers train their fish to feed from the top of ponds by distributing feed which floats rather than sinks to the pond's bottom. Although this process produces a fish that is both good-tasting and healthful, getting this message to consumers is the first task of those involved in the marketing of catfish.

Despite some sporadic efforts by catfish producers to promote their "crop," evidence suggests that these efforts are not reaching a very large number of potential catfish consumers. In fact, a limited survey by agricultural economists at M.S.U. reveals that perhaps as many as three of four consumers are unaware of the availability of catfish. The same survey, based on a taste test, indicated that about 95 percent of those tasting catfish would be willing to buy regularly if it were available in their area. So there are two related, major consumer characteristics impeding the expansion of catfish production: the widespread ignorance of how good catfish tastes and its value as a source of flesh protein.

Recently there has been a realignment of marketing duties among two industry organizations representing catfish growers and processors. This reshuffling of responsibilities appears to have been the solution to some intraindustry power struggles. The result is a new trade association, the American Catfish Institute, which is charged with the responsibility of conducting a marketing program aimed particularly at parts of the country where catfish consumption is very low. Initial plans call for spending approximately $2 million per year on the campaign. The function of the old organization, Catfish Farmers of America, will be largely educational. Its primary tasks are to be staging cooking contests featuring catfish dishes, putting on exhibitions at trade shows, and lobbying activities.[12] Many consumers see catfish as a commodity or generic product just as most other agricultural products are seen. So at least part of the thrust of future marketing programs will be to elevate catfish from commodity status. One industry observer underscores the importance of building a solid marketing program by saying: "With catfish production expected to double in the near future, the marketing push is considered essential to prevent a collapse in the price of catfish. . . ." An executive in the industry echoes the need for a cohesive marketing plan when he says such a plan ". . . is crucial because the industry is production and supply driven rather than marketing driven."[13]

Although modest attempts have been made to market catfish abroad, the efforts so far have met with little success. In the case of exporting to Japan, a country where fish is a dietary staple, a straightforward translation of the word catfish into Japanese causes problems. The term originally used for catfish apparently conjured up in the Japanese some images incompatible with something good to eat. In particular, a mythical monster in Japanese folk lore bears an unfortunate resemblance to the catfish. To circumvent this sort of problem, early plans are to market the product as American whitefish rather than catfish. In any case there appears to be substantial room for development in the area of export markets for catfish.

One knowledgeable banker who keeps abreast of developments in the industry observes:

> The outlook for the farm-raised catfish industry remains bright. The supply has been increasing nationwide 20 to 30 percent a year for the past few years without creating any long-term surpluses. While prices to the farmer and producers are down, total sales continue to increase. All things considered, the growth pattern which has been experienced is likely to continue.[14]

In considering the governor's mandate, the Director knew one facet of the industry was still missing from his report. Namely, what were the difficulties encountered?

Production Problems

Despite all the positives, several threats to catfish crops require constant monitoring and management, just as with conventional crops. Weather is a critical, but largely uncontrollable, factor in raising catfish commercially. Excessive rain, heat,

[12]"Coup Marks a Shift in Delta Catfish Industry," *Clarion Ledger,* August 3, 1986, p. 3G.
[13]"Swimming Uncharted Waters," p. 24.
[14]Deposit Guaranty National Bank, 1986.

and cold are especially troublesome to aquaculturalists. Aside from weather, the two most serious threats to a catfish crop are poor water quality and disease. The most important characteristic of water for fish farmers is its oxygen content. As a result, all ponds must be accessible to aeration (oxygen enhancing) equipment. Monitoring oxygen content is virtually an hour-by-hour job, particularly in very hot weather.

Ponds must be sufficiently oxygen-rich to support fish life and to prevent disease. Although disease can be present even if ponds are properly aerated, fish are more susceptible to disease in oxygen-deficient water. An infestation of any fish-borne disease can easily wipe out an entire pond's population of fish. With the cooperation of the Schools of Agriculture and Veterinary Medicine at M.S.U., programs for effective disease prevention and treatment have been developed. Modern pond management has drastically improved the chances of bringing to harvest a large fraction of the original number of fingerlings stocked. Under normal circumstances the mortality rate among fish in well-tended ponds can be held to around 10 percent.

The industry faces three other problems which are economical rather than natural. First, catfish farming uses the same resources as does conventional agriculture. Second, the domestic catfish industry faces competition from imported catfish. In 1985 about 7 million pounds of catfish were imported into the United States. The third economic problem is the status of catfish as a "down-scale" or inferior product (in the sense that consumers tend to buy less of it as their incomes rise).

Before completing the report, O'Shea suddenly realized he had not included the role of fish in the country's diet. His next task was to review that.

FISH IN THE AMERICAN DIET

The per person consumption of fish products has been very stable over the period from 1976 to the present. During that time the average American ate between 12.7 and 13.6 pounds of fish yearly, compared to the decline in red meat consumption from 153 pounds in 1976 to 143.7 pounds in 1984.[15] The beneficiary of that decline does not appear to have been fish, however. Fish's share of flesh protein consumption has remained fairly stable at about 7 percent for the last ten years.[16] That share amounts to annual per capita consumption of 1.33 to 2 pounds of fish per year. Catfish currently accounts for only about one-third pound of the annual per person consumption of whitefish in the United States. Increasing by just one ounce the amount of catfish eaten by the average American would generate demand for an added 14 million pounds of catfish yearly. As recently as 1970, catfish accounted for only 3.6 million pounds of total retail fish sales. In 1985, total production of catfish was 185 million pounds with a retail value of $250 million. Experts expect total production to top 200 million pounds by 1990.[17] Such phenomenal

[15] *Agricultural Statistics* 1985, USDA, 1985.
[16] Booz, Allen & Hamilton.
[17] Ibid.

growth suggests that catfish is overcoming one big hurdle on the road to respectability as a food—the general image of catfish as a bottom-dwelling scavenger unsuitable for human consumption appears to be diminishing. Catfish farmers specifically use feeding methods that train their fish to feed from the tops of carefully tended ponds. The result is a perfectly acceptable food fish which shares very little with its cousin living in the wild.

ECONOMIC DEVELOPMENT OF MISSISSIPPI

O'Shea finished his task, and within 48 hours the governor called for him to present the report to the legislature. At the completion of that presentation, the governor spoke:

> Ladies and Gentlemen—members of the House and Senate. As of 1983, the latest year for which complete data are available, Mississippi's per capita annual income was $8,072. Of the fifty states, the next lowest income per person was the $8,937 earned by the average West Virginian. The U.S. average annual income is $25,200. Despite our generally poor economic performance, Mississippi is not without enclaves of vital economic activity aside from its well-known agricultural base. For example, the Gulf Coast area of the state has extensive tourism, and the area is also a major benefactor of national defense expenditures. Mississippi's economic activity in 1984 generated gross state product (GSP) of $24.185 billion and in 1985, $25.479 billion. Estimates for GSP in 1986 are in the neighborhood of $27 billion.
>
> Whereas agriculture is by comparison a low value-added endeavor, Mississippi has some industry which boasts higher added values and incomes. There are five military bases in the state. Pascagoula has Ingalls Shipbuilding, a division of Litton Industries. Ingalls builds state-of-the-art warships such as the U.S.S. *Yorktown.* Partly because of the existence of the shipyard at Pascagoula, and partly because of the position of former Senator John Stennis (an influential member and former chairman of the Senate Armed Service Committee), Mississippi is in the running to become home port to segments of a naval task force being formed around the U.S.S. *Iowa,* which was refitted at Ingalls. In fact, total federal spending in the Pascagoula MSA is over $15,000 per person, highest of any MSA in the nation. Lockheed-Georgia has a similar operation at Meridian near a naval air station there. Under contract to the Defense Department, the firm refurbishes aircraft already in service. Another arm of the federal government, NASA, has a rocket engine test facility near Bay St. Louis on Mississippi's coast. Workers at the facilities earn well above the statewide average, if not above the national average. They also possess higher skill levels than does the average Mississippian. Although not selected as the site for the proposed semiconducting supercollider, the state was one of the finalists in the competition for that project.
>
> In addition to U.S. government sponsored employment, the state has some important, private, higher skilled, and higher value-added industry. Furniture manufacturing is important to Mississippi, particularly in the northeastern section of the state near Tupelo. In fact, Mississippi ranks second only to North Carolina in the making of furniture. Although not selected, one locale in the state was a finalist in a recent site selection competition for a Toyota assembly plan. The state was also reported to have had at least an outside chance to get the new GM Saturn plant that was ultimately located in

our neighboring state of Tennessee. The upshot of that could very well be the locating of some GM suppliers in Mississippi near the Saturn facility. GM's Packard Division already has one wiring harness plant in Canton, Mississippi.

Two industries within the state have already reached at least moderate levels of development, both of which may hold some promise for future advancement. The first of these is the tourism industry which has been a consistent provider of income for the state. Recently enhanced promotional campaigns are intended to attract visitors not only to traditional tourist destinations along the Gulf Coast but also the state's other areas of interest as well. We do have 27 state park areas which are promoted. The other area is banking and finance. As is often the case with developing regions, the capitol here in Jackson is the financial center for our state. With its already developed financial institutions, the state may be able to take advantage of the rapidly changing and growing financial network.

Despite all these factors, we still occupy the bottom rung of the economic ladder. Among candidates for providing an answer, the catfish industry seems to hold some promise. I want every member of the legislature to commit yourselves to reviewing its potential. Mississippi, as the leading grower and producer of catfish, has an opportunity to make inroads into its comparatively deficient income levels by furthering the development of this industry. I want each body—House and Senate—to set up a ten-member task force to study this industry and propose specifically what we can do to make sure it achieves its fullest potential.

The governor then posed to the legislature several questions concerning the state's future direction and the role catfish might play in that future.

The task force should consider, but not be limited to, the following:

1. Assess the perceived strengths and weaknesses and opportunities and threats for the advancement of economic development in Mississippi through catfish production.
2. From the perspective of producers, what do you see as threats and opportunities?
3. What are your suggestions for a strategy assuming that the catfish industry fits into the overall economic development program for the state?
4. Do we need to spend more money educating the state's farmers on growing catfish?
5. Should we be doing more to promote consumption of this fish?
6. If catfish is not really the best crop for Mississippi, what should we be doing to advance the economic development of the state?

He closed by saying, "While these are certainly not mutually exclusive, they give you some idea of the direction needed. I'd like results from your respective task forces in one month. Before we adjourn, let me take this opportunity to thank Mr. O'Shea and his staff for a good job."

Only then did the Director breathe a slight sigh of relief. Yet he knew the really tough task lay ahead—a task whose outcome could help determine the fate of the state and possibly his own.

K mart Corporation: Corporate Strategy at the Crossroads

In 1988, K mart, Inc. included discount department stores, variety stores, restaurants, financial services, home improvement centers, and specialty shops in the United States and several foreign countries, including Canada, Australia, China, and Puerto Rico. Measured in sales volume it was the second largest retailer and the largest discount department store chain in the United States.

By the mid 1980s, the discount department store industry was perceived to have reached maturity. In 1985, K mart, as part of that industry, had a retail management strategy that was developed in the late 1950s. The firm was at the crossroads in terms of corporate strategy. The problem was what to do during the next twenty years. Exhibits 16-1, 16-2, and 16-3 illustrate K mart's financial performance.

THE EARLY YEARS

K mart was the outgrowth of an organization founded in 1899 in Detroit by Sebastian S. Kresge. The first S.S. Kresge store represented a new type of retailing that featured low-priced merchandise for cash in low-budget, relatively small (4,000–6,000 sq. ft.) buildings with sparse furnishings. The adoption of the "5¢ and 10¢" or "variety store" concept, pioneered by F.W. Woolworth Company in 1879, led to rapid and profitable development of the then S.S. Kresge Company.

Kresge believed it could substantially increase its retail business through centralized buying and control, by developing standardized store operating procedures, and by expanding with new stores in heavy traffic areas. In 1917, the firm was incorporated. It had 150 stores and, next to Woolworth's, was the largest variety chain in the world. Over the next forty years, the firm experimented with mail order catalogues, full-line department stores, self-service, a variety of price lines, and the opening of stores in planned shopping centers.

By 1957, corporate management became aware that the development of supermarkets and the expansion of drug store chains into general merchandise lines had made inroads into market categories previously dominated by variety stores. It also became clear that a new form of store with a discount merchandising strategy was emerging.

This case was prepared by James W. Camerius, Northern Michigan University, as a basis for class discussion rather than to illustrate either effective or ineffective handling of an administrative situation. Used by permission from James W. Camerius.

Exhibit 16-1   **Financial Performance K mart/S.S. Kresge Company, 1960–1986**
                 (In thousands)

Year	Sales	Assets	Net Income[a]	Net Worth
1960	418,200	269,343	11,120	205,757
1961	432,838	274,293	8,863	205,791
1962	452,561	281,897	9,014	205,493
1963	510,531	315,265	10,278	209,109
1964	692,499	344,272	17,150	212,700
1965	862,441	394,015	23,470.	229,597
1966	1,102,688	442,740	28,609	251,803
1967	1,401,168	525,536	34,915	275,632
1968	1,757,750	657,825	47,611	319,450
1969	2,185,298	797,526	54,089	367,519
1970	2,595,155	926,227	66,994	456,761
1971	3,139,653	1,095,948	96,116	548,469
1972	3,875,183	1,383,439	114,674	779,726
1973	4,702,504	1,652,773	138,251	924,512
1974	5,612,071	1,896,110	104,772	1,016,600
1975	6,883,613	2,377,541	200,832	1,197,825
1976	8,483,603	2,865,572	266,574	1,441,793
1977	10,064,457	3,428,110	302,919	1,687,817
1978	11,812,810	4,836,260	343,706	1,915,666
1979	12,858,585	5,642,439	357,999	2,185,192
1980	14,204,381	6,102,462	260,527	2,343,172
1981	16,527,012	6,673,004	220,251	2,455,594
1982	16,772,166	7,343,665	261,821	2,601,272
1983	18,597,900	8,183,100	492,300	2,940,100
1984	20,762,000	9,262,000	503,000	3,234,000
1985	22,035,000	9,991,000	472,000	3,273,000
1986	23,812,000	10,578,000	570,000	3,939,000

[a]After taxes and extraordinary credit or charges.

Source: Fortune Financial Analysis and Annual Reports.

The Cunningham Connection

In an effort to regain its competitiveness and possibly save the company, Frank Williams, then President of the S.S. Kresge Company, nominated Harry B. Cunningham as General Vice-President in 1957. This maneuver was undertaken to free Mr. Cunningham, who had worked his way up the ranks in the organization, from operating responsibility. He was being groomed for the presidency and was given the assignment to study existing retailing business and recommend marketing changes.

In his visits to Kresge stores, and those of the competition, Cunningham became interested in discounting—particularly a new operation in Garden City, Long Island. Eugene Ferkauf had recently opened large discount department stores called

Exhibit 16-2   **K mart Corporation Consolidated Statements of Income (In millions)**

	Fiscal Year Ended		
	January 29, 1986	January 28, 1987	January 27, 1988
Sales	$22,035	$23,812	$25,627
Licensee fees and rental income	223	234	237
Equity in income of affiliated retail companies	76	83	92
Interest income	23	23	22
	22,357	24,152	25,978
Cost of merchandise sold (including buying and occupancy costs)	15,987	17,258	18,564
Selling, general and administrative expenses	4,673	4,936	5,296
Advertising	554	581	617
Interest expense:			
Debt	205	171	156
Capital lease obligations	181	178	174
	21,600	23,124	24,807
Income from continuing retail operations before income taxes	757	1,028	1,171
Income taxes	181	458	479
Income from continuing retail operations	472	570	692
Discontinued operations	(251)	28	—
Extraordinary item	—	(16)	—
Net income	$ 221	$ 582	$ 692
Earnings per common and common equivalent share:			
Continuing retail operations	$ 2.42	$ 2.84	$ 3.40
Discontinued operations	(1.27)	.14	—
Extraordinary item	—	(.08)	—
Net income	$ 1.15	$ 2.90	$ 3.40
Weighted average shares	197.4	201.5	203.5

Source: K mart *Annual Report,* 1987.

Exhibit 16-3   **K mart Corporation Consolidated Balance Sheets (In millions)**

	January 28, 1987	January 27, 1988
Assets		
Current Assets		
Cash (includes temporary investments of $134 and $296, respectively)	$ 521	$ 449
Merchandise inventories	5,153	5,571
Accounts receivable and other current assets	390	353
Total Current Assets	6,064	6,373
Investments in Affiliated Retail Companies	317	379
Property and equipment—net	3,594	3,744
Other assets and deferred charges	603	610
	$10,578	$11,106
Liabilities and Shareholders' Equity		
Current Liabilities		
Long-term debt due within one year	$ 4	$ 2
Notes payable	296	—
Accounts payable—trade	2,207	2,309
Accrued payrolls and other liabilities	639	606
Taxes other than income taxes	223	242
Income taxes	162	211
Total Current Liabilities	3,531	3,370
Capital lease obligations	1,600	1,557
Long-term debt	1,011	1,191
Other long-term liabilities	315	379
Deferred income taxes	182	200
Shareholders' Equity	3,939	4,409
	$10,578	$11,106

E.J. Korvette. They had a discount mass-merchandising emphasis that featured low prices and margins, high turnover, large free-standing departmentalized units, ample parking space, and a location typically in the suburbs.

Cunningham was impressed with the discount concept, but he knew he had to first convince the Board, whose support would be necessary for any new strategy to succeed. He studied the company for two years and presented it with the following recommendation:

> We can't beat the discounters operating under the physical constraints and the self-imposed merchandise limitations of variety stores. We can join them—and not only join them, but with our people, procedures, and organization, we can become a leader in the discount industry.

In a speech delivered at the University of Michigan, Cunningham made his management approach clear by concluding with an admonition from the British author, Sir Hugh Walpole: "Don't play for safety, it's the most dangerous game in the world."

The Board of Directors had a difficult job. Change is never easy, especially when the company has a proud heritage. Before the first presentation to the Board could be made, rumors were circulating and one shocked senior executive had said:

> We have been in the variety business for 60 years—we know everything there is to know about it, and we're not doing very well in that, and you want to get us into a business we don't know anything about.

The Board of Directors accepted H.B. Cunningham's recommendations. When President Frank Williams retired, Cunningham became the new President and CEO and was directed to proceed with his recommendations.

THE BIRTH OF K MART

Management conceived the original K mart as a conveniently located one-stop shopping unit where customers could buy a wide variety of quality merchandise at discount prices. The typical K mart had 75,000 square feet, all on one floor. It generally stood by itself in a high-traffic, suburban area, with plenty of parking space, and with a floor plan common to other units in the organization.

The firm made an $80 million commitment in leases and merchandise for 33 stores before the first K mart opened in 1962 in Garden City, Michigan. As part of this strategy, management decided to rely on the strengths and abilities of its own people to make decisions rather than employing outside experts for advice.

The original variety store operation was characterized by low gross margins, high turnover, and concentration on return on investment. The main difference in the K mart strategy would be the offering of a much wider merchandise mix.

The company had the knowledge and ability to merchandise 50 percent of the departments in the planned K mart merchandise mix, and contracted for operation of the remaining departments. In the following years, K mart took over most of those departments originally contracted to licensees. Eventually all departments, except shoes, were operated by K mart.

THE MATURATION OF K MART

By the late 1970s, corporate management at K mart considered the discount department store industry to be at a level of maturity. K mart itself was the largest discount department store organization, with 2,100 stores serving 80 percent of the population. The industry was characterized by a reduced number of store openings, reduced expansion of square feet of floor space, and similar product offerings by competitors. Although maturity was sometimes looked on with disfavor, K mart executives felt that this did not mean a lack of profitability or lack of opportunity to increase sales (Exhibit 16-4). The industry was perceived as being "reborn." It was in this context that a series of new marketing programs, designed to upgrade the K mart image, were developed.

By the mid 1980s, the discount department store industry began to undergo a series of fundamental changes. Nearly a dozen firms like E. J. Korvette, W. T. Grant, Arlans, and Atlantic Mills passed into bankruptcy or reorganization. Many regional firms such as Wal-Mart Stores, Target Stores and ShopKo Stores began carrying more fashionable merchandise in more attractive facilities and shifted their emphasis to more national markets. Specialty discounters such as Toys-R-Us were

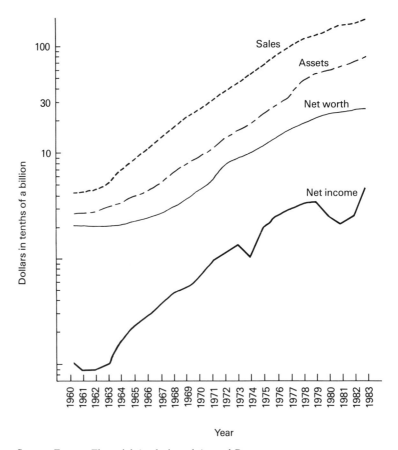

Source: Fortune Financial Analysis and Annual Reports

Exhibit 16-4   **Financial Performance K mart/S.S. Kresge Company 1960–1983**

making big inroads in toys, sporting goods, paint and other lines. The so-called "superstores" of drug and food chains were rapidly discounting more and more general merchandise. The discount divisions of other big retailers, for example, Gold Circle (Federated Department Stores), Calder (Associated Dry Goods), and Venture (May Department Stores) had emerged as well-financed and professionally managed organizations; and some firms like Woolworth (Woolco) withdrew from the field entirely after years of disappointment.

Many retailers such as Target, who adopted the discount concept, attempted to go generally after an upscale customer. The upscale customer tended to have a household income of $25,000 to $44,000 annually. Other "pockets" of population were being served by firms like Zayre, which targeted consumers in the inner city, and Wal-Mart, which served the needs of the more rural consumer in secondary markets. Senior management at K mart felt that all firms in the industry were facing the same situation. They were very successful five or ten years ago but were not changing and, therefore, were becoming somewhat dated. Management that had a historically successful formula, particularly in retailing, was perceived as having difficulty adapting to change, especially at the peak of success. Management would wait too long and then would have to scramble to regain competitiveness. Exhibits 16-5 through 16-8 illustrate K mart's performance compared to major competitors.

K mart executives found that discount department stores were being challenged by several new retail formats. Some retailers were assortment oriented, with a much greater depth of assortment with a given product category. To illustrate, Toys-R-Us was an example of a firm that operated 20,000-square foot toy supermarkets. Toys-R-Us prices were competitive within an industry that was highly competitive. When the consumers entered a Toys-R-Us facility, there was usually no doubt in their minds that if the product was not there, no one else had it.

Other retailers were experimenting with the "off price" apparel concept where name brands and designer goods were sold at 20 to 70 percent discounts; home improvement centers which were warehouse-style stores with a wide range of hardline merchandise for both do-it-yourselfers and professionals; and drug supermar-

Exhibit 16-5   **Performance Comparison K mart vs. Selected Competition, 1980**

	K mart	Sears	Wal-mart	Target	Caldor
Sales ($000)	$14,204,381	$25,194,900	$1,643,199	$1,531,700	$666,530
No. of stores	1,968	856	368	148	75
Sales per sq. ft.	$104	$145	$120	$154	$129
Sales growth	11.6%	2.6%	31.6%	36.7%	18.4%
Gross margin	26.7%	32.1%	21.6%	26.7%	22.2%
Overhead (% of sales)	23.4%	29.9%	15.3% est	20.5%	15.6%

Source: Company records.

Exhibit 16-6   **Financial Comparison Selected General Merchandise Organizations, 1980**

Retail Chain	Sales (In millions)	Earnings (In millions)	Number of Retail Units	Number of Employees	Strategic Thrust
Sears, Roebuck	$16,865	$209,000	854	390,000	Product/fashion leadership
K mart	$14,204	$260,500	1,885	250,000	Price leadership
J.C. Penney	$11,353	$233,000	2,119	190,000	Product/fashion leadership
F.W. Woolworth	$ 7,218	$161,000	6,061	196,527	Conventional mass merchandise
Federated Dept. Stores	$ 6,301	$219,600	358	116,000	Product/fashion leadership
Montgomery Ward	$ 5,500	$(162,000)	866	102,000	Product/fashion leadership
Wal-Mart	$ 1,643	$ 55,682	344	28,000	Price leadership
Zayre	$ 1,594	$ 18,015	531	27,000	Price leadership

Source: "$100 Million Club" © *Chain Store Age Executive,* August 1981, Lebhar-Friedman, Inc., 425 Park Ave., N.Y. 10022, 51–52.

kets which offered a wide variety of high-turnover merchandise in a convenient location.

In these cases, competition was becoming more risk oriented by putting $3 or $4 million in merchandise at retail value in an 80,000-square foot facility and offering genuinely low prices. The F & M stores in the Detroit market, Drug Emporium in the midwest, and a series of independents were examples of organizations using the entirely new concept of the drug supermarket.

Competition was offering something that was new and different in terms of depth of assortment, competitive price image, and format. K mart management perceived this as a threat because they were viable businesses and hindered the firm in its ability to improve and maintain share of market in specific merchandise categories.

Corporate research revealed that on the basis of convenience, K mart served 80 percent of the population. One study concluded that one of every two adults in the United States shopped at a K mart at least once a month. Despite this popular

Exhibit 16-7   **Physical Expansion: Net Square Footage Added Selected General Merchandise Organizations (In thousands)**

	1980	1981
1. K mart	10,200	7,850
2. Wal-Mart	3,000	4,000
3. Sears	2,200	3,300
4. Kroger	2,800	3,200
5. Dayton Hudson	3,388	2,790
6. City Products	2,338	2,500
7. Safeway	2,480	2,600
8. Federated	2,289	2,853
9. J.C. Penney	2,700	2,000
10. Jewel Cos.	1,300	1,800
11. Lucky Stores	2,500	1,526
12. 84 Lumber	1,050	1,500
13. Melville	1,045	1,340
14. Woolworth	2,000	1,300
15. Revco[a]	1,380	1,250
16. May	1,172	1,051
17. Albertson's	719	1,060
18. Rapid American	950	1,000
19. Carter Hawley Hale	1,250	1,000
20. Zayre	0	925
21. Allied Stores	259	823
22. American Stores	1,400	820
23. Winn-Dixie	800	800
24. W.R. Grace & Co.	800	700
24. Montgomery Ward	1,000	700

[a]Fiscal year

Source: Chain data and *Chain Store Age Executive* estimates.

appeal, strategies that had allowed the firm to have something for everybody were no longer felt to be appropriate for the 1990s. K mart found that it had a broad customer base because it operated on a national basis. Its strategies had assumed the firm was serving everyone in the market.

K mart was often perceived as aiming at the low-income consumer. The financial community believed the K mart customer was blue collar, low income, and upper lower class. The market served, however, was more professional and middle class because K mart stores were initially in suburban communities where the growth was occurring.

Although K mart has made a major commitment in more recent years to secondary or rural markets, these were areas that had previously not been cultivated. The firm, in its initial strategies, perceived the rural consumer as different from the

Exhibit 16-8   **Physical Expansion: Capital Expenditures Selected
General Merchandise Organizations (In thousands)**

	1980	1981
1. Safeway	$493,000	$500,000
2. Federated	313,300	450,000
3. Sears	344,000	300,000
4. Dayton Hudson	265,200	300,000
5. Kroger	239,000	275,000
6. J.C. Penney	295,000	250,000
7. K mart	275,000	250,000
8. Woolworth	150,000	240,000
9. May	180,000	200,000
10. Montgomery Ward	229,700	176,000
11. Carter Hawley Hale	150,000	170,000
12. Lucky Stores	147,000	150,000
13. Jewel Cos.	90,000	116,000
14. R. H. Macy	115,900	115,900
15. Allied Stores	60,000	115,000
16. A&P	90,000	110,000
17. City Products	89,600	90,000
18. Winn-Dixie	95,000	85,000
19. Supermarkets General	43,000	78,000
20. Grand Union	53,068	68,600
21. Super Valu	100,000	68,000
22. W. R. Grace	60,000	64,000
23. Wal-Mart	48,900	55,000
24. Melville	58,000	55,000
25. Albertson's	37,227	50,000

Source: Chain data and *Chain Store Age Executive* estimates.

urban or suburban customer. In readdressing the situation, it discovered that its assortments in rural areas were too limited and there were too many preconceived notions regarding what the Nebraska farmer really wanted. The firm discovered that the rural consumer did not always shop for bib overalls and shovels but shopped for microwave ovens and all the things everyone else did.

The goal was not to attract more customers but to get the customer coming in the door to spend more. Once in the store the customer was thought to demonstrate more divergent tastes. The upper income consumer would buy more health and beauty aids, cameras, and sporting goods. The lower income consumer would buy health and beauty aids, toys, and clothing.

In the process of trying to capture a larger share of the market and get people to spend more, the firm began to recognize a more upscale market. When consumer research was conducted and management examined the profile of the trade area and the profile of the person who shopped at K mart in the past month, they were found to be identical. K mart was predominately serving the suburban consumer in suburban locations.

In "life-style" research in markets served, K mart determined there were more two-income families, families were having fewer children, there were more working wives, and customers tended to be homeowners. Customers were very careful how they spent their money and were perceived as wanting quality. This was a distinct contrast to the 1960s and early 1970s, which tended to have the orientation of a "throw away" society. The customer had said, "What we want is products that will last longer. We'll have to pay more for them but we will still want them at the lowest price possible." Customers wanted better quality products but still demanded competitive prices. According to K mart's *Annual Report,* "Consumers today are well educated and informed. They want good value and they know it when they see it. Price remains a key consideration, but the consumer's new definition of value includes quality as well as price."

MARKETING STRATEGIES

Several new marketing programs emerged as the result of an overall reexamination of existing corporate strategies. The area receiving initial attention was improvement in product displays. Before 1980, the traditional K mart layout was by product category. Often these locations for departments were holdovers from the variety store past. Many departments would not give up prime locations. As part of the new marketing strategy, the shop concept was introduced. Management recognized that it had a sizable "do-it-yourself" store. As planning management discussed the issue, "nobody was aware of the opportunity. The hardware department was right smack in the center of the store because it was always there. The paint department was over here and the electrical department was over there." "All we had to do," management contended, "was put them in one spot and everyone could see that we had a very respectable 'do-it-yourself' department." The concept resulted in a variety of new departments such as "Soft Goods for the Home," "Kitchen Korners," and "Home Electronic Centers." The goal behind each department was to sell an entire life-style–oriented concept to consumers, making goods complementary so shoppers would want to buy several interrelated products rather than just one item.

The programs also involved using and revitalizing the space K mart already had under its control. This took the form of remodeling and updating existing stores. Initial effort was concentrated in key major markets such as Indianapolis, Atlanta, Denver, Chicago, Detroit, and Buffalo. Stores were also identified in smaller markets which had rapid growth and significant new competition. A key to implementing this program was remerchandising assortments, which required changing the firm's preconceived notions about what the customer would or would not buy and under what conditions. The new look featured a broad "poppy': new racks: round, square, and honeycombed that displayed the full garment; relocation of jewelry and women's apparel to areas closer to the entrance, and redesigning of counters to make them look more upscale and hold more merchandise.

Name brands were added in soft and hard goods as management recognized that the customer transferred the product quality of branded goods to perceptions of private label merchandise. In the eyes of K mart management, "If you sell Wrangler, then the private label must be in good quality."

Additional programs emphasized the quality image. In a joint venture with *McCall's,* a new magazine called *Betsy McCall,* aimed at girls ages 6 through 12, was launched. Pro golfer Fuzzy Zoeller was engaged to promote golf equipment and other associated products. Mario Andretti who races in the Championship Auto Racing Teams' Indy car series agreed to cosponsorship of his car with associated promotion. Dusty Lenscap, an animated marketing character, was introduced to promote photo developing equipment. K mart hired Martha Stewart, an upscale Connecticut author of lavish best-selling books on cooking and home entertaining, as its "life-style spokesperson and consultant." Martha Stewart was featured as a corporate symbol for housewares and associated products in advertising and in-store displays. Management visualized her as the next Betty Crocker, a fictional character created some years ago by General Mills, Inc., and a representative of its interest in "life-style" trends.

In the mid 1970s and throughout the 1980s, K mart became involved in the acquisition or development of several smaller new operations. K mart Insurance Services, Inc., acquired as Planned Marketing Associates in 1974, offered a full line of life, health, and accident insurance centers located in 27 K mart stores primarily in the South and Southwest.

In 1982, K mart initiated its own off-price specialty apparel concept called Designer Depot. Twenty-eight Designer Depot stores were opened in 1982, to appeal to customers who wanted quality upscale clothing at a budget price. A variation of this concept, called Garment Rack, was opened to sell apparel that normally would not be sold in Designer Depot. A distribution center was added in 1983, to supplement both of the above ventures. K mart unsuccessfully attempted a joint venture with the Hechinger Company of Washington, D.C., a warehouse home center retailer. However, after much deliberation, K mart chose instead to acquire Home Centers of America of San Antonio, Texas. The division would be building 80,000-square foot warehouse home centers named Builders Square. It would capitalize on K mart's real estate, construction, and management experience and Home Centers of America's merchandising expertise.

Waldenbooks, a chain of 877 book stores, was acquired from Carter, Hawley Hale, Inc. in 1984. It was part of a strategy to capture a greater share of the market with a product category that K mart already had in its store. K mart had been interested in the book business for some time and took advantage of an opportunity in the marketplace to build on its common knowledge base.

In 1987, K mart and Bruno's, Inc. formed a partnership to develop large combination grocery and general merchandising stores or "hypermarkets." The giant,

one-stop-shopping facilities of 225,000 square feet would trade on the grocery expertise of Bruno's and the general merchandise of K mart to offer a wide selection of
products and services at discount prices.

In 1988, the company acquired a controlling interest in Makro Inc., a Cincin-
nati-based operator of warehouse "club" stores. Makro, with annual sales of about
$300 million operated "member only" stores which were stocked with low-priced
fresh and frozen groceries, apparel, and durable goods in suburbs of Atlanta, Cincinnati, Washington, and Philadephia.

THE PLANNING FUNCTION

Corporate planning at K mart was the result of executives, primarily the senior
executive, reorganizing change. The role played by the senior executive was to get
others to recognize that nothing is good forever. "Good planning" was perceived
as the result of those who recognized that at some point they would have to get
involved. "Poor planning" was done by those who didn't recognize the need for
it. When they did, it was too late to survive. Good planning, if done on a regular
and timely basis, was assumed to result in improved performance. K mart's Director
of Planning and Research contended:

> Planning, as we like to stress, is making decisions now to improve performance tomor-
> row. Everyone looks at what may happen tomorrow, but the planners are the ones who
> make decisions today. That's where I think too many firms go wrong. They think they
> are planning because they are writing reports and are aware of changes. They don't
> say, 'because of this, we must decide today to spend this money to do this to accomplish
> this goal in the future.'

The Director of Planning and Research believed that K mart had been very
successful in the area of strategic planning. "When it became necessary to make
significant changes in the way we were doing business," he suggested, "that was
accomplished on a fairly timely basis." When the organization made the change
in the 1960s, it recognized there was a very powerful investment opportunity and
capitalized on it—far beyond what anyone else would have done. "We just opened
stores," he continued, "at a great, great pace. Management, when confronted with
a crisis, would state, 'It's the economy, or it's this, or that, but it's not the essential
way we are doing business.'" He continued, "Suddenly management would recognize that the economy may stay like this forever. We need to improve the situation
and then do it." Strategic planning was thought to arise out of some difficult times
for the organization.

K mart had a reasonably formal planning organization that involved a constant evaluation of what was happening in the marketplace, what competition was
doing, and what kinds of opportunities were available. Management felt a need to
diversify because it would not be a viable company unless it were physically growing.
Management felt it was not going to physically grow with the K mart format forever.

It needed physical growth and opportunity, particularly for a company able to open 200 stores on a regular basis. The Director of Planning and Research felt that, "Given a 'corporate culture' that was accustomed to challenges, management would have to find ways to expend that energy. A corporation that is successful," he argued, "has to continue to be successful. It has to have a basic understanding of corporate needs and be augmented by a much more rigorous effort to be aware of what's going on in the external environment."

A planning group at K mart reports directly to the chairman of the board through its director of planning and research. The group represents a number of functional areas of the organization. Management describes it as an "in-house consulting group" with some independence. It is made up of (1) financial planning, (2) economic and consumer analysis, and (3) operations research. The CEO is the primary planner of the organization.

THE CHALLENGE

On April 6, 1987, K mart Corporation announced that it agreed to sell most of its 55 Kresge and Jupiter variety stores in the United States to McCroy Corporation, a unit of the closely held Rapid American Corporation of New York. The move left the firm with approximately 4,000 retail units including discount department stores, restaurants, home improvement centers, financial and real estate service centers, and specialty shops in the United States and several countries including Canada, Australia, China, and Puerto Rico.

In the light of a corporate climate of asset disinvestment and asset redeployment, the firm was at the crossroads, in terms of corporate strategy. The question was, what to do now?

Goodyear Tire and Rubber: The Goldsmith Challenge

GOODYEAR HISTORY

When Frank A. Seiberling, a 38-year-old entrepreneur, founded Goodyear Tire and Rubber Company in 1898, he was barely solvent and was only modestly acquainted with the rubber and tire business. In 1899, the firm's first full year of operation, sales totaled $508,597 with generated profits of $34,621. By 1901 sales had climbed to $1,035,921. All profits, however, were placed in escrow until 1902 when the Federal Court of Appeals ruled that Goodyear had not infringed on the Grant patent. Goodyear was free to take the lead in the tire and rubber business.

New plants and factories were added to the growing list of properties. Goodyear employment in Akron increased from 22,000 in 1913 to 70,000 by 1920. Sales in 1920 reached $192 million, and profits topped $51 million. In April 1920, production of pneumatic auto tires reached 837,236 but by December had plummeted to 117,865, and sales had fallen to $105 million with a $5 million loss. With both rubber and fabrication production falling drastically, sudden layoffs dropped Goodyear's 1920 employment from 34,000 to only 8,000.

Frank Seiberling's historic reluctance to let Wall Street financiers gain any control over the firm handicapped Goodyear in its bid for new money. Temporary financing of $18 million from a banking syndicate headed by Goldman Sachs and Company was not enough. The book value of common stock ($75 million in early 1920) was wiped out entirely. Refinancing was essential, and Frank Seiberling had trouble raising funds from any source.

As receivership loomed in 1921, large-scale refinancing was undertaken. A banking group directed by Dillon, Read and Company of New York, developed a plan to take up Goodyear's loans, pay off creditors, and provide working capital. A reorganization of the company was completed on May 12, 1921. Goodyear's Seiberling era was over.

This case was prepared by Bernard A. Deitzer, Allan G. Krigline, and Thomas A. Peterson, The University of Akron, as a basis for class discussion rather than to illustrate either effective or ineffective handling of an administrative situation. Used by permission from Bernard A. Deitzer.

THE TIRE AND RUBBER INDUSTRY[1]

There are approximately 12 members of the tire manufacturing industry in the United States. Principal domestic competitors are Goodyear Tire and Rubber Company, The Firestone Tire and Rubber Company, the B.F. Goodrich Company, Uniroyal, Inc., and General Tire, Inc. Several major foreign-based tire manufacturing concerns, including Michelin (which has plants in the United States and Canada), Bridgestone (which has a plant in the United States), Continental, Pirelli, Toyo, and a few Korean tire companies are significant competitors in the market.

The Tire Market

Within the industry, motor vehicle tires (passenger car, truck, and bus) account for 85 percent of the total value of product shipments. Additional markets include tractor and implement tires (agriculture), industrial and utility pneumatic tires (manufacturers), motorcycle and moped tires (recreational), aircraft tires (military and civilian), solid and semipneumatic tires (small equipment), RV tires (recreational), and inner tubes. Exhibit 17-1 indicates the industry leaders' tire sales in all market segments.

Tire manufacturers not only produce tires for sale through their own dealers, but also to the specifications of such major retail outlets as Sears, Montgomery Ward, Atlas, K mart, and Western Auto Supply. These and other retailers market the tires under their established brand names. In 1985, independent tire dealers accounted for an estimated 55 percent of total retail tire sales, department and chain

---

Exhibit 17-1 **World's Largest Tire Makers in 1987 with Percent of Firm's Sales in Tires**

Firm	Percent
Goodyear (United States)	74
Michelin (France)	93
Bridgestone (Japan)	70
Sumitomo (Japan)	80
Firestone (United States)	68
Pirelli (Italy)	44
Continental (West Germany)	70
Uniroyal-Goodrich (United States)	82
Yokohama (Japan)	70
General Tire (United States)	N/A

---

[1]Data throughout this section are drawn with permission from multiple issues of *Standard & Poor's Industrial Surveys* and *U.S. Industrial Outlook*.

stores for 20 percent, stores owned by the rubber companies (mostly Goodyear and Firestone) for 10 percent, service stations for 10 percent, and auto dealers and miscellaneous units for the remaining 5 percent.

Of the two tire categories, replacements are much more important than original equipment (OE) units. Since an automobile tire sold in the replacement market commands about twice the price of a similar quality OE tire, an estimated 85 percent or more of dollar sales and an even higher percentage of operating profits in 1985 were likely derived from the replacement segment. Tire prices in the OE market are tight and thus reflect the close pricing policies of the domestic auto market as well as the desire of the leading tire producers to maintain their market shares.

In years when new car production volume is low, profit margins for tire manufacturers on OE tires are narrow, frequently absorbing only necessary overhead expenses. However, recently the OE business has become somewhat more profitable as premium-priced radials have become the dominant tires on new cars.

More durable radial tires, commanding premium prices, benefit both in dollar sales and profit margins vis-a-vis older bias-ply or bias-belted tires. In addition, the replacement market for radials is not subject to the pricing pressure typical of the OE market where the enormous buying power of an automaker dictates contract terms.

Radial tires accounted for 89 percent of the total passenger car replacement tire market in 1987, extending the strong uninterrupted trend that increased from 59 percent in 1981. The primary factor responsible for this upswing in the replacement market appears to be deceleration of the gains in average radial treadlife. Industry analysts believe treadlife is being held down by a shift in the product mix to all-season and high-performance tires. It appears that although these tires enhance traction and handling along with high speed capability, there is the attendant disadvantage of shorter treadlife.

Worldwide Tire Production

During the past 25 years, world motor vehicle registrations and tire production have changed drastically. In 1960, the United States claimed nearly two-thirds of the world's registered motor vehicles. By 1985, the U.S. share had fallen to slightly more than one-third. Meanwhile, foreign tire production had grown significantly during this period. The U.S. share of world tire production dramatically declined from 50 percent in 1960 to less than 30 percent in 1985.

The world motor vehicle tire production in 1985 was 665 million tires, distributed by origin of manufacture:

United States: 195 million

Canada and Mexico: 35 million

Central and South America: 45 million

Western Europe: 160 million

Africa and Asia (except China): 140 million

Eastern Europe and China: 90 million

There are three distinct groups of world tire producers numbering approximately 179 companies: a small number of important multinational producers; state-owned facilities of the centrally planned economies such as China with 22 plants and the Soviet Union with 17; and smaller independent tire producers. In 1987, there were 371 tire plants worldwide including 58 in the United States and Canada. The major multinational producers accounted for 72 percent of output in 1985; the centrally planned economies of Eastern Europe and China 14 percent, and the smaller independents 14 percent.

Altogether, the total value of U.S. shipments of tires and inner tubes reached $11.2 billion (current dollars in 1987), a constant dollar increase of about 6 percent over 1986.

Industry Influences

Several factors have adversely affected the industry. Motor vehicle production and OE tire sales have been depressed. One cause, longer lasting radial tires, has extended the tire replacement cycle from every two years to every three to four years. Additionally, the number of imported motor vehicles with foreign-made tires has grown substantially. Imports of replacement market tires correspondingly have risen from 17 million in 1976 to over 40 million in 1986.

In 1987, imports of passenger car radial tires rose 12.8 percent from those in 1986 and accounted for slightly more than 20 percent of total automobile radial tires shipped to the replacement market. Competition from foreign tires was predicted to be intense and to continue to exert strong pressure on prices in the domestic tire replacement market. Furthermore, lower wage rates characteristically gave foreign tire producers a decided cost advantage, certainly an important factor in the highly competitive pricing structure prevailing in the U.S. tire market. In 1987, major suppliers of tires and inner tubes to the U.S. market were Japan with 26.7 percent share of the import market, Canada with 23.3 percent, South Korea with 9.6 percent, and France with 6.4 percent share. Imports of passenger car radial tires rose 12.8 percent from those of 1986 and accounted for little more than 20 percent of the total automobile tires shipped to the replacement market.

Market Stagnation Factors

The U.S. tire and inner tube business in 1987, within an intensively competitive market, has shown little growth in the last several years. Annual tire production since 1983 has been between 180 and 200 million tires. Industry experts attribute several factors relevant to the industry's stagnation including:

- Relatively stable new car production.

- Continued growth in the use of longer lasting radial tires, which now account for nearly 80 percent of domestic tire production.
- Sizable imports of replacement tires (more than 40 million annually) and imports of motor vehicles with mounted foreign-made tires.

Industry Performance

In 1987, with the help of capacity reductions stemming from various plant closings (during the period 1975 through 1985 more than 25 tire plants in North America were closed permanently, eliminating about 25 percent of total tire capacity), the industry utilization of production capacity jumped to an estimated 91 percent from 83 percent in 1986. Subsequently, profits in the industry were up from the more efficient operating rate as well as from corporate fixed-cost reduction programs. In addition, those companies with extensive foreign operations (Goodyear and Firestone) enjoyed foreign exchange benefits from 1987's weaker dollar.

On the other hand, not everything went well with the major producers. Raw material costs had increased at an accelerated pace. Nevertheless, because of efficiency gains, fixed cost reductions, and benefits from the weaker dollar, industry operating earnings jumped 32 percent in 1987.

In the long run, expected growth will increase due to the increase in the number of drivers, and, in turn, the number of registered motor vehicles. This, analysts felt, should point toward greater long-term demand for tires. Other factors affecting future demand are, of course, the price of motor fuels and possible shifts in urbanization. It appears price will be the major determinant of relative growth of both domestically produced and imported tires.

Standard & Poor's forecasted a 1 percent decline in new auto assemblies for 1988. In the replacement tire market, shipments were forecasted to increase about 1 percent to 150 million units in 1988, following 1987's impressive gain of 5 percent. The Rubber Manufacturers Association (RMA) envisioned slightly different growth patterns as seen in Exhibit 17-2.

Beyond 1988, the future outlook for the tire and rubber industry appears cloudy. A modest decline in shipments is anticipated for 1989, including slippage of 1 percent in the passenger tire market and 2 percent in the truck tire market. The forecast for 1989 assumes a weak economic environment with real GNP growth of less than 1 percent. It further assumes a cyclical trough in new car and truck sales of 13.3 million units, down from 15 million units in 1988. For passenger tires, an 11 percent drop is anticipated in shipment to the OE market with the decline being offset by continued gains in the replacement market and in exports.

GOODYEAR PRIOR TO THE CHALLENGE

In 1985, Goodyear was the world's largest manufacturer of tires and rubber products with consolidated net sales of $10.9 billion and consolidated income of

Exhibit 17-2   Tire and Tube Consumption Forecast—RMA Industry Consensus (In thousands, includes imports)

	1988	1989	1990	1991	1992	1993	% Growth
Passenger tires							
OE tires	53,000	52,500	54,500	55,800	57,700	57,700	1.7
Replacement tires (new)	155,000	157,000	157,000	158,000	159,000	160,000	.6
Retreads	14,000	13,000	13,000	12,000	12,000	11,000	−4.7
Truck and bus tires							
OE tires	8,502	8,312	8,000	8,210	8,310	8,420	.2
Replacement tires (new)	34,790	34,690	34,600	34,710	35,141	35,810	.6
Retreads	17,710	18,812	18,910	19,520	20,120	20,220	2.7
Tractor—implement (front and rear)							
Original equipment	665	670	685	690	705	720	1.6
Replacement	2,650	2,780	2,810	2,835	2,855	2,875	1.6
Industrial and utility and garden tractor							
Original equipment	10,300	10,300	10,350	10,500	10,600	10,700	.8
Replacement	5,300	5,350	5,375	5,400	5,500	5,600	1.1
Passenger inner tubes							
Original equipment	10	5	1	1	1	1	−36.9
Replacement	8,500	8,200	8,600	8,300	8,000	7,700	−2.0
Truck and bus inner tubes							
Original equipment	1,300	1,200	800	700	600	500	−17.4
Replacement	12,000	11,700	11,500	11,100	10,700	10,300	−3.0
Tractor—implement inner tubes							
Original equipment	200	200	240	250	260	275	6.6
Replacement	3,500	3,000	2,750	2,600	2,500	2,400	−3.7
Industrial—utility and garden tractor inner tubes							
Original equipment	300	300	400	400	400	400	5.9
Replacement	7,000	7,000	6,100	6,100	6,200	6,200	.7

Source: RMA Industry Report, Rubber Manufacturers Association, 1400 K St., N.W., Washington, D.C. 20005, with permission.

$445 million. Goodyear manufactured its products in 57 plants in the United States and 45 plants in 27 foreign countries. Operations included more than 2,250 facilities around the globe for the sale and distribution of its products, seven rubber plantations in Brazil, Guatemala, Indonesia, and the Philippines, a resort hotel in Litchfield, Arizona, and a government-owned uranium enrichment plant. Goodyear was strategically positioned for expansion opportunities in four major areas: tires and rubber, general products, high-tech aerospace, and defense and energy.

Goodyear Tire and Rubber Executive Officers

Robert E. Mercer, 61, Chairman of the Board, CEO, and Director, joined Goodyear in 1947. After serving in various capacities in Goodyear's General Products and Tire Divisions, he was elected President on May 2, 1978. Mr. Mercer was elected Chairman and CEO on April 4, 1983.

Tom H. Barrett, 55, President and Chief Operating Officer (COO) and Director, joined Goodyear in 1953. After serving in various posts, he was elected Executive Vice-President on October 3, 1978, serving in such capacity as the executive officer responsible for manufacturing and related services. Mr. Barrett was elected President and COO effective December 31, 1982.

The other officers have had experience working at Goodyear or subsidiaries. The company's organization chart is presented in Exhibit 17-3.

Goodyear's Products and Services

Goodyear manufactures and markets a broad line of rubber tires and tubes for automobiles, trucks, buses, tractors, farm implements, earth-moving equipment, airplanes, motorcycles, industrial equipment, and other applications throughout the world. Its products are for sale to OE manufacturers and for sale in the replacement market. In addition, the company manufactures metals, synthetic rubber, several lines of chemicals, oil and gas, and high-technology products for aerospace, defense, and nuclear energy applications.

Goodyear offered three basic constructions of passenger tires: radial, bias-belted, and bias-ply. Several major lines of Goodyear-brand radial passenger tires are sold in the United States: the Vector, the Arriva, and the Tiempo all-season lines, the Double Eagle, the Custom Polysteel, the Eagle GT, ST, and VR50 lines, the Viva II, and the F32 All Winter Radial. Goodyear offers a line of bias-belted passenger tires marketed under the trade name Cushion Belt Polyglas. The principal line of Goodyear-brand bias-ply passenger tires is the Power Streak II.

Goodyear offered several passenger tire lines in various foreign markets. In Europe, where more than 95 percent of all tires sold are radials, Goodyear sells several radial lines, including the Vector, Eagle, the Grand Prix S, the high-performance Eagle VR and NCT, the GT and the NCT Ultral Grip, and the All Weather lines of winter tires. In other foreign markets, Goodyear offers both radial and bias-ply tires.

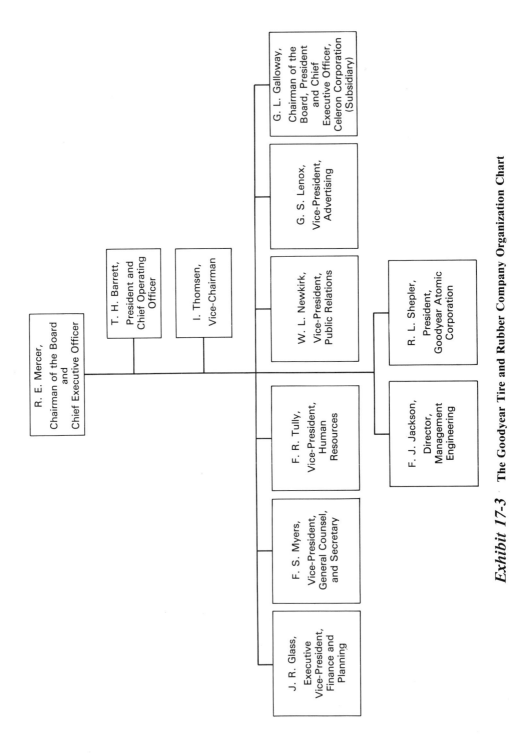

Exhibit 17-3 The Goodyear Tire and Rubber Company Organization Chart

The boxes in the chart contain:

R. E. Mercer, Chairman of the Board and Chief Executive Officer

T. H. Barrett, President and Chief Operating Officer

I. Thomsen, Vice-Chairman

J. R. Glass, Executive Vice-President, Finance and Planning

F. S. Myers, Vice-President, General Counsel, and Secretary

F. R. Tully, Vice-President, Human Resources

W. L. Newkirk, Vice-President, Public Relations

G. S. Lenox, Vice-President, Advertising

G. L. Galloway, Chairman of the Board, President and Chief Executive Officer, Celeron Corporation (Subsidiary)

F. J. Jackson, Director, Management Engineering

R. L. Shepler, President, Goodyear Atomic Corporation

Marketing Strategy

Goodyear has dominated every tire market in the United States. It has developed a successful strategy for selecting a profitable market niche in the high-performance tire business. In the last decade, Goodyear and its subsidiaries have increased their share of the U.S. replacement market from about 26 percent to 31 percent. In the OE market where Goodyear is a supplier to auto manufacturers, it has increased its share from about 27 percent to 32 percent (Exhibit 17-4).

Management at Goodyear in 1985 coordinated worldwide facilities and efforts to put competition on a global basis rather than tailor competition to local markets as a multinational firm. Goodyear's share of the U.S. tire market was one-third of the total, and its share of the foreign tire market was one-fifth of that total market. With one-third of all autos in the United States and two-thirds in foreign countries, the tire market shares translated into Goodyear having approximately one-fourth of the world's market for auto tires.

Goodyear's competitive advantage in tires had been enhanced by several distinct factors. First, it had concentrated on quality tire production, an area in which foreign makers lacked capital and technological prowess. Second, Goodyear had the largest system of dealerships in the industry. The company owned about 1,100 retail outlets and sold through more than 3,000 franchises and independent dealers. Third, Goodyear enjoyed highly sophisticated and highly guarded production methods. Fourth, Goodyear had always experienced positive relations with its work force. Despite these competitive advantages, Goodyear wanted to diversify into less cyclical and more profitable industries.

Manufacturing Strategy

As the rubber industry matured, competition became more intense. Recognizing that the key to lower costs was in improved production methods, Goodyear invested heavily in plant modernization. Conversely, its closest U.S. competitor chose to reduce costs (and reduce capacity) by closing older, less efficient plants. Goodyear expenditures for 1985 were nearly $1 billion to convert and modernize a number of tire and rubber products facilities. Goodyear's modernized plants were able to compete successfully with foreign plants which had only two-thirds of Goodyear's labor costs.

A critical factor in Goodyear's success has been its implemented production strategy. Predicated on sophisticated quality control systems, the strategy set perfection as a daily target and emphasized the importance of people involvement. Termed "Commitment to Perfection," it was a participative responsibility model that meant the individual workers, rather than management, were accountable for quality.[2] As an integrating mechanism to incorporate participative management and to increase

---

[2]Kenneth Labich, "The King of Tires is Discontented," *Fortune,* May 23, 1984, pp. 65–70.

Exhibit 17-4 Replacement Passenger Tire Market Segment Positions, 1984

Segment	Market Leaders (ranked by share)
High performance	Goodyear Goodrich[a] Pirelli
All-season radial	Goodyear (including Kelly-Springfield) Armstrong Firestone Goodrich Uniroyal
Other passenger car radial	Goodyear Firestone Michelin (Sears)
Passenger car bias	Goodyear (Sears) Firestone
Light truck radial	Goodyear Michelin Firestone Goodrich
Light truck bias	Goodyear Firestone GenCorp Goodrich Armstrong
Heavy truck tires (bias and radial)	Goodyear Michelin Firestone
Heavy truck radial	Michelin Goodyear Bridgestone

[a]Donaldson, Lufkin & Jenrette Securities Corporation makes a market in this security, has periodic positions in this security in connection with this activity, and may be on the opposite side of the public orders executed on the PSE in the stock.

Source: Alexandre, May 5, 1986. Reprinted with permission from the Donaldson, Lufkin & Jenrette Securities Corporation.

productivity and reduce labor costs, management inaugurated quality circle discussion groups to suggest ways to improve productivity.

Goodyear allocated significant amounts each year on basic and applied research for the development of new, and the improvement of existing, products and manufacturing processes and equipment. During 1985 the company expended, either directly or indirectly, $298.6 million on basic and applied research, an increase of $18.3 million over 1984. Goodyear budgeted $325 million for research and development activities in 1986.

Financial Strategy

Corporate financial goals were to reach sales of $15 billion in five years, with a 5 percent return on sales and a 15 percent return on shareholders' equity. To achieve these goals, it was recognized that Goodyear's heavy dependency on the slower growing and cyclical tire business would have to be reduced. Downturns in the auto manufacturing industry depressed OE tire demand, and technological improvements in tires, leading to increased mileage, lessened demand for replacement tires.

Chairman Mercer envisioned a day when a quarter of Goodyear's total earnings would come from Celeron, its energy production and distribution subsidiary, and another quarter from Goodyear Aerospace, its aerospace and aviation hardware component. Goodyear Aerospace, with sales of $742 million in 1985, had a history of producing an array of products for the armed services and space exploration programs, ranging from the well-known Goodyear blimps to superconductors and aircraft tires, wheels, and brakes.

However, Chairman Mercer confirmed that the company would remain dedicated to dominating the world tire market. Recent financial performance data seemed to support Goodyear's strategic intention (Exhibits 17-5 through 17-11).

Goodyear's Grand Strategy

In 1985, Goodyear's overall strategy was to have tire sales and general products bringing in one-half of total sales volume while one-fourth was to come from improved performance from Goodyear Aerospace Corporation. The remaining one-fourth of total sales volume was to come from the Celeron Corporation.

Celeron was purchased in 1983 for $825 million of Goodyear stock and was primarily involved in the transmission of natural gas through its approximately 2,700 miles of pipeline. Celeron also engaged in onshore and offshore oil exploration and production programs in 14 states. In 1982, the company had sales of $900.5 million and operating income of $119.4 million.

Celeron seemed to fit Goodyear's acquisition guidelines with sound management, a positive attitude toward Goodyear, and debt-to-equity ratio of 30 percent. Celeron also had plentiful gas and oil reserves. The company was in the process of building and oil pipeline to move oil from the west coast of California to the Gulf Coast oil refineries of Texas at a cost competitive with long distance and much slower shipment by oil tankers through the Panama Canal.

The best single advantage of the pipeline was a lower-cost means of transportation than the alternative—tankers. The estimated cost of shipping crude in an existing tanker was $4 to $6 per barrel. Industry analysts suggested that even if there were considerable cost overruns, the pipeline would be able to move each barrel at

Exhibit 17-5   **Goodyear Tire and Rubber Company Earnings Model, 1982–1986**
(In millions)

	1982	1983	1984	1985	1986
Sales					
Tires	$6,029	$5,959	$6,239	$6,364	$6,492
Transportation products	1,074	1,342	1,530	1,546	1,608
Gas and oil	901	762	700	685	680
Industrial, chemical, and plastic	987	974	1,003	1,043	1,085
Other products and services	600	699	768	861	955
Total sales	9,589	9,736	10,241	10,500	10,820
Other income	79	64	87	90	90
Total	9,668	9,799	10,328	10,590	10,910
Cost of goods sold	7,528	7,684	8,099	8,297	8,521
Selling, general and administrative	1,315	1,333	1,379	1,414	1,451
Interest	197	117	127	140	150
Plant closings or dispositions	0	74	−10	−10	0
Foreign currency exchange	44	56	46	35	30
Minority interest	10	6	6	9	9
Income before tax and extraordinary items	575	529	681	705	749
Taxes	262	259	270	288	304
Income before extraordinary items	313	270	411	417	445
Extraordinary items	17	35	0	0	0
Net income	330	305	411	417	445
Average shares outstanding	98.79	99.91	105.61	106.80	106.80
Earnings per share	$ 3.34	$ 3.06	$ 3.88	$ 3.90	$ 4.15
Ratios					
Cost of goods/sales	77.86%	78.4%	78.4%	78.4%	78.1%
Selling, general and admin/sales	13.60	13.6	13.3	13.4	13.3
Tax rate	45.60	48.9	39.6	40.9	40.6
Net income/sales	3.41	3.1	4.0	3.9	4.1
Operating profit					
Tires	528	464	505	516	532
Transportation products	54	74	103	102	106
Gas and oil	119	87	90	85	83
Industrial, chemical and plastic	64	53	92	95	100
Other products and services	69	88	94	108	119
Total	834	766	884	905	941

Exhibit 17-5   (continued)

	1982	1983	1984	1985	1986
Operating profit (%)					
Tires	8.75%	7.79%	8.10%	6.10%	8.20%
Transportation prod-					
ucts	5.00	5.50	6.71	6.60	6.60
Gas and oil	13.26	11.37	12.83	12.41	12.21
Industrial, chemical					
and plastic	6.48	5.48	9.12	9.10	9.20
Other products and					
services	11.57	12.58	12.26	12.50	12.50

Source: Alexandre, May 5, 1986. Reprinted with permission from the Donaldson, Lufkin & Jenrette Securities Corporation.

Exhibit 17-6   **The Goodyear Tire and Rubber Company and Subsidiaries Consolidated Balance Sheet (In millions)**

	December 31,			
	1982	**1983**	**1984**	**1985**
Assets				
Current assets				
Cash and short-term securities	$ 102.2	$ 111.1	$ 143.4	$ 139.0
Accounts and notes receivable	1,431.7	1,527.5	1,370.1	957.4
Inventories	1,305.0	1,218.9	1,333.4	1,378.5
Prepaid expenses	103.3	63.0	53.6	83.3
Total current assets	2,942.2	2,920.4	2,900.5	2,558.2
Other assets				
Investments in noncons. sub-				
sid. and affiliates, at equity	147.8	151.5	158.2	181.3
Long-term accounts and notes				
receivable	34.5	50.7	39.6	126.8
Investments and misc. assets,				
at cost	30.9	24.2	25.5	30.6
Deferred charges	12.3	19.5	33.8	31.6
Total Other Assets	225.5	245.9	257.1	370.3
Properties and plants	2,718.2	2,819.2	3,036.7	4,025.0
Total Assets	$5,885.9	$5,985.5	$6,194.3	$6,953.5
Liabilities and Shareholders' Equity				
Current liabilities				
Accounts payable-trade	$ 538.9	$ 593.4	$ 582.5	$ 657.4
Accrued payrolls and other				
compensation	257.0	281.1	298.4	347.4
Other current liabilities	168.7	204.0	192.4	219.1

(continued)

Exhibit 17-6   (continued)

	December 31,			
	1982	**1983**	**1984**	**1985**
United States and foreign taxes				
Current	213.1	178.8	204.6	173.2
Deferred	106.5	78.6	84.3	58.8
Notes payable to banks and overdrafts	4.8	154.6	157.4	116.3
Long-term debt due within one year	10.3	41.7	38.8	35.2
Total Current Liabilities	1,299.3	1,532.2	1,558.4	1,607.4
Long-term debt and capital leases	1,174.5	665.2	656.8	997.5
Other long-term liabilities	256.4	296.5	293.9	301.6
Deferred income taxes	312.1	413.9	448.9	475.3
Minority equity in foreign subsidiaries	66.4	61.5	65.0	64.3
Shareholders' equity				
Total Liabilities	3,108.7	2,969.3	3,023.0	3,446.1
Preferred stock, no par value Authorized, 50,000,000 shares				
Outstanding shares, none	—	—	—	—
Common Stock, no par value Authorized, 150,000,000 shares				
Outstanding shares, 106,492,709	84.9	91.5	92.5	94.1
Capital surplus	407.0	589.4	613.6	655.4
Retained earnings	2,509.9	2,678.8	2,931.1	3,172.2
Total Equity	3,001.8	3,359.7	3,637.2	3,921.7
Foreign currency transformation adjustment	(224.6)	(343.5)	(465.9)	(414.3)
	2,777.2	3,016.2	3,171.3	3,507.4
Total Liabilities and Shareholders' Equity	$5,885.9	$5,985.5	$6,194.3	$6,953.5

Source: The Goodyear Tire and Rubber Company Annual Reports of 1982–1985.

less cost than tankers. If the theoretical tariff were $3.50 per barrel using Celeron's throughput assumptions (allowing for 15% return on Goodyear's equity investment and assuming that the total cost of the project is $1 billion) the pipeline would be less expensive and profitable.[3]

[3]James L. Alexander, "Goodyear Tire and Rubber Company," Donaldson, Lufkin and Jenrette Securities Corporation, May 5, 1986, p. 6.

Exhibit 17-7   **The Goodyear Tire and Rubber Company and Subsidiaries Geographical Market Segments (In millions)**

	1982	1983	1984
Sales to unaffiliated customers			
United States	$6,252.8	$6,672.3	$ 7,091.5
Europe	1,157.8	1,088.9	1,070.7
Latin America	711.8	858.5	925.0
Asia-Africa	711.8	678.5	674.7
Canada	390.1	437.6	478.9
Net Sales	$9,589.2	$9,735.8	$10,240.8
Revenue			
United States	$6,361.2	$6,794.2	$ 7,273.7
Europe	1,188.5	1,131.0	1,114.3
Latin America	1,078.6	868.1	969.3
Asia-Africa	727.1	698.6	692.1
Canada	420.8	485.6	556.8
Adjustments and elimin.	(187.0)	(241.7)	(365.4)
Total	$9,589.2	$9,735.8	$10,240.8
Operating Income			
United States	$ 623.3	$ 576.6	$ 643.3
Europe	19.1	17.8	33.1
Latin America	140.3	119.4	141.8
Asia-Africa	60.4	43.5	46.9
Canada	(10.0)	10.7	16.3
Adjustments and elimin.	1.1	(1.9)	2.1
Total	$ 834.2	$ 766.1	$ 883.5
Assets			
United States	$3,534.5	$3,719.1	$ 3,896.7
Europe	745.7	720.4	696.6
Latin America	718.3	662.6	729.5
Asia-Africa	489.2	460.4	433.9
Canada	256.0	274.2	285.2
Adjustments and elimin.	(5.6)	(3.7)	(5.8)
Total Identifiable Assets	$5,738.1	$5,834.0	$ 6,036.1
Investments in affiliated co.	147.8	151.5	158.2
Assets at December 31, 1984	$5,885.9	$5,985.5	$ 6,194.3

Source: The Goodyear Tire and Rubber Company Annual Reports of 1982–1985.

Implementing the Strategy

As Goodyear proceeded with its grand strategy, a few dark clouds appeared. At the time of the Celeron purchase, crude oil had been selling at a level near $30 per barrel. Then crude oil fell to the $15 to $18 per barrel price range and had even dipped below $10 per barrel for a short time. This reduced the value of Goodyear's oil reserves.

Exhibit 17-8 Consolidated Statement of Income, The Goodyear Tire & Rubber Company and Subsidiaries (In millions)

	Year Ended December 31,		
	1985	1986	1987
Net sales	$8,341.1	$9,040.0	$ 9,905.2
Other income	114.2	121.0	179.9
	8,455.3	9,161.0	10,085.1
Cost and expenses			
Costs of goods sold	6,550.4	6,941.5	7,374.6
Selling, administrative and general expense	1,380.9	1,596.6	1,634.9
Interest and amortization of debt discount and expense	101.5	121.9	282.5
Unusual items	21.3	10.1	(135.0)
Foreign currency exchange	33.8	19.1	38.9
Minority interest in net income of subsidiaries	6.6	9.6	16.8
	8,094.5	8,698.8	9,212.7
Income from continuing operations before income taxes	360.8	462.2	872.4
United States and foreign taxes on income	133.7	245.4	358.5
Income from continuing operations	227.1	216.8	513.9
Discontinued operations	185.3	(92.7)	257.0
Net income	$ 412.4	$ 124.1	$ 770.9
Per share of common stock			
Income from continuing operations	$2.11	$2.02	$8.49
Discontinued operations	1.73	(.86)	4.24
Net Income	$3.84	$1.16	$12.73

Exhibit 17-9 Consolidated Balance Sheet, The Goodyear Tire & Rubber Company and Subsidiaries (In millions)

	December 31,		
	1985	1986	1987
Assets			
Current Assets			
Cash and short-term securities	$ 139.0	$ 130.5	$ 200.5
Accounts and notes receivable	957.4	1,986.5	1,501.3
Inventories	1,378.5	1,352.2	1,501.4
Prepaid expenses	83.3	82.7	101.3
Net assets held for sale	—	107.8	—
Total Current Assets	2,558.2	3,659.7	3,304.5

Exhibit 17-9 (continued)

	December 31,		
	1985	**1986**	**1987**
Other assets			
Investments in nonconsolidated sub-sidiaries and affiliates, at equity	181.3	32.9	107.6
Long-term accounts and notes re-ceivable	126.8	240.0	354.0
Investments and miscellaneous as-sets, at cost	30.6	34.4	53.8
Deferred pension plan cost	—	320.2	373.1
Deferred charges	31.6	72.1	74.6
Net assets held for sale	—	96.6	—
Total Other Assets	370.3	796.2	963.1
Properties and plants	4,025.0	4,583.4	4,128.3
Total Assets	$6,953.5	$9,039.3	$8,395.9
Liabilities and Shareholders' Equity			
Current liabilities			
Accounts payable—trade	$ 657.4	$ 749.5	$ 821.9
Accrued payrolls and other compen-sation	347.4	337.1	322.9
Other current liabilities	219.1	406.9	375.9
United States and foreign taxes:			
Current	173.2	168.5	268.7
Deferred	58.8	—	16.0
Notes payable to banks and over-drafts	116.3	304.2	244.0
Long-term debt due within one year	35.2	44.4	90.2
Deferred gain on sale of assets	—	134.7	—
Total Current Liabilities	1,607.4	2,145.3	2,139.6
Long-term debt and capital leases	997.5	2,914.9	3,282.4
Other long-term liabilities	301.6	317.5	376.7
Deferred income taxes	475.3	586.4	679.3
Minority equity in subsidiaries	64.3	72.6	83.5
Total Liabilities	3,446.1	6,036.7	6,561.5
Shareholders' equity			
Preferred stock, no par value			
Authorized, 50,000,000 shares			
Outstanding shares, none	—	—	—
Common stock, no par value			
Authorized, 150,000,000 shares			
Outstanding shares, 56,986,579			
(97,080,482 in 1986)			
(108,110,085 in 1985)	94.1	97.1	57.0
Capital surplus	655.4	104.2	11.2
Retained earnings	3,172.2	3,122.2	1,922.6
Total Equity	3,921.7	3,323.5	1,990.8
Foreign currency translation adjust-ment	(414.3)	(320.9)	(156.4)
Total Liabilities and Shareholders' Equity	3,507.4	3,002.6	1,834.4
	$6,953.5	$9,039.3	$8,395.9

Exhibit 17-10   **Consolidated Statement of Changes in Financial Position, The Goodyear Tire & Rubber Company and Subsidiaries (In millions)**

	Year Ended December 31,		
	1985	**1986**	**1987**
Funds provided from operations			
Income from continuing operations	$ 227.1	$ 216.8	$ 513.9
Non-cash items:			
Depreciation	268.3	349.0	349.9
Unusual items	28.5	(45.5)	4.1
Accounts and notes receivable reduction (increase)	—	(295.2)	485.2
Inventories (increase) reduction	(45.1)	26.3	(149.2)
Long-term accounts and notes receivable (increase)	(87.2)	(113.2)	(114.0)
United States and foreign taxes increase (reduction)	(59.3)	(64.2)	116.2
Deferred income taxes increase	26.4	111.1	92.9
Other items	138.6	170.7	118.7
Income (loss) from discontinued operations	185.3	(92.7)	257.0
Funds (used for) provided from financing	682.6	263.1	1,674.7
Notes payable to banks and overdrafts (reduction) increase	(41.1)	187.9	(60.2)
Long-term debt and capital lease reduction	(234.7)	(109.6)	(2,846.2)
Long-term debt and capital lease increase	982.4	1,455.7	3,259.5
Common stock issued	43.4	66.0	14.6
Common stock acquired	—	(614.2)	(2,027.2)
	750.0	985.8	(1,659.5)
Funds used for investment			
Capital expenditures	(1,098.2)	(1,130.8)	(665.6)
Property and plant dispositions	405.6	254.3	925.0
Discontinued operations—capital expenditures	(577.7)	(256.8)	(92.2)
Other transactions	(47.0)	(43.4)	(185.9)
	(1,317.3)	(1,176.7)	(18.7)
Dividends paid	(171.3)	(174.1)	(91.0)
Foreign currency translation adjustment reduction	51.6	93.4	164.5
Cash and short-term securities increase (reduction)	$ (4.4)	$ (8.5)	$ 70.0

Exhibit 17-11   Consolidated Statement of Shareholders' Equity, The Goodyear Tire & Rubber Company and Subsidiaries (In millions)

	Common Stock		Capital Surplus	Retained Earnings	Foreign Currency Translation Adjustment
	Shares	Amount			
Balance at December 31, 1984 after deducting 1,423,479 treasury shares	106.5	$92.5	$613.6	$2,931.1	$(465.9)
Net income for 1985				412.4	
Cash dividends paid in 1985—$1.60 per share				(171.3)	
Common stock issued (including 102,750 treasury shares)	1.6	1.6	41.8		
Foreign currency translation adjustment					51.6
Balance at December 31, 1985 after deducting 1,320,729 treasury shares	108.1	94.1	655.4	3,172.2	(414.3)
Net income for 1986				124.1	
Cash dividends paid in 1986—$1.60 per share				(174.1)	
Common stock purchased for treasury	(13.1)	(13.1)	(601.1)		
Adjustment of stated capital to $1.00 per share		14.0	(14.0)		
Common stock issued (including 547,196 treasury shares)	2.1	2.1	63.9		
Foreign currency translation adjustment					93.4

(continued)

Exhibit 17-11   (continued)

	Common Stock		Capital Surplus	Retained Earnings	Foreign Currency Translation Adjustment
	Shares	**Amount**			
Balance at December 31, 1986 after deducting 13,904,338 treasury shares	97.1	97.1	104.2	3,122.2	(320.9)
Net income for 1987				770.9	
Cash dividends paid in 1987—$1.60 per share				(91.0)	
Common stock purchased for treasury	(40.5)	(40.5)	(107.2)	(1,879.5)	
Common stock issued (including 383,800 treasury shares)	.4	.4	14.2		
Foreign currency translation adjustment					164.5
Balance at December 31, 1987 after deducting 54,005,825 treasury shares	57.0	$57.0	$ 11.2	$1,922.6	$(156.4)

More significantly, the low oil price gave foreign oil an advantage over domestically produced oil. The lower price depressed domestic production, which reduced the amount of oil on the west coast of California needing transport to the Texas Gulf Coast. Goodyear management considered this to be a short-term development in the oil market and proceeded with the construction of the hot-oil pipeline. However, management became less certain concerning Celeron's ability to contribute to sales volume and profits to reach the goal established in overall corporate planning.

On Wednesday, March 19, 1986, a full-page advertisement appeared in the *Akron Beacon Journal* as an open letter to Robert Mercer, CEO and Chairman. Signed by the Honorable Gonzalo Barrientos, Texas State Senator, the Honorable Mike Renfro, Texas Travis County Judge, and the Honorable Walter Burnett, Texas Hays County Judge, the letter was a plea for Goodyear to add 20 to 60 miles to its pipeline and change its route to divert it from the Edwards Aquifer to protect the water supply of over one million Texans. In addition, the letter requested that an environmental impact study be conducted. This action temporarily halted construction of the pipeline while the study was completed.[4] Goodyear quickly acknowledged the complaint and as a socially responsible corporate citizen promised to investigate and alleviate the aquifer problem as soon as possible.

CORPORATE RAIDER ACTIVITY IN THE TIRE AND RUBBER INDUSTRY

Goodyear's management, while working to resolve the unexpected downturn of events at Celeron, had also become aware that Goodyear might be an attractive target for a takeover attempt. Over a four-year period, the company had witnessed four attacks on the rubber industry by corporate raiders. In 1981, Loew's Corporation announced its intention to purchase up to 15 percent of Firestone stock. As shares rose from $10 to $13, Firestone purchased large blocks of shares on the market, including Loew's shares. Carl Icahn purchased Firestone shares in 1982, but was bought out by Firestone at the market price, which had risen about $2 per share.

Icahn then proceeded to purchase 1.2 million shares of Goodrich stock which was subsequently repurchased by Goodrich in 1984 at a premium of 25 percent over market price. The profit, now referred to as "greenmail," was about $7 million. The next target for Icahn in the rubber industry was Uniroyal in 1985. A tender offer was made for two-thirds of Uniroyal's stock at $18 per share. Uniroyal management was able to arrange a stock buyback for $22 a share. Icahn and his investment group subsequently made a profit of about $18 million.[5]

With the knowledge that it was a potential target for a raid, Goodyear management had taken some steps to reduce its attractiveness to corporate raiders. They conferred with investment analysts in an effort to boost the stock price to make Goodyear less of a target by making any acquisition attempt more costly. Goodyear's board of directors in July 1986 approved a shareholder rights plan, a "poison pill" tactic, that would make any acquisition attempt a prohibitive expense.

Under this arrangement, shareholders could exercise their rights by converting them into additional shares during a takeover attempt, thereby raising the purchase price of the company. Also, in July 1986, William Newkirk, Vice-President for Public Relations, directed his public relations staff to a takeover preparedness camp in Maryland for four days of preemptive tactical training. These steps were taken calmly, with no sense of urgency at the corporate office. At the time Goodyear's shares were trading, as they had for several years, in the low $30 per share range.[6]

---

[4]*Akron Beacon Journal,* March 19, 1986, p. A9.

[5]D. Oplinger, "Raiding the Rubber Industry," *Akron Beacon Journal,* December 1, 1986, p. C2.

[6]"The Goodyear War," *Akron Beacon Journal,* November 30, 1986, pp. B1–B10.

THE CHALLENGE BEGINS

At the end of September 1986, Goodyear's share price started rising in active trading on the New York Stock Exchange (NYSE). The share price continued to rise until by the week of October 20–24, 1986, it closed at $44 1/8 a share, up $2 5/8. More than $16 million shares (nearly 15% of Goodyear's outstanding shares) had changed hands. Rumors and takeover speculation intensified; however, a Form 13-D (required when any one investor accumulates 5% or more of the shares of a company) had not yet been filed with the Securities and Exchange Commission (SEC) by the close of business on Friday, October 24, 1986.[7]

The steady increase in volume and share price was viewed with alarm by Goodyear's management. Contributing to their apprehension was the difficulty of sorting out and identifying one buyer or group of buyers as the potential corporate raider.

Anonymous risk arbitrageurs accounted for much of the trading as Goodyear shares became the most actively traded on the NYSE. The arbitrageurs would buy Goodyear (or the shares of any rumored takeover target) in the hopes that the shares would quickly rise in value and make large short-term profits possible. It was not clear whether a corporate raider was accumulating stock to gain control of Goodyear, or whether a Wall Street "shark" was using timely rumor to drive up share price to later sell out at a greater profit.

In response to rumors, Robert Mercer, CEO and Chairman of Goodyear, pointed out the company's situation in a letter to Goodyear employees. Apparently a large block of stock, 1.7 million shares, was sold by an institutional investor through a Merrill Lynch broker to another Merrill Lynch broker acting for Merrill Lynch Capital Markets. When Goodyear contacted its local Merrill Lynch office to inquire about the transaction, the local analyst replied that he was not permitted to comment on the transaction.

Goldsmith Identified as the Challenger

On November 3, 1986, the *Wall Street Journal* broke the news. A group led by Sir James Goldsmith, a global financier holding both French and English citizenship, disclosed that it had acquired an 11.5 percent stake or nearly 12.5 million of Goodyear's approximately 109 million outstanding shares. The SEC filing disclosed that the group's ultimate goal was to obtain control of or make a business combination with Goodyear. Goldsmith's first purchase of Goodyear stock had been 33,000 shares at $31 7/8. The group had purchased 1.7 million shares on September 25, 1986, at $33 a share. Most of the group's purchases were in the $40 to $44 range. Between October 27 and 29, 1986, nearly 1.5 million shares were purchased at $48 a share, which seemed to be the highest price paid by the group.

In a separate SEC filing, Goldsmith indicated that he would receive $246.6 million from the sale of a container company he acquired when Crown Zellerbach Corporation was taken over by him earlier in 1986. In October 1986, Goldsmith

---

[7]"Regional Stock Report," *Akron Beacon Journal,* October 27, 1986, p. B5.

raised an additional $213 million by having another company, also acquired from Crown Zellerbach, issue an unusual stock dividend. These two moves would give Goldsmith about $460 million in cash for his "war chest" if he should decide to make a tender offer for Goodyear.

In a letter to Mercer, Goldsmith explained his delay in making a bid for Goodyear by saying, "It seemed to us that the market overreacted and that both the volume and price of Goodyear's shares have reached unexpected levels." In this same letter, he expressed a desire to discuss "possible ways to advance the interests of Goodyear's shareholders and employees" and he believed "a greater concentration on the core business would be more beneficial than major diversification efforts."[8]

A detailed look at the SEC filing for the acquisition of Goodyear shares revealed that Goldsmith reported a total of $3.1 billion available to gain control of Goodyear. After purchasing 11.5 percent of the company's stock, $2.6 billion in financing remained. Some of the financing was to come from the Wells Fargo Bank in San Francisco, First National Bank of Chicago, and Bank of Nova Scotia in Canada.

The combined 12.5 million shares held by the group represented an investment of $530 million. Based on the closing price of $48 5/8 on October 31, Goldsmith's holdings had appreciated to $610 million. At the same price, Goldsmith would need $1.14 billion more to acquire a 35 percent interest in Goodyear, the minimum amount regarded as necessary to have controlling interest in a company.

Goldsmith had paid Merrill Lynch Capital Markets $5 million to assist in the purchase of Goodyear shares and had contracted to pay from $7.5 million to $15 million more for continued assistance. The stock was held by General Oriental Ltd. Partnership of Bermuda, incorporated September 19, 1986. The two newly incorporated partnerships, the latest in the maze of Goldsmith's financial empire, were obviously located and designed to take advantage of tax laws which would maximize earnings.

Sir James Goldsmith

On February 26, 1933, James Michael Goldsmith was born into an affluent family known in Europe for banking and finance. His father owned forty-eight hotels, and James spent his early years in some of the grandest hotel suites in Europe. Uninterested and largely unsuccessful in his formal education, as well as being nonconforming in behavior, he had acquired a reputation as a playboy with a fondness for the gaming tables. His interest in business developed when he discovered that it was as exciting as gambling.[9]

---

[8]G. Stricharchuk and P. Miller, "Goldsmith Goodyear Stake Put at 11.5%," *The Wall Street Journal,* November 3, 1986, p. 8.

[9]G. Wansell, *Tycoon—The Life of James Goldsmith,* Chap. 3-4, Atheneum, Macmillan Publishing Co., New York, 1987.

James Goldsmith's genius for financing was aided by both timing and amazing good fortune. In his first business venture, he was saved from certain bankruptcy when the staff of every bank in France went on strike for the first time in twenty years. In England and in the United States, he was successful in his two most critical business takeovers because he expected the stock market to rise while they had been falling. When the markets quickly rebounded, he was able to sell stock at high enough prices to pay off his borrowings for the acquisitions.

The foundation for James Goldsmith's business empire was laid by acquiring failing companies, selling off unprofitable operations or closing them, and installing management teams capable of running the companies at above average profits. The assets of the companies were then parlayed for the next acquisition. The Goldsmith business empire eventually crystallized with his U.S. acquisitions of Diamond International and Crown Zellerbach. Up to this point, Goldsmith, the penultimate gambler, had always risked all in a "double or nothing" fashion; afterwards he would not have to risk everything to make an acquisition.

Goldsmith viewed himself as a change agent, an undiluted capitalist, who steadfastly maintained that the control of major U.S. corporations which began as capitalist enterprises was bound to evolve from traditional entrepreneurial founders to professional managers, and eventually and finally, to institutional investors and savers. And corporate raiders, catalysts of the change, were really breaking the vise of the managing class. Concurrently, with this dramatic change was the opportunity to advance one's own interest and those of others just as the "invisible hand" of Adam Smith guaranteed that the pursuit of individual interests resulted in an overall good.[10]

The very epicenter of the controversy, according to Goldsmith, was the relationship between the shareholder and the corporation:

> Although corporations belong to their shareholders . . . corporate managements sometimes believe that the business that employs them has become an institution and that they are the trustees of that institution. Some believe that they have developed some sort of proprietorial rights. Shareholders then become no more than an inconvenience. . . . The principal difference between a friendly merger and a hostile takeover is that management agrees to a merger. A hostile takeover is only hostile to established management. . . . The management of large, tired companies, fearful of the free market, plead with the government bureaucracy for special protection to protect the status quo and avoid change. Corporate raiders don't perform their useful function altruistically. But their self-interest usually leads to a collective good. . . . In a free economy, the inefficient are eliminated and the efficient—as long as they remain so—grow for the benefit of all. . . . [11]

[10]Ibid., Chapter 22.
[11]Ibid., pp. 314–315.

GOODYEAR AND THE COMMUNITY RESPOND

In the fall of 1986, as the price of Goodyear's stock rose, some employees and Akron residents sold their shares to cash in on the dramatic increase. However, within days, the local selling of Goodyear stock almost stopped as the workers and citizenry came to realize the consequences of such a change in Goodyear's ownership. The prevailing mood became defensive and placards and posters appeared in front of homes reading "Don't turn your back on family! Save Akron! Buy Goodyear stock!"

When it became known that Merrill Lynch Capital Markets was supporting Goldsmith with $1.9 billion of its own funds, Akronites set up a picket line at the local Merrill Lynch office. Clients with ties to Goodyear withdrew their funds from Merrill Lynch to demonstrate their displeasure for its part in the takeover.

In October 1986, Representative John Seiberling, the Democratic Congressman from Akron, a former 17-year employee of Goodyear, and the grandson of Goodyear's founder, requested that the Judiciary Committee hold hearings on the Goodyear takeover. The hearings were to be held in an effort to encourage the administration to enforce antitrust laws to stop the Goodyear takeover. Under the Clayton Antitrust Act, the government was empowered to prohibit any takeover that would weaken competition. Goodyear argued that its competitive position would be weakened if it were forced to cut spending for research and development or if it were forced to sell valuable assets.

Seiberling was also considering a request to the House Energy and Commerce Committee to hold hearings to ensure that the SEC properly monitored the trading of Goodyear stock. Seiberling, a senior member of the Judiciary Committee and its subcommittee, had grown up with the knowledge that Wall Street and similar financiers had forced Goodyear out of his grandfather's hands in the 1921 reorganization. He also felt that Congress should pass a law to prohibit the takeover of the company by a foreign investor because of Goodyear's defense work.

The *Akron Beacon Journal* carried the following editorial on November 2, 1986:

> What Goodyear has going for it in this fight is that, as analysts note, it is a very well-managed company. That such a company should be targeted for a hostile takeover makes a mockery of the argument that such corporate raids are a part of capitalism's sorting-out process. If so, it is certainly not the best use of the capitalist system.
>
> Corporate raiders are the most extreme manifestations of one common criticism of American corporations: that they focus too much on shorter-term profits.
>
> But, Goodyear has been playing the game the right way. To combat foreign and domestic competition, Goodyear has taken the long-range view, investing in productivity and improving its international market position, at the expense of short-range profits. These expenditures, say some analysts, may have made Goodyear an appealing takeover target, even though its plan is one that should be followed by other corporations.

> As U.S. Rep. John Seiberling said, "What kind of message does this send to management across the country?" . . . More general standards would be welcome that might prevent any corporation from being in danger, simply for making the right moves toward future planning. . . .

Goodyear encouraged all such public efforts and proceeded to lobby the Ohio legislature to enact laws preventing such unwanted takeovers for any corporation.

Goodyear's Legal Defense

During October 1986, after learning the identity and interest of the raider, Goodyear decided the best defense would be a good offense. The investment banking firm of Goldman Sachs and Company was hired as a primary adviser. The New York law firm of Cahill Gordon & Reindel was enlisted to assist Goodyear's own legal talent. The Carter organization, a proxy solicitation firm, hired more often than any other company of its kind for corporate-control battles, had been commissioned to identify the raider.

Another investment banking firm, Drexel Burnham Lambert Inc., which had pioneered the use of high-risk "junk bonds" as a tool for raiders in takeovers, was hired to advise Goodyear on a possible restructuring to maximize shareholder value. Moreover, their key executive, Martin Siegel, specialized in mergers and acquisitions. Drexel brought in Joe Flom, one of Wall Street's best known takeover artists. Goodyear management felt that if Siegel and Flom were not on Goodyear's side, they might be hired by the other side. Ironically, many of the outsiders on Goodyear's defense team were more accustomed to working for the raiders than for acquisition targets.

Goodyear's Mercer said:

> Whoever the raider was, we didn't want him to have Drexel and Flom. They knew what to say. They knew the language (in meetings). Whether or not it was worth the money to pay them, I don't know. But I do know this: You'd be severely criticized if you went into this kind of battle without hiring the best people in the business to advise you.

The best people would eventually cost Goodyear several million dollars.[12]

Goodyear's advisers presented three options. Goodyear could (1) repurchase the stock that Goldsmith had garnered, (2) sell off subsidiaries, trim operations, take on enormous debt, and thus elevate the stock price beyond Goldsmith's war chest, or (3) find a "white knight" who possibly might take the same actions, but in a much less brutal fashion. It was clear that Goodyear would emerge a smaller and more debt-ridden company. Moreover, the costs of buying back stock and paying investment bankers, lawyers, and public relations firms, in addition to interest payments on a mammoth debt, would almost certainly mean that significant employment cutbacks would be necessary.

---

[12]"The Goodyear War," *Akron Beacon Journal,* November 30, 1986, pp. B1–B10.

On November 3, 1986, the first business day after Goldsmith announced his intentions, Mercer initiated Goodyear's takeover defense by announcing a dramatic restructuring plan that included selling its oil and gas subsidiary, Celeron. Acquired in 1983 for $825 million, its Louisiana pipelines and processing plants had been sold by Goodyear for $447 million. Oil and gas reserves had been acquired from Chevron Corporation for $395 million, and Goodyear had invested $900 million in Celeron's All-American pipeline.

In 1986, Celeron's oil reserves were estimated at 100 million barrels worth $1.4 billion. Selling these reserves would allow Goodyear to repurchase about 30 percent of its outstanding shares, while maintaining the debt of $600 million for the pipeline. With a total debt of $1.9 billion, Goodyear would be a more highly leveraged company and a less desirable target.

Additionally, with fewer shares outstanding, the current earnings of $3 per share would increase to $4.50 or $5 per share. Just before Goldsmith began buying, Goodyear's stock was selling at ten to eleven times earnings. If that multiple were applied to the new earnings estimate, Goodyear stock could be selling for $50 per share, a price higher than Goldsmith was willing to pay.[13]

At noon on the same day that Goodyear announced the restructuring, Goodyear's stock was off 1 1/4 at $47 3/8 on a volume of 1.59 million shares. It closed off 3/8 at $48 1/4 on a volume of 3.9 million shares, which at the time, was the second most actively traded stock in the history of the NYSE.

The Goldsmith Interview

The *Akron Beacon Journal* interviewed Goldsmith on November 6, 1986. In that interview he indicated that he thought the Goodyear tire company, "the core business," was a great business. He felt the company (from an outside perspective) had weakened its position somewhat by losing its focus. He continued by stating that he felt the company could be improved by refocusing and working exclusively on developing the core business and releasing assets used in peripheral activities.

Goldsmith stated that he would not operate the company. "I'm not a manager and I don't pretend to know the tire business. The only input I can have is input in strategic terms—to avoid, for instance, diversification. We intend to stay. We would invest in the long term in improving Goodyear's core business."

When asked if he planned to keep the current management team, Goldsmith replied, "We call the shots. We would plan to work with current management, ask the questions, work out the plans with them. We have no alternative management team or any of that stuff."[14]

As the battle for Goodyear progressed, the first steps were taken in restructur-

---

[13]R. Winter and G. Stricharchuk. "Goodyear, Responding to Takeover Bid, Seeks Buyer for Its Oil and Gas Unit," *The Wall Street Journal,* November 4, 1986, p. 3.

[14]D. Oplinger, et al. Transcript of *Beacon Journal* interview with Goldsmith, *Akron Beacon Journal,* November 6, 1986, p. A14.

ing that Mercer had announced in his second meeting with Goldsmith on November 5, 1986. Goodyear retired its blimp "Europa" based near Rome. The annual cost to keep the four blimps aloft was $10 million.[15] The company closed its advanced tire building group at Howdine Ltd. in Britain, transferring the technology to existing centers in Luxembourg and Akron. A 26-year participation in Formula One Grand Prix racing was ended.[16] In addition, Goodyear announced an unspecified number of engineers would lose their jobs and an early retirement program for salaried employees was expanded.

U.S. House Judiciary Committee Testimony

Goldsmith, Mercer, Akron Mayor Tom Sawyer, and United Rubber Workers President Milan Stone were to testify on the takeover attempt. On November 10, 1986, Goodyear stock closed at $47 5/8, up 1/8. More than 6.2 million shares were traded, making it the most active stock on the NYSE.

The U.S. House Judiciary Committee's subcommittee on monopolies convened on Tuesday, November 18, 1986. Both Goldsmith and Mercer were ordered to testify. Sir James Goldsmith prefaced his testimony with the following opening statement:

> Paul W. Litchfield was Chief Executive Officer of Goodyear during the 30 years of its greatest prosperity and growth. He defined Goodyear's job quite clearly. It was, he said, "to build better tires, cheaper, and sell them harder."
>
> The current management of Goodyear forgot Mr. Litchfield's lesson. It strayed into industries (Celeron) about which it knew nothing, jeopardizing the very heart of Goodyear's business and the security of all those associated with it.
>
> The approximately $2 billion spent in the oil and gas business should have been invested to build the most modern, state-of-the-art, frontier-breaking industrial infrastructure to produce better tires, cheaper, and to ensure that Goodyear's operations could compete with anything, including imports, no matter what their origin.

Mercer's remarks preceding his testimony before the subcommittee were as follows:

> Mr. Chairman and members of the subcommittee, I am Robert E. Mercer, Chairman and Chief Executive Officer of the Goodyear Tire and Rubber Company, a corporation which is known to James Goldsmith and his partners, Merrill Lynch and the Hanson Trust of Great Britain, by the code name "Patience."
>
> I won't quibble over their choice of "Patience" as a code for a project to take over Goodyear. But I can tell you that our classic shareholders, our employees, our customers,

---

[15]T. Gerdel. "Goodyear Deflates European Blimp, Tire Works," *Cleveland Plain Dealer,* November 11, 1986, p. 1–A.

[16]L. Pantages and K. Byard, "Goodyear Will Lower Profile in Racing," *Akron Beacon Journal,* November 12, 1986, p. Al.

our suppliers, and the communities in which we operate are running out of patience—and pretty darned fast.

Look at it from their view: they have supported a corporation which for 88 years has made money the old fashioned way—we've earned it through a strong work ethic and solid commitment to our shareholders and all of our constituencies.

And what we've earned, we have shared with our shareholders. In the last six years, for instance, our stock has appreciated 250 percent, and we have maintained a yield of 5 percent.

It's high time the administration, Congress, and the appropriate regulatory bodies face up to what this unrestricted takeover activity is doing to the nation's economy, its industrial base, and the prospect of being any real force in the market in the years ahead, not only overseas but right here at home.

While there is still time for our nation, I urge you to put some reasonable curbs on the activity that is sapping more and more of America's industrial strength.

In my opinion, it is reasonable to require an individual, group, or partnership seeking to acquire control of a company to reveal that intent at the onset, rather than only after a significant position has been achieved in a company's shares.

I consider it reasonable to ask such an individual, group, or partnership to file a premerger notification under the Hart-Scott-Rodino Antitrust Improvement Act.

I consider it reasonable to require anyone who gets 5 percent or more of a company's shares to keep that position for at least one year.

And I consider it reasonable to require that anyone who considers control of a company discusses in advance his detailed description of his plans—including hard estimates on how he is going to cut employment, whether he plans to extract a lot of cash from the company's operations and force it to operate in a run-down and declining condition, and whether he will maintain the level of research and development that will enable the company to survive in its markets.

American industry deserves no less, in my opinion; the public will settle for nothing less.[17]

GOLDSMITH-MERCER NEGOTIATIONS

Goodyear Chairman Mercer was pessimistic about the likely outcome of the takeover after the subcommittee hearings. "If this guy has got the ability to buy the whole company, there is little we can do to stop him. I'm not sure where we go from here."[18]

It was Goldsmith who made the next move by inviting Mercer to a meeting on Tuesday, November 18, 1986. Goldsmith informed Mercer that he was proceeding with the tender offer the next day. Goldsmith was apparently concerned about the

[17]M. Calvey, "Excerpts of Goldsmith, Mercer Testimony," *Akron Beacon Journal,* November 19, 1986, p. A17.

[18]L. Pantages et al. "Board Meets as Goodyear Stock Falls," *Akron Beacon Journal,* November 19, 1986, p. A17.

passage of new laws by Ohio state legislature that would hinder takeovers. Mercer asked Goldsmith if he still had an open mind on the takeover, and when Goldsmith replied he was still open, Mercer suggested Goodyear buy back Goldsmith's holdings.

Representatives for both sides met through the night and reached an agreement by Wednesday morning. In addition to the new laws pending in Ohio, Goldsmith cited the changing climate of opinion on Wall Street and in Washington for terminating his efforts to take over Goodyear. "The Boesky scandal altered the environment, and at the same time, Congress went back to the Democrats. Things were so different. It was also not a good time for Europeans in America."[19]

In the agreement reached by the two sides, Goodyear was to buy all of Goldsmith's 12.5 million Goodyear shares for $49 1/2 each, or a total of about $619 million. In addition, Goldsmith would receive $37 million to cover his expenses. This last payment was referred to as "greenmail" by some observers. It was estimated that Goldsmith's group netted a profit of $94 million for their two-month effort. Goldsmith agreed, however, not to buy any Goodyear stock for a period of at least five years.

THE POST GOLDSMITH CHALLENGE

Goodyear announced that it would continue its restructuring and planned to spend $2 billion to buy 40.4 million of its shares, or about 41.5 percent of the total remaining shares, for $50 per share. It was this buyback of shares at a price higher than that paid to Goldsmith that circumvented the "greenmail" charge. The settlement would add $2.6 billion to Goodyear's total debt and double its debt-equity ratio to about 72 percent.[20]

On Friday, November 21, 1986, Goodyear stock closed at $42 1/8 on a volume of 2.9 million shares, down $5 1/8 for the week. On Thursday, November 20, 1986, the stock had closed at $43, on a volume of 7.6 million shares, the most active on the NYSE despite a freeze on its trading for some of the session.[21]

Goodyear, to generate enough funds needed for its tender offer to shareholders, began to both discontinue and downsize aspects of its business. On July 24, 1987, the company sold approximately 6.5 percent of its oil and gas reserves to a subsidiary of International Paper for $70 million. On December 4, 1987, the company sold substantially all of its remaining oil and gas reserves in the sale of all the shares of Celeron Oil and Gas Company to an Exxon subsidiary for $615 million.

Celeron's oil pipeline went on the block for $1.3 billion with the expectation

[19]G. Wansell, pp. 385–86.

[20]T. Gerdel, "Goodyear Tire Wins Takeover Fight," *Cleveland Plain Dealer,* November 21, 1986, p. 1–A.

[21]R. Reiff and G. Gardner, "Market Reaction Negative, Shareholders May Be Losers," *Akron Beacon Journal,* November 21, 1986, p. A1.

that a consortium of oil companies would come forward in a partnership agreement. The pipeline began in Santa Barbara, California, and its last leg from central Texas to the Gulf Coast was still under construction. Goodyear did not plan to sell until the line was a completely finished unit. A sale was expected in 1989 with the proceeds slated to reduce the corporate debt of $3.62 billion, as of September 30, 1988, which required interest payments of about $1 million every working day.

In December 1986, the company had sold the assets of two Arizona subsidiaries involved in agriculture products, real estate development, and a resort hotel for a total price of $220.1 million to the SunCor Development Company, a subsidiary of AZP Group of Phoenix, an electric utility with diversified operations.

On March 13, 1987, the company sold substantially all the assets of Goodyear Aerospace Corporation to Loral Corporation, an international, high technology company (ironically an earlier Goodyear takeover possibility) for $588 million. Earlier, on December 20, 1986, the company sold the capital stock of Motor Wheel Corporation for an aggregate selling price of $175 million, and on April 1, 1987, sold the capital stock of Motor Wheel Canada (MWC) and certain other assets, including three manufacturing plants, to a group at MWC.

During the summer of 1988, in an effort to eliminate overhead expenses, avoid job redundancies, and expendable support staff, Goodyear reorganized the firm into two major divisions—tire and nontire products. Formerly separated geographical business segments were combined in global divisions. Furthermore, the company reduced research and development expenditures, closed plants in Cumberland, Maryland and Toronto, Canada and cut 6,000 jobs through direct terminations and early retirement incentive plans. Additional cutbacks were gloomily predicted.[22]

In the climatic aftermath of hostile raider Sir James Goldsmith's takeover attempt, Chairman Robert E. Mercer found himself at several critical junctures. The challenges beyond Goldsmith were almost overwhelming. After drastic organizational restructuring and downsizing to accommodate debt, the company was shifting its corporate direction and grand strategy from one of intended deemphasis on the tire business to one of almost total dependency. Mercer's original plan had been to eventually reduce tire manufacturing to about 50 percent of Goodyear's overall business. In 1987, Goodyear was approximately 85 percent concentrated in tires— certainly a dramatic turnaround for a diversified conglomerate aspiring to worldwide greatness.

In the 1987 *Annual Report,* Chairman Mercer reported:

> This 1987 annual report contains striking confirmation of the fighting spirit of Goodyear's organization throughout the world.
>
> Fewer in number, working under the constraints and stress of restructuring, the people of all walks of Goodyear seized the opportunities that exist in the global marketplace and achieved outstanding returns on the prior investments that built our strength and durability. For that, I commend them and thank them.

---

[22]"Goodyear's New Boss Faces Tough Road Test," *Business Week,* December 12, 1988, p. 90.

Income from continuing operations reached an all-time high in 1987, as did sales and net income.

As the year closed, we were ahead of schedule in our program to reduce the added debt resulting from the restructuring. (Debt reached a peak of $5.61 billion in February 1987 and was $3.62 billion at year's end.) We will endeavor to maintain this momentum in 1988. To this end, our plans for our business segments include special emphasis on cash flow. We will continue our strides in cost reduction while maintaining research and development and other investments at levels designed to maximize the cost/benefit equation and maintain our technological edge in the future.

Case 18

LOTUS Development Corporation: Maintaining Leadership in the Competitive Electronic Spreadsheet Industry

With sales of microcomputers increasing faster than sales of minicomputers and mainframes, sales of microcomputer software have been growing at a fairly rapid rate. The growth rate for microcomputer software was a respectable 24 percent in 1987 compared with 23 percent in 1986, and microcomputer software revenues are expected to increase by 27 percent in 1988.[1]

According to Dataquest,[2] worldwide shipments of personal computer units declined slightly from 15 million units in 1984 to 14.7 million units in 1985, but increased to 15.2 million units in 1986 and to 17.4 million units in 1987 (estimated). United States packaged software revenues (in millions of dollars) have increased from $8,380 in 1984 to $9,300 in 1985, $10,935 in 1986, and $13,095 in 1987.[3] U.S. Data Corporation has estimated that worldwide revenues of microcomputer software firms are growing three times faster than microcomputer hardware sales.[4] Rev-

[1]U.S. Industrial Outlook, Department of Commerce, 1988.

[2]*Time,* May 11, 1987.

[3]*Standard & Poor's Industry Surveys,* May 1988.

[4]U.S. Industrial Outlook, 1988.

This case was prepared by William C. House, University of Arkansas, as a basis for class discussion rather than to illustrate either effective or ineffective handling of an administrative situation. Used by permission from William C. House.

enues of the top 50 independent software companies increased from $1,939 million in 1984 to $2,758 in 1985, $3,620 in 1986, and $5,231 in 1987.[5]

The microcomputer software industry has thousands of small independent suppliers with less than $1 million annual sales. The big three (LOTUS, Ashton-Tate, and Microsoft), currently hold about 50 percent of the market as represented by revenues of the top 100 vendors. The gap between these three companies and other companies seems to be widening as a transition is made from a cottage industry to one dominated by a very few suppliers. Barriers to entry are increasing as the industry experiences intense competition, a high degree of product similarity, and product changes geared to hardware innovations. Brand name recognition and increased marketing and product development/implementation costs also discourage the entry of newly formed companies.

The "Big Three" also have large user bases, strong customer loyalty, and large, well-developed research and development programs. These companies have sufficient financial resources to acquire competitors (e.g., Ashton-Tate's acquisition of Multimate), expand product bases, and to diversify into application areas not now covered. Ashton-Tate believes that price/performance, marketing and sales expertise, ease of use, product support, product line integration, and vendor financial strength are key factors in product success.[6] Although price competition has not been as important as brand name recognition and product improvements in product sales growth, an industry trend toward site licensing and volume discounts may make price more important in the future.

LOTUS COMPANY HISTORY

Mitchell Kapor, a disk jockey with an interest in transcendental meditation, developed LOTUS 1-2-3 in 1981 along with associate Todd Agulnick. At that time Kapor was president of Cambridge-based Micro Finance Systems, a small New England software company. Several years earlier, Dan Bricklin, a Harvard University dropout, introduced the first electronic spreadsheet, VisiCalc, which was designed for the Apple II computer.

LOTUS has grown astronomically since its inception in 1983. In that first year, LOTUS had sales of $53,000 and a staff of several dozen people. It has increased in size to the point that by 1987, revenues were just under $400 million, and the number of employees had increased to 2,400. Jim Manzi, a former newspaper reporter and a Greek and Latin scholar, joined the firm in 1984 as Sales and Marketing Manager. Kapor, an informal, undisciplined entrepreneur, came to rely increasingly on Manzi, who joined the company with a reputation as a hard-headed businessman.

[5]*Software News,* May 1986, 1987, 1988.

[6]*Standard & Poor's Industry Surveys,* May 1988.

Kapor left the company in 1986 and Manzi became President. The brash, aggressive, and competitive former newspaper reporter very quickly made it clear he expected LOTUS to continue to be the number one microcomputer software company in terms of size, sales, profits, and image. He was one of the highest paid chief executives in all industry, receiving more than $26 million in salary and stock options in 1987. Stock analysts have pointed out that LOTUS's current president, unlike the chief executives of other major companies such as Microsoft, Ashton-Tate, and Borland, had no prior software company experience.

In 1987 as sales and profit growth began to level off, Manzi issued orders to staff members to exercise close control over costs. After a series of negative articles appeared in a New England newspaper in response to published reports of Manzi's salary and a series of insider stock sales shortly before announcement of further delays in introducing an updated version of LOTUS, Manzi ordered company employees not to talk with the reporters of that newspaper. The order was later rescinded. LOTUS claimed that officer salaries were not out of line with those of other industry leaders and justified the stock sales as necessary to cover income taxes on stock options granted to key executives. Concurrently with these developments, a number of key executives left the company, and the stock price declined sharply.

Frank King, a 17-year IBM veteran involved in the development of the PC/2, became Senior Vice-President of Software Products in the spring of 1988. Due to his computer experience and engineering background, he has gained greater creditability with the LOTUS staff than his predecessor. Outsiders say the more highly organized work environment contrasts with the informal, individualistic environment fostered by Kapor. However, morale appears to be better and annual turnover had declined to 15 percent compared with an industry average of 20 percent.

PRODUCT DEVELOPMENT

LOTUS's goal is to be number one in the microcomputer software industry in terms of sales, profits, size, and reputation. It relies heavily on one product, LOTUS 1-2-3, which currently contributes 70 percent of its total revenues. Sales of its integrated package Symphony have been disappointing. The only new products introduced since 1984 have been add-ons or add-ins designed to speed up worksheet operation or to enhance such functions as data base management, word processing, and graphics display. Recently its sales and profits have lagged behind those of its number one competitor, Microsoft.

Spreadsheet

LOTUS desires to improve 1-2-3 while still retaining the familiar look of the present version. Competitors such as Borland, Microsoft, Computer Associates, and Paperback Software are offering improved programs with added features at the same price as 1-2-3 or, in some cases, at even lower prices. The company has indicated an intention to develop versions of LOTUS which will run on all types of computer hardware, including mainframes, minicomputers, and microcomputers. If this goal could be achieved, it would allow sharing of worksheets, files, and terminals while reducing training costs. However, achieving this objective is likely to be difficult. For example, writing one program which will work satisfactorily on the 8088, 80286, and 80386 microprocessor-based hardware presents formidable challenges.

Since its introduction in 1983, LOTUS has sold more than three million copies of its 1-2-3 program and holds 70-80 percent of the IBM PC-compatible spreadsheet market. In its early years, the only serious competitors were Microsoft's Multiplan and Sorcim's (now Computer Associates) SuperCalc. LOTUS sold 100,000 copies of 1-2-3 in its first year of operation and now sells that many copies in one month.

LOTUS has about 76 percent of the IBM compatible market, SuperCalc 4.1 percent, Multiplan 3.2 percent, and other spreadsheets about 16.7 percent in 1987. Microsoft's Excel holds about 75 percent of the Apple Macintosh market with LOTUS Jazz possessing 17 percent of the market and others 8 percent. LOTUS's introduction of 1-2-3 in the Apple market during 1988 was seen as negatively impacting sales of Jazz without having a significant effect on sales of Excel. As a result, LOTUS announced plans to phase out Jazz soon after the 1-2-3 program for Apple was implemented.

Exhibit 18-1 contains spreadsheet sales in units for the major spreadsheet suppliers for 1985, 1986, and 1987. LOTUS sales have continued to increase at a steady rate during this period while the sales of other spreadsheet companies have not kept pace. However, the effect of the introduction of two new competitors, Excel and Quattro, and revised versions of VP-planner (Plus) and SuperCalc (V) on LOTUS sales cannot be determined at this point.

LOTUS 1-2-3 is a relatively easy-to-use product with a broad user base. It is a familiar, proven package with established compatibility across company lines and with company divisions. Added power and utility come from LOTUS add-ins such as HAL (natural language interface), Freelance Plus (graphics), and Manuscript (word processing). In comparison with competitors' spreadsheet products, LOTUS

Exhibit 18-1	**Shipments of Major Spreadsheet Suppliers (in millions of units) for 1985, 1986, and 1987**		
	1985	**1986**	**1987**
LOTUS 1-2-3	680	750	900
Multiplan	221	275	250
Excel-IBM	—	—	120
V P-planner	—	100	60
Quattro	—	—	50
SuperCalc	34	65	40

Source: Dataquest, *Personal Computing,* October 1986, 1987, 1988.

has limited functions, poorer graphics, and a higher price in many cases. It has lost sales due to restrictive site licensing and copy protection provisions not attached to other spreadsheets. A lack of LAN (local area network) support has caused some users to switch to other spreadsheets such as SuperCalc.

Spreadsheet linking for 1-2-3 is cumbersome, and multiple spreadsheets cannot be displayed on the same screen. Graphics capabilities are limited, and printing is often unwieldy and time consuming. LOTUS's macro capability permits customization of the spreadsheet program to fit many different situations. Many users have invested a large amount of time, money, and effort in developing macros and templates for use with 1-2-3. This may inhibit switching to other products unless they are vastly superior to 1-2-3 and can clearly demonstrate file and macro compatibility.

To overcome some of its inherent limitations, LOTUS has developed several add-ins to perform functions not available on its 2.0 or 2.1 version. Speedup increases the effective operating speed of LOTUS by only recalculating cells affected by the previous command or command sequence. Learn gives LOTUS the capability of memorizing keystrokes for macrogeneration without the need to use complex series of commands. HAL, a natural language interface, provides an easier-to-use command structure and permits easier linking of multiple spreadsheets than possible with the original product.

LOTUS announced that after prolonged delay, version 3.0 of 1-2-3 would be made available during the fourth quarter of 1988. However, at that time, a further postponement was announced, moving the target date for version 3.0 to the second quarter of 1989. It is expected to add a number of performance features not possible with current versions of 1-2-3 such as the ability to link several worksheets, display up to three worksheets on the same screen, and to merge text and graphs in the same worksheet. Layered worksheets can be stored in main memory, faster recalculation of spreadsheet changes has been implemented, and the revised spreadsheet program can be automatically reconfigured to work with either DOS or OS/2 operating systems.

With all the new features added and an easier-to-use interface promised, the look and feel of version 3.0 may be considerably different from previous versions. If the new version requires considerable retraining, existing users of 1-2-3 may be reluctant to switch to the newer version or may even seriously consider adopting a competitive spreadsheet. Another problem is that version 3.0 will not run efficiently unless the user has the newer 286 or 386 microprocessor-based hardware. LOTUS had originally claimed that the new version of 1-2-3 would perform satisfactorily on 8088-based systems if users had 640K of internal memory and a hard disk.

LOTUS is striving to develop 1-2-3 versions that will run on both micros and mainframes, in distributed and nondistributed environments. New versions of 1-2-3 are being written in C language instead of assembler to ensure high portability. As part of its plans to push 1-2-3 as an operating environment, LOTUS has announced a high-level language for developing customized applications called Extended Applications Facility.

Integrated Software

Integrated software packages combine several functions such as word processing, spreadsheet, data base management, and communications all into one package. The major advantage is that a user can perform a number of computer-based functions with one program using a common command structure. Not having to switch from one program to another each time a different function is performed saves time and effort. The disadvantage is that normally a given integrated package will emphasize one or two functions such as spreadsheet or data base management and will provide only minimum capabilities for others (e.g., word processing, graphics). Some users are reluctant to pay the extra price for a package containing four or five functions when only one or two will be used continually.

Many users desire a "core" product which can be used for data base, spreadsheet, word processing, memo writing, desk calculating, scheduling, and so on. However, the market for individual applications (e.g., data base, word processing, spreadsheet) has grown faster than that for integrated software packages. It is estimated that integrated package sales grew 4 percent in 1986 over 1985 while sales of individual applications increased at a rate of 31 percent. Exhibit 18-2 shows actual and estimated individual application package revenues compared with those of integrated software packages for 1985 to 1989.

The major integrated software packages include LOTUS Symphony which has a strong spreadsheet, a fair data base, and a weak word processing capability, and Ashton-Tate's Framework, which has a strong data base, a good word processor, and a fair spreadsheet. Revenues from Symphony were estimated to be $36 million in 1986 (36% market share), and Framework generated $26 million for a 26 percent share. The other major players were Innovative Software's Smartware, which produced $14 million in revenues for a 14 percent share of the market and the Enable Group's Enable package which captured 3 percent of the market with $4 million in sales. More than forty other competitors divided the remaining 22 percent.

Exhibit 18-2 **Revenues for Individual and Integrated Software Packages for 1985–1989 (In millions)**

Year	Individual Applications	Integrated Packages
1985	625	103
1986	820	107
1987	967[a]	120
1988	1,150[a]	130[a]
1989	1,350[a]	140[a]

[a]Estimated
Source: PC Week.

At the lower end of the scale, Software Publishing Company (SPC) introduced First Choice in August 1986 and sold 70,000 units during the first six months of product life. It also sold 25,000 copies of its separate Professional Plan spreadsheet during 1986. It is estimated that SPC has sold 200,000 copies of First Choice at a list price of $195 through mid 1988. Version 2 of First Choice added graphics capabilities to other functions. Microsoft has converted its Macintosh integrated package "Works" for use on the IBM PC and compatibles and is expected to be a strong competitor with a price comparable to First Choice. A recent entry by Spinnaker Software is its Better Working Eight-In-One program. At $59.95, it provides outlining, word processing, spelling checker, spreadsheet, data base, graphics, communications, and a desktop organizer with a memo pad, address book, and calendar.

THE COMPETITIVE ENVIRONMENT

The electronic spreadsheet industry is growing less rapidly than other types of software and sales increases in recent years have not matched those of earlier years. Exhibit 18-3 shows the actual and expected unit sales of electronic spreadsheets from 1986 to 1990, according to one industry source. After levelling off in 1988, electronic spreadsheet sales are expected to grow at a slow but steady pace during the rest of the decade. However, the timing and magnitude of the impact of OS/2 based hardware on spreadsheet demand is very uncertain at this point.

Spreadsheets and word processing programs are the most widely installed applications and represent slower growth, mature markets. Data base managers have somewhat more potential with modest growth possibilities. Graphics, CAD/CAM, project management, and desktop publishing applications represent the fastest growing markets with considerable room to develop without saturation. The Sierra Group in a recent poll of over 1,500 users found that 60 percent of users surveyed planned to buy word processing packages, 54 percent planned to buy data base

---

Exhibit 18-3   **Actual and Estimated Sales of Electronic Spreadsheets (millions of units)**

Year	Number	Year	Number
1986	1.20	1989	1.80
1987	1.40	1990	2.00
1988	1.50		

Source: IDC Corporation, *Computerworld,* December 21, 1987.

managers, 51 percent spreadsheet purchases planned and 35 percent expected to buy graphics presentation packages.[7]

Exhibit 18-4 contains actual and estimated shipments of word processing, spreadsheet, graphics, communications, and data base management systems. With only modest sales growth expected from 1987 to 1988, for the period 1988 to 1992 spreadsheet sales are expected to increase at an average annual rate of 33 percent compared to 35 percent for word processing packages, 45 percent for graphics systems, 38 percent for communication packages, and 89 percent for data base managers.

Paperback Software introduced VP-planner as a LOTUS clone during the mid 1980s for $99, and Borland in 1988 introduced a lower priced LOTUS compatible for $195 that has more features than 1-2-3 and can access all LOTUS files and perform most LOTUS functions. In addition, Borland has acquired the rights to Surpass from Sergio Rubenstein, the developer of WordStar. Surpass is a higher priced LOTUS compatible spreadsheet selling for $495 that has many advanced features. In 1987, Microsoft introduced an IBM-PC compatible version of its popular Macintosh spreadsheet Excel for $495 which has a graphic interface characterized by ease of use. During 1988, LOTUS is expected to sell 1,200,000 copies of 1-2-3, Borland is estimating sales of 150,000 copies of Quattro, and industry analysts expect Excel sales to be at least 120,000 units. VP-planner and SuperCalc sales should level off or even decline.

LOTUS competitors such as SuperCalc, Multiplan, Excel, and Quattro can offer added features and ease of use along with function and file compatibility at the same or a lower price. However, other spreadsheets have the disadvantage that they must persuade buyers to undergo a retraining process for users, and 1-2-3 file compatibility must be demonstrated before the alternative products become viable contenders.

Exhibit 18-4   **Shipments of Applications Software Packages (in millions of units)**

	1987	**1988**[a]	**1992**[a]
Word processing	3.2	3.5	4.9
Spreadsheets	2.2	2.5	3.4
Graphics	1.4	1.8	3.3
Communications	2.1	2.5	3.8
Data base management	1.0	1.4	5.0

[a]Estimated.

Source: Dataquest, *Personal Computing,* October 1988.

---

[7]*Computerworld,* May 9, 1989.

Microsoft

Microsoft has two spreadsheet products: Multiplan and Excel. Multiplan has been a solid but nonspectacular software product with a slightly different formula and command structure than 1-2-3. It has data base capability with mouse support, runs under M/S Windows and on networks. Multiplan has 1-2-3 file read/write capability and can import files from dBase and R Base. Although the worksheet has no graphic capability, it can import graphs from Microsoft's Chart program.

Excel, a Microsoft worksheet program which proved popular on the Apple Macintosh, has a graphic interface and is more powerful that 1-2-3. It can operate on arrays, handle trend projection and optimization calculations, and display multiple spreadsheets on the same screen, linking them using a mouse or keystroke commands. The maximum spreadsheet size is two times that of LOTUS, and graphs can be printed from within the spreadsheet. The user may select from 42 different graph formats and numerous font, boldface, and italic sizes. Variable character heights, borders, shaded areas, and underlining are easy to implement. It is not copy protected and has flexible site licensing provisions.

Excel is designed for 286 or 386 personal computers with high-resolution graphics, at least 640K of internal memory, and a hard disk. It is fully compatible with 1-2-3 files and has a help facility which automatically gives the Excel equivalent when a 1-2-3 sequence is entered. However, Excel is not keystroke compatible with 1-2-3 and is only 95 percent compatible with LOTUS macros. It has a macro translator that translates 1-2-3 macros into Excel macros. Minimal recalculation is permitted and built-in auditing and data base capabilities are also provided.

Microsoft is emphasizing high-resolution graphics, mouse applications, and an easy-to-use pull down menu system interface in a package which can only be run on 286 and 386 machines. It expects the Windows interface and OS/2 Presentation Manager with which its program is compatible to become an industry standard. Excel is written in C language so portability is assured although it has no announced plans to make Excel available on the current generation of personal computers. Its greatest appeal is still to Macintosh users.

Borland—Quattro and Surpass

Quattro, at $195, is less expensive and more functional than 1-2-3. It provides selective recalculation, more types of graphs, and a wide variety of screen display and printing options. Graphs can be printed from within the spreadsheet and the program takes full advantage of EGA and VGA Graphics adapters. Quattro has full 1-2-3 file capability, improves macro development ability using a macro generator, and permits extensive customization of applications. For debugging purposes, individual commands within a macro sequence can be executed one at a time. It requires a minimum of 512K in internal memory and is not copy protected.

Surpass, at $495, will likely appeal to users who have reached the limit of LOTUS 1-2-3 capabilities. A subset of Surpass can be used to implement all 1-2-3 keystrokes, files, macros, and formulas, making it unnecessary for complete retraining of former LOTUS 1-2-3 users. It can handle multiple spreadsheets, align them in 3-D fashion, post changes from one spreadsheet to others automatically, and refer to a spreadsheet without requiring that it be in main memory. Dynamic links between spreadsheets are provided and a macro library contains command sequences which can be used on more than one spreadsheet. Multiple spreadsheets can be displayed on the screen, graphs may be displayed in 3-D format, and an undo command permits easy correction of mistakes. A built-in file manager can perform many common DOS functions.

Borland has imitated LOTUS by writing Quattro in assembly language, making it as fast and as compact as possible. Unlike LOTUS, the company is opposed to using one product for multiple computer architectures. It prefers to develop a lower priced package that will make the fullest possible use of a given type of machine. For users who want a higher level LOTUS look alike, the company can offer Surpass with more features than 1-2-3 at a comparable price.

SuperCalc

SuperCalc, acquired by Computer Associates when it absorbed Sorcim in the mid 1980s, permits use of larger spreadsheets than LOTUS (i.e., about 2,000 additional rows) and is not copy protected. The command structure differs somewhat from LOTUS, but a careful reading of menus will allow users to accomplish most of the functions possible with LOTUS. It reads and writes 1-2-3 files and can import or export VisiCalc, DIF, and ASCII files. Graphics and data base modules are included in the program and as many as nine graphs per spreadsheet can be saved in memory. It permits macrorecording, providing more financial and logical functions than LOTUS, and LAN support is also provided.

Version 5 of SuperCalc permits faster retrieval of information from cells with similar names or codes than previously possible and is menu, macro, and file compatible with 1-2-3. An optional 1-2-3 interface facilitates user transition from 1-2-3 and macros can contain both 1-2-3 and SuperCalc commands. Enhanced presentation graphics, a toggle on and off minimum recalculation feature, and an undo command for ease of use in correcting errors are provided. Macrodebugging and built-in auditing capabilities are also included. A version of Sideways is thrown in as a bonus feature with each SuperCalc purchase. Computer Associates has a volume discount and liberal site licensing policy for SuperCalc.

VP-planner

VP-planner, developed by Alex Osborne's Paperback Software, is a low-cost clone costing $99 that uses most LOTUS commands plus a few new ones. It will read and write dBase files, record macros, and open up to six windows. While working on one spreadsheet, users can print another one. VP-planner cannot run LOTUS add-ins but some add-ons will work with this program (e.g., 1-2-3 Forecast, Ready to Run Accounting, Goal Seeker). VP-planner has no built-in graphics capabilities but can develop graphs using the separate VP-graph program. Another drawback is that unlike other spreadsheet companies, it charges users for technical support.

The notoriety from the LOTUS lawsuit charging copyright infringement based on the look alike, feel alike quality of VP-planner has hurt sales. However, it is obvious that VP-planner is more than just a LOTUS clone. A new version, VP-planner Plus carries a slightly higher price tag ($179.99) and provides twice as many financial and logical functions as LOTUS, permits recalculation of selected cells, and is not copy protected. Graphics capabilities are only fair, not being in the same class as Quattro or Excel. An optional interface with pull down menus makes it easier to follow command sequences than possible with 1-2-3.

VP-planner's data base capability permits reading and writing dBase, VP-Info, and DIF files as well as viewing data in up to five dimensions. One obvious shortcoming of Paperback Software's marketing program is that it overstressed the value of VP-planner as a low-cost LOTUS clone and did not emphasize its strong data base capability. In its most recent annual report, Paperback reported a net loss of $354,000 or $0.12 per share on sales of $4.7 million compared to a net income of $77,000 or $0.02 per share on sales of $3.4 million in the previous year.

Ashton-Tate

Ashton-Tate, which gets 60 percent of its sales from dBase, its data base manager, is not an active player in the spreadsheet market although it does have an integrated package named Framework. However, its competitive position is eroding because its current programs will not work on the new 386 machines, and it is facing intense competition in the data base market from Oracle, Borland, and others. Both LOTUS and Microsoft are moving into the data base market with add-ins or built-in capabilities as part of their spreadsheet programs.

REVENUE AND INCOME ANALYSIS

Exhibit 18-5 contains revenues for LOTUS and five other companies that have developed and marketed electronic spreadsheets for the period 1984 to 1987.

Total spreadsheet industry revenues for the top six competitors have increased from $406.6 million to $1,338.7 million or 329 percent (1984 = 100). The average annual increase in revenues for the period under consideration was $310.7 million or 76.2 percent.

Exhibit 18-6 shows net incomes for the period 1984 to 1987. Total industry income increased from $70.4 million to $216.9 million, an increase of $146.5 million or 308 percent (1984 = 100). The average increase in net income for the period considered was 69.3 percent. Thus, total revenues increased 54 percent in 1985 over 1984, 35 percent in 1986 over 1985, and 59 percent for 1987 over 1986; net income increased 26 percent for 1985 over 1984, 29 percent for 1986 over 1985, and 90 percent for 1987 over 1986.

Exhibit 18-5   **Electronic Spreadsheet Company Revenues (In millions)**

Company	1984	1985	1986	1987
LOTUS	157.0	226.0	283.0	396.0
Ashton-Tate	$43.0	$82.0	$122.0	$211.0
Borland	1.1	11.6	29.7	38.1
Computer Associates	85.0	129.0	191.0	309.0
Microsoft	97.0	140.0	198.0	346.0
Software Publishing	23.5	37.2	23.7	38.6
Total Revenues	$406.6	$625.8	$847.4	$1,338.7

Source: Standard & Poor's Stock Reports, 1988.

Exhibit 18-6   **Electronic Spreadsheet Company Net Incomes (In millions)**

Company	1984	1985	1986	1987
LOTUS	$36.0	$38.2	$ 48.3	$ 72.0
Ashton-Tate	5.3	6.5	16.6	30.1
Borland	0.1	0.9	0.9	1.3
Computer Associates	9.5	13.3	18.5	36.5
Microsoft	15.9	24.1	39.3	71.9
Software Publishing	3.6	5.8	0.7	5.2
Total Income	$70.4	$88.9	$114.3	$216.9

Source: Standard & Poor's Stock Reports, 1988.

Exhibit 18-7   **Electronic Spreadsheet Company Assets (In millions)**

Company	1984	1985	1986	1987
		(In millions)		
LOTUS	$122.0	$186.0	$209.0	$ 318.0
Ashton-Tate	31.0	46.0	88.0	175.0
Borland	0.5	5.4	12.2	31.1
Computer Associates	118.0	148.0	245.0	439.0
Microsoft	48.0	65.0	171.0	288.0
Software Publishing	10.0	27.4	26.8	35.0
Total Assets	$329.5	$477.8	$752.0	$1,286.1

Source: Standard & Poor's Stock Reports, 1988.

Exhibit 18-7 shows total assets for the six spreadsheet companies for years 1984 to 1987. For the industry, assets increased from $329.5 million to $1,286.1 million or 390.3 percent, compared with a 329 percent increase in revenues and a 308 percent increase in net incomes. Assets increased 45 percent for 1985 over 1984, 57 percent for 1986 over 1985, and 71 percent for 1987 over 1986.

Exhibit 18-8 contains eaᵗ ings per share for 1986 and 1987 as well as research and development expenditures as a percent of sales revenues. Earnings per share increased at an average rate of 75 percent for the total industry compared to an average increase of 59 percent in total revenues and 90 percent in net income for 1987 compared to 1986. Four of the six companies increased research and development expenditures as a percent of sales slightly or not at all in 1987 while two companies (CAI and Software Publishing Company) significantly decreased their research and development outlays as a percentage of revenues. Also included are advertising expenditures as a percent of sales revenues[8] and sales per employee, which is sometimes used as a measure of productivity.

Exhibit 18-9 and 18-10 contain LOTUS financial statements since the company's inception in April 1982.

Exhibit 18-8   **Electronic Spreadsheet Earnings per Share, R&D Outlays, Advertising Expenses/Sales Revenues and Sales/Employee**

Company	EPS 1986	EPS 1987	R&D/Sales 1986	R&D/Sales 1987	Adv/ Sales 1986	Sales/Employee 1986	Sales/Employee 1987
LOTUS	$1.03	$1.58	13.8%	14.8%	0.26%	$135	$188
Ashton-Tate	0.85	1.26	9.3	9.2	2.12	111	191
Borland	0.02	0.03	9.0	9.3	9.22	54	102
Computer Associates	0.42	0.74	18.0	13.0	0.73	49	160
Microsoft	0.78	1.30	10.0	11.0	1.64	110	167
Software Publishing	0.10	0.69	24.9	19.9	4.81	100	162

Source: Standard & Poor's Stock Reports; Software News, October 1988; Computer Industry Encyclopedia, 1987.

---

[8]T. Juliussen et al. *Computer Industry Almanac,* 1987, latest data available.

Exhibit 18-9   **Lotus Development Corporation Consolidated Statements of Operations 1982–1987 (In thousands)**

	April 23, 1982 (Inception) to Dec. 31, 1982	December 31				
		1983	1984	1985	1986	1987
Net Sales	$ 174	$53,007	$156,978	$225,526	$282,864	$395,595
Costs and expenses						
Cost of sales	54	6,798	24,459	43,706	54,724	68,676
Research and development	341	2,201	14,752	22,324	39,167	58,420
Sales and marketing	575	12,086	43,139	76,376	87,455	126,848
General and administrative	408	5,923	15,941	22,189	37,662	46,546
Total Operating Expenses	1,378	27,008	98,291	164,595	219,008	300,490
Operating income (loss)	(1,204)	25,999	58,687	60,931	63,856	95,105
Interest income, net	55	944	3,826	3,932	3,311	3,960
Other income	4	489	3,025	2,540	3,863	3,853
Income before provision for income taxes	(1,145)	27,432	65,538	67,403	71,030	102,918
Provision for income taxes	—	13,115	29,492	29,253	22,730	30,875
Net Income	$(1,145)	$14,317	$ 36,046	$ 38,150	$ 48,300	$ 72,043
Net income per share	$(0.13)	$.98	$2.24	$.77	$1.03	$1.58
Weighted average common shares and common share equivalents outstanding	8,678	14,057	16,065	49,596	46,752	45,720

Exhibit 18-10   **Lotus Development Corporation Consolidated Balance Sheets, 1983–1987 (In thousands)**

	December 31,				
	1983	1984	1985	1986	1987
Assets					
Current assets					
Cash and short-term investments	$56,181	$ 58,800	$ 91,053	$ 93,157	$164,909
Accounts receivables, net	14,234	26,182	36,433	37,844	45,541
Inventory	1,846	10,176	9,147	6,794	9,210
Prepaid expenses	370	1,211	2,416	6,396	5,665
Total Current Assets	72,631	96,369	139,049	144,191	225,325
Property and equipment, net	4,689	24,413	38,203	40,964	51,920
Intangible assets associated with acquisitions, net	—	—	8,124	23,270	32,297
Marketable securities and other assets	1,023	1,429	427	584	8,111
Total Assets	$78,343	$122,211	$185,803	$209,009	$317,653
Liabilities and Stockholders' Equity					
Current liabilities					
Loans payable	$ 178	—	$ 3,514	$ 2,680	$ 7,736
Accrued employee compensation	271	778	3,914	11,350	15,287
Accounts payable and accrued expenses	5,938	12,745	17,085	30,554	31,685
Deferred revenue	—	2,908	3,550	6,221	11,734
Income taxes payable	12,796	3,110	12,287	7,926	17,381
Deferred income taxes, current	—	4,647	5,078	4,129	1,784
Total Current Liabilities	19,183	24,188	45,428	62,860	85,607
Deferred income taxes	320	1,724	1,833	1,556	—
Long-term debt	—	—	—	30,000	30,000
Commitments and contingencies	—	—	—	—	—
Stockholders' equity					
Preferred stock authorized, none issued	—	—	—	—	—
Common stock	166	169	171	526	546
Additional paid-in-capital	45,547	53,575	59,044	66,624	83,274
Retained earnings	13,172	49,218	87,368	135,317	207,360
Translation adjustment	—	268	(247)	(776)	243
Treasury stock	(3)	(3)	(3)	(83,135)	(87,743)
Deferred employee compensation	(42)	(6,928)	(7,791)	(3,963)	(1,634)
Total Stockholders' Equity	58,840	96,299	138,542	114,593	202,046
Total Liability and Stockholders' Equity	$78,343	$122,211	$185,803	$209,009	$317,653

Chaparral Steel Company

In 1973, Texas Industries, Inc. (TXI), a Dallas-based construction materials company, and Co-Steel International Ltd. of Canada agreed to build a steel mill as a joint venture in Midlothian, Texas. The initial attraction of the small town 25 miles south of Dallas was its proximity to a major population center, available power supplies, highways, and railroads.

Despite these assets, Midlothian (population 3,219) seemed an unlikely choice for a steel "mini-mill," but as the story goes, Co-Steel Chairman Gerald Heffernan saw a Midlothian Chamber of Commerce bulletin board notice which read: "Need money? Try working." He was convinced that they had found the sought-after site for their new mill. The farm and ranch lands in the area were populated with individuals deeply imbued with a work ethic that management was seeking. Few of the locals had ever worked in a steel mill, and as one manager observed, "We didn't want people who had learned bad work habits."[1]

Texas Industries, Inc.'s decision to start its own steel company, christened Chaparral Steel, was a natural outgrowth of its building materials business, since steel reinforcement is required in much of construction. In addition, the company forecasted a reinforcing bar (rebar) shortage that, unfortunately for the new company, never materialized. Observed one member of Chaparral's top management: "We had to diversify, and fast."[2]

Fortunately for the new manufacturer, flexibility, a trait that has virtually eluded domestic "big steel" firms, is one of the drawing cards for the mini-mill. Unlike the bigger, more complex "integrated" mills, the mini-mills are basically recycling plants, albeit technologically sophisticated ones. Having scaled-down operations and fewer steps in the manufacturing process, the mini-mill has significantly more tolerance for error and thus greater flexibility than the typical integrated mill.

Chaparral Makes Money in a Nongrowth Industry

Chaparral has been profitable and competitive in an industry which is facing perhaps the most difficult period in its history (Exhibit 19-2). When U.S. Steel (now

---

[1]Kurt Eichenwald, "America's Successful Steel Industry," *Washington Monthly,* February 1985, pp. 40–44.

[2]Ibid.

This case was prepared by John W. Simmons and Mark J. Kroll, The University of Texas at Tyler, as a basis for class discussion rather than to illustrate either effective or ineffective handling of an administrative situation. Used by permission from Mark J. Kroll.

Exhibit 19-1   **Streetscape of Midlothian at City Limits**

USX) lost $2.5 billion in 1982, Chaparral showed a profit of $11 million. In fiscal 1987, Chaparral produced and sold over 1.2 million tons of steel, representing over half of TXI's sales.

Pursuing market share amid its efforts to be the low-cost producer, Chaparral, in fiscal 1987, produced and sold more tonnage in a greater variety and over a wider geographical market than in any previous year. This record production was achieved in the face of what TXI's President and CEO, Robert D. Rogers, called "the most stagnant economic growth since before Texas Industries was founded in 1951."

In his letter to shareholders, dated July 15, 1987, Rogers announced that initial shipments of steel were made that same month to Western Europe and noted that Chaparral's impressive results were accomplished in "only an average market of structural products and a declining market during the year for bar products."

Chaparral is one of the most productive steel firms in the world in terms of labor, and it is the nation's tenth largest steelmaker, providing steel products to 44 states, Canada, and Western Europe. The firm has been the only U.S. mini-mill to

Exhibit 19-2   **TXI Business Segment Information (In thousands)**

	1986	1987	1988
Net sales			
Steel	$297,155	$318,807	$376,398
Cement/concrete	351,075	270,254	258,936
	$648,230	$589,061	$635,334
Operating profit			
Steel	$ 37,178	$ 42,171	$ 60,496
Cement/concrete	32,431	14,150	3,233
	69,609	56,321	63,729
Corporate expense (income)			
Administrative and general	14,836	16,912	14,605
Interest expense	41,880	38,740	38,043
Other income	(14,107)	(2,262)	(998)
Income before taxes and other items	$ 27,000	$ 2,931	$ 12,079
Depreciation, Depletion and Amortization			
Steel	$ 22,433	$ 23,567	$ 21,566
Cement/concrete	33,221	31,347	29,339
Corporate	790	510	634
	$ 56,444	$ 55,424	$ 51,539

Source: Annual Reports.

lower costs enough to make a profit in foreign markets.[3] Efforts have also been made to crack the bureaucratic obstacles of the Japanese market.

Since the first day of operations, Chaparral has used unorthodox managerial methods to achieve and maintain its competitiveness. According to Tom Peters, one of the authors of *In Search of Excellence:* "If you wrote down the ten most widely believed principles about managing in this century, you would find that Chaparral violates every one of them." Peters wrote that some business savants consider Gordon Forward, Chaparral's President and CEO, to be "the most advanced thinker in American management today."[4] Notwithstanding such hyperbole, the Midlothian steel firm has been ever watchful of its competitive environment and looks to the future rather than resting on its impressive early accomplishments.

Noting that this U.S. steel producer is "one of the few profitable ones," Peters explained that Forward managed his firm "more as a laboratory than as a factory." Forward, a native of Canada, earned a Ph.D. in metallurgy from the Massachusetts

[3]Tom Peters, *On Achieving Excellence,* Monthly Newsletter, San Francisco, TPG, May 1987.
[4]Ibid.

Institute of Technology. Company executives have credited Chaparral's success to Forward's leadership in three major areas: a marketing strategy attuned to customer needs, a relentless pursuit of technological improvement, and, perhaps most significantly, the application of participatory management techniques that encouraged employee creativity.[5]

At start-up in May 1975, Chaparral operated at an annual capacity of just over 400,000 tons, using the basics of a mini-mill plant: a single electric arc furnace, one continuous billet caster, and a rolling mill. By 1978, the firm was a leader in mini-mill technology. From 1978 to 1981, Chaparral earned a pretax average of $18 million per year.

Early in 1982, Chaparral brought on-line a second electric arc furnace, another continuous billet caster, and a larger rolling mill. This $180 million, largely debt-financed expansion could not have come at a worse time, paralleling the start of the worst steel recession in fifty years. Steel prices tumbled 20 to 50 percent, the industry's operating rate fell below 40 percent of capacity, and much of Chaparral's debt, at floating rates, floated out of sight. Fueled by high interest rates, the dollar climbed, imported steel flooded domestic markets, and Chaparral faced losses between 1982 and 1984.

Maintaining a long-term vision of its industry, the highly automated mini-mill tripled its annual capacity between 1982 and 1987. With its new product development program, the firm shipped approximately 1.3 million tons of steel to more than 900 customers in fiscal 1988. Furthermore, Chaparral added an average of 100,000 tons to its annual output during each of the past 13 years.

The attitude at TXI and Chaparral is that it is possible to make money in a nongrowth industry if you are good enough. As a result of its vision and diligence, the Midlothian firm currently produces and ships more tonnage than any other single U.S. steel mill constructed in the past 30 years.[6] Although future growth in the mini-mill segment is expected to slow, industry experts still see opportunities for additional mini-mill market growth. The "mini's" are expected to retain an advantage because of lower raw materials costs, utilization of new technology, efficient operation, plant location, perceptive marketing, flexible work rules, and consequent higher productivity. However, saturated markets and cheap imports are forcing the mini-mills to continue seeking new ways to grow.[7]

Prior to 1982, Chaparral was a part of the much publicized mini-mill phenomenon, but the future holds ever greater challenges. In 1985, four Sunbelt mini-mills closed their doors, and global overcapacity portends a continued threat of industry shake-out. Older, less technologically competent minis were particularly vulnerable. Producers of steel were differentiated mostly by price, product mix, and service.

---

[5]"Chaparral Steel Company," *Making America Competitive: Corporate Success Formulas,* Bureau of National Affairs Special Report, Washington, BNA, n.d.

[6]George Melloan, "Making Money Making Steel in Texas," *The Wall Street Journal,* January 26, 1988, southwest ed., p. 29.

[7]"Mini-Mills Up the Heat on the Maxis," *Fortune,* April 13, 1987, pp. 8–9.

Exhibit 19-3   Chaparral Steel Company Plant

State-of-the-art technology became so accessible around the world that quality was no longer optional.

The challenge which Chaparral has successfully faced up to this point is maintaining its responsive managerial style, marketing sensitivity, and technological currency and consequent productivity gains. It appears that Chaparral is not aspiring to become the new "big steel" but rather is striving to maintain its status as a highly competitive and successful niche-player.[8]

CHAPARRAL MANAGEMENT

Robert Rogers, a graduate of Yale and Harvard Business School, has been with TXI for 25 years. Mr. Rogers was serving as Chairman of the Board of Chaparral Steel Company as well as Chairman of the Board of TXI. A TXI director since 1970, he was also Chairman of the Board for the Dallas Chamber of Commerce and the immediate past Chairman of the 11th Federal Reserve District.

[8]Melloan, "Making Money."

In an interview, Mr. Rogers reflected on the unlikely success of an upstart company in a declining steel industry:

> We went into the carbon steel business when everyone else was going out of it. The biggest advantage we had was that we didn't have any plant, didn't have any customers, didn't have any employees or management and we didn't really know anything about how to make steel. We're still learning. Once we learn it, we're going to be in big trouble.

Pondering further the benefit of being the new kid on the block, Rogers observed:

> If we would have known the steel business, we would have known that the only way you could go forth with a company of any size would be to be unionized. Not knowing the steel business and being the largest non-union cement company in the U.S., we felt it was far better to represent the legitimate interests of employees ourselves rather than turn it over to some outside partner.

Concluding his remarks on Chaparral's unorthodox approach, Rogers said:

> Another thing was to hire employees who by and large did not come from industrial backgrounds. They came from rural backgrounds. The steel plant is next door to our largest cement plant and we have the same type of employees there. We knew they were hard-working and imaginative, so they didn't know you were supposed to spend three to four man-hours per ton of steel. When we got to 1.8 or 1.6 and were working to get down substantially less than that, they didn't know that there's a limit on how many tons of steel you can get per man hour.[9]

Despite recent economic setbacks for TXI as a whole, Chaparral remained strong and was moving forward. Rogers and the TXI Board were still planning for the long-term. Fiscal 1988 was the twenty-sixth consecutive year of increased cash dividends to TXI shareholders. Notwithstanding the virtual absence of earnings, due in large part to the regional construction slump and the dumping in TXI markets of imported cement, the Directors maintained cash dividends at the annual rate of $0.80 per year with a year-end stock dividend of 4 percent (Exhibit 19-4).

The Board of Directors

The Chaparral Board of Directors provided a wealth of educational, professional, and cultural experience. Past and present directors have served the community and most have other corporate affiliations. Co-Steel Chairman Heffernan, who has been involved with several Canadian mining and metallurgical professional groups, has been a TXI Director since 1986 and was also a Chaparral Director. In October 1987, the Chaparral Board was reduced in number and reorganized to have a non-TXI majority. New board members were John M. Belk, Chairman, Belk Stores Services, Inc., Charlotte, North Carolina; Dr. Gerhard Liener, Chief Financial Officer, Daimler-Benz AG, Stuttgart, West Germany; and William J. Shields, President and CEO, Co-Steel International Ltd., Toronto, Ontario, Canada.

[9]Ibid.

Exhibit 19-4 Selected Financial Data, TXI and Subsidiaries (In thousands except per share data)

	1981	1982	1983	1984	1985	1986	1987	1988
Results of operations								
Net sales	285,003	282,713	321,468	335,381	343,688	648,230	589,061	635,334
Net income	30,411	18,332	18,691	12,300	17,597	22,114	1,253	13,053
Return on common equity	22.4%	11.9%	11.4%	7.2%	9.9%	11.9%	0.6%	6.8%
Per share information								
Net income	3.22	1.96	2.00	1.32	1.93	2.26	—	1.09
Cash dividends	.60	.62	.64	.67	.70	.73	.76	.80
Stock dividends, distributions	4%	4%	4%	4%	4%	4%	4%	4%
Other information								
Avg. common shares outstanding (in 000s)	9,427	9,339	9,299	9,285	9,074	9,574	10,039	10,160
No. of common stockholders	6,785	6,605	6,286	6,111	5,811	5,508	5,975	5,632
Common stock price (hi/lo)	31–18	30–14	36–15	38–25	29–21	31–23	31–22	40–24

Source: Annual reports.

Gordon E. Forward, President and CEO

Gordon Forward has been described as the architect of the winning Chaparral formula and has received the lion's share of credit for making the formula a success. Displaying a great willingness to undertake managerial experiments, Forward claimed that the legendary Captain Bill "Scrap Heap" Jones, a nineteenth century steel mill superintendent, was a role model for his approach. Of Jones, Forward said:

> If there was a better machine to do a job, the old one went quickly on the scrap heap. He also fought for his men's welfare and inspired them to set world steel production records. And they loved him for it. I think the industry ought to take a new look at Captain Jones' ideas.[10]

Mr. Forward, a native of Vancouver, has been referred to as "a refugee from big steel bureaucracy."[11] He was hired as Chaparral's executive vice-president in 1974. A vocal critic of the stagnated domestic steel industry, Forward, in an interview, remarked:

> U.S. steel producers had no real competition after the war. Every time the unions demanded more wages or whatever, the managers said, "Fine, we'll simply pass the costs on to the consumer." Well, this went on for more than 20 years and had a real effect on how managers thought about staying on top technologically. . . . Of course, they spent money on improvement. But they went about it the way that bureaucracies are likely to go about something like that: they kept tacking new things on to their established operations.

As steel labor costs rose in the 1970s, the mini-mills, quickly adopting foreign technological improvements, were able to seize new markets and Chaparral was a leader of the pack.

NATURE OF THE STEEL INDUSTRY

Big Steel

The term "big steel" generally referred to the large, traditional, integrated steel mills, so named because they had the capability of processing coke and iron ore into a wide range of steel products. Steel mill products were consumed by industries touching virtually every aspect of daily life, but were sold principally to the transportation, construction, machinery, and container industries.

Prior to 1970, the United States had been the world's leading steel producer, but the domestic steel industry was declining. Most U.S. steel mills were of pre-World War II vintage, and, despite periodic renovation, the mills lacked the effi-

---

[10]*Making America Competitive.*

[11]Eichenwald, "America's Successful," p. 40.

cient layouts, the economies of scale, and the more productive technologies utilized in the "greenfield" mills of Japan and Western Europe.[12]

After World War II, negotiations with the United Steelworkers Union began an upward spiral for wage rates that were disproportionate to the growth of labor productivity, thereby increasing unit labor costs. Attempting to reduce escalating wage increases (which averaged 6.6% annually between 1947 and 1957, a period of relatively low inflation), big steel entered into a strike that lasted from July to November 1959. During the strike, foreign producers supplied American needs, and the United States became a net importer of steel in 1959. Imports grew to an average of 15 percent of consumption in the 1970s, 19 percent in 1981, and over 20 percent in 1982.[13]

The steel industry was becoming much more competitive and internationalized as world exports of finished steel products increased dramatically during the 1960s, prompted by declining raw material and shipping costs, and powered by foreign investment in modern facilities. American steel exports tumbled as Japanese and Western European exports shot skyward. State-of-the-art technology became available to any producer willing to pay for it, and product quality became essentially uniform across geopolitical boundaries.

During the 1970s, domestic steel production grew only modestly, profits remained depressed as competition from imports grew, and, as a result, the U.S. industry's ability to add new capacity was severely constrained. Domestic industry employment began a steady decline in 1972, and in 1982 reached the lowest levels since data collection began during the Great Depression.[14]

In 1982, the U.S. steel industry lost a record $3.2 billion.[15] By mid 1987 the industry's operating losses had reached $6 billion.[16] In March 1982, testifying before the U.S. Senate, Dr. Donald F. Barnett, speaking for the American Iron and Steel Institute (AISI) regarding international competitiveness in the domestic steel industry, stated:

> Perhaps the most significant determinant of international competitiveness is labor productivity. . . . However, even if labor productivity is low, a product can still be competitive if there are other compensating advantages, e.g., lower labor rates as persist in many developing countries. Alternately, an investment which raises productivity can actually decrease cost competitiveness if the capital cost of the investment outweighs the labor savings. Hence, improved labor productivity cannot be the ultimate goal in and of itself. International competitiveness in the steel industry, therefore, must

[12]United States Dept. of Commerce, *Critical Materials Requirements of the U.S. Steel Industry,* Washington, GPO, March 1983.

[13]Ibid.

[14]Ibid.

[15]Jack Robert Miller, "Steel Mini-Mills," *Scientific American,* May 1984, pp. 32–39.

[16]Julian Szekely, "Can Advanced Technology Save the U.S. Steel Industry?" *Scientific American,* July 1987, pp. 34–41.

also look at capital efficiency, e.g., capacity use, labor costs, raw material costs, yield rates, and energy efficiency . . . [17]

Regulatory costs and materials availability were other factors which determined industry competitiveness. Despite recent turmoil, the domestic integrated mills have increased their productivity in the last decade compared with Japanese mills (Exhibit 19-5). By 1986, AISI reported, the U.S. steel industry had become the most efficient in the world.[18] However, while the domestic steel industry was competitive in energy and materials costs and use, it was less competitive in terms of labor costs and productivity.[19]

Clearly, the integrated mills have been attempting to respond to the changing market conditions as indicated by increased productivity rates. The big mills have gradually improved their marketing techniques by specializing in limited ranges of higher quality, cost-competitive products so that big steel firms are no longer able to function as steel "supermarkets."[20]

Unfortunately, the stock market crash of October 19, 1987, occurred just as the moribund steel industry was reviving. Despite the 33 percent drop in steel stock prices, analysts predicted sharp increases in earnings, due to the falling dollar and steel import quotas legislated through September 1989.[21] Despite recent difficulties in earning, attracting, and borrowing sufficient investment capital, the domestic integrated firms have retained a large share of the U.S. market.

The growth of U.S. production is expected to remain relatively low due to trends in consumption and output. Projections of world steel production indicate a continuing malaise in the industrialized nations, contrasted with rapid growth in the developing countries. By the year 1990, steel production capacity is expected to in-

---

Exhibit 19-5   **Average Man-Hours to Produce One Ton of Steel**

	1977	1986	1988
U.S. integrated mills	10.04	6.91	—
Japanese integrated mills	8.94	8.61	—
U.S. mini-mills	—	2.00	—
Chaparral	—	1.60	1.50

Sources: "Chaparral Steel Company." *Making America Competitive: Corporate Success Formulas,* Bureau of National Affairs Special Report, Washington, BNA, n.d. and Karen Freeze, "From a Casewriter's Notebook," *HBS Bulletin,* June 1986, pp. 54–63.

---

[17]*Critical Materials Requirements.*

[18]*Making America Competitive.*

[19]*Critical Materials Requirements.*

[20]Tom Stundza, "Steel: Making More with Less," *Purchasing,* February 12, 1987, pp. 50–57.

[21]David Carey, "Forecast: Industry Analysis—Metals," *Financial World,* January 5, 1988, p. 40.

crease by 20 percent in developing countries and to erode by 3 percent in the United States.[22]

The hard times which domestic steel has been facing have many causes: poor management, labor squabbles, obsolete technology, foreign competition, and product substitutes such as aluminum and fiber-reinforced plastics. Many of U.S. big steel's problems can be attributed to their own sluggishness and complacency in technology and marketing matters, but the problems of integrated mills are proving to be somewhat systemic as the industries in Japan and Europe have begun to face problems similar to those of their American counterparts. As Dr. Barnett foresaw,[23] developing countries are entering the steel industry with relative ease and success, and some experts doubt whether the large, inflexible integrated mills will survive the twentieth century.

Mini-Mills

The steel industry can be divided into three segments of different economic and technical profiles: the integrated mills, the mini-mills, and the specialty steel mills. Domestically, the minis are the chief competitors of the integrated mills. The specialty steel mills accounted for only 5 percent of U.S. output, but they manufactured more expensive products than did the minis and accounted for a higher percentage of total revenues.[24] The minis and specialty steel mills have avoided the worst of the recent industry turmoil, but it is the mini-mills that are expected to make the greatest gains in the domestic market into the 1990s, and at the expense of the integrated mills.[25]

The mini-mill concept was relatively slow in arriving in the United States. The method thrived in Japan and Western Europe for over twenty years before Chaparral was founded in 1973. Interestingly enough, North America's first mini-mill was established in Canada in 1962 by a former manager of Co-Steel, the Canadian holding company that played a seminal role in the creation of Chaparral.[26] In the 1960s, 10 to 20 mini-mills shared roughly 2 percent of the domestic steel market. In 1988, the number of domestic mini-mills was around 55, with a market share just over 20 percent.

A "mini-mill" was so named, not because it was small, but because its operations entailed only a part of the integrated steelmaking process (Exhibit 19-6). The mini-mill avoided almost entirely the integrated mill's energy- and capital-intensive "front end" aspect of steelmaking, that is, the iron-smelting process, including the mining and preparation of raw materials, and the blast-furnace operation.

The mini-mill begins with steel scrap (Exhibit 19-7), flux, and occasionally

[22]Szekely, "Can Advanced Technology?"

[23]Ibid.

[24]Ibid.

[25]Stundza, "Steel: Making More."

[26]*Making America Competitive.*

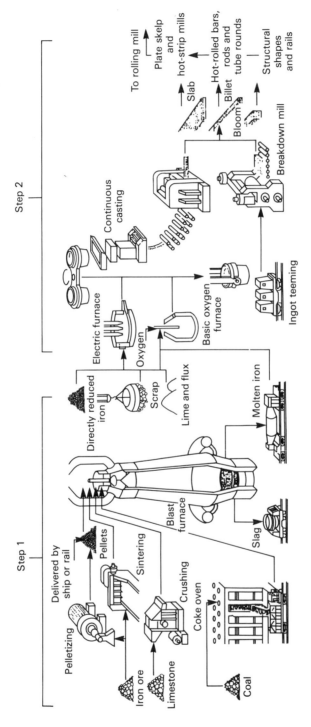

Step 1

Delivered by
ship or rail

Pelletizing

Pellets

Sintering

Iron ore

Limestone

Crushing

Coke oven

Coal

Blast
furnace

Slag

Molten iron

Directly reduced
iron

Scrap

Lime and flux

Electric furnace

Oxygen

Basic oxygen
furnace

Ingot teeming

Step 2

Continuous
casting

Breakdown mill

Bloom

Billet

Slab

To rolling mill

Plate skelp
and
hot-strip mills

Hot-rolled bars,
rods and
tube rounds

Structural
shapes
and rails

Exhibit 19-6 **Integrated Mill and Mini-Mill Steel Manufacturing**

Note: Integrated steel mills produce steel using both steps 1 and 2. Beginning with iron ore, coal and limestone, they go through most of the steps presented here. Mini-mills use scrap as their raw material, and complete step 2, using either an electric furnace or a basic-oxygen furnace. Most recently built mini-mills use an electric furnace and continuous casting technology.

Exhibit 19-7   Chaparral Steel Raw Material

directly reduced iron. The scrap is melted in an electric furnace, poured into ladles, and then transferred to a continuous-casting machine to be made into billets, looms, or slabs directly from the molten steel.

The success of domestic minis was due in part to the use of continuous billet-casting, which has been standard practice in minis since 1970. The continuous casting process can increase yield 18 percent over ingot-casting, the process common to conventional steel mills.[27] Only about half of the domestic integrated mills utilize continuous casters.[28] Continuing to emphasize innovation, Chaparral has a recently commissioned horizontal casting machine which came on line in 1988 and is expected to add materially to productivity (Exhibit 19-8).

All three segments of the domestic steel industry used scrap to some degree

[27]Miller, "Steel Mini-Mills."
[28]Szekely, "Can Advanced Technology?"

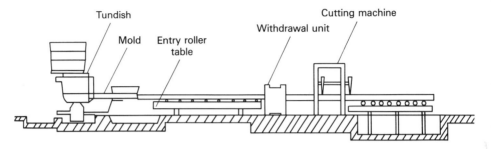

Exhibit 19-8   **Horizontal Continuous Caster**
Baltimore Works, Armco.

but the mini-mills were almost wholly dependent on it. Recycling scrap (processing or secondary materials) resulted in less waste and reduced overall raw materials requirements.[29] The United States was estimated to have had a scrap inventory of 620 billion metric tons in 1982, and, with annual accumulations, supply was expected to meet demand for at least several decades.[30] Chaparral processed some 300,000 cars per year, or one every 20 seconds, which provided roughly 30 percent of the firm's raw material. The use of steel substitutes (e.g., plastic) in automobiles caused some concern in the industry, but Mr. Forward maintained a sense of humor:

> There is a possibility we may have to go back to an iron ore base some day. For the moment, however, we are all right. We keep on importing Toyotas, which have a seven-year life. It takes us seven years to get a new Toyota into our furnace.

In the meantime, there was what some called a "ubiquitous availability" of domestically generated scrap.[31] Another dimension of the problem concerned the impurity content of the scrap, which prevented production of certain high-quality grades of steel,[32] another reason mini-mills have concentrated on relatively high-volume, low-cost steels.

The mini-mill segment has remained relatively profitable by restricting product range and therefore the level of capitalization required by utilizing locally generated scrap and thereby lowering transportation costs and by marketing in the vicinity of the mill.

Unlike big steel, the minis, in order to increase productivity, have relied on innovative processing technology copied from abroad and adapted to suit their individual purpose. In contrast, the specialty steel industry has typically developed its new technologies in-house,[33] while the integrated mill has been constrained by rela-

[29]*Critical Materials Requirements.*

[30]Miller, "Steel Mini-Mills."

[31]Ibid.

[32]Szekely, "Can Advanced Technology?"

[33]Ibid.

tively larger capital investment requirements and restrictive labor contracts. Operators of mini-mills have been able to invest capital in new technology, and recapture markets that big steel abandoned to imports.

The significance of potential foreign competition in the mini-mill segment has been mitigated by the dominant role played by transportation costs. On this topic, Mr. Forward has said of Chaparral:

> We adopt certain goals. In our beams, for instance, the Koreans are the most efficient producers. So we just adapt so that we will have a lower labor content than the shipping costs of beams from Korea to the West Coast. If they have zero labor costs, we'll still have a competitive advantage.

Furthermore, as mentioned earlier, the minis had the advantage of relatively low raw material costs and flexible work rules. Firms such as Chaparral, Nucor, and Birmingham Steel had much lower base wage rates, but provided generous bonus programs for high levels of team productivity.

The mini-mill products of the recent past have been simple and limited in variety. They have included wire rods, reinforcing rods, and various bar products. The bar forms, classified by cross-sectional shape, include flats, rounds, and squares. Mini-mills may also manufacture light I beams, T beams, angles (with 90 degree cross section), and channels (with a shallow "U" in cross section). A product is considered a light section if the longest part of a shape viewed in cross section is 75 mm or less; a heavy section measured greater than 75 mm. Merchant bars are bars made of carbon steel and rolled hot. An alloy steel was made when small amounts of manganese, chromium, nickel, and so on, singly or in combination, were added to the melt. Recently, mini-mills have been venturing into lines of higher-grade products. These items were mainly for the construction industry, but Chaparral and other minis also sold such products to the automakers.

Steel sheet and large structural girders have long been the mainstay of integrated steelmakers. Until recently, mini-mills had not been able to manufacture sheet, but Nucor Corporation, one of the most successful of the minis, was building a sheet mill that used a new technology to make sheet in mini-mill quantities and of mini-mill thicknesses.[34] Furthermore, Nucor, which already owned a number of mini-mills, announced a joint venture with Yamato Kogyo Co., a large Japanese steelmaker, to build a mill in Arkansas that would manufacture large structural girders. Similarly, Chaparral had voiced an interest in either buying or building a plant that can turn out large structural beams.[35]

With continued adaptation of new technologies, the mini-mill segment of the industry was expected to continue to increase market share at the expense of the less efficient, older mills. Estimates for the mini-mill share ranged as high as 40 percent

---

[34]George J. McManus, "Mini-Mill Report: The Honeymoon is Over," *Iron Age,* March 1, 1986, p. 26+.

[35]"Mini-Mills Up the Heat."

of domestic output by the end of the century.[36] The locations of many of the larger mini-mills are presented in Exhibit 19-9.

Clearly, mini-mills had natural cost advantages over integrated mills. Indeed, minis were sometimes referred to as "money-mills." The capital cost of building an integrated plant was approximately $1,600 per ton of annual capacity, whereas for a mini-mill it was only $200 to $300. The capital outlay for an integrated steel plant easily approached several billion dollars.[37] As mentioned, the man-hours per ton were also substantially different (Exhibit 19-5). Likewise, raw material costs and energy costs favored the minis. A comparison of mini-mill and integrated steel mill cost structures is seen in Exhibit 19-10.

THE CHAPARRAL WAY OF RUNNING A PROFITABLE BUSINESS

Market Responsiveness

In 1987, Gordon Forward proclaimed Chaparral's marketing goal: "to become the easiest steel company to buy from." The strategy for accomplishing that objective was to provide service by developing new products, raising quality levels, and extending shipping capabilities. Flexibility and responsiveness to changing customer needs were crucial. As an example, Forward recalled how the company quality control department introduced a microalloy steel production capability and be-

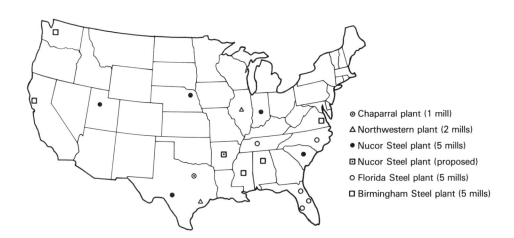

Exhibit 19-9   **Mini-Mill Sites in the United States**

[36]Ibid.
[37]Szekely, "Can Advanced Technology?"

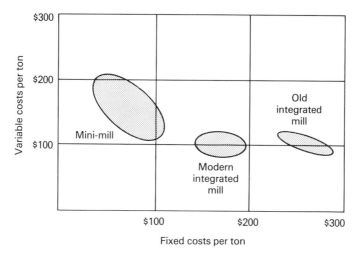

Typical range of costs per ton of annual capacity for an old integrated mill, a modern integrated mill, and a mini-mill can be expressed in terms of fixed and variable costs. Fixed costs are expenditures for such items as capital, manpower, and maintenance, which do not vary significantly once a plant is operating. Variable costs include expenditures for raw materials, other supplies, and energy, which may change from year to year. Since mini-mills do not have to wait as long as integrated mills to recoup the investment in setting up operations, they can consider replacing old equipment with new sooner.

Exhibit 19-10   **Comparison of Cost Structures**

gan marketing the resultant product in an unconventional way and thereby expanded the firm's customer base. As an additional service, Chaparral customers had full access to the marketing and quality control departments. Furthermore, the Midlothian firm offered flexible rolling schedules and newly developed remote shipping points.

The classic mini-mill concept was grounded in the strategy of locating where the mill could take advantage of locally available markets and sources of labor and scrap. Subcategories of mini-mills include the "neighborhood mill," the strategy of which was to locate in an area where the demand for steel was expected to grow, and the "market mill," which concentrated on one or two specific products to meet a given market.[38]

When Chaparral began operations 14 years ago, it was essentially a market mill, producing rebar for the regional construction market. Richard T. Jaffre, Chaparral's Vice-President for Raw Materials, noted that domestic and global mini-mill capacity was being overbuilt in the late 1970s:

It became clear that if Chaparral was to continue to prosper and grow, we had to rethink our place in the market. From the beginning, our focus has always been on

[38]Miller, "Steel Mini-Mills."

steel. We had no interest in diversifying into oil, insurance, or whatever. We believe
the steel business can and should be both profitable and fun. So, in 1979, Chaparral
decided that our primary opportunity for growth was to expand our product mix and
transcend the traditional mini-mill size range (structural shapes up to 6 inches in cross-
section). The problem with this strategy is that the cost of building a facility for larger
shapes can flatten a mini-mill's wallet. The price of steel mill equipment tends to rise
exponentially with the cross-sectional dimensions of its products.

Nevertheless, the perception of Chaparral as a market mill persisted at least
through the mid-1980s,[39] but a 1987 comment by Forward was quite revealing in
this respect:

> Although Chaparral is classified as a mini-mill, this year we began producing a range
> of steels traditionally supplied only by larger, integrated steel mills.

Furthermore, the president and CEO expected that the firm's recently commissioned horizontal casting machine, which came on-line in 1988, would provide the
firm with "even greater opportunities to serve customers more completely."

The horizontal caster was expected to facilitate getting Chaparral down to
"micro-mill" size.[40] Rejecting the prospect of making the Midlothian plant bigger
or increasing its 950-member employee roster, Forward asserted that his firm was
steadfast in its intent to remain relatively flat organizationally, acknowledging that
small was better in today's steel industry. After looking hard at microtechnology
and studying how McDonald's fast-food chain does what it does, Forward claimed:
"We figured out how to build something small enough you could literally put it on
a barge and run it with only 40 people." Says Forward: "We could almost franchise
it."[41]

Technological Currency

A scientist by training, Mr. Forward viewed his mill as a laboratory and encouraged experimentation. Saying that research was too often mistakenly isolated
as a staff position, Forward explained:

> We've tried to bring research right into the factory and make it a line function. We
> make the people who are producing the steel responsible for keeping their process on
> the leading edge of technology worldwide. If they have to travel, they travel. If they
> have to figure out what the next step is, they go out and find the places where people
> are doing interesting things. They visit other companies. They work with universities.

According to the AISI, the integrated steel industry has spent an average of 4
to 7 percent of annual sales on modernizing plants and equipment. Chaparral, by
contrast, spent 15 percent of annual gross profits on upgraded equipment and new

[39]McManus, "Mini-Mill Report."
[40]Ibid.
[41]Ibid.

technologies. As a matter of policy, the Midlothian firm had an annual summer shutdown to make the necessary capital improvements. Having labor costs at 9 to 10 percent of sales, compared with an integrated steel industry average of 40 percent, is another factor that made technology funding an easier task for Chaparral.[42]

Chaparral has fought to maintain a work environment that nourishes people, innovation, and accomplishment. The total involvement of the work force was critical, because, as Jaffre noted:

> This is really the heart of the matter, because high tech is something people create, implement, and maintain. You can't just go out and buy it. Bodies and dollar bills aren't enough. Big Steel went out and hired thousands of researchers, industrial engineers, corporate planners, and staff specialists and the world still passed them by.

What were typically staff functions at other mills were dove-tailed with line functions at Chaparral. For example:

> When there's a need for new production equipment, a line manager is put in charge of the entire project, including conceptual design, budgeting, purchasing, construction, installation, and start-up. Maintenance people are also included in the conceptual design stage, with the result that the equipment is easier to maintain. We've found that when forces shaping the design come from our production managers—when their egos get hooked—the odds of success are greatly enhanced. They make it work.[43]

People who are involved in the decision process are more likely to be committed to the decision reached.

Naturally, computer technology would be used by any steel mill striving for efficiency. According to Mr. Jaffre, Chaparral used computers in "planning, forecasting, inventory management, control of receipts, control of purchase orders, issuance of purchase orders, extensions, payables . . . the whole nine yards."[44] Because the Chaparral operation consumed 100 million tons of junk automobiles, refrigerators, stoves, and the like, per year, Jaffre noted that computers were most useful as repositories of historical cost-trend information.

Like most firms, Chaparral tried to minimize its investment of cash in inventory, but the mini-mill must buy numerous lots of scrap, frequently. Therefore, observed the vice-president, "We're bound by the market." In conclusion, Jaffre stated,". . . in the main, the computer was for short-, medium-, and long-term planning. It's the data base for our formal planning—the corporate financial forecast, typically done once a year with quarterly updates."[45] The firm not only relied on a talented, motivated work force but also invested in sophisticated computerized systems and production facilities.

[42]*Making America Competitive.*

[43]"Mini-Mills Up the Heat."

[44]Robert E. Lee, "How They Buy Scrap at Chaparral," *Purchasing*, August 22, 1985, pp. 98A1–98A4.

[45]Ibid.

Participatory Management

During the 1970s, U.S. Steel (USX) had as many as 11 layers of management. The quintessential big steel firm subsequently "evolved down" to four layers.[46] A key initial Chaparral decision was to create only four layers. Decision-making at Chaparral was forced down to the shop floor where the actual production takes place.

It has been said of Gordon Forward that he's "a man of many slogans," including: "Participatory management means taking decision making to the lowest competent level—and making the lowest level competent."[47] Says Chaparral's CEO: "We believe that people want to work and do a good job if you give them some responsibility and reward them with more than a paycheck."[48]

Chaparral's pioneering participatory management strategies appeared to benefit the firm as well as the employees. A clear indication was the fact that a 1977 attempt by the United Steelworkers of America to unionize the mill was soundly rejected by 73 percent of the 98 percent of the work force voting.[49] A former steelworker from U.S. Steel's South Works mill in Chicago was quoted as saying: "At the other mill I was stuck in a craft line. I couldn't help somebody in a different job, and he couldn't help me. That was because of the union. Here [at Chaparral] we do what we have to do to get the job done."[50]

Described by some in the business literature as a "maverick mini-mill," the "us-versus-them" mentality that haunts so many of the older mills was largely absent from the Midlothian firm. Rather than "steelworkers," some employees referred to themselves as "Chaparral people."[51] Chaparral was a people-oriented firm, whether dealing with employees or with customers. The Chaparral work force was governed by an esprit de corps which has been hospitable to risk-taking and forgiving of setbacks. Although such incidents were neither unique to Chaparral nor common there, one $15,000 mistake, which at a less dynamic firm might have cost the melt shop superintendent his job, was stoically dubbed a "$15,000 paperweight."[52]

The company has had a no-layoff policy and claimed never to have laid off an employee, not even during the difficult 1982 to 1984 period. In fact, during that time, employees with construction skills were lent to work on the construction of Chaparral's second mill, rather than bringing in outside builders and having to sack superfluous steelmakers.[53]

[46]*Making America Competitive.*

[47]Karen Freeze, "From a Casewriter's Notebook," *HBS Bulletin,* June 1986, pp. 54–63.

[48]*Making America Competitive.*

[49]Eichenwald, "America's Successful."

[50]Ibid.

[51]Ibid.

[52]Freeze, "From a Casewriter's Notebook."

[53]*Making America Competitive.*

Numerous other policies and programs distinguished Chaparral among steel-makers. For instance, the seniority system, common at big steel mills, was never adopted at the Midlothian firm, and promotions were made based on job performance. There were no time clocks to punch and all Chaparral employees have been salaried since 1981.[54] Furthermore, there were no assigned parking spots, no dress codes or color-coded hard hats, and no executive lunchroom. Claimed one Chaparral manager: "We've eliminated every barrier to communication, every barrier to identification with management and company goals." Tom Peters wrote:

> Imagine a $300-million company where the vice-president of administration fills in on the switchboard, where there are no formal personnel and purchasing departments and no personal secretaries. There isn't much for secretaries to do because executives are discouraged from writing memos. For that matter, there aren't that many executives.[55]

Moreover, Peters declared, "You won't find a corporate organization chart like that in any business text." Team spirit was further promoted by the company-wide practice of communication on a first-name basis, decentralized offices, and the minimization of formalized meetings.[56]

Although Chaparral workers have not been paid extravagant wages, job security and other benefits have taken up the slack. Bonuses and profit sharing were introduced from the start and together have run as high as 20 percent of wages.[57] Management further showed its trust in labor by delegating to every member of the firm responsibility for quality control and sales, thus removing what they saw in their company as two nonessential managerial layers. Said Forward:

> Everyone in the company pays attention to our customers. Everyone in the company is a member of the sales department. Literally. About four years ago, we made everyone in the company a member of the sales department. That means people in security, secretaries, everyone.

Actually, at Chaparral there was a conscious effort to "bash barriers between jobs."[58] Security guards, for example, were paramedics, ran the company ambulance, administered employee hearing tests, and entered safety and quality control data into the computer. Foremen remained responsible for hiring, education, training, and benefits. To prevent employee burnout, Chaparral had a compulsory annual sabbatical program that permitted people at the supervisor level to visit other mills, customers, and so on for a period from two weeks to six months.

[54]Ibid.

[55]Peters, *On Achieving Excellence.*

[56]Freeze, "From a Casewriter's Notebook."

[57]*Making America Competitive.*

[58]Peters, *On Achieving Excellence.*

THE FUTURE OUTLOOK FOR CHAPARRAL

Asked if Chaparral would "swallow hard and scrap unamortized equipment and put in new technology—even if (the firm) didn't feel competition nipping at (its) heels," Forward responded:

> Absolutely. We simply can't wait until we've been forced into a corner and have to fight back like alley cats. In our end of the business, we can't afford to act like fat cats. We have a system that's tough by its own definition. If we succeed in making our business less capital-intensive, we'd be naive not to expect a lot of others will want to get into it. If we succeed at what we are trying to do as a mini-mill, we'll also lower the price of entry. So we have to go like hell all the time. If the price of what we sell goes up too high, if we start making too much money on certain parts of our product line, all of a sudden lots of folks will be jumping in. And they can get into business in 18 months or so. They can hire our people away. . . . This makes us our own worst enemy. We constantly chip away the ground we stand on. We have to keep out front all the time. Our advantages are the part of the industry we're in, but also the kind of organization we have. We have built a company that can move fast and that can run full out. We're not the only ones—there are others like us. Nucor does many of the same things, but it has a slightly different personality. And there's Florida Steel. There are a number of quality mini-mills. We are all a bit different, but we all have to run like hell.

Today's steel industry has been increasingly dichotomized into two segments: the quick and the dead. CEO Forward likened firms that do not utilize ever-improving technologies with Forest Lawn: "Not because there are no good ideas there, but because the good ideas are dying there all the time."

Observing that mini-mills were no longer very labor-intensive, Forward, taking a cue from Dr. Barnett, believed that the next big step for Chaparral was to use new technology to drastically cut energy usage. Technological developments in the forging process were also receiving close scrutiny. Jaffre stated that Chaparral maintained a competitive edge by:

> . . . Never forgetting the magnitude and strength of international competition; by maintaining our capacity to anticipate and manage change; by continuously developing our skills in the application of new technology and the service of our markets; by providing an environment that taps our greatest natural resource—our people.

Furthermore, the Chaparral Vice-President asserted that the firm had ardently chosen not to be a party to any "de-industrialization" but rather to be a forceful player in the new "industrial renaissance."

Future growth was an issue for Chaparral management. Should they keep expanding the Texas facility, or expand into a new area and attempt to duplicate their success? With the opening of the Nucor plant in Arkansas, the competition in both the structural steel and the scrap markets in the North Texas–Eastern Oklahoma–Arkansas area would heat up. This was especially true given the reopening of a Houston plant by Northwestern Steel. The regional market might be reaching saturation with these additions.

With the dollar declining against other major currencies, both the domestic market and export opportunities would be expanding. For these reasons, the possibility of a new mill would have to be addressed.

Problems might develop if Chaparral continued expansion at the present plant. The firm would have to go further and further for scrap. More importantly, Chaparral's management felt that their success formula was susceptible to diseconomies of scale. As Forward pointed out, "small is beautiful in terms of the Chaparral formula." The firm could not continue both to grow and stay small indefinitely. By the same token, it might not be able to reproduce its magic everywhere it might go. At this juncture, the real question facing Chaparral was, "Which way to grow?"

Case 20

Zenith Data Systems: The Trials and Tribulations of a Corporate Repositioning Strategy

In one year, 1988, Zenith Electronics Corporation (ZEC) fought off a hostile takeover, introduced a new top-of-the-line microcomputer, announced it would enter the minicomputer market from the micromarket direction, partially quelled a retail distributor uprising, and prepared to bid on the largest government personal computer contract ever. At the same time they tried to find some way to make the last domestic television manufacturing operation in the United States profitable. As a strategic manager, Jerry K. Pearlman, Zenith's CEO, was very busy. How did all this happen at once, and what does the company face in the future?

In mid 1988 Zenith Data Systems (ZDS) announced its newest entry in the race for domination of the lucrative laptop computer market by introducing the TurbosPort 386. An 80386 microprocessor-based machine, the TurbosPort 386 was quickly hailed as a new standard for processing speed, capacity—2 megabytes of random access memory (RAM), and operating efficiency (over two hours of operations on a battery that recharges in two hours compared to competitors' eight hours). Following up on the highly successful SupersPort 286 design based on the

This case was prepared by Paul H. Meredith, University of Southwestern Louisiana, as a basis for class discussion rather than to illustrate either effective or ineffective handling of an administrative situation. Used by permission from Paul H. Meredith.

Intel 80286 processor, the TurbosPort 386 gave ZDS a top-end product to complement the mid-price/quality SuperSport 286 and the low-end Model 181 portable. The product mix placed the company squarely in the running for the fastest growing segment of the corporate PC market, face-to-face with IBM, Toshiba, Compaq, Hewlett Packard, and NEC.

Was this latest product introduction the result of a radical shift in product market strategy? Or was it a part of an ongoing pattern of product development and the implementation of a market penetration strategy?

THE FOUNDING OF ZDS

ZDS was formed in 1980, a wholly owned subsidiary of Zenith Radio Corporation (ZRC), ZEC's predecessor corporation. The parent corporation was a well-respected manufacturer of consumer electronics equipment, primarily color televisions and television-related products. The television/video equipment industry was entering a difficult period even as it was capturing an increasing percentage of U.S. disposable income. Massive numbers of low-cost, foreign-manufactured products were flooding the domestic market. Average prices paid by consumers were declining. The market mix was shifting toward low- to medium-priced products with consumers' buying patterns becoming typical of those in a commodity market.

Although management continued to expand their television production capacity, they were aware that they were facing a severe cost-price squeeze. As seen in the following comparisons of price and cost changes (Exhibit 20-1), ZRC's pretax profits had declined $163 million from 1976 to 1980 due to market based erosion in margins.

In 1979 ZRC made an effort to diversity its operations. For $65 million they acquired Heath Company, the best known manufacturer of home-assembly elec-

---

Exhibit 20-1   **Zenith Radio Corporation Cost and Price Changes, Impact on Pretax Income 1976–1980 (In millions)**

Years of Operation	Price Increase (Decrease)	Payroll and Material Cost (Increase)	Pretax Profit (Decrease)
1976–1977	$(25)	$(34)	$(59)
1977–1978	(1)	(35)	(36)
1978–1979	33	(59)	(26)
1979–1980	26	(68)	(42)
1976 vs. 1980	$33	$(196)	$(163)

Source: Annual Report, 1981.

tronics kits. Well respected by electronic hobbyists, Health commanded favorable margins on its high-quality products. A factor adding value to the Heath acquisition was the presence of a relatively new product in their traditional ham radio, diagnostic instrument, and television product mix. Since 1977 Heath had been producing a desktop computer kit, the H-89. This modest beginning in the emerging microcomputer industry became Zenith Data Systems in 1980.

The manufacturing and sale of assembled computer products became the sole responsibility of ZDS; Heath continued to make and market kit products. At the time of ZDS formation, the company was seeking to market integrated hardware and software solutions for the small businesses manufacturing and financial markets.

By the end of 1981 ZDS sales were $71 million. That same year, ZDS increased its distributors from 8 to 24, a 300 percent increase. ZDS was initiating distribution in Canada and seven European countries.

Also of significance in 1981 was a major enhancement to the ZDS sales/marketing function. John Frank was hired as national sales manager (Exhibit 20-2). Frank was to become the prime architect of the emerging ZDS product/market strategy. Up to the point of Frank's employment ZDS strategy was to avoid the home computer market and focus on "business," with no other real target market. Frank changed that almost immediately.

THE EVOLUTION OF THE ZDS NICHE STRATEGY

By 1983 Frank had advanced to the position of Vice-President of Marketing at ZDS. This was due primarily to his success in narrowing the focus of the expanding sales force toward two primary markets, the federal government and the university–education market. Heath/Zenith introduced its Z100 micro to these markets,

---

Exhibit 20-2   **John P. Frank Personal History**

John P. Frank is President of Zenith Data Systems (ZDS), the computer products subsidiary of Zenith Electronics Corporation. He was named to this post in August 1987.

Frank joined ZDS in 1981 as National Sales Manager. He was named ZDS Vice-President of Sales in March 1983 and Vice-President of Marketing in September 1983. Early in 1987, Frank was named ZDS Senior Vice-President of Sales and Marketing.

Frank was one of the chief architects of ZDS's successful "niche" marketing strategy—targeting Zenith computer products to the educational, government, *Fortune* 1000 markets, and to major retail accounts.

Before joining Zenith, Frank held key marketing positions with the Basic Four, Genesis One and Wordstream subsidiaries of Management Assistance, Inc.

A Chicago native, Frank earned a B.S. degree in marketing from DePaul University, Chicago.

seeking large defense contracts and mass distribution to students, faculty, and administrators on university campuses. They were successful.

Zenith outbid over 30 vendors for a three-year contract to supply the Air Force with computers, software, and peripherals. The contract, worth $29.3 million in revenue, called for purchases of at least 6,000 model Z100s. Subsequently, the Z100 was selected as the exclusive single-user general-purpose microcomputer for the Air Force, Navy, and Marines; the Z100 became the worldwide standard for those branches.

In the education market ZDS also achieved significant market penetration. By the end of 1983 over 200 universities were using their equipment. ZDS developed a unique symbiosis with several schools. All entering students were provided with a computer for use in classes.

As the dominant supplier to business markets, IBM had established the de facto standard microcomputer architecture. As other makers were forced to do, ZDS responded with its Z150 PC series of computers using the IBM PC architecture in 1984. The Z150 in a modified form was adopted that year by the military as their standard high security/cryptographic microcomputer. The five-year contract was valued at $99.8 million and entailed delivery of over 10,000 "Tempest" units.

ZDS had been able to maintain its position and in some cases had improved it. By early 1988 Zenith was ranked third in market share in the university market. Apple was still the clear leader, IBM was second, and Zenith was third, and challenging IBM. In the government market Zenith was the dominant supplier to the military. In 1987 the Department of Defense accounted for 68 percent of all government purchases. Zenith's Z248 model has been standard equipment for all the branches under Pentagon contract signed in 1986 and extending into 1989. The IRS used Zenith laptop computers for all its full audits. In addition the Z184 laptop, a lighter, customized version of the commercial Z183, was being purchased under a three-year contract by the military.

THE LAPTOP MARKET

Zenith's entrance into the laptop market, after IBM, was another example of their characteristic product design approach. First with the model 171, and later with the 181 and 183/184 models mentioned above, Zenith sought to overcome the biggest problems associated with all carryable micros. They sought a position of leadership in monitor functions. They focused on screen size, optical quality, and brightness. In machine operations they sought to extend the operating cycles by decreasing power consumption. Reduced recharge time and switchability to AC operations were also stressed. Interestingly, though weight is often mentioned in product reviews, ZDS has not tried to put its machines on a diet, seeking only to keep them in a competitive weight range; improving capacity for use seems to be more important to Zenith than does saving ounces.

With the second generation of laptops, ZDS focused on performance. As discussed earlier, the SupersPort 286 and TurbosPort 386 have continued to stress high-end performance.

ZDS portables have emerged as some of the hottest products in the corporate/business market. This demand has permitted ZDS to make its first serious entry into the corporate market with a differentiated, identifiable product line. When the company began to make serious efforts to enter the retail markets, most industry analysts suggested that retailers were already saturated with "clones" in a brand-oriented market. ZDS, as a low-profile brand name and entering the channel late, was predicted to encounter major resistance from retailers already concerned about low product turnover and minimization of inventory. Compaq, a national competitor in the retail channel was, by 1985, well identified in the market. They had directed their strategy toward being the prime retail competitor to IBM.

However, the analyst's predictions have been wrong. Major retail chains now carry Zenith's products. There are retail ads, discount houses, and mail order operations featuring and advertising ZDS equipment to the business market. With this entrance the company has tried to force retailers to carry more than the portable PC product lines.

CORPORATE DIRECTION

ZDS now identifies four target market niches. They are government, education, business (focused on the *Fortune* 1000 companies), and the OEM market. ZDS entered the OEM market by an agreement with Hewlett Packard (HP). HP is remarketing a customized version of the SupersPort 286 portable under its name. ZDS has reported negotiations with other manufacturers about possible reseller ventures. The company's selling points are clear. Flexibility and modularity in design along with high quality and strict adherence to software compatibility with other makers has been the ZDS approach to establishing an edge in selling to this market.

With the two large military contracts discussed earlier, ZDS has taken the lead in the government market. They were awarded the contracts because, first, they met specifications. They were willing and able to rethink hardware designs to the point that their equipment performs at or above the special purpose needs of the military branches served. Second, they contracted to provide large numbers of units, by fixed points in time subject to rigid specifications. This was important. They used the contracts to expand capacity and develop their ability to mass produce a high quality, reliable product. Third, they outbid the competition. They established a strong competitive position as the low price seller. Competitors know they will have to offer very deep discounts to underbid ZDS. The low margins which resulted were acceptable as they were necessary to establish an acceptable market share. Clearly ZDS was looking toward improving margins as they increased their factory utilization and moved up on the learning curve in manufacturing technology.

THE MINICOMPUTER/SUPERMICRO MARKET

As a major contractor for government and defense, ZDS must regularly monitor government bid specifications. The Department of Defense (DOD) specifications for the next generation of personal computing equipment were released in April 1988. Those specifications have forced a significant product strategy decision on the Zenith company. Is ZDS to be a personal computer manufacturer or the manufacturer of personal computer technology based systems? The 1988 DOD specifications are forcing the issue. The specs call for Desktop III equipment capable of operating under the UNIX operating system environment without jeopardizing the major investment in MS-DOS compatible software. Additionally, these specifications are for a networked, multi-processing, multitasked environment all consistent with the 80386, 32-bit microcomputer architecture.

Major contractors with experience in minicomputers seem to have the edge in this next round of DOD acquisitions. Tandy, Compaq, IBM, Wang, Sun, and a host of others appear to be directing their efforts toward capturing orders for what could be a total of 250,000 machines and $1 billion in revenue. In August Zenith announced a prototype of a machine directed at this market. The Z1000 is a hybrid micro/mini computer. It uses standard 80386 PC processors, has a standard buss (connector), and can use standard PC add-on boards. However, it is also a minicomputer. It has the capacity to run five separate concurrent processors each of which can support up to 32 separate serial ports (terminals). Packed into a nineteen inch cabinet the Z1000 has a maximum disk storage capacity of 2.4 gigabytes and operates in the 10 MIPS (millions of instructions per second) range in a 64-megabyte main memory. Company representatives say a production model will be available for release in the first quarter of 1989. Significant numbers of mini-market-experienced people will have to be acquired if the Z1000 is to be introduced commercially.

EFFECTS OF ZENITH EXPANDING
INTO THE RETAIL MARKET

Expansion into the retail market, while lucrative and desirable, has created major market strategy problems in Zenith's traditional channels of distribution. Retail dealer costs for equipment are usually above the sales price for equipment sold to the university and government channels. Dealers, depending on volume, may be competing with university contracts and bookstores selling equipment at 40 percent off list while the dealer discount is only 35 percent. Dealers have banded together to fight what they consider to be unfair pricing and product dumping by Zenith, IBM, and Apple. The microcomputer industry association (ABCD) brought pressure on Zenith to deal with this sensitive issue when it formed a task force on the problem. In August 1988 in a defensive move, Zenith responded by announcing the appointment of channel managers and advisory councils to deal with issues in the education, dealer, and major accounts channels. The stated purpose is to provide a forum for discussing marketing strategies and ways of implementing sales programs. This approach may permit Zenith to improve its image with small dealers and the 52 major national accounts which sell Zenith. However, questions arise as to how it will affect their long-term commitment to the education market.

CORPORATE TAKEOVER AND ZENITH'S LONG-RANGE DIVERSIFICATION

Zenith faces new challenges not only in the education, government, and retail markets, but also a takeover, could be on the horizon. ZEC has diversified but not divested itself of its television-related businesses. As seen in the table on facilities (Exhibit 20-3) and the financial statement from the *Annual Report* (Exhibit 20-4), large portions of their assets are devoted to losing operations. In addition, ZDS has traditionally sold at low margins as they established high market penetrations in education and government. A block of disgruntled shareholders headed by the Bookhurst Partners, an arbitrage firm, has been seeking to force ZEC to liquidate or sell the television-related businesses. With 7.1 percent of ZEC's shares, they are a potent force. Zenith has resisted the group's overtures, maintaining that television product prices will soon rise, returning Zenith to a position of having two profitable divisions rather than one, ZDS, supporting the other.

Zenith's response, as reported at its 1988 annual meeting, was to aggressively oppose any takeover. Zenith acknowledged it had a "poison pill" shareholders rights plan designed to make a takeover too expensive. In fact, the company lowered the point at which the "pill" would take effect from any raider holding 35 percent of ZEC's stock to 15 percent. The pill gives shareholders the right to buy more shares if the threshold is reached.

If earnings can be improved and a positive investment image can be created, the takeover can be more easily resisted. Yet Zenith is still positioned between its old business and its new one. Can it afford to wait for the turnaround in television or should it cut losses and leave the television market forever?

Exhibit 20-3 Zenith Electronic Corporation Summary of Operating Properties As of December 31, 1986

Location	Nature of Operations	Square feet (In millions)
Domestic		
Chicago, Illinois (including suburban locations)	Thirteen locations—primarily assembly of electronic components, production of cathode-ray tubes, and related marketing, engineering, development, and administration.	3.0
Springfield, Missouri	Assembly of color television sets and color monitors and production of portable color television cabinets and other plastic parts.	1.7
Evansville, Indiana	Two locations—manufacture of color television cabinets.	.7[a]
Brownsville, McAllen, and El Paso, Texas; Douglas, Arizona	Six locations—warehouses.	.2
St. Joseph, Michigan	Manufacturing, warehouse, and store facilities for Heath and computer products.	.7
Various	Eleven locations—domestic distribution of consumer electronics products.	1.0
Various	Sixty-one locations—retail outlets for Heath and computer products.	.3
Various	Four locations—regional manufacturing and marketing facilities for computer products.	.1
Foreign		
Taiwan	Assembly of video displays and electronic components.	.2
Mexico	Fifteen manufacturing and warehouse locations—manufacture of electronic components, chassis assemblies, and color television cabinets; assembly of color television sets, cable television sets, and cable television products.	1.8
Canada	Three locations—distribution of consumer electronics products.	.3
Canada	Five locations—retail outlets for Heath and computer products.	—
Europe	Six locations—office and warehouse support for computer products.	—
Ireland	One location—manufacture and marketing of electronic components and computer products.	.1
Total		10.1

[a]The company has announced that operations in Evansville, Indiana will cease by mid 1987. One plant of 0.3 million square feet is currently idle and being held for future sale.

Source: Company 10K (abbreviated).

Exhibit 20-4   Zenith Electronics Corporation Financial Statement

FINANCIAL REVIEW

Analysis of Operations

Earnings per Share (EPS): A loss of 78 cents per share was incurred in 1987, compared with a loss per share of 43 cents in 1986. In 1985, the loss per share was 33 cents.

	EPS Increase/ (decrease)	
	1986 vs. 1985	1987 vs. 1986
Reason for change		
Operating income	$0.39	$0.13
Interest expense, net	(.12)	(.31)
Disposition of properties and 1985 pension plan termination	(.26)	—
Tax effect, net (Note 7)	(.11)	(.19)
Issuance of new shares in 1987 (Note 8)	—	.02
Earnings per share change	$(.10)	$(.35)

Operating Results: The 1987 pre-tax loss was $29 million, compared with a pre-tax loss of $20 million in 1986 and $21 million in 1985.

	Increase/ (decrease)	
	1986 vs. 1985	1987 vs. 1986
	(In millions)	
Consumer Electronics	$11	$(51)
Computer Systems and Components	7	73
Special charges in 1987	—	(16)
Operating income	18	6
Interest, net	(5)	(15)
Disposition of properties and 1985 pension plan termination	(12)	—
Net change	$1	$(9)

Consumer electronics operating results in 1987 declined by $51 million, compared with a gain of $11 million in 1986. Price declines for color television and video products (video cassette recorders and camcorders) reduced profitability by $67 million in 1987 and $37 million in 1986. Declines in video products pricing are calculated net of significant price reductions received by Zenith from its suppliers.

Reduced sales volume in 1987 occurred mainly in the second half when Zenith briefly held its selling prices for TV and video products while competitors continued to lower their prices. Lower volume affected operating income by $27 million in 1987, compared with a gain of $12 million from higher volume in 1986.

Consumer electronics benefited by $43 million in 1987 (and $19 million in 1986) from net reductions in production and operating expenses, and as a result of gains from sales of cable products and from components shipped to other television manufacturers.

Operating results for computer systems and components improved by $73 million in 1987 (after absorption of more than $25 million of "flat tension mask" expenses), compared with $7 million in 1986.

The computer products group significantly increased revenues and operating income in 1987. Results from higher sales in 1986, however, were adversely affected by lower margins, principally on new government computer contracts.

In 1987, Systems & Components was profitable, excluding flat tension mask picture tube expenses, as a result of higher revenues and lower operating costs. Volume buildup of flat tension mask tubes and high-resolution color computer monitors was slower than planned in 1987.

Results for 1987 included special charges of $16 million (pre-tax), associated with salaried staff reductions and other adjustments made in response to business conditions in consumer electronics.

Financial Resources and Capital Structure

Total assets rose by $138 million during 1987, primarily due to increases in inventories and receivables to support higher sales throughout the year. Year-end data are summarized as follows:

(continued)

Exhibit 20-4 (continued)

	December 31,			% Increase	
				1986 vs. 1985	1987 vs. 1986
	1985	1986	1987		
	(In millions)				
Fourth-quarter sales	$484	$597	$686	23%	15%
Inventories	332	503	584	51	16
Receivables	283	378	418	34	10

Year-over-year rates of change in these key working capital assets were consistent with or lower than the percentage of increase in fourth-quarter 1987 sales, compared with the same period in 1986.

Investment in property, plant and equipment (net of accumulated depreciation) increased by $10 million in 1987. Capital expenditures of $55 million were made in 1987 (compared with $61 million in 1986 and $57 million in 1985), including $16 million to complete the start-up program for the flat tension mask picture tube, with the balance supporting ongoing improvements in computer and color TV operations. In 1987 and 1986, capital expenditures exceeded depreciation by $14 million and $21 million.

Reduced capital expenditures in 1988 of about $50 million will more closely approximate depreciation charges for the year. These expenditures primarily will be made for improvements in television, picture tube and computer operations. Expenditures in 1988 will be lower than in recent years principally due to the absence of such major programs as the cabinet plant in Mexico and the flat tension mask picture tube facility.

During 1987, the company entered into a $250 million revolving credit agreement with a group of banks to support commercial paper issuance and to provide short-term borrowing availability for seasonal requirements. The $200 million seasonal portion is scheduled to expire on April 30, 1988. Negotiations with the same group of banks are now in process to establish a new credit agreement of similar magnitude to provide for the company's 1988 short-term financing needs. (See Note 5.)

In 1987, Zenith sold 2.3 million shares of common stock for approximately $60 million, and borrowed $50 million in a private placement of 9.97% five-year promissory notes. The $110 million proceeds were used to reduce short-term borrowings. In 1986, the company issued $115 million of convertible subordinated debentures.

Year-end debt and equity are summarized as follows:

	December 31,		
	1985	1986	1987
	(In millions)		
Short-term borrowings	$ 26	$102	$120
Long-term debt	165	272	315
Stockholders' equity	437	432	478

As of year-end 1987, the company has fully utilized all available U.S. income tax net operating loss carrybacks, and has a balance of approximately $24 million to carry forward for application against future taxable earnings. For additional tax information, including comments on accounting for income taxes, see Note 7.

Exhibit 20-4   (continued)

FIVE-YEAR SUMMARY OF SELECTED FINANCIAL DATA

	1983	1984	1985	1986	1987
		(In millions, except per share amounts)			
Results of operations					
Net sales	$1,361.3	$1,716.0	$1,623.7	$1,892.1	$2,362.7
Net income (loss)	46.3	63.6	(7.7)	(10.0)	(19.1)
Net income (loss) per share					
Primary	2.26	2.88	(.33)	(.43)	(.78)
Fully diluted	2.11	2.88	(.33)	(.43)	(.78)
Financial position at December 31					
Total assets	739.0	908.9	927.3	1,235.0	1,373.0
Working capital	318.8	416.7	396.1	475.4	541.4
Long-term debt	104.6	172.4	165.1	272.4	315.4
Stockholders' equity	375.2	442.8	437.2	431.6	478.2
Book value per share	17.08	20.00	18.90	18.49	18.45
Other data					
Capital expenditures	31.4	66.3	56.5	61.0	55.4
Depreciation	29.8	31.8	36.7	40.0	41.5
Number of employees on December 31 (in thousands)	30	29	33	37	35

STATEMENTS OF CONSOLIDATED INCOME AND RETAINED EARNINGS

		Year Ended December 31,		
		1985	1986	1987
		(In millions, except per share amounts)		
Revenues	Net sales	$1,623.7	$1,892.1	$2,362.7
Costs, expenses and other	Cost of products sold	1,359.8	1,588.4	2,017.9
	Selling, advertising and administrative	187.4	202.7	239.3
	Engineering and research	96.0	99.7	103.4
	Other, net (Note 1)	(6.5)	(3.8)	(9.7)

(*continued*)

Exhibit 20-4   (continued)

STATEMENTS OF CONSOLIDATED INCOME AND RETAINED EARNINGS

		Year Ended December 31,		
		1985	**1986**	**1987**
		(In millions, except per share amounts)		
Income	Operating income (loss)	(13.0)	5.1	11.8
	Gain on disposition and valuation of properties	5.4	—	.4
	Gain on settlements of pension plans (Note 10)	7.3	.7	—
	Interest expense	(23.4)	(29.6)	(45.7)
	Interest income	2.8	3.6	4.6
	Loss before income taxes	(20.9)	(20.2)	(28.9)
	Income taxes (credit) (See Note 7)	(13.2)	(10.2)	(9.8)
	Net loss	$ (7.7)	$ (10.0)	$ (19.1)
	Net loss per share Primary and fully diluted	$ (.33)	$ (.43)	$ (.78)
Retained earnings	Balance at beginning of year	$ 355.9	$ 348.6	$ 338.6
	Net loss for year	(7.7)	(10.0)	(19.1)
	Effect of pooling of interests acquisition (Note 2)	.4	—	—
	Balance at end of year	$ 348.6	$ 338.6	$ 319.5

The accompanying Notes to Consolidated Financial Statements are an integral part of these statements.

CONSOLIDATED BALANCE SHEETS (In millions)

		December 31,	
		1986	**1987**
Assets			
Current assets	Cash	$1.1	$19.5
	Marketable securities (at cost, which approximates market)	1.8	—
	Receivables, less allowances of $6.9 and $6.2 (Note 7)	378.2	417.7
	Inventories (Note 4)	502.8	583.6
	Prepaid income taxes	58.8	51.4
	Prepaid expenses and other	23.7	17.3
	Total current assets	966.4	1,089.5

Exhibit 20-4   (continued)

		December 31,	
		1986	**1987**
Property, plant and	Land	13.3	12.4
equipment, at cost	Buildings	161.8	161.3
	Machinery and equipment	417.4	459.6
		592.5	633.3
	Less accumulated depreciation	(336.0)	(366.5)
	Property, plant and equipment, net	256.5	266.8
Other	Long-term receivables and other assets (Note 3)	12.1	16.7
	Total assets	$1,235.0	$1,373.0
Liabilities and Stock- **holders' Equity**			
Current liabilities	Short-term debt (Note 5)	$95.0	$113.0
	Current portion of long-term debt	6.9	6.9
	Accounts payable (Note 5)	199.0	220.5
	Compensation and retirement benefits (Note 10)	44.8	53.9
	Product warranties	43.0	42.9
	Co-op advertising and merchandising programs	35.8	36.4
	Income taxes payable (Note 7)	7.4	2.3
	Other accrued expenses	59.1	72.2
	Total current liabilities	491.0	548.1
Other	Long-term debt (Note 6)	272.4	315.4
	Deferred income taxes (Note 7)	40.0	31.3
Stockholders' equity	Common stock, $1 par value per share; 100,000,000 shares authorized; issued 25,920,280 and 23,345,227, respectively	23.3	25.9
	Additional paid-in capital	69.7	132.8
	Retained earnings	338.6	319.5
	Total stockholders' equity (Note 8)	431.6	478.2
	Total liabilities and stockholders' equity	$1,235.0	$1,373.0

The accompanying Notes to Consolidated Financial Statements are an integral part of these balance sheets.

(continued)

Exhibit 20-4   (continued)

STATEMENTS OF CONSOLIDATED CASH FLOWS (In millions)

		Increase (Decrease) in Cash Year Ended December 31,		
		1985	**1986**	**1987**
Cash flows from operating activities	Net loss	$ (7.7)	$ (10.0)	$ (19.1)
	Adjustments to reconcile net income to net cash provided by operating activities			
	Depreciation	36.7	40.0	41.5
	Changes in assets and liabilities (see below):			
	Current accounts	1.7	(159.5)	(67.4)
	Non-current accounts	9.9	(4.1)	(12.7)
	Net cash provided (used) by operating activities	40.6	(133.6)	(57.7)
Cash flows from investing activities	Capital additions	(56.5)	(61.0)	(55.4)
	Disposals	1.8	2.7	3.0
	Net cash used in investing activities	(54.7)	(58.3)	(52.4)
Cash flows from financing activities	Net short-term borrowings	13.7	76.0	18.0
	Proceeds from issuance of long-term debt	—	114.6	50.0
	Principal payments on long-term debt	(7.3)	(7.3)	(7.0)
	Issuance of common stock	.9	—	59.0
	Exercise of stock options and PAYSOP contribution	1.6	4.4	6.7
	Net cash provided by financing activities	8.9	187.7	126.7
	Increase (decrease) in cash and cash equivalents	$ (5.2)	$ (4.2)	$ 16.6
Cash and cash equivalents	At beginning of year	$ 12.3	$ 7.1	$ 2.9
	Increase (decrease) during year	(5.2)	(4.2)	16.6
	At end of year	$ 7.1	$ 2.9	$ 19.5
Changes in assets and liabilities	Increase (decrease) in cash attributable to changes in current accounts			
	Receivables, net	$ 1.3	$ (83.5)	$ (68.6)
	Current income taxes, net	(32.5)	(14.8)	31.4
	Inventories	15.2	(170.7)	(80.8)
	Other current assets	5.5	(14.3)	6.4

Exhibit 20-4   (Continued)

	Increase (Decrease) in Cash Year Ended December 31,		
	1985	1986	1987
Accounts payable and accrued expenses	12.2	123.8	44.2
Total current accounts	$ 1.7	$(159.5)	$ (67.4)
Increase (decrease) in cash attributable to changes in non-current accounts			
Long-term receivables and other	$ 0.1	$ (10.3)	$ (4.0)
Deferred income taxes	9.8	6.2	(8.7)
Total non-current accounts	$ 9.9	$ (4.1)	$ (12.7)

The accompanying Notes to Consolidated Financial Statements are an integral part of these statements.

NOTES TO CONSOLIDATED FINANCIAL STATEMENTS

Note 1—Significant Accounting Policies

Principles of Consolidation: The consolidated financial statements include the accounts of the company and all subsidiaries after elimination of intercompany accounts and transactions.

Inventories: Inventories are stated at the lower of cost or market. Costs are determined for the major portion of the inventories using the first-in, first-out (FIFO) method. The remaining inventories are valued by the last-in, first-out (LIFO) method.

Properties and depreciation: Additions of plant and equipment with lives of eight years or more are depreciated by the straight-line method over their useful lives. Accelerated methods are used for depreciation of substantially all other plant and equipment items, including shorter-lived high-technology equipment that may be subject to rapid economic obsolescence.

Substantially all tooling is charged to expense in the year acquired; the remainder is amortized over 24 months. Certain production fixtures are capitalized as machinery and equipment. A capital lease related to a manufacturing facility is included in plant and equipment.

Rental expenses under operating leases were $14.2 million in 1987, $12.3 million in 1986 and $12.3 million in 1985. Commitments for lease payments in future years are not material.

The company capitalizes interest on major capital projects. Such interest was not material in 1987, 1986 or 1985.

Engineering, Research, Product Warranty and Other Costs: Engineering and research costs are expensed as incurred. Estimated costs for product warranties are provided at the time of sales based on experience factors. The costs of co-op advertising and merchandising programs are provided at the time of sales.

Foreign Currency Translation: The accounts of foreign subsidiaries are translated in accordance with Financial Accounting Standards Board (FASB) Statement 52, with the U.S. dollar used as the "functional currency" for all subsidiaries. Foreign currency translation gains and losses are included in other income. Such gains were $5.0 million, $2.7 million and $2.6 million in 1987, 1986 and 1985.

Income Taxes: Prepaid income taxes result from timing differences on the recognition of ex-

(continued)

Exhibit 20-4   (continued)

penses (principally product warranty, co-op advertising, merchandising and certain insurance programs) and asset valuation reserves which are tax deductible in other periods. Deferred income taxes relate primarily to timing differences on tax depreciation and certain employee benefits. Investment tax credits have been recognized as a reduction of tax expense in the year eligible property was placed in service.

Earnings per share: Primary earnings per share (EPS) are based upon the weighted average number of shares outstanding and common share equivalents, if dilutive. Fully diluted earnings per share, assuming conversion of the $6\frac{1}{4}\%$ convertible subordinated debentures, are not presented because the effect of the assumed conversion is antidilutive. Amounts used to compute earnings per share were:

	Net Loss	Shares Used	EPS[a]
	(In millions, except per share data)		
1987	$(19.1)	24.5	$(.78)
1986	(10.0)	23.3	(.43)
1985	(7.7)	23.1	(.33)

[a]Primary and fully diluted

    Earnings per share for 1987 would have been $(.66) had the July 15, 1987, issuance of 2,300,000 shares of the company's common stock occurred on January 1, 1987, assuming that net proceeds would have been used to reduce short-term debt. (See Note 8.)

Reclassification: In connection with the 1987 adoption of FASB 95, Statement of Cash Flows, prior period amounts were restated to conform with the current year presentation.

Line of Business: The company's predominant business is the design, manufacture and distribution of electronics products.

Note 2—Acquisition
On May 30, 1985, the company acquired all of the outstanding shares of common stock of In-

teq Incorporated in exchange for 900,001 shares of the company's common stock. Zenith/Inteq develops, manufactures, modifies and markets microprocessor-based electronic products and associated peripheral products, most of which are designed to meet the security specifications of the U.S. government's "Tempest" program.

    The acquisition was treated for accounting purposes as a pooling of interests. The company's statements of consolidated income and retained earnings include Inteq's results of operations from January 1, 1985.

Note 3—Geographic Area and Major Customer Data
Foreign operations consist of manufacturing subsidiaries in Mexico, Ireland and Taiwan and distribution subsidiaries in Europe, Canada, Hong Kong and Australia. Sales to affiliates are accounted for principally at amounts based on local costs of production plus a reasonable return.

    Geographic area data are summarized below:

	1985	1986	1987
	(In millions)		
Net sales:			
Domestic companies:			
Sales to outside customers	$1,494.6	$1,745.4	$2,118.5
Sales to foreign affiliates	62.1	79.5	161.8
	1,556.7	1,824.9	2,280.3
Foreign companies:			
Sales to outside customers	129.1	146.7	244.2
Sales to domestic affiliates	113.9	121.7	144.1
	243.0	268.4	388.3

Exhibit 20-4 (continued)

	1985	1986	1987
		(In millions)	
Elimina-tions—affiliate sales	(176.0)	(201.2)	(305.9)
Total net sales	$1,623.7	$1,892.1	$2,362.7
Loss before income taxes:			
Domestic companies	$(14.5)	$ (17.8)	$ (28.3)
Foreign companies	(6.4)	(2.4)	(.6)
Loss before income taxes	$(20.9)	$ (20.2)	$ (28.9)
Assets:			
Domestic companies	$761.4	$1,035.2	$1,075.2
Foreign companies	165.9	199.8	297.8
Total assets	$927.3	$1,235.0	$1,373.0

During 1987, sales to the U.S. government, consisting principally of computer products and peripherals, exceeded 10% of consolidated net sales. Sales to the U.S. government were $529.2 million, $223.6 million and $140.5 million in 1987, 1986 and 1985, respectively.

The long-term portion of accounts receivable from installment sales to an agency of the U.S. government is included in long-term receivables and other assets as of December 31, 1987 and 1986.

Note 4—Inventories

Inventories consisted of the following:

	December 31,	
	1986	1987
	(In millions)	
Raw materials and work-in-process	$269.0	$277.4
Finished goods	253.9	322.9
	522.9	600.3
Excess of FIFO cost over LIFO cost	(20.1)	(16.7)
Total	$502.8	$583.6

At December 31, 1987 and 1986, $86.0 million and $107.2 million of inventories were valued using the LIFO method.

Note 5—Short-Term Debt and Credit Arrangements

In May 1987, the company replaced a $50 million revolving credit agreement with a combined revolving credit and seasonal borrowing facility. The new agreement provides revolving credit of up to $250 million through April 30, 1988, and thereafter up to $50 million through December 30, 1988, primarily for commercial paper backup. There were $153 million and $34 million unused under these agreements at December 31, 1987 and 1986, respectively.

In addition to restrictions similar to those contained in the company's long-term debt agreements, the new agreement requires that net worth and the ratio of adjusted income to interest expense be maintained at or above specified levels. As of December 31, 1987, the required minimum ratio was 1.10 and the actual ratio was 1.52; the required ratio will increase to 1.50 as of March 31, 1988, and thereafter. Additionally, no retained earnings were available for the payment of cash dividends as of December 31, 1987.

(continued)

Exhibit 20-4 (continued)

During 1986 and 1987, the company's credit agreements primarily supported commercial paper borrowings. Additional sources of funds, as needed, were supplied by money market borrowings and the banker's acceptance market.

Borrowing and interest rates were:

	1985	1986	1987
	(In millions)		
Maximum month-end borrowing	$135.0	$96.5	$224.0
Average daily borrowing	75.8	45.0	173.1
Weighted average interest rate	8.3%	6.7%	7.5%

As an alternative to short-term borrowing, the company sells certain receivables. Receivables were reduced by $20.8 million as of December 31, 1987 and 1986, as a result of such sales.

Several contracts with foreign suppliers permit the company to elect flexible, extended payment terms bearing interest at varying rates. At December 31, 1987 and 1986, $70.8 million and $33.3 million, respectively, were outstanding under these agreements.

Note 6—Long-Term Debt

The components of long-term debt were:

	December 31,	
	1986	1987
	(In millions)	
9.97% promissory notes due 1992	—	$ 50.0
12⅛% notes due 1995	$ 74.7	74.7
9.95% promissory note due 1999	89.4	82.6
6¼% convertible subordinated debentures due 2011	115.0	115.0
Capitalized lease obligations	.2	—
	279.3	322.3
Less current portion	6.9	6.9
Total long-term debt	$272.4	$315.4

On August 19, 1987, the company sold $50 million of 9.97% promissory notes due July 15, 1992. The notes are redeemable at the option of the company, in whole or in part, at any time after July 14, 1991, at the principal amount thereof together with accrued interest. The principal restrictive covenants in the note agreement require a minimum level of working capital and place restrictions concerning additional borrowing and retained earnings available for stock repurchases and payment of dividends.

On January 10, 1985, the company sold $75 million of 12⅛% notes due 1995. The notes are redeemable at the option of the company, in whole or in part, at any time after January 14, 1992, at the principal amount thereof together with accrued interest.

The terms of the 9.95% note include annual sinking fund requirements of $6.9 million. The note is redeemable at the option of the company, in whole or in part, at a premium subject to certain restrictions contained in the note agreement. Covenants in this note agreement are similar to those in the 9.97% note agreement.

On April 15, 1986, the company sold $115 million of 6¼% convertible subordinated debentures due 2011. The debentures are unsecured general obligations, subordinate in right of payment to certain other debt obligations, and are convertible into common stock at $31.25 per share. Terms of the debenture agreement include annual sinking fund requirements of $5.8 million, beginning in 1997. The debentures are redeemable at the option of the company, in whole or in part, at specified conversion prices provided, however, that the debentures cannot

Exhibit 20-4   (continued)

be redeemed prior to April 1, 1988, unless the company's common stock price equals or exceeds specified levels.

All of the company's loan agreements, including the revolving credit agreement described in Note 5, under certain circumstances permit acceleration of the company's obligations if the company is not in compliance with any agreement under which it has borrowed money.

Note 7—Income Taxes

Income tax provision (credit) components were:

	1985	1986	1987
	(In millions)		
Currently payable (refundable)			
Federal	$ (9.7)	$(23.8)	$(1.3)
State	.6	(1.5)	(1.1)
Foreign	(.3)	2.7	2.3
Investment tax credit	(3.0)	(.9)	—
Research and development tax credit	(.6)	(24.5)	(.1)
	(13.0)	(1.0)	—
Deferred (prepaid)			
Federal	(1.4)	13.5	(9.7)
State	—	1.8	—
Foreign	1.2	(1.0)	—
	(.2)	14.3	(9.7)
Total income taxes (credit)	$(13.2)	$(10.2)	$(9.8)

Items giving rise to deferred (prepaid) income taxes:

	1985	1986	1987
Timing differences on current income and expense items	$(1.2)	$(3.5)	—
Timing differences on tax depreciation and tooling	2.4	1.5	—
Timing difference on funding of certain employee benefits	—	5.8	—
Undistributed earnings of foreign subsidiaries	.8	1.4	(9.7)
Asset valuation reserves	(6.4)	4.3	—
Tax effect on foreign exchange gain	3.0	5.9	—
All other	1.2	(1.1)	—
	$ (.2)	$14.3	$(9.7)

The statutory federal income tax rate and the effective rate are compared below:

	1985	1986	1987
Statutory federal income tax rate	(46.0)%	(46.0)%	(40.0)%
Tax benefits not recognized subject to future realization	—	—	32.0
State income taxes, net of federal tax benefit	1.3	.9	(2.3)

(continued)

Exhibit 20-4 (continued)

	1985	1986	1987
Income taxes related to undistributed earnings of foreign subsidiaries	1.9	(.6)	(35.3)
Foreign subsidiaries' losses not tax-benefited (carry-forward utilized)	(4.0)	3.0	10.6
Investment tax credit	(14.1)	(4.4)	—
Research and development tax credit	(2.9)	(5.2)	—
Other	.6	1.8	1.3
Effective tax rate	(63.2)%	(50.5)%	(33.7)%

During 1987, the company recorded a $1.3 million income tax credit, which represents its U.S. income tax refund available through the utilization of net operating loss carrybacks. As of December 31, 1987, the company has U.S. net operating loss carryforwards for financial statement purposes of approximately $24 million, or $8 million of unrecorded future tax benefits. The $8 million consists of $2 million of U.S. net operating loss tax effects and $6 million of tax credit carryforwards that expire in years 2000 through 2002.

As of October 3, 1987, the company had undistributed earnings of approximately $45.2 million from certain of its foreign subsidiaries. Deferred U.S. income taxes, payable upon distribution, had been provided in prior periods at statutory rates on these earnings. Management reviewed the company's investment in these foreign subsidiaries during the third quarter of 1987 and determined that $32.7 million of such earnings will be invested indefinitely. Accordingly, income tax expense for 1987 includes the reversal of $9.7 million, or $.40 per share, of previously accrued deferred U.S. income taxes. At December 31, 1987, there were approximately

$41 million of undistributed earnings for which no taxes have been provided.

Changes in the tax law and year-end tax adjustments increased fourth-quarter 1986 income tax expense by $1.4 million and reduced fourth-quarter 1985 income tax expense by $1.2 million. No significant adjustments were made to fourth-quarter 1987 income tax expense.

Refundable federal and state income taxes of $3.9 million and $33.0 million are included in receivables at December 31, 1987 and 1986, respectively.

In 1987, FASB Statement 96 was issued, requiring the company to adopt the liability method of accounting for income taxes during 1989, or earlier, and providing for retroactive restatement or a cumulative adjustment in the adoption year. The company is currently analyzing the requirements of Statement 96 and, while the effects have not been quantified, it is anticipated that the amount by which prepaid taxes exceed deferred taxes may no longer be recognized, resulting in a corresponding reduction in retained earnings. Because this adjustment depends on circumstances at the time of adoption, it is not currently possible to determine the amount of the net tax assets that will be charged against retained earnings on the initial date of application or the impact on net income in subsequent years.

Note 8—Changes in Stockholders' Equity
Changes in stockholders' equity accounts are shown below:

	Common Stock ($1 Par)	Additional Paid-in Capital
	(In millions)	
Balance, December 31, 1984	$22.1	$64.8
Shares issued for pooling of interests acquisition	.9	(.8)
Exercise of stock options and PAYSOP contribution	.1	1.5

Exhibit 20-4   (continued)

	Common Stock ($1 Par)	Additional Paid-in Capital
	(In millions)	
Balance, December 31, 1985	$23.1	$65.5
Exercise of stock options and PAYSOP contribution	.2	4.2
Balance, December 31, 1986	$23.3	$69.7
Sale of common stock	2.3	56.7
Exercise of stock options and PAYSOP contribution	.3	6.4
Balance, December 31, 1987	$25.9	$132.8

At the company's annual meeting on April 28, 1987, stockholders approved a resolution increasing authorized common stock of the company from 50,000,000 to 100,000,000 shares.

On July 15, 1987, the company issued 2,300,000 shares of its common stock, $1.00 par value per share, at a price of $26.50 a share. Net proceeds of $59.0 million were realized.

On October 3, 1986, the company's board of directors declared a distribution of one common share purchase right for each outstanding share of common stock. Each right entitles the holder to purchase one-half of one share of common stock at an exercise price of $37.50, subject to adjustment.

The rights will not be exercisable until 10 days after a public announcement that a person has acquired beneficial ownership of 20% or more of the company's common shares (the "Stock Acquisition Date") or 10 days after a person commences or announces an intention to commence a tender offer, the consummation of which would result in such person owning at least 30% of the common shares. The rights expire October 14, 1996, unless redeemed earlier. The rights are redeemable at $.05 per right until the 20th business day (subject to extension) after the Stock Acquisition Date. If at any time after the rights become exercisable and not redeemed and the company is involved in a merger or other business combination transaction, the rights will automatically be modified so as to entitle the holder thereof (other than the acquiring person) to buy a number of shares of common stock of the acquiring company having a market value of twice the exercise price of each right.

Alternatively, if the company is the surviving corporation in a merger with an acquiring person or any associate or affiliate thereof and the common stock is not changed or exchanged, or such acquiring person were to engage in one of a number of self-dealing transactions, or if any person becomes the holder of 35% or more of the common stock, each right not owned by the acquiring person (including affiliates and associates thereof) would become exercisable for the number of shares of common stock which at the time has a market value of twice the exercise price of the right.

Note 9—Employee Stock Purchase Plan

The company has granted to key management personnel options to purchase common stock at the market price of the shares on the date of grant. Options expire 10 years from the date granted.

Certain stock options include stock appreciation rights (SARs) that are exercisable only to the extent of the related option. At December 31, 1987 and 1986, 3,450 and 16,150 stock appreciation rights were outstanding.

Transactions in 1987 are summarized as follows:

	Shares	Price
Options outstanding at January 1, 1987	1,163,658	$10\frac{3}{8}$–$26\frac{5}{8}$
Granted	877,800	$14\frac{1}{8}$–$23\frac{1}{8}$
Exercised	(244,881)	$10\frac{3}{8}$–$26\frac{5}{8}$
Surrendered under SARs	(3,400)	$13\frac{3}{4}$–$20\frac{3}{4}$

(continued)

Exhibit 20-4   (continued)

	Shares	Price
Canceled or ex-pired	(54,689)	$20\frac{3}{8}$–$26\frac{5}{8}$
Options outstanding at December 31, 1987	1,738,488	$10\frac{3}{8}$–$26\frac{5}{8}$
Options exercisable at December 31, 1987	748,181	
Shares available for grant: January 1, 1987	490,960	
Additional authorized	1,000,000	
Granted	(877,800)	
Canceled or expired	54,689	
December 31, 1987	667,849	

Note 10—Retirement Plans and Employee Benefits

Most domestic and Canadian employees are eligible to participate in noncontributory profit-sharing retirement plans after completing one full year of service. The plans provide for a minimum annual contribution of 6% of employees' eligible compensation. Contributions above the minimum could be required based upon profits in excess of a specified return on net worth. Profit-sharing contributions were $15.6 million in 1987, $15.1 million in 1986 and $14.1 million in 1985.

In 1987, the company terminated its participation in a multi-employer pension plan that covered union employees at a facility which ceased operation. The anticipated liability for this withdrawal was previously provided.

In 1986, a group annuity contract was purchased to settle pension obligations for certain retired participants of a pension plan, re-sulting in a gain of $.7 million that is reflected in the 1986 income statement.

In 1985, the company terminated its Heath Salaried Retirement Plan. All benefits earned under the terms of the terminated plan became fully vested. Current employees are now covered by the Zenith Salaried Profit-Sharing Retirement Plan. Excess plan assets of $7.3 million reverted to the company. This gain on plan termination is reflected in the 1985 income statement.

The company has three defined benefit plans. One plan covers hourly employees at the Heath Company. The other plans supplement profit-sharing benefits for certain salaried employees. Net periodic pension cost and unfunded accumulated benefit obligations were not material in 1987, 1986 or 1985.

Employees in Mexico and Taiwan are covered by government-mandated plans, the costs of which are currently accrued and partially funded by the company.

Note 11—Contingencies

In April 1987, the U.S. Supreme Court declined to review the opinion and judgment of the U.S. Court of Appeals for the Third Circuit, affirming dismissal of the company's antitrust and antidumping claims against defendant Japanese television manufacturers. Certain of the defendants in that litigation have counterclaims pending against the company, seeking substantial treble damages for alleged violations of the antitrust laws. One former defendant has filed a counterclaim, alleging violation of the Lanham Act in advertising that resulted in diversion of television sales. The company is also a defendant in various lawsuits and proceedings incidental to the conduct of its business. These generally relate to distributor terminations, patents, government contract and environmental matters, and product liability claims. The company's management believes that these various lawsuits and proceedings will be dismissed or otherwise disposed of without material effect on the company's financial position.

As a result of general conditions in the U.S. insurance market, the company has been unable to obtain, at acceptable cost, liability insurance at the levels of coverage historically

---

Exhibit 20-4   (continued)

maintained. However, the coverage obtained is in excess of losses previously incurred by the company.

AUDITORS' REPORT

To the Stockholders of Zenith Electronics Corporation:

We have examined the consolidated balance sheets of ZENITH ELECTRONICS CORPORATION (a Delaware corporation) and subsidiaries as of December 31, 1987 and 1986, and the related statements of consolidated income and retained earnings and cash flows for each of the three years in the period ended December 31, 1987. Our examinations were made in accordance with generally accepted auditing

standards and, accordingly, included such tests of the accounting records and such other auditing procedures as we considered necessary in the circumstances.

In our opinion, the consolidated financial statements referred to above present fairly the financial position of Zenith Electronics Corporation and subsidiaries as of December 31, 1987 and 1986, and the results of their operations and their cash flows for each of the three years in the period ended December 31, 1987, in conformity with generally accepted accounting principles applied on a consistent basis.

ARTHUR ANDERSEN & CO.

Chicago, Illinois,
February 22, 1988.

QUARTERLY FINANCIAL INFORMATION   (Unaudited)

	1986 Quarters Ended				**1987 Quarters Ended**			
	Apr. 5	**July 5**	**Oct. 4**	**Dec. 31**	**Apr. 4**	**July 4**	**Oct. 3**[a]	**Dec. 31**
				(In millions, except per share amounts)				
Net sales	$400.6	$380.6	$513.8	$597.1	$546.8	$538.5	$591.8	$685.6
Gross margin	67.0	56.0	89.1	91.6	86.7	85.6	72.9	99.6
Income (loss) before income taxes	(10.3)	(18.8)	5.4	3.5	1.9	0.3	(36.4)	5.3
Net income (loss)	(4.4)	(9.9)	3.9	.4	1.0	0.3	(25.1)	4.7
Net income (loss) per share[b]	(.19)	(.43)	.17	.02	.04	.02	(.99)	.18
New York Stock Exchange market price per share								
High	$26\frac{1}{4}$	$29\frac{7}{8}$	$25\frac{3}{4}$	$22\frac{1}{4}$	$27\frac{1}{8}$	$29\frac{3}{4}$	$33\frac{5}{8}$	$26\frac{5}{8}$
Low	18	$22\frac{1}{4}$	$19\frac{1}{2}$	$18\frac{7}{8}$	$21\frac{1}{2}$	$24\frac{1}{2}$	26	10

[a]Third-quarter 1987 net income benefited from a non-recurring tax adjustment of $9.7 million, or $.38 per share. See Note 7.

[b]A stock offering in July 1987 resulted in the issuance of 2.3 million shares.

Source: Zenith Electronics Corporation *Annual Report,* 1987. Reprinted with permission of Zenith Electronics Corporation.

Saunders System, Inc. (1916–1986): The End of a Tradition

Saunders System, Inc.'s 61-year-old Co-Chairman Harris Saunders, Jr. observed, "Selling a family-owned company can be like planning a wedding. By the time you get down to signing the papers and going through the ceremonies, it's kind of anticlimactic."

"You have emotions when you sell your business," added his younger brother and Co-Chairman, Bob Saunders. "After 70 years the company won't be in existence in the same form."

Saunders System, Inc., a $285 million-a-year truck transportation services company, had grown substantially over the last 70 years, survived the depression, vigorous competition, trucking industry deregulation, and was now being sold to the company's giant competitor, Ryder Systems of Miami, Florida. Ryder Systems had been acquiring smaller firms for several years, and early in 1986 offered to buy Saunders System. Ultimately, the offer was accepted and Saunders was integrated into Ryder Systems. The company that had built a tradition based on survival ceased to exist.

"Somebody offered a lot of money to buy the company," Harris Saunders commented. "The business has changed so significantly. It requires a whole new terminology, a whole new outlook, new management, and new thinking. I think we're from the old school."

SAUNDERS SYSTEM, INC.: BEFORE DEREGULATION

The Saunders Company was founded in 1916 by Warwick Saunders and his four sons: Warwick, Jr., Joe, Ellis, and Harris. It is credited as being the first car and truck rental business in the United States. Twenty-seven-year-old Joe Saunders had the idea when the family car broke down, and he borrowed a Model T Ford. Joe realized that if he could use a temporary vehicle, plenty of other people might also. Thus, Joe placed a seven-line classified advertisement in the *Omaha World*

This case was prepared by Peter M. Ginter, Linda E. Swayne, and John D. Leonard as a basis for class discussion rather than to illustrate either effective or ineffective handling of an administrative situation. Used by permission from Peter M. Ginter.

Herald offering a five-passenger Ford for rent. Joe is often credited with giving birth to the vehicle renting industry.

The fledgling Saunders Company soon owned a whole fleet of cars and eventually changed the name to Saunders Drive It Yourself System, with offices in major cities around the nation. The car rental company grew, but truck leasing grew faster and became the company's main line of business. By the early 1950s, automobile rentals were phased out in order to concentrate on leasing and renting heavy-duty vehicles.

Early Challenges

Throughout the 70 years of Saunders System's existence, several significant events challenged or changed the course of the company's development. The firm had to respond to the demands of World War I, the Great Depression, the post World War II recovery, the inflation of the 1970s, and trucking deregulation.

Very few firms were prepared for the crash of 1929 and the depression that followed. Saunders System was essentially wiped out and the Saunders family lost the business. The Saunders brothers were able to buy some rental facilities at auction when they could assume the mortgages, pay for the equipment, and negotiate an equitable lease with the owner of the building. Some operations, and the Saunders name, were able to continue in this fashion.

The Growth Era

The business was restructured in the 1930s. Four geographical divisions were formed, and a new, smaller company prevailed. It was during this time that the family realized that in addition to selling their service they needed to develop stronger balance sheet ratios and a better working capital position.

The post–World War II era was a time of economic boom. It was during this time that Saunders System deemphasized car leasing and concentrated on truck leasing. The truck leasing segment of the business was growing much more rapidly and became the company's major focus.

During the 1960s, the Saunders family considered the option of making Saunders System a public firm. The advantages of increased prestige, increased equity capital, and increased ability to use stock versus cash for other financial transactions weighed heavily in the decision. The costs of going public for Saunders included reduced managerial freedom, increased cost of accounting methods and reporting, increased time and money spent with underwriters, analysts, and others, and pressure to show improvements on a quarterly basis.

Finally in 1967, Saunders System made their first public stock offering. Additional offerings were made in 1972 and 1982. The family retained 51 percent ownership of the firm with a French firm building a 21-percent share. The balance of the outstanding shares was not consolidated in any other large holding.

Energy Crisis

The 1970s were a time of great pressure on costs. The emergence of OPEC created tremendous problems for the fuel industry. Subsequently, the trucking industry and related services suffered. High inflation also contributed to the economic pressures faced by business. Though Saunders itself was not a regulated business, pressure on the trucking industry was lessened somewhat by industry regulation. Escalating prices were passed on to customers, and price competition was dampened. Performance within the industry was generally maintained at status quo. Regulated prices were essentially the same, but firms were able to differentiate themselves by their service record and image. Saunders System continued to build a strong image of service during this time.

SAUNDERS SYSTEM INC.: AFTER DEREGULATION

The decade of the 1980s brought a new era for the trucking industry and Saunders System. Deregulation contributed to overcapacity within the industry and new methods of competition, which were formerly banned, became prevalent. Weaker firms were acquired or went bankrupt; stronger firms became larger and stronger.

By the mid 1980s Saunders had become one of the largest of the nation's full-service leasing companies with 141 service centers and freight terminals located across the United States and Canada. Saunders competed with such billion dollar giants as Ryder, Hertz, and Leaseway truck rental companies. As of 1986, Saunders had over 2,000 employees, a fleet of over 8,000 vehicles, and served more than 5,700 truck transportation clients. Saunders offered a full line of transportation services tailored to each client's needs. This diversification of services led to changing the name of the company from Saunders Leasing System, Inc. to Saunders System, Inc.

The deregulation of the early 1980s forced the industry to address a freer, more competitive market. While Saunders System remained competitive and profitable, the company did not show the strength of the industry leaders such as Ryder.

Organization and Reorientation

Prior to deregulation, the company's management, as with most trucking firms, was oriented toward trucking operations rather than marketing or company strategy. In 1985, Gordon Shelfer, Jr. became the first nonfamily member to become President and CEO in the history of Saunders. The competitive pressures of the market, the effects of trucking deregulation, and the company's attempt to emphasize marketing contributed to his nomination as CEO.

Shelfer focused Saunders on a functional basis with four primary departments—markets, operations, human resources, and finance and administration.

The resulting organization of Saunders System, Inc. is illustrated in Exhibit 21-1. In this organization the executive vice-president of marketing was responsible for carrier services, advertising, research and planning, and sales and field marketing. The vice-president for operations directed the driver central operations, the tire remanufacturing operation, and all company equipment maintenance. The executive vice-president of finance and administration was responsible for the management information system, budgeting, legal matters and accounting. The senior vice-president of human resources maintained labor relations, safety of facilities and vehicles, training, the in-house newspaper, and employment support.

Two additional directors reported to Mr. Shelfer—the director of properties and the director of internal audit. The director of properties was responsible for negotiating leases, buildings and facilities, and complying with EPA regulations. The director of internal audit examined the four primary functions to make sure they were following procedures and regulations.

In an attempt to make the company more competitive and reduce costs, Shelfer streamlined management and increased management's span of control. Shelfer felt that overhead had been allowed to grow unchecked. In the past, the firm added staff and enlarged budgets in order to meet projected sales volume, but would not cut back responsively when revenues fell short of expectations. The result was excessive overhead costs which increased each year. Not enough attention was paid to costs in a market which had become very cost competitive.

The reorganization of company operations reduced eleven area offices to seven, enabling management to improve coordination and to somewhat reduce overhead costs. The seven area offices and cities with facilities/terminals are shown in Exhibit 21-2.

In addition to the reorganization, Shelfer reinforced "client tailored services" in which a client's individual needs were identified, then services were tailored to meet those needs. In conjunction with tailored services, Mr. Shelfer encouraged top management to get out into the field to interact with customers and field personnel. Top management exposure strengthened client relations, Saunders' internal communications network, and increased employee loyalty and understanding of the business. Further, Mr. Shelfer managed the company with an emphasis on performance, cost reduction, maintenance of quality standards, and market segmentation.

Product Line

With deregulation of the trucking industry, Saunders had developed a wide line of products for its clients. Saunders' array of products included the following.

Full-Service Leasing.   As the company evolved, full-service leasing accounted for less and less of the Saunders business. In 1985, as illustrated in Exhibit 21-3, leasing comprised approximately 50 percent of the total revenue of Saunders. A

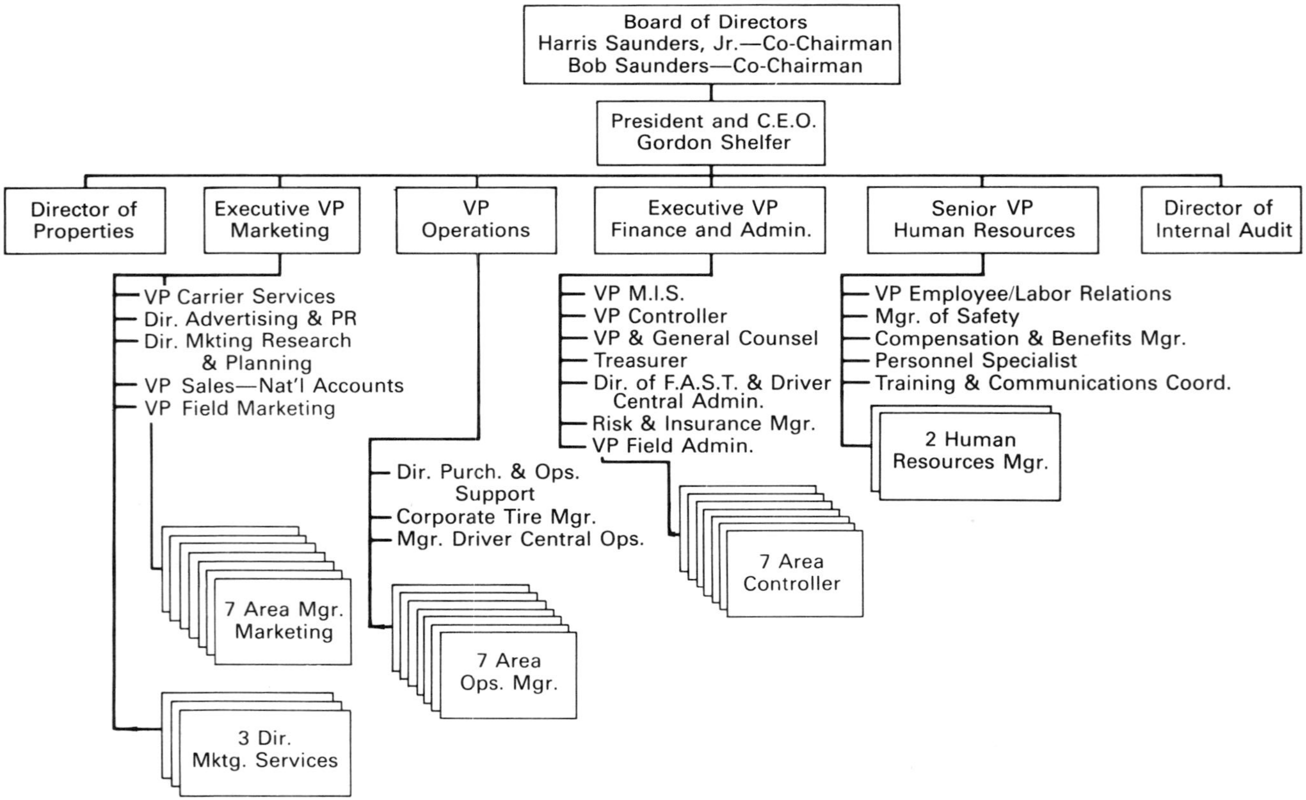

Board of Directors
Harris Saunders, Jr.—Co-Chairman
Bob Saunders—Co-Chairman

President and C.E.O.
Gordon Shelfer

Director of Properties

Executive VP Marketing
- VP Carrier Services
- Dir. Advertising & PR
- Dir. Mkting Research & Planning
- VP Sales—Nat'l Accounts
- VP Field Marketing
  - 7 Area Mgr. Marketing
  - 3 Dir. Mktg. Services

VP Operations
- Dir. Purch. & Ops. Support
- Corporate Tire Mgr.
- Mgr. Driver Central Ops.
  - 7 Area Ops. Mgr.

Executive VP Finance and Admin.
- VP M.I.S.
- VP Controller
- VP & General Counsel
- Treasurer
- Dir. of F.A.S.T. & Driver Central Admin.
- Risk & Insurance Mgr.
- VP Field Admin.
  - 7 Area Controller

Senior VP Human Resources
- VP Employee/Labor Relations
- Mgr. of Safety
- Compensation & Benefits Mgr.
- Personnel Specialist
- Training & Communications Coord.
  - 2 Human Resources Mgr.

Director of Internal Audit

Source: Company records.

Exhibit 21-1 Organization of Saunders System, Inc.

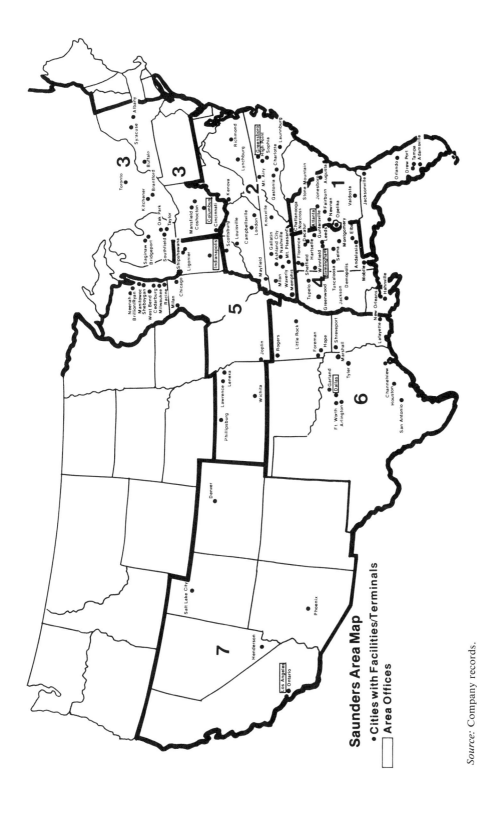

Saunders Area Map

- **Cities with Facilities/Terminals**
- **Area Offices**

Source: Company records.

Exhibit 21-2 **Saunders' Area Offices and Facility Locations**

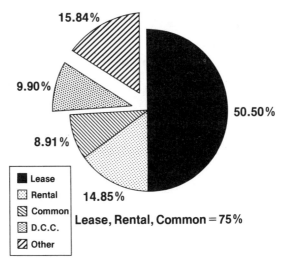

Source: Saunders Leasing System, Inc. *Annual Report,* 1985.

Exhibit 21-3   **Revenue Mix 1985**

full-service lease with Saunders included all parts, tires, maintenance, fleet driver, safety training, substitute vehicles, optional full-tax services, fuel, and insurance. In addition, the vehicle leased by Saunders was painted the colors desired by the client company.

The service was tailored primarily toward the client who wanted to control the distribution system, but did not want to handle daily operational and maintenance problems. Depending on the needs of the client, lease terms typically ranged from six months to three years. Two major clients with full service leasing arrangements were Nabisco and K mart Corporation.

Truck Rental.   Truck rental is the short-term use of tractors, trailers, and trucks. Short-term vehicle rental is often used for rush loads and during peak seasons. In the past, truck rental was the mainstay of Saunders System. Although truck rental diminished in relative importance in Saunders' revenue mix, as indicated in Exhibit 21-3, it still made up almost 15 percent of 1985 revenues. Two clients that used truck rental were Texas Instruments and Sears, Roebuck & Company.

Bulk Common Carriage.   Another important product in the Saunders line was common carriage, comprising approximately 9 percent of total revenue. Bulk common carriage provided shipping services including the shipping of general and specific commodities on flatbed trailers, vans, and dump and tank trailers.

Saunders Carriers, Inc., a part of the common carriage business, was organized as a subsidiary of Saunders System after its acquisition in 1980. This subsidiary specialized in the safe handling of bulk liquids and was recognized nationally for its safety record. Emergency response teams, trained to handle tank accidents, were stationed at each Saunders terminal. Special emphasis was given to preventing or reducing potentially harmful environmental consequences. In 1985, Saunders Carriers, Inc. built the nation's most technologically advanced terminal dedicated to the cleaning of bulk liquid trailers and the proper treatment of the resulting waste water. Two clients that used this service were Monsanto Company and Du Pont.

Dedicated Contract Carriage (DCC).   Although it began operations in 1984, dedicated contract carriage comprised almost 10 percent of Saunders' revenue in 1985. Saunders DCC handled the total transportation needs of a client, including an in-depth analysis of the client's service needs. Saunders DCC provided all required vehicles, a fully equipped truck maintenance facility, quality drivers, supervisors, mechanics, delivery scheduling, and all related paperwork. Saunders assumed total responsibility for the management and operation of the client's distribution system. In addition, Saunders' vehicles were painted with the client's corporate colors and logo. Two important clients for this service included AT&T and Goodyear Tire and Rubber Company.

Truck Maintenance.   Saunders offered truck maintenance to companies that owned their fleet but did not want to service their vehicles. Under this program, Saunders' personnel performed the same preventive maintenance, service, and repairs for a client's vehicles as they did for Saunders' owned vehicles. Two clients using this service were Weyerhaeuser and Royal Cup, Inc.

Driver Central (Road Breakdown and Driver Assistance).   Driver Central was an emergency dispatch system providing drivers with prompt road assistance any hour of the day, any day of the year. A computerized records system and a specialized communications system were used to access more than 19,000 service facilities in the United States and Canada. The facilities were no more than 30 miles apart, providing prompt service.

The communication system allowed for up to a six-way phone conference. Driver Central documented all actions taken so the client would know exactly what happened and how long it took to remedy the situation. This service was started in 1976 as a means to cut "down time" for leased fleets. In 1976, it reduced down time by 40 percent. Two clients using this service were W. R. Grace and Co. and Hammermill Paper Company.

Fuel and State Tax (FAST).   The FAST program was designed to help fleet operators with the complex task of state fuel and mileage tax reporting. The program helped customers get the best prices and services for fuel wherever they travelled. Because fuel is one of the largest cost factors in truck fleet operation, this was important.

Fuel taxes vary from state to state, not only in amount but in requirements regarding paying taxes on fuel used within a state although bought in another state. Some states allow tax refunds for overpurchases; some charge a tax on fuel used in the state even though tax was paid in the state of purchase. There are almost as many different fuel tax regulations as there are states. A customer of the FAST program did not have to keep up with the frequent changes in state laws; the client did not have to handle the complicated and time-consuming state fuel tax reports nor the annual audits made by the states. In addition, a client's fuel purchasing and use patterns could be analyzed periodically to make recommendations concerning the minimization of tax liabilities and other costs. Two clients for this service included Beatrice and Tom's Foods, Inc.

Fuel Management.   The Fuel Management System provided assistance in the management of over-the-road fleet fueling. Clients could choose between two types of credit cards which were computer linked to fuel stops and service centers in the United States and Canada. The "electronic fuel card" enabled a client's drivers to obtain fuel and service at over 500 fueling centers nationwide. The "cash card" enabled a client's drivers to select from over 1,500 fuel stops and 100 service centers in the United States and Canada. Both services provided a client with consolidated fuel billings and fleet management reports. Two clients using this service included Burger King and the Ship-N-Shore Division of General Mills.

Consulting and Safety Programs.   The consulting and safety programs assisted clients in the analysis and improvement of client distribution systems. The program included investigation and recommendations concerning intercorporate hauling, intermodel alternatives and distribution routes, driver training, and freight brokerage services. Transportation Industry Consultants, Inc., another Saunders subsidiary, specialized in helping companies analyze and streamline their distribution methods. The safety program offered audiovisual aids designed to instruct drivers to anticipate and handle all types of road problems. Two clients using this service were Coca-Cola Bottling Company and South Central Bell.

Remanufactured and New Tires.   Saunders operated its own facility for the remanufacture of long-lasting radial truck tires. Saunders' remanufactured brand was called the Long Rider. Truck Central, Inc., the tire supply subsidiary of Saunders, located in Birmingham, Alabama, sold more than 100 types and sizes of new major brand truck tires. In addition, Saunders would custom remanufacture a client's worn tire casings using state-of-the-art tire remolding equipment. Truck Central offered professional advice on the uses of radial and remanufactured tires. Two clients for this service were Avondale Mills and West Point Pepperell.

Used Vehicles.   Late model Saunders trucks, tractors, and trailers were available for sale at the end of their respective lease periods. These vehicles were sold by area rental account managers from strategically located centers across the nation.

Current Financial Condition

Revenues of 1985 were a record, surpassing 1984 revenues, the previous record year. As indicated in Exhibit 21-4, total revenues for 1985 increased by $6.2 million or 2.3 percent over those of 1984. This increase was due to a larger fleet size, a greater volume of used revenue equipment sales, and the company's successful expansion in dedicated contract carriage. Operating expenses for 1985, exclusive of

Exhibit 21-4   **Consolidated Statement of Income (In thousands, except per share)**

	1983	1984	1985
Revenues			
Vehicle lease	$138,622	$146,092	$147,610
Vehicle rental	27,367	33,215	29,528
Common carrier	34,198	29,744	18,809
Contract carrier	—	4,818	20,102
Other services	40,912	51,094	55,120
	241,099	264,963	271,169
Costs and expenses			
Operating expenses, exclusive of depreciation	192,793	210,764	209,914
Depreciation (net of gain on sale of revenue equipment, $4,422 in 1985; $5,003 in 1984; $2,793 in 1983)	27,054	28,584	33,989
	219,847	239,348	243,903
	21,252	25,615	27,266
Interest expense	16,207	18,755	21,234
Income before provision for income taxes	5,045	6,860	6,032
Provision for income taxes	790	1,125	895
Net income	$ 4,255	$ 5,735	$ 5,137
Net Income per Common and Common Equivalent Share	$ .61	$ .85	$ .58

Source: Saunders System, Inc. *Annual Report,* 1985.

depreciation, decreased by $850,000 from 1984; however, 1985 depreciation and interest expenses were higher than 1984.

Exhibit 21-5 shows Saunders' consolidated balance sheet. In 1985, total assets increased to approximately $274.9 million from $260.1 million in 1984 and $208.0 million in 1983. Long-term debt also increased to $157.6 million in 1985 from $153.0 million in 1984 and $116.1 million in 1983.

DEREGULATION OF THE TRUCKING INDUSTRY

One of the more significant events in the history of the trucking industry was the deregulation legislation passed in the early 1980s. Three recent pieces of legislation had great influence on the industry—the 1980 Motor Carriers Act, 1982 Surface Transportation Assistance Act, and 1982 Staggers Rail Act (See Motor Carrier Transportation, Case 22, for further details).

The Impact of Deregulation on the Industry

Deregulation directly affected the number of competitors entering the market, and eased operating restrictions for those already in service. The free market environment created a "buyer's market" where shippers were able to demand lower rates and improved service. Though it appears that the increased competition held down shipping costs, the failure rate of trucking firms escalated rapidly. In addition to business failures, acquisitions and intermodal mergers increased.

New Market Entries. The deregulation of the trucking industry facilitated ease of entry which resulted in overcapacity and subsequently price (rate) erosion. The American Trucking Association reported that from 1980 to 1982 some 43,000 new operating certificates were issued. Approximately 80 percent of these were issued to existing firms.[1] Between 1980 and 1984, the number of regulated motor carriers jumped 70 percent to over 30,000.[2] Additionally, private carriers were allowed generous back-haul options which reduced the available demand for existing firms and increased industry capacity.

In addition to new firms, many existing carriers moved swiftly to accelerate their long-term growth strategies. Five- and ten-year plans were executed in two years or less. Many trucking firms were overly optimistic concerning geographical expansion. Moreover, many firms had inadequate capital to support an expansion strategy, especially at the same time that margins were being squeezed because of falling prices.

---

[1]*Standard & Poor's Industry Surveys,* February 20, 1986, p. R–30.
[2]Ibid., p. R–29.

Most new firms entered the Truckload (TL) segment of the market. A single operator could secure a route with dedicated tonnage from a single source and operate profitably. Expanding into the Less Than Truckload (LTL) segment required substantial capital (terminals, equipment, etc.) and was an alternative for only the larger, stronger firms in the industry.

Rising Costs.   In addition to the pressure on operating margins, insurance premiums rose sharply as a result of deregulation. The U.S. Department of Agriculture surveyed nearly 700 general commodities carriers and found that between 1984 and 1985 the average premium increased 23 percent. Approximately 15 percent of the sample paid 100 percent more for insurance, while nearly a third paid 50 percent more. Increases of 1,000 percent have been publicized, while some firms could not secure insurance at any cost.[3]

Many firms searched for shortcuts through the price-cost squeeze. There were cutbacks on maintenance, training, and vehicle rehabilitation. Many drivers exceeded posted speed limits and violated shift limits (road time) in an effort to increase revenues. Some firms considered the alternative of self-insurance, but the ICC requires the posting of a $1 million line of credit for payment of claims. In 1986, approximately 90 percent of the industry could not meet this requirement.[4]

Industry Consolidation.   The trucking industry's responses to the new environment had both economic and social ramifications. Dun & Bradstreet indicated that in 1978 there were 162 trucking business failures, in 1984 there were 1,409, and in 1985 there were 1,533. An American Trucking Association official stated that 20 percent of all for-hire motor carriers (6,000 firms) could be forced out of business.[5] In addition, society had shown increasing concern for the actions of the trucking industry. Safety records were under scrutiny and trucking firms were required to take costly remedial action for spills, accidents, and so on.

As a result of low operating margins and acquisition strategies by the large firms, consolidation in the industry had occurred. Chairman George E. Powell of Yellow Freight System stated that "deregulation makes the big firms stronger, forces the smaller firms into niches, and allows the medium sized firms to get squeezed."[6]

Saunders' CEO, Gordon Shelfer, indicated that deregulation was more of an indirect force in the leasing segment of the business. He stated, "It may have quickened the inevitable, but the real issue facing the industry is cost control. Companies have to realize approaching a more competitive environment without having costs in line will tend to highlight weaknesses."

---

[3]*Standard & Poor's Industry Surveys,* May 29, 1986, p. R–1.
[4]Ibid., p. R–3.
[5]Ibid., p. R–3.
[6]*New York Times,* December 22, 1985, p. F-17.

Exhibit 21-5 **Consolidated Balance Sheet (In thousands)**

	1983	1984	1985
Assets			
Current assets			
Cash	$ 2,759	$ 2,850	$ 5,187
Accounts receivable			
Trade	23,670	25,772	29,927
Other	3,850	2,972	2,590
Inventories	6,547	5,288	5,448
Prepaid vehicle licenses and taxes	2,321	2,610	4,054
Other prepaid expenses	1,198	1,696	2,401
	40,345	41,188	49,607
Revenue equipment, at cost	241,061	292,413	289,739
Less accumulated depreciation	88,229	91,867	87,638
	152,832	200,546	202,101
Operating facilities, at cost	16,915	17,969	19,565
Less accumulated depreciation	7,198	7,735	8,323
	9,717	10,234	11,242
Unamortized leasehold improvements	1,847	2,330	3,464
	164,396	213,110	216,807
Deferred charges	648	3,110	5,902
Costs in excess of net assets of businesses acquired	2,378	2,437	2,392
Other assets	235	210	225
Total Assets	$208,002	$260,055	$274,933

Source: Saunders System, Inc. *Annual Report,* 1985.

Increasing Environmental Complexity

In addition to deregulation, the turbulent economy of the 1980s contributed to a more complex industry. Adding to the difficulty of management were the rise and fall of interest rates, the declining cost of new equipment and fuel, and the unpredictability of the used truck market.

During the era of double-digit interest rates, leasing had become an attractive alternative to ownership. As a result, Saunders' leasing business did well. However, when interest rates declined, many companies (both trucking and nontrucking) were able to finance purchases of equipment at rates competitive to Saunders' 12.5 percent cost of capital.

Exhibit 21-5   (continued)

	1983	1984	1985
Liabilities and Stockholders' Equity			
Current liabilities			
Current portion of long-term notes payable	$ 648	$ 612	$ 724
Notes payable—bank	3,500	2,400	3,400
Accounts payable, trade	8,494	8,722	8,325
Accrued liabilities	4,726	6,426	5,410
	17,368	18,160	17,859
Revenue equipment obligations due within one year	21,578	30,830	26,637
Long-term debt			
Revenue equipment obligations due beyond one year	112,864	149,925	155,226
Notes payable, net of current portion above	3,214	3,076	2,346
	116,078	153,001	157,572
Deferred income taxes	7,021	8,084	8,797
Other liabilities	434	449	459
Preference Stock—Redeemable			
Preference stock—redeemable, par value $1.00 per share, Series C, Cumulative Nonvoting. Liquidation value $2,920,000	4	3	3
Capital in excess of par value	3,636	3,277	2,917
	3,640	3,280	2,920
Common stock, preference stock— nonredeemable and other stockholders' equity			
Common stock, par value $1.00 per share:			
Class A, authorized 15,000,000 shares	3,222	3,248	3,353
Class B, authorized 6,500,000 shares	3,029	3,037	2,948
Preference stock, par value $1.00 per share, Series A, Convertible Voting Involuntary liquidation value $231,000	18	18	18
$1.20 Convertible Exchangeable Preference stock, par value $1.00 per share Cumulative Nonvoting. Involuntary liquidation value $12,995,000			1,300
Capital in excess of par value	92	142	10,728
Retained earnings, as annexed	35,769	40,045	42,581
	42,130	46,490	60,928
Less common stock in treasury, at cost, 95,308 shares, 1985 and 1984; 98,208 shares, 1983	247	239	239
	41,883	46,251	60,689
Total Liabilities and Stockholders' Equity	$208,002	$260,055	$274,933

Source: Saunders System, Inc. *Annual Report,* 1985.

In the late 1970s to the early 1980s there had been undercapacity in the trucking industry which enabled used vehicles to be sold at premium prices. Used truck sales were an important part of Saunders' business. As a result of the high used vehicle prices, Saunders raised the salvage value (and reduced the amount of depreciation) of its vehicles. Most of the used equipment inventory was "cab over" type trucks due to federal length laws.

Subsequently, two events had a substantial impact on the profitability of Saunders. First, federal legislation was enacted allowing longer vehicles on the highways (drivers tend to prefer the longer conventional cabs for safety and ride). Secondly, overcapacity occurred in the trucking industry.

The selling price of new trucks fell significantly, which made ownership more attractive. Furthermore, fuel prices began to fall. Cheaper equipment, lower interest rates, and lower fuel costs caused more manufacturers to opt for ownership, rather than leasing, to meet their transportation needs. Used equipment became more difficult to sell. Seemingly without warning, the bottom fell out of the used truck market and Saunders had a lot of underdepreciated and idle "iron."

The result of factors such as these made planning in the leasing segment of the industry extremely difficult. Consequently, planning tended to have a shorter and shorter focus. Mr. Shelfer indicated that "changes were taking place in the industry which had a tremendous impact on the business but were impossible to predict and thus by the mid 1980s we were reacting rather than planning."

SAUNDERS' STRATEGY

In 1986 Saunders System was in the final year of a five-year plan which focused primarily on geographical and product expansion. Through the strategy, Saunders had continued to be a national truck leasing firm with a wider variety of related services. Implementation of the strategy included the replacement of approximately 70 percent of the sales force with more aggressive, better trained people to meet the challenges of the new marketplace.

Changes to the management structure allowed for better communications and market assessment. Saunders had an advanced computer system and terminal network. They routinely replaced trucks on a set schedule. They kept up with the latest in new trucking technology and kept the fleet new and clean looking. Management felt they had laid the necessary groundwork for making the firm viable at least into the 1990s.

Commenting on the strategy, Gordon Shelfer, President of Saunders, stated, "The current strategy, which has been in place for about four years allowed us to hold our own in the industry. But we're not going to meet our objective of 16 percent rate of return." Mr. Shelfer continued, "We have a hard time competing against the big guys in the industry. They had a tremendous cost advantage because of their size. They can get better prices on fuel, parts, and capital through volume buying and the way they secure additional capital."

The president further reflected:

> Saunders had the opportunity to grow. In the early 1970's, the leasing portion of Ryder and Saunders were approximately the same size. Ryder went aggressively to the equity markets for financing and Saunders did not. Saunders had grown rapidly in the 1960s but we needed additional capital in order to continue on the same course. The Saunders brothers, however, made it clear that the dividend policy would not change and our operating results and capital structure probably aren't good enough to borrow money at a reasonable enough rate and our objective is to reduce, not add debt as a percentage of total capital. Moreover, equity financing is not acceptable because it would dilute the family's holdings. However, if we don't expand, I don't know how much longer we can compete given the nature of this business.

ON THE BLOCK

The Saunders brothers felt that the trucking industry had changed substantially in the decade of the 1980s. In addition, Saunders performance was sluggish, financial condition was weak, and future prospects for the company would continue to be marginal without a major revamping of the strategy. Therefore, in March 1986, "the boys" engaged Kidder, Peabody investment bankers to investigate the sale of Saunders System to a nontrucking firm. They knew such a sale could remove the Saunders brothers from the business, but the Saunders name and operations would be retained.

Several firms were initially interested in acquiring Saunders including Dart-Kraft and GECC. However, internal considerations within these companies (unrelated to Saunders) made the acquisition undesirable. News that Saunders System might be for sale instigated interest from other firms, including several firms within the trucking industry. As a result, Saunders' Board of Directors became concerned about generating the broadest base of interested buyers and avoiding minority stockholder law suits and therefore asked Kidder, Peabody to widen the search for possible acquisition alternatives.

Approximately 84 firms were contacted concerning the possible acquisition of Saunders System. Forty firms responded with requests for additional information. Seven of these indicated a more serious intent and visited Saunders System's main offices in Birmingham, Alabama for the purpose of viewing confidential presentations. Ryder Systems was one of these firms, and on June 20, 1986 offered approximately $10 per share for Saunders System. Negotiations between the two firms culminated in an agreement on June 26, 1986 whereby Ryder would buy Saunders for $12.50 per share.

Negotiation and Sale

The original plan was to sell to a noncompeting firm in order to maintain Saunders as an operating unit. Management at Saunders felt that the company could be sold for a price of $16 to $18 per share. As it developed, most interested buyers were competitors, and they were offering $10 to $12 per share.

Although the offers were not up to expectation, they were good offers in comparison to book value, market value, and earnings. Shelfer observed that once the process started it was difficult to stop, and that it would have been difficult both legally and economically to reject a fair bid. Shelfer explained that the difference in value expectation was due to the fact that the firm was holding tax carryover benefits that could no longer be carried into the future. Thus, prospective buyers reduced their offering price.

In retrospect, Shelfer was not sure whether the family would repeat the process, knowing the eventual price and buyer. From an investor's point of view, Shelfer felt that the decision was proper. The offer was a reasonable multiple of book, and it was the right time for the family to get out of the business. However, some of the original objectives of the sale had not been achieved.

Saunders System, Inc. would no longer exist. Much of Saunders' operations (those redundant with Ryder) were dismantled and the rest of Saunders System was absorbed into Ryder. In addition, the final selling price, though fair, was less than initially expected. Finally, and perhaps most importantly, Shelfer was never really given an opportunity to "make it work."

Case 22

Motor Carrier Transportation

Few industries in this decade have had as much change as the transportation industry. Deregulation, fluctuating prices for fuel and new vehicles, and escalating costs have contributed to making transportation much more competitive. Adaptations have had to occur in methods of operation and management philosophy. In many ways, transportation is very different from the industry it was in the 1970s.

This case was prepared by Peter M. Ginter and Linda E. Swayne as a basis for class discussion rather than to illustrate either effective or ineffective handling of an administrative situation. Used by permission from Peter M. Ginter.

Transportation is the movement of people or goods from one location to another. A number of distinct types of transportation can be identified:

- Passenger transportation—movement of human beings.
- Cargo transportation—movement of anything other than people by any of the five modes of transportation.
- Intracity (urban) transportation—movement between two points within a metropolitan area.
- Intercity transportation—movement beginning in one city and ending in another city.
- Intrastate transportation—movement between points in the same state.
- Interstate transportation—movement where the origin and destination are in two different states.
- Domestic transportation—movement between points within the United States and its territories.
- International transportation—movement between the United States or its territories and another country; or movement between two non-U.S.points.

Traffic or transportation managers are responsible for inbound and outbound transportation decisions for an organization. Specifically mode and carrier decisions are used to meet company objectives.

TRANSPORTATION MODES

The five modes of transportation include rail, water, pipeline, highway, and air. However, seldom does a shipper have the choice among all of the modes. For example, little water shipping occurs in Kansas. The nature of the cargo, characteristics of the mode (speed, cost, etc.), and availability of service are important in mode selection.

Transportation of cargo is measured in ton miles—one ton of cargo moved one mile. Although declining, railroads still are the dominant mode of transportation accounting for 30 percent of ton miles (Exhibit 22-1).

Specific modes are selected based on accessibility, reliability, speed, flexibility, control, and liability. Some carriers offer specialized equipment for products, such as flammable liquids or oversized construction materials, that provide access to a market that otherwise would be less accessible.

Reliability is often a major consideration in mode selection. Companies schedule a carrier to deliver at specific times in order to maintain supplies so that sales are not lost. However, too early delivery can be equally dissatisfying because the companies do not have excess warehouse space to store product delivered ahead of schedule. Shippers want reliable methods of transportation with delivery at the agreed upon time.

With time-sensitive goods, speed is the most important factor in determining mode selection. Control, or knowing where a shipment is at any point in time, is an

Exhibit 22-1   **U.S. Transportation by Mode**

	1975		1984	
Mode	**Ton-miles**	**Percent**	**Ton-miles**	**Percent**
Rail	759,000	36.74	936,000	36.65
Motor carrier	454,000	21.97	602,000	23.57
Water	342,000	16.55	404,000	15.82
Pipeline	507,000	24.54	605,000	23.69
Air	3,700	00.19	6,600	00.26

Source: U.S. Bureau of the Census, *Statistical Abstract of the United States: 1986,* p. 591.

important consideration for some shippers. Accuracy and timeliness in locating goods has become increasingly important as shippers attempt to maximize their customer service and minimize costs by diverting goods in transit. Moreover, the extent of damage and the loss record (liability) is a service consideration for mode and carrier selection.

Flexibility is a service variable important to some shippers. Meeting unusual needs such as unscheduled pick-ups or deliveries, "rush" deliveries, and so forth, are important mode-selection factors to the traffic manager in order to meet company objectives.

After determining the appropriate mode of transportation, carrier selection is determined by service and rate consideration. Carriers supply transportation services and can be private or for-hire carriers.

MOTOR CARRIER TRANSPORTATION

Motor carrier transportation provides a lifeline for our economy by fulfilling needs that are critical to any industrialized nation. Without trucking, shippers could not compete effectively in the marketplace and customers would not enjoy the magnitude of choice. As shown in Exhibit 22-1, trucking accounts for approximately 24 percent of total cargo ton miles in interstate movement of goods. Furthermore, trucking has the largest portion of intracity movement of goods.

The motor carrier industry is segmented by the type of goods transported, the geography covered, and the nature of service offered. Exhibit 22-2 outlines the major segments in the U.S. trucking industry.

There are four legal forms of carriage—common, contract, exempt, and private. Common carriers are for-hire transportation companies that are required to charge reasonable rates, to avoid undue or unjust discrimination, to serve the public, and to deliver. Common carriers are expected to serve all customers who request their services provided they have the equipment and operating authority to haul the commodity.

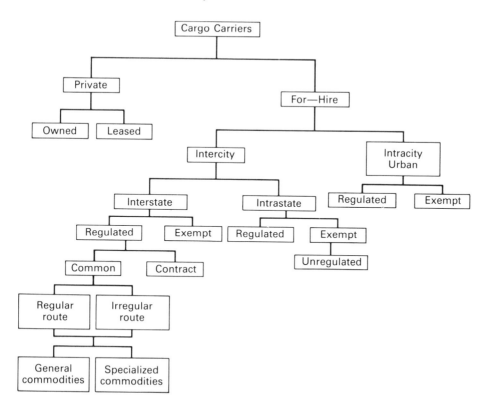

- Regulated refers to economic regulation either by the Interstate Commerce Commission (ICC) or by a specific state or city.
- Exempt refers to specifically identified commodities not subject to regulation (usually agricultural products such as livestock, grains, etc.).
- Unregulated means that a state has no economic regulation or has completely deregulated trucking.
- Contract carrier negotiates service levels and rates with a shipper.
- Regular route means regularly scheduled service over designated roads.
- Irregular route allows a carrier to service between points by any route cleared for safe operation.
- General commodities usually refers to packaged freight.
- Specialized commodities include heavy machinery, liquids, refrigerated products, forestry products, explosives, etc.

Source: Adapted from F. A. Stephenson, *Transportation USA,* Reading, MA: Addison-Wesley, 1987.

Exhibit 22-2   **Motor Carrier Segments for Cargo**

Contract carriers are for-hire carriers bound only by the agreement that they negotiate with the shipper that contracts for their service. Exempt carriers are for-hire carriers but are exempt from economic regulations. Private carriers are company owned/managed fleets of trucks to transport company products and are not required to follow economic regulations.

There are an estimated 150,000 private fleets in trucking.[1] Some firms by necessity acquire their own fleet because of specialized equipment needs. Others own their own fleets because of perceived rate or service advantages.

Motor Carrier Regulation

Historically the freight transportation industry was the first regulated sector of our economy beginning with the Interstate Commerce Act of 1887. The U.S. trucking industry has been regulated by the federal government since the enactment of the Motor Carrier Act of 1935.

The Motor Carrier Act was modeled after railroad regulation. Carriers were granted operating authority between cities. Since this system treated trucks identically to trains, the capability of trucks to travel anywhere that roads existed was not acknowledged.

The Motor Carrier Act required truckers to obtain federal "certificates of public conveniency and necessity" before offering their services to the public. The Act required approval of the routes truckers were to take (sometimes even specific roads to travel) and approval of the rates or tariffs to be charged. Proposed tariffs differing from the rest of the industry were rarely granted, and truckers were penalized if the prices they charged were lower or higher than those approved. Free of competition and protected by the ICC, the industry kept rates high. Consequently, truckers competed on the basis of service and not rates.

ICC approval was required for any mergers involving trucking companies. Additionally, the ICC prohibited two-way operating rights that resulted in trucks returning from their destination with an empty trailer (backhauling).

During this period, the only way for companies in interstate commerce to expand was to gain additional operating rights from other carriers who were ceasing operations. Excessive costs were associated with the purchasing of operating authority and the protection of rates.

Dramatic changes occurred with the passage of the Motor Carrier Act of 1980. The two major areas of change were the lessening of control over pricing and reduction in ICC interference in granting operating authority. No longer were truckers required to demonstrate public need in order to obtain operating rights. With additional carriers entering the industry and less rate restriction, price competition became a major factor in the market.

Specifically, the purpose of the Motor Carrier Act of 1980 was to reduce un-

---

[1]J. V. Strickland, "Private-Carriage Boosted by Deregulation," *Distribution,* September 1980, p. 30.

necessary government regulation of motor carriers. The major provisions of the Act include:

- Lifting the burden of proof from the applicant for an operating permit. Now a person objecting to the permit would have to prove that the service would be inconsistent with the public convenience and necessity.
- Granting truckers a "zone of rate-making freedom." Carriers were permitted to raise or lower rates by 10 percent a year without having to obtain ICC approval.
- Directing the ICC to repeal rules requiring truckers to take circuitous routes or to stop at designated intermediate points.
- Directing the ICC to reduce restrictions on the commodities that could be carried by a trucking firm and the territory that could be served.[2]

The 1980 Motor Carrier Act left much to the discretion of the ICC, and the members of the deregulation-minded commission went further than the law required.[3] They began to routinely approve applications for operating authority recognizing that new, competitive services are almost never inconsistent with the "public convenience and necessity." New rates (tariffs) have also been routinely approved, resulting in intense price competition.

The results of the deregulation have been an increase in the number of carriers, lower prices, and better service, including service to smaller communities. However, the large firms have grown larger, and some predict that greater concentration in the industry will eventually lead to higher prices.

Certainly those companies that can achieve economies of scale will be able to offer a lower price to customers and could eventually eliminate the inefficient producers from the industry. Industry statistics for selected motor carrier companies are included in Exhibits 22-3, 22-4, and 22-5.

In 1980 there were 18,945 general freight carriers in the United States. With deregulation, there were 30,481 general freight carriers by the end of 1984.[4] At the same time, there has been a significant increase in the number of failures in the industry. In 1979 there were 67 intercity trucking companies that ceased operations. In 1980 there were 125, in 1984 there were 549, and in 1986 the number of failures reached 1,533. The failures had been predicted as deregulation eliminated the inefficient and inept from the industry.

Individual firms have been affected by deregulation differently as each company chose strategies of expansion or contraction. For instance, RLC Corporation with over 50 percent of their revenues from bulk chemical shippers, and Leaseway who had over 50 percent of their revenue from two customers (General Motors and

---

[2]"Summary of Provisions of the Motor Carrier Act of 1980," Report of the National Motor Freight Traffic Association, Incorporated, June 20, 1980.

[3]"Time to Complete Trucking Deregulation," *Backgrounder,* The Heritage Foundation, Washington, D.C., January 16, 1986, p. 3.

[4]Ibid.

Exhibit 22-3 Selected Trucking Company Revenue and Net Income (In millions)

	1984		1985		1986	
	Operating revenues	Net income	Operating revenues	Net income	Operating revenues	Net income
General Commodity Motor Carriers						
Arkansas Best Corporation	$ 630.2	$ 12.3	$ 633.58	$ 18.29	$ 665.39	$ 20.31
Carolina Freight Corporation	468.8	12.1	554.90	16.89	572.11	17.42
Consolidated Freightways, Inc.	1,704.9	74.5	1,999.62	87.96	2,063.24	88.59
IU International Corporation	2,514.8	7.9	1,630.08	38.23	1,594.40	1.35
Overnite Transportation	415.0	33.9	507.63	44.55	523.66	46.75
Roadway Services, Inc.	1,461.5	100.0	1,688.73	79.04	1,709.01	75.39
Transcon, Inc. Calif.	326.0	5.4	336.49	1.74	344.26	2.04
Yellow Freight System-Del.	1,380.0	44.1	1,616.43	68.37	1,665.52	70.09
Contract Motor Carriers/Leasing						
Gelco Corporation	$ 929.0	$ 13.1	$1,016.39	$ (2.67)	$ 794.77	$(15.10)
Leaseway Transportation Corp.	1,348.5	42.3	1,440.66	32.25	1,451.90	33.10
RLC Corporation	374.5	15.2	406.58	7.85	419.52	13.37
Ryder System, Inc.	2,485.9	117.6	3,328.25	139.70	3,609.91	152.80
Saunders System, Inc.	265.0	5.7	271.17	5.10	n/a	n/a

Source: Standard & Poor's Industry Surveys, January 15, 1987.

Exhibit 22-4   Trucking Industry Selected Financial Information—Contract Motor Carriers/Leasing

Price-Earnings Ratio (high-low)	1983	1984
Gelco Corp.	[a]	25–14
Leaseway Transportation Corp.	15–12	11–7
RLC Corp.	36–17	15–8
Ryder System, Inc.	14–10	12–8
Saunders System, Inc.	13–7	7–5

[a]Not meaningful

Source: Standard & Poor's Industry Surveys, February 20, 1986.

Sears), had distinct areas of specialization. In contrast, management at Gelco decided to make the company smaller. They sold their European trailer division and attempted to sell a Puerto Rican trucking subsidiary.[5]

Ryder, on the other hand, had been rapidly expanding by acquisition and continued an expansionary strategy after deregulation. Other firms, overly optimistic concerning geographical expansion, had inadequate capital to support expansionary strategies, especially at the same time that margins were being squeezed because of falling prices.

While no uniform tracking of trucking industry rates is collected on a national scale, people involved either as shippers or as companies in the industry agree that the cost of moving goods has declined. One industry executive estimated the total savings to the economy from deregulation to be $50 billion annually.[6]

The savings have been a result of the truckers' abilities to institute cost reductions. For example, less paperwork (red tape) is involved, which reduces costs, and trucks no longer have to travel empty on backhauls, the return trip after a delivery. More efficient use of resources is accomplished when tariffs can be earned in both directions.

Increased competition has led to many companies offering discounts to shippers and negotiating lower-priced individual contracts with shippers. Most shippers reported better service since deregulation because shippers and truckers are free to determine the level and type of service to be provided.[7] More frequent service, delivery at specific locations, special care for certain fragile items, or merely faster service can be negotiated.

The fear that small communities would lose trucking service has not been real-

[5]Value Line Investment Survey, July 1986.

[6]Robert V. Delaney, "Managerial and Financial Challenges Facing Transport Leaders." *Transportation Quarterly,* January 1986, p. 32.

[7]David K. Lifschultz, "Some Deregulation Myths," *Traffic World,* August 26, 1985, p. 18.

Exhibit 22-5   **Trucking Industry Selected Financial Information—Contract Motor Carriers/Leasing**

	1980	1981	1982	1983	1984
Return on Equity (%)					
Gelco Corp.	29.0	28.6	14.5	*a*	6.3
Leaseway Transportation Corp.	19.5	17.8	9.9	13.3	14.3
RLC Corp.	22.3	13.5	6.1	6.8	15.1
Ryder System, Inc.	17.1	17.5	15.8	16.8	16.6
Saunders System, Inc.	11.0	13.4	4.7	9.6	12.2
Return on Assets (%)					
Gelco Corp.	2.7	2.5	1.3	*a*	0.5
Leaseway Transportation Corp.	5.5	5.6	3.2	4.2	4.3
RLC Corp.	6.1	3.9	1.6	1.6	3.5
Ryder System, Inc.	3.6	4.3	4.4	4.8	4.6
Saunder System, Inc.	2.2	2.5	1.1	2.1	2.5
Return on Revenues (%)					
Gelco Corp.	6.2	6.0	3.1	*a*	1.4
Leaseway Transportation Corp.	4.6	4.5	2.5	2.9	3.1
RLC Corp.	6.3	4.0	2.0	2.1	4.0
Ryder System, Inc.	3.3	3.8	4.0	4.2	4.7
Saunders System, Inc.	1.8	2.0	0.9	1.8	2.2
Debt/Capital Ratio (%)					
Gelco Corp.	78	81	82	83	84
Leaseway Transportation Corp.	43	42	46	39	48
RLC Corp.	49	50	56	58	61
Ryder System, Inc.	58	49	49	47	49
Saunders System, Inc.	74	71	70	69	73
Earnings per Share ($)					
Gelco Corp.	3.65	4.67	2.51	(2.38)	0.94
Leaseway Transportation Corp.	3.63	3.70	2.22	3.12	3.54
RLC Corp.	1.24	0.80	0.34	0.34	0.83
Ryder System, Inc.	1.47	1.76	1.81	2.15	2.47
Saunders System, Inc.	0.58	0.77	0.29	0.61	0.85
Book Value per Share ($)					
Gelco Corp.	(8.84)	0.27	2.88	1.86	3.37
Leaseway Transportation Corp.	19.15	21.44	21.19	22.40	23.41
RLC Corp.	5.51	5.81	4.73	4.95	5.61
Ryder System, Inc.	8.64	10.54	11.61	12.73	14.80
Saunders Leasing System, Inc.	4.72	5.25	5.30	5.79	6.51

*a*Not meaningful

Source: Standard & Poor's Industry Surveys, February 20, 1986.

ized. An ICC study indicated that only 2 percent of all shippers responding considered their service to be worse since deregulation, and a majority of shippers reported that the number of carriers serving them had increased or remained the same.[8]

Even with the reforms of the Motor Carrier Act of 1980, trucking companies are still required to file applications and forms with the ICC before offering a new service, discontinuing a service, raising or reducing their rates, and merging with another company. The paperwork is costly. In 1985 the ICC received almost 1.4 million tariff or rate filings.[9] Some in the industry argue that rate filings are necessary to enable customers and competitors to contest changes in rates. Others argue that in the competitive situation in today's market, dissatisfied customers can easily find another motor carrier that will satisfy their price and service needs.

Federal legislation has changed trucking regulation for interstate operations; however, approximately 40 states still heavily regulate intrastate trucking. There are substantial costs to customers. For example, it cost $612 to ship a truckload of detergent from Dallas to Houston—a 243 mile trip. The same truckload from Dallas to Tulsa, Oklahoma—a 275 mile trip—cost $375.[10]

Other Legislation Affecting Trucking

The 1982 Surface Transportation Assistance Act gave firms the authority to operate multiple trailer vehicles and wider and heavier trucks on designated federal highways. In addition, the act raised both federal and state road-use taxes.

The 1982 Staggers Rail Act allowed existing railroads the opportunity to consolidate and to compete with one another on pricing. Newly designed rail cars and greater efficiency in route scheduling increased carrying capacity. These efficiencies led to faster delivery and favorable rates for shippers, thus narrowing the price/service differential between rail and trucks.

An appropriate area of regulation for the ICC appears to be trucking safety. Competitive pressures may be causing companies to cut corners on maintenance and to keep their drivers on the road for extended time periods (regulations specify that one person cannot drive for more than ten hours in a day followed by eight consecutive off-duty hours, no more than 60 hours in a consecutive seven-day period and no more than 70 hours in a consecutive eight-day period). Either or both factors may account for the increase in the number of truck accidents—up 18 percent in 1984.[11] The Motor Carrier Safety Act of 1984 provided the ICC with specific powers to regulate safety.

---

[8]"ICC Says Deregulation Has Not Reduced Truck Service to Small Towns," *Traffic World,* September 20, 1982, p. 28.

[9]"Secretary Dole Pushes Deregulation as Beneficial to Trucking Industry," *Daily Traffic World,* September 30, 1985, p. 1.

[10]"Time to Complete Trucking Deregulation," p. 7.

[11]Ibid, p. 8.

PRIVATE TRUCKING

Deregulation has caused major changes within the industry. Private carriers have been given intercorporate operating rights that allow them to carry property of other subsidiaries of the parent company on backhauls. They can also apply for and be granted for-hire common carrier and contract carrier authority to haul goods for fees. Low start-up costs and deregulation have induced many companies to enter private trucking.

Advantages of private trucking include flexibility, control, speed, reduced loss and damage, and lower transportation costs. However, a company may not have the capital to invest in equipment or the management expertise in transportation. Added problems in scheduling and burdensome paperwork are required to seek and obtain the backhaul traffic necessary to keep private fleets working to desired levels of profitability. Furthermore, for-hire transportation costs seem to be falling rapidly, making private fleets less advantageous.

Successful use of a private fleet appears to be based on productive use of the equipment and cost efficiencies. Private carriers exist to haul the goods of the parent company. Therefore, less backhaul opportunity and seasonal variations may result in poor equipment utilization. Additionally, private fleets are required to pay state fuel taxes for fuel consumed by vehicles operating on each state's highways.

Furthermore, private carriers have to be concerned with liability for cargo and equipment, and injury to operators and bystanders. Unknown environmental factors can also have a detrimental effect on private carriage. Fuel costs may escalate rapidly or the demand for the company's product may decline, making private trucking far from being risk free.

Truck Leasing

Truck leasing has emerged as a way to obtain the advantages of private trucking while reducing some of the risks. Full-service leasing permits a shipper to utilize a fleet of trucks with minimal up-front capital and to avoid maintenance responsibilities. Skilled transportation managers employed by the leasing company operate the fleet. Risk is minimized since the company can easily exit from private trucking if cost/service objectives are not achieved.

With leasing, the company does not have to worry about mechanical failures, as the lessor totally maintains the fleet including routine maintenance and emergency repairs. Fuel costs are typically lower because of the quantity discounts for bulk purchasing by the lessor. One-way trips become more cost efficient as the lessor handles backhaul requirements.

Each service utilized is charged to the company and, over time, may mean that the cost of leasing is more than the cost of owning a fleet. However, the reduction in risk seems to be a determining factor, and many companies who otherwise would not have entered into private trucking are doing so through the lease option.

Single-Source Leasing

Since 1982, the ICC has allowed owner-operators to lease equipment and drivers to private carriers. Single-source leasing has increased the private carrier's ability to meet increased temporary demand for hauling at minimum cost and risk. Leases can be as short as 30 days and provide equipment and drivers. The private carrier has complete control over the equipment and driver for the period of the lease, but has no maintenance or labor responsibilities.

COMMON CARRIAGE

To become a common carrier in today's deregulated environment applicants must prove they are fit, willing, and able, and establish that the proposed service will fulfill a public purpose. Consequently, entry into common carriage has been eased substantially. With financial responsibility and a shipper that indicates the need for the carriage proposed, a new common carrier can enter the industry. And they have. In 1980 there were 18,045 carriers. That number increased to 30,481 in 1984, an increase of 69 percent.[12]

Regular-route common carriage is characterized by national, regional and local networks of terminals linked by long haul operations. This business is primarily built around less-than-truckload (LTL) shipments. Scheduled departures, pre-planned stops and destinations, and published rate schedules are common in the regular-route common carriage.

Less-than-truckload carriers have not been affected as much by deregulation, although the segment continues toward greater concentration. Because of the capital-intensive network of terminals required to bring small lots together and mix them into larger lots with the same destination, a natural barrier to entry exists. Small regional carriers used to supply service for short hauls to larger LTL carriers. Now the larger firms are buying out the regional supplier or expanding to develop their company into a national full-service carrier. The top five companies in LTL have increased their share of the business to 40 percent in 1984 (29% in 1978).[13]

Irregular-route-service companies have broad operating authority and freedom to use any routes to deliver goods. Irregular-route companies have concentrated on truck load (TL) shipping needs. Thus, they avoid small shippers, high variable costs, and capital intensive terminals required of the LTL shippers.

Irregular-route carriage is characterized by a large number of firms, reliance on owner-operators (independents who own and drive their own trucking equip-

[12]Ibid, p. 3.

[13]Charles R. Enis and Edward A. Morash, "Some Aspects of Motor Carrier Size, Concentration Tendencies and Performance After Deregulation," *Akron Economic and Business Review,* 18 (Spring 1987), p. 91.

ment), demand-activated schedules and many nonunionized firms. The major area of turmoil in the trucking industry appears to be in the TL sector.

Private carriers, both owned and leased operations, and contract carriers have attempted to capture market share in this profitable segment from the common carriers. Truckload shipping is less capital intensive. Only a rig and a driver are needed as compared to the many terminals required in the LTL segment. The specific carrier types are blending, and today irregular route carriage is more like contract carriage than a form of common carriage.

CONTRACT CARRIAGE

Contract trucking is TL oriented, door-to-door hauling. Entry has been facilitated because only a permit is required. A permit is granted when the applicants prove that they are fit, willing, and able, and the service would be consistent with the public interest.

Contract carriers have become more aggressive marketers since deregulation. Due to their lower labor costs, they have been able to favorably compete on a price basis with the more unionized common carriers. A large portion of truckload traffic that used to be moved by common carriage is now being moved by contract carriage.

INDUSTRY PROBLEMS

Deregulation has caused many carriers to redefine the business they are in. Lifting of restrictions has allowed many companies to expand from TL and common carriage to LTL and contract carriage.

Although many new carriers have entered the industry in every segment, many have also left the industry. It seems that the larger companies have become larger, and the smallest companies have left the industry.

Rapidly rising fuel costs, federal and state user's taxes, insurance expense, and labor expense have caused the collapse of many motor carriers—and not all of them are small. McLean Trucking, fifth largest carrier in 1984, filed for bankruptcy in January 1985.[14]

Escalation of Insurance Premiums

Carriers are responsible for the property they move. The ICC requires insurance for property loss/damage, as well as injury to bystanders and the environment. In 1985 alone, insurance premiums for carriers jumped 300 to 500 percent.[15] These

---

[14]John Cleghorn, "Fuel Prices, Economy to Keep Trucking Industry Rolling." *The Charlotte Observer,* January 18, 1987, p. 7K.

[15]F. A. Stephenson, Jr., *Transportation USA,* Reading, Massachusetts, Addison-Wesley Publishing Company, 1987, p. 330.

significant jumps in the cost of insurance were due to falling interest rates, poor insurance company investments of premiums, and high jury awards.

Lower premiums had been available to carriers as the insurance industry aggressively competed for market share. When the insurers finally realized that market share gains were coming at the loss of profits, they weren't terribly concerned because they could easily invest premiums at higher interest rates. But when the prime rate fell, the insurance industry suffered billions of dollars in losses. Although it was an insurance industry problem, it became a trucking problem as liability insurance is required by the ICC and higher premiums had to be paid.

In addition, the national trend of juries to award high settlements to victims has affected all insurance premiums and trucking is no exception.

If a carrier prefers the alternative of self-insurance, the ICC requires the posting of a $1 million line of credit for payment of claims. In 1986, approximately 90 percent of the industry could not meet this requirement.[16]

Price Competition

Competition, and in particular price competition and discounting, has caused carriers to manage their resources better. Equipment, labor and capital all have to be efficiently utilized. Greater cost control practices have been instituted throughout the industry. Shippers have benefitted by lower costs and more tailored services.

Intermodal Competition

Containerization by other modes of transportation, including air, water, and rail, and the use of private trucking to handle the containers after reaching the destination point is allowing other modes to be more competitive with trucking. Some of these competitors are purchasing or merging with trucking companies developing large, intermodal carriers.

Piggyback, fishyback, and airtruck are being offered to speed service and cut costs for shippers. Shippers are interested in dealing with a single carrier as deregulation makes it more difficult for the transportation manager to monitor the activities and rates of many carriers.

Knowledgeable Shippers

Traffic managers are searching for and finding ways to reduce transportation costs. They are shipping larger quantities to take advantage of volume discounts, taking advantage of backhaul rates, shipping items in concentrated form to reduce cargo weight, using off-peak periods, redesigning containers to permit more units to be loaded in a transport vehicle, shipping items in disassembled form to reduce

---

[16]*Standard & Poor's Industry Surveys,* May 29, 1986, p. R–3.

volume, and negotiating multiple shipments at one time to generate quantity discounts.

Lack of Marketing Orientation

Before deregulation, marketing was relatively nonexistent in the trucking industry. Motor carriers had sales departments and traffic departments. Traffic departments determined routes and rates, and the sales department attempted to convince shippers to use the company's services at the rate established. There was little or no price competition because all rates were approved by the ICC.

With deregulation, truckers are attempting to determine what customers want and to provide that level of service at a price that customers are willing to pay. Frequently however, truckers find that they cannot afford to supply service at the price customers are willing to pay. With many competitors and an emphasis on price, clearly new and innovative strategies were needed. Many firms, grasping for survival, have turned to marketing.

Pricing appears to be a major marketing variable in the trucking industry. Prices set too high will lose business; and prices set too low may mean that a carrier cannot cover variable costs. Market research has been used to find what services and prices customers are seeking. Market segmentation has highlighted some specific types of industries with unique service requirements. Segmenting variables used have included commodities shipped, customer type, size of shipment, speed of delivery, and length of haul.

Target marketing can help the carriers understand the necessity of focusing their efforts on profitable business. Targeting encourages companies to service those kinds of customers where the firm has a comparative price or service advantage.

Higher-priced companies have the opportunity to differentiate their service and convince customers that the service is worth the additional cost. More reliable service, better pick-up and delivery schedules, better credit terms, better-than-average loss and damage records, better tracing and control, faster delivery times, and simplified paperwork are ways that trucking firms can differentiate their transportation service.

George G. Morris, a finance analyst specializing in trucking firms, indicated three strategies for success in the industry: national distribution with a full line of differentiated products and emphasis on attractive service/price trade-offs, low cost producers, and specialty firms with services targeted toward profitable industry segments.[17]

[17]George G. Morris, ''Deregulation Benefits Shippers, the Public and Well-Run Truckers,'' *Investor News,* May 1983, p. 1.

Chili's Restaurant

THE STORY

It was 5:20 P.M. Norman Brinker left his office building, 6820 LBJ Freeway, Dallas, still worrying about the earlier meeting. Although Chili's had maintained its average store volumes at 1985 levels during 1986, market conditions were rather poor. With 66 percent of the restaurants located in the economically impacted energy-belt states, Chili's would have to concentrate its efforts on the future expansion of the company in order to grow.

Traffic was heavy on the freeway. Norman turned on the radio and tried to keep his mind away from the difficult two and a half hours he had just spent with his colleagues. Bruce Springsteen was singing again, the same song, over and over. "That's enough," Norman thought. "I have already heard this song three times today." He turned the radio off and directed his thoughts toward his business.

THE COMPANY

In 1975 brothers Larry and Jack Lavine opened the first Chili's restaurant on Greenville Avenue in Dallas. The Lavines were banking on a new niche in the industry between fast-food and midscale restaurants. They were committed to the quality burger. Their first restaurant offered the customer two new appealing attributes: fast, full service and quality hamburgers.

Through 1982 the Lavines opened up 17 more Chili's restaurants, primarily in the Southwest. During the period from 1975 to 1982 investors and restaurant analysts started following the growth of Chili's with interest. As of June 30, 1986 Chili's had expanded to 80 units in 12 states (Exhibit 23-1). Chili's initial expansion strategy was to establish restaurants in Sunbelt cities with somewhat of a "youthful" atmosphere—Dallas, Houston, Atlanta, Tampa, Orlando, Los Angeles, and San Francisco.

In 1983 Norman Brinker, a well-respected restaurant industry pioneer, paid $12 million for 35 percent of Chili's stock. Prior to this time the company was privately held by the Lavine brothers. In January 1984, Chili's had its first public stock offering on the over-the-counter exchange.

Since the initial public stock offering, the company had opened more than 50 restaurants. In 1986 Chili's had 65 company-owned units, 14 joint-venture–owned

This case was prepared by L. Miklichansky and B. Logan under the supervision of Sexton Adams, University of North Texas, and Adelaide Griffin, Texas Woman's University, as a basis for class discussion rather than to illustrate either effective or ineffective handling of an administrative situation. Used by permission from Sexton Adams.

419

Source: Chili's *Annual Report,* 1986.

Exhibit 23-1   **Chili's Restaurant Units Open as of June 30, 1986**

units, and one franchised unit.[1] Chili's had signed two primary joint-venture agreements, one with Sunstate Restaurant Corporation in the Southeast and one with Dunkin' Ventures Corporation in the Northeast.

In 1986 Chili's was a restaurant concept that appealed to winners. Fiscal year 1985 had been a landmark year for Chili's in terms of operating and financial results (Exhibit 23-2). Management felt that it had been able to leverage its talents toward the expansion processes it was undergoing. Menu introduction, new marketing efforts, and a 25 percent increase in total employment (to 4,500 employees from 3,600) occurred in 1986. Chili's at this point was considering the following nonexclusive alternatives:

- National expansion.
- Further existing market penetration.
- New product introductions.

Chili's Chairman and CEO Norman Brinker said, "We have an unusually dedicated and talented group. That's the difference. A company is simply the sum total of individual efforts towards a common goal."[2]

---

[1] Donald Smith, "Romancing the Burger," *Nation's Restaurant News,* February 10, 1986, p. F9.

[2] "The Restaurant Chain Industry," *Nation's Restaurant News,* August 11, 1986, pp. F3–F70.

Exhibit 23-2   Chili's Inc. Selected Financial Data (Dollar amounts in thousands)

	Year Ended June 30,		
	1984	**1985**	**1986**
Revenues	$43,157	$69,301	$106,990
Net income	$ 1,990	$ 4,131	$ 4,799
Working capital	($230)	$ 1,453	$ 2,375
Total assets	$22,209	$41,147	$ 63,110
Long-term debt	$ 3,528	$ 8,483	$ 10,739
Stockholders' equity	$12,535	$23,307	$ 38,500
Weighted average shares outstanding	3,983	4,714	5,230
Number of restaurants open at year end	28	45	65

Source: Chili's *Annual Report,* 1986.

THE ECONOMY

Industry observers saw 1986 as a year of considerable change within the restaurant industry. Oil prices had plunged, inflation was falling, and the stock market was soaring. Cheaper oil prices were hitting the Southwest harder and faster than expected. Energy companies were slashing capital spending budgets and laying off workers. Other industries, both directly and indirectly related to energy, were also suffering. Restaurant companies located in the economically impacted energy-belt states had reported sluggish market conditions.

Another element which presented a direct threat to the restaurant industry was the 1986 Tax Reform Act, which eliminated 20 percent of the expense-account write-off for business-related dining and also eliminated the investment tax credit. Industry analysts felt that fewer businessmen would eat out due to this reform. And, in the case of rapidly expanding companies, the investment tax credit had resulted in beneficial tax savings. Chili's recognized investment tax credits of over $1.5 million in 1985 and 1986.

As opposed to tightened economic conditions in the U.S. market, volatility of world politics and increased terrorism abroad persuaded many Americans to consider the advantages of traveling in the United States rather than in foreign countries. Industry experts considered this trend as an opportunity for U.S. hotel and restaurant businesses.

Demographers had pointed out the aging of the population. The baby boom generation had reached maturity. The tastes and values of upwardly mobile young professionals, less concerned with price than with variety and style, would benefit full-service sit-down restaurants and cafeterias, industry experts believed. These restaurant categories offered a wide selection of items and an atmosphere favored by a broad section of the population. The trend was toward the ''gourmet'' eating experience, coupled with nutrition and weight consciousness.

Also influencing the restaurant industry was consumer retrenchment. Spending on restaurant meals was one of the first areas to be affected by changes in the financial condition of consumers. Growth in real disposable income and employment, the two key supports for restaurant sales, had moderated in 1986. When combined with relatively high debt loads and a low savings rate, the customer's propensity to eat away from home had declined.[3]

Sales of hard goods had been relatively strong in early 1986. While purchases of autos, furniture, appliances, and other consumer durables obviously were not substitutes for restaurant sales, they channeled an amount of buying power away from meals eaten outside the home. However, their impact on restaurant sales was expected to be short-lived since much of the strength in hard goods sales had been promotionally induced and was probably not sustainable.[4]

The differential between the cost of food prepared at home and the prices in restaurants had widened. According to *The Nation's Restaurant News,* an industry journal, the average monthly increase in 1985 in the cost of food eaten away from home was 3.9 percent, whereas the average monthly increase in the cost of food eaten at home was 1.5 percent. In 1984 these figures were 4.2 and 3.7 percent, respectively.[5]

The restaurant industry had become more competitive. Competition was coming from nonrestaurant food retailers as well as from other restaurants. Convenience stores, deli counters, and salad bars at supermarkets and restaurants within department stores were among the nontraditional food outlets capturing more of the market for food consumed outside the home by providing new alternatives for the consumer.[6]

In addition to general economic trends and consumer demand influences, direct operation factors had an impact on restaurant companies. The industry was facing rising insurance costs. Third-party liability awards and workers' compensation claims were climbing, leading to substantially higher insurance premiums. Those operators whose restaurants had a high alcohol mix had been hit especially hard. Encouraging alcoholic beverage sales was no longer commonplace in the wake of consumer awareness (Mothers Against Drunk Driving, etc.).[7]

According to a report published by the National Restaurant Association

---

[3]Don Jeffrey, ''Smaller Dinnerhouses Rely on Local Marketing,'' *Nation's Restaurant News,* March 10, 1986, p. F8.

[4]Ibid.

[5]''The Restaurant Chain Industry,'' pp. F3–F70.

[6]Jeffrey, p. F8.

[7]Ibid.

(NRA), the nation's food-service industry would face a shortage of 1.1 million workers by 1994.[8] This industry, which employed 158,000 restaurant cashiers in 1984, would need 216,000 cashiers in 1995, a 36.7 percent increase. Cooks and chefs would expand to 435,000 in 1995 from 331,000 in 1984, a 31.4 percent increase. The need for bartenders would rise 29.8 percent to 353,000 in 1995 from 272,000 in 1984.

The industry labor shortages were exacerbated by high turnover rates in food service, according to the report, which was prepared in conjunction with the consulting firm of Arthur D. Little, Inc. Food counter and fountain workers and waiter and waitress assistants all demonstrated a 43 percent turnover rate, followed by the 32 percent rates of kitchen workers, waiters and waitresses in 1984. Even supervisors had a 24 percent turnover rate, the NRA said in its report. In addition, the industry was facing a labor crisis because its employment rate would swell 21.7 percent over the next ten years, to 8.9 million persons while overall employment would increase only 14.9 percent, according to the NRA report. Consequently, for most operators, wage rates were being bid up and recruiting and training had intensified.

THE INDUSTRY

As of January 1986, the restaurant chain industry consisted of approximately 100,000 outlets, an increase of 9 percent over the previous year. The largest of the ten different segments in the industry (Exhibit 23-3) was the burger segment, accounting for 40 percent of sales dollars.[9] However, the fastest growing was the pizza chain segment, registering an annual sales growth rate of 23 percent for 1985. Industry observers attributed this result to increased consumer demand for speed and convenience, home delivery, and variety of product. Contract feeders, snack chains, and fast-food chains were all growing and reaping market share gains. Dinnerhouses, chicken chains, family restaurants, family steakhouses, and cafeterias were showing slower sales growth than the industry as a whole (Exhibits 23-4 and 23-5).

Dinnerhouse Segment

Restaurant analysts considered Chili's within the dinnerhouse segment, defined as the niche between the fast-food and midscale restaurants. "It is one of the most effectively positioned restaurant concepts," said Donald Smith, Professor of Hotel Restaurant and Institutional Management at Michigan State University.[10] The late 1960s saw the development of the concept, representing the birth of the Ameri-

---

[8]"Food Service Facing Shortage of 1.1 Million Workers By 1995," *Nation's Restaurant News,* July 28, 1986, p. 61.

[9]"The Restaurant Chain Industry," pp. F3–F70.

[10]Smith, p. F9.

Exhibit 23-3   **Restaurant Chain Industry Segments**

Segment	Major Chains
Burger	McDonald's, Burger King
Contract	Marriot Food Service, ARA Services
Family restaurant	Denny's, International House of Pancakes
Pizza	Pizza Hut, Domino's
Chicken	Kentucky Fried Chicken, Church's
Dinnerhouse	Bennigan's, Red Lobster
Snack	Dairy Queen, Dunkin' Donuts
Family steakhouse	Ponderosa, Western Sizzlin'
Cafeteria	Luby's, Wyatt's
Fish	Long John Silver's, Captain D's

Source: Nation's Restaurant News, August 11, 1986.

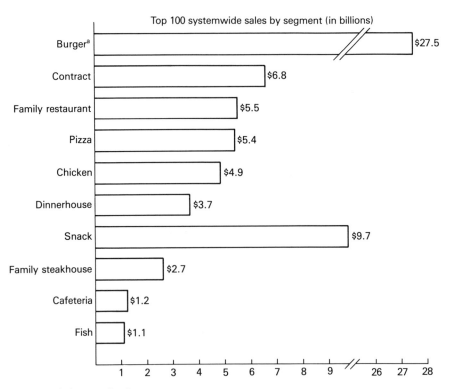

Top 100 systemwide sales by segment (in billions)

Burger[a] — $27.5
Contract — $6.8
Family restaurant — $5.5
Pizza — $5.4
Chicken — $4.9
Dinnerhouse — $3.7
Snack — $9.7
Family steakhouse — $2.7
Cafeteria — $1.2
Fish — $1.1

[a]Includes roast beef.
Source: Nation's Restaurant News, August 11, 1986.

Exhibit 23-4   **Burgers Do the Biggest Business . . .**

can tavern. These restaurants were neighborhood eating, drinking, and meeting places, right on target for the hungry, lonely young adult audience. They emphasized a casual dining atmosphere, good quality, and variety accompanied by alcoholic beverages at reasonable prices.

In 1985, the top ten dinnerhouse chains had an average of 182 units with annual sales of $2.1 million. The average guest check was $10.00 per person, up 0.8 percent from the previous year (Exhibit 23-6).

As a result of consumer awareness programs and governmental regulations concerning alcohol sales and consumption, the new strategy in the dinnerhouse segment was one of menu expansion to offset decreased sales of alcoholic beverages. Alcoholic beverage sales in this segment ranged from 15 percent of total sales to 40 percent, but with increased awareness the norm seemed to have declined to about 20 percent of total sales.

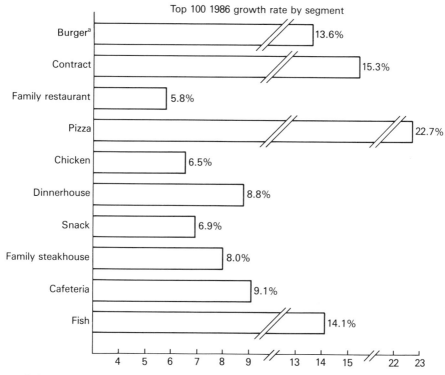

Includes roast beef.
Source: Nation's Restaurant News, August 11, 1986.

Exhibit 23-5   . . . **But Pizza is Growing the Fastest**

Exhibit 23-6   **1985 Dinnerhouse Segment Data**

	Systemwide Sales (In millions)	Number of Units	Dollar Market Share (%)	Average Guest Check
Red Lobster	$ 925	400	25.09	$10.75
Bennigan's	455	223	12.34	8.40
Chi-Chi's	435	217	11.80	7.82
El Torito	383	196	10.39	n/a
T.G.I. Friday's	366	123	9.93	10.00
Steak and Ale	295	190	8.00	13.00
Stuart Anderson's	275	120	7.46	n/a
Ground Round	220	201	5.97	n/a
Chili's	185	97	5.02	6.81
Brown Derby	148	56	4.01	n/a
	$3,687	1,823	100.00	

Source: Nation's Restaurant News, August 11, 1986. Copyright *Nation's Restaurant News.*

HUMAN RESOURCES

Restaurant analysts saw Chili's as a very well-managed company headed by experienced and creative restaurant veterans. This dynamic outlook filtered down to the restaurant level where there was an energy and attitude present about the employees. Chili's offered a comprehensive training program and an attractive compensation and benefits package to develop and keep talented restaurant management. As a result, Chili's boasted a 15 percent management turnover rate, one of the industry's lowest.[11] In 1986 Chili's had approximately 4,500 employees, up from 3,600 in 1985. Chili's organization was very structured in terms of operating autonomy, as seen in Exhibit 23-7.

THE KEY PLAYERS

A major turning point for Chili's came in 1983 when Norman Brinker and several other top executives were hired to replace the Lavine brothers. The new team was known in the restaurant industry for holding aggressive marketing philosophies and growth-oriented attitudes. The key executives averaged more than 13 years' experience in the restaurant industry.

Norman Brinker, 54, joined Chili's in 1983 as Chairman and CEO. He had 27 years of experience in the food-service industry. In 1966, he started the Steak & Ale

[11]Charles Glousky and Steven Rockwell, "Here Comes the Shakeout," *Nation's Restaurant News,* March 10, 1986, p. F37.

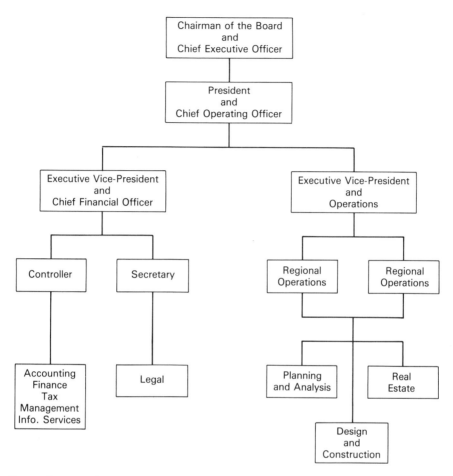

Source: Company data.

Exhibit 23-7   **Chili's Organization Chart**

restaurant chain. The Bennigan's chain followed in 1976. He sold both chains to Pillsbury in 1976 and went to work for that company as the Chairman of Steak & Ale. He also served as Chairman and CEO of Burger King Corporation, a subsidiary of Pillsbury.

Ron McDougall was named President and COO of Chili's in 1983, after serving as Senior Vice-President for Steak & Ale Restaurant Corporation, where he helped create the Bennigan's concept. His experience also included senior management positions with Burger King Corporation, the Pillsbury Company, Sara Lee, and Proctor & Gamble. Under his direction, Chili's corporate expansion strategy took on a more quantitative approach to market penetration, restaurant design and construction, site selection procedures, and advertising in the form of demographic studies, competitive studies, and site selection models.

Jim Parrish, Executive Vice-President and CFO, joined Chili's in 1983. His prior experience included serving as CFO for companies in the restaurant, agricultural processing, and oil and gas industries.

Creed Ford III, who had been with Chili's since 1976, was named Director of Operations in 1978 and promoted to Executive Vice-President of Operations in 1986. John Titus, a Real Estate and Construction Officer from Steak & Ale, was elected the Vice-President of Real Estate in 1983. Ed Palms, previously Steak & Ale Director of Design, also joined Chili's in 1983 as Vice-President of Design after serving Steak & Ale for nine years.

These executives were aggressive and risk-taking in their management styles according to restaurant analysts. Chili's had installed the right mixture of leadership and know-how to position itself for the future.

CHILI'S MENU CONCEPT AND SERVICE

Chili's distinctive buildings became well established and familiar landmarks in the markets in which the company operated. Market analyses, conducted in 1984 on management's behalf, indicated that, by making some design modifications to the Chili's standardized buildings, the company could increase the appeal of the existing restaurants while significantly reducing maintenance costs. Management decided to undertake a remodeling program, including the installation of effective signage, improved lighting, and custom-designed awnings. These changes made significant contributions to the exterior appearance and visibility of each Chili's location. Other key improvements involved a new kitchen layout to increase operational efficiency, a reconfiguration of the customer areas to raise table turnover, and a low-maintenance brick exterior.

In 1986 the decor of a Chili's restaurant consisted of booth seating, tile-top tables, hanging plants, and wood and brick walls covered with interesting memorabilia. Each restaurant had a casual atmosphere and was open seven days a week, for lunch, dinner, and late-night meals. Chili's restaurants featured quick, efficient, and friendly service. Most were free-standing units of approximately 6,000 square feet with 156 to 178 dining seats. Table turnover was 45 minutes.

Management placed emphasis on serving customers substantial portions of high-quality food and beverages at moderate prices. Full bar service was available, with frozen margaritas offered as a specialty drink. Draft and bottled domestic and imported beers were served in frosted mugs. In 1986, Chili's introduced a premium "Top Shelf" margarita and premium wines which were available by the glass or bottle. Because of these new drinks, liquor sales had held steady at about 20 percent of total revenues. Although Chili's did not downplay liquor, its focus was on food, and a substantial portion of alcohol sales was made to customers waiting for tables. As Ron McDougall said, "We are not a watering hole."[12]

Chili's menu was designed to be varied enough to accommodate a diverse customer group yet limited enough so that all offerings could still be "prepared from substantially fresh products each day on the premises," said Norman Brinker.[13] Thirteen varieties of half-pound hamburgers were available with a wide range of toppings. Other selections included the ever-popular "bowl of red," Mexican style specialties such as nachos, soft tacos, and quesadillas, and meal-sized salads (Exhibits 23-8 and 23-9).

In 1985, Chili's scored big gains with the introduction of chicken and beef fajitas, a chicken sandwich, and two new appetizers—Buffalo chicken wings and cheese fries. Seeking to broaden its market base, Chili's extended its menu early in 1986 by adding other nonburger items—the chicken Frisco salad, the Monterey chicken platter, the country fried steak, and the BBQ baby back ribs.

These products were targeted toward a growing consumer demand for variety, according to Chili's chairman. "Burgers are still king, but people just want more different things more often," Brinker said.[14] Burgers, which once accounted for more than 50 percent of sales, according to the company, made up less than 35 percent by 1986.[15] Also in response to customer requests, a children's menu and desserts, which included hot fudge sundaes and a cinnamon apple sundae delight, were introduced. New product introductions were well received and boosted Chili's per person check average from $6.50 to $6.81.[16]

At Chili's, a new item strategy was pursued, as long as the dishes would meet the goals of high quality, simple preparation, fast service, and outstanding price/value. Further, through a diversified menu, Chili's intended to maintain and enlarge its customer loyalty. Internal research had shown that more than half the customers visited Chili's restaurants an average of three times per month.

Advertising Campaign

Prior to the change in management at Chili's, almost no money was spent on advertising and promotion. Success, such as it was, was due almost exclusively to word-of-mouth. In October 1983, Chili's engaged New York-based McCann-Erickson to handle its advertising. However, in February 1984, the $1-million account was awarded to Dallas-based Levenson, Levenson, and Hill. McDougal attributed the change primarily to management's dissatisfaction with the advertising strategies

---

[12]Jeffrey, p. F8.

[13]Glousky and Rockwell, p. F37.

[14]Ibid.

[15]Ibid.

[16]Chili's *Annual Report,* 1986.

Exhibit 23-8 Chili's Menu

430

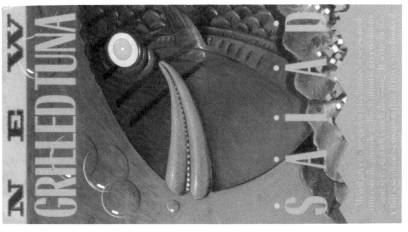

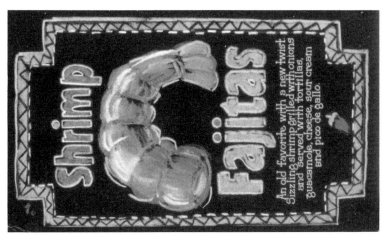

Exhibit 23-9   **Advertising Table-Tents**

taken by McCann-Erickson. Additionally, the change enabled Chili's executives to work with the top agency people as opposed to a branch office of a large agency.[17]

In mid 1984, the "No Place Else is Chili's" campaign debuted, in which phase one lasted about a year and focused on both television and radio spots. March 1985 began the second phase of the campaign with two national television commercials and four new radio spots. Chili's commercials took viewers inside Chili's restaurants to eavesdrop on conversations at various tables. Scenarios included a couple reminiscing over old times and mutual friends and a group of neighbors relaxing after a garage sale. According to the President of the ad agency, Bill Hill, "You can't do it by showing pretty food alone. You have to create a personality for them (the restaurants)." Levenson, Levenson and Hill conducted market research to answer the question "What is Chili's?" The agency concluded that Chili's was an original, rather than an imitator or a fad, thus the reason for the slogan "No Place Else."[18]

In February 1986, to make up for its concentration in the oil-depressed Southwest, Chili's launched a two-pronged plan of new product introduction and television advertising in an effort to stimulate sales. The advertising campaign was targeted at key oil-sensitive markets in Dallas, Houston, Austin, Denver, and Oklahoma City.[19]

Finance and Administration

Chili's became a publicly held company on January 6, 1984, after which the company posted sales gains exceeding 50 percent in each of the next two years. Same store sales in 1986 were relatively unchanged from 1985, although expansion of new restaurants boosted revenues. New menu items introduced in 1986 raised cost of sales by 0.4 percent from 27.2 percent in 1985. In 1984 cost of sales were 26.0 percent. Operating expenses, including marketing, had risen from 49.4 percent in 1984 to 52.5 percent in 1986. This cost increase was made up of first-year and start-up expenses associated with opening new restaurants and with rising insurance costs. In 1986 management believed it had positioned itself for future growth with adequate personnel and support functions in place. The growth throughout 1985 and 1986 resulted in lower general and administrative expenses as a percentage of sales. The largest operating expense by the company in 1986 outside of salaries was rent expense, totalling $8.5 million. This coupled with depreciation expense of $6.7 million represented 14.2 pecent of total sales. In 1984 the same expenses were 4.7 percent of sales. This 300 percent increase reflected 50 additional restaurant locations, a 267 percent increase in unit growth. Chili's profit margin in 1986 dropped

---

[17]D. S. Hansard, "Chili's Picks Dallas Ad Agency," *Dallas Morning News,* February 22, 1984, p. 2D.

[18]D. S. Hansard, "Chili's Expands Ad Campaign," *Dallas Morning News,* March 15, 1985, p. 1D.

[19]David Zuckerman, "Chili's Introduces New Products, Ads," *Nation's Restaurant News,* April 28, 1986, pp. 2, 59.

to 4.5 percent from 6.0 percent in 1985. Company officials believed that they could see lower profit margins during periods of heavy growth in return for higher margins in later years.

Management believed that financially Chili's was in relatively good shape in 1986. Total assets had experienced a 285 percent growth rate since 1984 and working capital was strong. Company officials believed that funds generated from operations, from built-to-suit agreements with landlords, and available under a revolving loan agreement and lines of credit with various Dallas banks were adequate to finance capital expenditures (Exhibits 23-10 and 23-11).

Expansion

Chili's expansion plan was twofold. First, it clustered restaurants in preexisting markets to obtain complete market penetration, and, second, it entered new geographical territories with one unit at a time or through joint-venture agreements with outside investors. Chili's had 20 units in Dallas/Fort Worth, ten units in Houston, nine units in Los Angeles and four to six units each in San Francisco, Denver, Atlanta, and Tampa/St. Petersburg by 1986. The biggest event in the story of Chili's expansion was an agreement signed in October 1985 with Dunkin' Ventures, operator of the world's largest donut shop chain. The 20-year agreement would allow the 50 percent joint venture to build and operate more than 50 Chili's in New England and Canada. Norman Brinker said that Chili's management was impressed with Dunkin's food service operations and expansion plans. The first unit was to open in the Boston area in fiscal 1987.[20]

In 1986 Chili's also had joint-venture agreements with Chesapeake Seafood Co. in the Washington, D.C., area and with Tampa-based Sunstate Restaurant Corporation. Chesapeake operated nine units and Sunstate operated ten units in 1986. This strategy behind the joint-venture agreements allowed Chili's to approach unfamiliar territories with limited financial risk.

At the start of fiscal 1986 Chili's plan was to grow to 80 restaurants by June 30, 1986. This goal was to be accomplished through a systematic, disciplined approach to expansion (Exhibits 23-12 and 23-13 document Chili's expansion). Chili's vice-presidents of design and construction and real estate used sophisticated site models in the selection of Chili's restaurant locations. In addition, rigorous financial analyses and experienced managerial instincts were used.

FUTURE DIRECTIONS

The future of the restaurant industry was not very glamorous by the fall of 1986. According to *Standard & Poor's,* profits of restaurants and lodging compa-

---

[20]J. Fine, "Chili's Franchise Agreement Fits in with Its Long-Range Expansion Plan," *Dallas Business Courier,* October 14, 1985, p. 3.

Exhibit 23-10 Chili's Inc. Consolidated Balance Sheet (In thousands)		
	June 30,	
	1985	**1986**
Assets		
Current Assets		
Cash and equivalent	$ 308	$ 2,581
Inventories	594	1,046
Other current assets	7,193	8,543
Total Current Assets	8,095	12,170
Property and equipment	34,117	54,933
Less: accumulated depreciation	(5,732)	(10,209)
Net property and equipment	28,385	44,724
Other Assets	4,667	6,216
Total Assets	$41,147	$63,110
Liabilities		
Current Liabilities		
Current portion of long-term debt	$ 586	$ 362
Accounts payable	3,558	5,842
Accrued liabilities	2,498	3,591
Total Current Liabilities	6,642	9,795
Long-term debt	8,483	10,739
Deferred income taxes	2,453	3,840
Deferred gain on sale and leaseback	262	236
Stockholders' Equity		
Common stock—authorized 20 million shares		
of $.10 par value; 5,222,818 and 4,661,038		
shares issued and outstanding in 1986 and		
1985, respectively	466	522
Additional paid in capital	15,509	25,847
Retained earnings	7,332	12,131
Total Stockholders' Equity	23,307	38,500
Total Liabilities and Stockholders' Equity	$41,147	$63,110

Source: Chili's *Annual Report,* 1986.

nies had dropped 22 percent during the 1986 third quarter in comparison with the same period in 1985. This result was due mainly to increased competition among restaurant chains and to an increase in the popularity of cheaper ready-made packaged foods that people could eat at home.[21] Some chains had been forced to close units;

[21]Laurie Baum, "Profits Look Muscular—But Not for Long," *Business Week,* November 17, 1986, p. 175.

Exhibit 23-11   Chili's Inc. Consolidated Statement of Income (In thousands)

	Year Ended June 30,		
	1984	1985	1986
Revenues	$43,157	$69,301	$106,990
Costs and Expenses			
Cost of sales	11,200	18,882	29,504
Operating expenses	21,320	34,891	56,165
General and administrative	4,880	5,887	7,483
Depreciation and amortization	2,040	3,378	6,730
Interest	774	301	470
	40,214	63,339	100,352
Income before taxes	2,943	5,962	6,638
Income taxes	953	1,831	1,839
Net Income	$ 1,990	$ 4,131	$ 4,799
Net Income per share	$ 0.50	$ 0.88	$ 0.92
Weighted average shares outstanding	3,982	4,714	5,230

Source: Chili's *Annual Report,* 1986.

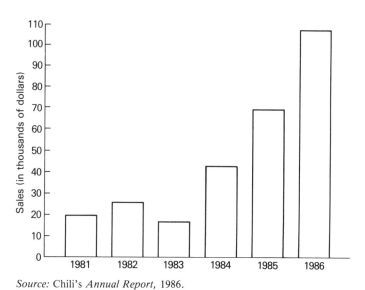

Source: Chili's *Annual Report,* 1986.

Exhibit 23-12   Chili's Inc. Sales Growth

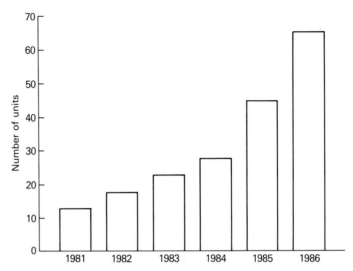

Source: Chili's *Annual Report,* 1986.

Exhibit 23-13   Chili's Inc. Unit Growth

others had reckoned on introduction of new menu items; and others were seeking geographical expansion.

Chili's plans for fiscal 1987 were the continuation of national expansion, clustering units in markets where the company already had restaurants, and entering new markets to develop broader national exposure. Chili's specific objectives were:

- Add approximately 35 new restaurants.
- Expand from 12 to 22 states.
- Maintain unit management turnover below 17 percent.
- Improve the ratio of sales to investment.
- Introduce an exciting new prototype for future Chili's restaurants.

The United States Army Health Services Command

Major General Tracy E. Strevey Jr., Commanding General (CG)[1] of the Army's Health Services Command (HSC), had a 0915 appointment for a haircut. He wished there were more hours in a day. The normal appointments, staff meetings, and trips to visit the many HSC facilities left little time for planning the future of Army medicine. Today, however, he was deeply concerned with that future. He was the physician in charge of providing complete health care to 3.5 million people. Those patients included the soldiers, their family members, retirees, and survivors of soldiers, residing on the mainland United States, in Alaska, Hawaii, Panama, Puerto Rico, and Guam and Johnston Island in the Pacific Basin. His command annually consumed $3.2 billion of the U.S. taxpayers' money. Congress wanted to reduce the dollar cost, ensure that combat readiness and quality of care were maintained, and achieve a high degree of patient satisfaction. General Strevey had to develop a strategic plan that would incorporate these three objectives.

The planning and budgeting of both military and civilian medicine was getting more difficult each year. General Strevey's civilian colleagues were concerned over the competition and cost pressures resulting from health maintenance organizations (HMO), preferred provider organizations (PPO), and the diagnosis-related groups (DRG) of the Medicare/Medicaid system. The HMOs and PPOs wanted to stem the rising costs of health care but retain high quality of care. The use of DRGs in prospective payment served to increase the pressure on that cost-quality relationship. Physicians faced increasing difficulty in maintaining the traditional management of their practices in the face of ever-increasing competition, threats from government interference, and possible takeover by corporate medicine.

General Strevey shared the challenges presented by DRGs and the cost-quality issue. He also had to consider a third-party payor: the Civilian Health and Medical Program of the Uniformed Services (CHAMPUS), which would adopt prospective DRG payment in 1988. In addition, HSC was spending tax money, and Congress, the Department of Defense (DOD), the Army Chief of Staff—General Strevey's immediate supervisor—and the taxpayers were demanding far greater efficiency from the Army health care system.

---

[1]Exhibit 24-1 provides an alphabetized list of acronyms used throughout this case.

This case was prepared by William F. Koehler, Jacksonville State University, as a basis for class discussion rather than to illustrate either effective or ineffective handling of an administrative situation. The views expressed in this case are those of the author and do not reflect the official policy or position of the Department of the Army, Department of Defense, or the U.S. government. Used by permission from William F. Koehler.

Exhibit 24-1   **Military and Health Care Acronyms**

AMEDD	Army medical department
CBO	Congressional Budget Office
CG	commanding general
CHAMPUS	Civilian Health and Medical Program of the Uniformed Services
COB	Command operating budget
CPA	contracted provider arrangement
CRI	CHAMPUS reform initiative
DA	Department of the Army
DCCS	deputy commander for clinical services
DCS	deputy chief of staff
DCSLOG	deputy chief of staff logistics
DENTACS	dental activities
DOD	Department of Defense
DRG	diagnosis-related group
FOA	field operating agencies
HCSSA	health care systems support activity
HMO	health maintenance organization
HSC	Health Services Command
HSC PPBES	HSC planning, programming, budgeting, and execution system
JCAHCO	Joint Commission for the Accreditation of Health Care Organizations
JMMC	Joint Military Medical Command
MEDCENS	Army medical centers
MEDDACS	Army medical department activities
MHCS	military health care system
MHSS	military health services system
NCO	noncommissioned officer
PARR	program analysis and resource review
PAS&BA	patient administrative systems & biostatistics activity
PPO	preferred provider organization
PRIMUS	primary care for the uniformed services

The HSC has never had enough doctors and nurses, even during a war. Facilities and equipment were always needing improvement or repair. Clinical technicians and other support personnel sought better salaries and working conditions in the civilian sector. Army medicine had to be prepared for war and maintain quality of care, modernize its equipment and facilities, and be on the "cutting edge" of technology—all with what seemed to be diminishing resources.

"Yes, the challenges have never been greater," the general thought. "We've developed the most technically skilled medical system in the world, and it is also the most expensive. Now that very sophistication has resulted in cost containment, competition, and concerns over access and quality that we hoped to avoid. Maybe we medical professionals have shot ourselves in the foot!"

The environment had changed for Army medicine. Until the late 1970s, there was minimal complaining about costs, and HSC facilities were fairly capable of keeping up with the patient load and providing high levels of satisfaction for care. The HSC mission—to remain prepared to transition to and operate during war and simultaneously provide high quality health care to the Army—had not changed. However, it had to be accomplished in an environment that now demanded continued readiness and high quality care at equal or reduced cost. General Strevey had to blend that environment and mission into the HSC strategic plan, which would be the operating framework for HSC in the coming five-year period, a period that promised decreasing resources with no reduction in mission. He would give the staff the job of developing such a plan.

While General Strevey was contemplating the current state of Army medicine, Colonel T. C. Munley, the HSC Chief of Staff, had been looking over the command's history regarding budget execution and performance. The HSC was budgeted for $3.9 billion to operate an organization containing 52,128 people. That made the command the Army's fifth largest civilian employer with a strength of 24,500 civilians. The military strength was 10,425 officers and 17,203 enlisted service members.

Colonel Munley's performance chart showed that on an average day HSC had 5,500 patient beds occupied, saw 50,000 patients in clinical visits, and provided 40,000 dental procedures to eligible beneficiaries (Exhibit 24-2). Exhibit 24-3 is a 1984–1988 summary of the command's annual operating budget.

The budget and patient data did not brighten Colonel Munley's day. He recognized the fact that HSC had more to do than resources would permit. He also knew that General Strevey was going to put the staff to work developing a strategic plan that would be executed in an environment of severe resource constraints.

"Well, thinking about it is not going to get the job done," Colonel Munley thought, as he put the papers down and left for the general's office. He needed to find out when General Strevey would be ready to provide guidance to the staff on the HSC strategic plan development. The plan was a top command priority, and

---

Exhibit 24-2   **Summary of an Average Day in HSC**

1. Patient beds occupied	5,500
2. Clinic visits	50,000
3. Dental procedures	40,000
4. Inpatients admitted	966
5. Immunizations	8,000
6. Births	87
7. X-ray procedures	38,000
8. Laboratory procedures	567,000
9. Veterinary procedures	5,000
10. Prescriptions filled	81,000
11. Pounds of food inspected	38,000,000

Exhibit 24-3 Health Services Command, Summary Budget, 1984–1988 (In millions)

	Fiscal Year				
Item	1984	1985	1986	1987	1988
1. Military Pay	$828	$902	$1,010	$1,109	$1,184
a. Physicians	488.52	532.18	595.9	654.31	698.56
b. Nurses	198.72	216.48	242.4	266.16	284.16
c. Technicians	107.64	117.26	131.3	144.17	153.92
d. Others	33.12	36.08	40.4	44.36	47.36
2. Civilian Pay	419	457	512	561	600
a. Physicians	104.75	114.25	128	140.25	150
b. Nurses	209.5	228.5	256	280.5	300
c. Technicians	71.23	77.69	87.04	95.37	102
d. Others	33.52	36.56	40.96	44.88	48
3. Supplies and Equipment	219.3	239	267.5	293.8	313.6
a. Pharmaceutical	175.44	191.2	214	235.04	250.88
b. Other medical	21.93	23.9	26.75	29.38	31.36
c. Nonmedical	21.39	23.9	26.75	29.38	31.36
4. Contracts	761	829	928	1,019	1,088
a. Physicians	68.49	74.61	83.52	91.71	97.92
b. Other medical	53.27	58.03	64.96	71.33	76.16
c. CHAMPUS	570.75	621.75	696	764.25	816
d. Others	68.49	74.61	83.52	91.71	97.92
5. Construction (MCA)	399	434	486	534	570
6. Miscellaneous	69.9	76.2	85.3	93.7	100
7. Total	$2,696.20	$2,937.20	$3,288.80	$3,610.50	$3,855.60

Note: This exhibit was developed by the author from very rough data on the 1988 expenditures of Health Services Command. It does not in any way reflect true or accurate budget data for the command. This exhibit should not be used or quoted as containing true financial data of HSC. It is to be used for academic purposes only in connection with the present case study.

the staff would have to do a great amount of preparation. Several of the staff officers were new to HSC and would have to learn the culture and strategy of the command to fully appreciate General Strevey's emphasis on strategic management.

With those thoughts, Colonel Munley arrived at Room 169, received Mrs. Tribbey's assurance that the general was free, and went in. "Good morning, Sir," Colonel Munley greeted his boss. "I need to find out when you'd like to discuss the preparation of our strategic plan with the staff. I've also been checking on the proficiency of our key staff in command strategy and planning. I see an immediate need for some review and study so we'll all be up-to-speed at the start of the planning cycle."

"I need to finalize my requirements for the strategic plan, and I've also got to go to Augusta to examine the plans for the new wing for Eisenhower," replied the general. "Why don't we meet three weeks from today? I'll be ready and the staff can review their needs and bone-up on strategic management and our environment. However, there are two points of guidance for our planning that you can pass on right now. We will plan on zero growth in terms of constant dollars for our annual operating budget, and a priority effort will be made to identify and plan for innovations that will maintain quality of care while simultaneously reducing costs. I believe that our most critical challenge in the coming decade will be our ability to control the quality-cost relationship in the face of the introduction of DRGs as the base for the financing of our subordinate facilities." With those comments General Strevey excused himself to leave for his haircut. Colonel Munley returned to his office and began preparation for the upcoming meeting.

THE MISSION OF HSC

The United States Army Health Services Command was born on April 1, 1973. The headquarters was established at Fort Sam Houston in San Antonio, Texas. The cost of modern health care, combined with the complexity of the Army health services system, and the rapidly increasing patient load made the command an organizational and economic necessity for the Army. The command consolidated Army medical department (AMEDD) resources in the United States and several selected overseas locations. Since its organization HSC has been faced with an ever-increasing patient load due to the aging of the retired Army population and a greater number of married active duty soldiers.

Mission, Values and Goals

The HSC has the mission to plan for and be prepared to implement all mobilization and contingency health services support requirements. The command must be ready to operate during war. An additional HSC mission is to provide health care to the Army. This mission includes medical, veterinary, and dental professional service, and education and training for AMEDD personnel. The first consideration in examining this mission is that medical and dental benefits are an important part of the overall employment package of the U.S. Army. Family member medical and dental care is secondary to care provided to active duty personnel and is subject to space availability. These provisions have been made a part of federal law in Title 10 US Code and appropriate Army regulations. The confidence that soldiers have that their families will have adequate medical and dental care has become an essential part of motivating them to serve in the Army and perform in combat.

The second consideration for the mission of AMEDD is the understanding that it has two major facets. It is responsible for maintaining the readiness of medical units and personnel to support the Army in war, and equally important, for maintaining the physical and mental health of American soldiers and their families. These are the functions of the fixed health facilities of the Army and are accomplished through patient care, training, research, and development. The mission of HSC is detailed in Exhibit 24-4.

The HSC mission has been implemented through a set of values and goals that have guided the planning, programming, budgeting, and execution of the command. The values which serve as the moral, ethical, and professional guideposts of HSC are: (1) integrity, (2) competence, (3) candor, (4) commitment, (5) courage, and (6) caring (Exhibit 24-5).

The command values are incorporated in a set of goals. Those goals are designed to serve as the base for implementing the command mission. They are also the framework for a series of command objectives used to structure planning for HSC. In effect, the HSC mission is accomplished through goals-based objectives that flow in an integrated manner from the top of the organization, through the chain-of-command, to all levels. The goals and objectives are integrated into HSC planning, programming, budgeting, and execution system (Exhibit 24-6).

THE HSC ORGANIZATION

Since 1973, HSC has grown to its current size of more than 80 separate subordinate commands. These include seven major Army medical centers (MEDCENS); 30 Army medical department activities (MEDDACS); 37 dental activities (DENTACS); four area dental laboratories; the Academy of Health Sciences; the Army Environmental Hygiene Agency, Fort Detrick, Maryland; and several field operat-

---

Exhibit 24-4   **The Mission of Health Services Command**

1. Provide peacetime health care for the Army in the continental United States, Alaska, Hawaii, Panama, Puerto Rico, and Guam and Johnston Island in the Pacific Basin.

2. Provide health care for other government agencies and organizations when directed by the Chief of Staff, U.S. Army.

3. Plan for and be ready for transition to war. Be prepared to implement all mobilization and contingency health services support requirements to transition and operate during war.

4. Provide the Army with health services training and education. Provide such training and education to the medical, veterinary, and dental professional personnel of the Army Medical Department.

5. Remain abreast of developing technology. Provide future concepts, doctrine, and systems of health services to support the Army.

Source: HSC Mercury, 15(7), Special Issue, 1988. United States Army Health Services Command 1988 Strategic Plan, May 10, 1988.

Exhibit 24-5   **The Values of Health Services Command**

---

1. **Integrity.** We hold to the highest standard of personal and professional ethics.
2. **Competence.** We act on our awareness of the need to continually acquire new knowledge and skills, to maintain our proficiency, and to willingly share our knowledge and experience with others in order to enhance the effectiveness of our team.
3. **Candor.** Sincerity, frankness, and openness characterize our communications.
4. **Commitment.** We are intellectually and emotionally bound to the achievement of our best personal performance of duty in order to enhance the effectiveness of the Army.
5. **Courage.** We are motivated by the moral conviction that what we do is right, worthy, and necessary. We take personal responsibility for challenging and correcting what we know to be wrong.
6. **Caring.** The work we do results in the provision of health services to our beneficiaries. Caring is the essence of our profession. We are a vital part of the Army medic team.

Source: United States Army Health Services Command 1988 Strategic Plan, p. 5.

---

ing activities. The MEDDACS and DENTACS provide the primary and some secondary patient care. The MEDCENS are the tertiary referral centers and teaching hospitals for Army medicine. Exhibit 24-7 shows the relationship of the MEDDACS and MEDCENS.

The Headquarters

Fort Sam Houston, where HSC is located, is the "Home of the Army Medical Department." It is also the home of the Brooke Army Medical Center and the Academy of Health Sciences. Brooke Army Hospital includes the Army's Burn Treat-

---

Exhibit 24-6   **The Goals of Health Services Command**

---

1. **Readiness.** To be a command that attains and maintains all facets of military medical preparedness and is ready to execute transition to a wartime posture to support the Army's mission.
2. **Sustainment.** To be a command that provides the base of health services knowledge, facilities, professional competence, and practice upon which the Army's mission capability depends.
3. **Modernization.** To be a command that forecasts needs, and develops, obtains, and uses up-to-date technology, techniques, organizational structure, and human potential to deliver quality health services.

Source: United States Army Health Services Command 1988 Strategic Plan, p. 6.

Exhibit 24-7   **Patient Service Relationship of MEDDACS and MEDCENS**

MEDCENS	Supported MEDDACS
1. Fitzsimmons Army Medical Center, Colorado (Aurora, Colorado)	1. Fort Carson, Colorado Fort Leavenworth, Kansas Fort Leonard Wood, Missouri Fort Riley, Kansas Fort Sill, Oklahoma
2. Eisenhower Medical Center, Georgia (Located at Fort Gordon, Georgia)	2. Fort Benning, Georgia Fort Campbell, Kentucky Fort Jackson, South Carolina Fort McClellan, Alabama Redstone Arsenal, Alabama Fort Rucker, Alabama Fort Stewart, Georgia Fort Polk, Louisiana Panama Puerto Rico
3. Madigan Army Medical Center, Washington (Located at Fort Lewis, Washington)	3. Alaska
4. Letterman Army Medical Center (Located at the Presidio of San Francisco)	4. Fort Irwin, California Fort Ord, California
5. William Beaumont Army Medical Center (Located at Fort Bliss, Texas)	5. Fort Hood, Texas Fort Huachuca, Arizona
6. Tripler Army Medical Center (Located in Honolulu, Hawaii)	6. Pacific Basin
7. Walter Reed Army Medical Center (Located in Washington, D.C.)	7. Fort Belvoir, Virginia Fort Bragg, North Carolina Fort Devens, Massachusetts Fort Dix, New Jersey Fort Drum, New York Fort Eustis, Virginia Fort Knox, Kentucky Fort Benjamin Harrison, Indiana Fort Lee, Virginia Fort Meade, Maryland Fort Monmouth, New Jersey West Point, New York

Source: HSC Mercury, 15(7), Special Issue, 1988.

ment Center of the Institute of Surgical Research, which is one of the world's leading burn treatment facilities. In early 1987, Brooke Army Medical Center, the Fort Sam Houston Dental Activity, Wilford Hall Air Force Medical Center and three Air Force clinics in the San Antonio area formed the first joint military medical command (JMMC). The JMMC reports directly to the USAF Air Training Command

and is a DOD innovation in organizational design. The JMMC concept is designed to provide more efficient use of existing resources, eliminate duplication, and increase efficiency of the military health services system (MHSS).

A diagram of the headquarters organization is presented in Exhibit 24-8. The HSC headquarters is organized along traditional functional lines. General Strevy,

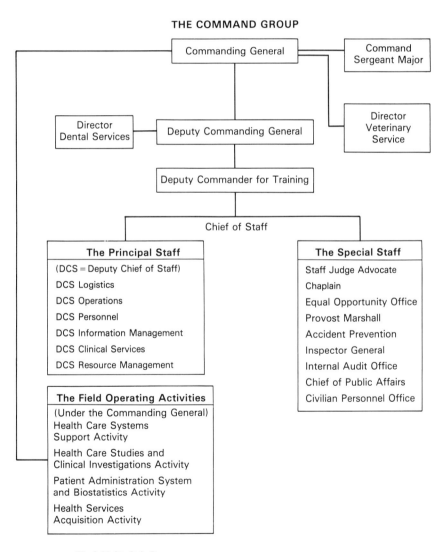

Exhibit 24-8   **The Organization of HSC Headquarters**

as commander, has three deputy commanders and a command sergeant major. The deputy commanding general is a dental officer and serves as the director of dental services for HSC. The deputy commander for training oversees the education, training, and combat development of the command and is also the commandant of the Academy of Health Sciences. The command sergeant major is General Strevey's personal advisor on non-commissioned officer (NCO) and soldier concerns and is the command's senior enlisted person. The deputy commander for administration/ chief of staff supervises the headquarters and coordinates the functioning of the HSC principal staff.

The Principal Staff

The HSC general (or principal) staff is organized to oversee the operating and staff functions of the command. Coordination and staff supervision of the general staff functions are the responsibility of six deputy chief of staff (DCS) sections: (1) DCS personnel, (2) DCS operations, (3) DCS logistics, (4) DCS information management, (5) DCS resources management, and (6) DCS clinical services.

The HSC has two staff sections that specialize in the coordination of two primary operating functions of the command: (1) director of dental services, and (2) director of veterinary services. The director of dental services has technical supervision of the 37 DENTACS. The director of veterinary services is responsible for food hygiene and quality assurance, care of government-owned animals, and animal disease prevention and control, as well as proficiency training of veterinary personnel in the HSC area.

The Special Staff

The special staff of an Army headquarters command consists of those staff sections with responsibilities of a sensitive nature or those not of a pure military nature under a general staff section. For HSC these sections are: (1) staff judge advocate (legal), (2) chaplain, (3) equal opportunity office, (4) provost marshall (military police), (5) accident prevention, (6) inspector general (complaints and compliance), (7) internal audit, (8) public affairs, and (9) civilian personnel.

Staff Responsibilities and Duties

The HSC staff provides coordination, policy, and advice to subordinate elements of the command. Each staff section has responsibilities that are executed on the authority of the chief of staff section. Actions that affect the command prerogatives of subordinate HSC commanders, or that establish primary command policy are referred to the HSC command section for decision. It must be remembered that staff officers do not have decision authority, but act only in the name of their commander. Actions that affect several staff sections are coordinated by the chief of staff.

For example, the DCS logistics (DCSLOG) has responsibility for the level of medical supplies permitted to be stocked at each subordinate HSC MEDDAC. Requests to raise or reduce these levels would be submitted to the DCSLOG from the subordinate hospital. Considering existing regulations and policy, together with the hospital's justification, the DCSLOG would make a decision in the matter and return the action to the requesting hospital. At this point, the affected hospital commander could appeal the decision to General Strevey if warranted. It should be noted that appeals on decisions of this nature are rare, as the primary duty of each general staff officer is to know and follow the regulations, policies, and command desires of the HSC commander.

The Field Operating Agencies

Any health care organization as large as HSC needs automated data support, medical research, and equipment acquisition. These needs are operationalized in the four HSC field operating agencies (FOAs): the patient administration systems and biostatistics activity, the health care systems support activity, the health care studies and clinical investigation activity, and the health services command acquisition activity. Although these activities are considered part of the HSC headquarters, they are staffed by operating personnel rather than staff personnel.

Patient Administration Systems and Biostatistics Activity (PAS&BA).   This activity collects, processes, and distributes recurring Army medical statistics, records of facility workloads, and results of substance abuse programs. The activity also updates current systems and conceives and develops new systems for record keeping.

Health Care Systems Support Activity (HCSSA).   This organization develops and maintains standard automated systems in support of the AMEDD worldwide. The systems used by the medical treatment facilities and other FOAs, such as PAS&BA, were developed and fielded by HCSSA. The developed systems are used for a variety of tasks from maintenance of workload data for all three services to the preparation of pharmacy labels in medical treatment facilities.

Health Care Studies and Clinical Investigation Activity.   This activity performs the worldwide mission of studying ways to improve the management and support of clinical and research programs throughout the Army. It is a central clearing house for monitoring research protocols procured by the clinical investigation personnel in the MEDCENs and MEDDACs. The activity is also responsible for ensuring that all investigations and research conform to current national research standards.

Health Services Command Acquisition Activity.   This organization has the mission of providing medical contracting support for certain of the medical centers as well as centralized command-wide service contracts and programs. The acquisition activity also oversees the HSC contracting and contract compliance mission.

THE MEDCEN

Eisenhower Army Medical Center is typical of the seven MEDCENs in HSC. Named in honor of former President Dwight David Eisenhower, the hospital was dedicated in 1975. The complex is accredited by the Joint Commission for the Accreditation of Health Care Organizations (JCAHCO) and is a member of the American Hospital Association. It includes a 14-story main building, a 36-chair dental care and research facility, a housing unit for more than 500 enlisted men and women assigned to the medical center, an animal research building, and several other outpatient and schoolhouse buildings. Eisenhower is located atop a hill at Fort Gordon, Georgia, just outside of Augusta. The hospital currently operates 423 beds with 16 of those for intensive care.

The hospital employs approximately 1,900 military and civilian workers and operates with an annual budget of $95 million. In addition to primary and tertiary health care, Eisenhower provides a six-week residential program for the treatment of drug and alcohol related problems for active duty persons. There are eight operating rooms and day surgery is also available.

This medical center offers graduate medical education programs in family practice, general surgery, psychiatry, internal medicine, orthopedic surgery, pathology, health care administration, clinical psychology, and child/adolescent psychiatry. Approximately 100 physicians are enrolled in these programs. Graduate nursing education is available in the center's clinical nurse anesthesiology program, and the Practical Nurse School graduates about 100 practical nurses annually. Enlisted medical specialists are also trained at Eisenhower. Courses are given for operating room specialists, physician assistants, and psychiatric mental health nurses.

In 1984, Eisenhower Medical Center was given the mission of supervising the clinical operations and quality of care at Army health care facilities in the southeastern United States and Puerto Rico. Thus, the commander and department chiefs must plan for delivering care on a regional basis. Commanders and department chiefs from all the hospitals meet quarterly. In addition, there are 14 consultants conducting annual seminars. These consultants and specialists from Eisenhower spend an average of 39 man-days each month in the nine community hospitals. These activities create a strong working relationship between the hospitals. Strong colleague relations have been established, and a regional quality assurance program exists. The regional approach to mission has enhanced the quality of health care provided to soldiers and their families.

THE MEDDAC

Noble Army Community is one of the hospitals in Eisenhower Medical Center's region. Noble is located at Fort McClellan, Alabama just outside of Anniston, and operates an extensive primary and secondary care facility. All clinics are quite busy. The military population of Fort McClellan is combined with an extensive retired population in Noble's catchment area (an area roughly 40 miles around a military hospital). Family members and retirees in this area may use CHAMPUS whenever they want for outpatient services. However, they must get prior permission from the local military medical commander for CHAMPUS payment of specific inpatient services. The hospital serves about 20,000 ambulatory patients per month and admits about 398 more. The hospital has 62 operational beds, 82 percent of which are occupied on average. The annual patient load of Noble Hospital is summarized in Exhibit 24-9.

The hospital clinics include surgery; eye, ear, nose, and throat; internal medicine; obstetrics and gynecology; pediatrics; urology; primary care; an emergency department; and a separate outpatient troop clinic that serves the post's basis training population.

As with all Army hospitals, Noble is commanded by an Army physician. The commander of an Army hospital equates to the CEO of a civilian hospital. The deputy commander for administration has the responsibilities associated with the job of administrator, or COO (chief operating officer) in a civilian sector hospital. Army hospitals also have a deputy commander for clinical services (DCCS) who equates to the chief of medical staff of a civilian hospital. The hospital staff functions are similar to those of HSC headquarters.

THE HSC OPERATING ENVIRONMENT

Changing Health Care

For several decades health care providers have concentrated on technical and structural development. From the 1940s to the 1960s health care focused on the

Exhibit 24-9 **Noble Army Community Hospital Clinic Visits, 1987**	
1. Medical/surgical	24,689
2. Nutrition	1,656
3. Urology	1,682
4. Obstetrics/gynecology	16,778
5. Pediatric	17,171
6. Orthopedic	7,748
7. Community mental health	5,267
8. Alcohol/drug abuse	4,486
9. Outpatient	23,010
10. Troop medical clinics	38,445
11. Physical examination	3,092
12. Eye, ear, nose, throat	11,136
13. Preventive medicine	14,240
14. Emergency room	23,435
15. Respiratory therapy	1,236
16. Physical therapy	28,704
17. TOTAL	222,775

construction of facilities consistent with the American policy of increasing public access to the health care system. From the 1960s to the early 1980s health care planning focused on medical services. In the civilian health care industry, physicians formed group practices, and community hospitals grew into large regional medical centers or became members of multihospital chains.

However, in today's highly competitive environment, a priority issue in health care is to balance quality with cost. The question is no longer whether there will be intervention in health care to ensure quality and contain costs, but who will intervene and what methods they will use. The JCAHCO has announced its intent to include outcome criteria as part of its accreditation process. At the federal level, Secretary of Health and Human Services Bowen has stated that health care providers must weigh two matters. One is concern for patients and the other is a recognition that extending the physician's healing touch must be tempered by the limit of society's resources. There is a clear challenge for health care providers to develop strategies that will control costs without sacrificing quality.

The Military Health Care System (MHCS)

The DOD funds a multibillion dollar health care system, one of the nation's largest. In the United States DOD has over 500 treatment facilities, including 129 hospitals and 350 clinics which provide care to 2.2 million men and women on active duty and about 7 million "nonactive" beneficiaries (defined as family members of active duty personnel, retired military personnel and their family members, and survivors).

In 1986 the three services spent about $5 billion to staff and operate their health care facilities; approximately $3.1 billion was for care of retirees and family members, the nonactive beneficiaries. Other functions such as education, training, and combat-readiness–related functions raised the total cost of the MHCS to $8.7 billion. Exhibit 24-10 summarizes some of these costs.

The number of beneficiaries and their diverse location created a demand for care beyond the capabilities of the system. Between 1956 and 1968 CHAMPUS was developed to provide health care to those nonactive beneficiaries who could not secure direct care. Currently, CHAMPUS costs over $2 billion per year for roughly 300,000 hospital admissions, six million outpatient visits, and several million ancillary procedures (laboratory tests and x-rays). The cost of direct care plus CHAMPUS is almost $11 billion.

CHAMPUS is the federal government financed health care plan for the armed services. It is the basis for MHCS beneficiaries to get care in civilian health care facilities when authorized care is not available in military facilities. CHAMPUS is intended as a supplement to benefits from a military hospital or clinic. Care under CHAMPUS is provided on an outpatient and inpatient basis, and the availability and costs to the beneficiary are conveniently divided into three large categories: active duty service members, active duty family members, and retired families. Active duty soldiers may not use CHAMPUS, but are afforded care in civilian facilities

---

Exhibit 24-10   Costs of Worldwide Military Health Care, 1986 (In millions)

Population and Source of Care	Inpatient	Outpatient	Total
1. Active duty, military facilities	$ 860	$1,055	$1,915
2. Nonactive duty, military facilities	1,395	1,715	3,110
3. Active duty, readiness and training costs			1,970
4. Total	$2,255	$2,770	$6,995

Source: J. Slackman, *Reforming the Military Health Care System,* Washington, D.C., U.S. Government Printing Office, 1988, p. 7.

---

when such care is essential to health through direct contract agreements with the civilian facilities. Families of active duty soldiers are eligible for CHAMPUS financed care only when comparable care is certified to be unavailable in a military facility. For such services they pay a small fee: $25 per day for inpatient care, and 20 percent of allowable outpatient charges after a small deductible is exceeded. Retirees and their families may use CHAMPUS at any time without a certificate of nonavailability. The retirees pay 25 percent of billed outpatient charges or $210 per day, whichever is less (the $210 is subject to change each fiscal year), and 25 percent of outpatient fees after exceeding a specified deductible. It is common for Army retirees to have private "CHAMPUS supplemental" health care policies to help with the payment of expensive inpatient services which become more probable as people age.

The high cost of military health care is driven by the high use of medical service and a heavy reliance on CHAMPUS. The average rate of outpatient visits for active duty family members in 1986 was seven per year, two more than their civilian contemporaries. For every 1,000 family members living inside a catchment area the DOD pays for 967 hospital days per year; 609, or 63 percent, are in military hospitals, with the rest in civilian hospitals under CHAMPUS. In comparison, the hospital rate for the general population was 521 days in 1986.

Echoing the concern of the health care industry for high quality care at affordable cost, Congress and the administration are searching for efficient means of cost containment in the MHCS. The administration developed the CHAMPUS reform initiative (CRI) and will begin testing it in California and Hawaii in August 1988. The CRI centers around several fixed-price contracts to provide care for beneficiaries not on active duty. An alternative to CRI would be to enroll the beneficiaries in specified established health care plans and pay the plans a capitation fee. These ideas are not new as can be seen by the application of principles now commonly in use in civilian HMOs and PPOs.

BACK AT FORT SAM HOUSTON

Two weeks later General Strevey had returned from his visit to the Eisenhower Medical Center, pleased with the plans presented for the expansion of that facility. The Army Corps of Engineers had created an outstanding design for the expansion. The HSC would improve technical quality of care, and Eisenhower would be better equipped for their consultation and education mission.

"Now, I must deal with the development of the command strategic plan," thought the general. He began formulating his guidance for the staff by considering the situation facing HSC in terms of the command's environments.

The General Situation

The DOD 1984 Beneficiary Study showed a significant degree of dissatisfaction among Army beneficiaries with care in military facilities compared to civilian care (Exhibits 24-11 and 24-12). The cost of CHAMPUS was $2.3 billion. A Congressional Budget Office (CBO) study on reforming the military health care system had increased the pressure on DOD to come up with specific plans and actions aimed at containing costs, maintaining quality, and assuring a system ready to provide care to military services fighting a war. The present challenge is to accomplish that mission.

Administration and DOD Cost Options. There had been progress toward a number of innovations to address the cost-quality challenge: the test of CRI, the opening of some civilian-run outpatient clinics, fixed-price contracts for mental

---

Exhibit 24-11　**Army Patient Satisfaction with Recent Military Health Care**

Dimension of Care	% Responding Positive	% Responding Negative
ACTIVE DUTY		
1. Quality and competence	63	37
2. Accessibility	57	43
3. Resources	56	44
4. Continuity of care	36	64
RETIREES AND SURVIVORS		
1. Quality and competence	77	23
2. Accessibility	63	37
3. Resources	82	18
4. Continuity of care	56	34

Source: A Reference Guide to the 1984 Military Health Services System Beneficiary Survey, Washington, D.C., Office of the Assistant Secretary of Defense (Health Affairs), December 1984, part V.

Exhibit 24-12   **Army Patient Satisfaction with Recent Civilian Health Care**

Dimension of Care	% Responding Positive	% Responding Negative
ACTIVE DUTY		
1. Quality and competence	89	11
2. Accessibility	82	18
3. Resources	94	6
4. Continuity of care	89	11
RETIREES AND SURVIVORS		
1. Quality and competence	86	14
2. Accessibility	79	21
3. Resources	92	8
4. Continuity of care	89	11

Source: A Reference Guide to the 1984 Military Health Services System Beneficiary Survey, Washington, D.C., Office of the Assistant Secretary of Defense (Health Affairs), December, 1984, part V.

health care, and special arrangements (similar to HMOs) with nonmilitary health care providers.

The Army's PRIMUS (Primary Care for the Uniformed Services) clinics are an example of civilian-run outpatient services. To date, four clinics have been established. Three are in the Washington, D.C. area and a fourth is in Savannah, Georgia. Experience with these clinics has been mixed. They serve as a "safety valve" for overloaded military facilities at a cost below CHAMPUS, enabling Army hospitals to treat more inpatients and make less use of CHAMPUS. Conversely, by expanding the access to free care, PRIMUS could increase total demand more than the savings indicated above.

The current test of "contracted provider arrangement" (CPA) in mental health care coverage has shown promise to reduce costs. Since military facilities offer limited psychiatric care, mental health benefits have made up a large part of CHAMPUS expenses. In 1986 CHAMPUS spent $330 million for mental health services. Essentially, CPA is a PPO, and has demonstrated potential for savings of 10 to 20 percent over CHAMPUS. Greater savings might be realized if CPA greatly reduces the rate of hospitalization.

Special arrangements with nonmilitary providers include the closing of small (less than 100 beds) military hospitals and transferring care to nearby civilian facilities and contracting directly with individual providers to provide care in military facilities. Closing of the small hospitals would eliminate inefficient operations and simultaneously increase competition among civilian hospitals. The increased competition should create opportunities to strike favorable deals. The contracting of individual providers for care in military facilities increases the efficiency of the military hospital and reduces the provider's costs by permitting them to use military equipment and facilities.

A fourth option is the full reorganization of the MHCS. This idea is not new. There have been several studies dealing with reorganization since the DOD was formed by the National Security Act of 1947. The options range from totally independent departments to a totally amalgamated medical service under DOD. Although the independent department option was prohibited under the 1947 organization act, the entire system could be legally dismantled in favor of complete civilian care. In addition to that option, four others are possible: (1) a laissez faire confederation, which is essentially the three medical departments operating within a guidance framework from a relatively weak central DOD entity; (2) a tightly integrated confederation under DOD, which would force cooperation of the three medical departments under a strong central entity; (3) a centralized command of all fixed treatment facilities, such as a defense health agency, with the surgeon general retaining the responsibility for the readiness mission; and (4) total consolidation into a "purple suit" or fully integrated DOD medical care organization. (This "purple suit option" comes from military slang that considers military persons working in DOD as wearing a "purple suit" since they were not working for the Army "green" or Navy "white" or Air Force "blue.")

The Army Cost Options. The Army is also pursuing four options in cost containment. These are (1) establish more PRIMUS clinics, (2) increase the capabilities of existing military primary care clinics, (3) increase capabilities of Army freestanding primary care clinics, and (4) make greater use of cost sharing or copayment by the beneficiaries of care.

Options (2) and (3) are similar. They represent the old way of doing business and would have to continue to compete with the rest of the Army for resources. Option (1) has been discussed earlier. Option (4), the use of a copayment for outpatient visits, assumes greater importance for cost containment in the present environment. The popular version of a copayment is to only charge family members of active duty persons and all retirees. Active duty soldiers would be exempt because of the health requirements for combat readiness. The size of payment ranges from $5 to $10 per visit with an annual cap of $200 per family.

Five criteria have been suggested to evaluate these options: accessibility, political feasibility, quality of care, efficiency, and readiness. Four of these have been cited previously as impacting the strategic management of HSC. Political feasibility underscores the importance of the political environment in military health care planning.

The HSC PPBES

"So much for the environment," thought General Strevey. "The next step for the command will be the formation of the HSC strategic plan within the HSC planning, programming, budgeting, and execution system (PPBES)." The PPBES provides HSC a means of ensuring effective use of resources. The command first develops a strategic plan covering the next ten years. Incremental resource requirements are then incorporated in the HSC program analysis and resource review (PARR). Annual requirements are planned for and tracked in the HSC command operating budget (COB). All planning and execution is a team effort and contains input from HSC subordinate commands.

The budget is a requirements-based document and the primary control of the HSC program. Budget execution is controlled by a series of reviews in which all HSC elements are examined for their rate of execution and fund obligation, together with changes in requirement priorities. Usually, a midyear review (March being the middle of the Army fiscal year) allows for redistribution of funds from slow-moving requirements and low-priority requirements to those whose importance has changed during the immediate fiscal year.

Thus, there is a cyclic planning and execution process for HSC. The strategic plan is updated annually, together with the PARR. Each COB provides a record of what is being done to follow the command's planning documents. This system embodies the principles of strategic management and has served HSC and the Army very well for almost 20 years. The form of and emphasis on this system has changed over the years. However, the principles used have permitted DOD to remain informed of changes in strategic threats to U.S. security and adjust the several service plans accordingly. The HSC strategic plan and PPBES play key roles in the Army's portion of the DOD PPBES.

General Strevey was ready for tomorrow's staff meeting. Colonel Munley had assured him the staff was ready also. The general turned off the lights, wished Mrs. Tribbey a "good evening" and departed.

THE GUIDANCE MEETING

On Thursday at 0930 in the HSC headquarters conference room, the staff officers were discussing business, forecasting next Saturday's football results, or trying to predict what the CG's guidance would be for the strategic plan. Colonel Munley quieted the conversation: "Ladies and gentlemen, the Commanding General." They all rose to their feet and came to attention. General Strevey entered, took his seat, invited everyone to do the same, and the meeting began.

The Commander first described the environment HSC was facing. He followed with information received from the Department of the Army (DA) that impacted upon their planning. That information reinforced the staff's opinion that both DA and DOD were very serious about high costs and maintenance of quality care.

"I know that Colonel Munley has given you my initial guidance concerning the strategic plan. I want to add a few things today which will permit you to begin work with some definite boundaries for options we need to be considering for the future of HSC." With this statement, General Strevey covered the following points:

1. The mission priorities are: (a) meet wartime requirements, (b) provide peacetime health care, and (c) educate and train HSC personnel.

2. All planning must be within the stated values and goals of the command.

3. Our most important resource is our people. Programs that provide excellence among our people are imperative for the high quality health care that we are committed to provide to our soldiers and their families.

4. The future promises fewer resources. Accordingly, we will assume an environment of zero-to-negative growth in resources. This means that any new programs and initiatives must be resourced through a trade-off of an existing initiative or program. Some programs may have to be eliminated. We must prioritize our programs, adequately resource the most important and indicate what cannot be done clearly, and in priority.

5. We must link goals, objectives, and tasks. This is especially important in today's environment of constant and rapid change. The future promises no resource growth and probably some reductions. I want you all to search out places where we can cut out the unnecessary, reduce the necessary, and begin new initiatives to maintain quality with increased efficiency for the U.S. taxpayers.

6. Finally, in our plan for patient care, I want to see some very specific people-oriented initiatives. Develop plans to implement good marketing strategies. Improve the management of access to care. Plan to promote a healthy lifestyle. Prevention of illness saves our operating resources. Finally, design ways for us to create and maintain a caring environment that enhances human worth and potential.

Case 25

Kraft, Inc.

Some of America's best-known brand names in food products are produced by Kraft. These include Kraft, Velveeta, Parkay, Miracle Whip, Philadelphia, Cracker Barrel, Sealtest, Light n' Lively, Breyers, and Breakstone's. The company's products are sold to stores and restaurants in 130 countries by over 5,000 salespeople.

This case was prepared by Charles W. Boyd, Southwest Missouri State University, as a basis for class discussion rather than to illustrate either effective or ineffective handling of an administrative situation. Used by permission from Charles W. Boyd.

Kraft ranks second only to General Foods in the food processing industry. The company is truly an industry giant that grew from very humble beginnings.

Even as Kraft has changed, so has the food processing industry. In the 1980s Kraft and its competitors have realized that the recent and projected slow population growth in the United States means that most future gains in market share must come at the expense of one another. As a result, the industry is being restructured through mergers and acquisitions as the major firms seek to strengthen their competitive positions. In order to remain at the top of the industry, Kraft's top managers must make correct strategic decisions regarding the company's product mix and the manner in which to structure the organization to best compete in the changing environment.

HISTORY OF THE COMPANY

James L. Kraft came to Chicago from Canada in 1903 and began wholesaling cheese from a rented, horse-drawn wagon. His four brothers—Fred, Charles, Norman, and John—joined the prospering business. By 1914, they were selling 31 varieties of cheese under the brand names Kraft and Elkhorn.

Kraft merged with a rival company, Phenix Cheese, in 1928. Kraft-Phenix accounted for 40 percent of U.S. cheese production and also had operations in Canada, Australia, Britain, and Germany. The company was acquired in 1930 by National Dairy. The new company ranked as one of America's largest, with annual sales of $375 million. For the next four decades, Kraft functioned as a separate entity in Chicago, while National Dairy functioned primarily as a holding company from its headquarters in New York City.

James L. Kraft died in 1953 at age 78. In 1969, the National Dairy company name was changed to Kraftco. Corporate headquarters was moved from New York City to the Chicago suburb of Glenview in 1972. In 1976, the company name was changed to its current title, Kraft, Incorporated.

Kraft, Inc. merged with Dart Industries in 1980 to form Dart & Kraft, Incorporated. Dart Industries had gone through significant restructuring of its business units during the few years preceding the merger with Kraft. In 1985, Dart & Kraft, Inc. operated in four major business segments, as seen in Exhibit 25-1. Results for 1985 were marked by strong growth for Kraft, Hobart commercial equipment, and the Wilsonart decorative laminate businesses. Success in these segments offset profit declines at Tupperware, Duracell, West Bend, and KitchenAid. Dart & Kraft ranked 34th among the 1985 *Fortune* 500 Industrials with annual sales of $9.9 billion and net income of $446 million.

Dart & Kraft acquired nine businesses at a cost of $300 million during 1985. These included Frusen Gladje superpremium ice cream; Invernizzi S.P.A., an Italian cheese company; and the Westman Commission Company, a full-line foodservice distributor. Top management expected these and the other 1985 acquisitions to be compatible with their strategy of maintaining a mix of high-quality, primarily consumer-oriented businesses. John Richman, chairman and CEO, stated in the

---

Exhibit 25-1   **Dart & Kraft, Inc., 1985**

Business Segments	Strategic Business Units
Food products	Kraft, Inc.
Direct selling	Tupperware (plastic storage, preparation, and serving-ware for food)
Consumer products	Duracell (batteries) KitchenAid (home appliances) West Bend (small appliances and physical fitness equipment) Health care businesses
Commercial products	Hobart (foodservice cooking equipment, cookware washers, refrigeration products, and supermarket weighing and wrapping equipment) Wilsonart (decorative laminates and disposable plastic and rubber items)

---

company's 1985 *Annual Report* that such acquisitions were likely to continue in 1986. In early 1986, the company signed an agreement to acquire Vulcan-Hart Corporation, a leading producer of gas cooking equipment, which was expected to add further competitive strength to Dart & Kraft's food equipment business.

Dart & Kraft recently took actions directed toward divesting most of the company's small health care operations and on January 31, 1986, the sale of KitchenAid to Whirlpool Corporation was consummated. Mr. Richman stated in his annual letter to the stockholders that this sale was opportunistic, rather than the result of strategic reappraisal. The sale resulted in an after-tax gain of $41 million to be recorded in the first quarter of 1986.[1]

Dart & Kraft's strategy in early 1986 was summarized by Chairman Richman and President Batts as follows:

> As to the longer term, our strategy will not be dramatically different. Contrary to the current industry trend, we continue to believe that there are benefits to be derived from our particular type of controlled and related diversification. For example, our ability to balance the cash-generating capacity of our retail food business and Tupperware with higher-growth, cash-using businesses like Duracell is an important benefit.[2]

OPERATIONS AT KRAFT, INC.

Michael A. Miles was President and CEO of Kraft, Inc. in 1985. Kraft's mission statement for that year is presented in Exhibit 25-2. Mr. Miles had publicly

---

[1]Dart & Kraft, Inc. *Annual Report* 1985, p. 31.
[2]Ibid., p. 4.

Exhibit 25-2   **Kraft, Inc. Mission**

Mission Summary

Kraft's mission is to become the leading food company in the world, based on achieving superiority versus competition in a balance of these factors:

- Outstanding overall quality of people, products, and business plans.
- Return on management investment (ROMI).
- Rate of growth in unit sales and operating income.
- Innovation.

Customers

Kraft's businesses will be built on the fundamental concept of achieving superiority versus competition in:

- Identifying the wants and needs of customers, both end-consumers and trade.
- Providing high-quality products and/or services to meet those needs in unique or advantageous ways.
- Marketing those products/services to reinforce their appeal and achieve superior acceptance.

Industries/Markets Channels of Distribution

Kraft will compete in any segment of the food business, in any geographic market, and in any channel of distribution, where:

- Participation can make a material long-term contribution to sales and income, while generating returns at or above corporate targets.
- The combination of product quality, management quality, and innovation provides us with a sustainable competitive advantage—or the prospect of same in a reasonable time frame.

Competition

Kraft has mass and resources that enable it to compete with any company in the world, and will utilize these resources to the fullest legal, ethical, and moral extent.

Kraft will engage any competitor in any geographical market, category, or channel of distribution of interest, where the combination of product quality, management quality, and innovation provides us with a sustainable competitive advantage.

Kraft will defend its established businesses ferociously.

People/Organization

Kraft recognizes that the quality of its people is the critical element in achieving the success of its mission.

Kraft's human resources policies and practices will be built on a standard of excellence and a total commitment to equal opportunity and fair treatment.

Kraft will promote based on merit and from within wherever possible.

Business Style

Kraft's business style will be characterized by:

- Overarching commitment to quality,
- Openness and honesty,
- Initiative,
- Innovation,
- Aggressiveness,
- Action orientation,
- Competitiveness,
- Efficiency,
- Risk acceptance,
- Superior analysis and planning,
- A standard of excellence in people.

What we say we do, we *do* do.

James L. Kraft

Source: Kraft, Inc. planning document.

identified five strengths and three weaknesses of Kraft. The five strengths and supporting reasons for them were:

1. Huge mass and resources—Kraft is one of the four largest food businesses
   in the world, and second only to General Foods in the United States.
2. Growth markets and growth categories—from 1979 to 1983, per capita consumption of cheese in the United States increased 23 percent, pourable
   dressings 14 percent, and premium ice cream 18 percent.
3. Extremely strong brand names and market share positions—Kraft is either
   the leader or a strong contender in virtually all of the major categories in
   which it competes.
4. Excellent customer relations—research indicates Kraft has the best reputation for quality in the food industry and that only Procter and Gamble
   compares with Kraft in sales force skill and effectiveness.
5. Worldwide infrastructure—the human and financial resources are in place
   to support new business initiatives anywhere in the world.

Mr. Miles also reported the following weaknesses:

1. No recent track record of success in developing significant new products.
2. Too conservative; need more challenges.
3. Increasing competition.

In addition, Mr. Miles outlined five broad strategies Kraft was currently pursuing:

1. To protect and build the existing businesses—for branded products, increased spending on advertising, competitive pricing, and more emphasis
   on advertisable product improvement—for commodity products, being the
   lowest-cost producer.
2. To gradually weight the business mix toward branded, value-added products and away from commodities.
3. To augment the growth of existing branded positions by a more active new
   business development effort.
4. To continue to pursue expense and asset minimization in all areas.
5. To increase organizational vitality.[3]

President Miles believed that these strategies would best capitalize on Kraft's
major strength: a quality reputation in producing and promoting branded food
products. As these branded products were expanded, the company planned to continue the retreat from fluid milk and certain private-label items, and from its bulk
cheese and edible-oil businesses in Europe.

___

[3]Warren L. Batts, President and Chief Operating Officer, Dart & Kraft, Inc., presentation to the
Consumer Analyst Group of New York, at St. Petersburg, Florida, February 21, 1984.

The fifth strategy—increasing organizational vitality—involved many actions. These actions included increasing employee communications, eliminating some excess layers of middle management, and a large-scale test of doubling the size of the U.S. retail sales force. The intent of these actions was to increase the sense of urgency and the timeliness of decision making. Some employees in Kraft's Retail Food Group dubbed this the M/B/F program, meaning more/better/faster.

KRAFT PRODUCT LINES

The key performers during 1985-1986 were the Retail Food, Food Service, and Dairy Groups. These and Kraft's other operating units and their principal products are identified in Exhibit 25-3.

Refrigerated Products Division. Kraft began the national distribution of Light Philadelphia Brand process cream cheese, another of several new products aimed at calorie-conscious consumers. The expansion of this product continued during 1986.

Grocery Products Division. Kraft experienced success with reduced-calorie versions of Miracle Whip Salad Dressing and Kraft Real Mayonnaise. Both products

---

Exhibit 25-3 **Key Performers During 1985–1986**

Group and Division	Principle Products
Retail Food Group	
Refrigerated Products Division	Process, natural, and cream cheese
Grocery Products Division	Salad dressings, mayonnaise, dry packaged dinners, and barbecue sauce
Venture Division	Bagels and herb teas
International Group	
Primary operations in Canada, West Germany, Italy, Australia, the Philippines, Latin America, and Mexico	Wide variety of products representing all Kraft divisions
Dairy Group	Ice cream, ice milk, lowfat yogurt, cottage cheese, and sour cream
Foodservice Group	Distributes products from the Retail Food Group to restaurants
Industrial Foods Group	Supplies food manufacturers with edible oils and edible-oil–based products, cheese items, snack seasonings, imitation cheese, flavorings, confections, dairy and nondairy proteins, and other ingredients

became the leading share brands in their categories. Velveeta Shells and Cheese Packaged Dinner, introduced in 1984, also experienced significant sales increases. Presto, a new Italian salad dressing, was introduced nationally during 1985. Even as volume declined, profitability on Parkay Margarine increased due to lower edible-oil costs.

Venture Division. This division completed two acquisitions during 1984— Lender's Bagel Bakery, Inc., and Celestial Seasonings, Inc. Both did well during 1985. The bagel business was geographically expanded beyond the Northeast during the year, necessitating the building of additional capacity which was scheduled for completion during 1986. Profit declined slightly in the Celestial Seasonings herb teas business due to costs incurred in creating new marketing programs and strengthening channels of distribution. In addition, four new tea flavors were added during 1985—Lemon Zinger, Raspberry Patch, Island Orange, and Cranberry Cove.

The Venture Division entered an agreement with DNA Plant Technology for the development and marketing of Vegisnax raw vegetables bred for superior taste and texture. The division also entered an agreement early in 1986 with San Francisco French Bread Company to market a line of sourdough products.

Foodservice Group. This group attempted to capitalize on the almost 50 percent of the American food dollar that is spent on meals away from home. The group accounted for 13 percent of Kraft's total sales, and experienced a 12 percent growth of tonnage sales during 1985. Many products, such as the familiar individual serving packets of Kraft's jams and jellies, are distributed by the Foodservice Group. The group engages in extensive research and development activity. Because the company manufactures nearly 50 percent of what the Foodservice Group sells, profit is captured from both production and distribution. This group also adds value to Retail Food Group acquisitions by broadening distribution of products such as Lender's Bagels and Celestial Seasonings herb teas.

Two acquisitions were completed by the Foodservice Group during 1985—the Westman Commission Company, a full-line distributor serving seven Rocky Mountain states, and Seaboard Foods, Inc., a broadline distributor in North Carolina. Letters of intent were signed in early 1986 to acquire distribution businesses in Kansas City, Chicago, Phoenix, and the New York areas.

The Foodservice Group developed innovations to add efficiency during 1985. A portable entry terminal for sales representatives shortened order-processing time and supported next-day delivery service. A computerized restaurant management system called "Kraft Link" connected customers with the nearest Kraft Foodservice location and assisted them with menu, food-cost and sales analysis, as well as order entry and inventory control. This system also provided customers with automatic price updating, on-line order verification, and other helpful services.

Dairy Group. This group accounted for 9 percent of total company sales. The group experienced market share and profit gains in almost every product line during 1985 due to an overall 10 percent sales increase.

The group's excellent year in ice cream was enhanced by the acquisition of Frusen Gladje, a superpremium ice cream line. This line's sales tripled following the acquisition as a result of a quick move to expand its sales territory and the creation of new television and print advertising.

Kraft's all-natural premium ice cream line, Breyers, expanded into nine western states during 1985. Sealtest ice cream celebrated its 50th anniversary with a 16 percent volume increase, aided by its new Cubic Scoops flavors. Double-digit sales gains were also registered by Polar B'ar ice cream squares and Light n' Lively ice milk. Sales increases were also achieved by Light n' Lively lowfat yogurt, Breakstone's, Sealtest, and Light n' Lively lowfat cottage cheese, and Breakstone's and Sealtest sour cream.

The only Dairy Group product to show a sales decline during 1985 was Breyers yogurt. This product was improved in late summer by adding larger chunks of fruit and more graphically appealing packaging.

International Group.   This group, which accounted for 24 percent of company sales, reported lower 1985 profits. This was primarily due to poor results in West Germany, Kraft's largest European market. Other European operations did well, especially Kraft S.P.A. in Italy, where the company acquired a major interest in Invernizzi S.P.A., a Milan-based producer and distributor of natural cheeses.

Kraft Australia acquired the Everest Group, a small, regional producer of pasta, ice cream, and frozen dinners. This acquisition was designed as a base from which Kraft could diversify from its dependence on cheese in the Australian market.

Anticipating that the poor economic conditions in Venezuela were going to persist, Kraft was in the process of introducing a new line of lower-cost products there. The company sold the small business interest it had in Brazil.

Industrial Foods Group.   This group accounted for 7 percent of Kraft's sales. Price declines in the edible-oil market during 1985 caused a significant decrease in group profits even though sales volume increased. The industrial ingredients business, however, achieved higher sales and profits.

Two important actions were taken in the Industrial Foods Group during 1985: the industrial emulsifier business was sold because it was not achieving satisfactory return, and the decision was made to phase out the California oil refining operations by September 1986. This latter action was designed to remove Kraft from the low-return bulk oils market. The company planned to continue supplying the West Coast with higher-margin specialty oil products from its two refineries located in Tennessee and Illinois.

All of these activities in Kraft's five groups were designed to move the company toward the major goal enunciated in its mission statement: to become the leading food company in the world. As Kraft's top management strives toward this goal, the U.S. food industry is changing. The dairy industry in which Kraft competes has witnessed changes in consumer preferences and consumption patterns during recent years. In addition, the larger food processing industry of which Kraft is a part is undergoing major restructuring.

THE U.S. DAIRY INDUSTRY

Three significant developments affected the dairy industry in 1985:

1. Cheese made a major comeback after three low-growth years.
2. The dairy farmers' advertising and promotional campaign completed its first year of operation.
3. Concern within the dairy industry intensified as Congress debated the dairy provisions of the 1985 farm bill.[4]

Four firms that operated in several segments of the dairy industry accounted for 18.3 percent of total 1985 sales, down 1 percent from 1984: Dart & Kraft, 6.8 percent; Beatrice, 4.6 percent; Borden, 3.7 percent; and Nestle, 3.2 percent.

Fluid Milk

Per capita consumption of two major fluid items—whole milk and cottage cheese—has declined consistently during recent years. Many consumers perceive that lowfat and skim milk are more healthful than whole milk. Lowfat and skim milk are also less expensive than whole milk. As a result, milk consumption patterns have changed. From 1980 to 1984, consumption of whole milk declined 3.4 percent annually, and it declined another 4 percent during 1985. Skim milk consumption rose by 8.8 percent during 1985, while lowfat milk use increased 3.9 percent. During 1980 to 1984, total per capita consumption of all milk declined 0.9 percent, and then remained unchanged during 1985.

Estimated per capita consumption of cottage cheese decreased 1.4 percent in 1985, while per capita consumption of lowfat cottage cheese (a yogurt rival) rose 5 percent. Per capita yogurt consumption increased 12.6 percent.

The four leading processors of fluid milk achieved 19.3 percent of total sales as follows: Southland, 6.8 percent; Beatrice, 4.6 percent; Borden, 4.3 percent; and Dairymen, a cooperative, 3.6 percent.

Cheese

Per capita consumption of all cheese declined an estimated 1.6 percent during 1985, but some product categories gained while others lost (Exhibit 25-4). For example, per capita consumption of American cheese declined 2.4 percent while that of Italian-type varieties increased 2.9 percent. One-half of cheese production is American cheese, whereas Italian varieties account for one-fourth of production.

Cheese substitutes fortified by the milk protein casein have appeared on the

---

[4]Facts relating to 1985 events and forecasts for the dairy industry are drawn from *1986 U.S. Industrial Outlook,* Department of Commerce/International Trade Administration, pp. 40-13 through 40-19.

Exhibit 25-4   U.S. per Capita Consumption of Cheeses (pounds)

Types of Cheese	1983	1984	1985[a]
American	11.62	12.02	11.77
Cheddar	9.13	9.73	9.53
Other American[b]	2.49	2.29	2.24
Italian	5.73	5.82	5.99
Mozzarella	3.71	4.06	4.20
Ricotta	.54	.58	.61
Provolone	.90	.55	.57
Other Italian varieties	.58	.63	.61
All other cheese	5.85	5.46	5.15
All cheese	23.20	23.30	22.91

[a]Estimated.

[b]Includes Colby, washed curd, stirred curd, and Monterey Jack.

Source: U.S. Department of Commerce: Bureau of the Census, and International Trade Administration (*ITA*); U.S. Department of Agriculture. Estimates by ITA.

market during recent years. For example, many brands of frozen pizza contain these less costly substitutes.

Producer prices for all natural cheese dropped 1.1 percent during 1985, while those for all processed cheeses declined 1.7 percent. Four producers of natural and processed cheeses accounted for 33 percent of total sales: Dart & Kraft, 21 percent; Schrieber Food, 5 percent; Land O' Lakes, 4 percent; and Beatrice, 3 percent.

Frozen Desserts

Consumption of ice cream and other frozen desserts had been quite steady during recent years. In 1985, estimated per capita consumption of ice cream melted 2.3 percent, while sherbet declined 3.9 percent. At the same time, per capita consumption of ice milk increased 2 percent and mellorine climbed 62.4 percent. Mellorine contains soy-based products such as frozen tofu, which many consumers consider to be more healthful than ice cream.

Along with mellorine, gelatin bars and frozen fruit bars are also gaining popularity among adults as well as children. Among the major food processors, Castle and Cooke now manufactures fruit bars and General Foods produces gelatin bars.

Several years ago, a few small companies began to achieve success in the premium ice cream market. Premium ice cream has a higher butterfat content than standard ice cream and is often produced with only natural ingredients, such as milk, sugar, and real fruit flavorings. Major food processors have now recognized the potential of this market segment. In 1983, Pillsbury acquired Haagen-Dazs, a popular regional producer of premium ice cream. In April 1985, Dart & Kraft acquired Frusen Gladje, a privately held manufacturer of premium ice cream.

In 1985, the average retail price for a half-gallon of ice cream reached $2.31, as producer prices edged up an estimated 2 percent. Four ice cream makers garnered 31 percent of the market for ice cream and frozen desserts: Southland, 11 percent; Dart & Kraft, 8 percent; Borden, 8 percent; and Beatrice, 4 percent.

Outlook for the U.S. Dairy Industry

Exhibit 25-5 summarizes the estimated and forecasted values of industry shipments of various dairy products for the years 1982 to 1986. The aggregate value of shipments for 1986 is expected to increase 0.7 percent, while total per capita consumption is expected to increase 0.8 percent, less than the predicted rate of population increase. Predictions for the real (inflation-adjusted) growth of specific products ranged from a 1.7 percent gain for cheese to a 1.6 percent decline for ice cream and frozen desserts.

Per capita consumption of all cheese may remain static, but consumption of Italian types is expected to increase 3 percent. Consumption of most other types of cheese is likely to be static or to decline.

Shipments of premium ice cream are expected to increase, thus preventing further decline in the real growth of frozen desserts. Novelty items and frozen tofu will continue to serve market niches. Demand for lowfat milk, skim milk, and yogurt are expected to continue to rise while demand for whole milk will continue to decline.

The volume of dairy shipments is expected to rise 0.2 percent annually from 1985 to 1990, while the population increases 0.9 percent a year. This slow expansion will be spread unevenly among the industry's product segments.

Ice cream and frozen desserts are expected to register slight declines. Shipments of fluid milk are likely to remain unchanged because the population of the prime consuming group, children aged 15 years and under, will expand only 0.2 percent annually. Expansion of the butter market will prove difficult as an increasing number of people reach maturity having used very little of it.

RECENT EVENTS IN THE FOOD PROCESSING INDUSTRY

The U.S. food market tends to grow pretty much in line with population growth. The population has been growing less than 1 percent annually, and per capita food consumption trends have been relatively flat. As a result, there has been low overall growth in the U.S. food market during recent years. U.S. food expenditures rose 3.2 percent in real terms during 1985, compared to 2.1 percent during 1984.

The increasing number of two wage earner households in the United States has resulted in higher disposable incomes and a growing need for convenience. Although Americans want more healthful meals, they have less time to prepare them, but more money to spend for them. As a result, spending for food away from home

Exhibit 25-5   **Recent Performance and Forecast: Dairy Products (In millions)**

| | 1982 | 1983 | 1984[a] | 1985[b] | 1986[c] | Percent change | | | |
						1982–1983	1983–1984	1984–1985	1985–1986
Value of shipments[d]	$39,063	$40,219	$40,832	$42,689	$43,879	3.0	1.5	4.5	2.8
Creamery butter	1,687	1,737	1,778	1,835	1,853	3.0	2.4	3.2	1.0
Cheese	10,763	10,907	11,064	12,332	12,785	1.3	1.4	11.5	3.7
Condensed and evaporated milk	4,731	5,746	5,673	5,603	5,631	21.5	−1.3	−1.2	0.5
Ice cream	2,855	2,963	3,126	3,244	3,302	3.8	5.5	3.8	1.8
Fluid milk	19,028	18,865	19,191	19,675	20,308	−0.9	1.7	2.5	3.2

[a]Estimated except for exports and imports.
[b]Estimated.
[c]Forecast.
[d]Value of all products and services sold by the dairy products industry.
Source: U.S. Department: Bureau of the Census, Bureau of Economic Analysis, International Trade Administration (ITA). Estimates and Forecasts by ITA.

has been increasing much faster than spending for food prepared at home. Although real food-at-home spending rose faster than real foodservice sales during 1985 (+2.6% versus +1.2%), the reverse was true for the 1983 to 1985 period (+11.3% for food away from home versus +6.6% for food at home).[5]

These two trends—slow growth in the food industry and a trend toward increased food consumption away from home—indicate that it will be difficult for competitors in the food processing industry to make continued large gains in the market simply through internal growth of existing products. For this reason, several large food processors have recently begun to reposition themselves into propitious product and geographical markets and to capitalize on the trend toward eating away from home. The slow-growing market means that the majority of future market share gains will result from taking existing market share away from competitors. Thus, the market has become, and is expected to remain, fiercely competitive. Food processors were second only to department stores in advertising expenditures during 1984 with outlays of $4.2 billion (Exhibit 25-6).[6]

Repositioning efforts also resulted in 315 mergers and acquisitions involving 260 firms in the food sector during the first six months of 1985. This is only a slight increase from the number of similar mergers during the same period of 1984.

Three mergers with a combined transaction cost approaching $14 billion achieved the most notoriety during 1985: R.J. Reynolds acquired Nabisco Brands for $5 billion; Phillip Morris spent $5.6 billion for General Foods Corporation; and Nestle S.A. purchased Carnation Company for $3 billion. In addition, Beatrice Foods agreed to a leveraged buyout that will take the company private. Food and beverage industry shipments account for about 60 percent of these four firms' annual sales, and together these companies sell 15 percent of total food and beverage industry shipments.[7] The slow growth of demand and the rapid change in consumer tastes may portend continued mergers in the food industry. In addition, food companies have been repurchasing their own stock at an unprecedented rate, partly to prevent becoming takeover targets. Stock held by the largest food processors as a percent of their total shares outstanding has increased from about 2 percent in 1981 to 15 percent by the end of 1985. These buybacks have added strength to the market price of these stocks. But financiers have also discovered the value of strong, established brand names in the food industry. The combination of realized market strength from good brand names and the stock buybacks caused food industry stock prices to jump 60 percent during 1985, even though industry profits declined 2 percent.[8]

[5]"Food, Beverages, and Tobacco: Current Analysis," *Standard & Poor's Industry Surveys,* vol. 54, no. 9, sec. 1, February 27, 1986, p. 1.

[6]"Advertising: Special Report," *Standard & Poor's Industry Surveys,* vol. 53, no. 40, sec. 1, October 3, 1985, p. 1.

[7]"Food and Kindred Products," *1986 U.S. Industrial Outlook,* U.S. Department of Commerce/ International Trade Administration, p. 40-1.

[8]Kenneth Dreyfack, "The Stage Is Set for More Megadeals," *Business Week,* January 13, 1986, p. 67.

Exhibit 25-6 Top 20 Spenders on Advertising—1984 (In millions)		
Company	**1983**	**1984**
Procter & Gamble	$915.0	$976.0
Sears	898.0	925.1
General Motors	823.5	892.3
Phillip Morris	810.6	892.0
Ford	787.2	808.5
Reynolds (R.J.)	633.0	702.0
Beatrice	288.0	680.0
Warner-Lambert	592.0	607.0
PepsiCo	488.3	595.9
Coca Cola	463.2	535.8
Sara Lee	456.0	513.0
Anheuser Busch	403.9	480.2
American Express	384.0	490.0
J.C. Penney	381.0	465.0
General Foods	395.9	431.8
Eastman Kodak	390.0	430.0
Ralston Purina	438.0	429.6
Dart & Kraft	339.6	418.6
American Home Products	409.9	412.0
General Electric	363.0	356.0

Source: Compustat Services, Inc.

Several indicators point to a good year for food processors during 1986:

1. Cost savings resulting from lower oil prices.
2. Stable prices for food commodities.
3. The average company's bottom line could be increased by 10 percent if proposed tax legislation being considered by Congress is passed.
4. Despite recent merger activity, there is no sign that the Justice Department is becoming concerned about concentration in the industry.[9]
5. Operating efficiencies and economies of size resulting from the recent mergers and acquisitions.[10]

The following statement regarding the food processing industry appeared in a January 1986 *Business Week* article: "As recently as five years ago, when high tech was king, the packaged-food industry drew nothing but yawns. Food companies themselves were weary of low margins and slow growth. But now a new ethic has taken hold, and the industry is alive and thriving. Boring had become beautiful."[11]

[9]Ibid.

[10]"Food and Kindred Products," p. 40-1.

[11]Dreyfack, *op. cit.*

Exhibit 25-7 Summary of Selected Financial Data (In millions, except per share)

	1982	1983	1984	1985	1986
Summary of Operations					
Net sales	$7,618	$7,425	$7,628	$7,920	$8,742
Costs and expenses					
Cost of products	5,754	5,395	5,442	5,478	5,970
Delivery, sales and administrative expense	1,399	1,475	1,550	1,727	2,055
Interest expense	87	68	94	79	71
Interest income	(58)	(63)	(70)	(50)	(39)
Other income, net	(33)	(19)	(37)	(34)	(25)
Total costs and expenses	7,149	6,856	6,979	7,200	8,032
Income from operations	469	569	649	720	710
Nonoperating items	(91)	—	—	—	—
Income from continuing operations before income taxes	378	569	649	720	710
Provision for income taxes	168	252	295	312	320
Net income from continuing operations	210	317	354	408	390
Net income from discontinued operations	140	118	102	58	23
Net income	$ 350	$ 435	$ 456	$ 466	$ 413
Net income per share					
From continuing operations	$1.27	$1.92	$2.33	$2.82	$2.77
From discontinued operations	.86	.72	.68	.40	.16
Total	$2.13	$2.64	$3.01	$3.22	$2.93
Dividends	$ 197	$ 210	$ 209	$ 219	$ 234
Per Share	$1.20	$1.28	$1.38	$1.52⅓	$1.68

Financial Position

Current assets	$2,286	$2,476	$ 2,339	$ 2,326	$ 2,475
Current liabilities	1,134	1,256	1,479	1,415	2,283
Working capital	1,152	1,220	860	911	192
Property, plant and equipment, net	901	900	948	1,075	1,350
Total assets	4,709	4,998	4,882	5,091	4,749
Long-term debt	574	549	508	439	232
Shareholders' equity	2,774	2,923	2,598	2,880	1,798[a]
Per share	$16.89	$17.77	$18.09	$19.95	$13.29

Statistical Information

Return on equity[b]	12.8%	17.7%	22.7%	22.3%	21.7%
Return on total capital[b]	11.0%	14.2%	17.0%	18.4%	15.4%
Long-term debt to equity[b]	34.9%	30.6%	32.6%	23.9%	12.9%
Total debt to total capital[b]	28.9%	27.2%	34.0%	24.5%	34.9%
Capital expenditures	$ 257	$ 137	$ 164	$ 181	$ 209
Depreciation	$ 116	$ 96	$ 104	$ 99	$ 113
Payroll and employee benefits	$1,104	$1,118	$1,114	$1,208	$1,386
Average number of employees	50,500	49,500	47,400	50,100	51,300
Number of shareholders at year-end	78,808	74,443	70,807	72,249	70,190
Number of shares of common stock outstanding at year-end (thousands)	164,237	164,483	143,627	144,334	135,279
Average number of common and common equivalent shares (thousands)	164,265	164,887	151,589	144,898	140,970

Note: Amounts have been restated to reflect the results from continuing operations, where appropriate. In 1986, Kraft adopted the new pension accounting standards issued by the Financial Accounting Standards Board. In 1985, Kraft adopted the LIFO inventory method of accounting for substantially all domestic inventories. Number of shares and per share data reflect a three-for-one stock split in 1985.

[a] Shareholders' equity for 1986 reflects the spinoff of Premark International, Inc. and the repurchase of shares.

[b] Equity and total capital are year end balances reduced by the net assets of discontinued operations for these ratios.

Exhibit 25-8 **Segments of Business by Classes of Products—Five-Year Summary (In millions)**

		1982	1983	1984	1985	1986
Net Sales	Food Products					
	Retail food	$3,259.2	$3,016.2	$3,182.3	$3,289.9	$3,365.0
	Dairy group	821.2	701.8	591.8	621.4	651.1
	Foodservice group	625.3	686.4	773.3	889.7	1,314.3
	Industrial foods group	437.9	486.3	576.0	531.3	441.6
	International group	1,897.5	1,769.7	1,707.2	1,733.0	2,007.7
	Total	7,041.1	6,668.4	6,830.6	7,065.3	7,779.7
	Consumer Products	576.9	764.4	797.8	854.2	962.5
	Net Sales	$7,618.0	$7,424.8	$7,628.4	$7,919.5	$8,742.2
Operating Profit	Food Products					
	Domestic	$ 365.4	$ 413.2	$ 467.7	$ 579.9	$ 613.9
	International	137.4	165.0	168.5	150.4	190.0
	Total	502.8	578.2	636.2	730.3	803.9
	Consumer Products	46.4	65.0	93.9	82.6	29.9[a]
	Total Operating Profit	$ 549.2	$ 642.2	$ 730.1	$ 812.9	$ 833.8
Identifiable Assets	Food Products					
	Domestic	$1,480.0	$1,430.3	$1,604.5	$1,607.8	$2,378.0
	International	772.7	680.9	701.1	786.4	849.6
	Total	2,252.7	2,111.2	2,305.6	2,394.2	3,227.6
	Consumer Products	493.0	576.1	661.3	757.7	849.6
	Corporate	833.8	1,182.3	875.3	891.3	672.1
	Total identifiable assets of continuing operations	$3,579.5	$3,869.6	$3,842.2	$4,043.2	$4,749.3

[a]After restructuring charges of $37.0 million.

The cost savings from lower commodity prices and possible tax legislation mentioned previously will help companies finance the advertising costs that will continue to be necessary in this highly competitive market. It appears that those firms that can most successfully identify and satisfy the rapidly changing customer needs with strong, high-value-added brands will be the winners in this slow-growth market during coming years.

DART & KRAFT BECOMES DART AND KRAFT

In July 1986, Dart & Kraft Chairman John M. Richman surprised the investment community by announcing that he would divide the corporation into two parts: a new Kraft, Inc., consisting of Kraft's food operations and the Duracell battery business, to be headed by Richman; and a corporation (later named Premark International, Inc.) composed of Tupperware, West Bend, Hobart, and Wilsonart, which would be spun off to shareholders and headed by Dart & Kraft President Warren L. Batts. Richman felt that the Kraft-Duracell combination would be more attractive on Wall Street. He was quoted as saying in reference to the former Dart & Kraft Inc., "Over time we feel Kraft would not be recognized for the power it is in the food industry."[12]

From 1980 to 1985, Dart & Kraft Inc.'s overall operating profit grew at a compound annual rate of 4 percent, while Kraft's rate was 10.3 percent, and Duracell's was 15 percent. During the same period, Tupperware's contribution to Dart & Kraft's earnings fell from 30 percent in 1980 to about 10 percent in 1985. Premark's management must contend with Tupperware's problems, the slow growth of its other units, and the loss of cash flow from the food business.[13]

When the announced spinoff raised questions about the wisdom of the 1980 merger, Richman pointed out that a $1 investment in Dart & Kraft at the time of the 1980 merger would have appreciated to $5.34 by mid June 1986. "The numbers tell it all," said Richman.[14]

FINANCIAL DATA

Exhibits 25-7 to 25-12 present a summary of Kraft, Inc.'s financial performance during recent years as presented in the firm's 1986 *Annual Report.* Inventories are valued at the lower of cost or market. In 1985, costing for virtually all domestic inventories was changed from the FIFO to the LIFO method. The FIFO method is used for other inventories, which represent approximately 43 percent of all inventories. Inventory cost includes cost of raw materials, labor, and overhead. Due to the nature of the business, management considers it impractical to segregate inventories into raw materials, work in progress, and finished goods.

---

[12]James E. Ellis, "Dart & Kraft: Why It'll be Dart and Kraft," *Business Week,* July 7, 1986, p. 33.

[13]Ibid.

[14]Ibid.

Exhibit 25-9 Common Stock Prices and Dividends

| | 1985 | | | 1986 | | |
	High	Low	Dividend	High	Low	Dividend
First quarter	$31 1/2	$27 7/8	$.35 1/3	$53 1/2	$38 7/8	$.39
Second quarter	36 5/8	29 3/4	.39	65 7/8	47 1/2	.43
Third quarter	38 3/8	33 5/8	.39	65	51 3/4	.43
Fourth quarter	44 7/8	36	.39	58 1/2[a]	47 1/8[a]	.43

[a]On October 31, 1986, Kraft, Inc. spunoff the businesses that make up Premark International, Inc.

Exhibit 25-10 Consolidated Statement of Changes in Financial Position (In millions)

	Year ending December 29, 1984	Year ending December 28, 1985	Year ending December 27, 1986
Cash provided from continuing operations			
Net income from continuing operations	$ 353.6	$ 408.0	$ 390.1
Items not resulting in cash flow			
Depreciation and amortization	111.3	112.2	135.5
Deferred income taxes	49.9	39.5	60.8
(Increase) decrease in working capital used in continuing operations (except cash, temporary investments, and borrowings) adjusted for translation	(73.1)	46.5	65.2
Cash provided from continuing operations	441.7	606.2	651.6
Investments			
Capital expenditures	(164.3)	(180.6)	(209.0)
Book value of properties sold	33.6	15.0	12.5
Business acquisitions and divestitures, net	(153.4)	(64.8)	(562.3)
(Increase) decrease in investments and long-term receivables	28.5	(62.2)	45.8
Other, net	9.9	5.7	11.3
Cash used for investments	(254.7)	(286.9)	(701.7)
Financing			
Dividends paid	(208.5)	(219.3)	(234.0)
Purchase of treasury stock	(531.7)	—	(597.7)
Decrease in long-term debt	(33.9)	(72.3)	(114.9)
Increase (decrease) in short-term borrowings	164.6	(135.0)	485.9
Cash used for financing	(609.5)	(426.6)	(460.7)
Cash provided from discontinued operations	167.9	65.6	356.0
Decrease in cash and temporary investments	$(245.6)	$ (41.7)	$(154.8)

Exhibit 25-11 Consolidated Balance Sheet (In millions, except par value)

	December 28, 1985	December 27, 1986
Assets		
Cash, time deposits and certificates of deposit	$ 160.9	$ 194.1
Temporary investments, at cost that approximates market	315.6	127.6
Total cash and temporary investments	476.5	321.7
Accounts and notes receivable, less allowances of $27.4 in 1986 and $19.1 in 1985	734.4	941.7
Inventories	1,115.3	1,211.3
Total Current Assets	2,326.2	2,474.7
Investments and long-term receivables	284.4	246.5
Prepaid and deferred items	115.7	139.6
Property, plant and equipment		
Land	32.6	45.1
Buildings and improvements	495.6	584.6
Machinery and equipment	1,249.5	1,504.7
Construction in progress	90.9	87.8
Total cost	1,868.6	2,222.2
Less—accumulated depreciation	(794.1)	(872.1)
Property, plant and equipment, net	1,074.5	1,350.1
Intangibles, net of accumulated amortization of $55.9 in 1986 and $35.5 in 1985	242.4	538.4
Net assets of discontinued operations	1,047.4	—
Total Assets	$5,090.6	$4,749.3
Liabilities and Shareholders' Equity		
Accounts payable	$ 434.3	$ 551.4
Short-term borrowings	130.0	615.9
Accrued compensation	169.4	193.7
Other accrued liabilities	333.5	447.7
Accrued income taxes	321.4	356.0
Current portion of long-term debt	26.0	118.3
Total Current Liabilities	1,414.6	2,283.0
Long-term debt	438.7	231.5
Deferred income taxes	228.6	284.8
Other liabilities	128.5	152.0
Shareholders' equity		
Preferred stock, $5.00 par value; authorized 150,000,000 shares; issued—none	—	—
Common stock, $1.00 par value; authorized 600,000,000 shares; issued 164,735,955 shares	164.7	164.7
Capital surplus	317.5	33.2
Retained earnings	3,191.8	2,810.9
Treasury stock, 29,457,022 shares in 1986 and 20,402,106 shares in 1985, at cost	(503.3)	(1,074.9)

(*continued*)

Exhibit 25–11　(continued)

	December 28, 1985	December 27, 1986
Unearned portion of restricted stock issued for future services	(1.0)	(.9)
Cumulative foreign currency adjustments	(289.5)	(135.0)
Total Shareholders' Equity	2,880.2	1,798.0
Total Liabilities and Shareholders' Equity	$5,090.6	$4,749.3

Exhibit 25-12　Segments of Business by Geographical Area—Three-Year Summary (In millions)

	1984	1985	1986
Net Sales			
United States	$5,581.1	$5,819.3	$6,278.3
Canada	673.1	638.6	628.6
Latin America	131.6	132.7	106.2
Europe and Africa	929.4	1,060.9	1,445.1
Pacific area	313.2	268.0	284.0
Net sales	$7,628.4	$7,919.5	$8,742.2
Operating Profit			
United States	$ 522.6	$ 623.7	$ 644.7
Canada	81.9	70.1	67.7
Latin America	16.9	18.1	15.2
Europe and Africa	76.8	67.9	69.7
Pacific area	31.9	33.1	36.5
Total operating profit	$ 730.1	$ 812.9	$ 833.8
Identifiable assets			
United States	$2,017.1	$2,060.7	$2,864.9
Canada	217.2	227.2	218.1
Latin America	90.9	75.2	65.5
Europe and Africa	411.8	594.2	710.3
Pacific area	229.9	194.6	218.4
Corporate	875.3	891.3	672.1
Total identifiable assets of continuing operations	$3,842.2	$4,043.2	$4,749.3

Purba-Paschim Trading Company: A Small Business Considers Expansion to Bangladesh

The Purba-Paschim Trading Corporation (PPTC), a Minnesota based small private firm, was established in 1973 with personal equity from Mr. George Fruth and Mr. Richard Fisher. Until 1986, PPTC was engaged in importing seasonal garments and frozen fish from a number of South Asian countries, primarily Bangladesh, India, Sri Lanka, and Thailand, to be sold to retailers located in the midwestern states of the U.S. market. Additionally, the company imported Italian wine to sell to several restaurant chains on a long-term contract basis.

Prior to 1985, company sales had increased about 10 percent per year, with peak sales reaching $13 million. Wine imports contributed 20 to 25 percent of the company's profit. However, with the increased competitive pressures for imported garments, especially those from Thailand, India, and Sri Lanka, it became evident that sales and profits were changing. Both Mr. Fruth and Mr. Fisher felt a need to reassess the changing situation and to develop a new strategy, given the emerging threats and opportunities facing PPTC.

Since Mr. Fruth was busy handling the Italian wine business, Mr. Fisher took the responsibility to study the current market for imported garments and to specifically identify the reasons that PPTC was now having difficulty obtaining favorable prices from the foreign manufacturers.

In his study, Mr. Fisher found that in 1986, PPTC had to buy merchandise from the manufacturers in Thailand, India, and Sri Lanka at higher average prices, which eventually reduced their 1986 profits from garment imports. PPTC was forced to pay higher prices because the local manufacturers of garments, particularly the larger firms, had gained sufficient international marketing expertise to begin exporting their own products without using a trading company.

Until the early 1980s, the local manufacturers in these less developed countries

This case was prepared by Hafiz G. A. Siddiqi, Mankato State University, as a basis for class discussion rather than to illustrate either effective or ineffective handling of an administrative situation. Used by permission from Hafiz G. A. Siddiqi.

(LDCs) preferred to market their products under some kind of joint-venture arrangements with established foreign multinational companies. They did not have the capital, distribution channels, or knowledge of the market to sell their products internationally. Recently the situation had changed and most of the local manufacturers did not need any help from foreign firms to market their merchandise.

Because the local manufacturers have developed their own marketing capability, the companies sell their total output, and thus the available sources of supply for a company like PPTC have been reduced. There are still some local firms who sell their merchandise to buyers like PPTC, although at higher prices. The price has gone up, not because of increased production costs, but because of increased demand. Mr. Fisher concluded, "Since PPTC is a relatively small buyer, we are likely to continue to loose ground against competition. This has already shown up in the reduction of our 1986 profit margin for garment imports from India, Thailand, and Sri Lanka."

Additionally, Mr. Fisher determined that if PPTC continued to depend on these countries for its garment imports, it would face another problem—quota restrictions. Recently, quota restrictions imposed by the U.S. government on the imports from nearly industrialized countries (NICs) and many LDCs, including the three countries that were major sources of supply for PPTC, have been tightened.

For quite some time, the NICs and LDCs enjoyed unrestricted privileges to sell their garments in U.S. markets with reduced import duties. These privileges were granted by many of the industrialized nations to the poor countries with the intent of increasing the latter's share in world trade under the generalized system of preferences (GSP) proposed by the general agreement on tariffs and trade (GATT).

The GSP granted by the United States was intended to help only the underdeveloped countries. Apart from the privilege of paying lower import duties during the initial stages, the United States had almost no restrictions on the quantity of garment imports from such underdeveloped countries as Bangladesh, India, Pakistan, Sri Lanka, and others. But as the number of countries clamoring for special treatment increased, the United States had to impose quotas for individual countries, so that the benefits were equally available to all who were eligible. As a result, countries like India, Thailand, Sri Lanka, and others were assigned a quota, a fixed amount of garments which they individually could export to the United States under GSP.

When Mr. Fisher had completed his description of the problems faced by PPTC, Mr. Fruth asked, "Why should the quota imposed by the U.S. government bother us? We can buy our merchandise in India and Sri Lanka and sell them here as we have been doing." Mr. Fisher responded:

> Although things vary from country to country, there is a typical pattern I can highlight. When the U.S. government assigns a quota to say, Sri Lanka, the Sri Lankan government or its designated agency allocates to the eligible manufacturers or exporters a certain quantity or percentage of the country's total quota for the year. To be entitled

to this allocation, a firm has to go through a very complex process. Foreign firms having wholly owned or joint-venture arrangements usually receive allocation; however in most cases, the amount is usually smaller than the company's capacity. Due to political and other contacts, there are some local firms who receive allocation much higher than their capability to produce. These firms sell their quota at a premium price in the "officially unrecognized market." The general impact of this transaction is a substantial increase in the merchandise prices a company like PPTC has to pay to the local suppliers.

"That means we need to look for new sources of supply in the very near future. We will not be able to compete with the large and established local exporting firms who have larger quotas. And the prices will be higher from the small firms because they can sell their quota to the large locals if we don't pay the higher prices," concluded Mr. Fruth.

"That's right," agreed Mr. Fisher. "As I see it we have two problems. First, the stronger bargaining power of the local manufacturers who have established their own marketing network, and second, the tightening of the quota restrictions imposed by the U.S. government. Our immediate problem is to identify what we're going to do to ensure PPTC's survival and growth."

Recently Mr. Fisher attended a seminar on U.S. trade relations with third world countries. In that seminar he learned that Overseas Private Investment Corporation (OPIC) was created by the U.S. government to extend financial and other assistance to U.S. firms interested in investments in LDCs. He became convinced that PPTC should become involved in direct foreign investment in manufacturing the garments that they were currently importing into the United States. If PPTC could manufacture its products in one of the third world countries, it could increase its margin, and in fact it could increase its sales by reducing prices, since the demand for garments is highly price elastic.

Through initial rough calculations, Mr. Fisher found that if PPTC could establish one garment factory by investing approximately $3 million under a joint-venture agreement with a local partner, the company could increase its present profit margin by 110 percent. Additionally, the joint venture should develop new opportunities for PPTC to expand its business.

Mr. Fisher thought it would be a good idea to find a country that was not subject to strict import quotas, where the labor was cheap, where there was no problem procuring the necessary raw materials and other accessories to keep the plant operational, and most importantly, where adequate government support and protection would be available. Bangladesh appeared to be a country that met the needs Mr. Fisher had outlined.

During the eight weeks that Mr. Fisher collected information on Bangladesh, he met Mr. Abdur Razzaque, an attorney who specialized in international business law. Originally from Bangladesh and now a U.S. citizen, Mr. Razzaque was familiar with the quota problems for garment imports. He had handled two cases of international commercial disputes between U.S. and Sri Lankan firms that had plants at Katunayake export processing zone in Sri Lanka.

While he was dealing with these cases, Mr. Razzaque studied conditions and regulations which are usually applied in the export processing zones in South Korea, Taiwan, Malaysia, India, and Bangladesh. After reviewing the data provided by Mr. Fisher, he was convinced that it was a commercially viable opportunity for PPTC to establish a joint venture plant in the Chittagong export processing zone (CEPZ) in Bangladesh. Mr. Razzaque found it so attractive that he offered to provide one-third of the financing. He also expressed his willingness to use his contacts in Bangladesh to obtain government approval to establish the joint-venture firm.

Mr. Fruth still had reservations and wanted to make certain that he and Mr. Fisher were thoroughly prepared before they met with Mr. Razzaque to discuss an investment in Bangladesh. Mr. Fisher agreed to develop a summary of everything he had learned about the opportunity.

MEMORANDUM

TO: Mr. George Fruth

FROM: Mr. Richard Fisher

SUBJECT: Summary of Information Gathered for Evaluating Joint-Venture Production in Bangladesh

INFORMATION FROM THE U.S. DEPARTMENT OF COMMERCE

Since PPTC is already engaged in the import business, we have had frequent contacts with the U.S. Department of Commerce (DOC). I knew that the International Trade Administration (ITA) of the DOC would have some information on the investment opportunities in Bangladesh.

After talking with officials of ITA/DOC in Washington, I learned that the government of Bangladesh has recently enacted a number of laws to encourage and attract foreign investment in their country. In 1980, the government of Bangladesh passed the Foreign Private Investment (Promotion and Protection) Act which established a legal framework for investment by guaranteeing protection against nationalization or expropriation, promising full indemnification, repatriation of investment, and fair treatment of all commercial claims. Additionally, the Bilateral Investment Treaty was signed in March 1986 between Bangladesh and the United States. It provided for unrestricted currency transfer, compensation for expropriation, dispute settlement procedures acceptable to the U.S. government, and the avoidance of double taxation. This bilateral agreement reduced both political and commercial risks for U.S. investors.

Further efforts have been made to encourage U.S. investment. The governments of the United States and Bangladesh have combined efforts to establish the Bangladesh–United States Business Council, located in Washington, D.C. The council acts as a chamber of commerce whose primary function is to gather and distribute information to American businesspeople who make inquiries concerning investment and other opportunities in Bangladesh.

In talking with the Business Council, I found confirmation for the opportunities in Bangladesh for PPTC. They suggested I contact Mr. James Novak, who has prepared a report on how U.S. investors could utilize the "excellent labor force" of Bangladesh. Mr. Novak worked as the representative of the Asia Foundation in Bangladesh from 1980 to 1984. I contacted the Asia Foundation office in San Francisco and gathered new insight from Mr. Novak. He suggested we consider establishing a factory in Bangladesh's CEPZ to take advantage of the special incentives the government of Bangladesh provides for U.S. investors.

INTRODUCTION TO BANGLADESH

Bangladesh, previously called East Pakistan, emerged as an independent state in 1971. Located in the northeastern part of the Indian subcontinent, it is one of the most densely populated countries of the world with more than 105 million people in a land area the size of Wisconsin. It is also one of the poorest countries, with a gross domestic product (GDP) of less than $15 billion and per capita gross national product (GNP) of approximately $160. About 50 percent of its GDP is generated in the agriculture sector. The industrial and manufacturing sectors in Bangladesh are modest in size, accounting for only about 15 percent and 9 percent of GDP, respectively. Like most of the LDCs, efforts are made to strengthen the country's industrial base. To implement its economic development plans, it is highly dependent on foreign aid, particularly from the United States.

Development of import substitution and export-oriented industries is given high priority. The government's industrial policies are geared to the growth and development of export-oriented and import-substitution industries which are considered essential for earning/saving scarce foreign exchange and the creation of new jobs.

In the past, Bangladesh had only three major exports: jute and jute goods, hides and skins, and tea. In an effort to reduce the dependence on the traditional exports, policy has shifted to accord higher priority to increasing exports of nontraditional items such as garments, shrimp, and leather goods. Industrial policies have recently been reformed under the guidance of the World Bank and the International Monetary Fund, the two major financing institutions for Bangladesh. The reforms include a more realistic exchange rate, import liberalization, and improved support for the private sector.

GOVERNMENT BUREAUCRACY: APPROVAL PROCEDURES

As in other LDCs, there is an incredible amount of time wasted in obtaining approval for an investment proposal. The government has taken special steps to speed the process and reduce bureaucratic red tape. In 1986, the investment approval system was liberalized and almost all restrictions on private investment were lifted. The revised industrial policy reserves only a few industries for the public sector. All other industries (125 of the total of 144) are now treated as free sectors which do not require prior approval, if the investment is funded from the investor's own resources.

FOREIGN INVESTMENT IN BANGLADESH

Because Bangladesh is a new and developing country, foreign investment is very low. As of 1984, total foreign investment was estimated to be as little as US$15.7 million, with an estimated annual average increase of US$4 million. According to the U.S. DOC, the government of Bangladesh recognizes that foreign investment could play a major role in the development of the country and has taken a number of important steps to improve the investment climate. As a result, foreign investors have started considering Bangladesh as a potential export platform.

If PPTC invests in Bangladesh, it would not be the first U.S. company to do so. Pfizer, Squibb, Singer, among others, already have direct investment in Bangladesh. The United States ranks ninth in investment in Bangladesh, behind the United Kingdom, France, Hong Kong, South Korea, Singapore, the Netherlands, Canada, and Sweden.

THE GARMENT INDUSTRY IN BANGLADESH

The garment industry is relatively new in Bangladesh. Although initiated in the 1960s, it did not gain visibility until the late 1970s. When the United States and Western European countries imposed quotas on the imports of garments from Singapore, Hong Kong, Taiwan, and other major suppliers of garments, manufacturers looked for countries which had cheap labor, but were not yet subject to quota restrictions. Bangladesh was such a country in the 1970s.

The country had abundant cheap and quality labor, but suffered from a high rate of unemployment. It was therefore natural for foreign investors to take advantage of the quota-free status of Bangladesh by setting up joint ventures in collaboration with Bangladeshi entrepreneurs. In most cases, the foreign partners had equity participation in hard currency and undertook the marketing responsibility. The local partners bore the primary responsibility for ensuring the needed supply of adequately trained workers who were able to perform the cutting, marking, and trimming activities.

Only labor from Bangladesh is used in manufacturing the garments. More than 80 percent of the garment factory workers are women. The employers prefer to hire female rather than male workers, which has created a cultural conflict in this Muslim dominated society. Most of the country's factories are located in Dhaka, the capital city, and Chittagong, the port city.

The Bangladesh garment industry is totally dependent on imported raw materials. To manufacture export-quality garments, a company needs high-quality fabrics, threads, buttons, and other accessories, including packing materials. None is manufactured in Bangladesh; everything has to be imported. Despite this dependence, the garment industry has experienced phenomenal growth during the 1980s (Exhibit 26-1).

The usual procedure is for a buyer, such as Sears or J.C. Penney's, to contact a garment manufacturer in Bangladesh to sign a contract for cutting, sewing, trimming, packaging, and shipping a series of orders at an agreed schedule. The buyer will provide the designs and detailed specifications for fabric, thread, buttons, and so on to the Bangladeshi firm. Additionally, the buyer will provide the sources (name of the countries and suppliers) from which the various components will have to be imported. If necessary, to procure the correct materials and components, the buyer helps the Bangladeshi firm to open back-to-back letters of credit against which the suppliers ship the materials to Bangladesh. The supplier is paid after the garments are manufactured with the imported materials and shipped to the original buyer. This kind of trade financing has been beneficial to Bangladesh.

Exhibit 26-1   **Exports of Garments from Bangladesh (In million taka)**

Year	Value
1980–1981	120
1981–1982	171
1982–1983	348
1983–1984	983
1984–1985	1,209

Note: The Bangladesh currency is the taka (Tk). The current exchange rate is US$1 = Tk 32. During the last five years the value of the taka depreciated by some 30 percent. One crore = ten million taka.

A NOTE ON EXPORT PROCESSING ZONES

An export processing zone (EPZ) is a legally demarcated geographical enclave in which an authorized firm can bring in imported inputs necessary for manufacturing or processing products exclusively for the purpose of exporting, without paying customs duties. The raw materials, components, accessories, packaging materials, plants, equipment, spare parts, and so on are imported to assemble, manufacture, or process the final products.

Although sometimes used interchangeably, an EPZ is somewhat different from a free trade zone. Although the former is exclusively for export promotion, the latter is used by both exporters and domestic importers. Usually strict application of customs regulations discourages a firm from engaging in the export business. On the other hand, almost all governments want to increase exports. One way to increase exports is to reduce customs barriers. By establishing EPZs, a government virtually removes many bottlenecks. Besides, since the exporters do not have to pay taxes, their cost of production decreases. They can therefore sell the product at a lower price which is likely to increase demand.

It should be noted that freedom from customs regulations is not the only incentive an EPZ provides. Within an EPZ, the host government generally develops required physical facilities and the necessary infrastructure such as readily available power and water supplies, a sewerage system, and telecommunications. In addition, most EPZs provide building facilities to house production, plant, equipment, and inventories. The EPZs are used mostly by the developing countries as a device to attract foreign investors. The EPZs offer to the investors from the United States, Western Europe, and Japan a wide range of support services as well as fiscal and financial incentives.

Fiscal incentives include tax holidays or reductions in corporate taxes and exemption from import duties, excise duties, sales taxes, among others. The financial incentives include the availability of easy loans and credits, freedom from exchange controls, and easy repatriation of capital invested. The host government's objectives are to increase foreign exchange earnings, to create employment, and to gain access to international markets through the multinational corporations who establish factories in the EPZ.

The EPZs are more common in LDCs. More than 30 developing countries have established EPZs. Within Asia, the governments of South Korea, India, Sri Lanka, Malaysia, Indonesia, Taiwan, China, and Bangladesh have authorized EPZs.

BANGLADESH EXPORT PROCESSING ZONE AT CHITTAGONG

In 1982, the Bangladesh government created a new organization, the Bangladesh Export Processing Zone Authority (BEPZA), to be responsible for developing and managing EPZs in Bangladesh. By 1988, BEPZA had established and developed one EPZ in the port city of Chittagong. The zone is located 2.41 km from the principal seaport and 7.24 km from the international airport.

Three types of investments can be made in CEPZ:

Type A: 100-percent foreign owned (including investments by Bangladesh nationals ordinarily residing abroad). For this type, the total investment in the project including the cost of construction, raw materials, and the working capital requirements are financed in foreign exchange from overseas.

Type B: Joint venture between foreign partners and Bangladeshi entrepreneurs residing in Bangladesh. Under this type, the total cost of capital machinery, spare parts, and raw materials may be provided by the foreign partners to be brought in from abroad. The Bangladeshi partners may contribute working capital in the local currency.

Type C: 100-percent Bangladeshi entrepreneurs residing in Bangladesh.

Fiscal and Financial Incentives

A number of fiscal and financial incentives are offered to companies who locate in the CEPZ.

1. Zone enterprises are allowed a five-year tax holiday for all industries. Upon expiration of the initial five-year holiday, rebates of 50 percent of income tax on export sales are allowed.
2. Exemption from income taxes on salaries of foreign technicians are allowed for up to three years.
3. Exemption from income tax on interest of borrowed capital from overseas.
4. For nonresident shareholders, the tax on dividend income is exempted during the period of the tax holiday, if the dividends are reinvested in the same project.

Free Import and Export

Import of capital machinery and spares, instruments, apparatus and appliances, including testing quality control equipment and parts thereof, materials and equipment for construction of building and factories in the zone as well as imported items such as raw materials and packaging materials destined for reexport are freely allowed into the zone. Additionally, complete exemption from excise tax and export duties on goods produced is offered.

Other Privileges

1. Remittance of approved royalties and technical fees.
2. Employment of foreign technicians wherever required.

Exhibit 26-2   Industries Approved March 1983–May 1987

Type	Total No. of Industries	Total Investment Proposed (000 US$)	Total No. of Jobs to Be Created
A	5	9,430	2,584
B	15	8,809	2,433
C	10	3,215	840

3. Exemption from national import policy restrictions.
4. No maximum or minimum ceiling on investment.
5. Freedom of sourcing raw materials, machinery, construction contractors, etc.
6. Freedom for appointing of shipping and C&F agents, etc.
7. Availability of "one window service" facility. The investors need to deal only with the BEPZA for all necessary correspondence.

Performance of the Chittagong Export Processing Zone

Exhibits 26-2 through 26-7 provide additional insights into the functioning of the CEPZ.

FACILITIES AT CEPZ

To facilitate the establishment of the export-oriented industrial units in the EPZ, the BEPZA developed the necessary infrastructure. The land is owned by

Exhibit 26-3   Industries Approved June 1987–September 1988

Type	Total No. of Industries	Total Investment Proposed (000 US$)	Total No. of Jobs to Be Created
A	3	2,033	434
B	1	2,500	270
C	1	354	194

Exhibit 26-4 **Descriptions of the Industries Approved after June 1987**

Banla-Thai Nishikawa Ltd., a wholly Bangladeshi-owned company, established at a
  cost of $1.54 million to manufacture imitation jewelry.
Tariq-Azim Textile Mills, a local-foreign joint-venture textile manufacturing enterprise,
  set up at a cost of $2.5 million.
Youngones Corporation, a wholly foreign-owned ready-made garments manufacturing
  company, established at a cost of $3 million.
Young An Hat Co., a wholly foreign-owned company, set up at a cost of $0.6 million
  to manufacture headwear.
International AAB, a wholly owned foreign electronics company, set up at a cost of
  $2.93 million.

Exhibit 26-5 **Distribution of Industries**

Category	No. of Units Approved	No. of Units in Operation
Garments	8	6
Textiles	3	1
Terrytowel	9	6
Steel chain	1	1
Electronics	5	1
Services	2	2
Acrylic sheet	1	—
Chemical and perfume	2	—
Footwear	2	—
Furniture	1	—
Imitation jewelry	1	—
Total	35	17

Exhibit 26-6 **Additional Information on the Units in Operation**

Type	No. of Units	Total Investment (000 US$)	No. of Jobs Created
A	6	10,330	2,297
B	7	5,500	977
C	4	1,458	76
Total	17	17,288	3,350

Exhibit 26-7 **Export Performance of Chittagong EPZ Enterprises**

Year	Export Value (in 000 US$)	Export Value in Crore Taka
1983–1984	2,164	0.51
1984–1985	4,450	13.79
1985–1986	7,400	22.94
1986–1987	16,474	51.07
1987–1988	23,811	73.80

the government, developed into factories and offices, and then handed over to the investors. The BEPZA constructs what they call "standard buildings" to house the factories for apparel and other industries approved by the government. Some companies construct their own factory buildings according to their own specifications. As of July 1988, eight local and foreign firms had constructed their own factory buildings and nine firms rented "standard buildings" provided by the BEPZA.

After reading the information in the memo provided by Mr. Fisher, Mr. Fruth thought the opportunities for PPTC in Bangladesh appeared to be favorable. Perhaps it was time for the company to grow. He decided to review the material one more time before he went to discuss it with Mr. Fisher. Their meeting with Mr. Razzaque tomorrow should be very interesting.

Case 27

Morningstar Bakery, Inc.

John Pollard was gathering the last of the chocolate cheesecakes so he could start delivery of that morning's bake to his customers. As he started out the door, he glanced at the tray of brownies on the cooling rack. A faint smile crossed his

This case was prepared by D. Michael Fields, The University of North Carolina at Charlotte, as a basis for class discussion rather than to illustrate either effective or ineffective handling of an administrative situation. Used by permission from D. Michael Fields.

face. After months of trying, he and his wife, Terri, had finally agreed on a recipe for a brownie they thought was better than anything presently on the market. Although he had no time to think about it now, he promised himself that he would make a decision by the end of the month on the amount of production time that would be allocated to this product. John knew it was a risk to commit total production to one product, but he was aware of several companies that had taken a single product and achieved a high level of success. John was aware this decision would play an important role in the future success of their bakery operation.

MORNINGSTAR BAKERY

In the 18 months since Morningstar had begun operations, the bakery had realized a moderate but steady increase in its customer base. "We started with no commercial baking experience, but a commitment to quality. I approached a number of restaurants and specialty shops and convinced them to add some of Morningstar's dessert items to their product line on a trial basis. Almost every one turned into a regular customer." John and Terri attributed this success to the consistently high quality of their products. When they began their business, the Pollards decided they would take no shortcuts in the baking of their products—they considered the quality of their products to be a personal reflection on them. In the development of the recipes, Terri insisted on only the highest quality of ingredients (e.g., using butter not margarine), limiting or eliminating preservatives, and hand mixing—rather than using their commercial mixer—when possible. The result was satisfied customers.

John and Terri were comfortable with the manufacturing/supplier role for their business. Neither desired the business to become a retail operation. Because they had no prior business experience, John and Terri were much more comfortable producing the product from guaranteed orders than trying to estimate varying customer demand. Additionally, their location was in the back of a building and was not conducive to pursuing retail sales.

Another area in which the owners took a great deal of pride was the degree of cleanliness of their bakery. Although few of their customers ever saw the bakery, those who did were usually impressed with the condition of the operation. As one person noted, "You know this place has never gotten dirty, because if it had, they could have never have got it this clean."

The couple had been receptive to the needs of their customers. On several occasions, customers had requested additional products the bakery was not presently making. "Most of the time, these 'special requests' are added to the product line since we spent time developing the product." However, this proved to not always be a good short-term business practice as John admitted "sometimes getting stuck making unprofitable items."

The product line being produced in the first quarter of 1988 can broadly be classified into five categories: cheesecake, coffee cake, other cakes, muffins, and miscellaneous snacks (Exhibit 27-1). Although all products were not being produced daily, all were being produced at least once a week and some were being baked several times each week.

The demands of the broad product line had lengthened the total production time and expanded the work day of John and Terri, the bakery's only two employees. "Most weeks, we work a six-day week and average 11 hours a day," said Terri. "There are some friends that could be called in an emergency, but we just don't get sick."

Like many new businesses, Morningstar did not make a profit in its first year of operation. The income statement for 1988 can be seen in Exhibit 27-2. Although the previous year's loss was not unexpected, John was concerned about the prospects for reaching profitability in the near term. He knew that increased volume would help the bakery achieve profitability, but he questioned how much more production time they could handle. Both were apprehensive about the potential impact on product quality if another shift were added. The decision on how to alter the

---

Exhibit 27-1   **Morningstar Bakery Product Line, May 1988**

Item	Unit Price	Ingredient Cost	Margin	Quantity Sold 1/1/88– 4/1/88
Cheesecake				
Plain	$12.00	$4.35	$7.65	95
Chocolate	13.00	6.47	6.53	60
New York	15.50	8.75	6.75	65
Amaretto	13.00	6.72	6.28	9
Coffee cake				
Plain	11.00	5.24	5.76	15
Chocolate chip	6.50	3.99	2.51	2
Other cakes				
Spice	6.50	3.74	2.76	4
Carrot	12.00	7.35	4.65	12
Truffle	8.25	4.93	3.32	36
Pound	10.00	5.13	4.87	80
Muffins				
Bran	6.00 (doz)	2.68	3.32	275
Blueberry	6.60 (doz)	3.25	3.35	80
Pumpkin	6.60 (doz)	3.25	3.35	80
Applenut	6.60 (doz)	3.25	3.35	40
Miscellaneous snacks				
Chocolate oatmeal bars	7.20 (pan)	4.01	3.19	300
Lemon bars	6.00 (doz)	3.68	2.32	35
Blonde brownies	10.00 (pan)	5.13	4.87	120
Cupcakes	4.80 (doz)	2.94	1.86	40

Exhibit 27-2 **Morningstar Bakery Income Statement, 1988**

Sales		$35,710.66
Cost of goods sold		
Ingredients	$13,352.48	
Bakery supplies	770.90	
Labor	123.00	
Samples	16.00	
Total		14,262.38
Gross margin		$21,448.28
Operating expenses		
Kitchen equipment	$ 1,968.39	
Delivery expense	1,917.52	
Salaries—officers	9,450.00	
Rent	3,250.00	
Utilities	2,091.00	
Interest expense	2,267.62	
Depreciation expense	2,978.35	
Amortization expense	857.94	
Insurance	1,384.13	
Advertising	291.50	
Bank charges	113.06	
Maintenance and repairs	308.03	
Office supplies	300.72	
Payroll taxes	878.86	
Taxes and licenses	240.00	
Telephone	799.99	
Miscellaneous	52.98	
Total Expenses		29,150.09
Net income (loss)		$(7,701.81)

product line was complicated by the fact that John believed the bakery was continuing to increase sales in the first quarter of 1988 with its present product line (Exhibit 27-1). Although sales for many retailers are traditionally slowest in the first quarter, John had found that the demand from his customers remained relatively consistent—making it proportionally representative for the year.

John believed the key to long-term profitability was trimming the product line. He knew that from a production standpoint, the optimal situation would be to identify a product with an acceptable contribution margin and dedicate all the production time to that product.

THE BROWNIE

Starting with an old family recipe, Terri began an almost endless series of alterations in an attempt to improve the product. With each iteration, she would test the result on numerous friends. Terri was convinced that their brownie, which drew the hearty approval of the testers, was better than anything available. It contained no preservatives, was made with all natural ingredients, and had a cakelike texture. In addition, the use of pure chocolate (rather than cocoa) gave the brownie a distinctive flavor. John's perceptions of how their brownie compared to some of the competitive products in the market can be seen in Exhibits 27-3 and 27-4.

As with their other products, the use of all natural ingredients created some drawbacks. First, their products were usually higher in calories. Second, they almost always were higher in price.

Initial calculations indicated that the physical cost of the brownie in a 2 × 3 × ¾-inch portion would be $.20 per unit. Individual "pocket" packaging that would need sealing on only one end was estimated to cost $.03 per unit. These costs, given the bakery's desired gross margin of approximately 50 percent and a range of selling costs and retail markup of between 30 and 50 percent, would generate a projected retail price to the consumer of $.75 to $.90 per brownie. The high relative cost not withstanding, the Pollards remained convinced that the quality of their product justified the price. In addition, they were certain that their product would gain easy acceptance in the marketplace.

John and Terri had purposefully not added the chocolate brownie to their product line. They had decided to wait until the decision was made concerning marketing and manufacturing the brownie. The couple wanted to avoid the possibility

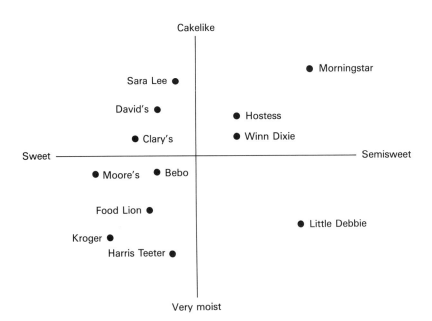

Exhibit 27-3 **Local Brownie Market Dimensioned by Sweetness and Texture**

Exhibit 27-4   **Brownie Product Comparison on Method of Preparation and Ingredient Types**

	Method of Preparation	
	Fully Prepared in Store	**Prepackaged**
All natural ingredients		
Bebo		Bebo
Clary's		Clary's
David's	David's	
Morningstar		Morningstar
Sara Lee		Sara Lee
Some artificial ingredients		
Food Lion	Food Lion	
Harris Teeter	Harris Teeter	
Hostess		Hostess
Kroger	Kroger	
Little Debbie		Little Debbie
Moore's		Moore's
Winn Dixie	Winn Dixie	

of having to discontinue the sale of the chocolate brownie at some point in the future to an existing customer. Nevertheless, a number of their customers had indicated a desire to handle the new product.

THE SNACK FOOD MARKET

The overall snack food industry has shown continued real growth in recent years. For example in 1986, *Business Week* reported that snack food sales have increased 54 percent to $16 billion since 1981. Similar growth has been noted in the sweet goods market, which has been projected at $15 billion for 1987. Total real shipments of bakery products, which are expected to increase 1.5 percent per year over the next four years, are expected to help continue to fuel this growth.[1]

Examples of other segments within the snack food area which have enjoyed recent growth include: (1) a 6 percent increase in cookie and cracker sales (to $5.2 billion) in 1985, (2) a 15 to 25 percent increase in upscale cookies in supermarkets in 1986, (3) the growth of the ice cream novelty market, which has doubled since 1981 and is expected to double again by 1991, and (4) the sale of potato chips growing two to three times faster than the overall population growth of 0.9 percent annually. However, not all snack food segments will enjoy uniform future growth. The

[1]Kimberly Carpenter and Christine Dugas, "Candy May Be Dandy but Confectioners Want a Sweeter Bottom Line," *Business Week,* October 6, 1986, p. 66.

past growth of cookies not withstanding, cookie consumption is expected to drop 0.03 percent in 1987, and a similar decrease is anticipated for the next four years.[2]

Changes in consumer's life-styles have had a dramatic effect on the development of new snack food products. Producers have responded to the national emphasis on health and fitness with snack products that are often high in fiber and low in fat and cholesterol. Ironically, the desire for "healthier" products does not necessarily mean the products will have fewer calories because studies have shown that people now consume 20 percent more calories per capita than they did ten years ago.

Finally, the snack food industry has been aided by the increasing number of women aged 20 to 44 who are working outside the home. In 1986, the total reached 60 percent, an increase of 10 percent since 1980. Because of the increased emphasis on convenience, these two-income families are spending more money per person on food and are particularly interested in prepared, prepackaged foods.

THE LOCAL BROWNIE MARKET

Typically, in each local market, a wide variety of brownies are available in supermarkets, convenience stores, bakeries, and similar type stores. In this market, retail prices ranged from $.99 per dozen for Little Debbie brownies to $.94 each for David's brownies (Exhibit 27-5). One competitor conspicuously absent from the local market was Rachel's Brownies. Rachel had started selling her brownies in 1975 in Philadelphia at a produce shop and an ice cream store. The company marketed an all natural product to those discriminating buyers who were willing to pay a premium for their brownies. By 1985, Rachel's employed 40 people and was producing five million brownies annually. The brownies at that time were being sold through 65 distributors in 35 states. They could be found in both supermarkets (in one-pound tins retailing at $3.79) and convenience stores (for $.75 each). In addition to their store sales, Rachel's had successfully pursued national distribution through mail order catalogs.

Rachel's management had indicated that "meeting the demands of growth is the biggest challenge, but we are determined to approach growth slowly, with deliberation and control, maintaining product quality. . . ." It had been rumored that Rachel's was close to signing an agreement with two distributors that serve the regional market—one operates in Morningstar's market.

THE DECISION

John and Terri Pollard were aware of the Rachel's story. They knew that 13 years ago Rachel's had been in a position not unlike their own and had developed

---

[2]Snack Food Association Management Report, 1987.

Exhibit 27-5   Sample of Competitive Brownies in Area Supermarkets/Convenience Stores

Brownie Name	Packaging Type	Weight (oz)	Price
Convenience Stores			
Bebo	Individual	3.00	$0.49
Clary's	Individual	1.75	0.49
Hostess	Individual	3.00	0.69
Moore's	Individual	1.60	0.49
Sara Lee	Individual	3.00	0.79
Supermarkets			
David's	David's Display	3.00	$0.94
Little Debbie	One dozen box	12.00	0.99
No Name (Food			
Lion)	None, display case	3.00	0.24
No Name (Harris			
Teeter)	None, display case	4.00	0.59
No Name (Kroger)	None, display case	3.00	0.33
No Name (Winn			
Dixie)	None, display case	3.00	0.50

a very successful business. Further, they were both aware that the success realized by Rachel's was not an isolated instance. Other small companies with "special" products had been able to realize substantial sales growth. For example in 1981, "Chipwich"—the popular ice cream and cookie combination—had been marketed from pushcarts on the streets of New York City. The couple felt that their gourmet brownie afforded them a similar opportunity, and they were both excited about the prospects.

John had collected some information to help with the impending decision. To begin with, he calculated the number of brownies that the bakery could produce with its present equipment. Given total dedication to brownies, Morningstar could produce 4,000 to 6,000 units each week. With the addition of a second shift, that initial total could be doubled. The purchase of a second oven (used, for an estimated $2,000) would increase production from 8,000 to 12,000 for one shift and 16,000 to 24,000 for two shifts. The addition of the second oven would necessitate the adding of a third baker to each shift. A second shift with the additional oven would probably be the maximum capacity in the current location.

Morningstar had a great deal more flexibility in its physical facilities than did most small businesses. Although the initial lease period was for three years, John had found the landlord to be "extremely laid back," and he felt that if the situation dictated it, the landlord would even allow Morningstar to break its lease without any penalty.

Existing customers, who had expressed an interest in selling the new brownie, had estimated the volume of the product that they would be able to retail. The

Exhibit 27-6 **Brownie Purchase Estimates of Existing Morningstar Customers**

Customer	Dozen Brownies/Week	Trays of 6 Doz. Brownies/Week
1. Out to Lunch (3 locations)	30	
2. Treats	8	
3. Reed's Supermarket	6	12
4. Wine Shop	2	
5. Eat Out	5	
6. Phil's Deli	9	
7. Berry Brook	2	
8. The Home Economist	4	
9. The Mill	3	12
10. Selwyn's	2	24
11. People's	3	12
12. The Fresh Market	8	
Total	82 doz	60 trays

Exhibit 27-7 **Street Vending Information**

Start-up Costs

Item	Cost
Mall vending packet	$ 5.00
Peddler's license	10.00
Application fee for location	35.00
Cost of purchasing cart	1,000.00
Uniforms for salesperson	150.00
Total	$1,200.00

Presently Licensed Street Vendors

Vendor	Products Sold
1. Halfpenny	Nacho's, baked potatoes
2. TCBY	Yogurt
3. Zackebobs	Shish kebob
4. LaLamas	Hot dogs, drinks
5. Purple Shop	Sundry items
6. John C's	German hot dogs
7. Kwik Way	Hot dogs
8. Larry's	Ice cream
9. Lemon Quench	Drink products
10. Jerry's	Ice cream

volume estimates, as noted in Exhibit 27-6, particularly pleased John since some of the customers had not yet had an opportunity to sample the final recipe.

John, remembering the success that the Chipwich product had enjoyed through the use of pushcarts, had investigated that possibility for Morningstar's new product. Although he had not favored the option initially, John found that the local chamber actually encouraged controlled street vending in areas adjacent to an outdoor plaza that had been developed to increase pedestrian traffic for downtown retailers. More than 40,000 people worked in the immediate area. An estimate of costs to develop a pushcart and those retailers that were already authorized to sell on downtown streets can be seen in Exhibit 27-7.

Two area food brokers had been contacted in an attempt to gauge their level of interest in adding Morningstar's gourmet brownie to their assortment of products. To John's surprise, both were somewhat cool to the idea. In fact, one had indicated that he "would not touch a product that could not guarantee a weekly volume of $6,000."

Finally, John considered the available funding to support the brownie project. John estimated they could get $10,000 from a family member. In addition, he was willing to take on as much debt as possible to get the brownie off the ground. He and Terri had a product they believed in and were willing to do whatever was necessary to succeed. The news that Rachel's might be moving into the market gave John an added sense of urgency.

"We think our gourmet brownie is better than anything on the market and we're willing to do whatever is necessary to get the job done," noted Terri. "We don't know if it's true that Rachel's is going to enter the market, but it probably won't be long."

"We need to be established in the market before Rachel's arrives," commented John. "We've got to make a product line decision soon so we can address the corresponding issues of increasing capacity and required capital. It's clear, if we're going to move, we're going to have to move quickly."

Golden Enterprises, Incorporated

COMPANY ORGANIZATION

Golden Enterprises, Incorporated, is a holding company that owns all of the outstanding shares of Golden Flake Snack Foods, Steel City Group, and the Sloan-Major Agency.

Golden Flake Snack Foods, Incorporated

The Golden Flake Snack Food Company accounts for 95 percent of Golden Enterprises's sales and over 96 percent of the operating profit. A full line of snack foods is manufactured including potato chips, corn and tortilla chips, cheese curls, popcorn, pork skins, roasted peanuts, onion rings, and cheese or peanut butter-filled crackers. Golden Flake snack products are manufactured in Alabama, Tennessee, and Florida and are sold in 13 states.

Steel City Group

The Steel City Group is comprised of Steel City Bolt & Screw, Incorporated, and Nall & Associates, a manufacturer's representative. Nall & Associates has only four employees and operates as part of Steel City Bolt & Screw. Steel City, founded in 1968 and acquired by Golden Enterprises in 1971, has become a leading manufacturer of custom-fabricated products, such as hot headed bolts, sag rods, anchor bolts, U bolts, pole line fasteners, and other bent and threaded items. Its products are sold and shipped nationwide, and some are exported.

Manufacturing is in a modern 80,000-square-foot plant in Birmingham, Alabama. A distribution warehouse in Greenville, South Carolina, was sold July 1986, to enable the company to concentrate its resources on manufacturing of specialty items. Customers include some of the leading American firms in such varied fields as electric utilities, lighting standard manufacturers, transmission towers, railroads, structured steel fabricators, farm equipment, metal buildings, and fastener distributors.

The Steel City Group contributed less than 5 percent to revenues and slightly over 3 percent in profit in 1986.

This case was written by Peter M. Ginter, Linda E. Swayne, and Patricia A. Luna as a basis for class discussion rather than to illustrate either effective or ineffective handling of an administrative situation. Used by permission from Patricia A. Luna.

Sloan-Major Agency

The Sloan-Major Agency is a full-service advertising agency with ten full-time employees. It was acquired by Golden Flake in 1980. Typical agency services are provided including media research and buying, creative development from concept to final copy (including package design), production, development and implementation of marketing programs, and public relations.

The account list for Sloan-Major has expanded from three to 30 clients, representing a variety of consumer, retail, industrial, and corporate accounts. Golden Flake Snack Foods has been its largest account; however Coke and Red Diamond Coffee represented substantial accounts as well. Billings for 1986 were $5 million, placing Sloan-Major among the top ten advertising agencies in the Birmingham area.

COMPANY HISTORY

Magic City Food Products was founded in 1923 in Birmingham, Alabama. Mr. Mose Lischkoff and Mr. Frank Mosher started the company in the basement of a Hills Grocery store in North Birmingham. Introduced as a new item, their fresh, kettle-cooked potato chips caught on quickly.

Helen Friedman was one of the first employees hired. Deemed the "Golden Flake Girl," she was the driving force in Magic City's rapid expansion. In fact, Helen and her mother financed the buy-out of Mr. Mosher's partner, Mose Lischkoff. Miss Friedman married Mr. Mosher in 1928, but later divorced him and received the company in settlement.

Under Helen Friedman's leadership, Magic City Food Products reached sales of almost $1 million by 1946. That year the company was incorporated and sold to the Bashinsky family. One of the first moves of the new owners was to officially change the name of the company to be more descriptive: Golden Flake, Incorporated.

Sloan Bashinsky, the current CEO, bought the company from his father ten years later in 1956. Although he had been one of the charter members of the board of directors and secretary-treasurer, Sloan Bashinsky had worked his way up through both route sales and production. He initiated the construction of Golden Flake's current Birmingham plant and later two additional plants in Nashville, Tennessee, and Ocala, Florida.

In 1968 the company became a public corporation and diversified into insurance, real estate, fasteners, and advertising. In 1977 Golden Flake Snack Foods became a wholly owned subsidiary of the holding company, Golden Enterprises, Incorporated. Exhibit 28-1 outlines company history.

The company has had steady sales growth. Since 1946 when $1 million in sales was achieved, Golden Flake Snack Foods has doubled sales every five years. In the

Exhibit 28-1	**Company History Summarized**
1985	Ocala, Florida manufacturing plant began operation
1979	Sloan-Major Advertising Agency formed as a wholly owned subsidiary
1977	Golden Enterprises, Incorporated, a holding company was formed; Golden Flake Snack Foods became a wholly owned subsidiary
1968	Became public corporation
1966	Don's Foods (Nashville company) purchased
1948	Renamed Golden Flake, Incorporated
1946	Incorporated and purchased by the Bashinsky family
1923	Magic City Foods started by Lischkoff and Mosher

1987 *Annual Report,* Golden Enterprises had total revenues of over $123 million (Exhibit 28-2).

THE SALTED SNACK FOOD MARKET: INDUSTRY PROFILE

Snack foods have been around for over two centuries. Snack is actually a Dutch word that means "to bite." Thus, snacks are bite-sized foods perfect for quick meals or quick energy. Sales of salted snack foods have steadily increased, and in fact, tripled over the last decade. However, projections are that sales will slow to a 9 percent increase over the next ten years. Sales volume for 1985 was $7.05 billion and increased 8.19 percent in 1986 to $7.63 billion.

The salted snack food market has been a relatively small portion of the total snack food market. Confectionary items (candy bars, candy morsels, etc.) constitute the greatest percentages of snack food sales (Exhibit 28-3).

Forty-seven percent of the salted snack food market was potato chip sales. Corn/tortilla chips represented 23.3 percent of industry sales. The remaining one-

Exhibit 28-2	**Golden Flake Snack Foods Sales and Income History** **(In thousands of dollars, fiscal year)**								
	1979	1980	1981	1982	1983	1984	1985	1986	1987
Total revenues	$42,831	$50,348	$58,681	$70,253	$81,218	$95,991	$112,289	$115,064	$116,617
Operating profit	$ 5,478	$ 5,026	$ 6,078	$ 9,560	$12,254	$15,664	$ 14,495	$ 11,608	$ 14,960

Exhibit 28-3   All Snack Food Sales 1986

	Sales 1986 (In millions)	Percent
Candy	$7,400	29.9
Cookies/crackers	5,627	22.8
Potato chips	2,977	12.0
Corn/tortilla chips	1,462	5.9
Snack cakes/pies	1,240	5.0
Nuts/meats	1,160	4.7
Frozen pizza	1,063	4.3
Imported and misc.	606	2.4
Dried fruit	508	2.1
Hot snacks	440	1.8
Extruded snacks	456	1.8
Meat snacks	400	1.6
Popcorn	382	1.5
Granola snacks	359	1.4
Pretzels	293	1.2
Other	396	1.6

Source: Snack Food Association, June 1987.

---

fourth of the market consisted of popcorn, cheese curls, pork rinds, pretzels, and salted nuts sales (Exhibit 28-4).

Sales volume in 1986 was up 8.19 percent over 1985, which had been a disappointing year in the industry. One regional executive speculated that the reason 1985 sales were "off" was the relatively prosperous economy. "The snack food market

---

Exhibit 28-4   Salted Snack Food Sales Volume by Product Type

Product	1985 Sales		1986 Sales	
	In Millions	Percent	In millions	Percent
Potato chips	$3,298.1	46.8	$3,580.0	47.0
Corn/tortilla chips	1,638.8	23.3	1,780.0	23.3
Salted nuts	930.7	13.2	986.8	12.9
Pretzels	341.8	4.8	366.4	4.8
Salted meat snacks	340.8	4.8	348.4	4.8
Extruded snacks	321.1	4.6	342.6	4.5
Popped popcorn	177.6	2.5	221.7	2.7
Total	$7,048.9		$7,625.9	

Source: Snack Food Association Management Report, 1987.

does well in recessionary times and suffers when the economy is better and people spend part of their greater disposable income to dine out." Fast-food restaurants are estimated to obtain approximately 48 percent of the $112 billion spent for food in the United States.

Potato Chips

Potato chip sales totaled $3.58 billion in 1986, an increase of 9.4 percent over 1985. Barbecue was the most popular flavored potato chip. Several new flavors such as cajun spiced and jalapeno were introduced but had not achieved much market share. Frito-Lay's "Jalapeno and Cheddar" pushed Lay's brand up 15 percent (Exhibit 28-5).

Corn/Tortilla Chips

Corn/tortilla chip sales were down in 1984 and 1985 but up 8.3 percent in 1986. Double-digit growth rates had occurred from 1980 through 1983. The product category seems to have matured and despite introductions of new flavors in 1985, sales grew less than anticipated. However, it is difficult to obtain accurate data for tortilla chip sales due to the number of small producers in California and the Southwest.

The total sales for the category were considered to be $1.78 billion, with tortilla chips accounting for two-thirds of that amount. It appears that corn chips and *not* tortilla chips have been responsible for the declining sales in this product category (Exhibit 28-6).

Exhibit 28-5   **Industry Averages: Potato Chips Sales by Flavor and Type**

Flavors	Percent in 1985	Percent in 1986
Salted/unsalted unflavored chips	70.8	61.0
Barbecue-flavored chips	11.5	19.1
Cheddar cheese-flavored	6.4	1.8
Sour cream and onion	5.9	3.1
Salt and vinegar	2.2	1.7
Others	3.2	3.3
Types		
Regular chips	60.4	55.6
Rippled/ridged	33.0	33.4
Thick homestyle	6.6	5.3
Kettle style	n/a	5.7

Source: Snack Food Association 1987 Management Report.

Exhibit 28-6   **Industry Averages: Corn/Tortilla Chip Sales by Flavor**

Corn Chips	Percent in 1985	Percent in 1986	Tortilla Chips	Percent in 1985	Percent in 1986
Unflavored (salted)	72.2	65.3	Nacho cheese	58.0	53.0
Barbecue	23.9	27.8	Unflavored (salted)	33.9	37.4
Nacho cheese	3.1	0.4	Other	6.1	3.6
Other	0.6	0.9	Cheddar cheese	2.0	0.2
Unflavored (unsalted)	n/a	5.7	Jalapeno	n/a	3.3
			Unflavored (unsalted)	n/a	2.7
Total Sales $614.0 million			Total Sales $1,170.0 million		

Source: Snack Food Association 1987 Management Report.

Extruded Snacks

Extruded snacks are products that have the shape defined as the product is pushed (extruded) through machinery. Although sales were up 6.7 percent in 1986, the extruded snacks share of the overall snack market declined slightly from 4.5 percent in 1985 to 4.4 percent in 1986 (Exhibit 28-7).

Salted Meat Snacks (Includes Pork Rinds)

Sales of salted meats increased from $340.8 million in 1985 to $348.4 million in 1986. Sales of pork rind products dropped 10 percent while other meat snack sales increased 5.3 percent. Salted meats account for 4.8 percent of the salted snack food market (Exhibit 28-8).

Exhibit 28-7   **Extruded Flavors**

	Percent of Market
Cheddar cheese	61.0
Unflavored	12.7
BBQ	8.2
Nacho cheese	5.1
Sour cream and onion	0.1
Other	12.9

Source: Snack Food Association 1987 Management Report.

Exhibit 28-8   **Pork Rind Flavors**

	Percent of Market
Unflavored	55.6
BBQ	29.1
Nacho cheese	1.1
Other	14.2

Source: Snack Food Association 1987 Management Report.

Popped Corn/Pretzels/Nuts

Popped popcorn is a salted snack product that had phenomenal growth in 1981 and has attempted to maintain double-digit increases each year. Sales in 1986 were up 25.7 percent over 1985, to $221.7 million.

Nationally, consumers are concerned about sodium intake which may have affected the sales of pretzels and salted nuts. Sales of these products were up slightly over 4 percent for 1985. In 1986, pretzels were up 7.9 percent to $366.4 million and nuts were up 6.7 percent to $986.8 million.

SALTED SNACK FOOD INDUSTRY AVERAGES

Companies with sales over $50 million reported pretax profit margins of 6.14 percent for 1986, down from 9.4 percent in 1985.

In the salted snack food industry, the average has been for cost of goods manufactured to be 55.2 percent of sales, selling and freight have been 23.9 percent, marketing and advertising averaged 9.3 percent of sales, general administrative expenses were 5.5 percent, and pretax income was 6.14 percent of sales.

Within the industry, companies averaged 6.4 percent of gross sales for promotional activities. Advertising accounted for 4.3 percent of gross sales. Promotions, both trade and consumer, accounted for 7.44 percent of gross sales (Exhibit 28-9).

It appears that most new product development in the industry is left up to Frito-Lay and other large, national manufacturers. Only 24.5 percent of the snack food manufacturers introduced a new product in 1985. However, 48.9 percent introduced line extension products (new size, new flavor of existing product, etc.).

The salted snack food market is growing at a rate of approximately 8.19 percent per year and reached $7.63 billion in total sales in 1986. The major products, such as potato chips and corn chips, have reached the maturity stage of the product

Exhibit 28-9	Average Allocation of Promotional Dollars in Snack Food Industry, 1985		
Promotional Activity	Percent of Gross Sales	Percent of Promotional Budget	
Advertising	3.1		
Print		45.2	
Radio		25.8	
Television		19.3	
Other		9.7	
Promotions	3.3		
Trade		60.6	
Consumer		39.4	

life cycle, although innovative products like granola balls and mixed snacks have been recently introduced.

Currently, the snack chip market is about 1.32 percent of the total food industry and is expected to keep growing. Snack chips are projected to make up 1.66 percent of food industry sales by 1995 (according to USDA statistics) as a result of rising per capita income and increasing snack food purchases.

Competition, especially from the large marketing-knowledgeable companies such as Frito-Lay, Borden, and Eagle, is expected to be strong in the future. Consolidation has occurred in the industry and is expected to continue.

Among consumers, health concerns and more meals eaten away from home will reduce the purchases of salted snack food products. Most meals eaten away from home are in fast-food restaurants that do not serve chips.

THE COMPETITION

Frito-Lay, a subsidiary of Pepsico, Incorporated, is Golden Flake's major competition through the Southeast. Such familiar names as Fritos, Lay's, Ruffles, O'Grady's, Cheetos, Doritos, and Tostitos are all Frito-Lay products. This formidable competitor owns 50 percent of the salted snack food market. The company has "state-of-the-art" manufacturing facilities in North Carolina, Connecticut, and Indiana, and has an extensive direct retail store delivery distribution system using company-owned, tractor-trailer trucks.

Other competitors have spikes of excellence, producing some very competitive brands for Golden Flake. Some are national in market coverage and others, like Golden Flake, are regionally oriented. A summary of Golden Flake's salted snack food competitors is presented in Exhibit 28-10.

Exhibit 28-10 Competitive Summary

Competitor	Sales (In millions)	Snack Brands	Market
American Brands, New York	$ 730	Sunshine, Bell, Bluebell Compadres, Squiggles, Humpty-Dumpty	United States and Canada
Anheuser-Busch, St. Louis	6,500	Eagle Snacks Cape Cod (Northeast, Florida)	National roll-out in 1987
Borden, Inc., New York	4,710	Cheez Doodles, Cottage Fries, New York Deli, Wise, Granny Goose	United States
Charles Chips (Mussers Potato Chips), Pennsylvania	*a*	Charles Chips	38 states and inter-national
Clover Club Foods, Vermont	50	Clover Club	Northeastern United States
Adolph Coors Company, Colorado	1,280	Coors Chips	7 western states
Culbro Corporation (Snacktime Co.—Indiana), New York	1,090	Tiras, Indian Corn, Chips, Cornies, Pepitos	14 midwestern states
Frito-Lay, Texas	2,500	Fritos, Lays, Ruffles, O'Grady's Muchos, Cheetos, Doritos, Tostitos, Funyuns, Rold Gold	United States
G. Heileman Brewing Co., Wisconsin	1,160	Barrell O'Fun, Red Seal	Southwestern states, Minnesota and Maryland
Keebler Company, Illinois	876	Krunch Twists, Potato Skins, Cheeblers	United States
Lance, Incorporated, North Carolina	355	Lance, Gold-n-Cheese, Lanchos	35 eastern states and D.C.
Mike-Sell's Tennessee	29	Mike-Sell's	Tennessee, Ohio
Moore's Inc., Virginia	*a*	Moore's chips	8 mid-Atlantic states
Nabisco Brands, Inc., New Jersey	6,370	Planters	United States
Procter & Gamble, Inc., Ohio	15,400	Pringles	United States

Exhibit 28-10   (continued)

Competitor	Sales (In millions)	Snack Brands	Market
Ralston-Purina Co., St. Louis	5,860	Chex Snack Mix	United States
Southland Corp., Texas	12,700	Pate, El-Ge, private labels	Northwestern, mid-western states
Zapp's, Louisiana	*a*	Zapp's	Louisiana, Mississippi, Florida
Tom's, Georgia	230	Tom's	United States

*a*Privately held, sales volume not available.

GOLDEN FLAKE SNACK FOODS, INCORPORATED

Corporate Goals

Although Golden Flake is the market share leader in Alabama, the company knows that being number one in other states is an unrealistic goal given the resources of the industry leader Frito-Lay. Generally, the corporate objective is to be the leader in Alabama and a very strong number two in all other markets.

Golden Flake's number one goal is quality. The company believes the quality goal can be achieved by setting the standard for the industry in production, taste, freshness, and productivity.

Another goal is to provide exceptional service and to deliver the freshest products. Despite its high cost, the direct-delivery distribution system is considered to be the best way to continue to accomplish this goal.

Further, Golden Flake has the objective to double sales dollars every five years. This was an original goal of the company that has been met since it was acquired by the Bashinsky family in 1946.

Finally, Golden Flake wants to attract and retain the best employees in the industry. Although over 1,700 people are employed by Golden Flake, the company has continued to emphasize a family atmosphere by including employees in stock purchase plans and quarterly small group meetings.

Management

Golden Flake's organizational chart illustrates the company's management philosophy (Exhibit 28-11).

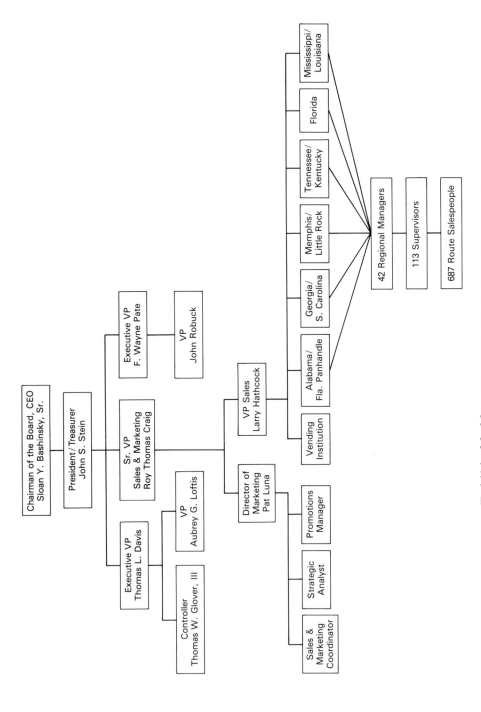

Exhibit 28-11   **Golden Flake Snack Foods Management**

508

Golden Flake 1987 Operating Results

Corporate income was down slightly in 1986 due to the small increase in revenues that were insufficient for the increased costs associated with the greater production capacity acquired over the last two years. Capital expenditures of $30.5 million during 1985 and 1986 were financed out of working capital. The company has no debt resulting from the capital expansion. The results for 1987 have shown improvement over 1986.

No major new products had been introduced in 1986 (although Cheese Puffs were included as a line extension). The company strategy was for market penetration-increased sales in existing markets with existing products. Southern Farms brand Mesquite potato chips were introduced in July 1987, and Ranch-flavored Tortilla Chips in October 1987.

Productivity

In 1985 significant expansion for Golden Flake was completed. A new snack food plant was constructed in Ocala, Florida, a corn tortilla line was added to the Nashville plant, and major renovations to conveying and packaging equipment were completed at the Birmingham facility. Three satellite warehouses were built in the Birmingham area. As a result of these expansions and improvements, Golden Flake is now in the strategic position to increase sales volume by up to 50 percent without any significant capital expenditures on plant or equipment.

Golden Flake has "state-of-the-art" processing and packaging equipment that allows for efficient use of raw materials. The new plant in Ocala, Florida utilizes the latest technologies. These modern facilities enable Golden Flake to compete with Frito-Lay in quality, taste, and freshness.

By establishing manufacturing plants in Ocala, Florida, and Nashville, Tennessee, Golden Flake has been able to provide quick delivery to customers in these areas. (See Exhibit 28-12 for location of manufacturing sites.) The Ocala plant can produce 2,100 pounds of potato chips per hour plus either 1,400 pounds of tortilla chips or 1,000 pounds of corn chips per hour.

A newly constructed potato warehouse in Birmingham will store 20 million pounds of potatoes in an atmosphere that is computer controlled for temperature and humidity. The warehouse utilizes hydraulic lifts, conveyer systems, and water flumes for unloading trucks and moving the potatoes to cleaning or storage. Potato warehouses help to ensure that temporary fluctuations in potato supply do not have a significant impact on company operations.

As capacity has increased, expanded markets have been sought. Originally selling only in the Birmingham area, Golden Flake now sells in 13 states in the Southeast.

Marketing Strategy

Golden Flake does not purport to be a leader in the snack food market. The company has been using a follow-the-leader strategy. For example, when Frito-Lay developed "O'Grady's" brand of cheese-flavored potato chip, Golden Flake introduced "au gratin" potato chips, which were withdrawn in late 1986 and replaced by a cheese-flavored chip.

The company feels that its distribution system will be useful for future growth. Company-owned trucks, driven by company employees, are important in providing outstanding service to customers and controlling distribution costs.

Moreover, the direct distribution system allows for expansion into new territories by what the company calls the "ink blot" method. Golden Flake has expanded its market territory gradually outward in every direction from Alabama. It is not willing to skip or jump over a large area of rural population to get to a city. Although the company is nearing Cincinnati and entered Louisville in the fall of 1986, it has not missed the potential customers in northern Kentucky or southern Ohio before reaching for the larger consumer markets.

Market Share.   Golden Flake represents only a small part of the total snack food market both in terms of geographical markets and sales volume. Nationally, Frito-Lay is the market leader with a 40-percent share. However, Golden Flake has had the largest market share in Alabama until 1987 (Exhibit 28-12). In the recent expansion states of Arkansas, Kentucky, Louisiana, and Ohio, the company's products are increasing in market share.

Positioning.   Research on consumer perceptions has developed a competitive price-quality positioning map (Exhibit 28-13) different from the map the company believes reflects the actual positions in the marketplace (Exhibit 28-14).

Although Golden Flake's positioning is similar to its competitors, its target market is different. Moore's is the only company with a similar target market; however it appears to be a significant competitor only in Tennessee at this time.

Target Market.   Demographically Golden Flake has defined the target market as:

- Women aged 20 to 44.
- Families with two or more children.
- Upper-lower to middle income.
- Blue and gray collar (homemakers, sales, clerical, craftpersons, farmers, manufacturing, service, etc.).
- High school graduate or college graduate.
- Rural roots, nontransient.

Exhibit 28-12   **Golden Flake Market Share by State**

	Percent in				Percent in		
	1986	**1987**	**1988**		**1986**	**1987**	**1988**
Alabama				**Tennessee/Kentucky**			
Golden Flake	40	36.3	44.3	Frito-Lay	60	57.4	49.8
Frito-Lay	35	43.8	36.2	Golden Flake	21	10.1	18.7
Pringles	7	7.2	6.4	Pringles	2	7.0	8.5
Tom's	5	6.2	3.8	Moore's	4	*a*	2.6
Eagle	1	2.6	3.0	Tom's	5	2.1	2.0
Others	12	3.9	6.3	Others	8	23.4	18.4
Georgia				**Florida**			
Frito-Lay	59	59.0	48.5	Frito-Lay	60	62.7	49.8
Golden Flake	21	11.2	18.4	Golden Flake	10	6.4	10.8
Pringles	5	7.6	7.1	Tom's	6	8.2	10.0
Wise	5	3.6	4.8	Pringles	3	*a*	7.3
Tom's	5	4.0	3.4	Eagle	2	*a*	6.8
Moore's	0	.4	.8	Wise	5	*a*	5.0
Others	5	14.2	17.0	Others	14	22.7	10.3
Louisiana/Mississippi[b]				**Memphis/Little Rock**[b]			
Frito-Lay		62.1	45.6	Frito-Lay		70.3	62.6
Golden Flake		13.0	18.8	Golden Flake		10.5	16.8
Tom's		2.9	3.6	Tom's		4.2	2.8
Others		22.0	32.0	Others		15.0	17.8

[a]Share changed, included with "others." ·
[b]New markets, 1986 data not available.
Source: Neilson Market Research Data, June 1, 1988.

The psychographic characteristics are very traditional:

- Two income, hard working.
- Strong work ethic, traditional values such as God, country, family, and home.
- Belongers, conformers.

Purchases are for a regular use occasion, and the dominant buying motive is value. The target customer is interested in quality (determined by taste, freshness, and crispness) at a reasonable price. Loyalty has been strong but is no longer necessarily true as higher discounting has made consumers more price sensitive. Approximately 75 percent of buyers purchase the same brand consistently. Children are purchase influencers. Over 87 percent of purchases are made in grocery stores.

The market potential for this segment is considered to be 35 to 42 percent of the salted snack food market.

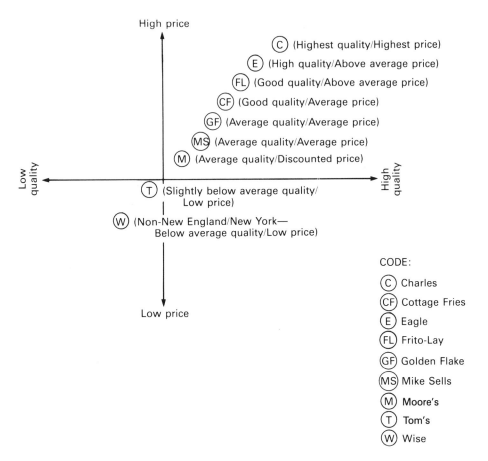

High price

C (Highest quality/Highest price)

E (High quality/Above average price)

FL (Good quality/Above average price)

CF (Good quality/Average price)

GF (Average quality/Average price)

MS (Average quality/Average price)

M (Average quality/Discounted price)

Low quality ← → High quality

T (Slightly below average quality/ Low price)

W (Non-New England/New York— Below average quality/Low price)

Low price

CODE:

C Charles
CF Cottage Fries
E Eagle
FL Frito-Lay
GF Golden Flake
MS Mike Sells
M Moore's
T Tom's
W Wise

Exhibit 28-13   **Competitive Positioning Price-Quality Customer Perception**

Geographically, Golden Flake has followed the "ink blot" strategy from Alabama to the surrounding states. The acquisition of the Tennessee plant and the construction of the Florida plant have enabled the company to increase its geographical market area. Exhibit 28-15 indicates the current geography served by Golden Flake.

Product.   Golden Flake's product line is characterized as mature products with low-involvement purchasing. Nearly 85 percent of snack products are impulse purchases.

Potato chips of various types make up over 54 percent of Golden Flake's product line. The next major contributor to sales volume has been tortilla chips, with approximately 9.6 percent of sales. Corn chips, cheese products, pork skins, pop-

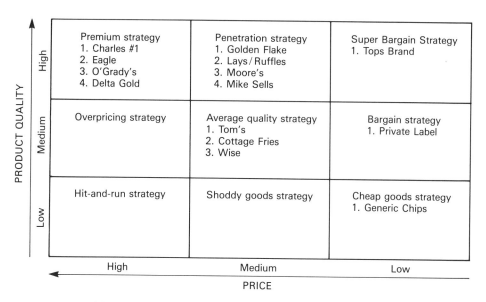

Exhibit 28-14   **Positions in the Market—Company Perception**

corn, and others contributed lesser percentages to sales volume (Exhibit 28-16). Snack foods in general are in the maturity stage of the product life cycle.

Golden Flake's cash cow is the potato chip. Golden Flake is considered to be an exceptional name by the company because it represents two very desirable attributes of a potato chip—golden in color and flaky in texture.

To make potato chips, a potato is washed, peeled, sliced, and then fried for about two minutes in vegetable oil. Although many might consider potato chips to be junk food or "empty" calories, potato chips do offer nutritional value in a diet.

Fresh potatoes are approximately 80 percent water. In the quick frying of chips, most of the water is boiled away, leaving a dehydrated potato much as a raisin is a dehydrated grape. A one-ounce bag of chips has most of the nutrient value of 3.5 ounces of fresh peeled potato. Specific nutrition information is included in Exhibit 28-17.

In addition, the company distributes a line of cake and cookie items and pretzels and nuts manufactured by others.

Product quality is a major criterion for Golden Flake. Quality testing is continuous. Chips are tested for color, size, amounts of salt, oil absorption, and the number of defective chips—those with brown spots or holes. Product testing is done in a very modern quality control laboratory and through live consumer taste tests.

Golden Flake is perceived to be of high quality and freshness by many customers. However, Frito-Lay is generally perceived to have higher quality. To illus-

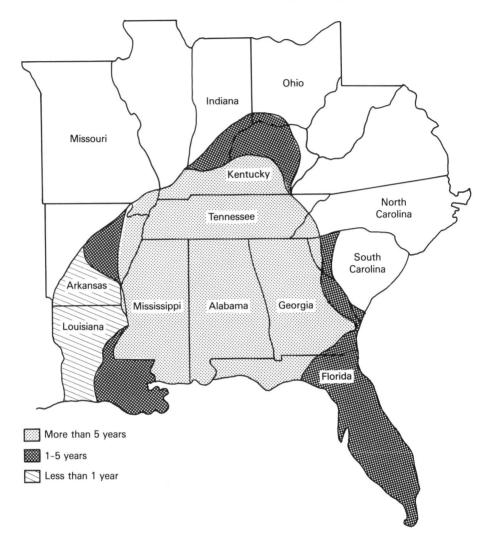

Exhibit 28-15   **Golden Flake Market Area**

trate, a study in Tennessee indicated that Golden Flake had 97 percent aided awareness but only 20 percent market share. Exhibit 28-18 shows results of a recent
consumer study in Tennessee. Using machine-controlled, scientific testing, Golden
Flake's product meets higher standards for color, size, amount of salt, oil absorption, and defective chips than Frito-Lay's Lay's brand, yet these factors are not
perceived by the market.

New product development is based on customer requests, competitive moves,

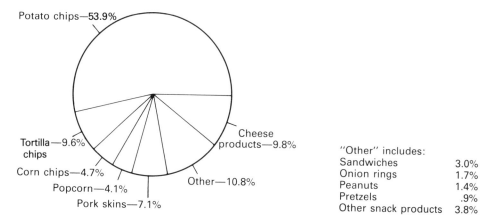

Potato chips—53.9%

Tortilla—9.6% chips

Corn chips—4.7%

Popcorn—4.1%

Pork skins—7.1%

Other—10.8%

Cheese products—9.8%

"Other" includes:
Sandwiches	3.0%
Onion rings	1.7%
Peanuts	1.4%
Pretzels	.9%
Other snack products	3.8%

Exhibit 28-16   **Golden Flake Sales by Product—as of June 30, 1987**

and sales force suggestions. Frito-Lay leads the industry in marketing effort and research and development. Recently, Frito-Lay spent $50 million to develop a new potato chip, "O'Grady's." Frito-Lay introduced Delta Gold in 1986–1987. It was thought to be aimed directly at Golden Flake, as it was introduced only in the Southeast.

Delta Gold has cannibalized sales of O'Grady's. Frito-Lay Cool Ranch Dorito Chips achieved first year sales of $100 million; General Foods introduced Ranch-Style Tortilla Chips in October 1987.

Acknowledging that Golden Flake cannot and does not expect to make that kind of research and development commitment, the company has elected a "follow-the-leader" strategy in product development. Golden Flake has introduced "au gratin" potato chips to compete with the O'Grady's brand. Almost nothing was

Exhibit 28-17   **Potato Chip Nutrition Information**

Nutrition Information per Serving		Percentage of U.S. Recommended Daily Allowances (U.S. RDA)			
Serving size	1 ounce	Protein	2	Calcium	*
Calories	150	Vitamin A	*	Iron	2
Protein	2 grams	Vitamin C	10	Vitamin B	4
Carbohydrate	14 grams	Thiamine	2	Phosphorus	4
Fat	10 grams	Riboflavin	*	Magnesium	4
		Niacin	6		

Source: Potato Chip/Snack Food Association, 1986.

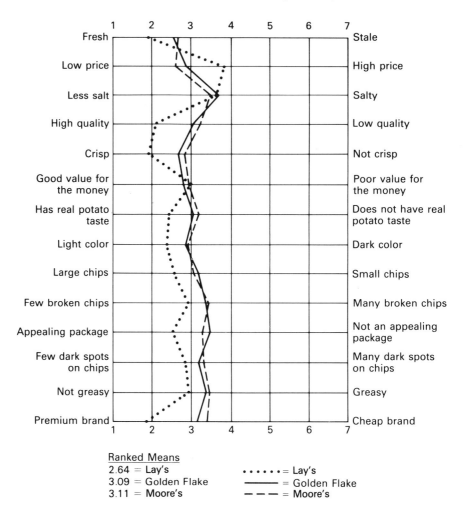

Ranked Means
2.64 = Lay's   •••••• = Lay's
3.09 = Golden Flake   ———— = Golden Flake
3.11 = Moore's   – – – = Moore's

Exhibit 28-18   **Average-Respondent Profile Comparisons of Golden Flake, Lay's, and Moore's—Knoxville, Tennessee 1985**

spent to develop au gratin chips as Frito-Lay's experience was used. Au gratin chips were discontinued in 1986 because of poor sales and replaced by cheese chips.

Golden Flake uses a metalized plastic bag or a foil bag that is heat sealed, providing product freshness for up to eight weeks. Freshness dating is stamped on the bag as a guarantee and to generate customer awareness of the freshness of the product. Packaging costs average approximately 11 percent of manufacturing costs at Golden Flake versus approximately 14 percent for the industry.

Several colors are used to differentiate the various flavors of chips and other snacks. The logo common to all packages is a "cloud" containing the Golden Flake name in block letters (Exhibit 28-19). The type face (style of type) differs for each product category.

Pricing.   Golden Flake prices its products to be competitive. Prices and package sizes are very similar to Frito-Lay and the rest of the industry. Pricing across the industry, especially in potato chips, is very standard. An audit of retail prices in Birmingham for several products indicates that Golden Flake's prices, at least at retail, are in line with competition. Exhibit 28-20 includes prices for selected Golden Flake products. Direct price comparisons by consumers is complicated by the great variety in package size—3 1/2 oz. versus 3 1/8 oz. for example.

Pricing for snack foods is complicated by the fluctuating costs of the commodity products (potatoes and corn) used as ingredients. Golden Flake buys raw materials used in manufacturing on the open market under contract through brokers and directly from growers. A large part of the raw materials used by the company are farm commodities and are subject to drastic changes in supply and price (Exhibit 28-21).

The company trades in farm commodity futures to reduce risk and control costs. Company costs and expenses have risen in part due to inflation, but efficient purchasing, increased volume, improvements in production, distribution, administration, and increased sales prices have allowed the company to maintain a profit margin above the industry average.

Distribution.   Distribution is concentrated in grocery stores and convenience stores with a minimal effort directed to mass merchandisers. Since snack products are perishable with a shelf life of approximately six to eight weeks, Golden Flake uses direct-to-retail-store delivery.

The direct-store-delivery system allows for quicker delivery, which maintains freshness, and less handling, which reduces damage to the product. In addition, the fact that company salespersons stock the racks in the store ensures that the rack looks right, the stock is rotated for freshness, and the display is prepared in a way most conducive to impulse buying by the customer.

Exhibit 28-19   **Golden Flake Package Design**

Exhibit 28-20 **Retail Prices for Selected Golden Flake Snack Foods in the Birmingham Market, October 1987**

Product	Golden Flake Suggested Retail Price
1¾ oz. corn chips	$0.39
7½ oz. corn chips	1.29
8 oz. cheese curls	1.29
1⅛ oz. potato chips	0.39
6½ oz. potato chips	1.39
10 oz. potato chips	1.89
16 oz. potato chips	2.49
6½ oz. tortilla chips	1.39
11 oz. nacho chips	2.09
1⅛ oz. peanuts	0.39
5 oz. popcorn	1.29
3½ oz. pork skins	1.39
11 oz. pretzels	1.19

Since the primary expense to any grocer is the cost of labor, the direct-delivery system provides the store substantial savings in labor cost as well as warehousing cost. To provide this service to retailers, the company has a chain of 20 company-owned sales warehouses with several others in various phases of development from planning to construction.

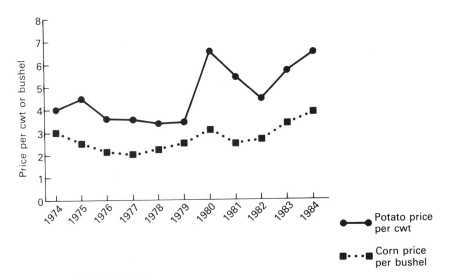

Exhibit 28-21 **Raw Material Price Trends—Potatoes and Corn**

The company warehouses range in size from 2,400 to 8,000 square feet. They are constructed in locations within a marketing area where there is a large enough concentration of routes to make ownership feasible (Exhibit 28-22). The leased warehouses in small areas are unmanned and each salesperson is assigned his or her own secured area. The salesperson is responsible for ordering and inventory control. The larger warehouses have a clerk to handle this function for the sales representatives assigned to the facility.

A fleet of over 1,000 company-owned and maintained vehicles is used to provide service directly to the retail stores. The direct-store-delivery system is considered to be one of the major strengths of the company because it ensures maximum profits and service for the accounts and maximum control for the company.

A minimum of 87 percent of snack foods are purchased in grocery stores. High volume supermarkets account for the largest portion of sales for all competitors in the industry (Exhibit 28-23).

Promotion.   Each salesperson/driver has an assigned territory and operates from the nearest company warehouse. Sales aids provided include price sheets, plan-o-grams for effective store settings (what the retail shelf should look like), trade promotions (discounts), at least quarterly price "deals" offered for upcoming time periods, copies of ads or storyboards for TV ads to illustrate company advertising,

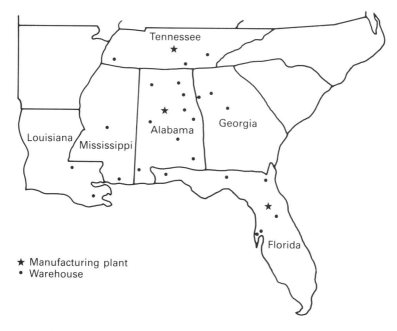

Exhibit 28-22   **Location of Company-Owned Warehouses and Manufacturing Facilities**

Exhibit 28-23   **Dollar Sales Share by Grocery Store Type/Size**

	Golden Flake (In percent)	Frito-Lay (In percent)	Others (In percent)
Supermarkets > $2 million	40.8	41.5	44.9
Chains > $2 million	30.2	34.4	37.5
Independents > $2 million	10.6	7.1	7.5
Chains < $2 million	7.5	4.4	1.1
Independents < $2 million	10.9	12.6	9.0
	100.0	100.0	100.0

and occasionally special incentives or "dealer loaders" (gifts) to offer store managers.

Salespeople are formally trained in-house by the regional manager. Following training, a newly hired driver will ride with an experienced driver until the end of the 12-week training program. Then a territory is assigned.

In Alabama, Golden Flake has high brand awareness, due primarily to a 25-year sponsorship with Coca Cola of the Bear Bryant football program. With the expansion of Golden Flake to other markets, advertising was needed to build awareness and develop the desired image. In 1987, Golden Flake cosponsored both Auburn University and University of Alabama football TV programs. In 1988, Golden Flake sponsored every major university football program in the Southeast as well as the basketball programs for the University of Alabama, Auburn University, and University of Louisville. Golden Flake became an official sponsor of the Southeastern Conference.

Golden Flake has developed a number of consumer promotions. Examples of these promotions are included in Exhibit 28-24. These promotions were developed to give added value to the trade and consumer in addition to integrating Golden Flake's entire marketing strategy from media to point-of-sale. Promotional media have been a useful way for stretching Golden Flake's marketing dollars.

The "World's Greatest Football/Basketball Machine" has been the most successful consumer promotion in Golden Flake's history. In 1988, 28 fully customized vans were given away, one for every major school in the Southeast and one for each of the coach's shows that Golden Flake sponsors.

Television, radio, and newspaper advertising was budgeted for 1986. The slogan, "Good as Gold" was used. When the advertising did not seem to be achieving desired results and budgets were tight, the television and radio ads were discontinued, and a new campaign was developed. Newspaper and FSIs (free standing inserts in newspapers) were maintained.

A new radio and television campaign "One Taste and You're Stuck—On Golden Flake" began in May 1987. Examples of in-store posters used to support the media campaign are included in Exhibit 28-25. Television advertising featured

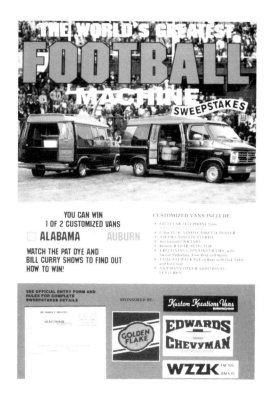

Exhibit 28-24   **Golden Flake Promotions**

historical figures "with a twist." Napoleon had his hand inside his jacket because he was eating Golden Flake potato chips and Venus de Milo with her missing arms in a Golden Flake bag were developed. Concept boards similar to the 1987 campaign are included in Exhibit 28-26.

All products are sold under the family brand of Golden Flake. Due to the regional nature and small advertising budget, the company had not attempted to develop individual brands as Frito-Lay had done with Ruffles, Cheetos, Tostitos, and so on. In June 1986 the first attempt at individual branding with "Southern Farms" brand kettle-fried potato chips resulted in Southern Farms generating 1.2 percent of total company sales in the first year.

Two-for-one deals are often offered to customers in new markets. The customer pays for one bag of Golden Flake potato chips and receives the second similar-sized bag for no additional charge. On-pack cents-off deals are also offered to consumers.

Golden Flake has an adopt-a-school program and provides plant tours for

Exhibit 28-25   **Golden Flake In-Store Posters**

school-aged children where the opportunity to sample a lot of potato chips is present. The company participates in five to eight trade shows each month.

Coupons are widely used by the company. The most effective vehicle for coupon distribution has been FSIs.

Financial Condition

Apparently Golden Flake's good-tasting quality product and competitive price has satisfied consumers. Satisfied customers and effective management have enabled the company to outperform the industry averages in both sales and profit in the last several years (Exhibits 28-27 and 28-28).

The conservative management of Golden Flake has kept the company in very good financial condition. Earnings per share have increased more than 25 percent per year over the last five years and the stock price has gone from a high of 4 $\frac{3}{16}$ in 1981 to a high of 21 in 1985. The 1986 EPS was down slightly as illustrated in Exhibit 28-29 but was improved in 1987 and held steady in 1988.

Exhibit 28-26   **Golden Flake Ad Campaign Concept Boards**

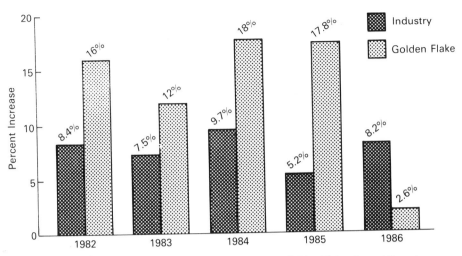

Source: Snack Food Association, 1987 Management Report; Golden Flake *Annual Report.*

Exhibit 28-27 **Golden Flake Sales Growth Compared to Industry Average**

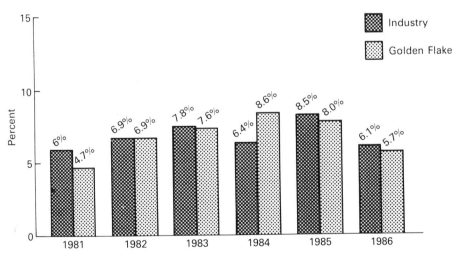

Source: Snack Food Association, 1987 Management Report; Golden Flake *Annual Report.*

Exhibit 28-28 **Golden Flake Profit as Percentage of Sales Compared to Industry Average**

Exhibit 28-29   Golden Enterprises, Inc.

Fiscal Year	Earnings per Share
1981	$0.46
1982	0.78
1983[a]	0.92
1984[b]	0.67
1985	0.73
1986	0.53
1987	0.61
1988	0.60

[a]In May 1983 the company effected a two-for-one stock split.
[b]In October 1984 the company effected a four-for-three stock split.

Exhibit 28-30   Consolidated Statements of Income Golden Enterprises, Inc. (Years ended May 31, 1985, 1986, 1987, and 1988)

	1985	1986	1987	1988
Revenues				
Net sales	$116,632,248	$119,978,611	$122,185,835	$128,649,399
Other income, including gain on sale of equipment of $263,791 in 1987, $268,060 in 1986 and $186,766 in 1985	463,297	495,635	685,478	619,755
Net investment income	653,488	288,976	469,404	817,315
Total Revenues	117,749,033	120,763,222	123,340,717	130,086,469
Costs and expenses				
Cost of sales	51,682,634	53,942,289	53,059,291	58,528,167
Selling, general and administrative expenses	49,618,452	53,185,862	54,237,335	59,215,493
Contributions to employee profit-sharing and employee stock ownership plans	1,566,272	1,476,827	1,596,279	1,620,105
Interest	192,458	238,867	88,499	57,369

(continued)

Exhibit 28-30 (continued)

	1985	1986	1987	1988
Total Costs and Ex-penses	103,059,816	108,843,845	108,981,404	119,421,134
Income before income taxes	14,689,217	11,919,377	14,359,313	10,665,335
Provision for income taxes				
Currently payable				
Federal	3,639,800	4,024,000	4,952,000	3,312,000
State	545,200	530,000	554,000	490,000
Deferred taxes	1,061,000	527,000	900,000	125,000
Total Provi-sion for In-come Taxes	5,246,000	5,081,000	6,406,000	3,927,000
Income before change in accounting principles	—	—	—	6,738,335
Change in account-ing for income taxes	—	—	—	1,025,000
Net Income	$ 9,443,217	$ 6,838,377	$ 7,953,313	$ 7,763,335
Per share of com-mon stock				
Income before ef-fect of account-ing change	—	—	—	$.52
Effect of change in accounting of income tax	—	—	—	.08
Net income	$.73	$.53	$.61	$.60

Exhibit 28-31 Consolidated Balance Sheets Golden Enterprises, Inc. (May 31, 1986, 1987, and 1988)

	1986	1987	1988
Assets			
Current Assets			
Cash and certificates of deposit	$ 2,071,883	$ 4,763,381	$ 5,992,720
Marketable securities	4,659,433	8,736,912	11,060,096
Receivables			
Trade notes and accounts	7,899,290	8,222,608	8,916,444
Other	188,615	589,061	568,901
	8,087,905	8,811,669	9,485,345

Exhibit 28-31 (continued)

	1986	1987	1988
Less: Allowance for doubtful accounts	20,000	20,000	20,000
	8,067,905	8,791,669	9,465,345
Inventories			
Raw materials	2,122,046	2,279,291	2,371,340
Finished goods	3,285,042	2,932,171	3,122,125
	5,407,088	5,211,462	5,493,465
Prepaid expenses	1,088,856	1,312,233	1,699,328
Total Current Assets	21,295,165	28,815,657	33,710,954
Property, plant and equipment			
Land	4,677,296	4,862,786	4,862,786
Buildings	17,934,962	18,241,400	19,386,724
Machinery and equipment	22,664,702	23,782,490	25,985,011
Transportation equipment	15,430,144	15,889,970	15,947,940
	60,707,104	62,776,646	66,182,461
Less: Accumulated depreciation	22,112,884	27,477,916	32,245,173
	38,594,220	35,298,730	33,937,288
Other Assets	1,585,046	1,336,389	709,495
Total	$61,474,431	$65,450,776	$68,357,737
Liabilities and Stockholders' Equity			
Current liabilities			
Checks outstanding in excess of bank balances	$ 829,429	$ 1,087,535	$ 1,921,879
Accounts payable	2,605,232	2,252,639	2,750,876
Accrued income taxes	895,579	—	269,603
Other accrued expenses	2,073,657	1,336,960	1,496,070
Deferred income taxes	294,004	324,607	317,139
Current installments of long-term debt	113,808	318,808	63,808
Total current liabilities	6,811,709	5,320,549	6,819,375
Long-term debt	573,088	254,280	190,472
Deferred income taxes	3,361,250	4,230,109	3,337,901
Stockholders' equity			
Common stock—$.66⅔ par value: Authorized 35,000,000 shares; issued 13,828,793 shares	9,219,195	9,219,195	9,219,195
Additional paid-in capital	5,416,498	5,623,673	5,939,261
Retained earnings	36,937,890	41,852,309	46,106,289
	51,573,583	56,695,177	61,264,745
Less: Cost of shares in treasury (757,581 shares in 1987 and 796,938 shares in 1986)	845,199	1,049,339	3,254,756
Total Stockholders' Equity	50,728,384	55,645,838	58,009,989
Total	$61,474,431	$65,450,776	$68,357,737

Exhibit 28-32   Golden Enterprises, Inc. and Subsidiaries, Summary of Business Segment Information (In thousands of dollars)

	Year ended May 31					
	1983	1984	1985	1986	1987	1988
Total Revenues						
Snack food products	$ 81,218	$ 95,991	$112,289	$115,064	$118,810	$124,710
Bolts and other fasteners	4,931	4,861	5,388	5,669	4,514	5,373
	$ 86,149	$100,852	$117,677	$120,733	$123,324	$130,083
Operating profit (loss)						
Snack food products	$ 12,254	$ 15,664	$ 14,495	$ 11,608	$ 14,228	$ 10,094
Bolts and other fasteners	(107)	68	319	442	21	521
	12,147	15,732	14,814	12,050	14,429	10,615
Elimination of inter-company items	(41)	(26)	(28)	(16)	(2)	(5)
Investment income of parent company and discontinued business	170	98	100	46	18	8
Interest expense	(193)	(158)	(192)	(239)	(88)	(57)
Parent company expense less than (in excess of) management fees from subsidiaries	(69)	(75)	(5)	78	182	104
Income before income taxes	$ 12,014	$ 15,571	$ 14,689	$ 11,919	$ 14,359	$ 10,665

Assets						
Snack food products	$ 38,089	$ 43,939	$ 54,192	$ 57,982	$ 62,201	$ 65,176
Bolts and other fasteners	2,642	2,927	2,941	2,960	2,409	2,821
Elimination of intercompany items	(290)	(320)	(265)	(150)	—	(88)
Corporate assets	1,887	1,859	1,063	682	841	449
Total assets at May 31	$ 42,328	$ 48,405	$ 57,931	$ 61,474	$ 65,451	$ 68,358
Depreciation and amortization						
Snack food products	$ 2,652	$ 2,990	$ 4,828	$ 6,414	$ 7,490	$ 7,292
Bolts and other fasteners	$ 111	$ 101	$ 89	$ 92	$ 92	$ 100
Consolidated	$ 2,780	$ 3,119	$ 4,922	$ 6,509	$ 7,586	$ 7,397
Additions to property, plant and equipment						
Snack food products	$ 3,935	$ 7,958	$ 21,680	$ 10,066	$ 3,462	$ 5,192
Bolts and other fasteners	$ 86	$ 67	$ 18	$ 57	$ 71	$ 123
Consolidated	$ 4,073	$ 8,025	$ 21,698	$ 10,123	$ 3,546	$ 5,315

Exhibit 28-33 **Golden Enterprises, Inc. and Subsidiaries Financial Review (In thousands, except per share data)**

	Year Ended May 31,					
	1983	1984	1985	1986	1987	1988
Operations						
Net sales and other operating income	$85,322	$99,692	$117,096	$120,474	$122,871	$129,269
Investment income	956	1,232	653	289	469	817
Total Revenues	86,278	100,924	117,749	120,763	123,340	130,086
Cost of sales	39,035	43,638	51,683	53,942	53,059	58,528
Selling, general and administrative expenses	35,036	41,557	51,185	54,663	55,834	60,836
Interest	193	158	192	239	88	57
Income before income taxes and cumulative effect of a change in accounting principle	12,014	15,571	14,689	11,919	14,359	10,665
Federal and state income taxes	5,449	6,904	5,246	5,081	6,406	3,927
Income before cumulative effect of a change in accounting principle	6,565	8,667	9,443	6,838	7,953	6,738
Cumulative effect on prior years of a change in accounting for income taxes	—	—	—	—	—	1,025
Net Income	6,565	8,667	9,443	6,838	7,953	7,763
Financial Data						
Depreciation and amortization	$ 2,780	$ 3,119	$ 4,922	$ 6,509	$ 7,586	$ 7,397
Cash flow (net income plus depreciation and amortization)	9,345	11,786	14,365	13,347	15,539	15,160
Capital expenditures	3,981	7,881	20,891	9,569	3,867	5,315
Working capital	17,277	19,943	12,317	14,483	23,495	26,892
Long-term debt	1,318	779	687	573	254	190
Stockholders' equity	32,358	39,246	46,481	50,728	55,646	58,010
Total Assets	42,328	48,405	57,931	61,474	65,451	68,358

Common Stock Data

Net income before cumulative effect of a change in accounting principle	$ .52	$ .67	$ .73	$ .53	$ .61	$ .52
Cumulative effect on prior years of a change in accounting for income taxes	—	—	—	—	—	.08
Net income	.92	.67	.73	.53	.61	.60
Dividends	.11	.14	.17	.20	.23	.27
Book Value	2.48	3.01	3.57	3.89	4.26	4.50
Price range (high and low bid)	$10\frac{1}{4}-3\frac{3}{4}$	$11\frac{11}{16}-8\frac{9}{16}$	$15\frac{3}{4}-8\frac{7}{16}$	$16\frac{1}{2}-10\frac{1}{4}$	$15\frac{1}{2}-11\frac{3}{4}$	$16\frac{1}{2}-9$

Financial Statistics

Current ratio	3.20	3.78	2.45	3.13	5.42	4.94
Net income as percent of total revenues	7.6%	8.6%	8.0%	5.7%	6.4%	6.0%
Net income as percent of stockholders' equity	23.3%	24.2%	22.0%	14.1%	15.0%	13.7%

Other Data

Weighted average common shares outstanding[a]	12,649,333	13,020,436	13,017,135	13,024,078	13,066,054	12,991,842
Common shares outstanding at year-end[a]	13,021,397	13,017,397	13,023,082	13,031,855	13,071,212	12,894,800
Approximate number of stockholders	1,600	1,600	1,700	2,100	2,100	2,100

[a]Adjusted for stock splits in years ended May 31, 1983, 1985 and 1986.

The consolidated income statement and balance sheets for Golden Flake for 1983 through 1988 are provided in Exhibits 28-30 and 28-31. Exhibits 28-32 and 28-33 are a business segment information summary and financial review.

According to the Robinson-Humphrey Investment Report on Golden Enterprises, with the completion of $30.5 million in expansion and renovation, Golden Flake is positioned for growth. Investment income dropped as expansion was funded from working capital. Higher cost of sales and higher sales and administrative expenses were associated with the new facilities start-up and increased promotional efforts. Robinson-Humphrey predicts a return to the company's previous high margins.

Case 29

PRINTECH Publishing Services, Inc.

Bob and Elyce Warzeski looked at the papers sitting on their dining room table with all kinds of mixed emotions. Six months earlier, those letters and announcements would have been a godsend. Now, in September 1987, they made life incredibly complicated. The field of geology had apparently begun to open up after a long dry spell. In the space of one week Bob had received three requests to interview for faculty and research positions and announcements of six other openings. Bob had been hoping for such a break ever since he had been laid off from a major oil company in May 1986. He was a bright and talented Ph.D. geologist with six years of industry experience. More than anything else he wanted to teach geology and do research at a good university. Now it seemed that it could happen. Even if any one of these particular jobs did not come through, there were enough openings in the geology market to convince Bob that he could be teaching by September 1988, if he so desired. The mixed emotions that he and his wife, Elyce, were feeling were generated by the fact that their own small desktop publishing business, PRINTECH Publishing Services, Inc., had recently begun doing very well, and showed every sign of doing even better in the near future. The letters and announcements had arrived just as Bob and Elyce were about to make a major investment, to the tune of $60,000, in PRINTECH.

This case was prepared by Elyce G. Warzeski under the direction of Jeffrey A. Barach, University of Tulane, as a basis for class discussion rather than to illustrate either effective or ineffective handling of an administrative situation. Used by permission from Jeffrey A. Barach. © J. Barach, Tulane University.

WHAT IS DESKTOP PUBLISHING?

Taking any idea from conception to printed word or graphic illustration was a complicated procedure. Because of the limitations of conventional typesetting equipment the procedure seemed like magic to many. Desktop publishing took the mystery out. With conventional "code-intensive" typesetting, a string of codes defined type styles, sizes, and typefaces, as well as column width, spacing, etc. What was entered into a computer bore no resemblance to what was finally printed. A string of columns would be printed, which would then have to be manually cut and pasted onto boards in the proper orientation. Desktop publishing operated along the concept of WYSIWYG (pronounced whi-see-wig) or "What you see is what you get." (This was a real piece of computer jargon that was used in most literature on the subject and almost all documentation for desktop publishing programs.) This meant that you saw, on the computer screen, exactly what you saw on the printed page.

The Macintosh computer, developed by Steven Jobs and once considered a toy, opened the door for desktop publishing with its capability for generating images of high resolution and variability. The Macintosh was introduced in 1984, along with the Imagewriter. The entire system cost less than $3,500, and the Imagewriter could produce copy with a resolution of 80 dots per inch (dpi).

In 1985 a series of announcements truly initiated the advent of desktop publishing. Apple introduced its new LaserWriter, with a resolution of 300 dpi. Allied Linotype Company (one of the most prestigious manufacturers and distributors of typesetting equipment and systems) made its typefaces available to Apple and Adobe so that those typefaces could be produced both on the LaserWriter and on Linotype's new Linotronic 300 (L-300) typesetter (with a resolution of 2,540 dpi). The International Typeface Corporation made similar provisions. Aldus Corporation introduced the Pagemaker program which would allow for both the formatting and composition of text and for generation and merging of graphics in a single document.[1]

"Desktop publishing" as a term requires some definition. It was originally proposed by Paul Brainerd, the president of Aldus Corporation. The word "desktop" had two meanings in this context. The Macintosh environment was set up much like a desktop. Icons which resemble the document they contain (dog-eared pages, books, initials of programs, etc.) represented files, which in turn reside in folders (designated by an icon which looks just like an office folder). These folders were located on disks (represented by a disk icon) and were discarded by placing them in a trash can (which looked like . . .). Also, all the equipment required to do desktop publishing took very little space—about the size of a normal desktop.[2]

---

[1]John Seybold and Fritz Dressler, *Publishing from the Desktop,* Bantam Books, 1987, pp. 1-2.
[2]Ibid., p. 3.

"Publishing" meant far more than simply typesetting. The Macintosh desktop publishing system could take documents from inception to camera-ready copy. Where the speed and paper size restrictions of the LaserWriter were not a problem, the system could go all the way to finished product. The process included text entry, editing, spelling checks, creation of and tailoring of graphics, and even some half-tone photographs.[3]

By 1987–1988, many of the recognized limitations of the Macintosh had disappeared. Its small screen could be upgraded to full-page and even double-page screens for a cost of between $1,000 and $2,000. This price had dropped significantly. Apple introduced the Mac II, a very high-powered rendition of the Macintosh with a larger screen and full color capabilities, and the Macintosh SE with an internal hard disk and greatly increased speed. Spooling software allowed the Macintosh to print while performing other tasks and was available and inexpensive. There were still problems and limitations, but the field of desktop publishing was well established by the fall of 1987.

BACKGROUND ON BOB AND ELYCE

Bob and Elyce met in 1981 when they both worked for Shell Oil Company in Houston, Texas, he as a geologist, she as a geophysical laboratory technician. Three years later they married. Bob was transferred to New Orleans shortly thereafter. One week before she arrived in New Orleans, Elyce discovered that she was pregnant. It was a happy but unexpected discovery since Elyce had been told she would probably not be able to conceive. Bob and Elyce found themselves in a situation where instead of two people living on two incomes, they would be three people living on one income. Shell never did find a position for Elyce in New Orleans. Money got very tight.

Elyce had been considering applying to business school while the Warzeskis were still in Houston. She and Bob decided that would still be the best course to take. Elyce worked some temporary secretarial jobs for the next eight months and applied to the business school at Tulane. She was accepted with a full fellowship, which was fortuitous, since otherwise, they would not have been able to afford the program.

That summer, shortly after the birth of their daughter, Rachel, Bob's grandmother passed away, leaving Bob about $250,000. A substantial portion of this money would not be cash in hand for several years, because it takes time for estates to be settled completely. Some of the money went into immediate and necessary home improvements, and the remainder Bob and Elyce invested in no-load mutual funds, which generated an average of 15 percent interest per year. This provided them with investment income of between $20,000 and $30,000 per year.

[3]Ibid., p. 4.

During Elyce's first year of the MBA program at Tulane, a crisis occurred in the oil industry. Oil companies began massive layoffs and hundreds of small companies folded. Although Bob had been doing quite well as an exploration geologist for his company, the crunch caught up with him in May 1986. He was provided a handsome severance package including several weeks' salary (with which Bob and Elyce purchased their first Macintosh computer).

Given the fact that they were more or less financially secure, Bob decided not to go job hunting right away. He had spent almost 15 years becoming a geologist and could not conceive of doing anything else. He had, however, become thoroughly disillusioned with the oil industry and wanted to do research and to teach. He spent the next year writing geology articles from his Ph.D. dissertation material, several of which were published in leading geology journals. Bob applied for university teaching positions which opened up during that year. Unfortunately, throughout 1986 and most of 1987, the geology market was glutted with highly qualified individuals in the same situation as Bob, and very few universities were hiring. On average, each position advertised received over 150 applications.

THE DECISION TO GO INTO BUSINESS

Elyce

> The summer after Bob was laid off I felt like I was going crazy, and I knew for a fact that my marriage was in trouble. Bob sincerely felt that the only career he could pursue was geology, and it was rapidly becoming obvious to me that he was not going to receive a faculty appointment any time soon. I knew that I could go out and secure a good job with my background and MBA, but Bob would suffer major anxiety if he felt that I was the sole support of the family. I remember how I felt when I didn't have a job and Bob was bringing home the only paycheck. I wouldn't wish that kind of helpless feeling on anyone.
>
> I started desperately trying to think of hobbies Bob had that he could capitalize on, but every suggestion I made he shot down. I was also stuck in a position where I really couldn't apply for jobs. Bob was ready to pick up and move on a moment's notice should a faculty position come through. How could I look for a job when I had no idea where we would be living and when?
>
> By April 1987 it had become apparent that no teaching positions were going to come Bob's way for the fall of 1987. I decided that even if something did come through for the spring of 1988, I would stay in New Orleans at least until the following September. (It would take that long just to pack up the house and try to get it either rented or sold.) I started thinking about perhaps opening our own business, but what kind of business? It would have to be something I could walk away from easily if a position for Bob did appear. Bob still felt that he could only do geology, but when I suggested businesses that were geology oriented, he balked.
>
> He did, at one point decide to design a particular font, or typeface, for the Macintosh that would designate fossils (a very useful tool for geologists who generally

have to draw them by hand). This started us thinking along the lines of making a business out of using the Macintosh. We had both become quite proficient with the machine since we had purchased it. Bob used it for all his geological papers and illustrations, and I had used it extensively in my school work. Bob also liked the idea of a high-tech, relatively new industry, in which he would have a valid reason for playing with all the latest equipment.

Bob

In the spring of 1987, Elyce and I had come to a point where decisions were required. I had been laid off in May 1986, after almost six years with a major oil company, four at their research center in Houston and two in offshore exploration in New Orleans.

Prior to getting laid off, the career I had envisioned involved becoming known throughout the company for expertise in my particular branch of geology, publishing various parts of my Ph.D. in professional journals, and probably going to a university teaching position after a few more years, so I could pick up on the research I'd done for my doctorate. I had reason to believe that I had done very good Ph.D. work, from reactions at talks I gave at professional meetings, and I felt that six or more years of industry experience could only enhance my hireability. Unsolicited requests that I apply for positions at three different schools (Ohio State, Tulane, and Oklahoma) confirmed my conception that I should be able to find a teaching job when I wanted to.

Being laid off was not part of the plan. Being laid off as the oil industry was falling apart and thousands of other geoscientists were also being put on the street was a major departure.

I made a decision that I would not seek work in the industry again, but would go after a university job. I set about getting the first pieces of my Ph.D. work (completed in 1983) published and started applying for jobs at universities when ads for positions starting in September 1987 began to appear.

By March 1987, I knew that the least desirable position I had applied for had received over 60 applicants. The really good ones had uniformly received "over 150 well-qualified applicants" as three different schools said. I had made the first cut at most of these schools, but was not on any of the "short lists" of people actually asked to interview.

I found that many of my friends, including some with extensive publication records, who had been actively doing research in our corner of geology and were known and respected, were in the same position I was and had had no better success.

Faced with the prospect of no job for September, I began to set my sights on September 1988, hoping that some of those "150 plus" other Ph.Ds would have either found jobs or decided to do something else with their lives. I knew by this time that the odds against my getting a position were very long.

When Elyce began pushing me to consider doing something else, I resisted and fought. I felt that I had no skills outside of my field, and couldn't imagine being anything but a geologist.

Of all the possibilities she brought up, only desktop publishing rang any bells. I had bought a Macintosh computer with part of my severance pay and had used its graphics capabilities to great effect in creating illustrations for my papers, in addition to writing the papers themselves on it. Plus, I was fascinated by the hardware and software that had grown up around the brand-spanking-new field of desktop publishing.

From the first, though, getting into desktop publishing was a stop gap, a way to pay the mortgage until a geology job came along. I had the uneasy feeling that a successful business could mean not only never being a geologist again, but being stuck in New Orleans in perpetuity.

THE FIRST STAGE

Bob and Elyce began researching the field of desktop publishing. They found that, although the genre had taken off like wildfire throughout most of the rest of the country, New Orleans was woefully behind the times. This gave them a wonderful opportunity to enter a wide-open market, while still being able to refer to established businesses for guidance.

They decided that for their purposes a Subchapter S Corporation would be most beneficial both because they would wind up paying less tax and because it would greatly simplify paperwork.

For legal purposes an S corporation is no different than other corporations. For tax purposes, however, an S corporation looks much like a partnership: corporate income and losses pass through to the shareholders' individual returns.

To qualify as an S corporation, a company must meet certain requirements. It cannot have more than thirty-five shareholders, it cannot have more than one class of stock, it cannot have any nonresident foreigners as shareholders, and it must properly elect S corporation status. [*Author's note:* This last is easily accomplished by any corporate lawyer. The total cost in legal and registration fees for the Warzeskis was $285 in March 1987. This figure includes registering a company name with the state.]

The distinct tax advantage the S corporation has over a regular corporation is that it pays tax on its income only once, and only at the shareholder level. Starting in 1987 this feature will make S corporations particularly attractive because individual tax rates will be lower than corporate rates.

Another reason to elect S corporation status is the new corporate alternative minimum tax. Beginning in 1987 tax reform imposes a more potent minimum tax on non-S corporations. The rate on this minimum tax jumps to 20 percent from 15 percent. And corporations must add back more tax preferences to income to compute tax. The new tax law excuses S corporations from the corporate alternative minimum tax.

A third argument in favor of S corporations is that the new tax law requires most corporations to recognize their gain or loss on liquidating sales and distributions just as if the assets had been sold. Certain small, closely held companies and S corporations are unaffected by this change.

Finally, a fourth argument in favor of S corporations is that they are permitted to use the cash method of accounting under the new law.

On the negative side: S corporations may not have corporate shareholders or subsidiaries, and deductions for retirement and fringe benefits paid to shareholders may be limited.

But overall, the advantages of S corporations after tax reform should greatly overshadow any negatives for qualifying corporations.[4]

The start-up cost for desktop publishing was quite low compared to other new businesses. The Warzeskis already had some equipment and needed about another $15,000 worth to really get things rolling. In April 1987, Bob and Elyce leased all the equipment they felt was required, and then borrowed $5,000 (personally guaranteed) from a large, conservative New Orleans bank, in order to cover operating expenses until the company got under way. They then spent about another $5,000 of their own money in miscellaneous start-up costs.

With this initial investment they had everything required to operate the business out of their home. Since they originally went into business to tide them over while Bob looked for a faculty position, desktop publishing appeared to fit their needs well. The commitment required on the part of Bob and Elyce at the start-up stage was small. The couple could work their own hours, which was convenient, especially while Elyce finished her MBA from Tulane University. The business should have been able to generate sufficient income to supplement their investments and provide a comfortable living. Finally, operating out of their home would give them an opportunity to spend more time with their two-year-old daughter.

The initial outlook for the company was bright. Everyone appeared to be excited about what desktop publishing could accomplish, and several organizations promised large accounts. Unfortunately, as is true with most small businesses, start-up took longer than anticipated. By the time their first loan came due in July, PRINTECH had generated less than $2,000 worth of gross revenue. Several large accounts had been promised but had not materialized. Advertising and promotion had been slow getting off the ground while Elyce, the marketing half of the team, finished school, and several pieces of equipment and software were slow in arriving and nonfunctional when they did appear.

At the end of three months they were still struggling along with only a few small jobs each week. Even though Elyce was just finishing up her MBA and had had little time for the business, she felt almost ready to give up. Bob, however, remained confident. They were still relying on word-of-mouth advertising which didn't seem to be getting them anywhere, and it took longer to get their promotional brochure ready than they had expected. Bob felt all that was to be expected so early on and was surprised that Elyce didn't have more patience.

[4]*The Price Waterhouse Guide to The New Tax Law,* Bantam Books, New York, 1968, pp. 244–245.

Preparing the brochure in and of itself turned out to be a major learning experience for Bob and Elyce and pointed out some of the problems that husbands and wives face when they go into business together. As an entrepreneurial couple they had to learn new ways to communicate with each other, because simple spousal relations did not suffice. As a case in point—note the following situation.

Illustrative Scenario

Bob had spent a great deal of time working on the advertising brochure while Elyce had been busily studying for exams. When he finally had what he considered to be a finished product, Elyce greeted it with ill-concealed dismay. She felt that it said the wrong things and was in a format that too closely resembled the brochure another desktop publisher had sent them. The anger and frustration she felt over what she considered to be wasted effort were obviously out of all proportion to the situation. She also knew that Bob would not take criticism from her very easily, especially for something he had put so much time and effort into.

Much of Elyce's frustration and anger were not directed at Bob but at a system which was not working. They realized that if the situation were not rectified soon, their business, and more importantly, their marriage would suffer.

Bob and Elyce decided that they needed to talk about communication issues rather than about specific problems. They recognized that the words "I don't want to talk about it right now," might be perfectly reasonable in the context of a marriage, but were not in a business situation. Elyce was careful to ask Bob how she should approach the situation knowing that her usual tendency to come on too strong would be a disaster.

Given the appropriate parameters for their talk, they recognized that they had both been under a great deal of pressure in their lives ouside of the business and that pressure had carried over. They had not spent anywhere near enough time discussing business matters, such as the brochure, and had never even set up guidelines for who was supposed to perform which tasks.

Without the appropriate guidelines, Elyce felt that she had not been consulted enough, and Bob didn't realize she had felt the need to be consulted at all. In turn, he felt that by the criticizing the brochure, Elyce was invading his territory. He had, after all, been forced to work largely on his own while she finished school. If they had taken a couple of minutes every morning to talk to each other, the problem would probably never have occurred.

The Warzeskis realized that neither one of them could run a business without the other. Both of them had to work on each project, at least in the planning stages. They had to confer often on important jobs, and constantly keep each other's strengths and weaknesses in mind. They also had to learn to express their feelings accurately, without unnecessarily putting the other on the defensive. Bob and Elyce used several tools to help them in these areas. Most importantly, they consulted with a professional therapist who helped them focus their discussions around basic needs rather than nit-picking arguments.

THE SECOND STAGE

Finally, in July, the brochure was completed and printed, and looked very impressive. At this time, their first loan came due, and the couple had to face their first round of business decisions; specifically, they had to decide whether or not it had been a mistake to go into business in the first place. Neither one wanted to give up. They knew they had a good product and a wide-open market. They just didn't know how to reach it. Besides, if they quit at that point they would have been right back where they started. Bob would still be unemployed, and it would be difficult for Elyce to find a job, since they had no idea where Bob might receive a faculty appointment should one materialize.

They decided to persevere and needed to determine whether or not to continue with their present loan or to increase the amount, and if so, by how much. They also had to decide just exactly how much of their own time and resources they were really willing to commit to the business. They had the resources to sink up to $100,000 of their own into the venture, but since that money was quite profitably invested, they were loathe to touch it.

Bob and Elyce asked for and received an additional $5,000. The entire $10,000 would come due in October 1987. Shortly after the bank extended them the additional money, things began to get interesting. Word-of-mouth advertising began to pay off. Suddenly they had one fairly large client using their services as typesetters as well as design and marketing consultants. He was recommending them to others. Within days, Elyce was talking to the marketing staff at a large psychiatric hospital, only blocks from where they lived. At a convention Bob met an out-of-state geologist who was very interested in working with PRINTECH. The theater group that Elyce worked with requested bids on some work and were very pleased with the answers, and two printers were using PRINTECH to do the typesetting referred to their shops . . . and all of this before PRINTECH's first advertisements hit the press!

Bob and Elyce had to come to some agreement about what PRINTECH meant to them and what they saw as the future of the company. This was a very complex issue because Elyce wanted to be in and stay in business, whereas Bob viewed it as a stopgap.

> Once the business started doing well, Bob really seemed happy for the first time in quite a while. I saw that the business had a great deal of potential, but I had to wait for Bob to suggest expanding. I didn't want a commitment to the business on Bob's part to be something I had talked him into since for Bob it would mean giving up so much. Even when Bob did start talking about expanding the business, I knew it was not a happy choice for him, but it seemed a determined one.

Elyce saw the company as growing to respectable proportions and promising rewards to both of them. Bob, who had initially considered it a way to pay the mortgage until something better came along, had become more involved.

Bob considered that:

> by midsummer, it was apparent that the business had considerable potential, and that
> we would need to commit ourselves and substantial amounts of our personal funds in
> order to take full advantage of the situation. It was apparent that we could choose to
> piddle along with the two computers and a LaserWriter in the extra bedroom while I
> wrote geology papers and applied for university positions for another year or two, or
> three, but that we would be passing up a major opportunity. In addition, each year
> that I was not actively involved in the field professionally (and I'm still not sure if
> publishing more pieces of the dissertation would count) would likely decrease my hire-
> ability.

Bob and Elyce both had some severe qualms (the heat, terrain, insects, and
mostly a terrible school system and a very high teenage alcoholism rate) about making New Orleans their permanent residence. They also had very different ideas about
the likelihood of Bob securing a tenure-track teaching position. Could the company
grow to the point where they could dispose of it profitably? PRINTECH was a
service company, with its size determined by its customer base. Could it be sold for
more than the value of the hardware? (Since "high-tech" equipment depreciates
very rapidly, Bob and Elyce could probably not expect to receive more than 50
percent of what they paid for the equipment after one year, and probably far less
than that amount thereafter.) Could they take the business with them to a new location? This could become a serious possibility if their advertisements in national geology journals were successful, since this would give them a national clientele, and
telecommunications could give them access to data from just about anywhere.

The Market

Local figures for typesetting were difficult to obtain, and marketing information on desktop publishing itself was completely unavailable, since the field was so
new. However, the Warzeskis were able to determine that there were hundreds of
small, commercial desktop publishing operations in cities such as Denver, New
York, Houston, and Los Angeles. There were only two or three operating in New
Orleans. In those cities in which desktop publishing was firmly established, most
businesses were small, but there were one or two large operations which dominated
the market. Bob and Elyce already had a business comparable to the small establishments, but no one in New Orleans had yet decided to go after major market share.
The companies in other cities which had done so had entered the market early,
stayed on top of the latest equipment and software, and aggressively marketed their
product.

In comparing the Denver or New York market to New Orleans, Bob and Elyce
realized that these other cities provided a far more sophisticated clientele. The Warzeskis would have to make some equipment decisions (see Equipment) concerning
output devices. These ranged in price from $5,000 for another LaserWriter to

$130,000 for the top-of-the-line, high-resolution Linotronic (L-300) with all its bells and whistles. The question was whether or not customers in New Orleans would be willing to pay anything for higher quality output. As of September, they had had no requests from their existing clientele for better resolution, and no indication that these customers would be willing to pay the $12 per page that L-300 would cost them.

How to advertise desktop publishing was another question Bob and Elyce had to face. Their advertisements in geology journals had not generated any new business. They recognized that magazine advertisements generally work with repetition, but that would be very expensive with no assurance of success.

Placing ads in the telephone yellow pages seemed more sensible, and much cheaper. New Orleans was divided into two major sections by the Mississippi River. PRINTECH was located on the "West Bank" near the Warzeskis' home. The West Bank had its own phone book and yellow page advertisements ran as little as $30 per month.

Bob and Elyce were also considering an advertising campaign which would focus not on PRINTECH *per se,* but on the advantages that desktop publishing had to offer in general. The ads would appear in local business journals and would be more instructional than sales oriented. Their experience had been that once people understood the versatility and capabilities of desktop publishing, their service sold itself.

STAGE THREE

By September 1987, it had become apparent that PRINTECH was either going to have to expand or refuse business. Expansion meant hiring additional help and purchasing new equipment. Specifically, they would need a high-quality printer, several additional computers, and some additional, more sophisticated software. With the business in its present condition, they could easily make enough money to cover their personal expenses, but growth potential would be severely limited. Keeping up with the latest technology would be crucial if PRINTECH were to survive for more than a year or two. This technology changed very rapidly. Each innovation was usually very expensive and generally maintained a corner on the technological market for about a year. By that time imitators would appear, and prices would drop rapidly. To maintain a share of the market, PRINTECH would constantly need to upgrade the equipment and software. This would become a very expensive proposition for a small company. For this reason, the Warzeskis believed that in its present state, PRINTECH would cease to be a viable operation in a fairly short time. On the other hand, if PRINTECH stayed at the leading edge of technology and captured enough market share early in the process, they could expect handsome profits and growth.

The Warzeskis felt that making the major investment decision would force Bob to choose between growing with PRINTECH or a geology career in the near future. Investments at this point would mean a commitment to the business of at least several years' duration. There would be little opportunity during that time for him to pursue his geological interests. Already, he was finding little time to work on his papers.

The decisions Bob and Elyce needed to face covered several fronts. First and foremost, they had to decide whether or not to take a major plunge. If they did decide to make a real play for a substantial business, the decisions required of them in the next few weeks would entail office space—where and what kind; finances— how much of their own money should they invest and how much more should they borrow; equipment—what kind and whether to buy or lease; and personnel—who to hire and when.

Office Space

One of their customers worked out of a cooperative office arrangement, where for $150 per month (and no lease) PRINTECH could rent office space with services provided, including receptionist, utilities, kitchen, maid, and courier service. If they moved in they would also have increased access to the client and therefore, in all likelihood, more business from that client. The main disadvantage to this office space was its location. It was several miles further from downtown than Bob and Elyce's home. This meant a bit longer to pick up and deliver jobs.

There were several other options for office space. Near their home was a high-rise office building with a special "executive suite" specially designed for new businesses. For between $200 and $600 per month, office space could be leased, with month-to-month terms. This rate would include utilities, receptionist services, phone instruments, kitchen and conference room facilities, security, and access to telex and fax machines. Office furniture, including drafting tables, could be rented directly from the building manager at extremely reasonable rates, and as the business grew, it could move into additional office space within the same suite. The manager was also interested in using PRINTECH's photocopier as the main copier for the office and would let PRINTECH charge $.10 per page for copies.

Upon discussing office space with the owner of a successful desktop publishing operation in Houston, Bob and Elyce were told that storefront space would be highly preferable to interior office space. It would generate a great deal more business simply on a walk-in basis, especially if the location were right. Within the area that Bob and Elyce considered feasible for their business, given proximity to several of their major accounts, were three or four such storefront locations. These locations would cost between $850 and $1,000 per month in rent and would require at least a one and a half year lease. PRINTECH would have to pay utilities of about $200 per month. The company would also have to provide all its own furnishings; a storefront facility would require better, and therefore more expensive, furniture because it would be constantly on public display.

Working from their home had several distinct advantages. PRINTECH paid no rent, and the company picked up a prorated portion of their mortgage, phone, and power bills. Since they would have to keep at least one computer at home, having the business there as well meant less equipment was necessary.

Bob and Elyce would soon need to hire additional help. They were both uncomfortable with the idea of having someone in their home as a full-time employee. If Bob and Elyce moved into the cooperative office space, this additional help could be postponed, since most of what they needed was available there. On the other hand, the hospital they had recently secured as a customer, and which was very happy with their work, considered their proximity a major advantage. This advantage, and quite possibly the customer, would be lost by taking space with the cooperative.

Equipment

Bob and Elyce were considering several pieces of equipment. A Linotronic 100 or 300 (L-100 or L-300) produced by Linotype Corporation could print images onto film or photographic plates at very high resolution. The sales representative quoted prices of $40,000 for the lower resolution machine and $70,000 for the higher resolution one. Linotype would arrange for lease purchase of either of these machines or sell the machines outright but would not rent them. These printers had extremely fine resolution for print and graphic design. Variable costs per page of output on photographic paper would run about $.70. These pages could be competitively charged to the customer at $8 to $24 per page. (Again, these were the Linotronic representative's figures.) Eight Linotronic machine could be purchased for cash or leased/purchased on a 60-month basis at between 18 and 20 percent interest. The Warzeskis were also told that the company was fairly flexible. Their interest rate would be higher than usual since their company was so new, but higher down payments, referral letters, a solid cash basis, and promises of yearly contracts would go a long way toward making the leasing arrangements more attractive.

The other type of machine would cost about $18,000 or could be rented for $750 per month. This machine, called a Varityper VT-600, would generate excellent quality images, many times the resolution of the LaserWriter, but not as fine as either Linotronic machine. The VT-600 was a plain paper copier, so cost per page for PRINTECH would be minimal. However, the Warzeskis could only charge $2 to $3 per page maximum to be competitive on this machine (simply for printing purposes, not typesetting and design) and there was some question as to how much demand there would be for such copies. (The demand would unquestionably be higher in a store-front situation than in an interior office.) Within a year Varityper Corporation expected to introduce a high resolution copier comparable to the L-300, and any lease-purchase agreement with Varityper could be upgraded at that time.

A high resolution machine would open up an entirely new market to PRINTECH. With such a machine they could do high quality work for advertising agencies. When coupled to a high resolution scanner (which would appear on the market within a few months), a printer such as the L-300 (the high-resolution machine) could generate high-quality black and white half-tone photographs as well as type and graphics.

Elyce spent several days on the telephone, talking to thriving desktop publishing companies in other cities. In the process of those conversations she learned that she might expect to pay close to $130,000 for the L-300 with all the necessary peripherals and that delivery time would likely be much faster than that quoted by the sales rep. She also learned that in a region of about 100,000 business establishments an L-300 could generate between $10,000 and $15,000 per month. New Orleans had about 30,000 business establishments in 1987. Another company told her that purchasing a high-resolution printer was silly and that the VT-600 was all the printer she would ever need. Very few of this latter company's customers could tell the difference between the 600 dpi resolution of a VT-600 and the 2540 dpi resolution of the L-300.

The intermediate Linotronic machine, the L-100, generated images of 1240 dpi. A desktop publisher in Baton Rouge was willing to make his L-100 available to the Warzeskis at a rate of between $6 and $8 per page. PRINTECH could then charge $12 per page. PRINTECH could send documents to Baton Rouge via modem, and receive the printed output the next day via either UPS, Greyhound, or Express Mail. Although the L-100 was not as high quality a machine as the L-300, no one that Bob and Elyce had spoken to who had an L-100 wanted to upgrade to the more expensive machine. In fact, those who were considering upgrading simply wanted to purchase another L-100. Also, according to these L-100 owners, the L-100 was a far simpler machine to use. The L-300 would probably necessitate PRINTECH hiring a technician just to deal with the machine. The L-100 apparently presented no such complications. The Baton Rouge publisher also said he would be interested in sharing the purchase of an L-100 in New Orleans should PRINTECH decide to go that route. Elyce found one other commercial L-100 in New Orleans and priced those copies at $11 per page.

Elyce spent some time visiting other desktop publishers, each of whom ran a very different operation. She came away from these visits with a wealth of new information and more questions than answers. It became apparent to her, after talking with a master typographer, that she and Bob had to learn a great deal more about the art of typography than they already knew. This gentleman had explained to her *why* high resolution was important, saying that clearer, sharper images apparently increase reading speed and comprehension dramatically, even if the difference in clarity is not visible to the naked eye. Elyce felt she might be able to market a high-resolution output, even in a market where customers did not recognize its importance. Again, marketing would involve educating the customers, more than selling.

Elyce also learned that desktop publishers made a substantial portion of their income by setting up systems for other people. The procedure for getting into this area of business was easy. PRINTECH simply needed to acquire a tax resale number and then contact the distributors of software and peripherals, like graphics boards and "mice." (A "mouse" was a device which allowed free movement of the cursor.

Exhibit 29-1A PRINTECH Publishing Services, Inc., Financial Projections with Linotronic–300, Actual and Projected Income Statements, Monthly April–December 1987, Quarterly 1988[a]

	April	May	June	July	Aug.	Sept.
Revenue	$ 227	$ 177	$ 220	$ 480	$1,172	$2,280
Less total variable costs	630	0	0	0	50	155
Contribution margin	− 403	177	220	480	1,122	2,125
Less fixed costs						
Tax accountant						75
Rent (office and furniture)	105	105	105	105	105	105
Utilities (phone and auto)			130	130	260	330
Interest expense	230	227	223	332	216	212
Insurance	200	200	200	200	200	300
Service Contracts						50
Wages						400
Advertising						200
Depreciation	626	640	640	640	640	640
Total fixed costs	1,161	1,172	1,298	1,407	1,421	2,312
Profit (before taxes)	− 1,564	− 995	− 1,078	− 927	− 299	− 187
Taxes (34%)						− 64
Profit after taxes						− 123

Exhibit 29-1B PRINTECH Publishing Services, Inc., Financial Projections with Linotronic–300, Actual and Projected Statement of Changes in Financial Position[a]

	Aug. 31	Sept. 30	Oct. 31	Nov. 30	Dec. 31
Assets					
Short-term assets					
Cash	$ 5,277	$35,686	$51,424	$47,550	$ 23,796
Accounts receivable	820	1,140	2,173	3,240	4,528
Inventory	500	500	500	500	500
Long-term assets					
Investment in chamber	225	225	225	225	225
Equipment	31,600	31,600	32,700	36,400	105,000
Furniture	1,000	1,000	1,000	1,000	1,000
Total Assets	39,422	70,151	88,022	88,915	135,049
Liabilities					
Notes payable	10,000	40,000	28,784	29,565	29,343
Leases payable	25,520	25,520	25,056	24,592	84,728
Total liabilities	35,520	65,520	53,840	54,157	114,071
Owner's equity	3,902	4,631	34,182	34,758	20,978
Liabilities and equity	39,422	70,151	88,022	88,915	135,049

[a]Statements and projections created by Elyse Warzeski—unaudited.

Oct.	Nov.	Dec.	Jan.–Mar.	Apr.–June	July–Sept.	Oct.–Dec.
$4,345	$6,480	$9,163	$39,853	$64,715	$87,091	$96,500
298	446	682	2,992	4,942	6,918	6,495
4,047	6,034	8,481	36,861	59,773	80,173	90,005
150	150	150	450	500	600	1,000
500	600	600	2,100	2,700	2,700	3,600
400	500	500	1,500	1,500	1,500	2,100
983	739	1,215	3,596	3,520	3,442	2,907
450	450	450	1,950	2,250	2,250	3,300
50	50	50	950	1,050	1,050	1,050
1,825	1,915	2,015	11,745	14,595	14,595	25,070
220	242	266	969	1,290	1,717	2,100
640	640	640	1,921	1,675	1,527	1,527
5,218	5,286	5,387	25,181	29,080	29,381	42,654
− 1,171	748	2,595	11,680	30,693	50,792	47,351
− 400	254	882	3,971	10,436	17,269	16,099
− 771	494	1,713	7,709	20,257	33,523	31,252

Jan.–Mar.	Apr.–June	July–Sept.	Oct.–Dec.
$ 24,091	$ 40,179	$ 68,433	$ 92,278
7,872	9,054	10,412	11,974
500	500	500	1,000
225	225	225	225
149,000	149,000	149,000	158,000
1,000	1,000	1,000	2,000
182,688	226,262	235,305	265,477
28,425	27,216	26,466	25,716
104,736	101,808	95,952	91,560
133,161	129,024	122,418	117,276
49,527	97,238	122,887	148,201
182,688	226,262	235,305	265,477

Exhibit 29-2A PRINTECH Publishing Services, Inc., Financial Projections with Varityper VT–600, Actual and Projected Income Statements, Monthly April–December 1987, Quarterly 1988[a]

	April	May	June	July	Aug.	Sept.
Revenue						
Total revenue	$ 227	$ 177	$ 220	$ 480	$1,172	2,280
Less variable costs	630	0	0	0	50	155
Contribution margin	−403	177	220	480	1,122	2,125
Less fixed costs						
Tax accountant						75
Rent (office and furni-ture)	105	105	105	105	105	105
Utilities (auto and phone)			130	130	260	330
Interest expense	230	227	223	332	216	212
Insurance	200	200	200	200	200	300
Service contracts						50
Wages						600
Advertising						200
Depreciation	626	612	612	612	612	612
Total fixed costs	1,161	1,144	1,270	1,379	1,393	2,484
Profit (before taxes)	−1,564	−967	−1,050	−899	−271	−359
Taxes (34%)						−122
Profit after taxes						−237

Exhibit 29-2B PRINTECH Publishing Services, Inc., Financial Projections with Varityper VT–600, Actual and Projected Statement of Changes in Financial Position[a]

	Aug. 31	Sept. 30	Oct. 31	Nov. 30	Dec. 31
Assets					
Short-term assets					
Cash	$ 5,227	$24,081	$ 42,336	$ 39,206	$ 38,011
Accounts receiv-able	820	1,140	2,173	3,740	5,282
Inventory	500	500	500	500	500
Long-term assets					
Investment in chamber	225	225	225	225	225
Equipment	31,600	42,600	63,537	63,537	63,537
Furniture	1,000	1,500	2,000	2,000	2,000
Total Assets	39,372	70,046	110,771	109,208	109,555
Liabilities					
Notes payable	10,000	40,000	29,770	29,537	29,302
Leases payable	25,520	25,520	25,056	24,592	24,128
Total liabilities	35,520	65,520	54,826	54,129	53,430
Owner's equity	3,852	4,526	55,945	55,079	56,125
Liabilities and equity	39,372	70,046	110,771	109,208	109,555

[a]Statements and projections created by Elyse Warzeski—unaudited.

Oct.	Nov.	Dec.	Jan.–Mar.	Apr.–June	July–Sept	Oct.–Dec.
4,345	7,480	10,563	41,984	62,457	84,188	97,141
298	517	732	2,912	4,337	5,846	4,245
4,047	6,963	9,831	39,072	58,120	78,342	92,896
150	150	150	450	500	600	1,000
400	742	640	2,180	2,700	2,700	3,600
400	500	500	1,500	1,500	1,500	2,100
1,009	880	823	2,369	2,228	2,928	2,173
450	450	450	1,950	2,250	2,250	3,300
50	50	50	250	300	300	300
2,173	5,880	5,904	23,382	26,452	26,879	28,643
220	242	266	969	1,290	1,717	2,100
894	894	894	2,682	2,351	2,247	2,135
5,746	9,788	9,677	35,732	39,571	41,121	45,351
−1,699	−2,825	154	3,340	18,549	37,121	47,545
−578	−960	52	1,136	6,307	12,621	16,165
−1,121	−1,865	102	2,204	12,242	24,500	31,380

Jan.–Mar.	Apr.–June	July–Sept.	Oct.–Dec.
$ 33,652	$ 24,275	$ 63,940	$ 63,453
7,979	11,561	15,388	16,174
500	500	500	1,000
225	225	225	600
68,037	68,037	68,037	68,037
2,500	2,500	2,500	3,000
112,893	125,298	150,560	152,264
28,524	27,847	27,085	26,336
45,936	43,344	40,752	38,160
74,460	71,191	67,867	64,496
38,433	54,107	82,753	87,768
112,893	125,298	150,590	152,264

For desktop publishing functions the mouse was essential.) A local computer shop was willing to deal with them and share the commission on sales of computer systems. PRINTECH could also provide training for new desktop publishers.

Armed with this information, Elyce prepared several financial projections (Exhibits 29-1 and 29-2). She kept her figures fairly conservative and knew that the set of projections which included the L-300 were far riskier than the projections which included the VT-600. Projections for an L-100 would fall somewhere between the two. The expenditures would be less, and the income generated would be less than with an L-300.

Bob described his feelings at this stage:

> Finally, in August, I decided that we had to make the effort to build the business. My reasons included a sense of fairness to Elyce, who was ecstatic at the chance to use all her MBA skills, a continuing fascination with the business, and I think, a realistic appraisal of the market for Ph.D. geologists for the next few years. We decided to move forward in September, hiring two employees, looking for office space, buying additional equipment, and arranging for a substantial loan from a bank. I felt ambivalent about the decision, but committed.

They hired a very qualified office manager and acquired some part-time help as well. They also had a salesperson ready to come on board at a moment's notice. The bank informed Elyce that the loan was assured. Everything was ready, but Bob and Elyce were still in a quandary as to which direction they should go!

As of September 1, they had an assurance of up to $30,000 which they could borrow from the bank at a floating interest rate of 2 percent above the bank's prime, which was then 10 percent, and had decided that they were ready to sink up to $30,000 of their own into PRINTECH. They learned that the price of the VT-600 had dropped from $18,000 to $13,500, and their Linotronic sales representative found them a factory reconditioned L-100 which would cost them about $35,000 if they decided to go that route. They had summed up their various options as follows:

(1) They could stay relatively small, perhaps operating out of their home or renting some small, inexpensive office space. They could stay with their present equipment, purchasing only enough to provide sufficient terminals for their new employees. This would amount to perhaps another $5,000 worth of equipment. This option would provide them with the most flexibility. Bob could take a position at any time. The equipment could either be sold, or the office manager that they had hired could be left with a small and easily run desktop publishing business which Bob and Elyce could supervise long distance. This option would not make PRINTECH a great deal of money, but it would pay expenses for itself and generate sufficient income to keep Bob and Elyce comfortable until a faculty position appeared for Bob.

(2) They could concentrate on the business entirely, and Bob would give up his ambition to teach, at least for several years. If they chose this option, all the decisions listed above about office space and machinery would come into play. The business had a great deal of potential. The Warzeskis also faced a great deal of risk

with this option. The industry was new, and high-tech industries often have a very short life span. The market was untested, and there was little research Bob and Elyce could do to test that market. They would have to sink a substantial portion of their own capital into the business, which would jeopardize their security, as well as their daughter's. Their free time would be sharply curtailed which would leave them less time with their daughter.

(3) Instead of concentrating the business in New Orleans and the virgin New Orleans market, they could try to capitalize on telecommunications and generate a national clientele. This would allow them to move whenever necessary. However, it would cause their employees some hardship should they leave, because they would not be leaving a business behind, but rather, taking it with them. Bob and Elyce both felt a major responsibility to the people working for them and were unwilling to leave them in the lurch. Venturing into this market would also expose them to an enormous amount of competition. Desktop publishing magazines were full of advertisements for high resolution output via modem. To pursue this option, they would have no choice but to purchase the most expensive machinery, just to keep pace with the rest of the industry.

THE DECISION

Bob and Elyce had all but decided to take the second option. Bob was enjoying the desktop publishing business and being his own boss. Elyce felt that their marriage was stronger than it had ever been. It was obvious that as an entrepreneurial couple, Bob and Elyce balanced each other very well. Other businessmen had predicted either a failed business or a failed marriage with a husband and wife working together. The Warzeskis were taking a great deal of pride in proving these people wrong. And then the letters and announcements of geology positions arrived.

The geology market had opened up substantially while Bob and Elyce had had their backs turned. There were, in fact, a number of very good schools advertising for geologists with Bob's background and expertise. The ones that specifically wanted to interview him were hooked into a fine network of research institutions as well as being in beautiful parts of the country with excellent school systems. Since it was now apparent that he could get a good position, if he decided to actively campaign for one, Bob needed to make a major career decision. The schools which had contacted him wanted to interview him within a week.

At the same time, Elyce had several very interesting meetings with people who were looking for high-resolution output in the New Orleans area. These accounts would be very large, but they would have to be secured soon. These potential customers were looking to sign yearly contracts with someone who had a Linotronic-100 or 300. Any one of these contracts would easily cover the overhead costs of the machine.

Suddenly everything that had seemed perfectly obvious a week earlier was as clear as mud. The Warzeskis felt that they were being pulled in many different directions. They found themselves snapping at each other for no reason, and Elyce would burst into tears at the slightest provocation. They had invested seven months, a lot of hard work, and a good deal of money into PRINTECH, but Bob had spent 15 *years* becoming a geologist. They felt that they could be happy with the business, but it wasn't Bob's lifelong dream. If Bob decided to wait a year or two and then look for a faculty position, he was likely to find that the field had passed him by.

If PRINTECH stayed small until Bob found out whether or not he could secure a faculty position by the fall of 1988, would industry have passed PRINTECH by? Having finally been invited to visit several prestigious colleges, Bob knew neither how many candidates were being asked to interview, nor his chances of landing the job, nor the likelihood of achieving secure long-term employment (tenure being problematical at prestigious institutions). The other advertised positions indicated that he could, perhaps effectively, campaign for a position which would commence in the fall of 1988. It was customary for universities to make hiring decisions between January and April. Bob and Elyce wondered if the New Orleans market would remain wide open that long, especially with their Baton Rouge contact already interested in a New Orleans connection.

Bob and Elyce felt thoroughly confused, but they knew they had to make their decisions within the next couple of days.

Appendix A

HOW TO ANALYZE A CASE

W. Jack Duncan

Cases represent real situations that a manager has faced. They exhibit different degrees of complexity in order to present future decision makers with opportunities to practice solving different kinds of management problems. Because cases represent real situations, no two are solved in exactly the same way.

In this chapter one approach to case analysis is presented. The importance of this approach, which is illustrated in Exhibit A-1, is that it offers a process or way of thinking about cases rather than prescribing a universally applicable approach that can be applied to all the situations presented in this book. This approach is based on logical analysis whereby we first do our homework in steps one and two. In step one the emphasis is on learning about the company in the case; step two ensures that we analyze the situation and learn about the economy, industry, society, and political systems within which the company under review operates.

In step three the emphasis is on defining the problem before we progress to generation, evaluation, and selection of the preferred action. Recommendations must then be presented and the rationale provided for the proposed action. Although the approach outlined here is logical, it is important to remember that each case must be approached and appreciated as a unique opportunity for problem solving.

VARIETY IN CASES

Cases are widely used in strategic management, and the best ones are real, like those in this book. Cases reconstruct actual decisions made by managers in organizations. Liz Claiborne, Apple Computers, Delta Airlines, Zenith, and many other familiar names fill the table of contents.

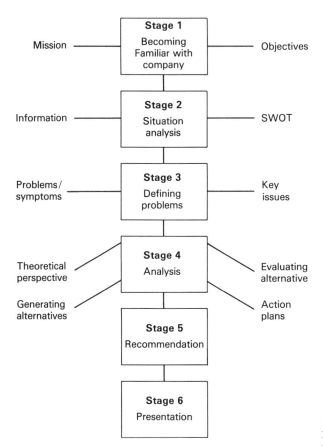

Exhibit A-1 **Overview of Effective Case Analysis**

Of course, less well-known cases have been selected because of the important issues they present to prospective managers. Sometimes the issues presented are not problems. Often the greatest challenge facing an organization is not solving a problem but recognizing and acting on an opportunity.

Cases rarely have obvious solutions upon which everyone will agree. This should not imply that there are no good or bad answers to the questions raised in cases. There are clearly bad, good, better, and best solutions to complex strategic cases, but typically the evaluation is based more on the logic or the way recommendations are derived than the specific actions suggested.

CASES STUDIED AND STRATEGIC MANAGEMENT

Cases add realism that cannot be achieved in customary lecture classes. Part of the realism results from the essential nature of cases. We may complain that cases do not provide enough information for making a decision. They rarely do. However, decision makers in real organizations seldom have all the information they want or need.

Dealing with Uncertainty

All decisions about the future involve uncertainty. John Kotter in *The General Managers* illustrates the nature of complex, executive level decision-making by stating that the managers he studied had "great difficulty explaining what it was they did, why, and why it worked as well as it did."[1] Strategic decision-making, because it is futuristic and involves judgment, is particularly challenging.

Because strategic decision-making deals with uncertainty, it also involves considerable risk. Cases help here as well because they allow us to practice making decisions in low-risk environments. As a student, you may not impress the professor or fellow class members if you fail to do your homework or prepare a case, but your failure will not force a company into bankruptcy. However, the lessons learned while solving cases and participating in discussions will begin to build problem-solving skills.

Unfortunately, few college students are familiar with how to analyze a case. Students get a lot of practice taking objective examinations, writing an occasional term paper, and crunching numbers on a computer but are rarely exposed to solving case problems. Therefore, this chapter is included—not to prescribe how all cases should be solved but to provide some initial direction on how to "surface" the real issues presented in the cases.

Solving Case Problems

In principle, solving a case is much like solving any other dilemma. The problems are defined, information is gathered, and alternatives are generated, evaluated, selected, and implemented. Although the student case analyst rarely has the opportunity to implement a decision, recommendations should be tempered by the limitations imposed on the organization in terms of its human and nonhuman resources. As the success or failure of the recommendations are analyzed and considered, lessons are learned that can be applied to future decision-making.

DIFFERENT ROLES AND CASE ANALYSIS

Diverse perspectives or roles can be assumed when analyzing cases. Some prefer to think of themselves as the president or financial officer in order to impose a perspective on the problems presented in the case. Others like to observe the case

---

[1]John P. Kotter, *The General Managers,* New York, Free Press, 1982, p. 9.

from the perspective of the consultant who has been invited into the organization to help solve a problem.

Any perspective can be imagined, but the first offers some unique advantages. Since there are no absolutely correct or incorrect answers to complex cases, one of the most important lessons to learn is why managers selected certain alternatives and pursued specific strategies under the conditions presented in the case. Becoming the manager, or at least mentally assuming the role, helps you learn the lessons case histories have to teach.

Consider Polaroid and its ill-advised decision to introduce the Polavision handheld, instant, home movie camera system. The detached consultant could easily point out that the product had serious limitations—its bright lights disturbed children, the pictures were grainy, and the show lasted less than three minutes.

The marketing consultant would no doubt suggest that movie cameras were losing out to video cameras even before the product was introduced. However, the case becomes more exciting when the role of the insider is assumed and the ego of Dr. Edwin Land, the company's founder, is experienced. Land was determined that Polavision would be the crowning achievement of his magnificent career and he, more than anyone else, was Polavision's champion.

Looking at a case from this perspective assists in moving beyond strategy to implementation and political issues, including the importance of interpersonal skills in decision making. How could those around Dr. Land have prevented the failure of the product? Who would have the courage to tell the founder that his ideas about Polavision were all wrong?

STEP 1. PREPARATION: BECOMING FAMILIAR WITH THE DETAILS

Effective case analysis begins with data collection. This initially means carefully reading the case, rereading it, and sometimes reading it again. Even the best students cannot absorb enough information from the first reading of a comprehensive case. Therefore, collect information and make notes as the details of the case problem unfold.

A Note on Information Sources

The data required to successfully solve a case comes in two forms. The first type of information is "given" as part of the case and customarily includes things like the firm's history, organization, management, and financial condition. Occasionally, a case will include information about the industry and maybe even some problems shared by all competing firms.

A second type of information is "obtainable." This information is not given in the case or by the instructor but is available from "secondary sources" in the library in familiar magazines and related publications. Obtainable secondary information helps us understand the nature of the industry, competing firms, and even some managers, past and present, who have made an impact on the industry. Detailed sources of this obtainable information are given in Appendix D.

If the case does not include industry information, your instructor may expect you to do some detective work before proceeding. Find out what is happening in the industry. Attempt to learn enough about trends to position the problems discussed in the case in a broader industrial context.

The culture of the organization or the style of the CEO may also constitute relevant information. An understanding of strategic decision-making at Beatrice Foods during the "reign" of its former CEO James Dutt, for example, required an appreciation of the philosophy of "Chairman James" as he was known in the company.

According to an article in *Fortune,* Dutt's style, among other things, was blamed for decreasing management and board involvement in key decisions, increases in corporate debt that threatened the security of the company, and a "mass exodus" of management personnel fleeing the chairman's wrath.[2] No serious case analysis could ignore such a significant factor in strategy making. All of this information becomes important as you become familiar with the organization and think about its purpose and objectives, its strengths and weaknesses, and the problems and opportunities facing the firm.

Purpose or Mission of the Company

Peter Drucker states that anyone who wants to "know" a business must start with understanding its purpose or mission.[3] If a mission statement is included in the case, does it serve the purpose of communicating to the public why the organization exists? Does it provide employees with a genuine statement of what the company is all about?

Mission statements provide valuable information, but they also leave much to be inferred and even imagined. Missions are broad, general statements outlining what makes the company unique. When the mission of the company is understood, a number of things are known that will help in arriving at a good solution to the case. Perhaps the greatest argument is made for a clear understanding of the company's mission by Chester Barnard in *The Functions of the Executive.* Barnard said that without a clear purpose or mission, an organization's environment is only a "mere mass of things" without meaning until this mass is reduced, organized, and structured according to the purpose of the organization.[4]

---

[2]Arthur M. Louis, "The Controversial Boss of Beatrice," *Fortune,* July 22, 1985, pp 110–116.

[3]Peter J. Drucker, *Management: Tasks, Responsibilities, and Practices,* New York, Harper & Row, 1974, p. 61.

[4]Chester I. Barnard, *The Functions of the Executive,* Cambridge, Harvard University Press, 1938, pp. 195–196.

A good ''sense'' of the company's mission, for example, should answer the following questions.

1. Who are the customers? The customers may be children, older adults, women, or pet owners. This group or these groups must be identified before any serious strategic analysis of the organization can be initiated.

2. What are the company's principle products or services? Does the company have its experience and expertise in consumer products, financial services, medical treatment, or some other area of specialization?

3. Where does the company intend to compete? Is the case about a company that competes only in one local market or is it a regional, national, or global economic force?

4. Who are the firm's competitors? Is the case about a company with a few well-known competitors or does it operate in a market along with hundreds of other similar firms? In other words, how much competition is actually present in the market(s) where the firm competes or intends to compete?

5. What is the preference of the company with regard to its public image? If the company wants to be perceived in certain ways it may have to limit its options when defining and solving strategic issues. Is it, for example, important to the company's leadership that the organization be regarded as a good citizen of the community or is the mere fact that it creates a large number of jobs sufficient?

6. What does the company want to be like in the future? Does the information in the case indicate the organization wants to continue to operate like it does at the present time or does it wish to expand its markets, product line, services offered, or even its own basic operating philosophy?

A good mission statement is invaluable in answering these questions. If a formal statement is not presented in a case, it is important to attempt to construct one from the information given.

Objectives: More Specific Directions

Whereas mission statements are broad and provide general direction, objectives should be specific and explicitly point out where the organization is expected to be in a year or so. Sometimes the case will indicate what the company plans to achieve in the next year, where it hopes to be in three years, or even its five-year goals. As with mission statements, if the objectives are not explicitly stated, there is a need to speculate about them since they will be the standards against which the success or failure of a particular strategy will eventually be evaluated.

When looking for or constructing company objectives, be sure they are as measurable as possible. This is important so decision makers can use them as a reflection of organizational priorities and as a way of determining how to set their own personal and professional priorities. Make sure that the objectives are motivational and inspirational, yet feasible and attainable. Moreover since strategic management is futuristic, and no one can predict the future with complete accuracy, objectives should always be adaptable to the changing conditions taking place in the company and in the industry. Sometimes a company can face a major strategic problem simply because it is unwilling to alter its objectives in light of changing conditions in the industry.

As a test of your own understanding of the case and the company under examination, before attacking any problems reflect on what your reading of the case has told you about the mission and objectives of the organization. Have you gained enough information and insight to comfortably:

- identify two or three of the primary values of the organization and speculate about the type of objectives it would like to accomplish;
- speculate about the kinds of measures that should be used to judge whether or not the values are being realized and the objectives are being accomplished;
- summarize the aspirations of the company's owners and managers realistically in view of the competition and the firm's strengths and weaknesses;
- evaluate whether or not the objectives being pursued are consistent with what you understand to be the mission of the company?

If you are not comfortable with your answers to this list of questions, another reading of the case is probably required.

Problems and Opportunities

Begin immediately identifying the strategic problems and opportunities faced by the company. When a problem is suggested, write it down and mark it for more detailed examination. Are the problems financial? Do the primary issues appear to be those of human resources, capital investment, or marketing? Perhaps there are few, if any, apparent problems. The strategic issue facing the company may be an opportunity to be exploited or at least investigated.

Federal Express, for example, was worried about the growing trend of electronically transferred messages. Instead of looking at the trend as a problem, the company chose to view electronic mail as an opportunity and entered the market with its ill-fated Zap Mail. Later this opportunity turned into a problem and after a loss of almost $350 million Zap Mail was dropped. Federal Express now hopes to do better with its recent acquisition of Flying Tiger Airlines and its plan to challenge United Parcel Service and other firms with its new capability for delivering services around the globe. Looking for the purpose, experimenting with objectives, and identifying problems and opportunities facing the company are all necessary first steps to understanding a case.

STEP 2. SITUATION ANALYSIS

After getting a fix on the company's mission and the initial impressions of the major strategic issues in the case the next step is gaining an understanding of where the firm, the industry, and the decision makers are at the time some type of strategic decision is needed. This is called *situation analysis* because the decision maker must understand the circumstances and the environment facing the organization.

Some Dimensions of Situation Analysis

Situation analysis is one of the most important steps in case analysis. The list below highlights some of the important areas that should be included in this stage of case analysis.

I. The Environment of the Company
   A. What is the size and growth trends in the industry?
   B. What is the nature of competition? How many direct competitors are there and is the competition increasing or decreasing? What are the relative market shares of the different competitors? Is there any significant pressure from foreign competitors?
   C. What macroenvironmental factors affect the company? What prevailing economic conditions, regulatory philosophies, life-style changes, demographic factors, and technological forces are likely to influence strategic decision making? What is the industry's and the company's history with respect to labor-management relations?

II. The Market
   A. Who are the company's primary customers? To what extent are they loyal to the firm's products and services? Is price the only major determinant in the purchasing decision of customers?
   B. What about products and services? Does the company offer a full range of products? Is the present product or service mix complementary? Does the company compete with itself in some areas?
   C. Are all products in the same stage of a product life cycle? Is the line a well-rounded mix of some products in the takeoff stage, some mature, and very few in the declining phase? Does this investigation suggest the need for new products or the need to trim down the product line?
   D. Is the market for the company's products or services geographically concentrated? regional? national? international?
   E. How sophisticated are the company's customers in terms of their buying habits and processes? What does this tell management about advertising and promotion?

  F. Are market segments easily identified? Are different strategies for each feasible or advisable?

III. The Firm

  A. Does the company have a clear sense of mission? Is there a mission statement and is it communicated to those responsible for accomplishing it? Are there well-developed and communicated long- and short-range objectives? Does the company have the human and nonhuman resources necessary to accomplish its mission?

  B. How sophisticated is the company in terms of marketing products and services? Has serious thought been given to advertising strategy? Has the appropriate channel(s) of distribution been identified and utilized? How flexible are the company's marketing policies—when was the last time management tried something new and innovative?

  C. Are the financial resources needed to compete available? Is the firm undercapitalized, too highly leveraged, or not leveraged enough? How do the key financial ratios of this firm compare with others in the industry and region?

Strengths, Weaknesses, Opportunities, and Threats

Once we have reviewed the situation, a better evaluation of the opportunities and threats facing the company can be made. Moreover, once we have done a good job of situation analysis, we should be able to look objectively at the firm and ask: "Given the company's apparent strengths and weaknesses how do we take advantage of opportunities and avoid the dangers in the environment?" One effective way of asking this type of question is with the use of SWOT (strengths, weaknesses, opportunities, and threats) analysis. An example of SWOT analysis is illustrated in Exhibit A-2.

Suppose in a case you are studying, there is an opportunity to buy a complementary company and thereby diversify the product line. SWOT analysis can be used to relate strengths, weaknesses, opportunities, and threats. Since the product produced by the other company uses similar technology, there is a strong possibility that our company can capitalize on its experience and skills in marketing present products and successfully run the acquired firm.

Unfortunately, a review of the financial statements presented with the case suggests that we have already borrowed too much money on a short-term basis and are experiencing problems generating the cash through operations to meet the interest payments each month. This is an internal weakness found in the information presented.

Because the company has borrowed a great deal of money, it must keep an eye on interest rates. If historical records show that during the time of the case interest rates were going up, this could be a serious threat to the continued growth

Exhibit A-2   **Strengths, Weaknesses, Opportunities, and Threats (SWOT) Analysis**

Potential Internal Strengths	**Potential Internal Weaknesses**
1. Expertise in what it does	1. No understood and communicated
2. Adequate financial resources	strategic direction
3. Good reputation in marketplace	2. Inadequate financing
4. Large enough to take advantage of	3. Limited R&D efforts
economies of scale	4. Limited marketing skills
5. Proprietary technology	5. Limited experience among managers
6. Proven management ability	
7. Balanced product line	

Potential External Opportunities	**Potential External Threats**
1. Possibility to diversify into new products	1. Likely entry of new competitors
2. Possibility to develop customer bases	2. Attraction of foreign competitors
3. Opportunity to vertically integrate and diversify	3. Poor economic outlook in related sectors
4. Complacency among competitors	4. Increased regulation
5. Excess capacity in present operations	5. Adverse demographic changes
	6. Popular substitutes

of the firm. Another potentially serious external threat is the competitors' need for good employees and their frequent attempts to hire our experienced employees rather than train their own work force.

We know this will be a continuing problem because our employees are experienced and much more productive than others in the industry. This is an internal strength given by the case.

With the use of an illustration like Exhibit A-2, we can "play around with" the possible outcomes resulting from internal strengths and weaknesses coming into combination with external threats and opportunities. A SWOT analysis helps better manage and organize information to facilitate decision-making.

STEP 3. DEFINING PROBLEMS

Situation analysis is designed to surface present and potential problems. In case analysis, problems include not only the usual idea of a "problem" but also situations where things may be working well but improvements are possible. As noted previously, the "problem" may actually be an opportunity that can be capitalized on by the firm if it acts consciously and decisively.

When analysis progresses carefully, patterns develop and discrepancies between what actually is and what ought to be become more apparent. In other words, core problems begin to emerge.

Looking for Core Problems Rather than Symptoms

It is important to realize that the events actually observed and "facts" provided in the case may not be the "core" or essential problems. Often what we see in an organization are the symptoms of more serious core problems. For example, increasing interest rates and cash flow discrepancies appear to be problems in many case analyses. In reality the core problem is the absence of adequate financial planning. The lack of planning is simply manifested as a cash flow problem.

Frequently, businesses conclude that they have operational problems in the area of marketing when sales are declining. Someone may suggest that the sales personnel are not working as hard as they should or the company is not spending enough on advertising. The real problem might be fundamental changes in the demographics of the market or outdated product lines that no amount of hard work or advertising will correct. Furthermore, in organizations as complex as the typical business firm, problems may have more than a single cause, so do not be overly confident when a single, simple reason is isolated.

Getting to core problems requires that the given and obtainable information be carefully examined and analyzed. Often quantitative tools can help. Financial ratio analysis of the exhibits included in the case will sometimes be helpful in the identification of real problems. Appendix B illustrates how financial analysis and information can be used to identify core problems of the organization.

In arriving at the ultimate determination of core problems, case analysis should never be "paralyzed by analysis" and waste more time than is necessary identifying problems. At the same time premature judgments about problem areas should not be made because of the risk of missing the "real" issues.

Always review the obtainable sources of data before moving to the next step in the analysis. One general guideline is that when research and analysis cease to generate surprises (when we can confidently say "I have seen that before") we can feel relatively, but not absolutely, sure that adequate research has been conducted, and the core problems have been identified.

The problem and opportunity discovery process should not become myopic. There is a tendency on the part of accounting students to focus exclusively on financial issues, marketing majors are tempted to look only at marketing, and management students see little more than management implications. This is too limited a view for effective strategic decision makers. Strategic analysis is the work of "general managers" or those who effectively transcend a single function.

Successful case analysis depends on correctly identifying the problems. Insistence on approaching case analysis exclusively from the viewpoint of one's own expertise and training is not likely to produce an accurate overall picture of the situation facing the company nor is this approach likely to improve the company's performance.

One final caution. Never blindly accept information, either given or obtained, at face value. The ratios on a company's financial statements may look strange, but are they? Before jumping to such a conclusion look at the company's financial ratios in a historical perspective. Even better, look at similar ratios of other companies in the same industry during the same time period.

Identifying Important Issues

Once the problems are identified they must be precisely stated and the selection defended. The best defense for the selection of core problems is the data set used to guide the problem discovery process. The reasons for selection of the problems and issues should be briefly and specifically summarized along with the supportive information on which judgments have been based.

Stating the Problem.   Problem statement is not a time for solutions. Focusing on solutions at this point will only reduce the impact of the problem statement. If the role of consultant has been assumed, the problem statement must be convincing, precise, and logical to the client organization, or credibility will be reduced. If the role of the strategic decision maker has been selected, you must be equally convincing and precise and perhaps even more sure that the correction of identified problems or pursuit of opportunities will put the company on the road to prosperity or at the very least on the road to recovery. After all, the manager will be the one responsible for ensuring things actually happen and that strategies are actually implemented.

Focus on Results.   Problem statements should relate only to those areas of strategy and operations where actions have a chance of producing important results. The results may be either increasing gains or cutting potential losses. Long- and short-range aspects of problems should also be identified and stated. In strategic analysis, the emphasis must always be on long-range problems rather than merely patching up emergencies and holding things together.

It is important to keep in mind that most strategic decision makers can deal with only a limited number of issues at a single time. Therefore, it is important to identify key result areas or critical success factors that will have the greatest positive impact on organizational performance.

STEP 4. ANALYSIS

When the problem(s) in the case are satisfactorily defined they must be analyzed. This involves: (1) developing a theoretical perspective; (2) generating alternative solutions or actions; and (3) evaluating the alternatives.

Developing a Perspective

One of the most serious mistakes made in case analysis is to attempt analysis inside a "theoretical vacuum." Although strategic management is not highly theoretical compared to other areas of management, it is important that the problems be defined and opportunities be evaluated according to some consistent theoretical perspective.

Are the problems the kind that cash flow analysis can assist in solving? Are the strategic issues facing the firm problems of leadership, organization, or control? For example, in order to understand the strategy followed by R. J. Reynolds since 1965 it is necessary to know something about the theory of diversification and also the theory of "sticking to one's own knitting."

Over the past two decades the American public has watched RJR Nabisco move from an almost exclusively tobacco company to a world leader in the consumer foods industry. The move has been accomplished by first attempting to spread risks in view of the surgeon general's report on the ill effects of smoking and the fitness trend among a large segment of society, as well as opportunistic investments.

After acquiring firms in the oil, transportation, and aluminum casting industries, management realized its real expertise was in consumer goods. In recent years the company has been involved in an attempt to move more directly and completely into consumer foods. There are sound practical reasons why this particular strategy has been initiated. RJR knows about consumers because of its success in making and marketing tobacco products for many years. The company's managers have been accustomed to keeping abreast of what is happening in consumer products; the organization itself appears more comfortable with its role in consumer goods.

Generating Alternative Actions and Solutions

If information has been managed and organized, the generation of alternatives will be a challenging but attainable task. To look at options, the given and obtained information must be matched with what is known about financial analysis, statistics, marketing, and management so that actions consistent with the company mission can be generated.

Good alternatives possess several characteristics. First, they should be *practical.* No one will seriously look at an alternative that is too theoretical and abstract to be understood by the people who have to accomplish it. Second, alternatives should be *carefully stated* with a brief justification of why they are believed to be practical ways of solving at least one of the core problems in the case.

Third, alternatives should be *specific.* Relate each alternative to the core problem it is intended to address. This is a good check on your work. If the alternatives generated do not directly address core problems ask how important they are to the case analysis.

Fourth, alternatives should be *implementable,* that is, they can be reasonably accomplished within the constraints of the financial and human resources available to the company. Finally, generated alternatives should be ones that can be *placed into action* in a relatively short period of time. If it takes too long to implement a proposed solution it is likely that the momentum of the recommended action will

566

Cases in Strategic Management and Business Policy

be lost. Of course, the implementation should always take place in light of the potential long-range effects of shorter term decision making.

After the alternatives have been generated and listed, each one must be: (1) evaluated in terms of the core problems and key result areas isolated in the prior analysis; (2) evaluated in terms of relative advantage or disadvantage compared with other possible solutions to core problems; and (3) justified as a potentially valuable way of addressing the strategic issues found in the case.

Evaluating Alternatives

Alternatives should be evaluated according to both quantitative and qualitative criteria. Financial analysis provides one basis for examining the impact of different courses of action. However, a good alternative course of action is usually more than merely the one with the highest payoff. It may be that the culture of the organization could not accommodate some of the more financially promising alternative courses of action.

For example, an established policy and practice in the firm may require that no more than a certain percentage of debt financing be tolerated. Although the financial analysis illustrates that additional debt is the low cost way to finance expansion, top management can be expected to reject the level of debt required, making other options necessary. On the more qualitative side, a company with a reputation for avoiding layoffs at all costs could be expected to reject any strategic alternative that involves plant closings and radical relocations.

Once the alternatives have been evaluated one must be selected. At this point it is *absolutely essential* to completely understand the criteria upon which the selection is being made and the justification for the criteria. Sometimes the key to identifying the criteria is in the case itself. The owner or CEO may have clearly stated the basis upon which decisions are to be made.

At other times it is necessary to look beyond the company to what is going on in the industry. Is price competition so fierce that capital investment decisions are likely to radically affect the ability to compete with other firms? If so, should the company intentionally postpone short-term actions and ensure enough resources are dedicated to modernization of plant facilities in order to improve the chances of long-range growth and development?

Action Planning

Once the strategic alternative(s) is selected an action plan is required. Action planning moves the decision maker from the realm of strategy to operations. Now the question becomes the very simple "how do we get all this done in the most effective and efficient way possible?"

The task of case analysis does not require that the student implement a decision in a real firm. However, because our alternatives must be "implementable," it is necessary that thought be given to how each alternative would actually be put into action in the company under review. This is called action planning and requires three important steps for each recommended alternative. First, the decision maker must decide what activities are needed to accomplish the alternative action. This involves thinking through the process and outlining all the steps that will be required.

Next, the list of required activities should be carefully reviewed and tasks should be grouped into logical patterns. Accounting functions go into one group, production activities go into another, and financial activities go into a third. Each itemized activity must be placed into such a group, and any activities that do not fit neatly into the existing organization of the company have to be placed in another category of tasks. If this "other" list is too long it may suggest that the organizational structure of the company needs revision.

Finally, the responsibility for accomplishing the different groups of tasks must be clearly assigned to the appropriate individuals in the organization. Although this is not always possible in case analysis, it is important that consideration be given to how, in a real organization, the recommendations will be accomplished. If, in the process of thinking about getting the different activities completed, it becomes apparent that the company does not have the resources or the organization to accomplish the recommendations other approaches should be proposed.

The process of action planning should never be neglected. Unfortunately, many organizations spend great amounts of money and resources developing strategic plans only to discover that they are not prepared to implement them in an effective manner.

STEP 5. RECOMMENDATIONS

Making good recommendations is a critical aspect of successful case analysis. If recommendations are theoretically sound and justifiable people will pay attention to them. If they are not, little is likely to result from all the work done to this point.

One effective method for presenting recommendations is to relate each recommendation to the firm's strengths. Or, if necessary, illustrate how a recommendation avoids known weaknesses. If the company under examination has obvious financial strengths the recommendations should highlight how each alternative action will capitalize on the financial condition of the company. If the marketing resources are limited, it will be important to avoid recommendations that rely on resources that are not available.

When making recommendations, it will be particularly useful to evaluate each suggested action by carefully looking at company resources that will be needed for implementation. For example, ask yourself the following questions with respect to each recommendation.

1. Does the company have the financial resources needed to make the recommendation work?

2. Does the company have the personnel to accomplish what will be required by each recommendation?

3. Does the company have the controls needed to monitor whether or not the recommendations are being accomplished?

4. Is the timing right to implement each recommendation? If not, when will the timing be right and can the company wait?

STEP 6. PREPARING THE REPORT

The preparation and presentation of the case report is the end result of case analysis. The report can be either written or oral depending on the instructions of the teacher. Although each is different, the goal is the same—to summarize and communicate effectively what the analysis has uncovered. This final section will only provide a brief outline of how to construct a written report. Appendix C provides guidance for making an oral presentation of the case analysis.

Decision-making is the intended result of the report. The analysis must be complete, but the emphasis should be on making the entire report brief enough that people will read it and at the same time comprehensive enough to ensure no major factors are overlooked that might adversely affect the decision. Below is a brief outline of the important sections of a written case analysis report.

Executive Summary

One of the most important things a written case analysis can teach prospective managers is how to organize and present ideas in a short, concise, hard-hitting manner. Always keep in mind that the reader is a busy person who needs information about the case. At the same time, the reader wants the essential facts fast.

In view of this, one of the most important parts of a case report is the executive summary. This brief section (usually not more than two pages) performs the function of an abstract. Its purpose is to provide a minimum amount of historical information to familiarize the reader with the firm and the industry. An equally important function of the executive summary is to force the writer to evaluate carefully what is really important in all the facts and data that have been accumulated.

The executive summary should clearly state the major problems or opportunities facing the organization. The outline of strategic issues should be followed by a list of recommendations and a brief justification for each. This summary will allow the reader to quickly see what has been done, help the reader see the logic of the following report, and force the analyst to think about the company's problems and formulate recommendations in a direct manner rather than hiding them away in the body of the case report.

Body of the Case Report

The body of the case analysis should be broken into several sections. The first section should report what you found in the *situation analysis*. What is the state of the firm today? What type of industry is it in and what is happening with regard to the competition?

The *strategic problems* should be introduced after the situation analysis. In this section the three to five most important strategic issues facing the firm should be listed and a justification provided for the inclusion of each. Consideration should also be given at this point to the *operational strengths and weaknesses* inside the firm and how they relate to the basic strategic problems.

It is a particularly good practice when matching the strategic issues and the company's strengths and weaknesses to think about the structure and the personnel of the firm. When the strategic issues are presented it is useful to outline them in terms of the functional areas of the organization most critical for the implementation of the recommendation. Therefore, the body of the report should include careful consideration of the production, financial, marketing, information processing, and human resource implications of the different recommended courses of action.

This final area is particularly important. All strategic actions must ultimately be accomplished by people. Therefore, the action plan for accomplishing recommended courses of action should include an audit of the individual capabilities required to insure the actions are taken. Who will be responsible for getting each of the recommendations accomplished? Is this individual likely to have the skills required to complete the task? If not, what actions will be necessary before the recommendation is fully implemented?

In view of the strategic problems and the operational condition of the company the *alternative* courses of action can now be generated and listed. Each of the alternatives can then be *evaluated*. When the evaluation is complete, the *recommendations* should be presented in considerable detail and particular attention given to the problem of *implementation*.

When writing a formal case analysis remember the following points:

1. Make the report look professional. Get a good typist or be sure you use a word processor with a reasonably good ribbon. If graphs and related tabular material are used, make sure the figures are drawn well, the words are spelled right, and the tables are neat. Face it, nothing is going to affect the creditability of your analysis more than how it looks!

2. Put yourself in the reader's place. It only takes a little extra effort to anticipate potential problems for those who read the analysis. The more problems that can be eliminated, the more favorable the ultimate evaluation will be. Make the sections as short as possible. Use subheadings to lead the reader through the text and make it more interesting.

3. Get the reader interested and never lose the initiative. It is a good idea to

have a hard-hitting or witty introduction so as to create a favorable initial impression. The careful use of charts, tables, and other visual aids is well worth the time, energy, and expense.

Always provide a list of sources that might be useful to decision makers so they can follow up on points made in the body of the report. Do not attempt to impress the professor with the length of the reading list used in compiling the references. To the contrary, find some very good sources that apply to the case analysis and list these valuable sources in a way that the reader can follow up on them if he or she wishes to do so.

It is particularly helpful to abstract the most useful sources. This will not do away with the reader's need to review the sources but it will help him/her decide precisely which sources need to be read in greater detail.

CONCLUSIONS

Case analysis is an art. There is no precise way to accomplish the task. Adapt the analysis to the particular case problem under review. The thing to keep in mind is that case analysis is a logical process that involves: (1) understanding of the company, industry, and environment; (2) clear definition of strategic problems and opportunities; (3) generation of alternative courses of action; (4) analysis, evaluation, and selection of the most promising courses of action; and (5) consideration of the operational aspects of how and by whom the recommendations will be accomplished.

The work of case analysis is not complete until a report or presentation of the recommendations is provided. Case analysis and presentation should always be approached and accomplished in a professional manner. Case problems provide a unique opportunity to integrate all you have learned about decision making and direct it toward specific problems and opportunities faced by real organizations. It is an exciting way to gain experience and decision-making skills. Take it seriously and develop your own, systematic, and defensible way of solving management problems.

REFERENCES

Barnard, Chester I., *The Functions of the Executive* (Cambridge, MA: Harvard University Press, 1938).

Drucker, Peter F., *Management: Tasks, Responsibilities, and Practices* (New York: Harper and Row, 1974).

Edge, Alfred G., and Denis R. Coleman, *The Guide to Case Analysis and Reporting,* 3rd ed. (Honolulu, HI: System Logic, Inc., 1986).

Kotter, John P., *The General Managers* (New York: Free Press, 1982).

Louis, Arthur M., ''The Controversial Boss of Beatrice,'' *Fortune,* July 22, 1985, pp. 110–116.

Pearce, John II, and Fred David, ''Corporate Mission Statements: The Bottom Line,'' *Academy of Management Executive,* May 1987, pp. 109–116.

Ronstadt, Robert, *The Art of Case Analysis* (Dover, MA: Lord Publishing, 1980).

FINANCIAL STATEMENT ANALYSIS: A PRACTICAL GUIDE

Bennie H. Nunnally, Jr.

INTRODUCTION

The purpose of financial analysis is to gain knowledge of the financial condition of the firm. That condition is represented by the firm's *profitability, liquidity, asset management,* and *financing pattern.* While profitability may be self-explanatory, the other concepts, which may be observed and analyzed from the firm's financial statements, will briefly be explained. Liquidity represents the firm's ability to pay its current liabilities (examples include accounts payable, wages/taxes payable) out of its current liabilities (which includes cash and accounts receivable). Asset management information reveals the firm's ability to make use of its cash, land and buildings, and equipment in order to increase the value of the firm. The firm's financing pattern refers to the amount of debt used by the firm to finance its assets, and how, if at all, that pattern compares to similar firms or to the firm's own operating history.

THE BASIC FINANCIAL STATEMENTS

The financial statements issued by for-profit firms are found in the annual report. The annual report is both an official (audited financial statement) and unofficial (management assessments and projections of a relatively nonquantitative nature) record of the company's position at that point in time. The annual report is issued by all firms whose stock is publicly traded. The financial statements found in the annual report are the balance sheet, income statement, statement of changes in financial position, and the statement of retained earnings.

To analyze financial statements it is necessary to understand the relationship among the statements. In order to understand such an interrelationship it is important to become familiar with each individual statement. A first step in becoming skillful in statement analysis is to learn the general format. If the format is familiar, it then becomes much easier to learn the techniques of analysis. We will see that there is a pattern to the structure or format of the balance sheet. Simply, the balance sheet items are arranged in descending order of liquidity. Familiarity with the statements will greatly contribute to the interesting, useful and, yes, marketable things which will be learned in this note.

Exhibits B-1, B-2, B-3, and B-4 illustrate the financial statements of the Ellison Manufacturing Company. The format of each statement is typical of those released by most firms. Ellison manufactures various paper and cardboard containers, and most sales are to the grocery industry.

The Income Statement

The firm's income statement, sometimes called a profit and loss statement, reflects the revenue less the expenses related to making those sales for a specific period of time. Taxes are also shown on the income statement, with a final figure being net income. In Exhibit B-1 the net income after-tax is divided by the number of common shares outstanding to reflect the earnings as it applies to each share of outstanding common stock (earnings per share or EPS). In addition, the amount of net income actually paid out as dividends is shown on Ellison's income statement. The dividends paid are based on a predetermined and relatively stable company policy but are declared by the board of directors in each dividend period.

Exhibit B-1   **Ellison Manufacturing Company Income Statement for Years Ended 1989–1990**

	1989	1990
Sales	$109,848	$126,540
Cost of goods sold[a]	68,065	72,834
Gross profit	41,783	53,706
Expenses (selling, administrative interest, depreciation)	27,462	31,044
Profit before tax	14,321	22,662
Taxes (45%)	6,444	10,198
Net income	7,877	12,464
Earnings per share (EPS)	7.88	12.46
Dividends per share (DPS 49%)	3.86	6.11
[a]Determined as follows:	**1989**	**1990**
Beginning inventory	$28,663	$ 27,462
Purchases	66,864	76,953
Goods available for sale	95,527	104,415
Ending inventory	27,462	31,581
Cost of goods sold	$68,065	$ 72,834

Exhibit B-2   **Ellison Manufacturing Company, Balance Sheet, December 31, 1989; December 31, 1990**

	1989	1990
Assets		
Cash	$ 6,925	$ 8,185
Accounts receivable	418	481
Inventory	27,462	31,581
Total current assets	34,805	40,247
Property, plant, equipment	14,328	16,477
Accumulated depreciation	1,194	1,374
Net property, plant, equipment	13,134	15,104
Total Assets	$47,939	$55,351
Liabilities and Equity		
Accounts payable	$ 4,537	$ 5,218
Accrued wages and taxes	2,448	2,815
Total Current Liabilities	6,985	8,033
Long-term debt (12%)	5,134	5,134
Common stock (1000 shares)	11,940	11,940
Paid-in-capital	5,970	5,970
Retained earnings	17,910	24,274
Total Liabilities and Stockholders' Equity	$47,939	$55,351

The Balance Sheet

A balance sheet (Exhibit B-2) shows the financial condition of the firm at a particular point in time. In the case of Ellison Manufacturing Company, the balance sheets are provided for the end of the calendar years 1989 and 1990. The calendar year and the firm's fiscal year (the accounting period which begins and ends at a particular time during the year, as determined by company management and at the end of which the annual reports are issued) may not coincide. The assets shown in Exhibit B-2 represent the means of production which are *owned* by the firm. The liabilities and equity, the right-hand side of the balance sheet, represent the claims on these assets. That section shows all current liabilities and other debt items and

Exhibit B-3   **Ellison Manufacturing Company Statement of Retained Earnings**

Retained earnings balance 12/31/89	$17,910
Plus net income—1990	12,464
Less dividends paid—1990	(6,100)
Retained earnings balance 12/31/90	$24,274

Exhibit B-4   **Ellison Manufacturing Company Statement of Changes in Financial Position, December 31, 1990**

Sources

Profit after tax	$12,464
Depreciation	179
Total sources	$12,643

Uses

Dividends	$ 6,100
Fixed assets	2,149
Net change in working capital	4,394
	$12,643

Analysis of Working Capital Changes

Increase (decrease) in current assets		Increase (decrease) in current liabilities	
Cash	$1,260	A/Payable	$ 681
A/Receivable	63	Accruals	368
Inventory	4,119	Total	$1,049
Total	$5,442		

Increase in current assets	= $5,442
Increase in current liabilities	= 1,048
Net change in working capital	= $4,394

---

the owner-supplied capital such as stockholders' equity. (The sum of common stock, retained earnings, and paid-in-capital, which is dollars received for common stock in excess of par value, equals stockholders' equity). The assets must equal the liabilities plus capital of the firm.

Statement of Retained Earnings

A firm has two uses for its profit. A portion is paid to the owners (equity holders) as dividends. The remaining profit is retained in the firm, thereby becoming a part, or all, of the financing for the assets of the firm. That part retained in the firm is added to the balance sheet item "retained earnings" at the end of each accounting period. This is an important way in which the income statement and balance sheet are interrelated.

Statement of Changes in Financial Position

A company's managers, its creditors, and other individuals or organizations will at some point be interested in a firm's *liquidity*. Liquidity refers to the ease with which an asset can be converted to cash. Such would be most important to creditors, say, if the firm were to become bankrupt. The change in financial position, as well as the current financial position, relates directly to the question of liquidity. Exhibit B-4 illustrates the *uses* of funds by Ellison Manufacturing Company, and the *sources* of funds between 1989 and 1990. The statement of changes in financial position is often referred to as a "source and use of funds" statement because it illustrates the origin or source of money used by the firm in a given time period. The following definitions may help to clarify the nature of sources and uses of funds.

A source of funds equals an increase in a liability or capital account or a decrease in an asset account.

A use of funds equals a decrease in a liability or capital account or an increase in an asset account. For example, in Exhibit B-2 Ellison Manufacturing had an increase in accounts receivable of $63 ($481–$418) between year-end 1989 and year-end 1990. That was a *use* of funds of $63 for that period because Ellison committed $63 in additional funds for that period to an asset. By contrast the $681 increase in accounts payable for the same period represents a source of funds for the firm because Ellison's suppliers financed Ellison's increased payables for that period.

The preparation of the sources and uses of funds statement begins with the selection of an interval of time, one fiscal year to the next, for example. Then the items which provide cash or require cash, for that time period, may be compared. The result will be the effect of the "cash movement" upon working capital. Working capital is current assets and current liabilities collectively; net working capital is current assets minus current liabilities.

A sources and uses of funds statement also permits the maturity of the sources and uses to be compared. It is necessary, in general, that the maturity of the source (short term such as an increase in accounts payable) be matched with the maturity of the use (short term such as increase in inventory). Such maturity matching will likely lead to improved control over the firm's working capital. That improved control will likely reduce the level of frequency of borrowed funds.

RATIO ANALYSIS

The analysis of financial statements involves recognizing the information conveyed by each statement and the interrelationship among the statements. In addition, the time for which the statement is analyzed should be consistent if more than one type of statement is being reviewed. The informational content of the financial statements can best be seen in terms of financial ratio analysis.

Financial ratio analysis is a means of reviewing financial data relative to some standard. That standard may be trend (activity over time) or industry comparison or both. The ratios may be divided into five categories: (1) liquidity ratios, (2) debt management ratios, (3) asset management ratios, (4) profitability ratios, and (5) market value ratios. The financial data presented for Ellison Manufacturing Company will be used to illustrate the computations and ideas in this section.

Liquidity Ratios

As noted previously, a firm's liquidity is a major concern for anyone who has dollars invested in that firm or if an investment is being considered. Liquidity ratios indicate whether a firm has enough cash or other liquid assets to meet its short-term obligations.

Current Ratio.   The current ratio is equal to current assets divided by the current liabilities. Current assets are those assets which will be converted to cash within the near future, usually a year or less. Current liabilities are those liabilities which will likely be paid within a year's time. The current assets and liabilities are liquidated as a normal part of the firm's business activities. The current ratio is a direct measure of the firm's liquidity. For Ellison Manufacturing the current ratios for 1989 and 1990 are as follows:

$$\text{Current ratio} = \frac{\text{Current assets}}{\text{Current liabilities}}$$

$$\text{Current ratio}_{1989} = \frac{\$34,805}{\$6,985} = 4.98 \text{ times}$$

$$\text{Current ratio}_{1990} = \frac{\$40,247}{\$8,033} = 5.0 \text{ times}$$

An interested party can immediately draw the following information from the company's current ratio: (1) If the firm had to liquidate (pay its creditors and cease operation) it would be able to cover each dollar owed in current liabilities with approximately \$5 of current assets. (2) Assuming an industry average of 4 times, then, Ellison is 25 percent more liquid than the average firm of its type, in its industry. Therefore, Ellison's current ratio is favorable.

Quick Ratio.   The items on the balance sheet are arranged in descending order of liquidity—if inventory (often the least liquid of the current assets) is not a part of the firm's liquidity then we can calculate a "quick" ratio for Ellison. The quick ratio is equal to the current assets, minus inventory, divided by total current liabilities.

$$\text{Quick ratio} = \frac{\text{Current assets} - \text{inventory}}{\text{Current liabilities}}$$

$$\text{Quick ratio}_{1990} = \frac{\$40,247 - \$31,581}{\$8,033} = 1.08 \text{ times}$$

Thus, if Ellison had to liquidate quickly it could still cover its current liabilities even if inventory were not readily convertible to cash. As with the current ratio, the quick ratio (sometimes called the acid-test ratio) can be compared to an industry average or to the firm's own performance during some prior period.

Debt Management Ratios

The debt management ratios provide information concerning the firm's use of funds supplied by creditors. The use of borrowed funds by a firm is often referred to as the use of leverage. In general, however, leverage is the use of fixed costs either in financing or operations. In financing, that fixed cost is interest, in operations the fixed cost is the use of automation versus human labor.

Debt Ratio.   The firm's total debt is the sum of current liabilities plus the firm's long-term debt. The long-term debt is clearly designated as such on Ellison's balance sheet. Long-term debt could also be shown as mortgages, or any of several types of debt. It is that portion of total debt that will not be paid in the current year. The *debt ratio* for the firm is as follows:

$$\text{Debt ratio}_{1990} = \frac{\text{Total debt}}{\text{Total assets}} = \frac{\$13,167}{\$55,351} = 23.8\%$$

For Ellison in 1990 the debt ratio was approximately 24 percent. That is, in 1990, 24 percent of the company's assets were financed with borrowed funds. The remaining 76 percent of assets were financed with common equity. Again, the trend or industry comparison or both applies to this ratio category—as indeed it does for all of the ratio categories.

Times Interest Earned.   Firms pay interest on the long-term debt which they carry, and on occasion there may be short-term debt which also requires interest. Such short-term borrowing will likely be shown as "notes payable" or "bank borrowing" and will be a current liability. In any case, the interest attached to the borrowed funds is a legal obligation. The inability of a firm to meet its interest payments could place a firm in bankruptcy. The ability to pay interest then is quite important, and the times interest earned ratio states directly how many times gross earnings will cover the firm's interest charges.

$$\text{Times interest earned} = \frac{\text{Earnings before interest and taxes (EBIT)}}{\text{Interest charges}}$$

$$\text{Times interest earned}_{1990} = \frac{\$23,302}{\$16} = 38 \text{ times}$$

The coverage of the interest charges of 38 times means that for each dollar of interest owed by the firm $38 of gross earnings is available to pay the interest. Certainly, with such a coverage ratio Ellison's creditors are secure.

Fixed Charge Coverage Ratio.   There are often other fixed, legally binding charges owed by the firm. These may include rent and lease payments. A measurement of the firm's ability to pay all such charges is called the fixed charge coverage ratio, computed as follows:

$$\frac{\text{EBIT} + \text{Leases}}{\text{Interest} + \text{Leases}}$$

Asset Management Ratios

The asset management ratios illustrate the firm's effectiveness (relative to an industry or trend comparison) in managing its assets. In order for a firm's performance to be at maximum, the assets should be neither too high nor too low in terms of their dollar value as shown on the balance sheet. Excessive asset levels will generally reduce the return on total assets, and inadequate asset levels may cause missed sales opportunities.

Average Collection Period (ACP).   The ACP provides a view of the firm's management of its accounts receivable. Specifically, the ratio answers the question "How long have the receivables, on average, been outstanding?" Thus the ratio provides an answer in a number of days.

$$\text{ACP} = \frac{\text{Accounts receivable}}{\text{Average sales per day}}$$

$$\text{ACP}_{1990} = \frac{\$481}{(\$126,540/360 \text{ days})} = 1.37 \text{ days}$$

The foregoing ACP implies that Ellison does virtually a "cash" business, meaning it has very little (1.37 days) lag time between the time a sale is made and the time of collection for that sale. If Ellison's terms of sale are cash, then its ACP corresponds very closely to those terms.

Inventory Utilization.   The inventory utilization ratio is sales divided by inventories.

$$\text{Inventory utilization} = \frac{\text{Sales}}{\text{Inventories}}$$

$$\text{Inventory utilization}_{1990} = \frac{\$126,540}{\$31,581} = 4.01 \text{ times}$$

Again, the ratio of 4 times for Ellison's inventory utilization may be compared to the industry average or to the company's trend data. It would be more representative of the month-by-month sales of the company's goods if the average inventory were used as the denominator in the foregoing ratio. Average inventory may be thought of as the addition of the beginning of the year inventory plus the end of year inventory divided by 2. Other averaging techniques could be used if sales follow a seasonal pattern or a pattern which is other than evenly spread throughout the year.

Fixed Asset Utilization. Many of the funds obtained by a firm to produce continued growth in sales and earnings are invested in fixed assets. The fixed asset utilization ratio tells us in very specific, comparative terms how well the fixed assets are being used as a means of generating sales. We see those assets shown as "property, plant, and equipment" on Ellison's balance sheet.

$$\text{Fixed asset utilization} = \frac{\text{Sales}}{\text{Net fixed assets}}$$

$$\text{Fixed asset utilization}_{1990} = \frac{\$126,540}{\$15,104} = 8.38 \text{ times}$$

Profitability Ratios

The firm's profitability is important to every individual or organization connected in any way to the success of that firm. In the business media we hear or read about "profits," return on equity, and other references to a company's profitability. There are several ways to measure profitability.

Profit Margin. One of the most commonly used measures is the profit margin on sales or the relationship of dollars of profit to dollars of sales.

$$\text{Profit margin on sales} = \frac{\text{Net income}}{\text{Sales}}$$

$$\text{Profit margin on sales}_{1990} = \frac{\$\ 12,464}{\$126,540} = 9.8\%$$

Thus, for each dollar of sales made by Ellison in 1990, 9.8 cents was profit after all expenses have been paid. The dividends to the firm's owners (stockholders) are paid from that 9.8 percent of profit, and the remainder becomes a part of the balance sheet item identified as "retained earnings." Retained earnings represent the accumulation of the dollars reinvested in the business over the entire life of the firm.

Return on Assets (ROA). This ratio measures company profitability as it related to the total assets of the firm. It answers the question, how much profit is earned on each dollar of assets?

$$ROA = \frac{\text{Net income}}{\text{Total assets}}$$

$$ROA_{1990} = \frac{\$12,464}{\$55,351} = 22.5\%$$

Each dollar of assets earned Ellison 22.5 cents in profit after-tax in 1990. That level of return may be assessed against an industry average.

Return on Equity (ROE).   Those who invest equity funds in the firm, the common stockholders, will obviously be interested in the profitability of their investment. If we are able to determine the profitability of assets (ROA) or of sales (profit margin), then it is also useful to compute the return on the equity portion of the firm's financing.

$$ROE = \frac{\text{Net income}}{\text{Common equity}}$$

$$ROE_{1990} = \frac{\$12,464}{\$42,184} = 28.5\%$$

From the profitability ratios then, we may view profitability in terms of sales, assets, or equity. As before, industry and trend comparisons allow an evaluation to be made as to the firm's effectiveness in any of these areas.

Market Value Ratios

A firm's market value usually refers to the price of each share of its common stock as it is publicly traded among investors. Common equity, the owner-supplied capital, is often shown under three separate balance sheet items: common stock, retained earnings, and paid-in capital. The sum of those three items equals common equity, as indicated above. Ellison's balance sheet shows $5,970 of paid-in-capital, which is funds received for issued common stock in excess of its par or stated value. The data which are obtained from the market value ratios are most useful for comparing *investor perception* of one company to that of another.

Price Earnings Ratio (P/E).   For example, if we assume that Ellison's common stock sells for $63 per share, its price-earnings ratio would appear as follows:

$$P/E = \frac{\text{Market price}}{\text{Earnings per share}}$$

$$P/E_{1990} = \frac{\$63}{\$12.46} = 5.06$$

Ellison's P/E is approximately 5 times, which means that investors are willing to pay $5 for each dollar of the company's earnings. There are two ways to assess the investor perception. (1) If other firms which are similar to Ellison (in terms of sales and earnings growth, dividends paid, earnings stability, and asset size) have a P/E of 4, we may conclude that Ellison's performance is perceived by investors as being superior to the other firms, since on average, investors will pay only $4 for each dollar of earnings from those firms. (2) The P/E of Ellison as compared to the other firms in its industry classification indicates investors believe Ellison will *continue* to do better than the others.

Market Value versus Book Value.   If a firm is liquidated, that is, it is no longer operated as a business but is "sold off" item by item, one measure of its worth at that time is *book value.* Thus, a firm's book value represents its worth at liquidation, if all assets are sold at their recorded value. After the settlement or payment of creditor-supplied capital, the remaining value must then be divided among the common stockholders.

$$\text{Book value} = \frac{\text{Stockholders' equity}}{\text{No. of common shares outstanding}}$$

$$\text{Book value}_{1990} = \frac{\$42{,}184}{1{,}000} = \$42.18$$

The common stockholders of Ellison would receive in effect, $42.18 for each share held at liquidation. Compared to our previously assumed market price of $63 per share. Therefore,

$$\frac{\text{Market value}}{\text{Book value}} = \frac{\$63.00}{\$42.18}$$
$$= 1.49$$

A number equal to or greater than one for the foregoing ratio is favorable for the equity holder because that represents a favorable market value (firm is worth more as a going concern) relative to book value.

LIMITATIONS OF RATIO ANALYSIS

The financial ratios which have been discussed in the preceding sections provide valuable, easily interpreted information concerning a firm and the industry in which it operates. We see that much of what is illustrated by the ratios-profitability, asset management, and so on, depend upon certain reasonable similarities between the firm's financial condition and the industry in which it operates, or between the firm's present and past operating environments, or both.

If inflation were severe in the early or later years of a trend analysis, the trend comparison will be less meaningful. For example, abnormally higher prices in a period may distort inventory values, and corresponding ratios, or more or less cash will be held based on the then prevailing economic environment.

If the age of assets owned by the company is less than is typical in the industry, certain ratios may also be affected. For example, if old assets, fully depreciated, are held by the industry, and the firm's assets are new, the firm's asset management ratios (total asset turnover, for example) cannot be meaningfully compared to industry ratios.

Therefore, when conducting a trend or industry comparison using financial ratios, the foregoing precautions must be taken into consideration. How to take such factors into consideration and to what extent requires judgment relative to each situation. Such judgment is developed by the "learning by doing" method based on the techniques presented in this note.

DuPont System of Financial Analysis

The DuPont system of financial analysis illustrates the interrelationship among the ratio categories. The various ratio categories may affect or determine a firm's profitability in combination rather than individually. The return on asset ratio (ROA) demonstrates this point.

Earlier we defined and described ROA, using 1990 data as:

$$ROA = \frac{\text{Net income}}{\text{Total assets}} = \frac{\$12,464}{\$55,351} = 22.5\%$$

Thus, we have, in the foregoing, an asset management ratio. The DuPont system, however, permits a view of the ROA which takes into account a profitability ratio *and* an asset management ratio.

$$ROA_{\text{DuPont}} = \frac{\text{Net income}}{\text{Sales}} \times \frac{\text{Sales}}{\text{Total assets}}$$

For Ellison's 1990 data we have:

$$\frac{\$12,464}{\$126,540} \times \frac{\$126,540}{\$55,351}$$

Separately, the Ellison "ROA Components" for 1990 appear as follows:

$$\text{Return on Sales} = \frac{\$12,464}{\$126,450} = 9.8\%$$

$$\text{Asset Turnover} = \frac{\$126,540}{\$55,351} = 2.29 \text{ times}$$

$$.098 \times 2.29 = 22.25\%$$

We are now better able to make an assessment of the strength or weakness in the ROA. Is that strength or weakness the result of one or both ratio categories, and how do the ratio categories which affect our ROA compare to trend or to an industry comparison? The foregoing questions provide greater insight into a ratio analysis than does the very useful but less powerful one-dimensional view of financial ratios.

Additional Useful Aspects of Financial Statement Analysis

When financial information is presented in the media it is often in terms of a time period comparison. How often do we hear the following: "Company XYZ's earnings have increased by 15 percent over the last four years." Does that mean there was a 15 percent increase in earnings from year-to-year for each of the previous four years? Probably not. An example may help to clarify this matter. We will again use Ellison's data in the illustration.

	1982	**1990**
Profit after tax	$3,300	$12,464

Steps necessary to calculate the compound average annual growth (CAAG) of Ellison's profit after tax for the period 1982 to 1990 (1982 data are assumed) are as follows:

1. Recognize that there are 9 periods involved but only eight compounding periods since profit figures are year-end.
2. Divide the 1990 amount by the 1982 amount; the resulting amount is a compound value interest factor (CVIF) which may be found in a "present value" table or by use of a financial calculator. Thus,

$$\frac{\$12,464}{\$3,300} = 3.777 \text{ CVIF}$$

A CVIF of 3.777 corresponds to a growth rate of approximately 18 percent, as found in the table. Hence, Ellison's profit growth for the period 1982 to 1990 has been, on average, 18 percent. The value of the growth rate number is in its use as a comparative figure. It may be compared to the industry or the national economy as possible benchmarks for Ellison.

In addition to being aware of growth rates, it is important to understand the earnings and dividend stability of a firm. Stability, the lack of significant variation from some mean or average, is important in financial management. Simply put, if items (earnings, sales, dividends) are not variable, their future level can be more accurately predicted and, presumably, better decisions can be made concerning future events (inflows/outflows of cash, for example). Earnings and dividends do vary, however, but firms generally attempt to maintain a stable (that is, predictable) dividend payment stream—even if earnings are volatile. If the firm's objective or plan is to bring the earnings volatility under control, such control will prevent a drain on the company's finances caused by paying dividends when earnings are less than adequate.

SUMMARY

The four financial statements most commonly released by firms are the balance sheet, the income statement, the statement of retained earnings, and the statement of changes in financial position. The financial statements are most readily found in the annual report of the public, for-profit firm. The financial statements may be assessed using ratio analysis. Such an analysis is facilitated by an assessment of the ratio for a firm as compared to the industry or the firm's past performance.

There are limitations to financial ratio analysis which must be kept in mind if the analysis is to be useful. When assessing a firm's performance it is beneficial to use the trend (time period) comparison and to be aware of the rate of change of financial statement items during the particular time period.

Questions

1. What do the liquidity ratios show?
2. What is trend analysis?
3. How does the age of assets affect ratio analysis?
4. What are retained earnings?
5. Without using the book, jot down the format of an income statement and a balance sheet.
6. What is meant by "a source of funds: a use of funds"?
7. How do a balance sheet and an income statement interrelate? (Hint: there is one income statement item which will be reflected on the balance sheet.)
8. What are the categories of financial ratios?
9. Illustrate one ratio from each of the categories.
10. How are financial ratios assessed or compared?
11. How does past or present inflation affect the reliability of financial ratio analysis?

PRESENTING A CASE ORALLY

Gary F. Kohut and Carol M. Baxter

Presenting a case is different from other speaking situations. First, some speaking situations require little research; however, cases require in-depth research and careful planning. Cases may lull you into believing that you have enough details to present an effective analysis. Until you start planning the presentation, you may be unaware of deficiencies in your material. Good case preparation is the key to good case presentation.

Second, in some speaking situations the material is very familiar to the speaker, so preparation for speaking is minimal. Cases, on the other hand, require careful planning, thoughtful organization of the main points, and a clear distinction between facts and conjecture.

Third, the oral presentation of cases requires a different organizational plan than a written analysis of the same case. For example, in a written report, the reader has the opportunity to refer back to information that may not have been understood the first time. In an oral presentation, if the listener does not hear a point, it is lost; the speaker will have gone on to another point. Therefore, good speakers must help the audience follow and remember main points about the case.

KNOWING YOUR AUDIENCE

Because you will give your presentation to a specific audience, you need to analyze that audience carefully before you plan your speech. Audience analysis is a method of examining the knowledge, interests, and attitudes of those who will hear your presentation. You will use that analysis to test the appropriateness of your material and to guide you in selecting supporting information, the pattern of organization for the information, the language you use, and even the type of delivery you choose. A key to ensuring that your points are understood is to know your audience's needs, values, expectations, knowledge of the subject, biases, and other background characteristics. The more you know about your audience, the better able you are to make your points clear to them.

Audience analysis involves asking yourself a series of questions about the audience.

1. Ask yourself if the audience is familiar with the material. Will they have read the case? Do they know about the industry? Do they have any related work experience? If the answers are no, you must include these background facts when planning the presentation.

2. Ask what kind of language they will best understand. Do they have knowledge of the jargon in the field? Will you have to use popular language or will you use jargon but define it as you go along?

3. Ask what background they bring to the case. Different people's experiences may cause them to perceive the case differently. For example, individuals with a liberal arts background may view the case differently from people with an engineering background. Being familiar with those in the audience allows you to make certain assumptions that can save considerable time in presenting the case orally. You may, for instance, be able to relate the case to their interests or you may have to find a creative approach to make the material interesting to them.

4. Ask what beliefs, attitudes, and feelings the audience has toward the subject matter. Will the listeners be sympathetic, apathetic, or hostile toward the topic? For example, some individuals have strong views about environmental issues, whereas others believe that providing jobs always takes precedence over environmental concerns.

If part of the audience is sympathetic, you must keep their sympathies. If part of the audience is hostile, you may be able to decrease their hostility or at least find ways not to increase it. If the audience is apathetic, look at their values and try to relate the issue to their concerns.

Your goal is to assess how the members of the audience are alike and how they differ. The extent to which you effectively analyze them will largely determine if you will be able to adapt your material to them.

ORGANIZING THE CASE MATERIAL

Once you understand your audience, you can begin to organize your material. An effective case presentation is the result of preparing a good outline of the points you want to cover. Your outline should follow these guidelines:

1. *Establish the objectives of your presentation.* Write a sentence that states the purpose of your presentation. Every other statement in your outline must refer back or support this thesis statement.

2. *Preview the main points to be covered.* Stating the key ideas you want to cover in the presentation prepares the audience for the information to come.

3. *Develop the main points in your presentation.* Write down the principle issues, problems (if any exist) or other concerns you want to bring before the audience. Your analysis should break down the case material and examine critically each of the parts. With this type of thinking, however, it is easy to concentrate on something wrong or why some proposed course of action should not be undertaken. To avoid this pitfall, be open to different perspectives on the case.

4. *Support your main points.* In this step, you must prepare definitions, descriptions, explanations, examples, statistics, and so forth to back up your main ideas. Of course, if the audience already understands the concept, do not insult their intelligence with needless definitions, explanations, or facts. Another method of supporting your main points is through the use of visual aids. This topic will be discussed in the next section of the chapter.

5. *Discuss alternatives, solutions, or conclusions.* Depending on the type of case analysis, you will be asked to present either viable alternatives, feasible solutions, or logical conclusions. Regardless of what they are asked to do, most individuals focus on this part of the presentation. Poor preparation of this part of the presentation will negate any earlier success you may have. Therefore, the development of this section requires a clear rationale for why you propose a certain course of action.

PREPARING VISUAL AIDS

Once you have a workable outline, you are ready to develop visual support for your presentation. Since our society is so visually oriented, we cannot rely solely on words to convey information and hold the audience's attention. We must find ways to show them as well as tell them the information.

When planning your visuals, first, determine the kind of visuals you will use. One type to consider is direct viewing visuals such as handouts, posters, flip charts, models, exhibits, and samples. A second type is projected visuals such as slides, overhead transparencies, and video tapes.

Your decision about the type of visual to use should be based on several factors.

1. *The amount of time you have to develop the visuals.* If you have little time, you may choose to use transparencies because they are quickest and easiest to make. On the other hand, if you have more time, you may want to use slides or a videotape since they can capture a process or show things to scale better than a transparency. Another example of the time factor involves making posters or charts. Freehand lettering takes little time, but may not be as neat as stencilled lettering. However, the latter requires considerably more time to produce.

2. *The cost of the visuals.* Although models and exhibits may better explain your points, the costs of preparing or obtaining them may be prohibitive to your budget. Some of the least expensive visuals are transparencies, flip charts, handouts, and samples.

3. *The site of the presentation.* The size, layout, fixtures, and furniture arrangement of the speaking site must be considered when selecting visuals. For example, you would not want to use a small model in a large room or slides in a very small room. You should explore the site of the presentation prior to delivering your speech to determine the type of visuals that will work best.

4. *The availability of equipment.* Slides are not effective if a screen is not available. Although you may try to improvise by using a wall as a screen, you run the risk of diminishing the positive effects of the slides. Similarly, a half-inch videotape is useless on a machine that plays three-quarter inch tape.

Some things should be avoided when using visual aids. Remember these guidelines; if ignored, they can wreak havoc on the most carefully developed visuals:

1. Avoid passing things around the room since they may become a distraction.

2. Avoid small lettering or crowded information that will be hard for the audience to read.

3. Avoid having too many or too many different kinds of visuals; there is a point of diminishing return.

4. Avoid showing your visuals to the audience while you are talking about something else. Cover them up until you are ready to refer to them.

5. Avoid overly detailed or overly complex visuals that will be hard for the audience to interpret.

6. Avoid talking to your visual aids; look at and talk to your audience.

DELIVERING THE PRESENTATION

Before delivering your case, you must prepare yourself mentally and physically for the task. First, practice the presentation aloud, preferably in the room where you will deliver it, using your visuals and your notes. This practice will allow you to estimate the amount of time you will need for the presentation.

Second, select clothing that is comfortable and appropriate for your audience and for the degree of formality in your classroom. Also be well-groomed since much of your credibility is based on your physical appearance.

Recognizing that you will be nervous for the presentation, you must take precautions not to exacerbate the situation. For example, do not drink alcoholic beverages to calm your nerves. Also, avoid carbonated beverages that may cause you to burp. Furthermore, avoid taking medications that will dry out the membranes of your mouth. If your mouth is dry, experienced speakers recommend lining the inside of your lips with petroleum jelly or sucking on a lemon—just before you speak—to increase production of saliva. Finally, avoid eating a heavy meal prior to delivering the presentation because it will sap your energy level.

Mental preparation is as important as physical preparation. Some people have found it valuable to visualize their entire presentation. Others picture themselves confidently standing before the audience delivering an excellent presentation. Such "psyching up" is valuable in building confidence. Mental preparation should also include addressing Murphy's law: if anything can go wrong it will. Consider what action you will take if you drop your notes, if the projector does not work, or if you forget what you want to say.

During the actual delivery of the case, you should display the traits of a credible speaker. You will appear confident if you:

1. Maintain eye contact with every member of the audience at some time during the presentation.

2. Avoid *reading* from notes or memorizing the entire presentation. Speak naturally and conversationally by using just an outline. If the entire presentation is written out, the temptation to read it may be too powerful to resist. However, be familiar with the outline or notes, so you won't "go off on tangents," a habit that wastes valuable time. Finally, do not be tempted to memorize the entire presentation: if you forget what you have memorized, no one can help you.

3. Use natural gestures; keep hands out of pockets, above the waist, and not behind the back. Do not pace back and forth and avoid leaning on the podium or sitting on the table. Often, case presentations are formal and your gestures should reflect that formality.

4. Be positive. Never make negative comments about your preparation, delivery, material, or visuals. Apologizing hurts your credibility. Once you have lost an audience, it is virtually impossible to regain your credibility with them.

5. Control your voice. For example, avoid numerous verbalized pauses such as "and uh," "you know," "ok," and so on. Successful speakers should follow these recommendations regarding the voice:
   a. Speak loud enough to be heard by everyone in the room.
   b. Speak slowly and enunciate the words clearly.
   c. Know how to pronounce all the words you plan to use in the presentation. When in doubt, consult a dictionary.
   d. Use vocal variety in the presentation. Research indicates that women have a problem with using too high a pitch, which can sound "screechy" or "sing-songy." Men, on the other hand, have problems with a monotonous voice. In such a voice, the pitch, rate, and volume remain constant—

no word, sentence, or idea sounds different from any other. The effect of a monotone is that the audience is lulled to sleep.

   e. Demonstrate some enthusiasm for the topic. During the presentation of the case, give emphasis to something in nearly every sentence. If you seem interested, the audience will be interested too. Even if your delivery is good, you must sustain your credibility during the question/answer period, which we will discuss next.

HANDLING QUESTIONS FROM THE AUDIENCE

Answering questions tests your understanding of the material. Here are some guidelines to assist you in preparing to answer questions.

1. Anticipate the kind of questions that may be asked.
2. Remain calm when asked a difficult question. You may restate the question to ensure your understanding of what is being asked. This technique also will "buy you some time" to think of the best way to answer the question.
3. Keep your answers brief and to the point. Trying to bluff or ignore the questioner will only make him or her more eager to "put you on the spot."
4. Admit that you do not know if you cannot answer a factual question. However, reassure the questioner that you will find the answer.
5. Avoid taking a defensive stance or an accusatory tone of voice when answering questions. Instead, turn a tough question into a positive one by complimenting or otherwise involving the questioner.

PRESENTING AS A TEAM OR INDIVIDUALLY

Most cases are either presented individually or in groups. Each type of presentation provides its own unique challenges. For example, individual case presentations require the speaker to plan how to present points, whereas, group presentations require some division of labor. In planning the division of labor, the group should work with the strengths of each person. For example, some people are good at incorporating visuals into the presentation but may have a difficult time explaining numerical information. Learn what each person *prefers* to contribute to the presentation and attempt to allow the individual responsibility for carrying it out.

Group presentations often require substantial preparation and coordination. Melding the views, opinions, or perspectives of several people is no easy task. Establishing open dialogue from the beginning can help immensely. In addition, good rehearsals can help the group develop a common "voice" where individual differences are minimized.

The amount of group contact is a function of the personality of its members. When planning your group case, we offer the following recommendations:

1. Try to meet regularly to track individual progress and avoid small problems that can escalate into major problems. Regular meetings also help identify strengths and weaknesses in group members.

2. Have specific goals that you want to achieve at each meeting to avoid wasting time and energy.

3. Decide who will be responsible for answering questions in a particular area. Keep in mind, though, that everyone has a stake in the presentation. Therefore, if a team member seems unable to answer a question, others in the group should help by answering.

4. Avoid monopolizing the presentation or the answers to questions. If the case is presented by a group, each person should have an almost equal share in presenting the information.

If you use the suggestions in this chapter, your case will probably be better prepared, organized, and delivered than many cases that are presented in today's classrooms.

Appendix **D**

STRATEGIC MANAGEMENT AND BUSINESS POLICY INFORMATION SOURCES

Peter M. Ginter and Linda E. Swayne

In case analysis it is often useful to perform at least part of the situation analysis by investigating secondary data. While each of the cases in this text have about as much information as the decision maker had at the time, further information could be obtained. However, it is wise to check your professor's preference for your investigating the company through library research. Some professors want students to use only the information provided in the case; others insist that students investigate the company and the industry using additional materials. Still others want students to research the company only up to the time of the decision point in the case.

Some students believe that a successful approach to case analysis will occur when they find an article about the company and the decision that was made. The student then writes up the decision that was implemented as the "correct" solution to the case. Knowing what the company did may prejudice your thinking and limit your ability to develop a creative solution. A question to consider: If the company had the opportunity to do it over, would management implement the same decision? If the results were impressive, a student might be tempted to say yes. But would a different decision have yielded even greater benefits?

As an aid to locating information, sources that are typically available in university libraries along with a brief description are listed. Organized by newspaper and periodical indexes, industry data sources, financial sources, databases, and guides to sources not described, this nonexhaustive list suggests sources that might be used in a situation analysis for the cases in this text.

The authors wish to express appreciation to Mark Sullivan, Business Librarian at The University of North Carolina at Charlotte, for his assistance in preparing this chapter.

NEWSPAPER AND PERIODICAL INDEXES

Business Index

This source is available on 16 mm computer-output-microfilm for viewing on a microfilm reader which provides more rapid availability and more complete cumulation of information. Over 375 business periodicals are indexed, as well as acquisitions, mergers, and corporate promotions from the *New York Times* and *The Wall Street Journal.*

Business Periodicals Index

BPI is a cumulative index to English language periodicals pertaining to business. Approximately 300 periodicals are indexed primarily by subject. Articles about a company are indexed under the name of the company. Volumes are issued monthly, with a cumulative quarterly update and a cumulative annual update published.

Funk and Scott (F & S) Index of Corporations and Industries

F & S is an excellent source to locate information concerning specific industries and companies. It indexes business related journals, some newspapers, trade publications, newsletters, and loose-leaf services. This index is divided into two sections, industry and company. The industry section is arranged by SIC number while the company section is arranged alphabetically by company name. To identify the SIC code for an industry, check the *Standard Industrial Classification Manual* usually kept at the reference desk at most libraries.

New York Times Index

Published semimonthly with quarterly updates and a yearly cumulative issue, the *NY Times Index* abstracts news and editorial matter classified by appropriate subject, geographical, organization, and personal name headings. Entries are by subject whenever possible and are alphabetized.

The Wall Street Journal Index

This index covers articles published in *The Wall Street Journal.* There are two sections: general news where articles concerning various subjects are arranged alphabetically and corporate news where articles about companies are arranged by company name.

INDUSTRY DATA

Almanac of Business and Industrial Financial Ratios

This source provides selected financial ratios for key U.S. industries such as transportation, communication, manufacturing, retail trade, financial services, and others. Most SIC categories are included.

Directory of Corporate Affiliation

The Directory lists 3,500 U.S. parent companies with their domestic and foreign divisions, subsidiaries, and affiliates, as well as 35,000 "corporate children" and their parent companies. Five bimonthly publications update personnel changes, acquisitions, address changes, and so forth.

Economic Census

The U.S. Bureau of the Census publishes an economic census every five years, in years which end in two or seven. This government document includes manufacturing, retail, wholesale, service construction, transportation, and mineral industries. The data include number of establishments, value of shipments or sales, cost of materials, employment, and payroll, arranged by line of business.

Financial Analyst's Handbook

The Handbook is in two volumes. Volume II contains discussions by specialists for a variety of industries. The orientation is toward economic, social, marketing, regulatory, taxation, or accountancy topics considered to be of significance to the industries.

Financial Research Associates' *Financial Studies* of Small Business

Most industry data is provided for larger business operations. FRA publishes ratios and norms for small businesses with total capitalization that is less than $1 million.

Forbes Magazine

Annually Forbes publishes a special issue (in January) which reviews the performance of major American industries and ranks the identified firms by profitability and growth.

Industry Norms and Key Business Ratios

Over 800 different types of business operations are included. Key industry ratios (including the common ROA, ROI, ROE, current ratio, quick ratio, and so on and some less common such as current liabilities to net worth, total liabilities to net worth) and industry norms are presented.

Robert Morris Associates' Annual Statement Studies

Robert Morris is an association of bank lenders that publishes composite financial data (activity, profitability, liquidity, market price ratios) on nearly 300 lines of business representing manufacturers, wholesalers, retailers, providers of services, and contractors. Financial ratios are computed for each industry included.

Standard & Poor's Industry Surveys

This source contains a wealth of data for 69 major, domestic industries. Examples include leisure time, computer and data processing equipment, liquor, photography, and so forth.

Statistical Abstracts of the United States

A standard summary of statistics on the social, political, and economic organizations of the United States, this source includes data from many statistical publications, both governmental and private. Emphasis is on national data, but regional, state, and metropolitan data are also included.

Survey of Current Business

This publication provides up-to-date leading economic indicators, as well as general business indicators, and analyses for selected industries.

Thomas' *Register of American Manufacturers*

Published annually in 12 volumes, each volume contains a comprehensive listing of American manufacturers. The first six volumes provide information by manufacturers according to product. Volume 7 lists branch offices, addresses, subsidiaries, and products. Volume 8 contains an index based on product classifications and a list of leading trade names. The remaining volumes (9–12) are catalogs of companies.

U.S. Industrial Outlook

Industries are profiled along with forecasts for industry activity for the next decade.

SOURCES OF FINANCIAL INFORMATION

Annual Reports

Most libraries maintain a file of annual reports for *Fortune* 500 and other public firms.

Q-File

An extensive microfiche file, this source contains corporate annual reports and 10-K reports for firms listed on the New York Stock Exchange (NYSE) or the American Stock Exchange (AMEX), and for public firms traded over-the-counter (OTC). The master index and updates are usually available in printed form in a loose-leaf binder as well as on microfiche.

Moody's Manuals

A subsidiary of Dun & Bradstreet, **Moody's** publishes manuals annually in five areas: industrial, bank and finance, public utility, transportation, and OTC industrial. Detailed financial information is provided for companies that represent investment opportunities. The information for the industries includes location and history of the firm, type of business, property, reserves, subsidiaries, officers, directors, annual meetings, balance sheets and income statements for several years, earnings, dividends, loans, debts, securities issued, market prices of securities, and related data. Similar information, tailored to other types of organizations, is provided in the different manuals. Each manual is updated by the loose-leaf *News Reports*.

Standard & Poor's Corporation Services

Standard & Poor's lists corporations and other organizations offering investment opportunities. Information is arranged alphabetically by company and includes capitalization, corporate background, financial statements, properties, officers, stock data, numbers of stockholders, price range of securities, dividends, and other data.

Value Line Investment Survey

While this source is designed to guide the private investor, professional analysts, corporate executives, purchasing agents, and sales managers, it does provide timely information on corporate developments and analysis of financial position as well as a brief industry overview. Over 1,500 companies in a variety of industries are covered in the weekly publication. Data include a 10-year statistical history of the firms in the *Survey,* estimates of the next three to five years' sales and estimates of quarterly sales, earnings, and dividends.

DATABASES

Many of these database services are available to "members" who have paid a membership or subscriber fee and then are charged for access time. Although the electronic databases are expensive to use, they offer speed and a comprehensive search.

ABI/Inform

ABI/Inform is the largest and oldest database of bibliographical business information. Over 680 business periodicals are indexed and a 150-word summary is included for each article. The database covers from 1971 to the present.

Business Periodicals Index

This database, available on CD-ROM, contains the same information as the hardcopy version previously described.

CompuServe

An on-line database, CompuServe offers a variety of services through a time-sharing computer system. Terminal access to the service can be made through the TYMNET system. There are two distinct services offered by CompuServe: Micronet and CompuServe Information Services (CIS). Micronet is designed for those who are familiar with programming and software. CompuServe is menu-driven and provides access to newspapers and specific topics such as finance, entertainment, communications, and so on.

Dow Jones News/Retrieval

Subscribers to this database can obtain the latest price quotations (no delay) for more than 6,000 stocks traded on nine different exchanges. It also allows for text searches for up-to-date news from the Dow Jones News Service Wires, *The Wall Street Journal, Barron's,* and *Washington Post.*

InfoTrac

Available on CD-ROM, InfoTrac indexes articles from 1,100 business and general interest periodicals and newspapers.

The Source

Also known as "American's Information Utility," The Source is a database service of Source Telecomputing Corporation. By dialing a Source access number and supplying a password, subscribers gain access to hundreds of databases. Some of the files included in the Source are: United Press International (UPI), *New York Times* News Summary, Aware Financial Services, and Business and Finance.

Standard & Poor's Corporate Descriptions

More than 9,000 publicly held U.S. corporations are included in this database which is available on CD-ROM. Descriptions include corporate background, income account and balance sheet figures, and stock and bond data.

GUIDES TO BUSINESS INFORMATION

If the preceding descriptions failed to suggest a suitable direction to obtain information, the following sources, which provide comprehensive listings, could be consulted.

Brownstone, David M. and Gorton Carruth, *Where to Find Business Information: A Worldwide Guide for Everyone Who Needs the Answers to Business Questions, 2nd edition,* New York: John Wiley Publishing Company, 1982.

Figueroa, Oscar and Charles Winkler, *A Business Information Guidebook,* New York: AMACOM, 1980.

Daniells, Lorna M., *Business Information Sources, Revised Edition,* Berkley, Calif.: University of California Press, 1985.

Woy, James, *Encyclopedia of Business Information Sources,* 7th ed, Detroit: Gale Research Company, 1988.